International Finance
The Markets and Financial Management of Multinational Business

McGraw-Hill Series in Finance

International Finance

The Markets and Financial Management of Multinational Business

THIRD EDITION

Maurice D. Levi

Bank of Montréal Professor
of International Finance
The University of British Columbia

McGraw-Hill, Inc.

New York St. Louis San Francisco Auckland Bogotá Caracas Lisbon
London Madrid Mexico City Milan Montreal New Delhi
San Juan Singapore Sydney Tokyo Toronto

This book was set in Times Roman by ComCom, Inc.
The editors were Michelle E. Cox and Judy Howarth;
the production supervisor was Paula Keller.
The cover was designed by Karen K. Quigley.
Project supervision was done by The Total Book.
Quebecor Printing/Fairfield was printer and binder.

Cover photos: *P. R. Production/Superstock;*
G. Kullenberg/Superstock.

INTERNATIONAL FINANCE
The Markets and Financial Management of Multinational Business

This book is printed on acid-free paper.

1 2 3 4 5 6 7 8 9 0 FGR FGR 9 0 9 8 7 6 5

ISBN 0-07-037687-5

Library of Congress Cataloging-in-Publication Data

Levi, Maurice D., (date).
   International finance: the markets and financial management of
multinational business / Maurice D. Levi.—3d ed.
      p.   cm.—(McGraw-Hill series in finance)
   Includes bibliographical references and index.
   ISBN 0-07-037687-5
      1. International finance.   2. International business enterprises—
Finance.   I. Title   II. Series.
HG3881.L455   1996
332'.042—dc20
                                                                    95-19667

About the Author

Since receiving his Ph.D. from the University of Chicago, Maurice D. Levi has taught and done research in a wide variety of areas of finance and economics. His broad range of research and teaching interests form the foundation for this book in international finance, a subject that he believes to be best treated as an application of economics and financial principles, rather than as a separate and isolated subject area.

Professor Levi has published research papers on the effectiveness of monetary and fiscal policy, the relationship between inflation and interest rates, the effect of taxes on capital flows, and the link between inflationary expectations and unemployment, as well as in the numerous areas of international finance that are reflected in this book. He has also written in the areas of econometric methods, macroeconomics, labor economics, environmental economics, money and banking, and regional economics. His papers have appeared in nearly every leading research journal in finance and economics, including *The American Economic Review; Econometrica; Journal of Political Economy; The Journal of Finance; Journal of Monetary Economics; Journal of Money, Credit and Banking; Journal of International Money and Finance; Journal of International Economics; Ecological Economics;* and *Journal of Econometrics.* He is also the author of *Economics and the Modern World* (Heath, Lexington Mass., 1994), *Economics Deciphered: A Layman's Survival Guide* (Basic Books, New York, 1981), and *Thinking Economically* (Basic Books, New York, 1985), and the coauthor, with M. Kupferman, of *Slowth* (Wiley, New York, 1980).

Since joining the Faculty of Commerce and Business Administration of the University of British Columbia, Professor Levi has held visiting positions at the Hebrew University of Jerusalem; the University of California, Berkeley; MIT; the National Bureau of Economic Research; the University of Exeter; and the London Business School. He has received numerous academic prizes and awards, including Killam and Nomura Fellowships and the Bronfman Award.

Maurice Levi is currently the Bank of Montréal Professor of International Finance at the University of British Columbia. His interests include astronomy, fishing, hiking, and enjoying his family: wife Kate and children Adam, Naomi, and Jonathan.

To Kate

"As for foreign exchange, it is almost as romantic as young love, and quite as resistant to formulae."

—H. L. Mencken

Contents

Part One
THE MARKETS FOR FOREIGN EXCHANGE

Part Two
DETERMINATION OF EXCHANGE RATES

*This chapter may be omitted without any loss of continuity.

Part Three
THE FUNDAMENTAL INTERNATIONAL PARITY
CONDITIONS

Part Four

MANAGING FOREIGN EXCHANGE RISK
AND EXPOSURE

*This chapter may be omitted without any loss of continuity.

Part Five
INTERNATIONAL INVESTMENT AND FINANCING

Part Six
INSTITUTIONAL STRUCTURE OF INTERNATIONAL
TRADE AND FINANCE

Preface

This book is intended for use in MBA and upper-level undergraduate business and economics courses in international finance which cover the management and markets of multinational business. The book is specifically designed for students who have taken introductory economics and finance and wish to build upon the basic economic and financial principles they have acquired. By assuming these prerequisites, this book is able to present a more in-depth study than competing textbooks in international finance and also to introduce the student to the new and exciting discoveries and developments in the dynamic and rapidly expanding field of international finance. These discoveries and developments, many of which have occurred during the last few years, are extensions of the central paradigms of economics and finance.

Of course, it is necessary to recognize that students of business, whether concentrating in finance or in international business, have a practical interest in the subjects they take. Consequently, any good textbook in international finance must cover real managerial topics such as where to borrow and invest, what different types of bonds can be used to raise capital, how exchange rates affect cash flows, what can be done to avoid foreign exchange exposure and risk, and the general financial management problems of doing business in the global environment. However, even these highly practical topics can be properly dealt with only by applying the basic financial and economic principles that are employed in this book, but which most other international finance textbooks seem reluctant to use. As a result of the "soft nature" of many other textbooks, despite adequate levels of preparation, generally including an introduction to economics and finance, the student often receives a rather descriptive treatment of these topics which fails to build on the foundations of previous courses. For this reason, many MBA students and undergraduate economics and business majors with solid backgrounds in, for example, the consequences of arbitrage or the principles of capital budgeting feel they move sideways rather than forward into international finance.

The topics in this text are covered from the perspective of a person who wishes to learn about the financial management of an internationally oriented business. However, it is important that managers also understand international financial developments on an overall macroeconomic level. Such an understanding enables managers to anticipate economic changes and adjust to what they expect to occur. Because of this double level of interest in the forces behind events and the consequences of these events for the firm, this book includes several chapters on the international finance of the economy. However, even at this macroeconomic level, a managerial perspective is taken, with the material linked closely to factors relevant to exchange-rate forecasting and the handling of volatility that has its roots in macroeconomic events.

This book represents a very major revision to the second edition of *International Finance*. Several new chapters have been included, and topics previously covered have been considerably rearranged and reintegrated. The new chapters include Chapter 4 on currency futures and options; Chapter 7 on modern theories of exchange rates; Chapter 13 on accounting exposure; Chapter 16 on speculation, market efficiency, and forecasting; and Chapter 22 on multinational banking. While these topics appeared in previous editions of *International Finance*, they were mixed in with other matters and were covered in less depth.

Other chapters have been reordered and reorganized. For example, operating exposure, Chapter 14, has been brought together with the other chapters dealing with exposure, while interest parity, which previously occupied two chapters, has been integrated into a single chapter, Chapter 11.

In addition to the inclusion of new chapters and reorganization of chapters, a number of real-life examples have been added to emphasize the practical value of the theory presented in the text. The guiding principle throughout this substantial revision has been to bring the book closer to the syllabus that seems to this author to be emerging in one-semester international finance courses in MBA and higher-level undergraduate business and economics programs. Most particularly, an attempt has been made to go beyond theory and into the vital and increasingly important real world of international finance. Of course, no book can escape the idiosyncrasies of its author, and so even this revised edition reflects what the author believes to be relevant. However, the author has taken more pains than in the previous two editions to suppress his own interests.

As with the second edition, a grand scale of revision has been necessary because the international financial developments that are occurring are nothing short of spectacular. For example, new markets and instruments are emerging at a frantic pace, in part as a response to exchange rates that at times have been so volatile they have grabbed the headlines, not just of the business section of the newspaper but also of the front page. Great fortunes have been made and lost in foreign exchange. News reports have also been full of exchange-rate crises in the United States and Europe, as well as the economic summits convened by world leaders to deal with these periodic crises. At the same time, there has been an explosion of published research in international finance and international financial management. The revisions to this book reflect these developments and the important research that has greatly sharpened the insights gained from studying this exciting subject.

This book has evolved over a number of years while I have been teaching at the University of British Columbia and also at the School of Business Administration of the Hebrew University, Jerusalem; the School of Business Administration of the University of California, Berkeley; the Department of Economics at the Massachusetts Institute of Technology; the London Business School; and the University of Exeter. I am indebted to all these institutions, especially the University of British Columbia, which has been my home base since I received my Ph.D. at the University of Chicago over two decades ago.

An author's debts are a pleasure to acknowledge, and in the course of three editions of this book I have incurred many I would find difficult to repay. The help offered by reviewers of the numerous drafts of this and previous editions has been immensely important in improving the final product. In preparing the first and second editions of *International Finance,* Carl Beidleman, Richard Bond, Richard Brealey, Kerry Cooper, Paul Fellows, Seymour Goodman, Roger Huang, James Hugon, Kenneth Kasa, David Leonard, Richard Levich, Bruce Resnick, and J. Fred Weston provided detailed and valuable advice. The major revisions in this third edition owe a lot to the perceptive comments of a long list of conscientious reviewers:

Steve B. Agahro, Jackson State University

Ward S. Connolly, Trinity University

A. Sam Ghanty, University of Wisconsin, Greenbay

C. Thomas Howard, University of Denver

Raymond M. Johnson, Auburn University at Montgomery

Shehzad Mian, Emory University

Prasad Padmanabhan, Pennsylvania State University

Marlene K. Puffer, University of Toronto

Siamack Shojai, Manhattan College

Andrew Solocha, The University of Toledo

Anant Sundaram, Dartmouth College

Gary Tallman, Northern Arizona University

Amir Tavokkol, Kansas State University

Jerome L. Valentine, St. Edwards University

Mark White, University of Virginia

Only the anonymity of the individual reviews prevents me from apportioning the vast amount of credit due collectively to them. The extensive nature of the improvements incorporated into this third edition are the result of the urging and encouragement of these reviewers and the editorial staff at McGraw-Hill. As with the preparation of the first and second editions, at every stage the work has been made easier by the unwavering help of the people at McGraw-Hill.

I would like to thank my colleagues at the University of British Columbia, especially Raman Uppal, who has provided advice on numerous topics. Last but not least, my research assistant, Jim Storey, has been a major help.

Khim Seow-Mah, Catherine Schittecatte, and my wife, Kate, have provided superbly professional and indispensable help in typing and preparing this manuscript. Too numerous to mention individually but of great importance were the students in my graduate and undergraduate courses in international finance at the University of British Columbia, whose reactions have had crucial influence on the various revisions of the text.

As with this and my other books, it is to my wife, Kate, that I owe my greatest and sincerest thanks. In addition to playing a vital role in preparing and checking the manuscript, she has provided the moral support and encouragement that have made this book a shared labor of love.

Maurice D. Levi

CHAPTER 1

The World of International Finance

The globe is not a level playing field.

—ANONYMOUS

WHAT IS UNIQUELY INTERNATIONAL IN FINANCE?

While tradition dictates that we continue to refer to the subject matter in this book as *international* finance, in a real sense the modifier "international" is redundant: today, with few remaining barriers to international trade and financial flows, and with important financial events impacting immediately around the globe, all finance is "international." Indeed, not only are domestic financial markets closely linked and internationally integrated, but the problems faced by companies and individuals in different lands are remarkably similar.

Even though most if not all finance must be viewed at the international level, there are special problems that arise from economic relations between nations. These are the problems addressed in this book. Many of these problems are due to the use of different currencies in different countries and the consequent need to exchange them. The rate of exchange between currencies is the amount of one currency received for another. Rates of exchange are set by a variety of arrangements, and both the rates and the arrangements themselves are subject to change. Changes in exchange rates between currencies can have profound effects on sales, costs, profits, and individual well-being. In addition to exchange-rate complications, other special, uniquely international problems that arise stem from the opportunities and risks involved in overseas borrowing and investment. Thus, the international subfield of finance has as its focus the problems managers face when exchange rates change and when they engage in overseas investment or borrowing.

THE BENEFITS OF STUDYING INTERNATIONAL FINANCE

A knowledge of international finance helps in two very important ways. First, it helps the financial manager decide how international events will affect a firm and

1

which steps can be taken to exploit positive developments and insulate the firm from harmful ones. Second, it helps the manager to anticipate events and to make profitable decisions before the events occur. Among the events that affect the firm and that the manager must anticipate are changes in exchange rates, as well as in interest rates, inflation rates, and asset values. Because of the close linkages between markets, events in distant lands—whether they involve changes in the prices of oil and gold, election results, the outbreak of war, or the establishment of peace—have effects which instantly reverberate around the earth. The consequences of events in the stock markets and interest rates of one country immediately show up around the globe, which has become an increasingly integrated and interdependent financial environment. The links between money and capital markets have become so close as to make it futile to concentrate on any individual part. These developments have made it imperative that every actual and aspiring manager take a good look into the exciting and dynamic field of international finance.

We are concerned with the problems faced by any firm whose performance is affected by the international environment. Our analysis is relevant to more than the giant multinational corporations (MNCs) that have received so much attention in the media and, in fact, is just as valid for a company with a domestic focus that happens to export a little of its output or to buy inputs from abroad. Indeed, even companies that operate only domestically but compete with firms producing abroad and selling in their local market are affected by international developments. For example, U.S. clothing or appliance manufacturers with no overseas sales will find U.S. sales and profit margins affected by exchange rates, which influence the dollar prices of imported clothing and appliances. Similarly, bond investors holding their *own* government's bonds, denominated in their *own* currency, and spending all their money at *home* are affected by changes in exchange rates if exchange rates prompt changes in interest rates. Specifically, if governments increase interest rates to defend their currencies when they fall in value on the foreign exchange markets, holders of domestic bonds will find their assets falling in value along with their currencies: bond prices fall when interest rates increase. It is difficult to think of any firm or individual that is not affected in some way or other by the international environment. Jobs, bond and stock prices, food prices, government revenues and other important economic variables are all tied to exchange rates and other developments in the global financial environment.

THE GROWING IMPORTANCE OF INTERNATIONAL FINANCE

While we shall emphasize the managerial issues of international finance in this book, it is important to reemphasize that the international flows of goods and capital that are behind the subject of international finance are fundamental to our well-being. Let us therefore pause to consider the evidence of the growth of the international movement of goods and capital. We shall also take a look at the sources of gains from the flows of goods and capital. We shall see that international finance is a subject of immense and growing importance.

International trade has a pervasive importance for our standard of living and our daily lives. In the department store we find cameras and electrical equipment from Japan and clothing from China and Hong Kong. On the street we find automobiles from Germany, Japan, Britain, Sweden, and France using gasoline from Nigeria, Saudi Arabia, Great Britain, Mexico, and Kuwait. At home we drink tea from India, coffee from Brazil, whiskey from Scotland, beer from Germany, and wine from France. We have become so used to enjoying these products from distant lands that it is easy to forget they are the result of the complex international trading and financial linkages discussed in this book.

Record on the Growth of Trade

Peoples and nations have been trading from time immemorial. During the period since records have been kept the amount of this trade between nations has typically grown at a faster rate than has domestic commerce. For example, since 1950, world trade has grown by about 6 percent per annum, roughly twice the rate of growth of world output over the same period. During the last century, international trade grew at an even more astounding rate, increasing by a factor of 25 times in the century leading up to World War I. Even in the period since 1970, a mere moment in the long history of international trade, the proportion of trade occurring between nations relative to total trade has almost doubled. This is seen in Table 1.1, which shows that global exports have risen from 9.9 percent of the global gross domestic product in 1970 to 15.8 percent by 1992. Indeed, if anything, the export figures and hence the percentages shown in Table 1.1 are understated. This is suggested by the fact that when the world's combined reported exports are compared to imports, global imports exceed exports. In the absence of extraterrestrial trade, this suggests reporting errors: properly calculated, global imports must equal global exports. The mechanisms for reporting imports are generally better than those for reporting exports—tax authorities keep track of imports for collection of duties—and therefore it is likely that exports are being understated rather than imports being overstated. Clearly, more and more economic activity is trade-related.

The growing importance of international trade is reflected in the trade statistics

TABLE 1.1. Aggregate International Trade versus GDP

Year	World Exports, Billion U.S.$	Exports/GDP, %
1992	3632.3	15.8
1990	3416.6	15.1
1985	1935.6	15.4
1980	1998.6	17.2
1975	875.5	14.1
1970	315.1	9.9

Source: National Account Statistics: Analysis of Main Aggregates, United Nations, New York, 1993.

of most industrialized nations. For example, Figure 1.1 shows that in the United States, the proportion of consumption consisting of imported goods and services has increased by almost 250 percent since 1962; it has increased from only 6.8 percent in 1962 to 16.28 percent in 1992. Figure 1.1, which shows the fraction of consumption consisting of imports, and Figure 1.2, which shows the fraction of gross domestic product (GDP) that is exported, reveal clearly that international trade is a matter of growing importance in the United States, Britain, Canada, Germany, France, and just about every leading country, whether we measure trade by imports or exports. It is worth pausing to consider why international trade and the international financial activity associated with that trade have grown relatively rapidly in recent decades.

Reasons for the Growing Importance of International Trade

There are two principal reasons why international trade has grown rapidly vis-à-vis overall economic activity:

1. A liberalization of trade and investment has occurred via reductions in **tariffs**, quotas, currency controls, and other impediments to the international flow of goods and capital.
2. An unprecedented shrinkage of "economic space" has occurred via rapid improvements in communication and transportation technologies and consequent reductions in costs.

Much of the trade liberalization has come from the development of free-trade areas, such as that containing the **European Union (EU)**, formally called the **Euro-**

FIGURE 1.1. Percentage of Consumption Consisting of Imports
In almost every country there has been a substantial increase in the dependence on imports, with a number of countries today importing more than half of what people consume. In the case of Japan, imports have declined, but this is because of a decline in *prices* of imported commodities, not a reduction in *quantities* of imports. (*Source:* International Monetary Fund, *International Financial Statistics,* November 1993.)

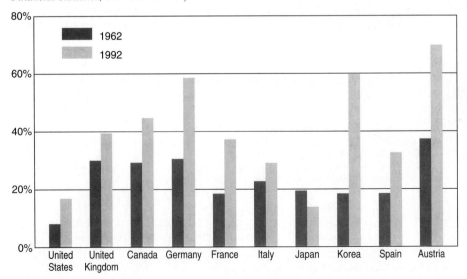

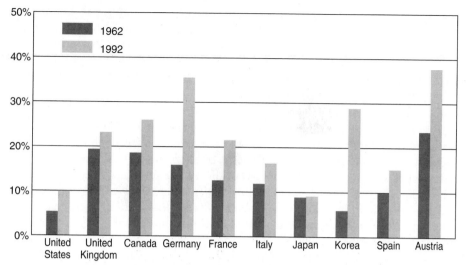

FIGURE 1.2. Percentage of GDP Arising from Exports
Today, foreign markets represent a more important part of demand for the products of almost
every country than in the past. For example, the fraction of U.S. GDP that is exported has
doubled since 1962, while the fraction of Korea's GDP that is exported has more than
quadrupled. (*Source:* International Monetary Fund, *International Financial Statistics,*
November 1993.)

pean Economic Community (EEC), consisting of 17 countries from Iceland to
Greece, and that of the United States, Canada, and Mexico, which signed the **North
America Free Trade Agreement (NAFTA)** in 1993. Similarly, rapid growth of
trade has occurred among the members of the **Association of South East Asian
Nations (ASEAN)**. Indeed, more and more of international trade is occurring within
regions. For example, Table 1.2 shows that between 1982 and 1992 the proportion
of U.S. trade with countries in North, Central, and South America increased from
29.3 percent to 37.1 percent, while Japan's trade with other Asian nations increased
from 19.7 percent to 34.6 percent. This trend toward regionalization of trade has

TABLE 1.2. The Growing Regionalization of Trade

	Percentage of Exports					
	U.S.		*Japan*		*Germany*	
	1982	1992	1982	1992	1982	1992
The Americas	29.3	37.1	33.8	35.0	9.4	9.1
Europe	26.9	25.4	14.9	21.0	63.7	76.6
Asia	20.1	27.2	19.7	34.6	4.1	7.5
Other	23.7	10.3	31.6	9.4	22.8	6.8
Total	100.0	100.0	100.0	100.0	100.0	100.0

Source: International Financial Statistics, International Monetary Fund, Washington, D.C., 1993.

important currency implications, making it of paramount importance to international finance. The Japanese yen is likely to become more dominant as the settlement currency in Asia, with the same being true for the **Deutschemark** in Europe. The role of the U.S. dollar, which has been the dominant global currency for price quotation and settlement of payments, may in the future be diminished outside the Americas.[1]

The second factor contributing to growing trade, namely, the shrinkage of "economic space" caused by a lower cost of communication and transportation, has had a profound effect. For example, in real terms, long-distance telephone costs have been reduced by more than 80 percent since the 1920s. Connection times have been reduced even more dramatically.[2] The cost of international business travel by air has dropped so substantially that it can cost little more for a U.S. executive to meet with a European client than to meet with another U.S. executive at the other side of the country. Air freight and ocean tanker costs for transporting goods have also fallen rapidly. This has resulted in a **globalization** of markets and consequent rapid growth in international financial activity.

Given the growing importance of international trade, it is worth briefly considering the rewards and risks that accompany it. This discussion will also allow us to introduce some of the matters discussed at length later in this book.

The Rewards of International Trade

The principal reward of international trade is that it has brought about increased prosperity by allowing nations to specialize in producing those goods and services at which they are relatively efficient. The relative efficiency of a country in producing a particular product can be described in terms of the amounts of other, alternative products that could be produced by the same inputs. When considered this way, relative efficiencies are described as **comparative advantages.** All nations can and do simultaneously gain from exploiting their comparative advantages, as well as from the larger-scale production and broader choice of products that are made possible by international trade.[3]

In the last few years it has become increasingly recognized that there is more to successful international trade than comparative advantages based on productive efficiencies.[4] These cannot explain distinct patterns of success, such as Hong Kong's growth with limited resources versus Argentina's slow advance despite abundant natural advantages. Also, comparative advantages do not explain why some regions *within* a country—for example, the region of northern Italy—grow faster than other regions in that country, or why parts of industries expand while others contract. Dynamic factors, rather than static production abilities, play a vital role in international trading success by offering countries **competitive advantages**. In particular,

---

[1]This possibility is discussed further in Chapter 2.

[2]See Ronald Abler, "Effect of Space-Adjusting Technologies on the Human Geography of the Future," in *Human Geography in a Shrinking World,* Ronald Abler, *et al.* (eds.), Duxberg Press, North Scituate, Mass., 1975, pp. 35–56.

[3]For those readers who have not learned or have forgotten the principle of comparative advantage, a summary is given in Appendix 1.1 at the end of this chapter. The gains from exploitation of comparative advantages are no different from the gains from specialization *within* a country.

[4]This recognition is in large part due to the influential book by Michael E. Porter, *The Competitive Advantage of Nations,* Harvard University Press, Cambridge, Mass., 1989.

countries typically are successful in products for which there are dynamic, discerning buyers at home. For example, French success in wine and cheese, German success in beer and finely engineered automobiles, British success in cookies, Italian success in fashion, and U.S. success in entertainment are in part due to the presence of consumers in the respective countries whose sophisticated tastes have forced firms to produce first-class products. After becoming successful at home, these firms have been able to succeed abroad. A further factor affecting success in international trade is the presence of suppliers and firms in supportive industries in the vicinity of exporting firms. For example, in Southern California the U.S. entertainment industry can call on lighting and camera engineers, actors and screen designers, and even such "extras" as exotic animal trainers and explosives experts. Other so-called "clusters" of supportive activities are found in the northern German chemical industry, the midwestern U.S. automobile industry, the northern Italian manufacturing industry, and the Tokyo-Osaka-based consumer electronics sector.

The Risks of International Trade

The rewards of trade come with accompanying risks. The most obvious additional risk of international versus domestic trade arises from uncertainty about exchange rates. Unexpected changes in exchange rates have important impacts on sales, prices, and profits of exporters and importers. For example, if a U.S. whiskey exporter faces an unexpected increase in the value of the dollar from DM1.6 (where DM stands for Deutschemark) to DM2.0, a bottle of whiskey sold for $10 will increase in price in Germany from DM16 to DM20. This will reduce sales, and since the U.S. exporter receives $10 *per bottle* before and after the change in the exchange rate, it reduces the exporter's revenue and profit.[5] Similarly, prices, sales, revenues, and profits of importers are also affected by unexpected changes in exchange rates.

Whether unexpected changes in exchange rates affect prices, sales, and profits of exporters and importers depends on whether changes in exchange rates really make a firm's goods cheaper or more expensive to buyers. For example, if an increase in the value of the dollar from DM1.6 to DM2.0 occurs while the price of a bottle of whiskey for export from the United States goes from $10 to $8, a bottle of whiskey will continue to cost DM16 in Germany. This is because the dollar price multiplied by the exchange rate, which gives the Deutschemark price, is unchanged. Our example shows that in order to determine the effect of changes in exchange rates, we must examine inflation and how inflation and exchange rates are related. This requires that we study international finance at the level of the economy as well as at the level of the individual firm.

The risk faced by exporters and importers resulting from the impact of exchange rates on prices, sales, and profits is only one, albeit probably the most important, of the additional risks of international trade versus domestic trade. Another risk of international trade is **country risk**. This includes the risk that as a result of war, revolution, or other political or social events a firm may not be paid for its exports. Country risk, which applies to foreign investment as well as to credit granted in trade, exists because it is difficult to use legal channels or seize assets when the

---

[5]Exhibit 1.1 provides some examples of export-oriented firms whose profits have been affected by exchange rates. The examples indicate that effects can be substantial.

The effects of changes in exchange rates on firms can be massive. The following excerpt from *The Economist* provides some notable examples:

Volkswagen recently held only a muted ceremony to mark the making of its 50 millionth car. Its party spirit was an indirect victim of floating exchange rates. The company had just found itself apparently defrauded of DM480m ($266m) by individuals whose job was to reduce Volkswagen's foreign exchange risk.

Consider some other, less criminal, prizes from the great exchange rate lottery:

- Eastman-Kodak reckons its pre-tax earnings were depressed by $3.5 billion between 1980 and 1985 because of the rising dollar. The dollar's subsequent fall revived its fortunes by adding 60 cents a share in 1986, but its market share abroad will take time to recover.
- Cadbury-Schweppes, a British drinks and confectionery firm, lost £10m in pre-tax profit in 1985 through sterling's appreciation against the dollar.
- Canon, Japan's largest camera firm, reported a 69% reduction in pre-tax profits for 1986, blamed largely on the climbing yen.
- BOC, a British industrial gases producer, banked a £16.8m windfall profit in 1985 from selling forward all its dollar revenues for the year at $1.09 to the pound sterling.*

It is worth mentioning that in the case of Volkswagen, the apparent fraud was the result of a failure of managers in charge of reducing the company's foreign exchange risk—or, more precisely, its "exposure," a term we define later—to take the steps they were supposed to. Indeed, forged documents were used to hide the absence of the appropriate steps. The Volkswagen experience is a vivid example of how costly it can be not to apply some of the principles in this book, although in Volkswagen's case top management knew very well what should be done. Indeed, Volkswagen had very strict rules that all foreign exchange exposure be "hedged."† Unfortunately, those responsible for putting the rules into effect ignored top management's instructions.

*Forward exchange is discussed in Chapter 3.
†Hedging is action taken to reduce foreign exchange exposure; it is discussed later at length, especially in Chapters 12 through 15.

Source: "Companies and Currencies: Payment by Lottery," *The Economist,* April 4, 1987, p. 81. © The Economist Newspaper Group, Inc. Reprinted with permission. Further reproduction prohibited. Also based on "Ex-VW Official Is Arrested in Fraud Case," *The Wall Street Journal,* April 8, 1987, p. 27.

buyer is in another political jurisdiction. Furthermore, foreign buyers may be willing but unable to pay because, for example, their government unexpectedly imposes currency exchange restrictions. Other added risks of doing business abroad include uncertainty about the possible imposition or change of import tariffs or quotas, possible changes in subsidization of local producers, and possible imposition of nontariff barriers.

Practices have evolved and markets have developed which help firms cope with the added risks of doing business abroad. For example, special types of foreign exchange contracts have been designed to enable importers and exporters to **hedge,** or **cover,** some of the risks from unexpected changes in exchange rates. Similarly, export credit insurance schemes have been established to help reduce country risk, and **letters of credit** have been developed to reduce other risks of trade. With international trade playing an increasingly important role in just about every nation, it is increasingly important that we learn about these risk-reducing practices. It is also increasingly important that we learn about the fundamental causes of the special risks of trade. These are two important topics of this book.

Increased Globalization of Financial and Real-Asset Markets

Alongside the growing importance of international versus domestic trade, there has been a parallel growth in the importance of foreign versus domestic investment in the money market, the bond market, the stock market, the real-estate market, and the market for operating businesses. At times, the importance of overseas investments and investors has swelled to overshadow that of domestic investment and investors. For example, there have been periods when purchases of U.S. government bills and bonds by Japanese, German, and other foreign investors have exceeded purchases of these instruments by Americans. Foreign buyers can be so crucial to the successful sale of securities that the U.S. Treasury and private brokerage firms must watch overseas calendars to ensure they do not launch a major sale when, for example, Japanese or European financial institutions are closed for an official holiday. The horizons of investors and borrowers have clearly become global.[6]

In response to the expanding horizons of investors, there has been an explosion of internationally oriented financial products such as internationally diversified, global, and single-foreign-country mutual funds. The popularity of these products is a sign of the internationalization of financial markets. Some examples of these funds are shown in Table 1.3. In this table, international funds are those with foreign components but no U.S. component, while global funds include U.S. and foreign assets. Those referred to as "emerging" are in smaller economies such as Thailand, Turkey, Malaysia, the Philippines, and Indonesia. Exhibit 1.3 illustrates the startling expansion of interest in such overseas investment instruments.

The buying of foreign securities directly by individuals without the use of mutual funds has also enjoyed explosive growth in recent years and has helped transform the international departments of securities firms into major profit-growth centers. Real-estate and other markets have also experienced transformations from the phenomenal pace of globalization. For example, foreign ownership of U.S. real estate expanded by an average rate of 39 percent per annum during the period 1976–1986.

The growth in globalization of investment viewed from a U.S. perspective can be seen in Figure 1.3. In the period 1970–1992 Americans increased their investments abroad by over 600 percent. During that same period, foreigners increased their investments in the United States by 1700 percent. A similar picture emerges in other countries. However, as with the expansion of the relative importance of international versus domestic trade, the increased globalization of investment has brought both rewards and risks.

Rewards of Globalization of Investment

Among the rewards of the globalization of investment has been an improvement in the global allocation of capital and an enhanced ability to diversify investment portfolios. The gain from the better allocation of capital arises from the fact that international investment reduces the extent to which investment opportunities with high returns in some countries are forgone for want of available capital while low-return investment opportunities in other countries with abundant capital receive

---

[6]Exhibit 1.2 provides some vivid illustrations of the astounding growth in international capital flows.

EXHIBIT 1.2
Getting a Grip on Globalization

After asking the question "What does 'globalization' mean?" *The Economist,* in its 1992 survey of the world economy, provides an answer which motivates a substantial part of the topic selection for this book: "The term can happily accommodate all manner of things: expanding international trade, the growth of multinational business, the rise in international joint ventures and increasing interdependence through capital flows—to name but a few."

When focusing on the last of these, increasing capital flows, *The Economist* provides a variety of measures of the dramatic rate at which globalization has occurred. Consider the following, including the caveat at the outset, taken directly from the survey in *The Economist.*

All the estimates that follow must be treated with caution. But even allowing for that, the story they tell is startling.

- In 1980 the stock of "international" bank lending (i.e., cross-border lending plus domestic lending denominated in foreign currency) was $324 billion. By 1991 it had risen to $7.5 trillion. To put these figures in perspective, the combined GDP of the 24 OECD [Organization for Economic Cooperation and Development] industrial countries in 1980 was $7.6 trillion; in 1991 it was $17.1 trillion. So during the past decade the stock of international bank lending has risen from 4% of the OECD's GDP to 44%. (See Figure E1.2.)

- In 1982 the total of international bonds outstanding was $259 billion; by 1991 it was $1.65 trillion. (See Figure E1.2.)

- Domestic bond markets have also been invaded by foreigners. Between 1970 and 1988 the proportion of American government bonds owned by foreigners went up from 7% to 17%—a growing share of a massively rising total. Between 1974 and 1988 the proportion of West Germany's official debt held by foreigners went up from 5% to 34%.

- As recently as 1986 the global stock of the principal derivatives (i.e., options, futures and swaps involving interest rates and/or currencies) was $1.1 trillion. In 1991 it was $6.9 trillion.

- Turnover in foreign exchange, including derivatives, is

FIGURE E1.2. Getting a Grip on Globalization
(*Source:* Bank for International Settlements.)

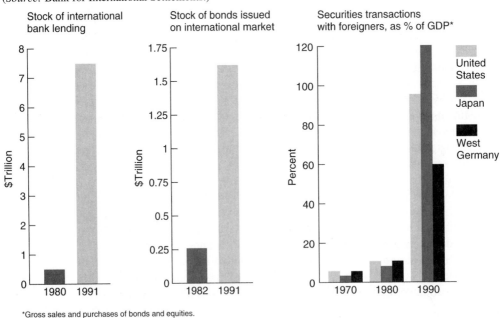

*Gross sales and purchases of bonds and equities.

funding. The flow of capital between countries moves rates of return in different locations closer together, thereby offering investors overall better returns. There is an additional gain from increased international capital flows enjoyed via an enhanced ability to smooth consumption over time by foreign lending and borrowing: countries can borrow abroad during bad years and pay back in good years. The analytical basis of the gain from consumption smoothing, along with the gain from a better international allocation of capital, are described in Appendix 1.2.

Cost of Globalization of Investment

The benefits of the globalization of investment have not come without a price. The price is the addition of exchange-rate risk and country risk.

Unanticipated changes in exchange rates cause uncertainty in investors' home-currency values of assets and liabilities. For example, if the exchange rate is $2 per British pound (£), a bank balance of £100 in London is worth $200 to a U.S. investor. If the British pound unexpectedly falls in value to $1.5, the U.S. investor's bank balance falls in value to $150. If instead of having an asset the U.S. investor has a debt or liability of £100, the unexpected change in exchange rate from $2 per pound to $1.5 per pound means a reduction in the dollar value of what the American owes. The dollar value of the liability will decline from $200 to $150.

In the case of a foreign-currency-denominated bank balance or debt, exchange-rate risk is due to uncertainty in the future exchange rates at which the asset or liability will be **translated** into dollars. Any asset or liability for which the home-currency value is affected by unexpected changes in exchange rates is subject to

11

TABLE 1.3. The Largest Overseas Stock Funds Trading in the United States

International	Pacific
Morgan Stanley Emerging Market	Morgan Stanley Instl: Asian Equity
Fidelity Emerging Markets	Dean Witter Pacific Growth
Gam: International	Merrill Dragon Fund;A
Govett: Emerging Market	Merrill Dragon Fund;B
Templeton Developing Markets	Wright Equity: Hong Kong
Merrill Developing Capital Market	Eaton Vance China Growth
GT Global Emerging Markets;A	T. Rowe Price International: Asia
Lexington Worldwide Emerging	World Funds: Newport Tiger
Montgomery: Emerging Markets	59 Wall St: Pacific Basin
Govett: International Equity	John Hancock FR Pacific Basin

Global	Japanese
Gam: Global	GT Japan Growth;A
Prudential Global;A	Capstone Nikko Japan
Prudential Global;B	The Japan Fund
GT Global Telecommunication;A	T Rowe Price International: Japan
Oppenheimer Global FD;A	Fidelity Investment TR: Japan
Morgan Stanley Instl;Global Equity	DFA Group: Japan Small Company
Paine Webber Atlas Global Growth;A	GT Japan Growth;B
Dean Witter Worldwide Investments	
Paine Webber Atlas Global Growth;B	
Paine Webber Atlas Global Growth;D	

European	Latin American
Dean Witter European Growth	Scudder Latin America
Alliance New Europe;A	Merrill Latin America;A
Alliance New Europe;B	Merrill Latin America;B
Paine Webber Europe Growth;A	GT Latin America Growth;A
Merrill Eurofund;A	TCW/DW Latin America Growth
Paine Webber Europe Growth;B	UST Mstr; Emerging America
Paine Webber Europe Growth;D	Hercules: Latin America Value
Putnam Europe Growth	GT Latin America Growth;B
DFA Group;UK Small Company	Fidelity Latin America
Merrill Eurofund;B	

	Canadian
	Mackenzie Canada Fund
	Fidelity Investments TR: Canada
	Alliance Global: Canadian

Source: "1993 Year-End Mutual Fund Report," *USA Today,* January 5, 1994, p. 5B. Copyright © 1994, USA TODAY. Reprinted with permission.

exchange-rate risk. This means that foreign stocks, bonds, property, and accounts receivable and payable may be subject to exchange-rate risk if their value in home currency (the U.S. dollar for a U.S. investor) is affected by exchange rates. However, as we shall see later, the mere fact that an asset or liability is in a foreign country does not mean that it is subject to exchange-rate risk, and the mere fact that an asset or liability is at home does not mean that it is *not* subject to exchange-rate risk.

Contributing to the increased importance of exchange-rate risk resulting from

EXHIBIT 1.3
The Incredible Interest in International Investment

Mutual funds catering to investors interested in participating in the rapid economic advance of so-called "emerging economies" such as Turkey, Thailand, Chile, Indonesia, and India have been among the hottest financial products of the 1990s. So too have mutual funds in the more established economies such as those of Europe and Japan. Consider, for example, a few of the following growth measures:

- According to the Investment Company Institute, the amount U.S. investors poured into international stock funds increased by 4 times in the 1-year period between 1992 and 1993.
- The number of international stock funds trading in the United States increased from 138 to 188 between 1992 and 1993.

- Assets in U.S.-traded international stock funds grew by 150% in 1993 alone.
- According to fund research firm Morningstar, assets in stock and bond mutual funds specializing in emerging markets grew from $1.2 billion in 1992 to $9.2 billion in 1993.
- At the start of 1994 there were 39 emerging market funds in the United States versus 21 a year earlier; 39 more were waiting for Securities and Exchange Commission approval.

Source: John Waggoner, "Foreign Stock Funds Hot, but Risky," *USA Today,* January 5, 1994, p. B1, and Eric D. Randall, "International Funds Leap Forward," *USA Today,* January 5, 1994, p. 5B. Copyright © 1994, USA TODAY. Reprinted with permission.

the globalization of investment is the interdependence it has created between financial markets in different countries. An interpretation of the circumstances surrounding the "Black Monday" stock-market crash of October 1987 illustrates this interdependence. The U.S. dollar had declined substantially in value in the two years preceding the crash, but the U.S. trade deficit had stubbornly refused to show any

FIGURE 1.3. International Investment Position of the United States
In the mid-1980s the United States switched from being an international net creditor nation to an international net debtor. (*Source: Survey of Current Business,* U.S. Department of Commerce, Office of Business Economics, June 1985 and June 1993.)

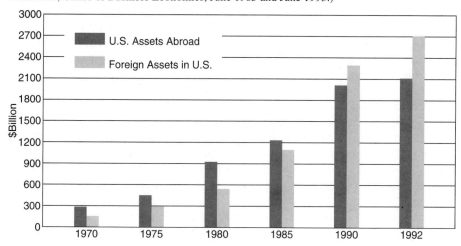

improvement. Indeed, the U.S. trade balance had worsened even while the dollar declined. It is believed by many economists that people were worried that, in anticipation of a further decline in the value of the dollar, foreign investors might sell the large volume of U.S. stocks and bonds they had accumulated; this large volume of U.S. stocks and bonds held abroad was itself a result of the globalization of investment. While other explanations of the crash are plausible, one view is that the release of the U.S. balance-of-trade statistics in the week before Monday, October 19, 1987, which were far worse than expected, turned market fear into panic. Furthermore, few would argue with the view that the globalization of investment contributed to the worldwide panic selling.

The globalization of investment has not only meant foreign exchange risk that has been exacerbated by the resulting increased interdependence; the increase in ownership of foreign assets has also meant that investors face increased country risk. As we have already mentioned, country risk involves the possibility of expropriation or confiscation of property, or its destruction by war or revolution. It also involves the possibility of changes in taxes on foreign income or the imposition of restrictions on repatriating income from abroad. As in the case of foreign exchange risk, this book is devoted to showing how practices and institutions have evolved to help reduce country risk.

Increased Volatility of Exchange Rates

The more rapid growth of international trade versus domestic trade and the expanded international focus of investment that we have documented offer more-than-adequate reason why it is increasingly important for students of business to study international finance. There is, however, an additional reason why knowledge of this exciting discipline has become imperative.

Exchange-rate risk has risen even more than the amount of foreign trade and overseas investment, because exchange rates have become increasingly volatile. This volatility has been so substantial that at times the plight of the dollar or the soaring or sinking value of some other major currency has become headline material even outside of the business press. Prompted at times by tensions in Russia, the Middle East, or some other politically sensitive part of the world, and at other times by news on the economic health or malaise of some major country, exchange rates have jumped and dropped by startling amounts. Billions of dollars—and yen, marks, pounds, and francs—are made and lost in a day as a result of these currency swings. Never before have exchange rates darted around as much as they have in recent years, and therefore never before has exchange-rate risk been so important.

Table 1.4 reveals the increased volatility in exchange rates that occurred during the postwar period. The volatility is measured by computing the standard deviation of month-to-month exchange rates and dividing by the mean to allow comparison. This statistic is called the **coefficient of variation.** The table shows how exchange-rate volatility has generally risen and how much more risk is consequently faced even on a constant amount of international trade and investment. If we add to the higher volatility the fact that international trade and investment are both far more important than they used to be, we can see why it has become so essential to understand the nature of exchange-rate risk and how to manage it.

There is no consensus as to why exchange rates have become more volatile than

TABLE 1.4. The Volatility of Exchange Rates

Period	Volatility, %			
	Can$	UK£	DM	Jap ¥
1950–1959	4	0*	0*	0*
1960–1969	4	8	8	0*
1970–1979	6	13	22	15
1980–1989	5	14	22	34
1990–1993	5	7	9	21

*Less than 0.5 percent.
Source: Standard deviation of month-end-to-month-end exchange rates as published in *International Financial Statistics,* divided by the mean exchange rate over the period 1950–1993. (*International Financial Statistics,* International Monetary Fund, Washington, D.C.)

in the past. Some analysts attribute the increased volatility to **flexible exchange rates**, which were adopted around 1973. However, others say the previous **fixed-exchange-rate** system could not have coped with the larger shocks that have occurred since that time—jumps and drops in oil prices, international conflicts, and so on. What is fairly certain is that the increased globalization of investment played a role by being associated with more **hot money** skipping from financial center to financial center in search of the highest return. Another factor may have been the technology for moving money and transmitting information, which has allowed both to move at the speed of light. Whatever the reason, a consequence of the greatly increased exchange-rate volatility has been a parallel increase in the importance of understanding the methods of managing foreign-exchange risk, as well as the other topics covered in this book.

Increased Importance of Multinational Corporations and Transnational Alliances

In addition to the growth of international trade, investment flows, and the riskiness of international trade and investment due to country risk and increased volatility of exchange rates, interest in international finance has grown with the increased importance of **multinational corporations (MNCs).** While the multinationalization of business is no easier to measure than the globalization of financial markets, corporate investment across borders, which is the essence of corporations' becoming multinational, grew 4 times faster than global output and 3 times faster than international trade between 1983 and 1990.[7] By 1993, the United Nations estimated that there were 35,000 multinational corporations, with the largest 100 of these possibly being responsible for $3.1 trillion, or approximately 16 percent, of the world's productive assets.[8] The power held by these massive, stateless enterprises has long been a source of governmental and public concern. The fear has been that by extending their activity they could influence governments and exploit workers and consumers, especially in smaller nations that might control fewer resources than the corpora-

[7]See "Multinationals: A Survey" in *The Economist,* March 27, 1993, p. 5.
[8]*Ibid.,* p. 6.

tions themselves. Indeed, concern over the extension of control by foreign multinationals has been voiced even in the world's largest economy, the United States, where the number of foreign-affiliate operations increased from 2999 in 1977 to 6857 in 1990, an increase of 129 percent, while in the same period total employment at these affiliates increased by 4 million, or 289 percent.[9]

Concern has also been expressed about the dominance of multinationals in international trade. For example, according to the U.S. Bureau of Economic Analysis, U.S.-based multinationals were associated with 80 percent of U.S. exports and 40 percent of imports.[10] Because of the importance of this issue, we shall discuss why multinationals have grown in relative importance and whether there really is any reason for concern. This is done in Chapter 20. We shall also discuss **transnational alliances**, which consist of separately owned corporations in different countries working in cooperation (to be distinguished from multinational corporations, which are commonly owned business operations in different countries). Let us briefly review how the discussion of multinationals and transnationals fits with the other topics in this book before we begin our exploration of the exciting and dynamic world of international finance.

TOPICS COVERED IN THIS BOOK

Part One, consisting of Chapters 2, 3, and 4, describes the organization of the foreign exchange markets. An introduction to the structure of the markets and the form in which currencies are exchanged is essential background to the study of international financial management. Chapter 2 explains the nature of the bank-note market and bank-draft market, the former involving the paper currency in our wallets and the latter involving checks. The chapter shows, for example, that the ability to choose direct or indirect exchange between currencies allows us to compute all exchange rates from exchange rates versus the U.S. dollar. Transaction costs are shown to cloud the link between currencies. Chapter 3 turns to the so-called "forward exchange market" and explains how it works. This is the market in which it is possible to contract for future sale or purchase of a foreign currency so as to avoid being affected by unanticipated changes in exchange rates. Chapter 4 introduces two other instruments for reducing exchange-rate risk, namely, currency futures and options. We explain their similarities and differences as well as the organization of the markets in which these "derivative" instruments trade.

Part Two, consisting of Chapters 5 through 9, examines the determination of exchange rates. The purpose of these chapters is to give the reader a solid understanding of the factors which can make exchange rates move up and down in various international financial systems. Such an understanding is essential for successful financial management in the international environment. Chapter 5 looks at the structure and meaning of the balance-of-payments account, where the factors behind the supply of and demand for a country's currency are recorded. Indeed, the balance-of-payments account is viewed as a record of the causes of the supply of and demand

---

[9]*Chicago Fed Letter,* The Federal Reserve Bank of Chicago, October 1993.
[10]See F. Steb Hipple, "The Measurement of International Trade Related to Multinational Companies," *The American Economic Review,* December 1990, pp. 1263–1270.

for a currency. Chapter 6 examines the supply and demand curves for currencies and the nature of the equilibrium they determine. It also shows that there is a real possibility that the exchange-rate equilibrium is unstable. This possibility is related to a phenomenon known as the J curve, whereby changes in exchange rates have unexpected effects. For example, a depreciating currency—a currency with a falling foreign exchange value—can actually make the balance of trade worse. (Normally, one would think depreciation would help a country's trade balance.)

Chapter 7 considers several new theories of exchange rates when exchange rates are flexible, while Chapter 8 describes a variety of international financial systems based on fixed exchange rates—rates set and maintained by governments. The discussion of fixed rates involves accounts of the now-defunct gold standard, the Bretton Woods standard, target zones, and the European Monetary System. This leads us into a discussion of the automatic adjustment mechanisms which help to correct payments imbalances between countries, especially those involving prices. While it is less important to study fixed exchange rates today than when exchange rates were formally fixed, we should pay some attention to issues concerning fixed exchange rates, both because the international financial system has moved away from complete flexibility in exchange rates since 1985 and because fixed rates still exist in a number of countries. Furthermore, the international financial system could well return to fixed exchange rates.

Chapter 9 looks at the historical events which have shaped the international financial system and at the problems the system faces today. In the course of considering the possible future evolution of the international financial system, we consider the pros and cons of fixed and flexible exchange rates and discuss the international financial institutions charged with charting the course through trade imbalances, mounting debts, and fundamental shifts in global economic power.

The discussion of exchange-rate determination in Part Two is self-contained and can be covered at any point in the study guided by this book. However, the most appropriate place for this segment is in the position it appears, that is, after introducing the foreign exchange markets and before describing the fundamental parity conditions that underpin international finance. The material in Part Two can be used in full or in part, depending on the extent to which the course covers the financial markets and the environment of multinational business. Chapter 7 contains material which might be heavy going for students without an intermediate-level background in economics. However, omission of this chapter does not affect the students' ability to comprehend the remainder of the book.

Part Three, consisting of Chapters 10 and 11, introduces two central principles of international finance, the purchasing-power parity (PPP) principle and the covered interest parity principle. The PPP principle states that exchange rates reflect the relative local currency prices of products in different countries, and that changes in exchange rates reflect differences in countries' inflation rates; countries with relatively rapid inflation should have depreciating currencies, and vice versa. Chapter 10 examines both the theory behind the PPP condition and its empirical validity. Chapter 11 is devoted to the covered interest parity condition. This condition says that when exchange-rate risk is avoided by using forward exchange contracts, investment yields and borrowing costs are the same in different currencies. If there really were no differences in investment yields and borrowing costs between currencies, it would not matter how or where investment or borrowing occurred. However, there *are* differences in yields and costs, and the reasons they exist are explained in Chapter 11. It is important that we understand why these yield and borrowing-cost differences exist, because they have implications for international cash management. Indeed, in the course of explaining why yield and borrowing-cost differences exist, we show how to decide on where to invest and borrow in the international context.

Part Four, consisting of Chapters 12 through 16, considers the nature of foreign exchange risk and exposure and how exposure may be hedged by the use of forward, futures, and options contracts, as well as by borrowing or investing in the money market via so-called "swaps." Chapter 12 is concerned with the definition and measurement of foreign exchange exposure, which is the amount which is at risk to changes in exchange rates. Different types of exposure and the factors determining the size of each type of exposure are described. In addition, exchange-rate *exposure* is carefully distinguished from exchange-rate *risk*. Because the accounting conventions that are used can affect exposure as it appears in financial statements, Chapter 13 examines accounting procedures for international transactions. This chapter also explains the concept of real changes in exchange rates and its relation to exposure.

Most discussions of the effects of exchange rates emphasize the gains or losses on assets or liabilities, not the effects on the ongoing profitability of a firm's operations. Chapter 14 deals with the underdiscussed area of operating exposure by applying the standard tools of microeconomics to discover the factors affecting how product prices, sales, production costs, and profits of exporters and importers are affected by unexpected changes in exchange rates.

Chapter 15 then deals with the important question of whether managers should take steps to reduce a firm's exposure to risk from unanticipated changes in exchange rates, or whether managers should leave hedging to individual shareholders. The consequences of different hedging techniques are described and compared. These include forward, futures, and options contracts, as well as swaps. A simple graphical technique known as financial engineering is used to compare the consequences of using the different hedging techniques.

Chapter 16 considers the extent to which foreign exchange markets reflect available information, as well as the closely connected question of whether it is possible to profit from speculation. This leads into a discussion of exchange-rate forecasting and the record of attempts to forecast exchange rates and to profit from such forecasts.

Part Five examines international investment and financing. Chapter 17 includes a discussion of short-term cash management and explains why a multinational corporation might want to centralize the management of its working capital. The chapter shows that the same factors causing differences in investment yields and borrowing costs between currencies (described in Chapter 11) are the factors which must be considered in cash management. Chapter 18 deals with portfolio investment and explains how investors can choose between investments in different countries' stock and bond markets. Attention is paid to the benefits of an internationally diversified portfolio of securities. The chapter shows that because economic conditions do not move in a perfectly parallel fashion in different countries, it pays to diversify internationally. The theory and evidence on whether securities are priced in an internationally integrated or a segmented market setting are examined within the context of the capital asset pricing model.

Chapters 19 and 20 focus on direct investment, which is what occurs when, for example, a company builds a manufacturing plant in another country. Chapter 19 shows how to evaluate foreign direct investments, including the **discount rate** and tax rate to employ, the way to handle concessionary financing, restrictions on repatriating income, and so on. Chapter 20 looks at the factors behind the growth of the giant multinational corporations (MNCs), which have been the result of **foreign direct investment**. It also considers problems caused by the growth of MNCs, and how costs and earnings can be allocated among divisions of an MNC by internal transfer prices for items exchanged between corporate divisions. Since a primary concern of MNCs is the country risk of foreign facilities being seized and of taxes being imposed on repatriated earnings, Chapter 20 looks at the measurement of and avoidance of country risk. Associations between corporations in different countries, forming so-called transnational corporations, are one such means of reducing country risk, and so transnational corporations are also discussed in Chapter 20.

Chapter 21 is concerned with the financing of overseas investment. The chapter covers equities, bonds, bank and government lending, and the choices between them that result in alternative possible financial structures, including the question of whether overseas subsidiaries should follow the financing practices of the parent company or those of the overseas destination of investment.

Part Six considers the institutional structure of international trade and finance. We begin with a discussion of the important role played by commercial banks. Today, large commercial banks offer deposits and make loans in a variety of currencies other than the currency of the country in which they are located. Such deposits and loans are called offshore currencies, of which Eurodollars are the best-known example. Chapter 22 explains why the offshore-currency market has developed and how it works. This leads naturally into a discussion of international banking. We explain the organizational structure of international banking, including the reasons why banks are among the largest multinational corporations that exist, often having an office or other presence in a hundred or more countries.

As well as covering trade financing, Chapter 23 looks at the practical side of exporting and importing. It describes the documents that are involved in international trade, the methods of insuring trade, and so on. Among the matters discussed are letters of credit and bills of exchange. Because a substantial part of international trade takes a special form known as countertrade, an account is also given of the nature of and possible reasons for this practice.

The preceding overview of the contents of this book, along with the earlier parts of this chapter, indicate the broad range of increasingly important issues addressed in this most globalized of all subject areas of business, international finance. Having sketched the main features of the world we are to explore, let us begin our journey with a tour of the fascinating markets for foreign exchange.

SUMMARY

1. Every good or service reaching us from abroad has involved international finance. Knowledge of the subject can help managers avoid harmful effects of international events and perhaps even profit from these events.

2. International trade has grown more quickly than trade in general. This has brought both rewards and costs.

3. The principal reward for international trade is the gain in standard of living it has permitted. This gain comes from exploiting relative efficiencies of production in different countries.

4. The costs of international trade are the introduction of exchange-rate risk and country risk. Methods and markets have evolved that allow firms to avoid or reduce these risks, and since international trade has become more important it has become more important to learn about these methods and markets.

5. International finance has also become a more important subject because of an increased globalization of financial markets. The benefits of the increased flow of capital between nations include a better international allocation of capital and greater opportunities to diversify risk. However, globalization of investment has meant new risks from exchange rates, political actions, and increased interdependence of financial conditions in different countries.

6. Adding to the increase in relevance of exchange-rate risk from the growth in international trade and the globalization of financial markets has been an increase in the volatility of exchange rates and a growth in importance of multinational and transnational corporations. All these factors combine to make it imperative that today's student of business study the factors behind the risks of international trade and investment, and the methods of reducing these risks.

REVIEW QUESTIONS

1. In what ways has the importance of trade to most countries grown in recent decades?
2. Why has international trade grown more rapidly than domestic trade?
3. What is a comparative advantage?
4. What helps provide a competitive advantage?
5. What is country risk?
6. What does it mean to "hedge"?
7. What are the principal benefits of international investment?
8. What are the principal costs of international investment?
9. What is "hot money"?
10. What is the difference between a multinational corporation and a transnational corporation?

ASSIGNMENT PROBLEMS

1. In what ways might the following be affected by sudden, unexpected changes in exchange rates?
   a. An American holder of U.S. Treasury bonds
   b. An American holder of GM stock
   c. An American on vacation in Mexico
   d. An American holder of Honda stock
   e. A Canadian on vacation in the United States
2. What is meant by a shrinkage of "economic space"?
3. What are the possible implications of the increasing regionalization of international trade?
4. What may be behind the success of a particular industry in international trade?
5. Why have some governments been concerned with the growing importance of multinational corporations?

ALIBER, ROBERT Z., and REID W. CLICK: *Readings in International Business,* MIT Press, Cambridge, Mass., 1993.

BRANDER, JAMES A.: "Comparative Economic Growth: Evidence and Interpretation," *Canadian Journal of Economics,* November 1992, pp. 792–818.

EVANS, JOHN S.: *International Finance: A Markets Approach,* Dryden Press, Fort Worth, 1992.

HARRIS, RICHARD G.: "Globalization, Trade and Income," *Canadian Journal of Economics,* November 1993, pp. 755–776.

KRUGMAN, PAUL R.: *Currencies and Crises,* MIT Press, Cambridge, Mass., 1991.

———: *Geography and Trade,* MIT Press, Cambridge, Mass., 1991.

———: *Rethinking International Trade,* MIT Press, Cambridge, Mass., 1990.

——— and MAURICE OBSTFELD: *International Economics: Theory and Policy,* HarperCollins, New York, 1991.

OHMAE, KENICHI: *The Borderless World: Power and Strategy in the Interlinked Economy,* HarperCollins, New York, 1990.

PILBEAM, KEITH: *International Finance,* Macmillan, Basingstoke, U.K., 1992.

PORTER, MICHAEL E.: *The Competitive Advantage of Nations,* Harvard University Press, Cambridge, Mass., 1989.

REICH, ROBERT B.: *The Work of Nations: Preparing Ourselves for the Twenty-First Century,* Alfred A. Knopf, New York, 1991.

The Economist: "Multinationals: A Survey," March 27, 1993.

VERNON, RAYMOND, and LOUIS WELLS, JR.: *Manager in the International Economy,* 5th ed., Prentice-Hall, Englewood Cliffs, N.J., 1986.

Parallel Material for Case Courses

CARLSON, ROBERT S., H. LEE REMMERS, CHRISTINE R. HEKMAN, DAVID K. EITEMAN, and ARTHUR STONEHILL: *International Finance: Cases and Simulation,* Addison-Wesley, Reading, Mass., 1980.

DUFEY, GUNTER, and IAN H. GIDDY: *Cases in International Finance,* 2d ed., Addison-Wesley, Reading, Mass., 1993.

FEIGER, GEORGE, and BERTRAND JACQUILLAT: *International Finance: Text and Cases,* Allyn and Bacon, Boston, 1982.

PONIACHEK, HARVEY A.: *Cases in International Finance,* Wiley, New York, 1993.

RUKSTAD, MICHAEL G.: *Corporate Decision Making in the World Economy,* Dryden, Fort Worth, 1992.

APPENDIX 1.1
The Gains from Trade in Goods and Services:
The Principle of Comparative Advantage

Comparative advantage is not one of the most intuitive concepts in economics, and it can require a little extra thought by the reader to achieve an understanding of why countries gain from exploiting their comparative advantages. Discovered by the English stockbroker-millionaire David Ricardo, the concept of comparative advantage can help answer questions such as the following:

> Suppose that Japan is much more efficient than the United States in producing steel and marginally more efficient than the United States in producing food, and that steel and food are the only items produced and required in both countries. Would both countries be better off by having free trade between them than by prohibiting trade?

When faced with this question, it is not uncommon to hear people say that while Japan would be better off from free trade because it is more efficient at producing both products, the United States would be worse off. The reasoning behind this view is the presumption that Japan would be able to undercut U.S. prices for both products and thereby put Americans out of work. What the principle of comparative advantage shows is that in fact *both* countries are better off from free trade than no trade, and that it is *relative* efficiencies rather than *absolute* efficiencies of production that determine the pattern and benefits of trade. These relative efficiencies of production are referred to as "comparative advantages." Let us explain and clarify this important principle of comparative advantage by giving an example.

Suppose that the amounts of labor needed to produce a ton of steel and food in the United States and Japan with the given stock of land and capital with which the labor can work are as shown on the top of Table 1A.1. These numbers assume that Japan can produce

TABLE 1A.1. The Situation with No International Trade

Output	United States	Japan
NUMBER OF PEOPLE EMPLOYED PER TON OF OUTPUT		
Food	25	20
Steel	10	4
OPPORTUNITY COST PER TON OF OUTPUT		
Food	2.5 tons steel	5.0 tons steel
Steel	0.4 tons food	0.2 tons food
MILLIONS OF PEOPLE EMPLOYED		
Food	75	40
Steel	75	40
OUTPUTS, MILLIONS OF TONS		
Food	3	2
Steel	7.5	10

both products with less labor than the United States, which means that Japan has an **absolute advantage** in both products.

If the United States were to produce one more ton of food by moving labor from producing steel, the forgone output of steel—that is, the opportunity cost of food in terms of steel—would be 2.5 tons of steel.[11] On the other hand, if the United States were to produce one more ton of steel by moving labor from producing food, the opportunity cost would be 0.4 tons of food. Similarly, in Japan the opportunity cost of one more ton of food is 5.0 tons of steel, and the opportunity cost of one more ton of steel is 0.2 tons of food. These numbers are shown in Table 1A.1. We see that the United States has a lower opportunity cost for producing food, while Japan has a lower opportunity cost for producing steel. These relative opportunity costs are the basis of the definition of comparative advantage.

A comparative advantage in a particular product is said to exist if, in producing more of that product, a country has a lower opportunity cost in terms of alternative products than the opportunity cost of that product in other countries. Table 1A.1 shows that the United States has a comparative advantage in food and Japan has a comparative advantage in steel. It should be clear that as long as relative efficiencies differ, every country has some comparative advantage. This is the case even if a country has an absolute disadvantage in everything. What we will demonstrate next is that by producing the good for which the country has a comparative advantage (lower opportunity cost) and trading it for the products for which other countries have a comparative advantage (lower opportunity cost), *everybody* is better off.

Table 1A.1 shows the number of workers (available labor power) in the United States and Japan. The table also gives the outputs of food and steel in each country, assuming half of the working population in each country is employed in each industry. For example, 75 million Americans can produce 3 million tons of food when 25 workers are required per ton, and the other 75 million who work can produce 7.5 million tons of steel. In this example, the total world output of food is 5 million tons, and the total world output of steel is 17.5 million tons.

Suppose now that 28 million Japanese workers are shifted from agriculture to steel, while at the same time 50 million American workers are shifted from steel to agriculture. The effect of this on the outputs of both countries is shown in Table 1A.2. We find that with Japan emphasizing steel production and with the United States emphasizing food, the outputs for the two countries combined are 5.6 million tons of food and 19.5 million tons of steel. The combined outputs of both items have increased by 10 percent or more merely by having Japan concentrate on its comparative advantage, steel, and the United States concentrate on its comparative advantage, food.

The United States and Japan can both be richer if they trade certain amounts between themselves. One such trading division would be for the United States to sell to Japan 1.8 million tons of food and to buy from Japan 5.5 million tons of steel, giving a **terms of trade** of approximately 0.3 tons of food per ton of steel. The United States and Japan would then end up consuming the amounts shown in the bottom rows of Table 1A.2, all of which exceed what they could consume without trade as shown in Table 1A.1.

The gains shown by comparing Table 1A.2 with Table 1A.1 are due to specializing production according to the countries' comparative advantages. The benefit of specializing production is only one of the gains from trade.

FURTHER GAINS FROM INTERNATIONAL TRADE

Given our assumption that Japan is relatively more efficient in producing steel than food and the United States is relatively more efficient in producing food than steel, under autarky

---

[11]Of course, it is individuals, not nations, that make production decisions. However, referring to countries as if they make production decisions is a convenient anthropomorphism.

TABLE 1A.2. Input/Output under Free Trade

Output	United States	Japan
MILLIONS OF PEOPLE EMPLOYED		
Food	125	12
Steel	25	68
TOTAL OUTPUT, MILLIONS OF TONS		
Food	5	0.6
Steel	2.5	17
CONSUMPTION AMOUNTS UNDER TRADING DIVISION		
Food	3.2	2.4
Steel	8	11.5

we can expect food to be cheap relative to steel in the United States, and steel to be cheap relative to food in Japan. This suggests that by exporting food to Japan, where food is relatively expensive in the absence of trade, the United States can receive a relatively large amount of steel in return. Similarly, by exporting steel to the United States, where steel is relatively expensive in the absence of trade, Japan can receive a relatively large amount of food. Therefore, via exchange of products through trade, both countries can be better off. The gain is a **pure exchange gain** and would be enjoyed even without any specialization of production. That is, there are two components to the gains from trade: the gain from adjusting the pattern of production (the gain from specialization) and the gain from adjusting the pattern of consumption (the pure exchange gain).[12]

The number of people required to produce the food and steel in our example is assumed to be the same whatever the output of these products. That is, we have implicitly assumed **constant returns to scale**. However, if there are **increasing returns to scale** it will take fewer people to produce a given quantity of the product for which the country has a comparative advantage as more of that product is produced. In this case of economies of scale there are yet further gains from international trade. Returns to scale can come in many forms, including pure technological gains, benefits of learning by doing, and so on. In addition, if there is monopoly power within a country and that monopoly power is removed by trade, consumers enjoy an additional benefit in terms of lower prices due to increased competition.[13] Yet a further gain from trade comes in the form of an increase in product variety. In addition, international trade can make a broader range of inputs and technology available and thereby increase economic growth.[14] Therefore, the gain from exploiting comparative advantages is only part of the total gain from free trade.[15]

[12]The pure exchange gain that comes from adjusting consumption cannot be shown in terms of our numerical example because demonstration of this gain requires measurement of relative satisfaction from the two products. This in turn requires the use of utility theory. Formal separation of the specialization gain from the pure exchange gain is best left to courses in the pure theory of international trade.
[13]For evidence on this effect of trade, see James Levinsohn, "Testing the Imports-as-Market-Discipline Hypothesis," National Bureau of Economic Research, Working Paper No. 3657, 1991.
[14]See Gene M. Grossman and Elhanan Helpman, "Product Development and International Trade," National Bureau of Economic Research, Working Paper No. 2540, March 1988, and "Growth and Welfare in a Small Open Economy," National Bureau of Economic Research, Working Paper No. 2970, May 1989. For an alternative view see Meir G. Kohn and Nancy P. Marion, "The Implications of

SOME COSTS OF INTERNATIONAL TRADE

While the numerous benefits of international trade are believed by most economists to exceed the costs of trade, there are possible costs to be weighed against the gains. These costs are in addition to the risks individual enterprises face, which are described in the text of this chapter.

One possible cost of free international trade occurs when a country finds its own firms put out of business and thereby exposes itself to exploitation by a foreign monopoly. This is the flip side of the gain from competition described above, and it is likely to occur only in oligopolistic markets with very few players.[16] For example, it has been argued that it can be advantageous to protect aircraft production in Europe so as to reduce prices faced on imported aircraft.[17] Another possible drawback of trade is the reduction in economic diversity a country might face. This is the flip side of the gain from specialization. Finally, some people have decried international trade because of the homogenization of culture and possible political domination it has brought to the planet, while others have questioned trade because of possible impacts on the global environment.[18] It is clear that as in most things in economics, there is no free lunch: trade-offs always exist.

Knowledge-Based Growth for the Optimality of Open Capital Markets," National Bureau of Economic Research, Working Paper No. 2487, January 1988.

[15]An account of the numerous sources of gains from trade can be found in Cletus C. Coughlin, K. Alec Chrystal, and Geoffrey E. Wood, "Protectionist Trade Policies: A Survey of Theory, Evidence and Rationale," *Review,* Federal Reserve Bank of St. Louis, January/February 1988, pp. 12–26.

[16]See Elhanan Helpman and Paul R. Krugman, *Trade Policy and Market Structure,* MIT Press, Cambridge, Mass., 1989.

[17]See James A. Brander and Barbara Spencer, "Export Subsidies and International Market Share Rivalry," *Journal of International Economics,* February 1985, pp. 83–100.

[18]For a discussion of the effects on culture and political domination see J. J. Servain-Schreiber, *The American Challenge,* Hamish Hamilton, London, 1968. For the connection between trade and the environment see Alison Butler, "Environmental Protection and Free Trade: Are They Mutually Exclusive?" *Review,* Federal Reserve Bank of St. Louis, May/June 1992, pp. 3–16.

APPENDIX 1.2
The Gains from the International Flow of Capital

In the previous appendix we showed that everybody can simultaneously benefit from international trade in goods and services. In this appendix we show that everybody can also simultaneously gain from the international flow of financial capital. Between them, the international flow of goods and services and the international flow of capital constitute the sum total of reasons for the supply of and demand for foreign exchange. Indeed, as we shall show in Chapter 5, the two major subdivisions of the balance-of-payments accounts—the current account and the capital account—report, respectively, the demand for and supply of a country's currency due to trade in goods and services, and the supply of and demand for the currency due to the flow of capital. Therefore, what this and the previous appendix do is show that the very bases of the study of international finance—the flow of goods and services and the flow of capital—are both important contributors to our well-being. It is not, as is often thought, just the international flow of goods and services from which we benefit.

We have already noted in the text of this chapter that the international flow of capital means that a project with a very high yield in one country is not forgone for want of funds while a low-yield project in a country of abundant capital goes ahead. This flow of capital benefits everybody because the investors in the country with the low-yield project can enjoy some of the high return offered in the other country, while the country with the high-yield project gets to fund what might otherwise be postponed or forgone. This is potentially a very important gain from the international flow of capital and is illustrated graphically in Figure 1A.1.

The heights of the curves I_A and I_B in Figure 1A.1 gives the rates of return on investment in countries A and B at different rates of investment. The curves slope downward because countries run out of good investment projects as their rates of investment increase.[19] The curves labeled S_A and S_B give the amounts saved at different rates of return on savings. If there is no flow of capital between countries, the equilibrium returns in A and B are r_A^0 and r_B^0.

The first dollar to flow from A to B means a forgone investment return in A of r_A^0 for a return in B of r_B^0. This is a net gain of $r_B^0 - r_A^0$. After *CD* dollars of capital have moved from A to B, an extra dollar of capital flow produces a net gain of $r_B^1 - r_A^1$. It should be clear from the figure that there is a global gain in return from investment until enough capital has moved to equalize returns in the two countries. Indeed, if the interest rate in countries A and B is r_E, where by assumption the excess of investment over saving in B matches the excess of savings over investment in A, then the gain from a better capital flow is at a maximum. This maximum gain can be shown in the figure by recognizing that the *total* return from investment can be measured from the area under the investment curve for that amount of investment. For example, the return on the investment between *C* and *E* on the right-hand side of Figure 1A.1 is the shaded area: each *incremental* dollar of investment has a return given by the height of the investment curve, so adding all incremental gains between *C* and *E* gives the area beneath the curve. Against the return in B from imported capital is the forgone return in A from which capital is being exported. This lost return is given by the area beneath I_A between *C* and *E* on the left-hand side of Figure 1A.1. The difference between the two areas is at a maximum at interest rate r_E.[20]

[19]The height of I_A or I_B is referred to as the **marginal efficiency of investment.**
[20]This is not the place to describe the distribution of the benefits from the international flow of capital between savers in the two countries. However, by representing interest receipts and payments as areas in Figure 1A.1, and comparing these to project returns, it can be shown that *both* countries gain from the flow of capital.

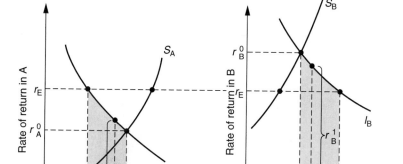

FIGURE 1A.1. The Gain from the Better Allocation of Capital
The heights of the curves I_A and I_B give the rates of return on an extra dollar's
worth of investment in countries A and B. The curves S_A and S_B give savings at
different returns on savings in the two countries. With no flow of capital
between the countries, returns will be r_A^0 and r_B^0. Each dollar moving from A to
B will result in a forgone return in A given by the height of I_A, and a return in B
given by the height of I_B. For example, after CD dollars have left A for B, the
added global return from *another* dollar is $r_B^1 - r_A^1$. The maximum gain from
reallocating capital occurs at r_E and is given by the difference between the two
shaded areas; the shaded area in B is the *total* return on investment between C
and E, while the shaded area in A is the forgone *total* return on investment
between C and E.

There is a further benefit of the international flow of capital that comes from the smoothing of consumption that is permitted by lending and borrowing. This gain comes from the
fact that if a nation were unable to borrow from abroad it would have limited scope to maintain consumption during temporary declines in national income.[21] Similarly, if the nation
were unable to invest abroad, it would have limited scope for dampening temporary jumps in
consumption during surges in national income.

It is frequently assumed that people are subject to diminishing marginal utility of income
and consumption. Indeed, this is a basic rationale for the postulate of risk aversion, which is
essential to much of the theory of finance. Diminishing marginal utility of consumption
means that a more even path of consumption over time is preferred to a more erratic path
with the same average level of consumption. The reason for this preference for a smooth
path of consumption over time is illustrated in Figure 1A.2.

The curve labeled TU shows the total utility derived from different rates of consumption. Because the curve slopes upward throughout its range, it shows that higher levels of

---

[21]National income, which is roughly equivalent to the gross national product and is usually denoted by
Y, can be classified into consumption C, investment I, government spending G, and exports minus
imports $(Ex - Im)$. This classification is met frequently in macroeconomics as the national income identity, $Y \equiv C + I + G + (Ex - Im)$. We see that for a decline in Y not to involve a decline in consumption it
would be necessary to suffer a decline in investment, government spending, or exports minus imports.
All these alternatives involve costs.

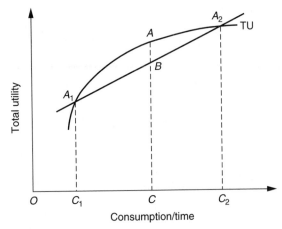

FIGURE 1A.2. Utility from Different Consumption Patterns

If a country faces variable consumption, being with equal frequency C_1 and C_2, the average total utility level that it enjoys is distance BC. This is the average of distances A_1C_1 and A_2C_2. If the country borrows from abroad during bad times and lends abroad during good times, and thereby enjoys consumption at C every period, it enjoys a utility level given by distance AC. The gain from smoothing consumption via borrowing from abroad and lending abroad is distance AB. This is a gain from the international flow of capital.

consumption are preferred to lower levels; that is, total utility from consumption increases as consumption increases. However, the rate at which total utility increases with consumption diminishes as consumption expands. This is revealed by the lower slope of curve TU as consumption increases, that is, as we move to the right along TU. The slope of TU gives the increase in total utility per unit of added consumption and is called the **marginal utility**.[22]

If a nation is forced to vary consumption from year to year because it cannot borrow and invest internationally and prefers not to vary other components of its national product, it may find itself consuming C_1 in one year when national income experiences a decline, and C_2 in the following year when national income experiences a favorable fluctuation. The total utility from consumption of C_1 is given by the distance A_1C_1, while the total utility from C_2 is given by A_2C_2. The average of A_1C_1 and A_2C_2, which is the average utility enjoyed in the 2 years, can be found by drawing a straight line between A_1 and A_2 and finding the height of this line at its center. This follows because the height of the line halfway between A_1 and A_2 is the average of A_1C_1 and A_2C_2. We find that the average utility from the 2 years of variable consumption is BC.

If the nation can borrow it might borrow the amount of C_1C during the economic down-

---

[22]Most introductory finance textbooks deal with the notion of diminishing marginal utility of consumption and its role in risk aversion. See, for example, Richard Brealey and Stewart Myers, *Principles of Corporate Finance,* 3d ed., McGraw-Hill, New York, 1988.

turn, allowing it to consume *OC*. The nation might then lend amount CC_2 during the upturn and therefore also consume amount *OC* during this time.[23] With consumption of *OC* in both periods and with total utility given by the distance *AC* in both periods, the average total utility is simply *AC*. It is immediately clear by inspecting Figure 1A.2 that the utility when consumption is smoothed by international borrowing and lending is higher than when borrowing and lending does not occur. Intuitively, this outcome is because the added or marginal utility of income during the period of higher consumption is smaller than the marginal utility lost during the period of lower consumption.

The empirical relevance of the preceding argument has been examined by Michael Brennan and Bruno Solnik.[24] They start by calculating what consumption would have been without international capital flows. This is determined by subtracting private capital flows from actual consumption during years when there was a net capital inflow to the country and by adding private capital flows to actual consumption during years of net capital outflow. This approach tells us what would have had to happen to consumption if borrowing and lending had not occurred.[25] All consumption data are put in per capita terms and adjusted for inflation.

Brennan and Solnik compute the standard deviations of the growth rates of consumption adjusted for capital flows and compare these with the standard deviations of the growth rates of actual consumption. This comparison is made for eight countries. They find that on average the standard deviations of actual consumption growth rates, which include international capital flows, are less than half the standard deviations of adjusted consumption growth rates, which exclude international capital flows. The reduction in standard deviation due to international capital flows is apparent in every country they examined and for all measures of capital flows they considered.[26]

Investment in new capital could, like consumption, be smoothed via international capital flows. The empirical evidence suggests, however, that relatively little investment smoothing occurs. This has been concluded from studies of the connection between saving and investment *within countries*. In completely integrated capital markets, a dollar increase in domestic saving would leave domestic investment unchanged and instead result in a dollar of exported capital. What has been shown, however, is that each dollar increase in domestic saving is, on average, associated with a 79-cent increase in net domestic investment.[27]

A gain from international capital flows that is closely related to the gains from consumption and investment smoothing is the gain from increased diversification of investment portfolios. This gain exists because the economic ups and downs in different countries are not

[23]Borrowing and lending involves paying and receiving interest. However, if the amount borrowed equals the amount subsequently lent, and if the periods are close together so that time value of money is unimportant, payments and receipts of interest cancel and thus can be ignored.
[24]See Michael J. Brennan and Bruno Solnik, "International Risk Sharing and Capital Mobility," *Journal of International Money and Finance,* September 1989, pp. 359–373.
[25]This assumes all borrowing and lending affects consumption and not the other components of national product. Of course, borrowing and lending do in reality affect government spending and investment. However, a smoother pattern of government spending and investment should contribute to smoother consumption. Furthermore, consumption is often considered as the end purpose of economic activity. This supports the case for concentrating on consumption.
[26]The implications of consumption smoothing for welfare are overstated in Brennan and Solnik, *op. cit.* See Maurice Obstfeld, "International Risk Sharing and Capital Mobility: Another Look," *Journal of International Money and Finance,* February 1992, pp. 115–121, and Michael J. Brennan and Bruno Solnik, "International Risk Sharing and Capital Mobility: Reply," *Journal of International Money and Finance,* February 1992, pp. 122–123.
[27]See Martin Feldstein and Phillippe Bachetta, "National Saving and International Investment," National Bureau of Economic Research, Working Paper No. 3164, 1990.

perfectly synchronized, allowing investors to achieve a higher expected return for a given degree of risk, or a lower risk for a given expected return. We do not discuss this here as it is discussed extensively in Chapter 18 of the text. However, it should be clear that diversification gains depend on different countries' having different economic conditions and experiences, which the other gains from the free movement of capital which we have described in this appendix depend on as well.

PART ONE

The Markets for Foreign Exchange

The foreign exchange market, which has several connected but nevertheless different parts, is the most active market on earth. Along with the size of the market come massive profits and losses of speculators and governments, as well as substantial income and employment in banks, currency brokerages, and specialized futures and options exchanges.

Part One introduces the reader to the different components of the foreign exchange market. Chapter 2 begins by considering the exchange of bank notes, such as the exchange of U.S. Federal Reserve notes ("greenbacks") for British pounds. Chapter 2 also explains how money in the form of bank deposits is exchanged via the interbank spot foreign exchange market. An understanding of what actually happens when a person calls a bank to buy a foreign currency requires that we know how customers are debited and credited, how the banks trade with each other, and how the banks settle transactions between themselves. This is all explained in Chapter 2. The chapter ends by showing why knowledge of exchange rates of each currency against the U.S. dollar allows us to calculate

all possible exchange rates. For example, it is shown why we can calculate the exchange rate between Deutschemarks and British pounds by using the Deutschemark–U.S.-dollar exchange rate and the British-pound–U.S.-dollar exchange rate. It is also shown why this ability to compute so-called "cross exchange rates" is nevertheless limited in reality by the presence of foreign exchange transaction costs.

Chapter 3 describes another component of the foreign exchange market, the forward exchange market, which plays an important role throughout the remainder of the book. Forward exchange involves a contractual arrangement to exchange currencies at an agreed exchange rate on some date in the future. The forward market plays an important role in the avoidance of foreign exchange risk (hedging) and in the selective taking of risk (speculating). Chapter 3 provides the necessary background so that we can show in later chapters how forward exchange can be used for hedging and speculating.

After explaining the forward market we turn our attention to currency derivatives which, as their name suggests, *derive* their values from underlying values of currencies. The two derivatives discussed in Chapter 4 are currency futures and currency options.* Currency futures are similar to forward exchange contracts in that they help fix exchange rates for future transactions. However, currency futures trade on formal exchanges such as the Chicago International Money Market, have only a limited number of value dates, come in particular contract sizes, and can be sold back to the exchange. There are also a few other institutional differences that we describe. These differences make forward contracts and currency futures of slightly different value as vehicles for hedging and speculation.

Chapter 4 also describes currency options. Unlike forward contracts and currency futures, options allow buyers discretion over whether to exercise (complete) an exchange of currencies. Different types of currency options are described, along with the factors which affect market prices, or premiums, on options. The advantages of using options versus futures and forwards when hedging and speculating are only briefly covered in Chapter 4; we save the details of using forwards, futures, and options for the chapters in which hedging and speculation are covered in greater depth. In Part One the purpose is primarily to introduce the reader to the institutional details of these fascinating and vital markets for foreign exchange.

---

*Forwards are also derivatives in that, as we shall see, their value depends on expected underlying future exchange rates. However, because forward contracts are themselves instruments for exchanging currencies, they differ in important respects from futures and options, which are bets on exchange rates.

CHAPTER 2

An Introduction to Exchange Rates

The market in international capital . . . is run by outlandishly well-paid specialists, back-room technicians and rows of computer screens. It deals in meaninglessly large sums of money. It seems to have little connection with the "real" world of factories and fast-food restaurants. Yet at times . . . it seems to hold the fate of economies in its grasp. The capital market is a mystery and it is a threat.

—*The Economist,* September 19, 1992

To the ordinary person, international finance is synonymous with exchange rates, and indeed, a large part of the study of international finance involves the study of exchange rates. What is not always known to those with a limited knowledge of international finance is the variety of exchange rates that exist at the same moment between the same two currencies. There are exchange rates for **bank notes,** which are, for example, the Federal Reserve notes with pictures of former U.S. presidents and the equivalent Bank of England notes displaying pictures of the Queen. There are also exchange rates between checks stating dollar amounts and those stating amounts in pounds or other currency units. Furthermore, the rates on these checks depend on whether they are issued by banks (as **bank drafts**) or by corporations, on the amounts they involve, and on the dates on the checks. Exchange rates also differ according to whether they are for the purchase or sale of a foreign currency. There is a difference, for example, between the number of U.S. dollars required to *purchase* a British pound and the number of U.S. dollars received when *selling* a pound.

We will begin by looking at exchange rates between bank notes. While the market for bank notes is only a small proportion of the overall foreign exchange market, it is a good place to begin because bank notes are the form of money with which people are most familiar.

THE FOREIGN BANK-NOTE MARKET

The earliest experience that many of us have of dealing with foreign currency is on our first overseas vacation. When not traveling abroad, most of us have very little to do with foreign exchange, which is not used in the course of ordinary commerce, especially in the United States. The foreign exchange with which we deal when on vacation involves bank notes and, quite frequently, foreign-currency-denominated traveler's checks. Table 2.1 gives the exchange rates on bank notes facing a traveler on February 18, 1994. Let us take a look at how these retail bank note rates are quoted.

The first numerical column of Table 2.1 gives exchange rates in terms of the number of units of each foreign currency that must be *paid to the bank* to buy a U.S. dollar. The column is headed "Bank buys foreign currency (sells U.S.$)" because when a bank buys foreign currency from a customer, it pays, or sells, the customer U.S. dollars. Table 2.1 shows, for example, that it takes 1.36 Canadian dollars (Can$1.36) or 0.69 British pounds (£0.69) to buy a U.S. dollar from the bank. The second numerical column gives the number of units of each foreign currency that a customer will *receive from the bank* for each U.S. dollar. For example, the traveler will receive Can$1.29 or £0.66 for each U.S. dollar.

The rates of exchange posted for travelers in bank and currency exchange windows or international tourist centers are the most expensive (unfavorable) that exist. They are expensive in the sense that the buying and selling prices on individual cur-

TABLE 2.1. Exchange Rates on Foreign Bank Notes
(Traveler's dollar—February 18, 1994)

	Foreign Currency per U.S. Dollar	
	Bank Buys Foreign Currency (Sells U.S.$)	Bank Sells Foreign Currency (Buys U.S.$)
Australia (dollar)	1.44	1.36
Austria (schilling)	12.50	11.50
Belgium (franc)	36.50	34.50
Britain (pound)	0.69	0.66
Canada (dollar)	1.36	1.29
China (renminbi)	8.95	8.40
Denmark (kroner)	7.05	6.60
Finland (markkaa)	5.85	5.50
France (franc)	6.22	5.85
Germany (mark)	1.75	1.65
Greece (drachma)	260.10	245.00
Hong Kong (dollar)	8.15	7.70
India (rupee)	33.10	31.30
Ireland (pound)	0.72	0.68
Israel (shekel)	3.10	2.90
Italy (lira)	1750.00	1650.00
Japan (yen)	108.50	102.50
Mexico (peso)	3.21	3.02
Netherlands (guilder)	1.96	1.84
Norway (kroner)	7.62	7.20
South Africa (rand)	3.60	3.32
Spain (peseta)	145.50	135.90
Sweden (krona)	8.17	7.72
Switzerland (franc)	1.48	1.41

Source: Compiled from various bank and currency exchange quotations, February 18, 1994.

rencies can differ by a large percentage—frequently more than 5 or 6 percent. The difference between buying and selling prices is called the **spread.** Table 2.1 shows that, for example, the 0.10 (1.75 − 1.65) difference between the buying price and the selling price on the German mark is a spread of approximately 6 percent.

Our experience changing currencies on vacation should not lead us to believe that large-scale international financial transactions encounter similar costs. The bank-note market used by travelers involves large spreads because generally only small amounts are traded, which nevertheless require as much paperwork as bigger commercial trades. Another reason why the spreads are large is that each bank and currency exchange must hold many different currencies to be able to provide customers with what they want, and these notes do not earn interest. This involves an opportunity, or inventory, cost, as well as some risk from short-term changes in exchange rates. Furthermore, bank robbers, in which the United States does not have a monopoly, specialize in bank notes; therefore, those who hold large amounts of them are forced to take security precautions, especially when moving bank notes from branch to branch or country to country. A further risk faced in the exchange of bank notes is the acceptance of counterfeit bills, which frequently show up in foreign financial centers. It is worth noting that because banks face a lower risk of theft of traveler's checks and because the companies that issue them—American Express, VISA, Thomas Cook, MasterCard, and so on—will quickly credit the banks that accept their checks, many banks give a more favorable buyer exchange rate on checks than on bank notes. Furthermore, issuers of traveler's checks enjoy the use of the money paid for the checks before they are cashed, and the banks selling the checks to customers do not face an inventory cost; payment to a check issuer by a check-selling bank is made only after checks have been purchased by a customer. The benefits to the issuers and sellers of traveler's checks keep down the spread.

While the exchange of bank notes between ordinary private customers and banks takes place in the retail market, banks trade their surpluses of notes between themselves in the wholesale market. The wholesale market involves firms which specialize in buying and selling foreign bank notes with commercial banks and currency exchanges. These currency-trading firms are **bank-note wholesalers.**

As an example of the workings of the wholesale market, during the summer a British bank might receive large numbers of Deutschemarks from Germans traveling in Britain. The same British bank may also be selling large numbers of Italian lire to British tourists leaving for vacations in Italy. The British bank will sell its surplus Deutschemarks to a bank-note wholesaler in London, who might then transport the mark notes back to Germany or to a non-German bank in need of mark notes. The British bank will buy lire from a wholesaler, who may well have transported the lire from Italy or else bought them from banks which had purchased lire from vacationing Italians. The spreads on the wholesale level are less than retail bank-note spreads, generally well below 2 percent, because larger amounts are generally traded.

THE SPOT FOREIGN EXCHANGE MARKET

Far larger than the bank-note market is the **spot foreign exchange market,** which is involved with the exchange of currencies held in different currency-denominated bank accounts. The **spot exchange rate,** which is determined in the spot market, is the number of units of one currency per unit of another currency, where both currencies are in the form of bank deposits. The deposits are transferred from sellers' to buyers' accounts, with the instructions to exchange currencies taking the form either of electronic messages or of bank drafts, which are checks issued by banks. Delivery, or **value,** from the electronic instructions or bank drafts is "immediate"—usually in 1 or 2 days. This distinguishes the spot market from the forward market (discussed in the next chapter), which involves the planned exchange of currencies for value at some date in the future—that is, after a number of days or even years.

Spot exchange rates are determined by the supplies of and demands for currencies being exchanged in the gigantic global interbank foreign exchange market.[1] This market is legendary for the frenetic pace at which it operates and for the vast amount of money which is moved at lightning speed in response to minuscule differences in price quotations.

Organization of the Interbank Spot Market

The interbank foreign exchange market is by far the largest financial market on earth. After correcting for double-counting, so that a purchase by one bank and the corresponding sale by a second bank is counted only once, average daily turnover is almost one trillion dollars.[2] The phenomenal size of this market can be put in perspective by noting, for example, that foreign exchange market turnover exceeds that of all the world's stock markets combined. Indeed, it takes over 2 months average trading on the New York Stock Exchange to match 1 day of trading in foreign exchange. Furthermore, foreign exchange volumes have roughly doubled every 3 years since the 1970s.[3]

The largest part of trading, 27 percent of the global total, occurs in the United Kingdom. Indeed, the amount of foreign currency trading conducted in London is so large that a larger share of currency trade in U.S. dollars (26 percent) and Deutschemarks (27 percent) occurs in the United Kingdom than in the United States (18 percent) or Germany (10 percent), respectively. Table 2.2 shows that the United States has the second-largest foreign exchange market, followed by Japan, Singapore, and Switzerland. Just about every market has shared the rapid growth of activity, with trading growth for the United States shown vividly in Figure 2.1.

The foreign exchange market is an informal arrangement of the larger commercial banks and a number of foreign exchange brokers. The banks and brokers are linked together by telephone, telex, and a satellite communications network called the **Society for Worldwide International Financial Telecommunications (SWIFT).** This computer-based communications system, based in Brussels, Belgium, links banks and brokers in just about every financial center. The banks and brokers are in almost constant contact, with activity in some financial center or other 24 hours a day.[4] Because

---

[1] In Chapter 6 the supply and demand curves for currencies are derived and used to explain the economic factors behind exchange rates.

[2] See *Central Bank Survey of Foreign Exchange Market Activity in April 1992,* Bank for International Settlements, Basle, Switzerland, March 1993.

[3] See Mark D. Flood, "Microstructure Theory and the Foreign Exchange Market," *Review,* Federal Reserve Bank of St. Louis, November/December 1991, pp. 52–70.

[4] Indeed, in the principal centers like New York, London, Tokyo, and Toronto, large banks maintain 24-hour operations to keep up with developments elsewhere during other centers' normal working hours.

TABLE 2.2. Geographical Distribution of Average Daily Foreign Exchange Turnover, April 1992

Country	Net Turnover, * Billion U.S.$	Percentage Share
United Kingdom	300	27
United States	192	17
Japan	126	11
Singapore	76	7
Switzerland	68	6
Hong Kong	61	5
Germany	57	5
France	36	3
Australia	30	3
Other	185	16
Total	1131	100

*Net of local double-counting; no adjustment for cross-border double-counting.
Source: Central Bank Survey of Foreign Exchange Market Activity in April 1992,
Bank for International Settlements, Basle, Switzerland, March 1993, p. 14.

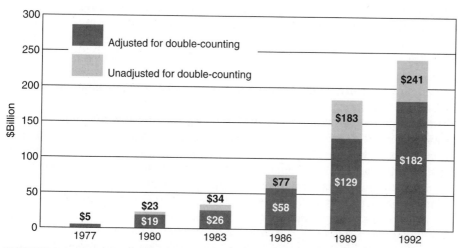

FIGURE 2.1. Daily Turnover in the U.S. Foreign Exchange Market, 1977–1992
The U.S. foreign exchange market has grown at a phenomenal pace. Globally, foreign exchange turnover has doubled every 3 years since 1970, a remarkable growth experience. (*Source: Summary of Results of the U.S. Foreign Exchange Market Survey Conducted in April 1992,* Federal Reserve Bank of New York, 1993, p. 1.)

of the speed of communications, significant events have virtually instantaneous impacts everywhere in the world despite the huge distances separating market participants. This is what makes the foreign exchange market just as efficient as a conventional stock or commodity market housed under a single roof.

The efficiency of the spot foreign exchange market is revealed in the extremely narrow spreads between buying and selling prices. These spreads can be smaller than a tenth of a percent of the value of currency exchanged and are therefore about one-fiftieth or less of the spread faced on bank notes by international travelers. The efficiency of the market is also manifest in the electrifying speed with which exchange rates respond to the continuous flow of information that bombards the market. Participants cannot afford to miss a beat in the frantic pulse of this dynamic, global market. Indeed, the bankers and brokers that constitute the foreign exchange market can scarcely detach themselves from the video monitors that provide the latest news and prices as fast as the information can travel along the telephone wires and radio waves of business news wire services such as Dow Jones Telerate and Reuters.

In the United States, as in most other markets, there are two levels on which the foreign exchange market operates, a direct **interbank** level and an indirect level via **brokers.** In the case of interbank trading, banks trade directly with each other, and all participating banks are **market-makers.** That is, in the direct interbank market, banks quote buying and selling prices to each other. This is known as an open-bid double auction. Because there is no central location of the market and because trading is continuous, the direct market can be characterized as a **decentralized, continuous, open-bid, double-auction market.**[5]

In the case of foreign exchange brokers, of which there were 16 versus over 150 commercial banks in the New York market in 1994, so-called **limit orders** are placed with brokers by banks. For example, a commercial bank will place an order with a broker to purchase £10 million at $1.5550/£. The broker puts this on the "books" and attempts to match the purchase order with sell orders for pounds from other banks. While the market-making banks take positions on their own behalves and for customers, brokers deal only for others, showing callers their best rates, called their **inside spread**, and charging a commission to both buying and selling banks. Because of its structure, the indirect broker-based market can be characterized as a **quasi-centralized, continuous, limit-book, single-auction market.**[6]

Figure 2.2, which depicts the United States foreign exchange market, shows that currencies are also bought and sold by central banks. Central banks enter the market when they want to change exchange rates from those that would result only from private supplies and demands, and in order to transact on their own behalves; central banks buy and sell bonds and settle transactions for governments which involve foreign exchange payments and receipts. Exhibit 2.1 provides a succinct summary of the players in the foreign exchange market, while Figure 2.3 illustrates the relative importance of market-making banks versus brokers, as well as the rapid growth of the U.S. market.

In the direct interbank market, which is the largest part of the foreign exchange market, bankers call foreign exchange dealers at other banks and "ask for the market." The caller does not say whether he or she wants to buy or to sell, nor does the caller state the amount to be traded. The caller might say, "Your market in **sterling**, please." This means, "At what price are you willing to buy and at what price are you willing to sell British pounds for U.S. dollars?" (British pounds are called sterling.) In replying, a foreign exchange dealer must attempt to determine whether the caller really wants to buy or to sell and must relate this to what his or her own preferred position is. This is a subtle and tricky game involving human judgment. Bluff and counterbluff are used. A good trader, with a substantial order in pounds, may first ask for the market in Canadian dollars. After placing an order he or she might

[5]Flood, *op. cit.*, p. 57.
[6]*Ibid.*

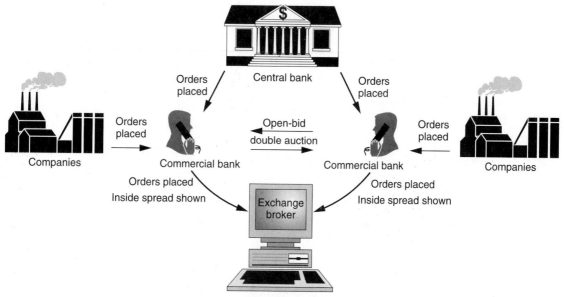

FIGURE 2.2. Organization of the Spot Foreign Exchange Market
The market-makers are commercial and investment banks that are in continuous contact with each other, openly quoting "bid" and "ask" exchange rates. They trade on their own accounts to affect the inventories of currencies they hold, as well as on behalf of customers. The market-making banks also place limit orders with brokers who try to match trades between the market-makers, and charge a fee to both. Central banks enter the market periodically, buying and selling to influence exchange rates or performing transactions for the government.

say, "By the way, what's your market in (British) sterling?" Dealers sometimes have their assistants place really large orders, in an effort to obtain favorable quotes: anticipation of a very large order might cause a quoting bank to increase its spread. A difference in quotation that shows up in the fourth decimal place can mean thousands of dollars on a large order. It is rather like poker, with massive stakes.

If a banker who has been called wants to sell pounds, he or she will quote on the side that is felt to be cheap for pounds, given this banker's feel of the market. For example, if the banker believes that other banks are selling pounds at \$1.6120/£, he or she might quote \$1.6118/£ as the selling price, along with a buying price that is also correspondingly low. Having considered the two-way price, the caller will state whether he or she wishes to buy or sell, and the amount. Once the rate has been quoted, it must be honored whatever the decision of the caller, up to a predetermined limit set by convention among market makers. The caller has only seconds to decide. Good judgment of the counterparty and good judgment of the direction of the market are essential in this multibillion-dollar game. It is important to be accurate and constantly in touch with events.

Delivery Dates and Procedures for Spot Exchange

Whereas bank notes of the major Western countries are exchanged for each other instantaneously over the counter, when U.S. dollars are exchanged in the New York interbank spot market with non-North American currencies, funds are not generally

The following excellent account of the foreign exchange market appeared in the *Review* of the Federal Reserve Bank of St. Louis:

The foreign exchange market is the international market in which buyers and sellers of currencies "meet." It is largely decentralized: the participants (classified as market-makers, brokers and customers) are physically separated from one another; they communicate via telephone, telex and computer network. Trading volume is large, estimated at $128.9 billion for the U.S. market in April 1989. Most of this trading was between bank market-makers.

The market is dominated by the market-makers at commercial and investment banks, who trade currencies with each other both directly and through foreign exchange brokers. Market-makers, as the name suggests, "make a market" in one or more currencies by providing bid and ask prices upon demand. A broker arranges trades by keeping a "book" of market-maker's limit orders—that is, orders to buy (alternatively, to sell) a specified quantity of foreign

currency at a specified price—from which he quotes the best bid and ask orders upon request. The best bid and ask quotes on a broker's book are together called the broker's "inside spread." The other participants in the market are the customers of the market-making banks, who generally use the market to complete transactions in international trade, and central banks, who may enter the market to move exchange rates or simply to complete their own international transactions. Market-makers may trade for their own account—that is, they may maintain a long or short position in a foreign currency—and require significant capitalization for that purpose. Brokers do not contact customers and do not deal on their own account; instead, they profit by charging a fee for the service of bringing foreign market-makers together.

Source: Mark D. Flood, "Microstructure Theory and the Foreign Exchange Market," *Review,* Federal Reserve Bank of St. Louis, November/December 1991, pp. 52–70.

FIGURE 2.3. U.S. Foreign Exchange Market Turnover, April 1992 (not adjusted for double-counting)
The foreign exchange market has two tiers, a direct interbank tier and a tier operating via brokers. Both segments have grown rapidly, with the interbank component remaining substantially larger than the broker component. (*Source: Summary of Results of the U.S. Foreign Exchange Market Survey Conducted in April 1992,* Federal Reserve Bank of New York, 1993.)

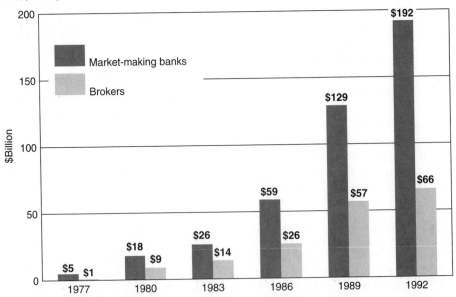

received until 2 business days after the initiation of the transaction. With the currencies of the North American continent, the U.S. and Canadian dollars and the Mexican peso, delivery is slightly quicker, with an exchange providing value after 1 business day. Whether the delay is 1 day or 2, it creates a distinction between the value date and the initiation date of a transaction. The distinction can be illustrated by an example.[7]

Suppose that a financial executive of an American corporation, Amcorp, calls his or her bank, Ambank National, a large currency-dealing bank in New York City, to buy £1 million. Suppose that the call is placed on Thursday, May 18, and that the British pounds are to be used to settle Amcorp's debt to Britcorp. Ambank will quote an exchange rate at which it will sell Amcorp the £1 million. If Amcorp approves of this rate, then the foreign exchange department of Ambank will request details for making the payment in Britain. These details will include the bank at which Britcorp is to be paid and the account number.

The details provided by Amcorp to Ambank will typically be conveyed to the designated bank in Britain, Britbank, by sending a message on the day of ordering the pounds, May 18, via SWIFT. The SWIFT network, which has been available since 1977, has grown so rapidly that it has virtually replaced the preexisting methods of conveying messages, namely, the mail and telegraphic transfer. SWIFT uses satellite linkages and transmits messages between banks in a standard format to minimize errors which can easily occur due to different languages and banking customs. SWIFT has been so successful that banks in just about every country, including Russia and other communist countries, have joined or applied to join.[8]

The spot exchange rate that is agreed upon by Ambank National on Thursday, May 18, will be binding and will not be changed even if market conditions subsequently change. A confirmation of the order for £1 million at the agreed exchange rate—for example, $1.6000 per pound—will be sent out to Amcorp on Thursday, May 18. Because of the intervening weekend, the value date, which is 2 business days later, is Monday, May 22, and on this day Ambank will debit Amcorp's account at the bank by $1.6 million, the dollar price of the £1 million at $1.6000 per pound. On the same value date, May 22, Britbank will credit Britcorp's account £1 million. The transaction is complete for the payer and payee, with the payee, Britcorp, being credited £1 million in Britain, and Amcorp, the payer, being debited the dollar equivalent, $1.6 million, in the United States.

Our description of the transaction in the example is complete only for the payer and the payee. We have not yet described the settlement between the banks. Specifically, the bank that has purchased foreign currency will have to pay the bank that has sold the foreign currency. This payment generally takes place via a **clearing house.** A clearing house is an institution at which banks keep funds which can be moved from one bank's account to another's to settle interbank transactions.

When foreign exchange is trading against the U.S. dollar, the clearing house that is used is called **CHIPS,** an acronym for the **Clearing House Interbank Payments System.** CHIPS is located in New York and, as we shall explain below, transfers funds between member banks. Currencies do also trade directly with each other

[7]It is possible to send money for value sooner than 2 days outside of North America and sooner than 1 day within North America. However, this occurs in the retail market, not the interbank market.
[8]Since 1987, nonbanking financial institutions such as brokerage firms have also been given access to SWIFT.

without involving the dollar—for example, Deutschemarks for British pounds, or Italian lire for Swiss francs. In these situations a European clearing house will be used. However, because a substantial volume of transactions is settled in dollars, we describe here how CHIPS works, although we can note that settlement between banks is similar in other financial centers.

Bank Settlement via CHIPS

CHIPS is a computerized mechanism through which banks hold U.S. dollars to pay each other when buying or selling foreign exchange. The system is owned by the large New York clearing banks; has over 150 members, including the U.S. agencies and subsidiaries of many foreign banks; and handles over 150,000 transactions a day, worth together hundreds of billions of dollars.

We can see how CHIPS works by extending the situation considered earlier, in which Amcorp initiated payment to Britcorp on Thursday, May 18, and Britcorp was credited at Britbank 2 business days later, on Monday, May 22, after the intervening weekend. The extension is to assume that immediately on agreeing to sell Amcorp £1 million, Ambank enters the interbank market to replenish its pound account at Britbank.

Let us suppose that after placing a few telephone calls Ambank finds the cheapest rate on pounds to be at UKbank. (Perhaps UKbank has just paid out U.S. dollars for a client and wants to replenish its dollar holdings.) On agreeing to buy £1 million from UKbank, Ambank gives instructions to deliver the pounds to its account at Britbank.[9] Ambank's payment to Britbank will be effected when Ambank enters into its CHIPS computer terminal its own code, that of UKbank, and the number of dollars to be paid. Similarly, UKbank enters its code, Ambank's code, and the number of dollars to be received. This is all done at the time the two banks agree on the purchase/sale, assumed to be the same day as Amcorp orders the pounds, May 18.

CHIPS records the information received from Ambank and UKbank and keeps track of other amounts to be paid or received by these banks and the many other CHIPS members. On the **value date** of the transaction, May 22, settlement reports are sent to the banks for gross and net amounts to be paid or received on that day. These reports are sent to members' CHIPS terminals at 4:30 P.M., Eastern time. Assuming Ambank and UKbank have no dispute over the reports they receive, the debtor bank, in our case Ambank, must send instructions to the Federal Reserve Bank of New York by 5:30 P.M. to debit Ambank's account there, called its **escrow account,** and to credit the escrow account of UKbank. The instruction from Ambank is sent via Fedwire, a system also used for settlement of domestic transactions. All transfers between escrow accounts are normally completed by 6:00 P.M. on the value date of the transactions.

The informal, doubled-tiered structure of the U.S. foreign exchange market, with direct interbank dealing coexisting with indirect brokered transactions, is similar to that of markets in Canada, Britain, and many other countries. In France, Germany, and some other countries, including those in Scandinavia, the procedure is more formal, with bank representatives, including a representative of the central

---

[9]The pounds will be moved from UKbank to Britbank as part of the normal settlement between banks provided by the clearing house in London.

bank, meeting daily face-to-face. Contracts are exchanged directly, although an informal market coexists in which many of the transactions occur. The formal meeting provides official settlement exchange rates for certain transactions.

Exhibit 2.2 gives a lively and vivid account of a typical transaction in the U.S. interbank market and also of a transaction made indirectly via a broker. The exhibit introduces some of the jargon that is involved.

Retail versus Interbank Spot Rates

While it is only exchange rates between banks that are determined in the interbank market, exchange rates faced by banks' clients are based on these interbank rates. Banks charge their customers slightly more than the going interbank selling rate, or **ask rate,** and pay their customers slightly less than the interbank buying rate, or **bid rate.** The extent of a bank's markup or markdown from the going interbank rate depends principally on the size of the retail transaction. Banks might not actually enter the interbank market, especially for small transactions, using instead currency they already own or adding to the amount they own. However, banks still base their retail spot rates on the interbank rates, and a bank might revise these once or twice each day for small transactions of up to a thousand dollars, while telephoning the bank's own foreign exchange trading room before quoting on large transactions. Larger banks have tellers' terminals linked to the banks' foreign exchange trading rooms for more frequent updating of retail rates.

Customer Drafts and Wire Transfers

When a customer requests foreign exchange from a bank, with this to be paid to a creditor in a foreign country, the bank sells the customer a draft payable to the creditor. This draft will be drawn against an account the bank holds with a bank in the country in which the payment is to be made. For example, if an American needs to make a Canadian dollar payment to a Canadian, he or she can buy a draft from a U.S. bank, where this draft is drawn against the U.S. bank's Canadian dollar account at a Canadian bank. A speedier settlement can be made by buying a **wire transfer**: instead of mailing a draft, the instructions are sent via SWIFT or some similar electronic means. The customer pays the U.S. bank a charge for the draft or transfer, with wire transfers costing slightly more.

When one bank maintains an account at another bank, the banks are called **correspondents** (this term originates from the mail instructions that used to be sent between such banks). Commercial banks keep accounts at correspondents in all major countries to help their customers make payments in these countries and to earn the fees charged for their services.

Conventions for Spot Exchange Quotation

In virtually every professional enterprise, especially in the realm of finance and economics, there are special conventions and a particular jargon. This is certainly true in the foreign exchange market, where practices in the quotation of exchange rates make the quotes difficult to interpret unless the jargon and conventions are well understood.

EXHIBIT 2.2
An Exchange on the Exchange
A Conversation between Market-Makers in the Foreign Exchange Market

The following account of an exchange between currency traders appeared in the *Review* of the Federal Reserve Bank of St. Louis. In this account, Mongobank and Loans 'n Things are two market-making banks. Interpretations of jargon are given as the jargon is used. For example, we are told that "Two mine" means to purchase $2 million of value of the foreign currency. "One by two" means being willing to buy 1 million units of a currency and sell 2 million units of the same currency.

In the direct market, banks contact each other. The bank receiving a call acts as a market-maker for the currency in question, providing a two-way quote (bid and ask) for the bank placing the call. A direct deal might go as follows:

Mongobank: *"Mongobank with a dollar-mark please?"*
(Mongobank requests a spot market quote for U.S. dollars (USD) against German marks (DEM).

Loans 'n Things: *"20–30."*
(Loans 'n Things will buy dollars at 2.1020 DEM/USD and sell dollars at 2.1030 DEM/USD—the 2.10 part of the quote is understood.)

Mongobank: *"Two mine."*
(Mongobank buys $2,000,000 for DEM 4,206,000 at 2.1030 DEM/USD, for payment two business days later. The quantity traded is usually one of a handful of "customary amounts.")

Loans 'n Things: *"My marks to Loans 'n Things Frankfurt."*
(Loans 'n Things requests that payment of marks be made to their account at their Frankfurt branch. Payment will likely be made via SWIFT.)*

Mongobank: *"My dollars to Mongobank New York."*
(Mongobank requests that payment of dollars be made to them in New York. Payment will most likely be made via CHIPS.)†

Spot transactions are made for "value date" (payment date) two business days later to allow settlement arrangements to be made with correspondents or branches in other time zones. This period is extended when a holiday intervenes in one of the countries involved. Payment occurs in a currency's home country.

*The Society for Worldwide Interbank Financial Telecommunications (SWIFT) is an electronic message network. In this case, it conveys a standardized payment order to a German branch or correspondent bank, which, in turn, effects the payment as a local interbank transfer in Frankfurt.
†The Clearing House Interbank Payments System (CHIPS) is a private interbank payments system in New York City.

The other method of interbank trading is brokered transactions. Brokers collect limit orders from bank market-makers. A limit order is an offer to buy (alternatively to sell) a specified quantity at a specified price. Limit orders remain with the broker until withdrawn by the market-maker.

The advantages of brokered trading include the rapid dissemination of orders to other market-makers, anonymity in quoting, and the freedom not to quote to other market-makers on a reciprocal basis, which can be required in the direct market. Anonymity allows the quoting bank to conceal its identity and thus its intentions; it also requires that the broker know who is an acceptable counterparty for whom. Limit orders are also provided in part as a courtesy to the brokers as part of an ongoing business relationship that makes the market more liquid. . . .

A market-maker who calls a broker for a quote gets the broker's inside spread, along with the quantities of the limit orders. A typical call to a broker might proceed as follows:

Mongobank: *"What is sterling, please?"*
(Mongobank requests the spot quote for U.S. dollars against British pounds (GBP).)

Fonmeister: *"I deal 40–42, one by two."*
(Fonmeister Brokerage has quotes to buy £1,000,000 at 1.7440 USD/GBP, and to sell £2,000,000 at 1.7442 USD/GBP.)

Mongobank: *"I sell one at 40, to whom?"*
(Mongobank hits the bid for the quantity stated. Mongobank could have requested a different amount, which would have required additional confirmation from the bidding bank.)

Fonmeister: [A pause while the deal is reported to and confirmed by Loans 'n Things] *"Loans 'n Things London."*
(Fonmeister confirms the deal and reports the counterparty to Mongobank. Payment arrangements will be made and confirmed separately by the respective back offices. The broker's back office will also confirm the trade with the banks.)

Value dates and payment arrangements are the same as in the direct dealing case. In addition to the payment to the counterparty bank, the banks involved share the brokerage fee. These fees are negotiable in the United States. They are also quite low: roughly $20 per million dollars transacted.

Source: Mark D. Flood, "Microstructure Theory and the Foreign Exchange Market," *Review*, Federal Reserve Bank of St. Louis, November/December 1991, pp. 52–70.

Let us concentrate on the spot exchange rates and consider Figure 2.4. The table in the figure quotes rates from *The Wall Street Journal* of February 18, 1994. These rates are the previous day's exchange rates, quoted at approximately 3:00 P.M., Eastern time. Since, as the table states, the rates are those charged by Bankers Trust Company of New York on sales of more than $1 million to other banks, the rates are interbank rates. As we have indicated and the explanation in the figure heading confirms, retail rates to corporate clients will be less favorable than these interbank rates.

FIGURE 2.4. Interbank Spot and Forward Exchange Rates
Exchange rates can be quoted as U.S. dollars per foreign currency or as foreign currency per U.S. dollar. The latter form, for example, DM1.7259/$, is referred to as "European terms." This is the way all rates are quoted in the interbank market, except for the British pound. The pound is quoted as U.S. dollar equivalent. Newspapers quote selling rates on foreign currencies, whereas interbank quotes involve both buying and selling rates. (*Source:* Reprinted by permission of *The Wall Street Journal,* © 1994 Dow Jones & Company Inc. All rights reserved worldwide.)

EXCHANGE RATES

Thursday, February 17, 1994

The New York foreign exchange selling rates below apply to trading among banks in amounts of $1 million and more, as quoted at 3 p.m. Eastern time by Bankers Trust Co., Telerate and other sources. Retail transactions provide fewer units of foreign currency per dollar.

Country	U.S. $ equiv. Thurs.	U.S. $ equiv. Wed.	Currency per U.S. $ Thurs.	Currency per U.S. $ Wed.
Argentina (Peso)	1.01	1.01	.99	.99
Australia (Dollar)	.7177	.7134	1.3933	1.4017
Austria (Schilling)	.08241	.08253	12.13	12.12
Bahrain (Dinar)	2.6518	2.6518	.3771	.3771
Belgium (Franc)	.02816	.02817	35.51	35.50
Brazil (Cruzeiro real)	.0017528	.0018237	570.50	548.33
Britain (Pound)	1.4780	1.4755	.6766	.6777
30-Day Forward	1.4761	1.4736	.6775	.6786
90-Day Forward	1.4725	1.4699	.6791	.6803
180-Day Forward	1.4685	1.4657	.6810	.6823
Canada (Dollar)	.7482	.7403	1.3365	1.3508
30-Day Forward	.7481	.7401	1.3368	1.3511
90-Day Forward	.7477	.7397	1.3375	1.3519
180-Day Forward	.7469	.7390	1.3388	1.3531
Czech. Rep. (Koruna)				
Commercial rate	.0334001	.0333778	29.9400	29.9600
Chile (Peso)	.002394	.002394	417.73	417.73
China (Renminbi)	.114943	.114943	8.7000	8.7000
Colombia (Peso)	.001217	.001217	821.73	821.73
Denmark (Krone)	.1487	.1482	6.7258	6.7475
Ecuador (Sucre)				
Floating rate	.000492	.000492	2033.02	2033.02
Finland (Markka)	.18014	.17949	5.5514	5.5712
France (Franc)	.17049	.17043	5.8655	5.8675
30-Day Forward	.17010	.17003	5.8789	5.8813
90-Day Forward	.16936	.16927	5.9046	5.9076
180-Day Forward	.16856	.16840	5.9325	5.9381
Germany (Mark)	.5794	.5802	1.7259	1.7235
30-Day Forward	.5782	.5790	1.7295	1.7272
90-Day Forward	.5761	.5768	1.7359	1.7337
180-Day Forward	.5739	.5745	1.7424	1.7407
Greece (Drachma)	.004002	.004011	249.85	249.30
Hong Kong (Dollar)	.12930	.12925	7.7342	7.7370
Hungary (Forint)	.0095997	.0096015	104.1700	104.1500
India (Rupee)	.03212	.03212	31.13	31.13
Indonesia (Rupiah)	.0004728	.0004728	2115.01	2115.01
Ireland (Punt)	1.4230	1.4189	.7027	.7048
Israel (Shekel)	.3348	.3348	2.9870	2.9870
Italy (Lira)	.0005966	.0005958	1676.31	1678.26
Japan (Yen)	.009586	.009631	104.32	103.83
30-Day Forward	.009594	.009640	104.23	103.73
90-Day Forward	.009616	.009662	103.99	103.50
180-Day Forward	.009659	.009705	103.54	103.04
Jordan (Dinar)	1.4495	1.4495	.6899	.6899
Kuwait (Dinar)	3.3544	3.3544	.2981	.2981
Lebanon (Pound)	.000586	.000586	1706.00	1706.00
Malaysia (Ringgit)	.3596	.3591	2.7810	2.7850
Malta (Lira)	2.5478	2.5478	.3925	.3925
Mexico (Peso)				
Floating rate	.3221649	.3221649	3.1040	3.1040
Netherland (Guilder)	.5165	.5172	1.9360	1.9334
New Zealand (Dollar)	.5755	.5754	1.7376	1.7379
Norway (Krone)	.1342	.1343	7.4543	7.4486
Pakistan (Rupee)	.0332	.0332	30.13	30.13
Peru (New Sol)	.4770	.4770	2.10	2.10
Philippines (Peso)	.03676	.03676	27.20	27.20
Poland (Zloty)	.00004566	.00004562	21901.00	21922.00
Portugal (Escudo)	.005744	.005733	174.11	174.42
Saudi Arabia (Riyal)	.26665	.26665	3.7502	3.7502
Singapore (Dollar)	.6290	.6281	1.5898	1.5920
Slovak Rep. (Koruna)	.0301386	.0298954	33.1800	33.4500
South Africa (Rand)				
Commercial rate	.2895	.2900	3.4538	3.4478
Financial rate	.2186	.2160	4.5750	4.6300
South Korea (Won)	.0012330	.0012333	811.00	810.80
Spain (Peseta)	.007127	.007085	140.32	141.14
Sweden (Krona)	.1253	.1246	7.9780	8.0263
Switzerland (Franc)	.6863	.6878	1.4570	1.4540
30-Day Forward	.6859	.6872	1.4580	1.4551
90-Day Forward	.6853	.6866	1.4593	1.4564
180-Day Forward	.6853	.6865	1.4593	1.4567
Taiwan (Dollar)	.037844	.037844	26.42	26.42
Thailand (Baht)	.03926	.03926	25.47	25.47
Turkey (Lira)	.0000561	.0000564	17832.15	17741.24
United Arab (Dirham)	.2723	.2723	3.6725	3.6725
Uruguay (New Peso)				
Financial	.222717	.222717	4.49	4.49
Venezuela (Bolivar)				
Floating rate	.00918	.00918	108.90	108.90

Figure 2.4 gives rates in two ways—as the number of U.S. dollars per foreign currency unit, which is called **U.S.$ equivalent,** and as the number of units of foreign **currency per U.S. dollar.** To a close approximation, the figures in the second two columns are merely the reciprocals of the figures in the first two columns. With the exception of the British pound, which is quoted in U.S.$ equivalent, that is as U.S. dollars per pound, all other rates are quoted in the interbank market as foreign currency per U.S.$. The quotation, number of units of foreign currency per U.S. dollar, is known as **European terms.** For example, on February 17, 1994, in the interbank market, the dollar would have been quoted in European terms as 8.7000 Chinese renminbi (¥8.7000).[10]

Figure 2.4 gives the rates only for selling and not for buying foreign exchange. It is customary for newspapers to quote only the banks' selling rates, or ask rates, but as we have seen, interbank traders give two-way quotations. In order to obtain the buying rates, or bid rates, newspaper rates must be adjusted, and we must guess the amount of adjustment required in Figure 2.4 since data for both sides of the market are not made available. For example, Bankers Trust might have been buying German marks at DM1.7264 per U.S. dollar while selling German marks at the quoted DM1.7259 per U.S. dollar. Because the conventional form of quotation of marks and almost every other currency is in European terms, that is, foreign currency per U.S. dollar, it is easier to think of exchange rates as the buying and selling prices of U.S. dollars, rather than as the selling and buying prices of the foreign currency. For example, we can more easily think of Bankers Trust as buying U.S. dollars for DM1.7259 and selling U.S. dollars for DM1.7264. Note that the price Bankers Trust is paying for U.S. dollars (its buying, or bid, price on dollars, DM1.7259) is slightly lower than the price it is charging for U.S. dollars (its selling, or ask, price on dollars, DM1.7264). The difference between the two rates is the bank's spread. More generally, the European terms exchange rates can all be thought of as bids and asks on the U.S. dollar since they are in terms of amounts of foreign currency per U.S. dollar. For example, the Can$1.3365 entry in Figure 2.4 can be thought of as the bid on a U.S. dollar (ask on the Canadian dollar): Bankers Trust would pay Can$1.3365 for a U.S. dollar. The ask for the U.S. dollar (bid on the Canadian dollar) might be Can$1.3370 per U.S. dollar.

In the case of the British pound, which unlike all other currencies is conventionally quoted as U.S. dollars per pound, it is easier to think of the $1.4780 in Figure 2.4 as the selling price of pounds, that is, Bankers Trust's ask on pounds. The buying price of pounds, Bankers Trust's bid on pounds, might be $1.4775/£. Of course, an ask on pounds is a bid on the dollar, and a bid on pounds is an ask on the dollar. Because the convention is to quote sterling as U.S. dollars per pound, it is easier to think of rates as buying and selling prices of the pound. That is, just as we can most easily think of European terms as buying and selling prices of U.S. dollars—the rates are amounts of foreign currency per dollar—in the case of the British pound we can most easily think of rates as buying and selling prices of pounds.

In quotations on the interbank market bids always precede asks. This is why it is suggested above that you think of European terms as bids and asks on the dollar, and of U.S. dollar equivalent terms used for the pound as bids and asks on the pound. For example, in the case of quoting U.S. dollars versus marks the rates would

---

[10]Renminbi means "the peoples' money."

be quoted as DM1.7259/64. This means DM1.7259 bid for a U.S. dollar, and DM1.7264 asked for a U.S. dollar. Indeed, as Exhibit 2.2 indicates at the outset of the conversation it describes, the DM1.72 part might be assumed to be understood, and the quote might be simply 59/64. The pound would be quoted as $1.4775/80, or simply 75/80, with the bid on the pound preceding the ask.

Whichever way rates are quoted, the last digit of the quotation is referred to as a **point.** For example, the difference between the bid on the U.S. dollar of DM1.7259 and the ask for U.S. dollars of DM1.7264 is $1.7264 - 1.7259 = 0.0005$, or five points. Similarly the assumed bid on British pounds of $1.4775 differs from the ask of $1.4780 by five points. A point always refers to the last digit convention-ally quoted, whether the total number of digits in the quotation is 5, as in the case of marks and pounds; 4, as in the European terms quotations on Taiwanese and Thai-land dollars; or 6, as in the case of the Italian lire.

It is important that we distinguish between bid and ask exchange rates, even if it seems that the differences are so small as to be almost irrelevant. There are two reasons for this. First, the bid-ask spread provides banks with their incomes, earned by charging their customers, from dealing in foreign exchange. For example, even if the banks charge only 0.0002 (2×10^{-4}) of the value of each transaction, the rev-enue to the market-making banks on their transactions of over $880 billion ($880 \times 10^9$) each day is $880 \times 10^9 \times 2 \times 10^{-4} = \$176$ million. This is not all profit for banks, because much of this revenue merely moves between banks doing interbank trans-actions and also because banks themselves face operating costs. However, the amount does indicate the importance of spreads to banks, and to the banks' cus-tomers who face the spreads. Second, spreads may seem small but can have a sub-stantial effect on yields when the spreads are faced on investments made for only a short period. For example, if a company invests abroad for 1 month and must there-fore buy the foreign currency today and sell it after 1 month, a 0.1 percent spread on buying and selling the foreign currency, when put on an annual basis by multiplying by 12, involves an annualized cost of 1.2 percent. If the extra interest available on foreign securities versus domestic securities is smaller than 1.2 percent, the spread will eliminate the advantage. The shorter the period for which funds are moved, the more relevant bid-ask spreads on foreign exchange become.

DIRECT VERSUS INDIRECT EXCHANGE AND CROSS EXCHANGE RATES

Indirect Exchange and the Practice of Quoting against the Dollar

With more than 150 currencies in the world, there are over $150 \times 149 = 22,350$ dif-ferent exchange rates. This is because each of 150 different currencies has an exchange rate against the remaining 149 currencies. Fortunately for the people who work in the foreign exchange market, many of the more than 22,350 possible exchange rates are redundant. The most obvious cause of redundancy is that once we know, for example, the price of dollars in terms of pounds, this immediately sug-gests knowing the price of pounds in terms of dollars. This reduces the number of relevant exchange rate quotations by one-half. However, there is another cause of redundancy: it is possible, for example, to compute the exchange rate between the German mark and the British pound from the exchange rate between the mark and the dollar and the exchange rate between the pound and the dollar. Indeed, if there were no costs of transacting in foreign exchange, that is, no bid-ask spreads, with 150 currencies all 22,350 possible exchange rates could be computed from the 149 exchange rates of each currency versus the U.S. dollar. Let us show why by beginning with a simple situation in which the only currencies are the German mark, the British pound, and the U.S. dollar.

The procedure we are going to use is to consider people wanting to exchange marks for pounds or pounds for marks. These exchanges can be made directly, or indirectly via the dollar. For example, it is possible to sell marks for dollars and then sell these dollars for pounds. We will argue that for banks to attract business involving the direct exchange of marks and pounds, the exchange rate they offer cannot be inferior to the exchange rate implicit in indirect exchange via the U.S. dollar.[11] We will see that when there are no foreign exchange **transaction costs**, the constraint of competing with indirect exchange will force banks to quote a direct exchange rate between the mark and pound that is exactly equal to the implicit indirect exchange rate via the dollar. This means that, if there are no transaction costs, we can find all possible exchange rates by taking appropriate exchange rates versus the dollar. When there are transaction costs, we will see that direct exchange rates are not always those that are implicit in rates against the dollar; however, in that case there are limits within which direct quotations can move, set by exchange rates versus the dollar.

Zero Foreign Exchange Transaction Costs

Let us begin by defining the spot exchange rate between the dollar and pound as $S(\$/\pounds)$. That is:

> $S(\$/\pounds)$ is the number of U.S. dollars per British pound in the spot exchange market. More generally, $S(i/j)$ is the number of units of currency i per unit of currency j in the spot exchange market.

First, consider a person who wants to go from marks to pounds. In terms of Figure 2.5, this is characterized by the dark, rightward-pointing arrow along the base of the triangle between DM and £. If a bank is to attract business selling pounds for Deutschemarks, the exchange rate it offers directly between the Deutschemark and pound must be no worse than could be achieved by going indirectly from the Deutschemark to the dollar and then from the dollar to the pound. In terms of Figure 2.5, the indirect route involves traveling from DM to £ via $, that is, along the dark arrows from DM to $, and then from $ to £.

If the person buys pounds directly for Deutschemarks, the number of pounds received per Deutschemark is $S(\pounds/DM)$ pounds, the spot number of pounds per mark, as shown on the side of the triangle in Figure 2.5 with the dark arrow pointing from DM to £. If instead the indirect route is taken from DM to £ via $, then on the

[11]As we shall see, banks in Britain and Germany do indeed quote direct exchange rates between the mark and pound, and the pound and mark. Furthermore, these rates are at least as favorable as the implicit rates calculated from rates vis-à-vis the U.S. dollar.

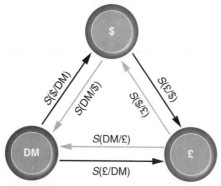

FIGURE 2.5. Direct versus Indirect Exchange: Zero Transaction Costs
It is possible to buy pounds with marks directly or else to do this indirectly, using marks to buy dollars and then dollars to buy pounds. Similarly, it is possible to buy marks with pounds directly or to do this indirectly by buying and then selling dollars. The possibility of indirect exchange via dollars forces banks to quote a cross rate between marks and pounds given by the mark and pound rates vis-à-vis the dollar. With zero transaction cost, $S(DM/£) = S(DM/\$) \cdot (\$/£)$, precisely.

first leg of the exchange, that going from DM to \$, each Deutschemark buys $S(\$/DM)$ dollars. Then on the second leg, that going from \$ to £, each of these $S(\$/DM)$ dollars buys $S(£/\$)$ pounds. Therefore, from the two legs, $S(\$/DM) \cdot S(£/\$)$ pounds are received for each mark.[12]

As we have said, a bank offering to exchange Deutschemarks directly for pounds at $S(£/DM)$ pounds per Deutschemark must offer at least as large a number of pounds as would be obtained via the indirect route. That is, for the bank's exchange rate to be effective in attracting direct Deutschemark-pound business it must be such that

$$S(£/DM) \geq S(\$/DM) \cdot S(£/\$) \tag{2.1}$$

Let us next consider a person who wants to exchange pounds into Deutschemarks. This person can go from £ to DM directly along the lightly-shaded leftward pointing arrow in Figure 2.5. This would result in $S(DM/£)$ Deutschemarks for each pound. Alternatively, the person can go from £ to DM indirectly along the lightly-shaded arrows, going from £ to \$, and then from \$ to DM. This route gives $S(\$/£)$ dollars for each pound, and then each of these dollars buys $S(DM/\$)$ Deutschemarks. Therefore, the number of Deutschemarks received per pound from the indirect route is $S(\$/£) \cdot S(DM/\$)$.

---

[12]It is worth noting that the units of measurement follow the usual rules of algebra. That is, (\$/DM) × (£/\$) = £/DM, with the dollar signs canceling.

A bank posting an exchange rate for directly converting pounds into Deutschemarks must offer at least as many marks as would be obtained by using the indirect route via the U.S. dollar. That is, for the bank to attract business, the exchange rate must satisfy

$$S(DM/£) \geq S(\$/£) \cdot S(DM/\$) \qquad (2.2)$$

We can compare inequality (2.2) with inequality (2.1) by noting that in the absence of transaction costs, by definition,

$$S(£/DM) = \frac{1}{S(DM/£)}, \quad S(£/\$) = \frac{1}{S(\$/£)}, \quad \text{and} \quad S(\$/DM) = \frac{1}{S(DM/\$)} \qquad (2.3)$$

That is, for example, if there are 0.25 pounds per Deutschemark, there are 4 Deutschemarks per pound. Using the equations in (2.3) in inequality (2.1) gives

$$\frac{1}{S(DM/£)} \geq \frac{1}{S(DM/\$)} \cdot \frac{1}{S(\$/£)} \qquad (2.4)$$

Inverting both sides of inequality (2.4), and therefore necessarily reversing the inequality, gives

$$S(DM/£) \leq S(DM/\$) \cdot S(\$/£) \qquad (2.5)$$

Inequality (2.5) is consistent with (2.2) only if the equalities rather than the inequalities hold. That is, the ability to choose the best way to go from Deutschemarks to pounds and from pounds to Deutschemarks ensures that

$$S(DM/£) = S(\$/£) \cdot S(DM/\$) \qquad (2.6)$$

Equation (2.6) tells us we can compute the exchange rate between Deutschemarks and pounds from the pound-dollar and Deutschemark-dollar exchange rates. For example, if there are 1.5 dollars per pound and 2.0 Deutschemarks per dollar, there are 3.0 Deutschemarks per pound. What we have shown in deriving equation (2.6) is that this follows because there is always the possibility of indirect exchange via the dollar in going from Deutschemarks to pounds or from pounds to Deutschemarks. However, recall that so far we have assumed zero transaction costs.

The exchange rate $S(DM/£)$ is a **cross rate.** More generally, cross rates are exchange rates directly between currencies when neither of the two currencies is the U.S. dollar. For example, $S(Can\$/£)$, $S(¥/Can\$)$, $S(¥/DM)$, $S(DM/SFr)$ are all cross rates. What we have derived in equation (2.6) generalizes for any cross rate as

$$S(i/j) = S(i/\$) \cdot S(\$/j) \qquad (2.7)$$

Of course, since $S(\$/j) = 1/S(j/\$)$, we can also compute the cross rate $S(i/j)$ from

$$S(i/j) = \frac{S(i/\$)}{S(j/\$)} \qquad (2.8)$$

The cross-rate formula in equation (2.8) uses exchange rates in European terms, that is, as units of currency per U.S. dollar. For example, if we know $S(Can\$/\$) = 1.33$ and $S(FFr/\$) = 5.85$, we can calculate the Canadian dollar per French franc rate as

$$S(\text{Can\$/FFr}) = \frac{1.33}{5.85} = 0.23$$

or alternatively, since $S(\text{FFr/Can\$}) = \dfrac{1}{S(\text{Can\$/FFr})}$

$$S(\text{FFr/Can \$}) = \frac{5.85}{1.33} = 4.40$$

Typically, the rule for calculating cross rates is based on **triangular arbitrage,** which involves a different line of argument than is employed above. We can use Figure 2.5 to explain the difference between triangular arbitrage and the argument we employed.

Triangular arbitrage is based upon the notion that if you started with $1 and went clockwise from $ to £ to DM and then back to $ in Figure 2.5, you could not end up with more than $1 from this triangular journey or there would be an **arbitrage profit.** Similarly, you would not be able to take the reverse counterclockwise route, going from $ to DM to £ and back to $, and end up with more than $1 if you started with $1. This argument based on triangular arbitrage gives the correct result when there are no transaction costs. However, it gives an inaccurate answer when there are transaction costs, for the following reason.

The choice of direct versus indirect exchange of currencies that we employed in deriving equation (2.6) involves selecting between one (direct) transaction and two (indirect) transactions. This means just one extra transaction cost when taking the indirect route rather than the direct route. On the other hand, clockwise triangular arbitrage is based on three transactions, and hence three transaction costs—for converting $ to £, for converting £ to DM, and converting DM to $. There are also three transaction costs for the reverse, counterclockwise arbitrage. The approach we have taken, which may be called **one-way arbitrage**, gives a narrower permissible bid-ask spread for a cross-rate transaction than is found by triangular arbitrage. In a market where a few points may translate into thousands of dollars, it is important that we derive the correct permissible spread, and this requires one-way arbitrage, not the more circuitous triangular arbitrage.[13]

Nonzero Foreign Exchange Transaction Costs

Defining the Costs of Transacting

As we have already noted, in reality the price that must be paid to buy a foreign currency is different from the price at which the currency can be sold. For example, the U.S. dollar price a person must pay a bank for a Deutschemark will exceed the U.S. dollar price received from the sale of a Deutschemark. In addition, the buyer or seller of a currency might have to pay a lump-sum fee or commission on each transaction. For our purpose, we can think of both the bid-ask spread and the exchange dealer's fee as two parts of the total cost of transacting. They both provide revenue for dealers in foreign currencies and cause those who need to

---

[13]Transaction costs become especially important in the context of interest arbitrage, which is covered in Chapter 11.

exchange currencies to lose in going back and forth. Let us define buy and sell rates:

> $S(\$/\text{ask}£)$ is the price that must be *paid to the bank* to buy one pound with dollars. It is the bank's offer or ask rate on pounds. $S(\$/\text{bid}£)$ is the number of dollars *received from the bank* for the sale of pounds for dollars. It is the bank's bid rate on pounds.

Instead of writing $S(\$/\text{ask}£)$ we could write $S(\text{bid}\$/\text{ask}£)$, because if a bank is offering to sell pounds for dollars, it is offering to buy dollars for pounds; these are two sides of the same transaction. Similarly, instead of writing $S(\$/\text{bid}£)$ we could write $S(\text{ask}\$/\text{bid}£)$. We need label only one currency because, for example, if we are talking of the bank's ask rate for pounds in terms of dollars, $S(\$/\text{ask}£)$, we know this is also the bank's bid rate on dollars. That is, once we have stated what is done with one currency, stating what is done with the other currency is redundant.

Because of transaction costs, we must be careful when taking the inverse of an exchange rate. When there are transaction costs, instead of writing

$$S(\$/£) = \frac{1}{S(£/\$)}$$

as in equations (2.3), we must write

$$S(\$/\text{ask}£) \equiv \frac{1}{S(£/\text{bid}\$)} \quad \text{and} \quad S(\$/\text{bid}£) \equiv \frac{1}{S(£/\text{ask}\$)}$$

More generally,

$$S(i/\text{ask}j) \equiv \frac{1}{S(j/\text{bid}i)} \quad \text{and} \quad S(i/\text{bid}j) \equiv \frac{1}{S(j/\text{ask}i)} \tag{2.9}$$

These rules follow immediately from the extended notation described above.

Cross-Rate Spreads and Transaction Costs

Figure 2.6 shows the exchange rates when going from DM to $ to £ when transaction costs are included. If a person were to buy pounds directly with Deutschemarks, he or she would receive $S(£/\text{bidDM})$ pounds from the bank; this is what the bank bids for Deutschemarks in terms of pounds, as is shown along the horizontal dark arrow in Figure 2.6. If instead the person goes indirectly from DM to $ to £ along the dark arrows, on the first leg each Deutschemark buys $S(\$/\text{bidDM})$ dollars; this is the bank's buying or bid rate for Deutschemarks in terms of dollars. On the second leg, each dollar buys $S(£/\text{bid}\$)$ pounds—the bank's buying or bid rate on dollars for pounds. Therefore, the indirect route gives $S(\$/\text{bidDM}) \cdot S(£/\text{bid}\$)$ pounds per Deutschemark.

The bank's direct quote for $S(£/\text{bidDM})$ will not be accepted by customers if it gives fewer pounds than the indirect route. This requires

$$S(£/\text{bidDM}) \geq S(\$/\text{bidDM}) \cdot S(£/\text{bid}\$) \tag{2.10}$$

Next, consider a person wanting to exchange pounds for Deutschemarks, the reverse of the previous situation. That person can exchange directly, as along the lightly-shaded arrow between £ and DM in Figure 2.6, receiving $S(\text{DM}/\text{bid}£)$

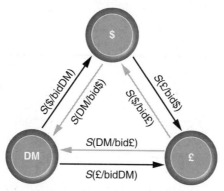

**FIGURE 2.6. Direct Versus Indirect
Exchange: Nonzero Transaction Costs**
One-way arbitrage ensures that the number of
DM received for each pound sold directly for
DM, S(DM/bid£), must be no less than the
number of DM received indirectly via the
dollar, which is S($/bid£) · S(DM/bid$).
Similarly, the number of pounds received for
each DM sold directly for pounds,
S(£/bidDM), must be no less than the number
of pounds received indirectly, which is
S($/bidDM) · S(£/bid$). In this way, one-way
arbitrage imposes a trading range on the
possible cross rates between Deutschemarks
and pounds.

Deutschemarks per pound—the rate the bank pays for, or bids on, pounds. Alternatively, he or she can exchange via the dollar, receiving S($/bid£) · S(DM/bid$)
Deutschemarks per pound; this is seen from the two lightly-shaded arrows from £ to
$ and from $ to DM in Figure 2.6. The direct rate will attract business only if it
gives at least as many Deutschemarks per pound as buying Deutschemarks indirectly. Therefore, for the direct exchange rate to attract business it is required that

$$S(\text{DM/bid£}) \geq S(\text{\$/bid£}) \cdot S(\text{DM/bid\$}) \tag{2.11}$$

By using the equations (2.9) in the inequality (2.10) we have

$$\frac{1}{S(\text{DM/ask£})} \geq \frac{1}{S(\text{DM/ask\$})} \cdot \frac{1}{S(\text{\$/ask£})} \tag{2.12}$$

Taking reciprocals, and therefore reversing the inequality in (2.12), gives

$$S(\text{DM/ask£}) \leq S(\text{DM/ask\$}) \cdot S(\text{\$/ask£}) \tag{2.13}$$

By comparing inequalities (2.11) and (2.13), we find what we do and do not
know about cross rates when there are transaction costs. We no longer know exactly
what the cross rates are from rates against the dollar. Instead, we know the smallest
number of Deutschemarks a bank can offer on pounds, as given by inequality (2.11).
We also know the maximum number of Deutschemarks it can ask for a pound, as

given by inequality (2.13). However, we do not know where in between these limits the actual direct exchange rates are. The exact bid and ask cross rates depend on the competition between banks for direct exchange between the currencies. If there is a lot of competition because there is a lot of business, the spread in the cross rate between Deutschemarks and pounds will be small, perhaps on the order of the size of the bid-ask spread between the dollar and one of these foreign currencies. If there is little competition, the spread could be quite large, perhaps as much as double the size of the bid-ask spread in the Deutschemark rate or pound rate vis-à-vis the dollar.

For example, suppose that rates on the mark and pound vis-à-vis the U.S. dollar are quoted as:

S(DM/bid$)	S(DM/ask$)	S($/bid£)	S($/ask£)
1.7259	1.7264	1.4775	1.4780

Then, for cross transactions to occur between Deutschemarks and pounds we know from inequality (2.11) that

$$S(DM/bid£) \geq 1.4775 \times 1.7259 = 2.5500 \tag{2.14}$$

and from inequality (2.13) that

$$S(DM/ask£) \leq 1.7264 \times 1.4780 = 2.5516 \tag{2.15}$$

The percentage spread on the Deutschemark-dollar rate is $\dfrac{1.7264 - 1.7259}{1.7259} = 0.00029$, or 0.029 percent. The percentage spread on the pound is $\dfrac{1.4780 - 1.4775}{1.4775} = 0.00034$, or 0.034 percent. On the other hand, the maximum possible percentage spread on the cross rate between Deutschemarks and pounds, given from inequalities (2.14) and (2.15), is $\dfrac{2.5516 - 2.5500}{2.5500} = 0.00063$, or 0.063 percent. This is much larger than for either of the spreads of rates versus the dollar. However, there is a large volume of exchange between Deutschemarks and pounds, and therefore spreads in quoted cross rates are likely to be less than 0.063 percent. With the pound-Deutschemark market being very active, the cross-rate spread might be bid down close to the 0.029 or 0.034 percent spreads of the Deutschemark and pound versus the dollar.

What do we learn from the above? We learn that when going from one foreign currency to another—for example, from Canadian dollars to pounds, or from Mexican pesos to Japanese yen—it pays to call a number of banks. The worst you could find are exchange rates as unfavorable as on two separate transactions, going into and out of the U.S. dollar. Generally, however, you will find a better situation. Different banks may have quite different direct quotes depending on whether or not they are market-makers in the direct exchange you are considering, and you might as well find the best deal.

Another thing we have learned is that, if there were no transaction costs, we could find all the possible exchange rates between n currencies from $n-1$ exchange rates, those against the U.S. dollar. However, since in reality there are transaction costs, the situation is very different. Not only are there $2(n-1)$ rates against the U.S. dollar, that is, a bid and an ask for each rate, but there are also a number of other bid and ask rates for direct exchanges. The major currencies of the **Organization for Economic Cooperation and Development (OECD)** countries trade directly against each other with, for example, quotations in Britain for direct purchase or sale of Canadian dollars, German marks, French francs, Japanese yen, and so on. In Tokyo there are quotes in yen against British pounds, Canadian dollars, and so on. There are consequently far more than $2(n-1)$ different quoted exchange rates.

It is worth pointing out that there is no rule that exchange rates must always be expressed only against the U.S. dollar. Any currency would do from a conceptual point of view. However, as a practical matter, it is important that the currency of quotation be one that is widely traded and held. At the beginning of the twentieth century, the pound sterling was widely used, but after the 1944 Bretton Woods agreement (which is described in Chapters 8 and 9), the U.S. dollar emerged as the standard for stating other currencies' values.[14] We might also note that it is possible to find all exchange rates even without knowing the values of currencies against an nth currency. Instead, we can use the values of all currencies against a commodity such as gold, or even against a purely international money such as Special Drawing Rights (SDRs), which are described in Chapter 9.

The conditions we have derived are valid not only for conventional or spot exchange rates, but also for forward exchange rates, which are explained in the next chapter. That is, if we replaced the $S(i/j)$'s in this chapter with forward exchange rates, everything would still be valid.

SUMMARY

1. The bid-ask spread on foreign bank notes is high because of inventory costs and the costs and risks of note handling. Bank notes are exchanged at a retail and at a wholesale level.
2. The spot foreign exchange market is the market in which currencies in the form of bank deposits are exchanged. In this market, currencies are received 1 or 2 business days after an exchange of currencies has been agreed upon.
3. The interbank foreign exchange market is the largest market on earth. It consists of a complex international network of informal linkages between banks and foreign exchange brokers. When banks are dealing with each other, they quote two-way exchange rates. The interbank market can be characterized as a decentralized, continuous, open-bid, double-auction market. When banks deal with a foreign exchange broker, they state their intentions. The broker quotes the inside spread to prospective counterparties.
4. Banks settle between themselves on the same day their customers receive and pay for foreign exchange. Messages between banks are sent via SWIFT.
5. Banks use clearing houses like CHIPS to clear balances between themselves. Banks also maintain correspondent accounts with each other for settling customers' accounts in foreign currencies.
6. Exchange rates are generally quoted in European terms, that is, in units of foreign currency per U.S. dollar. Newspapers generally quote only selling rates. When exchange rates are quoted in European terms, it is easier to think of rates as bids and asks on the

---

[14]There is some evidence that the attractiveness of quoting in the U.S. dollar is diminishing, especially in the European and Asian trading blocs. See Stanley W. Black, "Transaction Costs and Vehicle Currencies," *Journal of International Money and Finance,* December 1991, pp. 512–526, and Jeffrey Frankel and Shang-Jin Wei, "Trade Blocs and Currency Blocs," National Bureau of Economic Research, Paper Number 4335, 1991.

U.S. dollar. The British pound is still quoted in U.S. dollar equivalent. The dollar-pound rate is best thought of as bids and asks on the pound. Bid rates are typically quoted before ask rates.

7. Transaction costs in the form of bid-ask spreads on exchange rates are important because they can greatly influence returns on short-term foreign investments. They also provide large incomes for banks and represent a cost to businesses.

8. A cross rate is an exchange rate which does not involve the U.S. dollar, for example, Japanese yen per British pound. In the absence of transaction costs, cross-exchange rates can be obtained from exchange rates vis-à-vis the U.S. dollar.

9. In the absence of transaction costs, the many possible cross-exchange rates between n different currencies can be obtained by just knowing the $n - 1$ values of the currencies against the remaining nth currency. Any standard will do for measurement.

10. In the presence of transaction costs, we cannot compute cross rates precisely from rates versus the dollar. Instead, we can compute a range within which cross rates must be quoted.

REVIEW QUESTIONS

1. What is a bank draft?
2. What is an exchange rate spread?
3. What does a bank-note wholesaler do?
4. What is a spot exchange rate?
5. What is the interbank spot market?
6. What is SWIFT, and what does it do?
7. What is CHIPS, and what does it do?
8. How does the interbank spot market differ from the brokered market?
9. What do we mean by the "bid" rate and "ask" rate on a foreign currency?
10. What is the difference between the U.S.$ equivalent and European terms methods of quoting exchange rates?
11. What do we mean by a "point" in quotation of exchange rates?
12. What is triangular arbitrage, and how does it differ from one-way arbitrage?
13. What is a cross rate?

ASSIGNMENT PROBLEMS

1. Do you think that because of the costs of moving bank notes back to their country of circulation, buying bank notes could sometimes be cheaper than buying bank drafts? Could there be a seasonal pattern in exchange rates for bank notes? [*Hint:* Think of the cost involved in shipping U.S. dollars arising from Americans spending summers in Europe back to the United States.]

2. How can companies that issue and sell traveler's checks charge a relatively low fee? How do they profit?

3. Compute the percentage spread on South African rands and Canadian dollars from Table 2.1. Why do you think the spread on Canadian dollars is lower?

4. What steps are involved in settling a purchase made in Britain with a credit card issued by a U.S. bank? How do you think the spread between rates used in credit-card payments compares with that for foreign bank notes?

5. Does the use of U.S. dollars as the principal currency of quotation put U.S. banks at an advantage for making profits? Why do you think the U.S. dollar has become a principal currency of quotation?

6. Why do you think that banks give bid and ask rates when dealing with each other? Why don't they state their intentions as they do when dealing with foreign exchange brokers?

7. Check a recent business newspaper or the business page for spot exchange rates. Form an $n \times n$ exchange-rate matrix by computing the cross rates, and check whether $S(\$/£) = 1/S(£/\$)$, and so on.

8. Complete the following exchange-rate matrix. Assume that there are no transaction costs.

Currency Sold	Currency Purchased				
	$	£	SFr	DM	¥
$	1	2.0	0.6	0.5	0.005
£		1			
SFr			1		
DM				1	
¥					1

BIBLIOGRAPHY

ALIBER, ROBERT Z. (ed.): *The Handbook of International Financial Management,* Dow Jones Irwin, Homewood, Ill., 1989.

DEARDORFF, ALAN V.: "One-Way Arbitrage and Its Implications for the Foreign Exchange Markets," *Journal of Political Economy,* April 1979, pp. 351–364.

EINZIG, PAUL: *A Textbook on Foreign Exchange,* St. Martin's, London, 1969.

FLOOD, MARK D.: "Microstructure Theory and the Foreign Exchange Market," *Review,* Federal Reserve Bank of St. Louis, November/December 1991, pp. 52–70.

KRUGMAN, PAUL R.: "Vehicle Currencies and the Structure of International Exchange," *Journal of Money, Credit and Banking,* August 1980, pp. 513–526.

KUBARYCH, ROGER M.: *Foreign Exchange Markets in the United States,* Federal Reserve Bank of New York, 1978.

REIHL, HEINZ, and RITA M. RODRIGUEZ: *Foreign Exchange Markets,* McGraw-Hill, New York, 1977.

SYRETT, WILLIAM W.: *A Manual of Foreign Exchange,* 6th ed., Sir Isaac Pitman, London, 1966.

CHAPTER 3

Forward Exchange

The future is not what it used to be.

—Paul Valéry

It would be difficult to overstate the importance of the forward market for foreign exchange. Indeed, a financial manager of a firm with overseas interests may find himself or herself as much involved with this market as with the spot market. This importance is confirmed by the aggregate turnover statistics given in Table 3.1, which show the market share of forwards to be essentially the same as for spots. Table 3.1 also makes it clear that despite the substantial attention paid to futures and options markets, the forward market is far more active. (Futures and options are discussed in Chapter 4.) The forward market is valuable for reducing risks arising from changes in exchange rates when importing, exporting, borrowing, and investing. Forwards are also used by speculators. This chapter explains the nature of this extremely important market, while later chapters (Chapters 12 and 17) describe the role forward exchange plays in foreign exchange management.

WHAT IS FORWARD FOREIGN EXCHANGE?

The 1- or 2-day delivery period for spot transactions is so short that when comparing spot rates with forward exchange rates we can usefully think of spot rates as exchange rates for undelayed transactions. On the other hand, forward exchange rates involve an arrangement to delay the exchange of currencies until some future date. A useful working definition is:

> The **forward exchange rate** is the rate that is contracted today for the exchange of currencies at a specified date in the future.

If we look back at Figure 2.4 on page 45, we note that for Britain, Canada, France, Germany, Japan, and Switzerland we are given exchange rates for 30-day, 90-day, and 180-day forwards. Although they are not quoted in the table, forward rates are also available for other currencies and for other maturities. Forward exchange contracts are drawn up between banks and their clients or between two banks. The market does not have a central location but instead is similar to the spot

TABLE 3.1. Foreign Exchange Net Turnover by Market Segment
(Daily Averages, April 1992)

Market Segment*		Turnover, Billion U.S.$		Percentage Share
Spot market		393.7		47
Forwards		384.4		46
Outright	58.5		7	
Swaps	324.3		39	
Futures		9.5		1
Options		37.7		5
Total turnover		832.0		100

*Totals do not sum owing to incomplete reporting of market segment breakdowns.
Source: Central Bank Survey of Foreign Exchange Market Activity in April 1992, Bank for International Settlements, Basle, Switzerland, March 1993.

market, being a decentralized arrangement of banks and brokers linked by telephone and the SWIFT network. Furthermore, the interbank component of the market involves continuous two-way open bidding between participants, that is, a so-called "continuous open-bid double auction": each bank continuously quotes a bid and ask to other banks. Foreign exchange brokers play a similar role as they do in the spot market, serving to indirectly match buy and sell orders between banks that prefer that their identities and intentions not be known by potential counterparties.

Figure 2.4 tells us that on Thursday February 17, 1994, a bank dealing in over $1 million could have purchased spot Japanese yen from Bankers Trust at ¥104.32/$. This would have meant delivery of the yen to the buying bank's designated account on Monday, February 21, 1994, 2 business days after the agreement was reached. If, however, the purchaser wanted to have the yen in 180 days rather than "immediately," then the rate would have been ¥103.54/$, or 0.78 (104.32 − 103.54) fewer yen per dollar than the rate for spot delivery. This means more dollars per yen for forward than for spot delivery. Figure 2.4 gives the exchange rate for the delivery of British pounds in 30 days at $1.4761/£. In the case of the pound, the forward value is lower than the spot value of $1.4780 by 19 points (1.4780 − 1.4761).

FORWARD EXCHANGE PREMIUMS AND DISCOUNTS

When it is necessary to pay more for forward delivery than for spot delivery of a foreign currency, as is the case for the Japanese yen in Figure 2.4, we say that the foreign currency is at a **forward premium**. When a currency costs less for forward delivery than for spot delivery, as is the case for the British pound in Figure 2.4, we say that the foreign currency is at a **forward discount**.

In order to show how to calculate forward premiums and discounts, let us first express the forward exchange rate in terms similar to those used for the spot rate:

$F_n(\$/£)$ is the n-year forward exchange rate of dollars to pounds. More generally, $F_n(i/j)$ is the n-year forward exchange rate of currency i to currency j.

For example, in Figure 2.4, $F_{1/4}(\$/£) = \$1.4725/£$, and $F_{1/2}(\$/£) = \$1.4685/£$. With the help of the definition of the forward rate we can define the n-year forward exchange premium or discount of British pounds versus U.S. dollars, on an annual basis, as[1]

$$\text{Premium/discount}\ (£\text{ vs.}\$) = \frac{F_n(\$/£) - S(\$/£)}{nS(\$/£)} \tag{3.1}$$

When the value of expression (3.1) is positive, the pound is at a forward premium vis-à-vis the dollar, because in this case the pound costs more dollars for forward delivery than for spot delivery. When expression (3.1) is negative, the pound is at a forward discount vis-à-vis the dollar. In this case the pound is cheaper to buy forward than to buy spot. In the event that the forward rate and spot rate are equal, we say that the forward currency is **flat.**

Forward premiums and discounts are put into annual terms by dividing by n because interest rates are quoted in per annum terms, and it is useful to be able to compare interest rates and forward premiums in these same terms.[2] Often, forward premiums and discounts are put in percentage terms by multiplying by 100. Using the values in Figure 2.4, we find that for the 180-day forward pound, expression (3.1) is negative and equal to

$$\text{Percentage premium/discount}\ (£\text{ vs.}\$) = \frac{1.4685 - 1.4780}{\frac{1}{2} \times 1.4780} \times 100 = -1.286$$

This is a discount on the pound versus the dollar of 1.286 percent per annum; the pound costs approximately 1¼ percent per annum less for forward delivery than for spot delivery. Table 3.2 gives the forward premiums and discounts for all forward currencies quoted in Figure 2.4.

When the pound is at a forward discount vis-à-vis the dollar, the dollar is at a forward premium vis-à-vis the pound. This follows because when pounds cost fewer dollars for forward delivery than for spot delivery, dollars must cost more pounds for forward delivery than spot delivery. Indeed, the n-year annualized forward premium/discount of the dollar versus the pound is

$$\text{Premium/discount}\ (\$\text{ vs.}£) = \frac{F_n(£/\$) - S(£/\$)}{nS(£/\$)} \tag{3.2}$$

For example, the 180-day premium/discount of the U.S. dollar versus the pound is given by

---

[1]More generally, the n-year premium/discount of currency i versus currency j is

$$\text{Premium/discount}\ (i\text{ vs. } j) = \frac{F_n(j/i) - S(j/i)}{nS(j/i)}$$

Note that for the premium/discount of i versus j, the j and i are reversed in the exchange-rate terms.
[2]When n is large, the per annum premium or discount on a compound basis is more accurately written as the nth root rather than via division by n. Specifically, the per annum premium/discount on currency; versus currency: is

$$\text{Premium/discount}\ (i\text{ vs.}.j) = \left(\frac{F_n(j/i) - S(j/i)}{S(j/i)} \right)^{\frac{1}{n}} - 1$$

TABLE 3.2. Per Annum Percentage Premium (+) or Discount (−) on Forward Foreign Exchange vis-à-vis the U.S. Dollar*

Currency	Premium or Discount	Forward Period		
		30 Days	90 Days	180 Days
Pound sterling	£ discount	−1.54	−1.49	−1.29
	U.S.$ premium	+1.60	+1.48	+1.30
Canadian dollar	Can$ discount	−0.16	−0.27	−0.35
	U.S.$ premium	+0.27	+0.30	+0.34
French franc	FFr discount	−2.75	−2.65	−2.26
	U.S.$ premium	+2.74	+2.67	+2.28
German mark	DM discount	−2.49	−2.28	−1.90
	U.S.$ premium	+2.50	+2.32	+1.91
Japanese yen	¥ premium	+1.00	+1.25	+1.52
	U.S.$ discount	−1.04	−1.27	−1.50
Swiss franc	SFr discount	−0.70	−0.58	−0.29
	U.S.$ premium	+0.82	+0.63	+0.32

*This table is derived from Figure 2.4 on page 45 using the formula premium/discount (i vs. j) = $\{[F_n\ (j/i) - S(j/i)]/nS(j/i)\} \times 100$, where n is the number of years forward. The discounts/premiums on the U.S. dollar versus the foreign currencies (bottom row of each pair) do not precisely equal the negatives of the forward exchange premiums/discounts of the foreign currencies versus the U.S. dollar (top row) because of the base-selection problem in computing percentage differences and because of bid-ask spreads.

$$\text{Premium/discount (\$ vs. £)} = \frac{0.6810 - 0.6766}{\frac{1}{2} \times 0.6766} = 0.01301$$

This is an annualized premium on the dollar (since the value is positive) of 0.01301, or 1.301 percent per annum.[3]

The fact that most currencies are quoted in European terms (number of units of foreign currency per U.S. dollar rather than the other way around) does not affect our definition of premiums or discounts. The n-year annualized premium/discount of, for example, the dollar versus the Deutschemark is

$$\text{Premium/discount (\$ vs. DM)} = \frac{F_n(\text{DM/\$}) - S(\text{DM/\$})}{nS(\text{DM/\$})} \tag{3.3}$$

FORWARD RATES VERSUS EXPECTED FUTURE SPOT RATES

As we shall explain in more detail in Chapter 16, if we assume that speculators are risk-neutral, that is, speculators do not care about risk, and if we ignore transaction

---

[3]There is a small difference between the numerical value of the pound-versus-dollar discount and the numerical value of the dollar-versus-pound premium, that is, −1.28 versus 1.30. This is because of bid-ask spreads and because of the base-selection problem in taking percentage differences.

costs in exchanging currencies, then forward exchange rates equal the market's expected future spot rates. That is, if we write the market's expected spot rate of currency j in terms of currency i as $S_n^*(i/j)$, where the * refers to "expected" and n refers to the number of years ahead, then

$$F_n(i/j) = S_n^*(i/j) \tag{3.4}$$

Equation (3.4) follows because if, for example, the market in general expected the dollar to be trading at DM1.80/$ in 1-year's time and the forward rate for 1 year were DM1.78/$, speculators would buy the dollar forward for DM1.78 and expect to make DM0.02 (DM1.80 − DM1.78) on each dollar when the dollars are sold at DM1.80 each. In the course of buying the dollar forward, speculators would drive up the forward price of the dollar until it was no longer lower than the expected future spot rate. That is, forward buying would continue until the forward price of the dollar were no longer below the expected spot rate. This can be written as

$$F_n(\text{DM/\$}) \geq S_n^*(\text{DM/\$}) \tag{3.5}$$

where inequality (3.5) means that the forward price of the dollar cannot be below the expected spot price for the date of forward maturity.

Similarly, if the market expected the dollar to be trading at DM1.80/$ in 1-year's time and the forward rate for 1 year were DM1.82/$, speculators would sell dollars forward. They would expect to profit from subsequently buying dollars at their expected spot price of DM1.80/$, which is DM0.02/$ less than the price at which they have sold dollars forward. In the course of selling dollars forward speculators would drive down the forward dollar price until it were no longer above their expected spot price. This can be written as

$$F_n(\text{DM/\$}) \leq S_n^*(\text{DM/\$}) \tag{3.6}$$

where inequality (3.6) means that the forward price of the dollar cannot be above the expected spot rate for the date of forward maturity.

Inequalities (3.5) and (3.6) are consistent only if the equalities of both relationships hold, that is

$$F_n(\text{DM/\$}) = S_n^*(\text{DM/\$}) \tag{3.7}$$

More generally, we have the condition presented in equation (3.4), recalling again that we are at this stage assuming risk neutrality and zero transaction costs—assumptions we relax later in the book.

PAYOFF PROFILES ON FORWARD EXCHANGE

While the price paid for a forward currency equals the future spot rate expected by the market at the time of purchase, when the forward contract matures, its value is determined by the realized spot rate at that time. The greater the extent to which the eventually *realized* spot rate differs from the spot rate that was *expected* at the time of buying the contract, the larger the change in the value of the forward contract vis-à-vis the purchase price. Stated differently, the larger the unexpected change in the spot exchange rate, the greater the change in the value of a forward contract. If the spot rate is as was expected, there is no change in the value of the forward contract. However, if the spot rate is higher or lower than expected, there is a gain or loss on the contract.

It is possible to plot the gain or loss on a forward contract against the unanticipated change in the spot exchange rate, where the unexpected change in the spot rate is the difference between the anticipated spot rate and the eventually realized spot rate. Such a plot is called a **payoff profile** and is useful for comparing the consequences of buying different instruments—forwards versus futures versus options—and for the management of foreign exchange risk, which we discuss in later chapters. Let us develop a payoff profile by considering an example. Suppose that the market's expected spot rate between the Deutschemark and dollar for 1-year's time is DM1.80/$ at the time of buying a 1-year contract to purchase $1 million with marks. With the forward rate equal to the expected future spot rate, the forward contract costs DM1.8 million. Let us now consider the gain or loss on the forward contract when the eventually realized spot rate is different from the originally expected rate.

As Table 3.3 shows, if the realized future DM value of the dollar is DM1.79/$ instead of the originally expected DM1.80/$, the unanticipated decline in the dollar by DM0.01/$ (DM1.80/$ − DM1.79/$) causes a decline in the value of the contracted $1 million by DM0.01/$ × $1 million, or DM10,000. (Note that the $ signs cancel, giving a Deutschemark amount.) On the other hand, if the eventually realized DM value of the dollar is DM1.81/$, the DM value of the contracted $1 million increases by DM0.01/$ × $1 million = DM10,000. Similarly, at a realized spot rate of DM1.82/$, the value of the $1 million to be received under the forward contract provides a gain of DM20,000 (DM0.02/$ × $1 million). These and other values for different realized spot rates are shown in Table 3.3.

We plot the unanticipated change in the spot rate along the horizontal axis of Figure 3.1 and the gain or loss on the forward contract to purchase $1 million at DM1.80/$ on the vertical axis. The unanticipated change in the expected spot rate is written symbolically as $\Delta S^u(\text{DM}/\$)$, where Δ is the Greek letter delta, for "difference," and the "u" superscript represents "unanticipated." The gain (+) or loss (−) on the contract is written as ΔV. We see from the figure that the payoff profile is an upward-sloping straight line. To the right of the vertical axis where $\Delta S^u(\text{DM}/\$)$ is positive, that is, the DM has unexpectedly gone down in value, or **depreciated,** there is a gain on the forward contract to buy the U.S. dollar. To the

TABLE 3.3. Unanticipated Changes in the Spot Exchange Rate and Gains or Losses on Forward Purchase of $1 Million at DM1.80/$

Realized Spot Rate	Unanticipated Change in Spot Rate	Gain (+) or Loss (−) on Contract
DM1.77/$	−DM0.03/$	−DM30,000
DM1.78/$	−DM0.02/$	−DM20,000
DM1.79/$	−DM0.01/$	−DM10,000
DM1.80/$	0	0
DM1.81/$	DM0.01/$	DM10,000
DM1.82/$	DM0.02/$	DM20,000
DM1.83/$	DM0.03/$	DM30,000

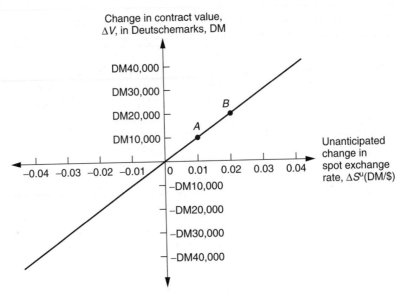

FIGURE 3.1. Payoff Profile on a Forward Contract to Purchase $1 Million at DM1.80/$

A payoff profile plots the unexpected change in the spot exchange rate against the gain or loss on an asset or liability. In this case the asset is a forward contract to purchase $1 million at DM1.80/$. We see that if the realized spot rate is DM1.81/$ when the expected rate had been DM1.80/$, the unexpected change in the spot rate is DM0.01/$ and there is a gain of DM10,000 (DM0.01/$ × $1 million) on the forward contract. This is plotted as point A. Similarly, if the spot rate is DM1.82/$, the unexpected change in the spot rate is DM0.02/$ and there is a gain of DM20,000. This gives point B. Plotting these and other points give an upward-sloping payoff profile line for the forward contract.

left of the vertical axis where $\Delta S^u(DM/\$)$ is negative, that is, the DM has unexpectedly gone up in value, or **appreciated,** there is a loss on the forward contract to buy the dollar.

A forward contract to *sell* $1 million at DM1.80/$ has a payoff profile that is opposite to that shown in Figure 3.1. In order to construct the profile, we again plot the gains or losses on the contract against the unanticipated change in the spot exchange rate. These gains and losses, and the associated unexpected changes in the spot exchange rate, are shown in Table 3.4. For example, selling $1 million for the contracted DM1.8 million when the realized exchange rate at maturity is DM1.79/$ means having a gain of DM10,000 [(DM1.80/$ − DM1.79/$) × $1 million]; the forward contract provides DM1.8 million for $1 million at the contract rate DM1.80/$, whereas $1 million would provide only DM1.79 million at the realized spot exchange rate. However, if the realized spot rate became DM1.81/$, the forward sale of $1 million at DM1.80/$ means having a loss of DM10,000: at DM1.81/$ the $1 million is worth DM1.81 million versus the DM1.80 million for which the dollars were sold. When these and the other values in Table 3.4 are plotted as they are in Figure 3.2, we obtain a downward-sloping profile.

TABLE 3.4. Unanticipated Changes in the Spot Exchange Rate and Gains or Losses on Forward Sale of $1 Million at DM1.80/$

Realized Spot Rate	Unanticipated Change in Expected Spot Rate	Gain (+) or Loss (−) on Contract
DM1.77/$	−DM0.03/$	DM30,000
DM1.78/$	−DM0.02/$	DM20,000
DM1.79/$	−DM0.01/$	DM10,000
DM1.80/$	0	0
DM1.81/$	DM0.01/$	−DM10,000
DM1.82/$	DM0.02/$	−DM20,000
DM1.83/$	DM0.03/$	−DM30,000

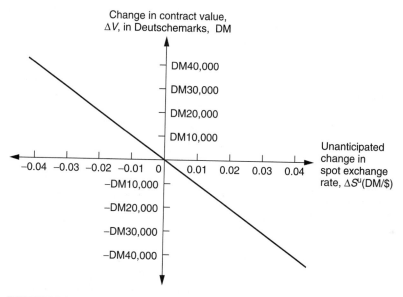

FIGURE 3.2. Payoff Profile on a Forward Contract to Sell $1 Million at DM1.80/$

The payoff profile from the forward sale of a currency has a slope that is the opposite of the slope for a forward purchase: compare Figure 3.2 to Figure 3.1. Figure 3.2 shows, for example, that if the realized DM price of the dollar is DM0.01/$ higher than had been expected, there is a loss on the forward sale of $1 million equal to DM0.01/$ × $1 million, or DM10,000. This is because the dollar has been sold forward for less than it subsequently becomes worth. This and other points on the payoff profile are obtained from Table 3.4.

The payoff profiles are useful for comparing the consequences of different foreign exchange management techniques. Before we turn in the next chapter to the profiles from other instruments, specifically, futures and options, let us consider a few other matters relating to the forward exchange market.

The Meaning of Outrights and Swaps

As Table 3.1 on page 59 shows, of the $384.4 billion daily turnover of forward exchange, the majority, $324.3 billion, takes the form of so-called **swaps.** The balance consists of **outright forward contracts.** As the name suggests, an outright forward exchange contract consists simply of an agreement to exchange currencies at an agreed price at a future date. For example, an agreement to buy Canadian dollars in 180 days at a rate of Can$1.3388/$ is an outright forward exchange contract. A swap, on the other hand, has two components, usually a spot transaction and a forward transaction in the reverse direction, although a swap could involve two forward transactions or borrowing one currency and lending another. For example, a **swap-in** Canadian consists of an agreement to buy Canadian dollars spot and sell Canadian dollars forward. A **swap-out** Canadian consists of an agreement to sell Canadian dollars spot and to buy Canadian dollars forward. An example of a swap involving two forward transactions would be a contract to buy Canadian dollars for 1 month forward and sell Canadian dollars for 2 months forward. This is a **forward-forward swap.** When the purchase and sale are separated by only 1 day, the swap is called a **rollover**. A definition of swaps that covers all these forms is:

> A swap is an agreement to buy and sell foreign exchange at prespecified exchange rates where the buying and selling are separated in time, or borrowing one currency and lending another.

The Uses of Swaps

Swaps are very valuable to those who are investing or borrowing in foreign currency. For example, a person who invests in a foreign treasury bill can use a spot-forward swap to avoid foreign exchange risk. The investor sells forward the foreign currency maturity value of the bill at the same time as the spot foreign exchange is purchased to pay for the bill. Since a known amount of the investor's home currency will be received according to the forward component of the swap, no uncertainty from exchange rates is faced. In a similar way, those who borrow in foreign currency can buy forward the foreign currency needed for repayment of the foreign currency loan at the same time that they convert the borrowed foreign funds on the spot market. The value of swaps to international investors and borrowers helps explain their growing popularity.

While valuable to investors and borrowers, swaps are not very useful to importers and exporters. Payments and receipts in international trade are frequently delayed. However, it is an outright forward purchase of foreign exchange that is valuable to the importer, not a swap. Similarly, the exporter needs to make an outright forward sale of foreign exchange. This is not, however, the place to present the details of these uses of forward exchange or the details of the value of forward exchange to borrowers and investors. That must wait until Part Four.

Swaps are popular with banks because it is difficult to avoid risk when making a market for many future dates and currencies. For some dates and currencies a bank will be **long** in foreign exchange, which means that it has agreed to purchase more of the foreign currency than it has agreed to sell. For other dates and currencies, a bank will be **short,** having agreed to sell more of these currencies than it has agreed

The following excerpt from the *Review* of the Federal Reserve Bank of St. Louis explains the difference between outright forwards and swaps, as well as the different users of these "products":

Participants in the foreign exchange market also deal for future value dates. Such dealing composes the forward markets. Active forward markets exist for a few heavily traded currencies and for several time intervals corresponding to actively dealt maturities in the money market. Markets can also be requested and made for other maturities, however. Since the foreign exchange market is unregulated, standard contract specifications are matters of tradition and convenience, and they can be modified by the transacting agents.

Forward transactions generally occur in two different ways: outright and swap. An outright forward transaction is what the name implies, a contract for an exchange of currencies at some future value date. "Outrights" generally occur only between market-making banks and their commercial clients. The interbank market for outrights is very small.

A swap is simply a combination of two simultaneous trades: an outright forward contract and an opposing spot deal. For example, a bank might "swap in" six-month yen by simultaneously buying spot yen and selling six-month forward yen. . . .

In practice, the vast majority of foreign exchange transactions involve the U.S. dollar and some other currency. The magnitude of U.S. foreign trade and investment flows implies that, for almost any other currency, the bilateral dollar exchange markets will have the largest volume.

Source: Mark D. Flood, "Microstructure Theory and the Foreign Exchange Market," *Review,* Federal Reserve Bank of St. Louis, November/December 1991, pp. 52–70.

---

to buy. Swaps help the bank to economically reduce risk. For example, if bank A is long on spot British pounds and short on 30-day forward pounds, it will find another bank, bank B, in the opposite situation. Bank A will sell pounds spot and buy pounds forward—a swap-out sterling—to bank B. In this manner, both banks balance their spot-versus-forward positions while economizing on the number of transactions required to achieve this balance. The use of only standard-length contracts, or so-called **even-dated contracts,** leaves some exposure to remaining long and short positions from day to day: exposure persists *within* the month-long intervals of even-dated contracts. This can be covered with **rollover swaps.** In this way swaps allow banks to exchange their surpluses and shortages of individual currencies to offset spot and forward trades with their customers and with each other. It should be no surprise that matching customer trades with appropriate swaps is a complex and dynamic problem.[4] Exhibits 3.1 and 3.2 summarize the different uses of swaps and outrights and some of the characteristics of the forward market.

THE FLEXIBILITY OF FORWARD EXCHANGE

The forward market offers more flexibility than Figure 2.4 on page 45 might indicate. For example, as Table 3.5 shows, while the majority of contracts involve the

---

[4]The reader is referred to the many accounts of this dynamic market. *Foreign Exchange Markets in the United States,* by Roger Kubarych, Federal Reserve Bank of New York, 1978, is an excellent account of the New York foreign exchange market. Other valuable sources include Paul Einzig, *A Dynamic Theory of Forward Exchange,* Macmillan, London, 1966, and Raymond G. Connix, *Foreign Exchange Today,* revised ed., Wiley, New York, 1980.

EXHIBIT 3.2
Differences between Outright Forwards and Swaps

The following excerpt from the biannual survey of foreign exchange markets by the Basle-based Bank for International Settlements highlights the important differences between outright forwards and swaps. For example, it explains how much more "international" are swaps.

The forward market comprises two distinct segments, the outright forward market and the swap market. Outright forward deals are similar to spot transactions except that they are for settlement more than two days hence. Swap deals on the other hand have two separate legs. The two counterparties agree to exchange two currencies at a particular rate at one date and to reverse the transaction, generally at a different rate, at some future date. Most swaps have a spot and a forward leg but forward/forward transactions also take place. Swap transactions in the exchange market involve the exchange of principal. In this they differ from other currency swaps (for example interest rate swaps) which entail the exchange of cash flows. . . .

The maturity of most forward business is quite short. Nearly two thirds of all transactions have a maturity of seven days or less, and only 1% have a maturity of more than one year. There is some variation across countries, with shorter maturities tending to account for a larger share of business in the countries with the most active markets. . . .

The outright forward market is strikingly different from other market segments. Firstly, a far larger share of this type of business is with "customers," particularly in countries which do not host major trading centers. In the market as a whole, almost half of all outright forward deals are with customers. . . . Many of the deals are undertaken to hedge exposures arising from foreign trade rather than to manage financial risks arising from funding and portfolio decisions.

A second notable feature of the outright forward market is that trading is less international than in other market segments. Almost 56% of all deals are concluded with counterparties located in the same country, with the share of local deals being higher, sometimes much higher, in countries with small markets. The domestic orientation of the outright forward market owes much to the importance of business with customers, which tends to be more local in character.

The swap market is the second largest market segment after the spot market and one of the fastest growing. It is capable of being used to a considerable degree for the purpose of hedging financial risk—in contrast to the use of outright forwards mainly for commercial risk hedging. . . . The swap market is heavily concentrated on the U.S. dollar. This currency is involved on one side in 95% of all transactions. . . . Swap business is quite international, with about 57% of transactions being concluded with counterparties located abroad. The pattern of cross-border trading is not much different from that of the market as a whole. Dealers tend to do more of their business with counterparties located abroad while customers conclude the bulk (71%) of their deals with local counterparties.

Source: Central Bank Survey of Foreign Exchange Market Activity in April 1992, Bank for International Settlements, Basle, Switzerland, March 1993, pp. 18–20.

U.S. dollar versus the major currencies, there are contracts against less important currencies and also **cross forwards** between other major currencies.[5] Furthermore, while Figure 2.4 suggests only a few specific and rather short maturities of forward contracts—30 days, 90 days, and 180 days—contracts can actually be arranged for bank customers for any period from a couple of days up to several years. On February 17, 1994, a corporate buyer of sterling might well want to take delivery of pounds on May 28, 1995, to meet a sterling obligation that will come due on that date. Forward currency can be bought or sold for the value date, May 28, 1995. Since for most currencies the spot market value date is already 2 business days in the future, the shortest forward contracts are for 3 days.

[5]Table 3.5 also shows currency pairs for futures and options, which are discussed in Chapter 4. The table makes it clear that futures and options are more concentrated in the mark and yen versus the U.S. dollar than is the forward market.

TABLE 3.5. Currency Pairs in Forward Contracts
(Percent of daily turnover in April 1992)

Currency Pair	Outright Forward	Swaps	Futures	Options
U.S. dollar/German mark	21.7	19.4	41.5	34.3
U.S. dollar/Japanese yen	20.4	25.0	29.9	27.9
U.S. dollar/British pound	9.4	11.5	11.1	4.1
U.S. dollar/Swiss franc	6.1	6.8	7.2	3.3
U.S. dollar/Canadian dollar	2.9	4.9	2.9	2.7
German mark/British pound	3.1	0.7	0.1	5.8
German mark/Japanese yen	3.5	0.3	0.1	6.0
U.S. dollar/Australian dollar	2.1	3.4	2.0	2.2
U.S. dollar/French franc	2.3	3.8	0.1	1.3
German mark/Swiss franc	1.6	0.2	0.1	2.4
Other intra-EMS* currencies, excluding DM/£	4.0	1.0	0.2	1.4
All other	23.0	23.1	4.9	8.5

*EMS stands for European Monetary System, described in Chapter 8.
Source: Central Bank Survey of Foreign Exchange Market Activity in April 1992, Bank for International Settlements, Basle, March 1993.

Sometimes buyers and sellers of forward exchange are not precisely sure when they will need their foreign currency or when they will receive it. For example, a U.S. importer may know that he or she must pay a British producer 30 days after delivery of the goods, but the exact day of delivery may not be known because of possible shipping delays. To take care of this, banks also sell forward exchange with some flexibility, allowing buyers to take delivery of foreign exchange on any day during the last 10 days of the contract period, or according to some other flexible scheme. Flexibility will cost the buyer a little more, the exchange rate being the most unfavorable for the customer during the period of possible delivery. However, it can relieve the buyer of considerable worry.

FORWARD QUOTATIONS

Swap Points and Outright Forwards

Even though some forward contracts are outright, the convention in the interbank market is to quote all forward rates in terms of the spot rate and the number of **swap points** for the forward maturity in question. For example, the 180-day forward Canadian rate would conventionally be quoted as

Spot	180-Day Swap
1.3365–70	23–27

The quote on the spot is the way spot transactions themselves are quoted and is in Canadian dollars per U.S. dollar. The spot rate means that the bid on U.S. dollars is Can$1.3365 (the quoting bank is willing to pay Can$1.3365 per U.S. dollar) and the ask on U.S. dollars is Can$1.3370 (the quoting bank will sell U.S. dollars for

Can$1.3370 per U.S. dollar). The swap points, 23–27 in this example, must be added to or subtracted from the spot bid and ask rates. The need to add or subtract depends on whether the two numbers in the swap points are ascending or descending. Let us consider an example.

When the swap points are ascending, as they are in the example, the swap points are added to the spot rates so that the implied bid on U.S. dollars for 180 days ahead is

$$Can\$1.3365/\$ + Can\$0.0023/\$ = Can\$1.3388/\$$$

That is, the quotation "Spot 1.3365–70; 180-day swap 23–27" means the quoting bank is bidding Can$1.3388 on the U.S. dollar for 180 days forward. In other words, the quoting bank is willing to buy 180-day forward U.S. dollars—sell Canadian—at Can$1.3388 per U.S. dollar. (This is the 180-day outright forward rate in Figure 2.4 on page 45.) Similarly, the above quote, "Spot 1.3365–70; 180-day swap 23–27," is an implied outright ask on U.S. dollars for 180 days of

$$Can\$1.3370/\$ + Can\$0.0027/\$ = Can\$1.3397/\$$$

This means the quoting bank is willing to sell forward U.S. dollars—buy Canadian—for Can$1.3397/$. The need to add the swap points in this case is due to the ascending order of the swap points: 27 is larger than 23. If the numbers were reversed, the points would have to be subtracted. For example, suppose the Canadian dollar had been quoted as

Spot	180-Day Swap
1.3365–70	27–23

The bid and ask on the U.S. spot are the same as before: the market-maker bids Can$1.3365 on the U.S. dollar and asks Can$1.3370. However, the implied outright bid on the U.S. dollar for 180 days forward is

$$Can\$1.3365/\$ - Can\$0.0027/\$ = Can\$1.3338/\$$$

That is, the market-maker is willing to buy U.S. dollars for delivery in 180 days for Can$1.3338/$. Similarly, the implied ask on the U.S. dollar for 180 days forward is

$$Can\$1.3370/\$ - Can\$0.0023/\$ = Can\$1.3347/\$$$

The need to add or subtract points based simply on the order of the swap points—ascending or descending—is a matter of convention. There is, however, a simple way of checking whether the arithmetic has been done correctly. Specifically, we note in the first case where we had

Spot	180-Day Swap
1.3365–70	23–27

that there are 5 basis points in the spot spread, Can$1.3365/$ versus Can$1.3370/$. However, the implied 180-day forward spread is larger because we calculated the 180-day bid on the U.S. dollar as Can$1.3388/$ and the ask on the U.S. dollar as Can$1.3397/$. This is a spread of 9 points (1.3397 − 1.3388). Similarly, in the second case where we had

Spot	180-Day Swap
1.3365–70	27–23

the spot has the same 5-point spread. The implied 180-day outright forwards are recalculated as a 180-day bid on the U.S. dollar of Can$1.3338/$ and an ask of Can$1.3347/$. The spread on the 180-day forward rate is larger than on the spot rate, again being 9 points (1.3347 − 1.3338) on the forward versus 5 points on the spot. The simple test of the outright calculation arithmetic is that spreads widen with maturity.

The same rule of adding swap points when they are in ascending order and sub- tracting them when they are in descending order applies whether exchange rates are quoted in foreign currency per U.S. dollar, as are all currencies except the pound, or as U.S. dollars per foreign currency, as for the pound. For example, suppose a market-making bank is quoting British pounds as

Spot	30-Day Swap	90-Day Swap	180-Day Swap
1.4780–85	19–17	55–50	95–85

that is, with the forward swap points descending in magnitude. In this case the swap points must be subtracted, giving the implied forward outrights quoted in Table 3.6.

While the rule for adding or subtracting points depending on whether they are ascending or descending is the same whether rates are quoted in currency per U.S. dollar (European terms) or as U.S. dollar per unit of foreign currency (U.S. dollar equivalent), the interpretation of whether the foreign currency is at a forward pre- mium or discount is different. In the case of the foreign currency per U.S. dollar quotation used for currencies other than the British pound, adding points means that the foreign currency is at a forward discount; there is more foreign currency per dol- lar for forward than for spot delivery. This means that for a quotation stated as for- eign currency per U.S. dollar, an ascending order of swap points means the foreign currency is at a forward discount, and a descending order means the foreign cur- rency is at a forward premium. This is the opposite of the situation with U.S. dollar equivalent quotation, as with the British pound. Clearly, it is necessary for foreign currency traders to think quickly and accurately.

Bid-Ask Spreads and Forward Maturity

The validity check that we have suggested—that is, of seeing whether implied out- right rates have wider spreads with increasing forward maturities—is based on spreads observed in the market. The reason banks quote larger spreads on longer- maturity contracts is not, as some people seem to think, that longer-maturity con- tracts are riskier to the banks because there is more time during which spot exchange

TABLE 3.6. Bids and Asks on Pounds

	U.S. Dollars/£ Sterling		
Type of Exchange	Bank Buys Sterling (Bids)	Bank Sells Sterling (Asks)	Spread (Points)
Spot	1.4780	1.4785	5
30-day	1.4761	1.4768	7
90-day	1.4725	1.4735	10
180-day	1.4685	1.4700	15

rates might change. As we have seen, banks tend to balance their forward positions by the use of swaps and rollovers, and since they can simultaneously buy and sell forward for every maturity, they can avoid losses from changes in exchange rates during the terms of forward contracts; what the banks gain (lose) on forward contracts to *sell* they lose (gain) on offsetting forward contracts to *buy*. Rather, the reason spreads increase with maturity is the increasing **thinness** of the forward market as maturity increases.

Increasing thinness means smaller trading volumes, which in turn means greater difficulty offsetting positions in the interbank forward market after taking orders to buy or sell forward; since banks state their market and are then obligated if their bid or ask is accepted, they may have to enter the market immediately themselves to help offset the position they have just taken; the market-makers cannot count on receiving offsetting bids and asks and simply enjoying their spreads. The longer the maturity, the less likely are unsolicited offsetting orders, and therefore the more likely the market-maker is to face other market-makers' spreads. The difficulty of offsetting longer-maturity forward contracts makes them riskier than shorter-maturity contracts, but the extra risk involves uncertainty about the price of an offsetting forward contract immediately after quoting, rather than uncertainty about the path of the spot exchange rate during the maturity of the forward contract.

Maturity Dates and Value Dates

Contracts traded on the interbank forward market are mostly for even dates—1 month, 6 months, and so on. The value date of an even-dated contract such as, for example, a 1-month forward, is the same day in the next month as the value date for a currently agreed spot transaction. For example, if a forward contract is written on Monday, May 18, a day for which spot transactions are for value on Wednesday, May 20, the value date for a 1-month forward is June 20, the value date for a 2-month forward is July 20, and so on. A 1-year forward contract agreed to on May 18 is for value on May 20 in the following year. However, if the future date is not a business day, the value date is moved to the next business day. For example, if a 1-month forward contract is agreed on Tuesday, May 19, a day for which spot value is May 21, the 1-month forward value date would not be Saturday, June 21, but rather the following business day, Monday, June 23. The exception to this rule is that when the next business day means jumping to the following month, the forward value date is moved to the *preceding* business day rather than the *next* business day. In this way, a 1-month forward always settles in the following month, a 2-month forward always settles 2 months later, and so on.[6]

It makes no difference whether the terminology used is "1-month," "2-months," and so on, or "30 days," "60 days," and so on: the same rules for determining the value dates for forward contracts apply whichever way we refer to even-dated contracts.

---

[6]When holiday dates differ between countries so that the value date in one country is a business day and in the other it is not, the value date is determined by the business days of the bank making the market, that is, the bank which was called to quote its market.

1. A forward exchange contract is an agreement to exchange currencies at a future date at a precontracted exchange rate. Forward contracts are written by banks and trade between banks in the interbank market and are sold to banks' clients.
2. As with the spot market, the forward market is a decentralized continuous open-bid double-auction market. Forward exchange trades in both outright and swap form, where the latter involves the purchase and subsequent sale of a currency.
3. A forward premium on a foreign currency means that the forward value of the foreign currency exceeds the currency's spot value. A forward discount means the forward value is less than the spot value.
4. If speculators are risk-neutral and transaction costs are not considered, the forward exchange rate equals the expected future spot rate.
5. Payoff profiles show the change in value of an asset or liability that is associated with unanticipated changes in exchange rates. For forward contracts, payoff profiles are upward- or downward-sloping straight lines.
6. Swaps, which involve a double-direction exchange—usually a spot exchange subsequently reversed by a forward exchange—are traded between banks so that individual banks can efficiently manage their foreign exchange risk.
7. Swaps are also valuable to international investors and borrowers, whereas outright forwards are valuable to importers and exporters.
8. In the interbank-market forward exchange rates are quoted as the spot rate plus or minus swap points. The swap points are added to or subtracted from the spot rate depending on the ascending or descending order of the swap points.
9. It is possible to tell from the order of swap points whether a currency is at a forward premium or discount.
10. Forward bid-ask spreads widen with increased maturity because of the increasing thinness of markets as maturity increases.

REVIEW QUESTIONS

1. What is a forward rate?
2. What is a forward premium?
3. What is a forward discount?
4. Why and under what conditions is the forward rate equal to the expected future spot rate?
5. What goes on the axes of a payoff profile for a forward exchange contract?
6. How does an outright forward contract differ from a swap?
7. What does it mean to be "long" in a currency?
8. What does it mean to be "short" in a currency?
9. What is meant by an "even-dated" forward contract?
10. What is the meaning of the "value date" on a forward contract?

ASSIGNMENT PROBLEMS

1. Why are forward spreads on less-traded currencies larger than on heavily traded currencies?
2. Why do banks quote mainly even-dated forward rates—for example, 30-day rates and 90-day rates—rather than uneven-dated rates? How would you prorate the rates of uneven-dated maturities?

3. Compute the outright forward quotations from the following swap quotations of Canadian dollars in European terms:

Spot	30-Day Swap	90-Day Swap	180-Day Swap
1.3910–15	10–9	12–10	15–12

4. Under what condition(s) would spreads widen quickly as we move forward to longer maturities in the forward market?

5. Could a bank that trades forward exchange ever hope to balance the buys and sells of forward currencies for each future date? How do swap contracts help?

6. Why do banks operate a forward exchange market in only a limited number of currencies? Does it have to do with the ability to balance buy orders with sell orders, and is it the same reason why they rarely offer contracts of over 5 years?

7. Why is risk neutrality relevant for the conclusion that forward exchange rates equal expected future spot exchange rates?

8. Why is it necessary to assume zero spreads when concluding that forward exchange rates equal expected future spot rates?

9. Plot the payoff profile for a forward contract to buy $1 million U.S. at Can$1.3500/$.

10. Plot the payoff profile for a forward contract to sell $1 million U.S. at ¥100/$.

BIBLIOGRAPHY

Burnham, James B.: "Current Structure and Recent Developments in Foreign Exchange Markets," in Sarkis J. Khoury (ed.), *Recent Developments in International Banking and Finance,* volume IV, Elsevier, Amsterdam, 1991, pp. 123–153.

Chrystal, K. Alec: "A Guide to Foreign Exchange Markets," *Review,* Federal Reserve Bank of St. Louis, March 1984, pp. 5–18.

Einzig, Paul A.: *The Dynamic Theory of Forward Exchange,* 2d ed., Macmillan, London, 1967.

Flood, Mark D.: "Microstructure Theory and the Foreign Exchange Market," *Review,* Federal Reserve Bank of St. Louis, November/December 1991, pp. 52–70.

Glassman, Debra: "Exchange Rate Risk and Transaction Costs: Evidence from Bid-Ask Spreads," *Journal of International Money and Finance,* December 1987, pp. 479–490.

Kubarych, Roger M.: *Foreign Exchange Markets in the United States,* Federal Reserve Bank of New York, New York, 1983.

Riehl, Heinz, and Rita M. Rodriguez: *Foreign Exchange and Money Markets: Managing Foreign and Domestic Currency Operations,* McGraw-Hill, New York, 1983.

CHAPTER 4

Currency Futures and Options Markets

Futures and options on futures are derivative assets; that is, their values are derived from underlying asset values. Futures derive their value from the underlying currency, and options on currency futures derive their values from the underlying futures contracts. . . .

—*Chicago Fed Letter,* November 1989

CURRENCY FUTURES

What Is a Currency Future?

Currency futures are standardized contracts that trade like conventional commodity futures on the floor of a futures exchange. Orders to buy or sell a fixed amount of foreign currency are received by brokers or exchange members. These orders, from companies, individuals, and even market-making commercial banks, are communicated to the floor of the futures exchange. At the exchange, **long positions** (orders to buy a currency) are matched with **short positions** (orders to sell). The exchange, or more precisely, its **clearing corporation,** guarantees both sides of each two-sided contract, that is, the contract to buy and the contract to sell. The willingness to buy versus the willingness to sell moves futures prices up and down to maintain a balance between the number of buy and sell orders. The market-clearing price is reached in the vibrant, somewhat chaotic-appearing **trading pit** of the futures exchange. Currency futures began trading in the International Money Market (IMM) of the Chicago Mercantile Exchange in 1972. Since then many other markets have opened, including the COMEX commodities exchange in New York, the Chicago Board of Trade, and the London International Financial Futures Exchange (LIFFE).

In order for a market to be made in currency futures contracts, it is necessary to have only a few value dates. At the Chicago IMM, there are four value dates of contracts: the third Wednesday in the months March, June, September, and December. In the rare event that contracts are held to maturity, delivery of the underlying foreign currency occurs 2 business days after the contract matures to allow for the normal 2-day delivery of spot currency. Contracts are traded in specific sizes—£62,500, Can\$100,000, and so on. This keeps the contracts sufficiently homogeneous and

75

few in variety that there is enough depth for a market to be made. The currencies that are traded, along with their contract sizes, are shown in Figure 4.1.

Figure 4.1 shows that in the IMM of the Chicago Mercantile Exchange, futures prices of foreign currencies are quoted as U.S. dollar equivalents, that is, as U.S. dollars per unit of foreign currency. On the other hand, forward rates, except for the British pound, are quoted in European terms, that is, as foreign currency per U.S. dollar. In the case of the Japanese yen the first two digits of the U.S. dollar price of the yen are omitted. This is the meaning of the (.00) in the heading above the yen futures prices. For example, the contract maturing in March has a settle price of $0.009593 per Japanese yen.

FIGURE 4.1. Currency Futures Quotations on the International Money Market of the Chicago Mercantile Exchange, February 17, 1994

Futures prices are quoted in U.S. dollar equivalent terms. Prices are per unit of foreign currency, so that prices of contracts are the contract sizes—shown above the respective quotations—multiplied by the exchange rates. In the case of the Japanese yen, it is necessary to put 0.00 in front of the unit price. Alternatively, yen prices are for 100 yen. (Reprinted by permission of *The Wall Street Journal*, © 1994 Dow Jones & Company Inc. All rights reserved worldwide.)

CURRENCY

	Open	High	Low	Settle	Change	Lifetime High	Lifetime Low	Open Interest
JAPAN YEN (CME) – 12.5 million yen; $ per yen (.00)								
Mar	.9645	.9680	.9580	.9593	– .0052	.9930	.8700	93,575
June	.9672	.9708	.9616	.9628	– .0053	.9945	.8540	8,404
Sept	.9695	.9695	.9670	.9672	– .0056	.9895	.8942	838
Est vol 34,958; vol Wed 33,716; open int 102,818, –313.								
DEUTSCHEMARK (CME) – 125,000 marks; $ per mark								
Mar	.5794	.5796	.5756	.5785	– .0005	.6205	.5642	125,531
June	.5745	.5765	.5726	.5755	– .0004	.6162	.5607	10,354
Sept	.5739	.5739	.5715	.5735	– .0004	.6130	.5600	332
Est vol 55,181; vol Wed 52,404; open int 136,284, +679.								
CANADIAN DOLLAR (CME) – 100,000 dlrs.; $ per Can $								
Mar	.7408	.7487	.7408	.7474	+ .0072	.7860	.7394	37,947
June	.7419	.7485	.7419	.7468	+ .0072	.7805	.7365	2,829
Sept	.7435	.7460	.7435	.7465	+ .0072	.7740	.7330	669
Dec	.7430	.7455	.7430	.7463	+ .0072	.7670	.7290	577
Mr95	.7425	.7429	.7425	.7463	+ .0072	.7605	.7376	370
Est vol 10,215; vol Wed 4,059; open int 42,404, + 1,184.								
BRITISH POUND (CME) – 62,500 pds.; $ per pound								
Mar	1.4746	1.4796	1.4720	1.4764	+ .0022	1.5550	1.3950	40,094
June	1.4700	1.4738	1.4670	1.4714	+ .0024	1.5300	1.4350	2,540
Sept	1.4640	1.4670	1.4630	1.4676	+ .0026	1.4950	1.4570	437
Est vol 13,348; vol Wed 15,878; open int 43,083, +1,417.								
SWISS FRANC (CME) – 125,000 francs; $ per franc								
Mar	.6868	.6882	.6836	.6858	– .0013	.7195	.6470	40,407
June	.6845	.6872	.6830	.6849	– .0014	.7081	.6590	1,625
Est vol 27,966; vol Wed 14,605; open int 42,080, +407.								
AUSTRALIAN DOLLAR (CME) – 100,000 dlrs.; $ per A.$								
Mar	.7127	.7175	.7127	.7174	+ .0050	.7175	.6380	6,989
Est vol 787; vol Wed 813; open int 7,049, –129.								
U.S. DOLLAR INDEX (FINEX) – 1,000 times USDX								
Mar	95.31	95.70	95.17	95.33	– .01	98.00	91.78	4,297
June	94.96	96.16	95.96	95.95	– .02	99.04	92.70	1,374
Est vol 3,200; vol Wed 2,090; open int 5,879, –690.								
The index: High 95.45; Low 95.00; Close 95.15 – .01								

The prices in Figure 4.1 are U.S. dollar prices *per unit* of foreign currency. To convert these *per-unit* prices into futures *contract* prices it is necessary to multiply the prices in the table by the contract amounts. For example, the Japanese yen contract is for ¥12.5 million. With the settle price per yen for March delivery of $0.009593, the price of one Japanese yen March contract is

$$\$0.009593/¥ \times ¥12,500,000 = \$119,912.50$$

Note that as always, the currency symbols can be canceled, so that ¥ disappears, leaving a price in U.S. dollars. Similarly, a March 1995 Canadian dollar contract has a settle price of

$$\$0.7463/Can\$ \times Can\$100,000 = \$74,630$$

As with forward exchange contracts, if we assume risk neutrality, the per-unit price of futures equals the market's expected future spot rate of the foreign currency. Otherwise, if, for example, the expected March 1995 spot rate of the Canadian dollar were above $0.7463/Can$, speculators would buy Canadian dollar futures, pushing the futures price up to the expected future spot level. Similarly, if the expected March 1995 spot rate were below the futures price of $0.7463/Can$, speculators would sell Canadian dollar futures until they had forced the futures price back to the expected future spot rate. It follows that it is changes in the market's expected future spot exchange rate that drive futures contract prices up and down.

Both buyers and sellers of currency futures must post a **margin** and pay a transaction fee. The margin is posted in a margin account at a brokerage house, which in turn posts a margin at the clearing corporation of the exchange. The clearing corporation, in turn, pairs buy and sell orders, that is, matches each buy order with a sell order. As we have said, all buy and sell orders are guaranteed by the clearing corporation. Margins must be supplemented by contract holders and brokerage houses if the amount in a margin account falls below a certain level, called the **maintenance level.** For example, the IMM's required *minimum* margin on sterling (British pounds) is currently $2000 per contract, and its maintenance level is $1500.[1] This means that if the market value of the contract valued at the settle price falls more than $500, the full amount of the decline in value must be added to the clients' and the brokers' margin accounts. Declines in contract values which are small enough to leave more than $1500 of equity do not require action. Increases in the values of contracts are added to margin accounts and can be withdrawn. Margin adjustment is done on a daily basis and is called **marking to market.** Let us consider an example of marking to market.

Marking to Market: An Example

Suppose that on day 1, a British pound June contract is purchased at the opening price of $1.4700/£. This means that one contract for £62,500 has a market price of

$$\$1.4700/£ \times £62,500 = \$91,875$$

---

[1]Brokers who trade on the IMM are required to set the IMM's minimum initial margin and maintenance level for clients, but they may, and often do, require more. Brokers face the minimum levels. All futures trading in the United States is regulated by the Commodities Futures Trading Commission (CFTC).

The settle price, which is the price at the end of the day used for calculating settlements with the exchange, is $1.4714/£; this is the market's expected future spot price for June at the end of day 1. At this price, the June pound contract to buy £62,500 is worth

$$\$1.4714/£ \times £62,500 = \$91,962.50$$

The purchase of the pound futures contract has earned the contract buyer

$$\$91,962.50 - \$91,875 = \$87.50$$

We assume this is left in the purchaser's margin account and added to the $2000 originally placed in the account. This is all shown in Table 4.1.

Suppose that on day 2 the June pound futures rate falls to $1.4640/£. The contract is now worth

$$\$1.4640/£ \times £62,500 = \$91,500$$

Compared to the previous settle contract price of $91,962.50 there is a loss of

$$\$91,500 - \$91,962.50 = -\$462.50$$

When this is deducted from the margin account the total is $1625 ($2087.50 − $462.50). The margin remains above the maintenance level of $1500 so nothing needs to be done.

Suppose that on day 3, because of a decline in the expected future spot rate, the settle price on June pounds falls to $1.4600. The contract is now valued at

$$\$1.4600/£ \times £62,500 = \$91,250$$

The loss from the previous day is

$$\$91,250 - \$91,500 = -\$250$$

This brings the margin account to $1625 − $250 = $1375, which is below the maintenance level of $1500. The contract buyer is asked to bring the account up to $2000, requiring that at least $625 be put in the buyer's account.

If on day 4 the June futures rate settles at $1.4750, the contract is worth

$$\$1.4750/£ \times £62,500 = \$92,187.50$$

This is a gain over the previous settlement of

TABLE 4.1. Settlements on a Pound Futures Contract

Day	Opening or Settle Price	Contract Price	Margin Adjustment	Margin Contribution (+) or Withdrawal (−)	Margin Account
1 Opening	$1.4700/£	$91,875.0	0	+$2000.00	$2000.00
1 Settle	$1.4714/£	$91,962.5	+$87.50	0	$2087.50
2 Settle	$1.4640/£	$91,500.0	−$462.50	0	$1625.00
3 Settle	$1.4600/£	$91,250.0	−$250.00	+$625.00	$2000.00
4 Settle	$1.4750/£	$92,187.5	+$937.50	−$937.50	$2000.00

$$\$92,187.50 - \$91,250 = \$937.50$$

The margin account becomes $2937.50, and the contract owner can either withdraw the $937.50 or use it toward the margin on another futures contract. We assume it is withdrawn. All this is summarized in Table 4.1.

We have seen that with risk neutrality, the futures price equals the market's expected future spot exchange rate. Therefore, the example indicates that futures can be thought of as daily bets on the value of the expected future spot exchange rate, where the bets are settled each day. In particular, on the other side of the margin adjustments to the futures *buyer's* account described above and in Table 4.1 are the adjustments to the margin account of the *seller* of June pounds. When the buyer's account is adjusted up, the seller's account is adjusted down the same amount. That is, what buyers gain, sellers lose, and vice versa. The two sides are taking daily bets against each other.

Futures Contracts versus Forward Contracts

The daily settlement of bets on futures means that a futures contract is equivalent to entering a forward contract each day and settling each forward contract before opening another one, where the forwards and futures are for the same future delivery date.[2] The daily marking to market on futures means that any losses or gains are realized as they occur, on a daily cycle. With the loser supplementing the margin daily and in relatively modest amounts, the risk of default is minimal. Of course, with the clearing corporation of the exchange guaranteeing all contracts, the risk of default is faced by the clearing corporation. Were the clearing corporation not to guarantee all contracts, the party winning the daily bets would be at risk if the losing party did not pay. Let us consider how this differs from the forward market.

In the forward market there is no formal and universal arrangement for settling up as the expected future spot rate and consequent forward contract value move up and down. Indeed, there is no formal and universal margin requirement.

Generally, in the case of interbank transactions and transactions with large corporate clients, banks require no margin, make no adjustment for day-to-day movements in exchange rates, and simply wait to settle up at the originally contracted rate. A bank will, however, generally reduce a client's existing line of credit. For example, if a bank has granted a client a $1 million line of credit and the customer trades $5 million forward, the bank is likely to reduce the credit line by, perhaps, $500,000, or 10 percent of the contract. For a customer without a credit line, the bank will require that a margin account be established. The procedure for maintaining the margin on a forward contract depends on the bank's relationship with the customer. Margin may be **called** on customers without credit lines, requiring supplementary funds to be deposited in the margin account if a large, unfavorable movement in the exchange rate occurs. In deciding whether to call for supplementing of margin accounts, banks consider the likelihood of their customers honoring forward contracts. The banks exercise considerable discretion, which is in sharp contrast to the formal daily marking to market of the futures market.

---

[2]See Fischer Black, "The Pricing of Commodity Contracts," *Journal of Financial Economics,* January/March 1976, pp. 167–179.

As with the situation of banks calling margin, many banks are also very flexible about what they will accept as margin. For example, stocks, bonds, and other instruments may be accepted in order to ensure that customers honor contracts, although it may be necessary to post more than 10 percent of the value of a forward contract if the instruments that are posted are risky. In the case of futures-exchange brokers' margins at the futures exchange, a substantial part of initial margins may be accepted in the form of securities, such as treasury bills, but subsequent maintenance payments are typically in cash. This means that while with forward contracts there is no opportunity cost of margin requirements, there may be such an opportunity cost with futures contracts, especially when contract prices have fallen and substantial cash payments have consequently been made into the margin account.

Unlike the case for forward contracts, when the buyer of a futures contract wants to take delivery of the foreign currency, the currency is bought at the going spot exchange rate at the time delivery is taken. What happens can be described by considering an example.

Suppose a futures contract buyer needs British pounds in August and buys a September pound futures contract.[3] In August, when the pounds are needed, the contract is sold back to the exchange, and the pounds are bought on the spot exchange market at whatever exchange rate exists on the day in August when the pounds are wanted. Most of the foreign exchange risk is still removed in this situation because if, for example, the pound has unexpectedly increased in value from the time of buying the futures contract, there will be a gain in the margin account. This gain will compensate for the higher-than-expected spot exchange rate in August. However, not all exchange-rate risk is removed, because the margin account will not in general *exactly* compensate for the unexpected movement in the spot exchange rate. The remaining risk is due to unpredictable variations in interest rates, which leave uncertainty in the amount in the account or in the cost of maintaining the account. Specifically, the amount in the margin account or paid to maintain it depends on the entire path of the futures price from initial purchase, and on interest rates earned in the account or forgone on cash contributions to the account. The risk due to variability in interest rates is called **marking-to-market risk,** and it makes futures contracts riskier than forward contracts, for which there is no marking to market.[4] Even in the very rare circumstance that delivery is taken on the maturity date of a futures contract, there is still marking-to-market risk because the margin account does not provide exact compensation for any unexpected change in the spot exchange rate.[5] This is again due to variations in interest rates. We see that a problem with futures in comparison with forwards is that futures contracts leave some risk when used as a risk-reducing vehicle, whereas forwards do not.

Another problem with using futures contracts to reduce foreign exchange risk is that the contract size is unlikely to correspond exactly to a firm's needs. For example, if a firm needs £50,000, the closest it can come is to buy one £62,500 contract. On the other hand, forward contracts with banks can be written for any desired amount. The

---

[3]Alternatively, a June contract might be purchased and delivery of the pounds taken. The pounds could then be held, earning interest until needed.

[4]While marking to market adds risk vis-à-vis forwards, the guarantee of the futures exchange to honor all contracts reduces risk.

[5]Statistics from the IMM show that fewer than 1 percent of futures contracts result in delivery. See *Currency Trading for Financial Institutions,* International Monetary Market, Chicago, 1982.

flexibility in values of forward contracts and in margin maintenance, as well as the absence of marking-to-market risk, make forwards preferable to futures for importers, exporters, borrowers, and lenders who wish to precisely hedge foreign exchange risk and exposure. Currency futures are more likely to be preferred by speculators because gains on futures contracts can be taken as cash and because the transactions costs are small.[6] As we have mentioned, with forward contracts it is necessary to buy an off-setting contract for the same maturity to lock in a profit and then to wait for maturity before settling the contracts and taking the gain. For example, if pounds are bought forward in May for delivery in December and by August the buyer wants to take a gain, in August it is necessary to sell pounds forward for December and then wait for the two contracts to mature in December to collect the gain.[7]

The extent to which futures are used to speculate rather than to hedge is indicated, albeit imperfectly, by the statistics on **open interest.** Open interest refers to the number of outstanding two-sided contracts at any given time. (Recall that orders to buy are matched with orders to sell, so each contract has two sides.) The statistics on open interest in Figure 4.1 indicate that most of the activity is in the nearest maturity contracts. While not apparent from Figure 4.1, open interest also falls off substantially just prior to maturity, with delivery rarely being taken. This does not necessarily mean that futures are used by speculators. However, the lack of delivery is consistent with futures being used for speculative purposes.[8]

Payoff Profiles on Currency Futures

It should come as little surprise that because currency futures are similar to forward contracts, the payoff profiles are also similar. The similarities between the profiles, as well as the minor differences that exist, can be clarified by considering an example similar to that used in Chapter 3 for a forward contract. The situation is summarized in Table 4.2 and in the associated payoff profile in Figure 4.2. Both the table and the figure describe the consequences of unanticipated changes in the spot exchange rate on the contract value and margin account of a purchaser of Deutschemark futures.

We assume that at the time of buying the futures contract the market's expected future spot rate for the maturity date of the contract is DM1.80/$ in the usual European terms. At this expected spot rate the futures market price per Deutschemark will be $0.5556/DM (1 ÷ DM1.80/$). Therefore, a futures contract for DM125,000 has a market price of

$$\$0.5556/DM \times DM125,000 = \$69,450$$

The purchaser is betting on the outcome vis-à-vis this price. Let us compare this contracted price with the realized value of DM125,000 to find the outcome of the bet.

If the eventually realized spot exchange rate in the usual European terms for

---

[6]A spread of 10 points on a forward contract for approximately $100,000 translates into $100, compared to a typical combined cost of a comparably valued futures purchase and subsequent sale of $20 to $40.

[7]Banks will sometimes offer to pay gains out early by discounting what is to be received. This is done to make forward contracts more competitive with futures as a speculative vehicle.

[8]See James Tobin, "On the Efficiency of the Financial System," *Lloyds Bank Review,* July 1984, pp. 1–15.

TABLE 4.2. Unanticipated Changes in Spot Rates and Futures to Buy Deutschemarks

Realized Spot Rate	Unexpected Change in Spot Rate	Per-Unit Futures Price at Maturity	Maturity Value of Contract	Accumulated Marking-to-Market Gain (+) or Loss (−)
DM1.77/$	−DM0.03/$	$0.5650/DM	$70,625.00	$1175.00±
DM1.78/$	−DM0.02/$	$0.5618/DM	$70,225.00	$775.00±
DM1.79/$	−DM0.01/$	$0.5587/DM	$69,837.50	$387.50±
DM1.80/$	0	$0.5556/DM	$69,450.00	0±
DM1.81/$	DM0.01/$	$0.5525/DM	$69,062.50	−$387.50±
DM1.82/$	DM0.02/$	$0.5495/DM	$68,687.50	−$762.50±
DM1.83/$	DM0.03/$	$0.5464/DM	$68,300.00	−$1150.00±

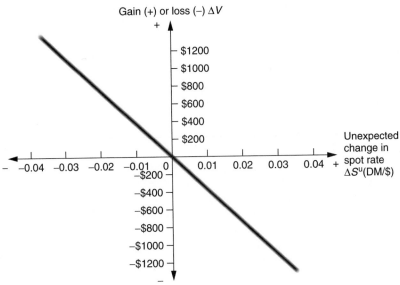

FIGURE 4.2. Payoff Profile on Purchase of Deutschemark Futures
An unexpected increase in the Deutschemark price of the dollar causes a loss on a futures contract to buy Deutschemarks. The exact loss depends on the time path of the expected future spot rate. Similarly, an unexpected decrease in the Deutschemark price of the dollar causes a gain on a futures contract to buy Deutschemarks, but again of an uncertain amount. Consequently, the payoff profile on a futures contract to buy Deutschemarks is a downward-sloping, somewhat fuzzy line, where the fuzziness reflects uncertainty about the exact gain or loss on the futures contract due to marking-to-market risk.

quoting Deutschemarks is DM1.79/$, the price per DM on the futures market at maturity will be $0.5587/DM (1 ÷ DM1.79/$). Therefore, a Deutschemark contract will be worth $0.5587/DM × DM125,000 = $69,837.50.[9] This represents a gain over the initially contracted price of $387.50 ($69,837.50 − $69,450). That is, the futures contract buyer has won $387.50 on the bet. However, depending on the actual time path of the expected future spot rate between the initial purchase of the contract at

DM1.80/$ and the contract's maturity, the gain, properly calculated, might not be *exactly* $387.50. For example, if it has been necessary to make many cash contributions to the margin account which have an opportunity cost, the true gain, including this cost, would be less than $387.50. Alternatively, if money has been withdrawn and invested, there might be more than $387.50 in margin plus interest earnings. The uncertainty is the result of marking-to-market risk and is shown in Table 4.2 by the ± in the last column.

Table 4.2 also shows that if the realized spot rate is DM1.82/$, the futures price per DM at maturity is $0.5495/DM ($1 \div$ DM1.82/$), and the DM purchase contract is worth $68,687.50 ($0.5495/DM × DM125,000). This is a loss vis-à-vis the contracted price of $69,450. The bet has resulted in a loss of $762.50 ($68,687.50 − $69,450). However, because of marking-to-market risk, the properly calculated loss might differ slightly from this amount. Other values in Table 4.2 are calculated in similar fashion. The table shows that as the eventually realized spot value of the Deutschemark increases—reading up the table from bottom to top—there is a larger and larger gain on the futures contract to buy Deutschemarks. The exact gain depends on the time path of the future's price from buying the contract to the contract's maturity, and on interest rates along this time path.

The unexpected change in the spot rate from purchase to maturity is the realized spot rate at maturity minus the expected spot rate at the time of buying the futures contract, DM1.80/$.[10] The unexpected change is plotted against the associated gain or loss on the contract in Figure 4.2. We see a downward-sloping line, akin to that plotted for the forward purchase of Deutschemarks in Chapter 3 (see Figure 3.2 on page 65). However, the downward-sloping line here is made purposely "fuzzy" because of uncertainty in precise payoffs that arise from marking-to-market risk.

The opposite side of the purchase of Deutschemark futures is the sale of Deutschemark futures. The payoffs for the sale of such futures are the numbers in the final column of Table 4.2, with the signs reversed, and the consequent payoff profile is an upward-sloping fuzzy line, with the same absolute value of slope as the downward-sloping line in Figure 4.2.

The Link between the Futures and Forward Markets

As Table 3.1 on page 59 shows clearly, the market for currency futures is small compared with the market for forwards, with over 40 times more forward than futures transactions, measured by value. However, despite the large difference in the sizes of the two markets, there is a mutual interdependence between them; each one is able to affect the other. This interdependence is the result of the action of arbitragers who can take offsetting positions in the two markets when prices differ.

---

[9]A minimum change in price per unit of currency—or **tick**—for the Deutschemark is $0.0001/DM, which for a contract of DM125,000 is worth $0.0001/DM × DM125,000 = $12.50. For the other currencies traded on the IMM the minimum price changes per unit and the associated contract price changes are Japanese yen ($0.000001/¥; $12.50); Canadian dollar ($0.0001/Can$; $10); British pound ($0.00002/£; $12.50); Swiss franc ($0.0001/SFr; $12.50); Australian dollar ($0.0001/A$; $10).

[10]We measure the unexpected change in the spot rate in European terms, that is, as DM per dollar, because this is the way rates on the spot market are conventionally quoted, and we want to make the payoff profiles comparable throughout the book. It is only for futures and options that Deutschemarks are quoted in U.S. dollar equivalent terms.

The most straightforward type of arbitrage involves offsetting outright forward and futures positions.[11]

If, for example, the 3-month forward buying price of pounds was \$1.5000/£ while the selling price on the same date on the Chicago IMM was \$1.5020/£, an arbitrager could buy forward from a bank and sell futures on the IMM. The arbitrager would make \$0.0020/£, so that on each contract for £62,500, he or she could make a profit of \$125 (\$0.0020/£ × £62,500). However, we should remember that since the futures market requires daily maintenance, or marking to market, the arbitrage involves risk which can allow the futures and forward rates to differ a little. It should also be clear that the degree to which middle exchange rates on the two markets can deviate will depend very much on the spreads between buying and selling prices. Arbitrage will ensure that the bid price of forward currency does not exceed the ask price of currency futures, and vice versa. However, the prices can differ a little beyond this due to marking-to-market risk. We should also note that the direction of influence is not invariably from the rate set on the larger forward market to the smaller futures market. When there is a move on the Chicago IMM that results in a very large number of margins being called, the scramble to close positions with sudden buying or selling can spill over into the forward market.

CURRENCY OPTIONS

What Is a Currency Option?

Forward exchange and currency futures contracts must be exercised. It is true that currency futures can be sold and margin gains can be withdrawn, and that forward contracts can be offset by going into an offsetting forward agreement. However, all forward contracts and currency futures must be honored by both parties. That is, the banks and their counterparties, or those holding outstanding futures, must settle. There is no option allowing a party to settle only if it is to that party's advantage.

Unlike forward and futures contracts, **currency options** give the buyer the opportunity, but not the obligation, to buy or sell at a preagreed price—the **strike price**, or **exercise price**—in the future. As the name suggests, an option contract allows the buyer who purchases it the option or right either to trade at the rate or price stated in the contract, if this is to the option buyer's advantage, or to let the option expire, if that would be better. That is, options have a throwaway feature.

Exchange-Traded Options

Futures Options versus Spot Options

At the IMM in Chicago, the currency options that trade are options on currency futures. Such options give the buyers the right but not the obligation to buy or sell currency futures contracts at a preagreed price. Options on futures derive their value

---

[11]We can note that even without any arbitrage via offsetting outright forward and futures positions, the rates for forward contracts and currency futures will be kept in line because users of these markets will choose between them if the rates differ. This is analogous to one-way arbitrage in the case of cross rates in Chapter 2.

from the prices of the underlying futures. The futures, in turn, derive their value, as we have seen, from the expected future spot value of the currency. Therefore, *indirectly,* options on futures derive their value from the expected future spot value of the underlying currency.

Currency options also trade on the Philadelphia Exchange. Unlike the IMM options, which are on currency futures, the Philadelphia options are on spot currency. These options give the buyers the right to buy or sell the currency itself at a preagreed price. Therefore, options on spot currency derive their value *directly* from the expected future spot value of the currency, not indirectly via the price of futures. However, ultimately, all currency options derive their value from movements in the underlying currency, and so in what follows, we can focus on the more direct linkage involving **spot option** contracts. Much of what we say also applies to **futures options**, which, as they approach maturity, become more and more like spot options.[12]

Characteristics of Spot Currency Options

We can illustrate the features of spot options by considering the quotations in Figure 4.3. The figure shows the wide variety of currency options trading on the Philadelphia Stock Exchange on February 28, 1994.

The first thing we notice in Figure 4.3 is that options trade on the same currencies as do futures on the Chicago IMM in Figure 4.1, namely, the British pound, German mark, Australian dollar, Canadian dollar, French franc, Japanese yen, and Swiss franc, plus the European Currency Unit (ECU).[13] The sizes of contracts are half of those of IMM currency futures. This is to help expand the number who feel they can afford to trade in options, while allowing options to be used in conjunction with futures.

If we examine the table, we see that quotations for "European style" option contracts are given for most currencies. The term "European style" has nothing to do with European terms for quotation; rather it has to do with when the option buyer can exercise the option, that is, buy or sell the currency at the strike price. **European options** can be exercised only on the maturity date of the option. They cannot be exercised before that date.

The alternative to the European option is the **American option.** The majority of options, those where it is not declared otherwise, are American options. American options offer buyers more flexibility in that they can be exercised on any date up to and including the maturity date of the option. Buyers would therefore pay no more for a European option of a given kind than for an American option.

The expiry months for options are March, June, September, and December, plus one or two near-term months. In Figure 4.3, March is one of the two near-term months, so the only other near-term month is April. No options in the table extend beyond June, making it clear that as yet, currency options are short-term.[14] Most

---

[12]As we have seen, if delivery on futures is taken, the currency is purchased at the spot rate. This means that at maturity of the futures contract, an option on currency futures is an option on the spot currency itself.

[13]The European Currency Unit is a basket of European currencies. It is described in the context of the European Monetary System in Chapter 8.

[14]Plans exist on the Philadelphia Exchange to introduce options with maturities of 13 to 24 months and 25 to 36 months as part of a much wider range of options products.

OPTIONS
PHILADELPHIA EXCHANGE

	Calls Vol.	Calls Last	Puts Vol.	Puts Last
BPound				**148.65**
31,250 British Pound EOM-European				
142½ Apr	...	...	600	0.50
145 Mar	...	...	400	0.45
145 Apr	...	...	1300	1.00
155 Mar	400	0.10	...	...
155 Apr	1900	0.55	...	...
DMark				**58.60**
62,500 German Mark EOM-European style.				
57 Mar	...	...	50	0.24
62,500 German Marks EOM-European style.				
54½ Mar	...	...	125	0.01
56½ Mar	...	...	275	0.12
59½ Mar	100	0.32	...	...
Australian Dollar				**71.32**
50,000 Australian Dollar EOM-cents per unit.				
69 Mar	...	...	10	0.08
73 Mar	10	0.20	...	...
50,000 Australian Dollars-cents per unit.				
68 Apr	...	...	10	0.08
70 Mar	...	...	20	0.08
70 Apr	...	...	5	0.56
72 Mar	20	0.27	...	...
72 Jun	2	1.09	...	...
73 Mar	...	...	5	1.50
74 Apr	10	0.20	...	...
British Pound				**148.65**
31,250 British Pounds-European Style.				
155 Apr	350	0.35	...	...
31,250 British Pounds-European units.				
145 Apr	...	...	350	0.80
31,250 British Pounds-cents per unit.				
142½ Apr	...	...	720	0.37
145 Mar	5	3.55	...	...
145 Apr	...	...	200	0.81
145 Jun	...	...	64	2.07
147½ Mar	76	1.60	...	...
147½ Apr	...	...	2	1.60
150 Mar	10	0.50	2	2.00
150 Apr	224	1.32	...	...
155 Apr	120	0.30	...	...
157½ Apr	600	0.14	...	...
British Pound-GMark				**253.13**
31,250 British Pound-German Mark cross.				
252 Mar	16	2.30	...	...
256 Mar	...	...	16	2.30
Canadian Dollar				**73.97**
50,000 Canadian Dollars-European Style.				
74½ Mar	...	...	1	0.68
50,000 Canadian Dollars-cents per unit.				
73½ Jun	...	...	30	0.72
74 Jun	...	...	12	1.00

	Calls Vol.	Calls Last	Puts Vol.	Puts Last
74½ Apr	15	0.36	10	0.95
75 Mar	...	...	13	1.05
75½ Mar	...	...	15	1.55
ECU				**113.49**
62,500 European Currency Units EOM-cents per unit.				
116 Mar	5	0.30	...	...
French Franc				**172.74**
250,000 French Francs-10ths of a cent per unit.				
17½ Mar	20	0.44	...	...
GMark-JYen				**61.19**
62,500 German Mark-Japanese Yen cross.				
60 Mar	10	1.03	...	...
60½ Mar	50	0.77	...	...
61 Mar	...	...	8	0.75
61½ Mar	...	...	10	1.05
German Mark				**58.60**
62,500 German Marks-European Style.				
56 Jun	...	...	25	0.53
57 Mar	...	...	25	0.09
57½ Mar	...	...	765	0.13
58 Mar	...	...	600	0.26
58½ Mar	100	0.37	...	...
59 Mar	556	0.31	...	...
59½ Mar	110	0.19	...	...
60½ Mar	60	0.05	...	...
62,500 German Marks-cents per unit.				
56 Mar	40	2.75	...	...
56 Apr	5	2.36	1030	0.18
56 Jun	...	...	150	0.49
56½ Apr	...	...	46	0.22
57 Mar	31	1.76	...	...
57 Jun	5	1.95	1209	0.78
57½ Mar	100	1.07	160	0.13
57½ Apr	...	...	360	0.48
58 Mar	207	0.85	32	0.26
58 Apr	...	...	1027	0.71
58 Jun	18	1.57	27	1.15
58½ Mar	6038	0.60	31	0.39
58½ Apr	...	...	360	0.89
59 Mar	406	0.36	28	0.66
59 Apr	913	0.71	...	...
59½ Mar	296	0.20	...	...
59½ Apr	32	0.51	...	...
60 Mar	130	0.11	...	...
60 Apr	546	0.40	...	...
60 Jun	2	0.78	...	...
60½ Apr	...	...	5	2.24
61 Apr	1350	0.18	...	...
61 Jun	5900	0.39	...	...

	Calls Vol.	Calls Last	Puts Vol.	Puts Last
Japanese Yen				**95.79**
6,250,000 Japanese Yen EOM-100ths of a cent per unit.				
92 Mar	...	...	535	0.26
6,250,000 Japanese Yen-100ths of a cent per unit.				
88 Mar	100	8.04	...	...
89 Mar	10	7.07	...	...
91 Mar	...	...	35	0.10
91 Apr	...	...	46	0.38
92 Jun	...	...	69	1.00
92½ Mar	...	...	50	0.20
93 Mar	10	3.31	5	0.22
93 Jun	...	...	169	1.28
93½ Mar	...	...	50	0.29
94 Apr	...	...	36	1.05
94 Jun	...	...	33	1.60
94½ Mar	...	...	60	0.50
95 Mar	4	1.73	7	0.65
95 Apr	2	2.62	5	1.39
95 Jun	...	...	12	2.00
96 Mar	1	1.00	...	...
96 Apr	...	...	5	1.87
96 Jun	1	2.84	35	2.50
97½ Mar	20	0.54	...	...
98 Mar	10	0.42	...	...
99 Mar	503	0.25	...	...
99 Apr	120	0.94	...	...
100 Mar	10	0.06	75	4.12
102 Apr	46	0.35	...	...
6,250,000 Japanese Yen-European Style.				
91 Mar	5	5.10	...	...
91 Jun	5	6.11	...	...
96½ Mar	16	0.85	...	...
Swiss Franc				**70.14**
62,500 Swiss Francs-European Style.				
66½ Mar	...	...	140	0.03
62,500 Swiss Francs-cents per unit.				
67 Apr	5	3.06	...	...
67 Jun	...	...	54	0.69
68 Jun	...	...	2	0.43
68 Jun	...	...	50	0.96
68½ Mar	...	...	40	0.14
69 Apr	80	1.12	...	...
69 Apr	...	...	4	0.73
69 Jun	...	...	16	1.30
70 Mar	25	0.75	10	0.52
70 Apr	11	1.13	...	...
70½ Mar	10	0.50	...	...
71 Mar	1	0.36	...	...
71 Apr	...	...	1	1.82
72 Apr	...	...	5	2.35
Call Vol 25,455			**Open Int ... 620,824**	
Put Vol 14,447			**Open Int ... 555,617**	

FIGURE 4.3. Foreign Currency Options Premiums, February 28, 1994
Options on the Philadelphia Exchange are options on spot currency. Some are European options, which are exercisable on the maturity date. Other options are American options, exercisable on or before the maturity date. Some mature on the Friday before the third Wednesday of the month. Others, marked "EOM," are end-of-the-month options which expire on the last Friday of the month. Calls are an option to buy and puts are an option to sell. (Reprinted by permission of *The Wall Street Journal*, © 1994 Dow Jones & Company Inc. All rights reserved worldwide.)

options expire on the Friday before the third Wednesday of the expiry month. This makes them essentially mid-month options. Figure 4.3 also shows some end-of-month options, identified by "EOM." These expire on the last Friday of the month. End-of-month options never extend beyond 3 months maturity.

The bold numbers directly across from the name of the currency give the spot exchange rate. This is in U.S. dollar equivalent terms and is given as U.S. cents per

86

unit of foreign currency. The exception is the quotation of cross-rate options. Figure 4.3 shows British-pound–German-mark cross options, for which the price is in hundredths of Deutschemarks, or pfennigs, per pound, and German-mark–Japanese-yen cross options, for which the price is in Japanese yen per Deutschemark.

The numbers in the first column of each segment of Figure 4.3 give strike prices. As we have stated, the strike price gives the exchange rate at which the option buyer has the right to buy or sell the foreign currency; it is also known as the exercise price. We can see that on each currency there are options at numerous strike prices, with gaps of 1 or 2 cents on the Australian dollar, 2½ cents on the British pound, and so on. When a new set of options is introduced, which occurs as an old set expires, the new options are written at the rounded-off value of the going spot exchange rate and at a slightly higher and slightly lower exchange rate. New strike prices are subsequently introduced if the spot rate changes by a large amount.

Whether the option gives the buyer the right to buy or sell the foreign currency is identified by whether the option is listed in one of the columns headed "Calls" or one of the columns headed "Puts." A **call option** gives the buyer the right to buy the foreign currency at the strike price or exchange rate on the option, and a **put option** gives the buyer the right to sell the foreign currency at the strike price.

We can illustrate the concepts so far introduced, and at the same time explain how options work, by considering a couple of options on German marks in the middle of Figure 4.3. We note first that the going spot price of the mark is 58.60 U.S. cents. That is, the exchange rate is $0.5860/DM on the spot market. Reading down below the spot rate we first have the European style options on 62,500 marks. Strike prices run from 56 U.S. cents per mark to 60½ cents per mark. Let us consider the meaning of the "58 Mar" option for which we see 600 contracts as the volume ("Vol.") and a last trading price of the put option of 0.26 U.S. cents per German mark; see the 0.26 in the last column of the middle segment of Figure 4.3.

A "58 Mar" European put option gives the buyer the right to sell the mark at 58 U.S. cents. The price of the option, 0.26 U.S. cents per mark, means that for the contract of 62,500 German marks the option buyer must pay[15]

$$\$0.0026/DM \times DM62,500 = \$162.50$$

This means that by paying $162.50, the option buyer acquires the right to sell the 62,500 marks for 58 U.S. cents ($0.58) each at the expiry date of the option, which is the Friday before the third Wednesday of March; the option is European style, so it is valid only for the expiry date. The option will not be exercised if the spot rate on the mark on the expiry date is above $0.58 because in these circumstances it would be better to sell marks spot. However, if the spot rate is below $0.58, the option has value because it gives the holder the right to receive $0.58 per mark, which is more than the mark's market value.

In actual fact, rather than exercise the option the buyer is likely to accept the difference between the exercise price and the going spot rate from the option **writer.** The writer is the person selling the put option, who received the $162.50 from the sale of the option.

Consider next the "58½ Mar" option, 12 lines below the heading "62,500 German Marks-cents per unit." Because it does not say "European Style," the options

---

[15]As always, the currency symbols can be canceled.

under this heading are American options. Therefore, they can be exercised on any date prior to maturity. Reading across the row for the "58½ Mar" option we see 6038 call options—the highest option volume in the table—and 31 put options at this strike price of 58½ U.S. cents per mark, that is, an exchange rate of $0.5850/DM. The call option costs 0.60 U.S. cents, or $0.0060, per mark. Therefore, a call option contract costs

$$\$0.0060/DM \times DM62,500 = \$375$$

This means the buyer of the 58½ March call acquires the right to buy DM62,500 for 58½ U.S. cents per mark up to the expiry date in March for $375. If the mark is above $0.5850 on the spot market, the option will be exercised on or before expiry or its value will be collected from the option writer or another buyer. If the spot value of the mark is below $0.5850 it does not pay to exercise the option. It is thus thrown away, and there is a loss of $375. The $375 can be thought of as an insurance premium for which if unfavorable events do not occur, the insurance simply expires.

If we compare the spot exchange rates shown in the top line of each type of option with the strike prices below, we see that for each currency there are options with higher and lower strike exchange rates than the spot exchange rate. A call option that gives the buyer the right to buy a currency at a strike exchange rate that is below the spot exchange rate is said to be **in the money.** This is because the option holder has the right to buy the currency for less than it would cost in the spot market. For example, the German mark call option at 58½ is in the money, with the exercise price of $0.5850 being a little below the spot rate $0.5860. Indeed, all the mark call options for which the strike price is 58½ or lower, which is about half of the American options shown at the bottom of the center segment of Figure 4.3, are in the money.

A call option with a strike price that is above the spot exchange rate is said to be **out of the money.** This is because the option holder would find it cheaper to buy the foreign currency on the spot market than to exercise the option. For example, all the German mark calls with strike prices of 59 cents or higher are out of the money. With the spot rate of 58.60 U.S. cents per mark, the right to buy the mark at 59 U.S. cents has no value *if exercised immediately.* However, the fact that a call option might be out of the money does not mean the option has no value. As long as there is a possibility that the spot exchange rate might move above the strike price during the maturity of the option, people will be willing to pay for the option contract.

A put option that gives the buyer the right to sell the foreign currency is said to be in the money when the strike exchange rate is higher than the spot exchange rate. This is because the option holder has the right to sell the currency for more than it could be sold on the spot market. A put option is out of the money when the strike exchange rate is lower than the spot exchange rate. This is because the option holder wanting to sell foreign exchange immediately would be better off not to exercise the option, but rather to sell at the spot exchange rate. As with call options, the fact that a put option is out of the money does not mean it has no value. It has value as long as there is a possibility that the spot rate might move below the strike exchange rate during the life of the option.

The extent to which an option is in the money is called its **intrinsic value.** For example, with the spot exchange rate $0.009579 per Japanese yen—see the 95.79 at the very top of the right-hand segment of Figure 4.3—the "93 Mar" yen (or $0.009300) call has an intrinsic value of 0.0279 U.S. cents ($0.009579 – $0.009300) per yen. That is, the intrinsic value is how many cents per yen would be gained by exercising the option immediately. As can be seen from Figure 4.3, the market value of the "93 Mar" Japanese yen call option is higher than its intrinsic value; the option is priced at 0.0331 cents per yen, where we note in the figure that prices are in 100ths of a cent per unit. This is because there may be an even larger gain for exercising the option during the remainder of its maturity. While call options have intrinsic value when the strike price is *below* the spot exchange rate, put options have intrinsic value when the strike price *exceeds* the spot exchange rate.

The amount paid for the option on each unit of foreign currency—for example, for each British pound or for each Canadian dollar—is called the **option premium.** This premium can be considered to consist of two parts: the intrinsic value, if there is any, and the **time value** of the option. The time value is the part of the premium that comes from the possibility that, at some point in the future, the option might have higher intrinsic value than at that moment. For example, the time value of the "93 Mar" yen call option is 0.0052 (0.0331 – 0.0279) U.S. cents per yen, the difference between the market value and the intrinsic value. When an option is **at the money,** which occurs when the strike price exactly equals the spot rate, all of the option premium is the option's time value. For example, the Canadian dollar option "74 Jun" is almost exactly at the money; the spot rate of 73.97 (or $0.7397/Can$) is almost exactly the strike price.

Quotation Conventions and Market Organization

Option dealers quote a bid and an ask premium on each contract, with the bid being what buyers are willing to pay and the ask being what sellers want to be paid. Of course, a dealer must state whether a bid or ask premium is for a call or put, whether it is for an American or European option, the strike price, and the month the option expires.

After the buyer has paid for an option contract, he or she has no financial obligation. Therefore, there is no need to talk about margins for option *buyers.* The person selling the option is called the writer. The writer of a call option must stand ready, when required, to sell the currency to the option buyer at the strike price. Similarly, the writer of a put option must stand ready to buy the currency from the put option buyer at the strike price. The commitment of the writer is open throughout the life of the option for American options, and on the maturity date of the option for European options. The option exchange guarantees that option sellers honor their obligations to option buyers and therefore requires option *sellers* to post a margin. On the Philadelphia Exchange, this is 130 percent of the option premium plus a lump sum to a maximum of $2500 per contract, depending on the extent the option is in or out of the money.[16]

As in the case of futures contracts, an exchange can make a market in currency options only by standardizing the contracts. This is why option contracts are written for specific amounts of foreign currency, for a limited number of maturity dates,

---

[16]For more details on margins see *Foreign Currency Options: The Third Dimension to Foreign Exchange,* Philadelphia Stock Exchange, undated.

and for a limited number of strike exchange rates. The standardization allows buyers to resell contracts prior to maturity. It also allows writers to offset their risks more readily because, for example, the writer of a call option can enter the market as a buyer of a call option to limit losses or to lock in gains.[17] However, as Figure 4.3 indicates in the volume columns, relatively few of the possible options are active.

Determinants of the Market Values of Currency Options

The factors that influence the price of an option are:

Intrinsic Value. As we have said, the premium on an option can be considered to be made up of the time value and the intrinsic value. (We recall that the intrinsic value is the extent to which the spot rate exceeds the strike price on a call option and the extent to which the strike price exceeds the spot rate on a put option. Alternatively, it is what the option would be worth if it had to be exercised immediately.) Therefore, the more the option is in the money (that is, the higher is the intrinsic value), the higher is the option premium.

Volatility of the Spot or Futures Exchange Rate. *Ceteris paribus,* the more volatile the underlying rate, the greater the chance that an option will be exercised to the benefit of the buyer and to the cost of the seller.[18] That is, the higher the volatility of the underlying exchange rate, the greater the possibility that it will at some time exceed the strike exchange rate of a call or be below the strike exchange rate of a put. Consequently, buyers will pay more for an option, and sellers will demand more, if the volatility of the exchange rate is higher.

Since Philadelphia options give the buyer the option to buy or sell spot foreign exchange, it is the volatility of the spot exchange rate that determines the value of Philadelphia options. With Chicago IMM options being on currency futures contracts rather than on spot exchange, it is the price and volatility of IMM futures contracts that determine the value of IMM currency options. However, because the spot exchange rate is the principal factor affecting futures contract prices, it is still the volatility of the spot rate that matters. (We might note that on the Chicago IMM, whether options are in the money or out of the money depends on the strike price versus the futures price, not the strike price relative to the spot exchange rate.)

Length of Period to Expiration. The longer the maturity period of the option, the greater is the chance that at some time the exchange rate will move above the strike price of a call or below the strike price of a put. Therefore, *ceteris paribus,* the longer the period to expiration, the higher the option premium a buyer is prepared to pay, and the higher the option premium a seller wants to be paid.

---

[17]The ways that options can be used for hedging and speculating are described in Chapter 15.

[18]The effects of volatility and the other influences listed here on *stock* options were first described by Fischer Black and Myron Scholes, "The Pricing of Options and Corporate Liabilities," *Journal of Political Economy,* May/June 1973, pp. 637–659. The effects of volatility and other factors on *currency* options have been described by Mark B. Garman and Steven W. Kohlhagen, "Foreign Currency Option Values," *Journal of International Money and Finance,* December 1983, pp. 231–237, and by J. Orlin Grabbe, "The Pricing of Call and Put Options on Foreign Exchange," *Journal of International Money and Finance,* December 1983, pp. 239–253.

American or European Option Type. The greater flexibility of American options as compared to European options means buyers will not pay more for a European option than for an American option of the same strike price and maturity. (Recall that American options can be exercised at any time before the expiry date, while European options can be exercised only on the expiry date.) Indeed, for a given strike price, exchange-rate volatility, and period to expiration, American options are typically more valuable than European options.[19]

Interest Rate on Currency of Purchase. The higher the interest rate on the currency paid for an option, the lower the present value of the exercise price. A higher interest rate consequently has the same effect on an option as does a lower exercise price, namely, it increases the market value of a call and reduces the market value of a put.[20]

The Forward Premium/Discount or Interest Differential. Because of very different rates of inflation, balances of trade, and so on, there can be trends in exchange rates that are to an extent predictable. For example, the foreign exchange values of currencies of countries with very rapid inflation tend to decline vis-à-vis those with slow inflation. *Ceteris paribus,* the greater the expected decline in the foreign exchange value of a currency, the higher the value of a put option on that currency because there is a greater chance the put option will be exercised. Similarly, the more a currency is expected to increase in value—because of low inflation, consistently good international trade performance, and so on—the higher is the value of a call option on that currency. Again, this is because, *ceteris paribus,* the more the currency is expected to increase in value, the more likely it is that a call option will be worth exercising.

Because the forward rate, under the assumption of risk neutrality, equals the expected future spot rate, currencies that are expected to decline in value tend to trade at a forward discount, while currencies expected to increase in value tend to trade at a premium.[21] Indeed, the more a currency is expected to decline/increase in value, the larger the forward discount/premium tends to be. It follows that, *ceteris paribus,* the greater the forward discount on a currency, the higher the value of a put option and the lower the value of a call option on that currency. Similarly, the greater the forward premium, the higher the value of a call option and the lower the value of a put option on the currency.[22]

An alternative way of stating the effect of expected decreases or increases in exchange rates on the value of options is in terms of interest rates. Countries with currencies that are expected to decline in value tend to have high interest rates relative to other countries. (Such high rates are necessary to compensate foreign investors for the expected decline in exchange rates.) Therefore, put options tend to be worth more when interest rates are higher than elsewhere; the relatively high

---

[19]Occasionally, "last" prices violate these rules. This can happen when the last quotes are for different times of the day.

[20]This is because other things are assumed constant as the interest rate changes. See John C. Cox and Mark Rubinstein, *Options Markets,* Prentice-Hall, Englewood Cliffs, N.J., 1985, p. 35.

[21]This was explained in Chapter 3.

[22]There is an arbitrage relation between option prices and the forward exchange rate that can be used to find the effects we have only verbally described. See Cox and Rubinstein, *op. cit.,* pp. 59–61.

interest rates suggest an expected decline in the value of the currency and, consequently, an increased chance that a put will be exercised. Similarly, call options tend to be worth more when interest rates are lower than elsewhere because relatively low interest rates suggest an expected increase in the currency's value and, consequently, an increased chance the call will be exercised.

Over-the-Counter (OTC) Options

Well before options began trading on formal exchanges in 1981, there had been an active **over-the-counter option market** in Europe, the options being written by large banks.[23] Indeed, the over-the-counter option market remains larger than that of the formal option exchanges. Amounts traded tend to be large, generally over $1 million. The banks that write over-the-counter options often use formal exchange options to hedge their own positions.

Many over-the-counter options written by banks are contingent upon such outcomes as whether a corporate takeover or bid on a foreign project is accepted.[24] That is, the buyer of the option purchases the opportunity to buy a foreign currency at a given strike exchange rate if, for example, a particular takeover occurs. An example of such an over-the-counter option is the option on sterling purchased by U.S. insurance broker Marsh and McLennan Company. Marsh and McLennan made a cash and share offer for C.T. Bowring and Company, a member of Lloyds of London, that required Marsh and McLennan to pay £130 million if the offer was accepted. Rather than take a chance on the exchange rate that might prevail on the takeover settlement date, Marsh and McLennan wanted to buy a call option for £130 million that it could exercise only if its takeover effort succeeded.[25] Bankers Trust agreed to provide an option which could be exercised up to 6 months after the original takeover offer. The takeover bid did succeed and the option was duly exercised.

The reason the over-the-counter market coexists alongside the formal options market is that options that trade on option exchanges are not perfectly suited for contingencies such as whether a takeover bid is accepted, whether an export contract is signed, and so on. Exchange-traded options are imperfectly suited for such contingencies because, even though the option buyer can choose whether to exercise, the value of exchange-traded options is contingent upon what happens to exchange rates rather than on whether a deal is consummated.[26]

An option that is contingent upon completion of a takeover might be cheaper than a traditional exchange-traded option because the writer of a call contingent on completion of a takeover or a bid on a foreign project does not deliver foreign exchange if the foreign currency increases in value but the deal is not completed. That is, there are outcomes where the deal-completion-contingent option writer does not lose, but where the writer of an exchange option would lose; an exchange call

---

[23]Currency options had also been traded in an unorganized fashion in the United States until this was ruled illegal. See David Babbel, "The Rise and Decline of Currency Options," *Euromoney,* September 1980, pp. 141–149.

[24]As Exhibit 4.1 explains, there are many other possible ways of designing options.

[25]This interesting case is described in "Marsh and McLennan Insures Takeover Exposure with Call Provision," *Money Report,* Business International, June 13, 1980.

[26]See Nalin Kulatilaka and Alan J. Marcus, "Hedging Foreign Project Risk," working paper, Boston University School of Management, April 1991.

EXHIBIT 4.1
The Scope for Writing Options

It is possible to write options based on more than just the eventually realized spot exchange rate. Among the various currency options that are used are the following:

PATH-DEPENDENT OR "ASIAN" OPTIONS

These pay out according to the average spot rate that has prevailed over a stated previous period of time. For example, an Asian option might have an exercise price equal to the average end-of-day spot rate for the previous year. Such an option is useful for hedging risk when a company is converting its foreign-currency income into domestic currency continuously throughout the year. For example, to avoid incurring foreign exchange losses, an exporter can buy Asian puts on each of the foreign currencies it earns. Then, if a foreign currency, on average, falls in value over the year, the option holder makes a gain on that option equal to its loss on foreign exchange earnings in that currency.

LOOK-BACK OPTIONS

These options give buyers the right to enjoy the best exchange rate that has occurred during a preceding period of time. For example, a 3-month look-back call on the Japanese yen gives the option buyer the right to buy yen at the lowest price of the yen in the previous quarter of a year. Similarly, a look-back yen put gives the owner the right to receive the best selling price of the yen in a given previous period of time. Of course, the premiums charged by writers of such options are higher than for regular options; in a sense the option provides discretion over whether to exercise, as well as over the exercise price within the range it has traveled.

OPTION-LINKED LOANS

An option can be written to repay a loan in the currency of the borrower's choice, where the different amounts of the alternative currencies which can be paid are stated in the contract. Multinational companies earning various foreign currencies find these useful since they can pay back with the less valuable currencies. The cost of the loans does, however, reflect the borrower's option. Alternatively, discretion over currency of repayment can be given to the lender. In this case the cost of the loan—the interest rate—is low, to reflect the lender's option.

OPTION-LINKED BONDS

An extension of the option-linked loan is a bond for which the buyer has the choice of currency for paying coupons and possibly also for repayment of principal. As with option-linked loans, the amounts of alternative currencies required on the coupons or principal are stated on the bond, with the borrower deciding what to pay based on spot exchange rates when payments occur. Payments will be in the least valuable currency at the time. This makes the bond yields high to compensate the lender. Alternatively, discretion over the currency in which coupons or principal are received can be given to the lender. This reduces yields as the lender stands to benefit and the borrower stands to lose.

Source: "The Look-back and the Linkage," *Euromoney,* special supplement, *Risk Management; Taming the Demon,* April 1989, p. 51.

option will be exercised if the option has value on the options exchange, even if the deal is not completed. Banks that write over-the-counter customized options frequently "reinsure" on an options exchange, so it is the bank rather than the option buyer that gains when the foreign currency increases in value but, for example, the takeover offer is rejected. The bank gains because it reinsures by buying an exchange-issued call option to cover the call it has written, and the exchange call increases in value without the need to deliver the foreign currency if the takeover offer is rejected.

Payoff Profiles for Currency Options

By plotting the payoff profiles for currency options we can graphically compare the consequences of using options for hedging and speculation with the alternative methods involving forward and futures contracts. Let us begin by considering a call option.

Payoff Profile for Call Option Buyers

Let us assume that the market's expectation of the spot value of the German mark for the maturity date of a call option is DM1.80/$, which we can approximate for simplicity as $0.5550/DM. Suppose that the price of a 55½ U.S. cents per DM call is 0.20 cents, so that the cost of one contract is $0.0020/DM × DM125,000 = $250.

If at maturity of the option the realized spot exchange rate is as expected, namely DM1.80/$, or $0.5550/DM, the option is at the money with zero exercise value. This is shown in Table 4.3, where we see zero exercise value per mark and for the contract. Because the contract has cost $250, the net gain/loss on the contract is a loss of $250, shown in the final column. The net loss is plotted in Figure 4.4 at the zero value of the horizontal axis because with the assumed expected spot rate and the realized spot rate being equal—both are DM1.80/$—the unexpected change in the spot rate is zero.

If the realized spot rate at maturity is more than DM1.80 per dollar, that is, the dollar price of the mark is below $0.5550, the call option will not be exercised; the right to buy marks at 55½ cents has no exercise value if the spot rate is below 55½ cents. We see this with the zero exercise values in Table 4.3 at DM1.80/$ and below. The net loss with these realized rates is the $250 paid for the option. The unexpected changes in the exchange rate in European terms are the realized values minus DM1.80/$, which are shown along the positive segment of the horizontal axis in Figure 4.4. Plotting the loss of $250 in this segment gives the horizontal segment of the payoff profile shown in the figure.

At a realized spot rate of DM1.79/$, or $0.5587/DM, the exercise value of the call is $0.0037 ($0.5587 − $0.5550) per mark, or $0.0037/DM × DM125,000 = $462.50 on the contract. After deducting the original $250 cost of the contract the net gain is $212.50. This, along with the gains at realized spot rates DM1.78/$, DM1.77/$, and so on, is shown in Table 4.3 and plotted in Figure 4.4. The figure

TABLE 4.3. Payoffs on a 55½-Cent Deutschemark Call Option

Realized Spot Rate, European Terms	Spot Rate, U.S. Dollar Terms	Exercise Value per Mark	Exercise Value of Contract	Gain (+) or Loss (−)
DM1.77/$	$0.5650/DM	$0.0100/DM	$1250.00	+$1000.00
DM1.78/$	$0.5618/DM	$0.0068/DM	$850.00	+$600.00
DM1.79/$	$0.5587/DM	$0.0037/DM	$462.50	+$212.50
DM1.80/$	$0.5550/DM	0	0	−$250.00
DM1.81/$	$0.5525/DM	0	0	−$250.00
DM1.82/$	$0.5495/DM	0	0	−$250.00
DM1.83/$	$0.5464/DM	0	0	−$250.00

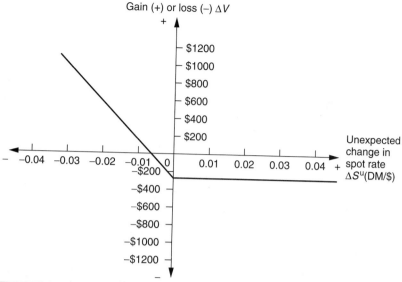

FIGURE 4.4. Payoff Profile for Buyer of a 55½-Cent Deutschemark Call Option

We assume the expected spot rate is DM1.80/$, which is approximately 55½ cents per DM, and that the cost of the call option is 0.20 cents per DM; $0.0020/DM × DM125,000 = $250. At DM1.80 per dollar and higher—or 55½ cents per DM and lower—the call is not exercised and the net loss on the option is the option price $250. This is the flat section of the payoff profile. The option has exercise value at fewer than DM1.80 per dollar, with the value increasing as the Deutschemark price of the dollar declines. This is the downward section of the profile, showing more exercise value as the Deutschemark increases in value, that is, as the dollar decreases in value. The profile shows that by buying the option, a gain is enjoyed if the Deutschemark has a high realized value, while losses are limited to the option price if the opposite occurs.

shows a downward-sloping profile to the left of the vertical axis, as is also the situation for buying Deutschemark futures or forward contracts. However, unlike futures and forwards, the call option profile does not continue to slope down to the right of the vertical axis, which is the region where the Deutschemark ends up being worth less than was expected. This is the important difference between futures and forwards on the one hand, and options on the other hand. With options, it is possible to avoid the bad outcomes, or "states." For a price of $250, the option buyer in our example can benefit if the mark ends up at a high value (as would a buyer of futures or forward contracts) but avoid losing if the mark ends up at a low value (unlike a buyer of futures or forward contracts).

Payoff Profile for Writers of Calls

The gains or losses of buyers of currency options are the losses or gains of the writers of the options. Therefore, we can obtain the payoff profile for the writer of a 55½-cent call on the Deutschemark by reversing the signs on the values in the last column of Table 4.3 and plotting these as in Figure 4.5. The profile shows that the

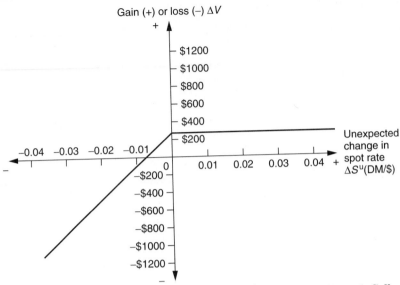

FIGURE 4.5. Payoff Profile for the Writer of a 55½-Cent Deutschemark Call Option

Along the right-hand segment of the horizontal axis the call option is not exercised: the realized spot dollar price of the Deutschemark is less than the strike price. Along the left-hand segment the call option is exercised and the writer has to deliver Deutschemarks for a price less than their realized spot value. The higher the realized spot value of the Deutschemark—that is, the lower the DM price of the dollar—the more the writer loses when honoring the call option. Note that the payoff profile for the writer is the opposite of that of the buyer: compare this profile to that in Figure 4.4.

writer earns the $250 paid for the option when the realized exchange rate is DM1.80 per dollar or higher, which by assumption means a positive unexpected change in DM/$. In these situations the option is not exercised. At realized rates lower than DM1.80 per dollar the writer loses what the buyer gains.[27] Figure 4.5 shows that a writer of a call option on the Deutschemark is hoping for the Deutschemark to end up at a low value in U.S. dollar terms, that is, worth less than 55½ cents; the call option writer gambles on the market's having overestimated the future value of the mark.

Payoff Profile for Put Option Buyers

Table 4.4 shows the payoffs on a 55½-cent Deutschemark put option. We see that when the Deutschemark ends up above 55½ cents—the DM/$ rate is below DM1.80/$—the right to sell the Deutschemark at 55½ cents has no value; it is better to sell the Deutschemarks at the going spot rate. The net loss is the cost of the option, assumed to be $250. When the Deutschemark ends up below 55½ cents—the DM/$ rate is above DM1.80/$—the option has exercise value. The lower the spot value of the Deutschemark, the higher the option value. When plotted as a payoff profile in Figure 4.6, we see the buyer of the option gaining when the

[27]We have ignored the transaction fees for writers and buyers.

TABLE 4.4. Payoffs on a 55½-Cent Deutschemark Put Option

Realized Spot Rate, European Terms	Spot Rate, U.S. Dollar Terms	Exercise Value per Mark	Exercise Value of Contract	Gain (+) or Loss (−)
DM1.77/$	$0.5650/DM	0	0	−$250.00
DM1.78/$	$0.5618/DM	0	0	−$250.00
DM1.79/$	$0.5587/DM	0	0	−$250.00
DM1.80/$	$0.5550/DM	0	0	−$250.00
DM1.81/$	$0.5525/DM	$0.0025/DM	$312.50	+$62.50
DM1.82/$	$0.5495/DM	$0.0055/DM	$687.50	+$437.50
DM1.83/$	$0.5464/DM	$0.0086/DM	$1075.00	+$825.00

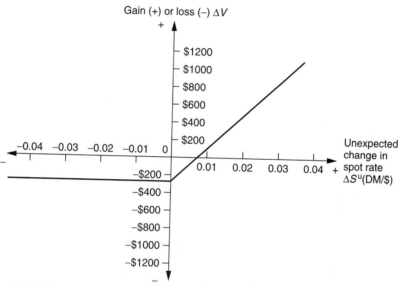

FIGURE 4.6. Payoff Profile for Buyer of a 55½-Cent Deutschemark Put Option

When the Deutschemark ends up above 55½ cents, that is, the DM value of the U.S. dollar ends up being less than DM1.80/$, which is the expected spot rate, a 55½-cent put is not exercised; it is better to sell at the realized spot rate. The put buyer's loss is the price paid for the option. Below 55½ cents per mark—that is, above DM1.80 per dollar—the option is exercised. The lower the realized value of the mark, the higher the gain on the put. This is the upward-sloping section of the payoff profile.

Deutschemark is low in value—the DM price of the dollar is high—and losing only the price paid for the option when the Deutschemark is high in value.

Payoff Profile for Put Option Writers

What option buyers gain option writers lose, and vice versa. Therefore, the payoffs facing the put writer are the values in Table 4.4 with signs reversed. These values are plotted against the associated unanticipated changes in the spot rate in Figure 4.7. The put writer is seen to gain the option price when the Deutschemark ends up

97

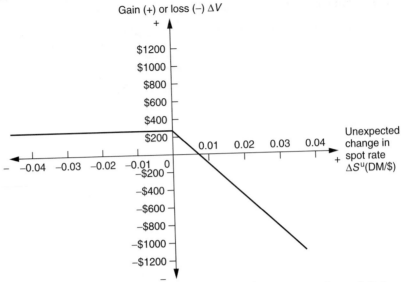

FIGURE 4.7. Payoff Profile for Writer of a 55½-Cent Deutschemark Put Option
If the realized spot value of the Deutschemark is above 55½ cents, the put option is not exercised; it is better for the option owner to sell at the spot rate. Therefore, at above 55½ cents per DM—or below DM1.80/$, in European terms—the option writer has a gain equal to the option price. If the realized spot rate is below 55½ cents per Deutschemark—that is, above DM1.80/$—the put is exercised and the writer loses; the option owner is receiving more for the Deutschemarks than their spot value. The more the realized spot rate is above DM1.80/$, that is, the further it falls to the right along the horizontal axis, the greater is the option writer's loss.

above 55½ cents, that is, the spot rate ends up below DM1.80/$. The option writer loses when the Deutschemark ends up below 55½ cents, that is, the spot rate ends up above DM1.80/$.

FORWARDS, FUTURES, AND OPTIONS COMPARED: A SUMMARY

While forwards, futures, and options can all be used both to reduce foreign exchange risk (that is, to hedge) and to purposely take foreign exchange risk (that is, to speculate), the differences between forwards, futures, and options make them suitable for different purposes. An explanation of which type of contract would be most appropriate in different circumstances must wait until we have dealt with many other matters, including further ways of hedging and speculating, so at this point we can do little more than list the differences between forwards, futures, and options. This is done in Table 4.5. The table notes the primary users of the markets, as well as the institutional differences between forwards, futures, and options. The reasons the different markets have different primary users can be explained with the payoff profiles we have constructed and are covered more fully in Chapter 15.

TABLE 4.5. Forwards, Futures, and Options Compared

	Forward Contracts	Currency Futures*	Currency Options†
Delivery discretion	None.	None.	Buyer's discretion. Seller must honor if buyer exercises.
Maturity date	Any date.	Third Wednesday of March, June, September, or December.	Friday before third Wednesday of March, June, September, or December on regular options. Last Friday of month on end-of-month options.
Maximum length	Several years.	12 months.	9 months.
Contracted amount	Any value.	£62,500, Can$100,000, etc.	£31,250, Can$50,000, etc.
Secondary market	Must offset with bank.	Can sell via exchange.	Can sell via exchange.
Margin requirement	Informal; often line of credit or 5–10% on account.	Formal fixed sum per contract, e.g., $2000. Daily marking to market.	No margin for buyer who pays for contract. Seller posts 130% of premium plus lump sum varying with intrinsic value.
Contract variety	Swap or outright form.	Outright.	Outright.
Guarantor	None.	Futures clearing corporation.	Options clearing corporation.
Major users	Primarily hedgers.	Primarily speculators.	Hedgers and speculators.

*Based on Chicago IMM contracts.

†Based on Philadelphia Stock Exchange contracts which are on spot foreign exchange. IMM options are on futures, and contracted amounts equal those on futures contracts.

SUMMARY

1. Currency futures are a bet on what will happen to the spot exchange rate. The bets are settled every day.
2. Futures are traded in specialized markets in standard contract sizes. There are relatively few maturity dates.
3. Because of their low transaction costs and easy settlement, currency futures appeal to speculators.
4. The payoff profiles for futures are similar to those for forward contracts, except that futures' outcomes are a little uncertain because of marking-to-market risk.
5. Marking-to-market risk is the result of uncertainty in the path of the future's contract value between purchase and sale and the volatility of interest rates.
6. Futures and forward exchange rates are linked by arbitrage.
7. Currency options give buyers the right or opportunity, but not the obligation, to buy or

99

sell foreign exchange at a preagreed exchange rate, the strike exchange rate. Call options give the buyer the right to purchase the foreign currency at the strike exchange rate, and put options give the buyer the right to sell the foreign currency at the strike exchange rate.

8. American options allow the buyer to exercise at any time prior to the expiry of the option, while European options allow the buyer to exercise only on the expiry date of the option.

9. The value of an option depends on the extent to which it is in the money, that is, the extent to which the option has intrinsic value, and also on the volatility of the underlying exchange rate, the length of time to expiration, the interest rate on the currency paid for the option, and the forward exchange premium or discount. Alternatively, the value of the option depends on the interest differential, which, like the forward premium or discount, reflects the expected path of the exchange rate.

10. An over-the-counter customized options market coexists with the exchange-based currency options. Over-the-counter options are written by banks.

11. Options allow their owners to gain from favorable outcomes but to lose only the price paid for the option when outcomes are unfavorable. Buying an option is like buying insurance against an unfavorable change in the exchange rate.

12. Payoff profiles for options have sloped segments like those of forwards and futures, but they also have horizontal segments. For buyers, the horizontal segments represent the limit of any loss to the amount paid for an option contract.

REVIEW QUESTIONS

1. What is a currency futures contract?
2. How are futures contracts cleared?
3. What is the meaning of "margin" on a futures contract?
4. What is meant by a margin's "maintenance level"?
5. What is meant by "marking to market"?
6. What causes marking-to-market risk?
7. What is meant by the "strike" or "exercise" price on an option?
8. How do American options differ from European options?
9. What is a put option on a currency?
10. What is a call option on a currency?
11. What is an option writer?
12. What does it mean to be "in the money"?
13. What does it mean to be "out of the money"?
14. What is an option premium?
15. What is meant by the "time value" on an option?
16. What factors influence options prices?
17. What is an over-the-counter option?
18. What goes on the axes of a payoff profile for a currency option?

ASSIGNMENT PROBLEMS

1. Why do you think that futures markets were developed when banks already offered forward contracts? What might currency futures offer which forward contracts do not?
2. To what extent do margin requirements on futures represent an opportunity cost?
3. How does the payoff profile of a futures sale of a currency compare to the profile of a purchase of the same currency?

4. Why is a futures contract similar to a string of bets on the exchange rate, settled every day?

5. Do you think that a limit on daily price movements for currency futures would make these contracts more or less risky or liquid? Would a limitation on price movements make the futures contracts difficult to sell during highly turbulent times?

6. How could arbitrage take place between forward exchange contracts and currency futures? Would this arbitrage be unprofitable only if the futures and forward rates were exactly the same?

7. Does the need to hold a margin make forward and futures deals less desirable than if there were no margin requirements? Does your answer depend on the interest paid on margins?

8. How does a currency option differ from a forward contract? How does an option differ from a currency future?

9. Suppose a bank sells a call option to a company making a takeover offer where the option is contingent on the offer being accepted. Suppose the bank reinsures the option on an options exchange by buying a call for the same amount of foreign currency. Consider the consequences of the following four outcomes, or "states":
   a. The foreign currency increases in value, and the takeover offer is accepted.
   b. The foreign currency increases in value, and the takeover offer is rejected.
   c. The foreign currency decreases in value, and the takeover offer is accepted.
   d. The foreign currency decreases in value, and the takeover offer is rejected.
   Consider who gains and who loses in each state, and the source of gain or loss. Satisfy yourself why a bank that reinsures on an options exchange might charge less for writing the takeover-contingent option than the bank itself pays for the call option on the exchange. Does this example help explain why a bank-based over-the-counter market coexists with a formal options exchange market?

10. What is the payoff profile from buying *and* writing a call option? Ignore the transaction costs.

11. What type of option(s) would speculators buy if they thought the Deutschemark would increase more than the market believed it would?

12. What type of option would speculators write if they thought the Deutschemark would increase more than the market believed it would?

BIBLIOGRAPHY

BORENSZTEIN, EDUARDO R., and MICHAEL P. COOLEY: "Options on Foreign Exchange and Exchange Rate Expectations," *IMF Staff Papers*, December 1987, pp. 643–680.

EINZIG, PAUL A.: *The Dynamic Theory of Forward Exchange*, 2d ed., Macmillan, London, 1967.

GARMAN, MARK B., and STEVEN W. KOHLHAGEN: "Foreign Currency Option Values," *Journal of International Money and Finance*, December 1983, no. 3, pp. 231–237.

GIDDY, IAN H.: "Foreign Exchange Options," *The Journal of Futures Markets*, summer 1983, no. 2, pp. 143–166.

GRABBE, J. ORLIN: "The Pricing of Call and Put Options on Foreign Exchange," *Journal of International Money and Finance*, December 1983, no. 3, pp. 239–253.

INTERNATIONAL MONETARY MARKET OF THE CHICAGO MERCANTILE EXCHANGE: *The Futures Market in Foreign Currencies*, Chicago Mercantile Exchange, Chicago, undated.

————, *Trading in International Currency Futures*, Chicago Mercantile Exchange, Chicago, undated.

————, *Understanding Futures in Foreign Exchange*, Chicago Mercantile Exchange, Chicago, undated.

KUBARYCH, ROGER M.: *Foreign Exchange Markets in the United States,* Federal Reserve Bank of New York, 1978.

LEVY, EDMOND: "Pricing European Average Rate Currency Options," *Journal of International Money and Finance,* October 1992, pp. 474–491.

PHILADELPHIA STOCK EXCHANGE: *Understanding Foreign Currency Options: The Third Dimension to Foreign Exchange,* Philadelphia Stock Exchange, undated.

SMITH, CLIFFORD W., JR., CHARLES W. SMITHSON, and D. SYKES WILFORD: *Managing Financial Risk,* Harper & Row, New York, 1990.

PART TWO

Determination of Exchange Rates

An exchange rate can be thought of as the price of one country's money in terms of another country's money. Therefore, it should come as little surprise that exchange rates are the result of supply and demand. As with traditional supply and demand, we can construct curves for currencies which show how quantities supplied or demanded depend on price. We can then determine the equilibrium price, or exchange rate. This is the theme of the following chapters. Special consideration is given to how different types of exchange-rate systems result in different supply and demand curves, largely as a result of the responses of central banks or international financial institutions to movements in exchange rates.

Chapter 5 begins by describing why the balance-of-payments account can be considered as a listing of the reasons a currency is being supplied and demanded. The chapter explains that all positive or credit items listed in the account give rise to a demand for the country's currency and all negative or debit items give rise to a supply of the currency. After explaining the basic principles of balance-of-payments accounting, each major entry

in the account is examined to provide an understanding of what factors can make each entry increase or decrease, and thereby change the exchange rate. This introduces the student to how such factors as inflation, interest rates, foreign debt, political risk, and expectations about future values of these factors can affect exchange rates. The purpose of the chapter is to provide a framework for thinking about what makes exchange rates change.

Chapter 5 includes a brief account of the different interpretations of the balance of payments with fixed and flexible exchange rates. It is shown that with flexible exchange rates the balance of payments is achieved without any official buying or selling of currencies by governments, whereas with fixed exchange rates there are changes in official foreign exchange reserves. The chapter also shows how to interpret imbalances in the current-account and capital-account components of the balance of payments. This is illustrated by drawing an analogy between a country's balance-of-payments account and the income statement of a firm. The chapter concludes with a discussion of a country's net indebtedness and a brief account of recent developments in the balance of payments and indebtedness of the United States.

Chapter 6 builds the supply-and-demand picture of exchange rates that is suggested by the balance-of-payments account. This involves deriving the supply curve for a country's currency from that country's demand curve for imports, and the demand curve for a country's currency from that country's supply curve of exports. Using the knowledge about balance-of-payment entries developed in Chapter 5, Chapter 6 shows how inflation and other factors can shift the currency supply and demand curves and therefore make exchange rates change. It is also shown, however, that a currency supply curve can slope downward rather than upward as might normally be expected, and that if this happens, exchange rates may be unstable. The chapter explains that the conditions resulting in an unstable foreign exchange market are the same conditions that result in the so-called "J curve." (A J curve occurs, for example, when a depreciation makes a country's balance of trade worse, rather than better as would normally be expected.)

The currency supplies and demands considered in Chapter 6 are *flows,* being amounts per period of time. We learn that exchange rates change until flow supplies and demands are equal. Chapter 7, which is optional, takes an alternative perspective, one which recognizes that *stocks* of currencies, being amounts at each point in time, must be held. We learn that stock supplies of currencies, represented by money supplies, must equal the demands to hold these stocks. The chapter begins with the simplest stock-based theory, known as the "monetary approach to exchange rates." This is extended to the "asset approach," which considers how expectations about the future affect today's exchange rates, and then to the "portfolio-balance approach," which considers the need for bonds as well as money to be held. Chapter 7 ends with a discussion of how stock-based theories can explain volatility in the form of exchange-rate "overshooting."

The emphasis in Chapters 6 and 7 is on the determination of exchange rates when they are flexible, meaning that they are determined by the forces of private supply and demand. Chapter 8 considers alternative fixed-exchange-rate systems including the classical gold standard, the so-called "Bretton Woods system," the European Monetary System, and the cooperative system operated by the Group of Seven (G7) since the mid-1980s. The focus is both on the mechanics of these systems of fixed exchange rates and on how imbalances in private currency supplies and demands are corrected. The mechanisms for correcting imbalances of currency supplies and demands with fixed-exchange-rate systems are compared with the balance-of-payments adjustment mechanism with flexible exchange rates. Indeed, the chapter ends with an account of the many arguments used in favor of or against fixed and flexible rates.

Armed with an understanding of the different ways the international financial system can be organized and with an appreciation of the pros and cons of the different systems, we consider in Chapter 9 why international financial history has weaved the path it has. We describe the flaws in the gold standard, the Bretton Woods system, and the European Monetary System that eventually brought about the collapse of each. We also examine some of the problems the international financial system has had to cope with, from recycling "petrodollars," to reserve shortages, to widely different inflation and employment experiences, to massive debts of developing nations, to the contemporary problems of trade imbalances and shifting economic power. We shall see how international institutions such as the International Monetary Fund (IMF) and World Bank have been devised and adapted to deal with these problems.

Part Two is designed to familiarize readers with the ever-changing international financial environment in which corporate and even individual decisions must be made. The twists and turns of the twentieth century—from gold, to Bretton Woods, to flexible rates, to cooperative intervention—tell us that if anything is predictable, it is that change in the international financial system can be counted on to continue into the twenty-first century. Only by considering where we have been and analyzing how previous international financial systems have worked can we understand whatever new and perhaps untried systems we might someday face. While it is possible to omit Part Two in its entirety, what is sacrificed is the context in which international business is done.

CHAPTER 5

The Balance-of-Payments Accounts

Money is just something to make bookkeeping convenient.

—H. L. HUNT

THE BALANCE OF PAYMENTS AS A RECORD OF CURRENCY SUPPLY AND DEMAND

As with the price of any commodity, the price of a country's currency depends on the supply of and demand for that currency, at least when exchange rates are determined in a free, unregulated market.[1] It follows that if we know the factors behind the supply of and demand for a currency, we also know what factors influence exchange rates. Any factor increasing the demand for the currency will, *ceteris paribus,* increase the foreign exchange value of the currency, that is, cause the currency to appreciate. Similarly, any factor increasing the supply of the currency will, *ceteris paribus,* reduce the foreign exchange value of the currency, that is, cause the currency to depreciate.[2] Clearly, then, there is considerable interest in maintaining a record of the factors behind the supply of and demand for a country's currency. That record is maintained in the **balance-of-payments account**. Indeed, we can think of the balance-of-payments account as an itemization of the factors behind the demand for and supply of a currency.

Of course, the motivation for publishing the balance-of-payments account is not a desire of government statisticians to maintain a record of the factors behind the supply of and demand for a currency. Rather, the account is published to report the country's international performance in trading with other nations and to maintain a record of the volume of capital flowing in and out of the country. However, reporting on a country's international trading performance and capital flows involves measurement of all the reasons a currency is supplied and demanded. This is what makes the balance-of-payments account such a handy way of thinking about what should

---

[1] When exchange rates are fixed, they are still determined by supply and demand, but there is an official supply or demand at the fixed exchange rate to keep rates from changing. Fixed exchange rates are discussed in Chapter 8.

[2] When exchange rates are fixed and the foreign exchange value of a currency is deliberately set by the authorities at a lower value, the currency is said to have been **devalued.** When the exchange rate is refixed at a higher value, the currency is said to have been **revalued.** These terms replace "depreciate" and "appreciate," which are the terms used with flexible rates.

105

be considered in a theory of exchange rates. This chapter shows why the balance-of-payments account can be thought of as a list of items behind the supply of and demand for a currency. We begin by examining the principles guiding the structure of the balance-of-payments account and the interpretation of the different items that are included. We then consider the different ways that balance can be achieved between supply and demand. As we shall see, the balance-of-payments account is designed to always balance, but the way that it is balanced tells us how well a country is doing in its transactions with other countries.

PRINCIPLES OF BALANCE-OF-PAYMENTS ACCOUNTING

The guiding principles of balance-of-payments accounting come from the purpose of the account, namely, to record the flow of payments between the residents of a country and the rest of the world during a given time period. The fact that the balance of payments records the flow of payments during a given time period makes the account dimensionally the same as the national-income account—a **flow** of so much per year or per calendar quarter—and indeed, the part of the balance-of-payments account that records the values of exports and imports appears in the national-income account.

Balance-of-payments accounting uses the system of **double-entry bookkeeping,** which means that every debit or credit in the account is also represented as a credit or debit somewhere else. An easy way of seeing how this works is to take a couple of straightforward examples.

Suppose that an American corporation sells $2 million worth of U.S.-manufactured jeans to Britain and that the British buyer pays from a U.S. dollar account that is kept in a U.S. bank. We will then have the following double entry in the U.S. balance of payments:

	Million Dollars (Credits +; Debits −)
Export (of jeans)	+2
Foreign assets in the U.S.: U.S. bank liabilities	−2

We can think of the export of the American jeans as resulting in a demand for dollars, and the payments with dollars at the U.S. bank as resulting in a supply of dollars. The payment reduces the liability of the U.S. bank, which is an asset of the British jeans buyer. We see that the balance-of-payments account shows both the flow of jeans and the flow of payments.

As a second example, suppose that an American corporation purchases $5 million worth of denim cloth from a British manufacturer and that the British company puts the $5 million it receives into a bank account in the United States. We then have the following double entry:

	Million Dollars (Credits +; Debits −)
Imports (of cloth)	−5
Foreign assets in the U.S.: U.S. bank liabilities	+5

We can think of the U.S. import of cloth as resulting in a supply of dollars, and the deposit of money by the British company as resulting in a demand for dollars. The deposit of money increases U.S. bank liabilities and the assets of the British company. In a similar way, every entry in the balance of payments appears twice.

The balance-of-payments account records *all* transactions that affect the supply of or demand for a currency in the foreign exchange markets. There is just as much demand for dollars when non-Americans buy U.S. jeans as there is when they buy U.S. stocks, bonds, real estate, bank balances, or businesses, and all of these transactions must be recorded. Since all sources of potential demand for dollars by foreigners or supply of dollars to foreigners are included, there are many types of entries. We need a rule for determining which are credits and which are debits. The rule is that any international transaction that gives rise to a demand for U.S. dollars in the foreign exchange market is recorded as a credit in the U.S. balance of payments, and the entry takes a positive sign. Any transaction that gives rise to a supply of dollars is recorded as a debit, and the entry takes a negative sign. A more precise way of expressing this rule is with the following definition:

> Credit transactions represent demands for U.S. dollars and result from purchases by foreigners of goods, services, goodwill, financial and real assets, gold, or foreign exchange from U.S. residents. Credits are recorded with a plus sign. Debit transactions represent supplies of U.S. dollars and result from purchases by U.S. residents of goods, services, goodwill, financial and real assets, gold, or foreign exchange from foreigners. Debits are recorded with a minus sign.[3]

The full meaning of our definition will become clear as we study the U.S. balance of payments in Table 5.1. Let us consider each of the items and the factors that influence them.

BALANCE-OF-PAYMENTS ENTRIES AND THE FACTORS THAT INFLUENCE THEM

Exports of Goods, Services, and Income

In order for overseas buyers to pay for U.S. goods and services which are invoiced in dollars, the overseas buyers must purchase dollars. In the rare event that U.S. exports of goods and services are invoiced in foreign currency, it is the American exporter that will purchase dollars when selling the foreign currency it receives. In either case, U.S. exports give rise to a demand for U.S. dollars in the foreign exchange market and are recorded with a plus sign. (If the foreign buyer of a U.S. good or service pays with foreign currency which the U.S. exporter chooses to hold rather than sell for U.S. dollars, the balance-of-payments account records the value of the export and an increase in U.S. private bank assets. In this case the U.S. export is considered to give rise to a demand for U.S. dollars, and the increased U.S. private holdings of foreign currency is considered to give rise to an equal increase in the supply of U.S. dollars.)

---

[3]The item with the least obvious meaning in this definition is "goodwill." As we shall explain later, goodwill consists of gifts and foreign aid. In keeping with the double-entry bookkeeping system, the balance-of-payments accountant assumes that gifts and aid buy goodwill for the donor from the recipient.

TABLE 5.1. Summary Format of the U.S. Balance of Payments, 1st Quarter, 1993

Line #	(Credits, +; Debits, −)		Billions of U.S. Dollars
1	Exports of goods, services, and income		+185
2	Merchandise, excluding military	+112	
3	Services	+45	
4	Income receipts on U.S. assets abroad	+28	
5	Imports of goods, services, and income		−191
6	Merchandise, excluding military	−136	
7	Services	−29	
8	Income payments on foreign assets in U.S.	−26	
9	Unilateral transfers (net)		−8
10	U.S. government	−4	
11	Private	−4	
12	U.S. assets abroad (net)		−5
13	U.S. official reserve assets	−1	
14	U.S. government assets other than official reserves	0	
15	U.S. private assets abroad	−4	
16	Direct investment	−11	
17	Foreign securities	−27	
18	U.S. non-bank assets	0	
19	U.S. bank assets	+34	
20	Foreign assets in the U.S. (net)		+19
21	Foreign official assets in U.S.	+11	
22	Other foreign assets in U.S.	+8	
23	Direct investment	+5	
24	U.S. Treasury securities	+14	
25	U.S. securities other than Treasury securities	+11	
26	U.S. non-bank liabilities	0	
27	U.S. bank liabilities	−22	
28	Allocation of SDRs		0
29	Statistical discrepancy		0
	Memoranda		
30	Balance on (merchandise) trade (lines 2 + 6)		−24
31	Balance on services (lines 3 + 7)		+16
32	Balance on goods and services (lines 30 + 31)		−8
33	Balance on investment income (lines 4 + 8)		+2
34	Balance on goods, services, and income (lines 1 + 5)		−6
35	Unilateral transfers (net) (line 9)		−8
36	Balance on current account (lines 1 + 5 + 9)		−14
37	Balance on capital account (lines 12 + 20)		+14

Source: U.S. Department of Commerce, *Survey of Current Business,* June 1993.

U.S. exports of goods, which are also referred to as **merchandise exports,** include wheat and other agricultural commodities, aircraft, computers, automobiles, and so on. The factors affecting these exports and hence the demand for U.S. dollars include:

1. *The foreign exchange value of the U.S. dollar.* For a particular level of domestic and foreign prices of internationally traded goods, the higher is the foreign exchange value of the dollar, the higher are U.S. export prices facing foreigners, and the lower is the quantity of U.S. exports and the demand for dollars. Normally, we single out the exchange rate as the principal factor of interest and put this on the vertical axis of a supply-and-demand figure. Then, all other factors listed below *shift* the currency demand curve. Changes in the exchange rate cause movements *along* the demand curve.

2. *U.S. prices versus the prices of comparable goods abroad.* If inflation in the United States exceeds inflation elsewhere, then, *ceteris paribus,* U.S. goods become less competitive and thus the quantity of U.S. exports declines. U.S. inflation therefore tends to reduce the demand for U.S. dollars at each given exchange rate.[4] This is a leftward shift in the demand curve for dollars.

3. *World prices of products that the U.S. exports.* Changes in the worldwide prices of what the United States exports shift the demand curve for dollars. Higher world prices shift the demand curve to the right, and vice versa. This effect is different from that described in point 2, above. Here we refer to terms of trade effects: an increase in U.S. export prices versus U.S. import prices—where imports are *different* goods than exports—is an improvement in the U.S. terms of trade. On the other hand, in point 2 we refer to prices of U.S. goods versus *comparable* goods abroad which compete with U.S. exports.

4. *Foreign incomes.* When foreign buyers experience an increase in their real incomes, the result is an improvement in the export market for American raw materials and manufactured goods. *Ceteris paribus,* this increases U.S. exports and therefore also increases the demand for dollars.

5. *Foreign import duties and quotas.* U.S. exports are reduced by higher foreign **import tariffs** (taxes on imported goods), lower foreign import **quotas** (the quantity of imports permitted into a country), and higher foreign **nontariff trade barriers,** such as quality requirements and red tape.

Alongside exports of goods are exports of services. These service exports are sometimes called **invisibles.** U.S. service exports include spending by foreign tourists in the United States. Service exports also include overseas earnings of U.S. banks, insurance companies, and engineering, consulting, and accounting firms; overseas earnings of U.S. holders of patents; overseas earnings of royalties on books, music, and movies; overseas earnings of U.S. airlines and shipping, courier, and freight services; and similar items. These service exports give rise to a demand for U.S. dollars when the foreign tourists buy U.S. currency, when the U.S. banks repatriate their earnings, and so on. U.S. earnings on these "performed service" exports respond to the same factors as affect exports of goods: exchange rates, U.S. prices versus foreign prices of comparable goods, world prices of U.S. exports, incomes abroad, and restrictions on trade.

The final category covered by "exports of goods, services, and income," namely, "income," is the earnings U.S. residents receive from past investments made abroad. These earnings can come in the form of interest on bills and bonds,

---

[4]The *value* of exports could, however, increase, because the reduced *quantity* of exports comes as a result of higher prices. As we shall show in the next chapter, values increase from higher prices when demand is inelastic so that the quantity of exports falls less than export prices increase.

dividends on stocks, rent on property, and profits on operating businesses. Sometimes these various sources of investment income are, for convenience, simply referred to as **debt-service exports.** These export earnings are derived from past foreign investments and therefore depend principally on the amount Americans have invested abroad in the past. Debt-service exports also depend on the rates of interest and sizes of dividends, rents, and profits earned on these past foreign investments. Unlike the situation with goods and services exports, the exchange rate plays only a minor role in the income received from abroad. Exchange rate changes can affect the **translated value** of foreign-currency income, but the *foreign-currency income* is not affected by exchange rates.

Imports of Goods, Services, and Income

U.S. imports of goods include such items as oil, automobiles, TVs, clothing, wine, coffee, and so on. U.S. imports respond to the same factors that affect exports, the direction of response being reversed. *Ceteris paribus,* the value of U.S. imports of goods is higher when the U.S. dollar is higher in the foreign exchange markets, when U.S. prices are higher relative to foreign prices of the same goods, when world prices of U.S. imports increase, when U.S. tariffs are lower, and when U.S. import quotas are higher.[5] U.S. imports of performed services (such as American tourists' spending abroad; American use of foreign banks and consulting firms; American use of foreign patents, airlines, and shipping; and American purchases of foreign movies and books) also depend on exchange rates, relative prices, U.S. incomes, and U.S. import restrictions. In the case of income imports, which consist of payments by Americans of interest, dividends, profit, and rent abroad, the principal relevant factor is past foreign investments; the higher have been foreign investments in U.S. government bonds, foreign purchases of corporate bonds and stocks, and past foreign investments in U.S. real estate and operating businesses, the higher are U.S. income imports. Income imports also depend on the rates of return foreigners earn on their investments in the United States.

Until 1986, the United States earned more on its investments abroad than foreigners earned on U.S. investments. That is, U.S. investment income from abroad (income exports) exceeded U.S. investment income paid abroad (income imports). This was because until 1986, the value of U.S. investments abroad exceeded the value of foreign investments in the United States. Because of considerable borrowing by the U.S. government from overseas lenders and because of considerable foreign private investment in the United States, especially in the 1970s and 1980s, in 1986 the United States went from being a net creditor nation to a net debtor nation. Indeed, in a matter of only a couple of years after that turning point, the United States became the largest debtor on earth. This means that the United States has become a net payer of investment income abroad.

Table 5.1 shows that on the merchandise side of trade, the United States ran a large balance-of-payments deficit in the first quarter of 1993. U.S. exports of mer-

---

[5]As with the effects of exchange rates and inflation on exports, we should really distinguish between the *quantity* and *value* of imports. For example, an appreciation of the U.S. dollar could reduce the *value* of U.S. imports even if it increases the *quantity* of U.S. imports. This occurs if the demand for imports is inelastic. We discuss this possibility in Chapter 6.

chandise amounted to $112 billion during the quarter, while U.S. imports of merchandise amounted to $136 billion. This is a **balance-of-trade deficit** during the quarter of $24 billion ($136 billion − $112 billion). This is shown on line 30 of Table 5.1, where it is referred to as the **balance on (merchandise) trade.**

On the service side, U.S. exports of performed services were $16 billion ($45 billion − $29 billion) larger than U.S. imports. There is also a $2 billion ($28 billion − $26 billion) surplus on income. This is despite the U.S. indebtedness, and it could reflect a higher *rate* of earnings on U.S. investments abroad than on foreign investments in the United States.[6] When the $18 billion combined services and income surplus is added to the merchandise trade deficit, we find that the United States had a **balance on goods, services, and income** that was in deficit by $6 billion. This is shown on line 34 of Table 5.1.

Unilateral Transfers (Net)

Unilateral transfers include such items as foreign aid, nonmilitary economic development grants, and private gifts or donations. These items are called *unilateral* transfers because, unlike the case of other items in the balance of payments where the item being traded goes in one direction and the payment goes in the other direction, in the case of gifts and aid there is a flow in only one direction, the direction of payment. However, unilateral transfers must be included somewhere in the account because receipt of a gift or aid gives rise to a demand for the country's currency in the same way the export of goods and services does.[7] Similarly, gifts or aid to foreigners gives rise to a supply of the country's currency in the same way the import of goods and services does. What the balance-of-payments accountant therefore does is treat unilateral transfers as if the donor were buying goodwill from the recipient. That is, the granting of aid is considered as a purchase or import of goodwill, a debit entry under "unilateral transfers." Similarly, a receipt of aid is considered a sale or export of goodwill, and is consequently recorded as a credit entry. By including transfers as a trade in goodwill, we preserve double-entry bookkeeping, since the payment for or receipt from the transfer, which will appear elsewhere in the account, is matched by the transfer entry.

The value of unilateral transfers depends both on a country's own generosity and on the generosity of its friends. It also depends on the number of expatriates who send money to relatives or receive money from relatives. Poorer countries, from which large numbers typically leave for job opportunities elsewhere, receive net earnings on unilateral transfers. India and Pakistan, for example, receive net inflows on transfers. Richer countries—such as the United States, Canada, Britain, and Australia—which have foreign aid programs and many recent immigrants, generally have net outflows on transfers.

When we compute the subtotal up to and including unilateral transfers we obtain the **balance of payments on current account.** That is, the balance of pay-

---

[6]It could also reflect an overstatement of U.S. net indebtedness because U.S. overseas investments are generally older than foreign investments in the United States, and may be undervalued.

[7]If the gift or aid must be spent in the donor country, so that the money never leaves the country, the goods or services received appear elsewhere in the account. In this case it is as if the donor country had an export which automatically matched the transfer.

ments on current account consists of exports and imports of goods, services, and income, plus net unilateral transfers: lines 1, 5, and 9 in Table 5.1. The current account is in deficit by $14 billion, as shown on line 36. The reason the balance of payments on current account is reported is that it shows how much the country will have to borrow or **divest**—sell off its past investments—to finance a current-account deficit, or how much the country must lend or invest if it has a current-account surplus. Borrowing or divesting is necessary if a country has a deficit in its current account, because it is necessary to pay for the extent to which its imports exceed its exports or to which it gives away more than it earns or receives from abroad. Similarly, lending or investing must occur if the country has a current-account surplus, since what the country earns and does not spend or give away is not destroyed but rather is loaned or invested in other countries. In summary:

> The current account of the balance of payments is the result of the export and import of goods, services, income, and goodwill (or unilateral transfers). A deficit in the current account must be financed by borrowing from abroad or by divestment of foreign assets, while a surplus must be loaned abroad or invested in foreign assets.

A country can finance a current-account deficit by selling to foreigners the country's bills, bonds, stocks, real estate, and operating businesses. A country can also finance its current-account deficit by selling off its previous investments in foreign bills, bonds, stocks, real estate, and operating businesses, that is, via divestment. Before we examine how the United States financed the $14 billion current-account deficit shown in Table 5.1, we should recall that there is nothing to distinguish the demand for a country's currency when foreigners buy its financial and real assets from the demand when foreigners buy the country's currency to buy that country's goods and services; a check or draft for the country's currency must be purchased regardless of what is being bought. Similarly, a country's currency is supplied in the same way whether residents of a country are buying foreign financial or real assets or are importing goods and services. Of course, different factors influence the purchase and sale of financial and real assets than influence the purchase and sale of goods and services, and, as we shall see, there are different long-run implications of trade in assets than of trade in goods and services; today's trade in stocks, bonds, real estate, and businesses affects *future* flows of dividends, interest, rents, and profits.

U.S. Assets Abroad (Net)

There are several components to this item, which are best considered separately. We see from Table 5.1 that collectively, the items under this heading added to the U.S. borrowing requirement: the United States added $5 billion to its foreign assets, meaning a net additional supply of $5 billion U.S. dollars.

The first subcomponent of U.S. assets abroad is **U.S. official reserve assets.** Official reserves are liquid assets held by the U.S. Federal Reserve and the Department of the Treasury; the Federal Reserve Bank of New York buys and sells foreign exchange on behalf of the Federal Reserve System and the U.S. Treasury. These liquid assets include gold, foreign currency in foreign banks, and balances at the **International Monetary Fund (IMF).**[8] We see in line 13 of Table 5.1 that there is

---

[8]The IMF is a place where many countries hold funds for financing balance-of-payments deficits. We discuss this institution in Chapter 9.

an entry of −$1 billion for changes in official reserves. The negative sign means a supply of U.S. dollars because the U.S. Federal Reserve or Treasury bought gold, foreign currency, or balances held at the IMF. Whatever is bought, the United States is accumulating foreign assets and is supplying U.S. dollars. This is done when the U.S. government is trying to prevent an appreciation of the dollar vis-à-vis other currencies: adding to the supply of dollars tends to push the price of the dollar down. On the other hand, the U.S. government buys dollars—reducing foreign assets—when it wishes to prop up the dollar in the foreign exchange market. The main influence on the size of the official reserve entry is the extent to which the U.S. government wishes to influence exchange rates. The harder the government is trying to support the dollar, the larger is the positive entry.

The next item under the heading "U.S. assets abroad (net)" is "U.S. government assets other than official reserves," line 14 of Table 5.1. This item shows new loans and loan repayments involving the U.S. government. When the U.S. government makes a foreign loan or repays a loan, this item shows a negative entry because there is a supply of dollars. When the U.S. government borrows from foreign governments, there is a positive entry and a demand for dollars. In the first quarter of 1993, the net supply of dollars under this heading is zero, indicating the U.S. government made no net new loans. As with the U.S. official reserve assets entry, a major factor influencing the size of this item is U.S. government efforts to influence the foreign exchange value of the dollar.

After the two entries reflecting U.S. government activity are four items which together constitute "U.S. private assets abroad." These entries show the extent to which U.S. private firms and individuals have made investments in foreign bills, bonds, stocks, real estate, and so on, or have divested themselves of such investments by selling assets purchased in the past.

The first subcategory of U.S. private assets is **direct investment.** By definition, direct investment by Americans occurs when the ownership of a foreign operating business is sufficiently extensive to give Americans a measure of control. Government statisticians have chosen the level of 10 percent or more ownership of a company's voting shares to constitute control. Original as well as incremental investments where 10 percent or more ownership is involved are considered direct investment (or divestment when funds are brought home). A typical example of direct investment would be the building of a factory in a foreign country by a U.S. multinational corporation. Line 16 of Table 5.1 shows that there was a supply of $11 billion of U.S. currency to the foreign exchange market from U.S. direct investment during the period. This supply of U.S. dollars adds to the supply of dollars from the deficit in the current account and the dollar sales of the U.S. government. This means that further down the balance-of-payments account there must be entries showing the U.S. borrowing and/or divestment that is financing the current-account deficit, U.S. government sales of dollars, and U.S. direct investment abroad.

Direct investment depends on the expected return from investing in plant and equipment, real estate, and so on in foreign countries relative to the opportunity cost of shareholder capital. The expected return net of the opportunity cost must be sufficient to compensate for the unavoidable risk of the direct investment.[9] Expected

---

[9]Because the opportunity cost of capital involves the alternative of investing at home rather than abroad, direct investment can also be considered to depend on expected returns abroad versus expected returns at home. The details of factors affecting direct investment are described in Chapters 19 and 20.

returns abroad may be high if foreign real wage rates are low, if raw materials are cheap, if corporate taxes are low, if borrowing rates are low—perhaps because of subsidized loans—and so on. The risks of overseas direct investment includes both business and political risks.

The next private investment item is titled "foreign securities." This shows the supply of or demand for U.S. dollars from the purchase or sale by U.S. residents of foreign stocks and bonds.[10] When U.S. residents add to their holdings of these assets, there is a supply of dollars and a negative entry in the balance-of-payments account. When U.S. residents sell these assets and repatriate the proceeds, there is a demand for dollars and a positive entry. Line 17 shows that during the first quarter of 1993 U.S. residents moved $27 billion into foreign stocks and bonds. This is a large, further supply of dollars, adding to the net supply of dollars from direct investment, U.S. government dollar sales, and the deficit in the current account.

The amount of foreign security investment depends on the difference in expected returns between foreign stocks and bonds and domestic stocks and bonds, and on relative risks. The expected return on a foreign security depends on the expected dividend on the stock or interest on the bill or bond, the expected change in the security's local-currency market value, and the expected change in the exchange rate. Because funds flow between countries until the expected returns in different locations are equal, the advantage that exists for investing in a particular location will be more obvious from statistics in the balance-of-payments account on the amounts flowing than from statistics on yields.[11] In addition to the difference between expected returns abroad and expected returns at home, U.S. residents' purchases of foreign securities depend on diversification benefits from foreign investment. We shall discuss these benefits in Chapter 18.

The next two items, shown in lines 18 and 19, give the supply of and demand for U.S. dollars due to short-term lending abroad. Line 18 gives lending by non-bank firms, including credits extended by U.S. firms in commercial transactions, where the receivables on the credits are assets of U.S. firms. A negative entry means an increase in outstanding loans and credits during the reporting period and a consequent supply of dollars. A positive entry means a reduction in outstanding loans and credits and a demand for dollars from repayment. There was little reported supply of or demand for U.S. dollars from this source during the first quarter of 1993.

Line 19 shows the change in the amount loaned to foreign borrowers by U.S. banks. The large positive entry for this item tells us that U.S. banks reduced their lending abroad during the reporting period. This occurred partly because U.S. banks' dollar claims on their own offices abroad declined and partly because of loan repayments by foreign borrowers. A reduction of U.S. bank claims on their own offices abroad occurs when the banks find it more profitable to make dollar loans in the United States than to make dollar loans in the **Eurodollar market**.[12] Banks find it more profitable to lend in the United States than abroad when there are higher inter-

---

[10]Of course, when a U.S. resident holds 10 percent or more of the voting stock of a foreign company, the flow of U.S. dollars for the foreign stock appears as a direct investment.

[11]This point is made, for example, by Fischer Black in "The Ins and Outs of Foreign Investment," *Financial Analysts Journal,* May/June 1978, pp. 1–7.

[12]Eurodollars are U.S.-dollar-denominated bank deposits in banks located outside the United States. The U.S.-dollar loans that appear in line 19 are made out of Eurodollar deposits. The reasons for the emergence of the Eurodollar market are given in Chapter 22.

est rates in the United States than in the Eurodollar market. Even a small interest-rate advantage can move a vast amount of money between nations. The speed with which the money can move is so rapid that funds moved between banks and bank offices have been called "hot money." This money needs only an internal bank real-location or an order sent via SWIFT (see Chapter 2) if the money is moving between unrelated banks. The effect on exchange rates can be as fast as the money itself can move, which in turn is as fast as the transmission of a satellite signal. For this reason, changes in interest rates can cause very large and sudden changes in exchange rates.

Foreign Assets in the United States (Net)

The next set of items in the balance of payments, those on lines 20 to 27, are the same as those described above and shown in lines 12 to 19 except that lines 20 to 27 give the supply of and demand for U.S. dollars due to borrowing, lending, invest-ment, and divestment by foreigners rather than by U.S. residents. The entry "for-eign official assets in U.S." gives the increase or decrease in U.S. dollar assets held by foreign governments in the United States. The positive entry shows that there was a demand for U.S. dollars due to dollar buying by foreign governments. This occurs when there is a cooperative effort of the governments of the leading industrial nations to prop up the U.S. dollar. The principal factor determining the size of this item is the extent to which foreign governments are committed to the stabilization of exchange rates.

When exchange rates are fixed, central banks buy whatever amount of dollars is necessary to prevent the dollar from falling. When exchange rates are flexible, or **floating**, governments are not supposed to buy or sell foreign currencies at all, instead leaving exchange rates to be determined by the forces of supply and demand. What then do we make of the positive entry on line 21? The answer is that exchange rates were not completely flexible in 1993. Rather, there was an effort to stabilize exchange rates, which took the form of a so-called **dirty float.** If exchange rates had been truly flexible, there would have been no buying or selling of U.S. dollars by governments, and line 21 would have been zero.

Line 23 shows the amount of direct investment made by foreigners in the United States. As with U.S. direct investment abroad, this is determined by the expected rate of return on the direct investment relative to the shareholders' oppor-tunity cost of capital and by the amount of unavoidable risk of the investment. The expected rate of return is a function of market opportunities in the United States, including the possibility of facing quotas and other forms of protectionism if the direct investment is not made. We find a demand for U.S. dollars from direct invest-ment by foreigners in the United States during the reporting period. This helps finance the current-account deficit but means profit repatriation within the income payments component of *future* current accounts.

Line 24 shows substantial purchases of U.S. Treasury securities by overseas investors; the entry is positive when foreigners increase their holdings of U.S. Trea-sury securities and negative when they reduce them. Similarly, in line 25 we see a substantial increase in foreign holdings of U.S. stocks and bonds during the report-ing period, augmenting the demand for dollars by foreign governments and for direct investment. The principal factors influencing foreign investment in U.S. Trea-sury securities, as well as stocks, bonds, and other securities, are U.S. versus foreign yields, and expected future changes in exchange rates. *Ceteris paribus,* the higher are U.S. versus foreign yields and the more the dollar is expected to increase in value, the greater is the demand for U.S. securities and dollars. Expected changes in exchange rates tend to be reflected in forward exchange premiums or discounts. Therefore, we can also think of the demand for U.S. securities in lines 24 and 25 as depending on yield advantages, plus the forward premium or discount on the U.S. dollar. We might note that a large number of U.S. Treasury bills and bonds issued to finance the U.S. fiscal deficit helped to fuel the demand for dollars during the first quarter of 1993.

Line 26 shows no effect of nonbank liabilities (nonbank credits granted by foreign firms to U.S. firms) on the demand for dollars. However, line 27 shows a large supply of dollars due to U.S. bank liabilities. U.S. bank liabilities consist of deposits by foreigners in U.S. banks. We see that deposits were withdrawn during the reporting period. This could have occurred because of fear of an expected decline in the value of the U.S. dollar, or because foreign investors preferred to shift their dollars from U.S. bank accounts into U.S. securities.[13]

Allocation of Special Drawing Rights (SDRs)

In line 28 of Table 5.1 we find the entry "Allocation of SDRs." The specific details of SDRs, or Special Drawing Rights, are discussed in Chapter 9. However, we can say here that SDRs are reserves created by the International Monetary Fund (IMF) and allocated by making ledger entries in the countries' accounts at the IMF. In 1993 the United States did not receive any SDRs. When SDRs are allocated, they appear as a positive entry, as would any other inflow of unilateral transfers.

Statistical Discrepancy

Until 1976 the **statistical discrepancy** was called "errors and omissions," which gives a better idea of its meaning. A discrepancy can exist because of errors in estimating many of the items in Table 5.1. Errors might appear because of differences between the time that current-account entries are made and the time that the associated payments appear elsewhere in the balance-of-payments account. It is customary for the U.S. Department of Commerce to collect data on exports and imports of goods and services from customs agents; the data on these current-account items are reported as the goods cross the border or as the services are rendered. The payments for these goods or services, which are financial flows, appear only afterward. This may be in a subsequent report of the balance-of-payments statistics.

Another reason for errors is that many entries are estimates. For example, data on travel expenditures are estimated from questionnaire surveys of a limited number of travelers. The average expenditure discovered in a survey is multiplied by the number of travelers. A further reason for measurement error is that illegal transactions, which affect foreign exchange supply and demand despite their illegality, do not explicitly enter the accounts. We can therefore have flows of funds without any associated measured flows of goods or services. As Exhibit 5.1 explains, error also

---

[13]It is possible that foreigners moved funds out of U.S. banks because of higher interest rates elsewhere; however, this does not seem likely in light of the positive entries in lines 19 and 24.

EXHIBIT 5.1
Extraterrestrial Trade or the Ether?
Data Difficulties in the Balance of Payments

While we remain earthbound, the current-account balances of all the countries in the world should themselves balance. That is, surpluses in some countries should exactly match deficits in others, with the sum of positive and negative balances being zero. So much for the theory. As the following excerpt from the *Review* of the Federal Reserve Bank of St. Louis explains, in practice, balance-of-payments accounting does not quite fit the theory. It turns out that the underreporting of service exports is probably the principal culprit.

In late 1987, the U.S. Commerce Department announced that in its monthly trade reports, exports to Canada would henceforth use Canadian customs data on imports from the United States rather than U.S. export data. The rationale for this procedure is the documented inaccuracy since 1970 of U.S. customs data for exports to Canada. The discrepancies between the U.S. and Canadian data have become substantial both in absolute terms—nearly $11 billion in 1986—and in terms of their effect on the U.S. trade balance—a 42 percent reduction in the 1986 U.S. trade deficit with Canada. While these errors are corrected in the annual reconciliation of U.S.-Canadian trade data, their persistence raises a broader question: Are U.S. exports to other countries similarly understated?

This possibility raises some important political and economic issues. In recent years, the trade balance has been the focus of much economic policy debate, rivaling or complementing such traditional domestic issues as employment, inflation and growth. In this context, isolating large under-statements in U.S. merchandise export data is clearly a topic with important policy implications. . . . Any exported good from the country of origin is an imported good for the country of destination. As a consequence, if the data are complete and accurate, the world can have neither a trade deficit nor surplus; it must have a balance. Yet, the world trade data do not yield a balance on current account.

Throughout the first half of the 1980s, world merchandise trade was in "surplus," substantially so in 1980 and 1981, and negligibly so since then. More broadly throughout the 1980s, the current account—the sum of merchandise and service trade minus transfers—has been in substantial deficit with no clear trend toward balance. The implication of these statistical discrepancies is that substantial export income is not being reported; that is, exports of services are understated.

The world current account balance discrepancy can be accounted for by a negative service account balance, with unreported shipping income, unreported direct investment income and unreported portfolio investment income the largest contributors. Shipping income is irrelevant for the United States; the IMF working party found it attributable to "several economies with large maritime interests (notably those of Greece, Hong Kong and Eastern Europe)." The other two discrepancy items, direct and portfolio investment income, were found to be attributable in large part to U.S. investors' unreported or misreported foreign income.

Source: Mack Ott, "Have U.S. Exports Been Larger than Reported?" *Review,* Federal Reserve Bank of St. Louis, September/October 1988, pp. 3–23.

arises from unreported or misreported income on investment and shipping, although the latter is not a problem in the U.S. account. Finally, we can have unreported flows of capital.

An obvious question is how the balance-of-payments accountant knows the size of the statistical discrepancy, since, by definition, it is due to inaccurate data. The answer is that due to the use of double-entry accounting principles, all the entries in the account must add to zero. (We saw this at the beginning of the chapter: every positive entry is matched by a negative entry.) If the balance-of-payments entries do not sum to zero, errors must have been made equal to the extent to which the sum of entries differs from zero. If you check by adding the numbers in the far-right column of Table 5.1, excluding memoranda items, you will see they do indeed add to zero in this particular period. However, the statistical discrepancy can sometimes be large, with a $20 billion discrepancy not uncommon.

The fact that the balance of payments must sum to zero means that it is subtotals such as the balance on current account that are of interest. Furthermore, the fact that the overall balance is zero can provide very useful insights into, for example, why a country has a current-account deficit.

IMPLICATIONS OF THE BALANCE-OF-PAYMENTS ACCOUNTING IDENTITY

Interpreting the Accounts with Fixed and Flexible Rates

We can offer an interesting explanation of why a country can run a current-account deficit if we consider the following accounting identity:

$$B_c + \Delta R + B_k + \varepsilon \equiv 0 \tag{5.1}$$

Here B_c is the balance of payments on current account, which is the sum of lines 1, 5, and 9 in Table 5.1. The next term, ΔR, is the change in official reserves of both the U.S. and foreign governments, that is, the sum of line 13 and line 21. The next term, B_k, is the sum of all the remaining entries in the balance of payments except the statistical discrepancy. This means that B_k is the sum of lines 12 and 20. B_k is the **balance of payments on capital account.** This balance is shown on line 37 in Table 5.1. The balance of payments on capital account, B_k, is the net result of all the borrowing, lending, investment, and divestment of nonbank firms, banks, and individuals, as estimated by the balance-of-payments accountant. The final term, ε, is the statistical discrepancy. In summary:

$$B_c = \text{balance on current account}$$
$$\Delta R = \text{changes in official reserves}$$
$$B_k = \text{balance on capital account}$$
$$\varepsilon = \text{statistical discrepancy}$$

Equation (5.1) is a fundamental balance-of-payments identity. It is useful to consider the implications of this identity separately for fixed and flexible exchange rates.

Flexible Rates

We have said that if exchange rates are truly flexible, there cannot be any changes in official reserves because central banks do not buy or sell currencies and gold. This means that if exchange rates are truly flexible,

$$B_c + B_k + \varepsilon \equiv 0$$

Assuming that we can calculate balances without error, this means

$$B_c \equiv -B_k \tag{5.2}$$

Equation (5.2) says that with flexible exchange rates, the correctly measured current-account deficit/surplus is exactly equal to the correctly measured capital-account surplus/deficit. It is equation (5.2) that is behind the view of many economists that the large U.S. current-account deficits of the 1980s were the result of too much foreign borrowing. Let us consider this view.

Some people tend to think that the direction of causation runs from the current account to the capital account. They would argue that having a deficit in the current account from spending more abroad than is earned from abroad causes a country to have to borrow abroad or divest itself of assets. This suggests a direction of causation from B_c to B_k. However, an equally valid way to view the situation is that an inflow of capital, such as occurs when the U.S. government sells its bills and bonds to foreign lenders to finance the U.S. fiscal deficit, forces the country to run a deficit in the current account equal to the net import of capital. Indeed, flexible exchange rates are the mechanism that ensures that a current-account deficit results from the capital imports. What happens is that the demand for dollars resulting from the foreign purchases of U.S. bills and bonds increases the value of the dollar, thereby reducing U.S. exports and increasing U.S. imports, causing a current-account deficit.

Fixed Rates

When exchange rates are fixed, there is no simple link between the correctly measured current and capital accounts as in equation (5.2). However, we can still use the fundamental accounting identity in equation (5.1) to reach some important conclusions.

If we again assume the current and capital account balances are correctly measured, we can rearrange equation (5.1) to state

$$\Delta R \equiv -\left(B_c + B_k\right)$$

This tells us that when exchange rates are fixed, as they were for most currencies during the so-called "Bretton Woods era" from 1944 to 1973, the increase/decrease in official reserves equals the combined surplus/deficit in the current and capital accounts.[14] Indeed, the mechanism for fixing exchange rates ensured that this happened. If a country had a combined deficit on its current and capital accounts, the net excess supply of the country's currency would have forced down its exchange rate if the government did nothing. Only by buying an amount of its currency equal to the excess supply could the country keep its exchange rate from falling. That is, governments had to demand whatever excess amounts of their currencies were supplied if they were to prevent their exchange rates from falling. Similarly, governments had to supply whatever excess amounts of their currencies were demanded if they were to prevent their exchange rates from increasing. Therefore, ΔR had to be equal and opposite in sign to the combined balance on current and capital account, $B_c + B_k$.

Long-Run versus Short-Run Implications of Payments Imbalances

Flexible Rates

If $B_c + B_k = 0$, but B_c is large and negative and B_k is large and positive, the country is likely to run into trouble eventually. This is because with B_c negative and B_k positive a country is paying for its excess of imports over exports of goods, services, income, and goodwill by borrowing abroad or divesting itself of investments made in the past. This is not sustainable in the long run, because B_c includes income

---

[14]The Bretton Woods fixed-exchange-rate system is described in more detail in Chapters 8 and 9.

payments and receipts. If the country is borrowing or divesting, the size of its income payments will grow faster than its income receipts and so therefore will the deficit on current account. That is, if B_c is negative and B_k is positive, then B_c will become more negative in the future via the additional net payments of interest, dividends, rents, and profits. This will make it necessary to borrow or divest more, thereby making B_c even more negative in the future, and so on. As we explain in Chapter 9 when discussing international debt crises, such a pattern has occurred in the past with nearly catastrophic consequences.

Fixed Rates

If $B_c + \Delta R + B_k \equiv 0$ with $B_c + B_k$ negative and ΔR positive, this means the government is buying up its own currency to offset the net excess supply due to the current-account plus capital-account deficits. The government buys its own currency by selling gold and foreign exchange reserves. This can occur in the short run if the government has a large stock of reserves. However, eventually reserves will run out. Official reserves can sometimes be borrowed from foreign governments, but the income payments to official foreign lenders due to borrowing causes higher future current-account deficits, requiring even more borrowing, still higher future current-account deficits, and so on. Eventually the country is likely to run out of credit.

What we discover is that only temporary deficits should be allowed in the current account, or else a country is likely to fall deeper and deeper into debt. With fixed exchange rates, it is possible to have a deficit in the combined current and capital accounts, but again, if this is not temporary, the country will run out of reserves, fall into debt, and eventually run out of credit.

The Firm versus the Economy: An Analogy

We can illustrate the importance of correcting imbalances of payments by considering an analogous situation of imbalances in the current and capital accounts of an individual firm. This analogy also helps us push our understanding of the balance of payments a little further.

The analogous account to the balance of payments on current account for the firm is the firm's income statement. In the case of the firm, the credit entries are revenues from sales and earnings on past investment such as interest received on bank accounts. The debit entries are the firm's payments for wages, salaries, rent, raw materials, equipment, and entertainment/advertising—the buying of goodwill—plus interest and dividend payments. If the firm has a surplus on its income statement, it can add to its investments or build up a reserve in the bank against possible losses in the future. If the firm has a deficit in its income statement, it must borrow, raise more equity, or divest itself of assets purchased in the past.

In the case of a surplus, the addition to investments means higher future income and, *ceteris paribus*, ever-larger future surpluses in its income statements. In the case of borrowing or divesting to cover losses, the extra debt or reduced income base of assets suggests even larger future losses. However, when we consider an individual firm, we recognize that having payments that exceed receipts is acceptable when it occurs because the firm is updating or otherwise improving its capital stock. This situation is acceptable because the firm is increasing its potential to generate future revenue or reducing its future costs of production. Provided the investment is a good investment, the extra revenue or saving in production costs will service any added debt incurred in making the investment. Therefore, having a deficit in the income statement, the analogous account to the current account of the balance of payments, is not necessarily a matter of concern. It depends on whether the deficit is the result of current operating and debt costs exceeding current revenue or whether the deficit results from capital investment.

It follows from what we have just said that it is not necessarily bad for a country to have a current-account deficit and a capital-account surplus. If the country is borrowing from abroad to finance the building of important infrastructure, the development of natural resources such as oil reserves, the purchase of state-of-the-art robots or construction equipment, and so on, then an excess of imports over exports in the current account may be due to the import of capital equipment. This is far healthier than a trade deficit from importing consumer goods such as VCRs, expensive wine, clothing, and automobiles. Indeed, if the imported capital equipment offers a return in excess of future interest or dividend payments incurred in financing the capital, this is a very healthy and sustainable situation. We see that we need to know the composition of the current-account deficit as well as whether the account is in deficit.[15] Unfortunately, no accounting distinction is made between the import of capital goods and the import of consumer goods. Both appear in the current account and contribute to a deficit even though they have different implications for future living standards and financial viability.

THE NET INTERNATIONAL INVESTMENT POSITION

The capital account of the balance of payments presents the record of the *flows* of funds into and out of a country. Capital inflows result from the sale of financial and real assets, gold, and foreign exchange to foreigners. Outflows result from the purchase of these assets from foreigners. The inflows and outflows are added to and subtracted from **stocks** of outstanding international assets and liabilities. The account that shows the stocks of assets and liabilities is called the **international-investment-position account.** This account is analogous to a firm's balance sheet. Table 5.2 gives the international investment position of the United States at the end of 1992.

When capital leaves the United States for investment overseas, it is added to U.S. assets abroad. The debit that appears in the balance of payments therefore corresponds to an increase in the value of U.S. assets in Table 5.2. Similarly, when capital flows into the United States, the credit that appears in the balance of payments corresponds to an increase in foreign assets in the United States, as shown in Table 5.2.

The inflows and outflows of investments are categorized into official/government and private components, with further divisions within these major categories. The listed items correspond to those in the balance-of-payments account, and indeed, in principle, an outflow of capital in the balance of payments should increase

---

[15]This point has been made by K. Alec Chrystal and Geoffrey E. Wood, "Are Trade Deficits a Problem?" *Review,* Federal Reserve Bank of St. Louis, January/February 1988, pp. 3–11.

TABLE 5.2. International Investment Position of the United States, Year-end 1992
(Billions of U.S. dollars)

U.S. Government assets abroad:				231	
U.S. official reserve assets			150		
U.S. government assets other than official reserves			81		
U.S. private assets abroad: direct investment at current cost				1772	
Direct investment at current cost			666		
(Direct investment at market value			776)		
Foreign securities			327		
Bonds		149			
Stocks		178			
Assets of U.S. non-banks			112		
Assets of U.S. banks			667		
(U.S. private assets abroad: direct investment at market value				1882)	

Foreign official assets in U.S.:				443	
Foreign private assets in U.S.: direct investment at current cost				2081	
Direct investment at current cost			492		
(Direct investment at market value			692)		
U.S. securities:			842		
Treasury securities:		225			
Bonds		317			
Stocks		300			
Liabilities of U.S. non-banks			46		
Liabilities of U.S. banks			701		
(Foreign private assets in U.S.: direct investment at market value				2281)	
Net international investment position of U.S.: direct investment at current cost				−521	
(Net international investment position of U.S. with direct investment at market value				−611)	

Source: U.S. Department of Commerce, *Survey of Current Business*, June 1993.

the corresponding "U.S. asset abroad" item in the net-international-investment-position account. Similarly, an inflow of capital should increase the corresponding "foreign assets in the U.S." item in the investment-position account. However, while there is a close correspondence between the balance-of-payments account and the net-international-investment-position account, that correspondence is imperfect. One of the main problems arises from changes in values of existing assets. Such changes in values do not appear in the balance of payments but should be reflected in a country's investment position.

An attempt is made to deal with changes in values of existing assets for direct investment but not for stocks, bonds, and other investment items. We see in Table 5.2 that the market value of U.S. direct investments abroad exceeds their "current cost"—the value at the time of the investment—by $110 billion ($1882 billion − $1772 billion). In the case of foreign direct investment in the United States the discrepancy is even larger, a whopping $200 billion ($2281 billion − $2081 billion). The use of these two measures of direct investment means there are two different measures of national net indebtedness. Table 5.2 shows that the United States is a net debtor by more than one-half trillion dollars. For the United States, net indebtedness is foreign assets in the United States minus U.S. assets abroad. The debt represents approximately 1 month of the U.S. GDP. Therefore, while substantial, the U.S. foreign debt problem is not as serious as the debt problems faced by many Latin American and Eastern European economies in the 1980s, for which debts were often equal to several years of the debtors' GDPs.[16]

One of the most important items in the net international investment position is the official reserve position of the government. This position is very important during times of fixed exchange rates or dirty floats for judging how long a country can influence exchange rates. A government can defend its currency only as long as it has sufficient reserves. If, for example, a government can afford many years of substantial deficits with its stock of reserves, a devaluation—an official reduction in the fixed exchange rate—can be considered unlikely. On the other hand, if reserves will meet existing deficits for only a few months, a devaluation is quite possible.

OBJECTIVES OF ECONOMIC POLICY

Even when it is pointed out that a trade deficit can be healthy if it is due to importing capital equipment that increases future output and exports, it is difficult for many people to give up the idea that it is better to try to achieve trade surpluses than trade deficits. This presumption that trade surpluses are an appropriate policy objective has a long history, being the opinion of a diverse group of writers of the sixteenth, seventeenth, and eighteenth centuries known as **mercantilists.** The mercantilists believed that trade surpluses were the objective of trade because, during that time, surpluses resulted in increased holdings of gold, the medium of exchange against which internationally traded products were exchanged. Today, a version of mercantilism is that trade surpluses are an appropriate objective because they result in accumulations of foreign assets, as reflected in the net international investment position. This seems so eminently reasonable that it is worth asking why indefinitely running trade surpluses is not a good policy objective.

---

[16]The debt problem of these nations is discussed in Chapter 9.

Consider what it means to have a trade surplus, with merchandise exports exceeding imports, and to have this surplus continue indefinitely. It means that a country is producing more goods for foreigners to enjoy than foreign countries produce for the country's own residents. But why should one country manufacture goods for the pleasure of another in excess of what it receives in return? Indefinite surpluses mean a country is living below its means. The country could enjoy more of its own production and still keep trade in balance.

One of the most direct ways of exposing the modern-day mercantilist fallacy is by considering the **national-income accounting identity** which is met in macroeconomics. This identity is written as

$$Y \equiv C + I + G + (Ex - Im) \tag{5.3}$$

where
$$Y = \text{gross domestic product (GDP)}[17]$$

$$C = \text{consumption}$$

$$I = \text{gross investment}$$

$$G = \text{government expenditures}$$

$$Ex = \text{exports of goods and services}$$

$$Im = \text{imports of goods and services}$$

By rearranging equation (5.3) we can state the balance of payments on goods and services as

$$Ex - Im \equiv Y - (C + I + G) \tag{5.4}$$

Equation (5.4) makes it immediately clear that having a surplus in trade, with $(Ex - Im)$ positive, means that what is produced (that is, Y) is more than what is "used" or "absorbed" by the economy in the form of consumption, business investment, and the provision of services by the government (that is, $C + I + G$). Interpretation of the balance of trade as expressed in equation (5.4) has been called the **absorption approach** to the balance of payments.

Just as surpluses mean a country is living below its means, deficits mean a country is living above its means. In terms of equation (5.4), a deficit means producing less than the country absorbs, that is, $Y < C + I + G$. A deficit means enjoying the products and resources of other nations in excess of the products the country in turn provides for other countries. This is marvelous as long as a country can get away with it, but as with individuals or firms that live beyond their means, a day of reckoning eventually comes when the credit runs out. This makes continuous deficits as undesirable as continuous surpluses. Indeed, in the case of deficits the situation is not easily sustainable.

In order to live within its means, a country does not need to balance its trade each and every year. Rather, it can have temporary surpluses and temporary deficits that on average leave its trade balanced.

---

[17]Gross domestic product, GDP, is the value of goods and services produced *within a nation*. Gross national product, GNP, is the value of goods and services produced by factors of production *owned by residents of a nation*. GNP includes net income earned by residents from abroad via having made investments, working abroad, and so on. If we write Y as GDP, then we exclude income earned abroad or paid to foreigners in Ex and Im in equation (5.3).

Temporary trade surpluses followed by temporary trade deficits, or temporary deficits followed by temporary surpluses, are a very different matter than continuous surpluses or deficits. During temporary trade surpluses, the country increases its holdings of foreign assets such as stocks, bonds, real estate, operating businesses, and so on. The income on these foreign assets allows the country to run trade deficits in the future without the country slipping into debt; interest, dividends, and other earnings in the current account can offset the merchandise deficit. Even if there is an overall current-account deficit because interest, dividends, and other "invisibles" do not fully offset the trade deficit, a country can sell off some of its past investments.

When a country has a trade surplus, it is saving, that is, acquiring foreign assets which can add to future income or which can be sold to finance future spending. It follows that indefinitely running trade surpluses is analogous to a family saving, and neither themselves nor their descendants ever dissaving. Saving is a reasonable choice for people who are patient, but only if it means that at some point in the future they or their descendants enjoy the benefits of past saving by consuming more than they earn. That is, it is appropriate to save sometimes and dissave sometimes, as long as on average over a long interval of time the savings are approximately equal to the dissavings. Similarly, it is appropriate to sometimes have trade deficits and sometimes have trade surpluses. The objective of economic policy should be to aim to have balanced trade over a long period, perhaps as long as a decade or more.[18]

What we have said is important because people tend to look at relatively short periods of trade statistics and become seriously alarmed without considering the trade pattern of earlier years, or the likely trade pattern of future years. Such alarm was voiced, for example, in the 1990s in response to the large U.S. trade deficits and corresponding large Japanese trade surpluses. Few people stopped to recall that in the 1970s the situation was the reverse, with the United States running trade surpluses, and Japan, importing expensive oil and other resources, running trade deficits. This is not to suggest that the situation in the 1990s was desirable or that it could continue indefinitely.[19] It does, however, warn us to take a long-term perspective.

SUMMARY

1. The balance-of-payments account is a record of the flow of payments between the residents of one country and the rest of the world in a given period. Entries in the account that give rise to a demand for the country's currency—such as exports and asset sales—are identified by a plus sign. Entries giving rise to a supply of the country's currency are identified by a minus sign. Therefore, we can think of the balance-of-payments account as a record of the supply of and demand for a country's currency.

2. The balance-of-payments account is based on double-entry bookkeeping. Therefore, every entry has a counterpart entry elsewhere in the account, and the account must balance. What is important, however, is *how* it balances. Anything tending to increase the size of positive entries, such as higher exports or increased sales of bonds to foreigners, will cause the account to balance at a higher exchange rate.

---

[18]The conclusion that an appropriate objective of policy is to balance the current account on average by borrowing sometimes and lending at other times is supported by the gain from consumption smoothing that is described in Appendix 1.2, Chapter 1. In that appendix, it is shown that there is a gain in expected utility from borrowing and lending.

[19]Indeed, we consider the problem of growing bilateral imbalances in Chapter 9.

3. Credit entries in the balance of payments result from purchases by foreigners of a country's goods, services, goodwill, financial and real assets, gold, and foreign exchange. Debit entries result from purchases by a country's residents of goods, services, goodwill, financial and real assets, gold, and foreign exchange from foreigners.

4. The current account includes trade in goods and services, income, and unilateral transfers. The goods or merchandise component alone gives the balance of trade as the excess of exports over imports. If exports exceed imports, the balance of trade is in surplus, and if imports exceed exports, it is in deficit. Income includes the flow of interest and dividend receipts and payments. Unilateral transfers are flows of money not matched by any other physical flow, and double-entry bookkeeping requires that we have an offsetting flow that can be marked down as goodwill.

5. A current-account deficit can be financed by selling a country's bills, bonds, stocks, real estate, or businesses. It can also be financed by selling off previous investments in foreign bills, bonds, stocks, real estate, or businesses. A current-account surplus can be invested in foreign bills, bonds, stocks, real estate, or businesses. The principal factors influencing investments in foreign financial and real assets are rates of return in the foreign country versus rates of return at home, and the riskiness of the investments.

6. Purchases and sales of financial and real assets result in a supply of or demand for a country's currency in the same way as do purchases and sales of goods and services.

7. Changes in official reserves occur when governments intervene in the foreign exchange markets to influence exchange rates. When exchange rates are truly flexible, changes in official reserves are zero.

8. Since all entries in the balance of payments should collectively sum to zero, the balance-of-payments accountant can determine the errors that were made, which together are called the statistical discrepancy.

9. With flexible exchange rates, the correctly measured deficit/surplus in the current account equals the correctly measured surplus/deficit in the capital account. With fixed exchange rates, the combined increase/decrease in official reserves of the domestic and foreign governments is equal to the combined surplus/deficit of the correctly measured current and capital accounts.

10. It is equally valid to consider a current-account deficit/surplus to be the cause of, or to be caused by, a capital-account surplus/deficit.

11. The balance-of-payments account is analogous to a firm's income statement. Deficits are equivalent to corporate losses and can be financed by selling bonds or new equity or by divesting assets. If there is a net outflow from a firm or country due to acquiring new productive capital, this might not be unhealthy. Unfortunately, the balance-of-payments account does not distinguish imports of capital goods from imports of consumption goods.

12. The international investment position is a record of the stock of foreign assets and liabilities. It is relevant for determining the likelihood of a currency devaluation.

13. It is not a good idea to run persistent deficits or persistent surpluses in the balance of trade. Rather, a country should balance its trade on average over the long run.

REVIEW QUESTIONS

1. Does the balance-of-payments account record stocks or flows?
2. Are transactions giving rise to the demand for a country's currency recorded as debits or credits in the balance of payments?
3. What economic variables might affect the value of a country's merchandise exports?
4. What are a country's terms of trade?
5. What are "invisibles" in the balance of payments?
6. What are debt-service exports?
7. How are interest earnings from abroad included in the balance of payments?

8. What is a balance-of-trade deficit?
9. What is a unilateral transfer?
10. What are official reserve assets?
11. What is direct investment?
12. What is a Special Drawing Right (SDR)?
13. What is a current-account surplus?
14. What is a capital-account deficit?
15. What is the identity linking the current account, capital account, change in official reserves, and statistical discrepancy?
16. What does the net-international-investment-position account show?
17. What did the mercantilists think?
18. What is the chief characteristic of the absorption approach to the balance of payments?

ASSIGNMENT PROBLEMS

1. Since gold is a part of official reserves, how would the balance-of-payments statistics show the sale of domestically mined gold to the country's central bank? What happens if the mining company sells the gold to foreign private buyers?
2. Can all countries collectively enjoy a surplus, or must all surpluses and deficits cancel against each other? What does gold mining and creation of paper reserves (such as SDRs) at the IMF mean for the world's balance?
3. Under what conditions would inflation increase the value of exports?
4. Even if inflation did increase the value of exports, would the balance of trade and the exchange rate necessarily improve from inflation that is higher than in other countries?
5. How do we know that an exogenous increase in exports will cause a currency to appreciate even though the balance of payments is always zero? How does your answer relate to the law of supply and demand whereby supply equals demand even after demand has increased?
6. What is the difference between the immediate effect and the long-run effect of the sale of bonds to foreigners?
7. What is the difference between the immediate effect and the long-run effect of direct investment by foreigners when the direct investment is in a heavily export-oriented activity such as oil exploration and development? Would it make any difference if the industry into which direct investment occurred were involved in the production of a good the country previously had been importing?
8. If the balance of payments of Alaska were prepared, what would it look like? How about the balance of payments of New York City? What do you think the net investment positions of these locations are? Should we worry if Alaska is in great debt?
9. If the overall level of interest rates in all countries went up, how would this affect the balance of payments of the United States as a net debtor nation?
10. Which item(s) in the balance-of-payments account, Table 5.1, would be most affected by an expected appreciation of the U.S. dollar, and how would the item(s) and the current spot value of the dollar be affected by the expected appreciation? Do you believe that the higher expected future value of the U.S. dollar could increase the spot value immediately?

BIBLIOGRAPHY

BALDWIN, ROBERT E.: "Determinants of Trade and Foreign Investment: Further Evidence," *Review of Economics and Statistics,* fall 1979, pp. 40–48.

BAME, JACK J.: "Analyzing U.S. International Transactions," *Columbia Journal of World Business,* fall 1976, pp. 72–84.

CAVES, RICHARD E., and RONALD W. JONES: *World Trade and Payments: An Introduction,* 4th ed., Little, Brown and Company, Boston, 1984, Chapter 5.

CHRYSTAL, K. ALEC, and GEOFFREY E. WOOD: "Are Trade Deficits a Problem?" *Review,* Federal Reserve Bank of St. Louis, January/February 1988, pp. 3–11.

COOPER, RICHARD N.: "The Balance of Payments in Review," *Journal of Political Economy,* August 1966, pp. 379–395.

GRUBEL, HERBERT G.: *International Economics,* Richard D. Irwin, Inc., Homewood, Ill., 1977, Chapter 13.

HELLER, H. ROBERT: *International Monetary Economics,* Prentice-Hall, Inc., Englewood Cliffs, N.J., 1974, Chapter 4.

KEMP, DONALD S.: "Balance of Payments Concepts—What Do They Really Mean?" *Review,* Federal Reserve Bank of St. Louis, July 1975, pp. 14–23.

MUNDELL, ROBERT A.: "The Balance of Payments" in David Sills (ed.), *International Encyclopedia of the Social Sciences,* Crowell-Collier and Macmillan, Inc., New York, 1968. Reprinted as Chapter 10 in Robert Mundell, *International Economics,* The Macmillan Company, New York, 1968.

OHMAE, KENICHI: " 'Lies, Damned Lies, and Statistics': Why the Trade Deficit Doesn't Matter in a Borderless World," *Journal of Applied Corporate Finance,* winter 1991, pp. 98–106.

"Report of the Advisory Committee on the Presentation of the Balance of Payments Statistics," in U.S. Department of Commerce, *Survey of Current Business,* June 1976, pp. 18–25.

SALOP, JOANNE, and ERICH SPITALLER: "Why Does the Current Account Matter?" *Staff Papers,* International Monetary Fund, March 1980, pp. 101–134.

STERN, ROBERT M.: *The Balance of Payments: Theory and Economic Policy,* Aldine Publishing Company, Chicago, 1973, Chapter 1.

———, et al.: "The Presentation of the U.S. Balance of Payments: A Symposium," Essays in International Finance, no. 123, International Finance Section, Princeton University, Princeton, N.J., August 1977.

WILSON, JOHN F.: "The Foreign Sector in the U.S. Flow of Funds Account," International Finance Discussion Papers, Board of Governors of the Federal Reserve System, no. 239 (undated).

CHAPTER 6

Supply-and-Demand View of Exchange Rates

The evolution of international currency arrangements from the Gold Standard to the Louvre agreement, spanning fifty years, has had a profound impact on business developments. We would therefore expect the management of an investee company to have a historical perspective of the present international currency order, and to have a view regarding the next step in its evolution.

—Charles Nichols

In the preceding chapter we explained that when exchange rates are flexible, they are determined by the forces of supply and demand.[1] In this chapter we consider these forces of supply and demand by deriving the supply and demand curves for a currency and using them to explain what makes exchange rates change. As we might expect, this involves consideration of the effects of items listed in the balance-of-payments account on the supply and demand curves. With the balance-of-payments account recording flows of payments into and out of a country, the explanation of exchange rates based on the account emphasizes *flow* demands and supplies of a currency.[2] However, as we shall see, in the case of currencies there is no assurance that the supply-and-demand situation will have the form that is familiar from the applications of supply and demand in other markets. In particular, there is no assurance that the supply curve of a currency will be upward-sloping.

The possibility that a currency supply curve slopes downward is not a mere curiosity with little practical relevance. Rather, it is a realistic possibility that is critical to explaining why foreign exchange markets may be unstable. This possibility has attracted increased interest because of the volatility of exchange rates in recent years vis-à-vis the quarter century following World War II (see Table 1.4 on page 15). It is also of interest because the condition for exchange-rate instability helps explain the so-called "J curve" whereby, for example, a depreciation of a currency worsens rather than improves a country's balance of trade. Considerable attention

---

[1] When exchange rates are fixed, as they were under the gold standard, the Bretton Woods standard, and the European Monetary System, they are also determined by supply and demand. The difference between fixed and flexible rates is that with fixed rates there is official demand or supply at the fixed rate, and this is adjusted to ensure that the exchange rate stays at or near the chosen rate. The determination of fixed exchange rates is explained in Chapter 8.

[2] In Chapter 7 we describe theories of exchange rates which emphasize *stock* demands and supplies.

has been given to the J curve since the decade-long, almost-relentless depreciation of the U.S. dollar after 1985 was observed to accompany a worsening of the U.S. trade deficit. The cause of the J curve and of exchange-rate instability can be understood via the central economic paradigm of supply and demand.

The traditional approach to supply and demand is to begin by explaining why the supply and demand curves slope the way they do, and then to consider the effects of shifts of the curves. Our approach here is the same, but in the case of exchange rates we write the exchange rate (the price of a country's currency expressed in terms of some other currency) on the vertical axis. In order to establish the slopes of the supply and demand curves for currencies, we consider the effects of exchange rates on the values of imports and exports. This is similar to considering the effect of price on quantity supplied and demanded.[3] We then show that all other factors in the balance-of-payments account can be considered as shifting the supply or demand curves, with effects on exchange rates that depend on the slopes of the curves.

IMPORTS, EXPORTS, AND EXCHANGE RATES

Deriving a Currency's Supply Curve

As with supply curves in general, the supply curve of a currency shows the amount of that currency supplied on the horizontal axis and the price of the currency, given by the exchange rate, on the vertical axis. However, when we draw the supply curve of a currency, we do not plot *quantities* on the horizontal axis—for example, so many bushels of wheat or automobiles produced per month—as we do with normal supply curves. Rather, we plot *values* on the horizontal axis—so many British pounds or Deutschemarks. Values involve the multiplication of prices and quantities, and they respond differently than do quantities. Indeed, as we shall show, it is the fact that values are on the horizontal axis that explains why the currency supply curve can easily slope downward rather than upward with respect to the foreign exchange value of the currency.

The supply curve of a currency derives, at least in part, from a country's demand for imports. This is because when paying for imports that are invoiced in foreign currency, the country's residents must sell their currency for the needed foreign exchange, and when imports are invoiced in domestic currency, the foreign recipient of the currency sells it. In either case, imports result in the country's currency being supplied.[4] The amount of the currency supplied is equal to the value of imports. Let us see how to plot the value of currency supplied against the exchange rate by considering British imports of wheat, which, for simplicity, we assume is the only import.

The quantity of pounds supplied equals the value of British wheat imports. This involves multiplying the pound price of wheat by the quantity of wheat imported.

---

[3]The pattern is similar, but it is different in that currencies involve *values* of exports and imports, not *quantities* of goods or services as in traditional supply and demand. We have far more to say about this as the chapter progresses.

[4]If imports are invoiced in the importer's currency, and the foreign recipient of the currency chooses *not* to sell it, we still consider that the currency is supplied via imports. This is matched, however, by a demand for the currency in the capital account.

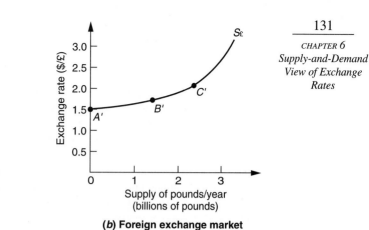

Figure 6.1. Deriving the Supply of Pounds
A currency is supplied in the course of paying for imports. If we limit consideration to goods
and services, the supply of a currency equals the value of imports. We find the currency supply
curve by taking each possible exchange rate and finding the price of imports at that exchange
rate. We then determine the quantity of imports at that price from the demand curve for imports
and calculate the value of imports by multiplying the price and the quantity of imports. We then
plot the value of imports against the exchange rate at which it occurs.

The product is the number of pounds Britain spends on wheat imports and thus also
gives the number of pounds supplied to the foreign exchange market. Let us suppose
that the world price of wheat is $3 per bushel, that wheat is traded without tariffs or
other restrictions, and that Britain buys such a small proportion of global wheat output that the world price of wheat is not influenced by Britain's imports.

At an exchange rate of $1.5/£, the pound price of wheat is $3 ÷ $1.5/£ = £2 per
bushel. Figure 6.1*a,* which shows the British import demand curve for wheat,
reveals that at £2 per bushel the quantity of wheat imports is zero, point *A.* That is,
at £2 per bushel Britain's production of wheat equals Britain's consumption of
wheat so that Britain is self-sufficient at this price. With zero imports the number of
pounds supplied is therefore zero at the exchange rate $1.5/£. This is shown by point
A′ on the supply curve of pounds, $S_£$, in Figure 6.1*b.* If the exchange rate is $1.7/£,
the pound price of wheat is $3 ÷ $1.7/£ = £1.76 per bushel. The import demand
curve in Figure 6.1*a* shows that at this price wheat imports are approximately 0.75
billion bushels, point *B.* The number of pounds supplied at exchange rate $1.7/£ is
therefore £1.76 × 0.75 billion = £1.32 billion per year. This quantity and pounds
supplied is plotted against the exchange rate $1.7/£, point *B′* on $S_£$ in Figure 6.1*b.*[5]
Similarly, at the exchange rate $2/£ the pound price of wheat is $3 ÷ $2/£ = £1.5 per
bushel. Figure 6.1*a* shows import demand of 1.5 billion bushels at this price, point
C, which involves an expenditure of £1.5 × 1.5 billion = £2.25 billion. This gives
point *C′* on $S_£$ in Figure 6.1*b.* By continuing in this way we can construct the supply
curve of pounds, which in this case happens to slope upward. (We consider the condition for a downward-sloping currency supply curve, and the implications of such
a curve, later in the chapter.)

[5]We see that we are calculating the *area* under D_{UK}^m in Figure 6.1*a* and plotting this as the *distance* along
the horizontal axis in Figure 6.1*b.*

Deriving a Currency's Demand Curve

The demand curve for a currency shows the value of the currency that is demanded at each possible exchange rate. Because the need to buy a country's currency stems from the need to pay for the country's exports, the currency's demand curve is derived from the country's export supply curve, which shows the quantity of exports at each price of exports.

Figure 6.2*a* shows the supply curve of British exports. For simplicity of reference we assume that Britain exports only oil. The demand for pounds to pay for Britain's oil exports is equal to the value of these exports. Therefore, in order to construct the demand curve for pounds we must calculate the value of oil exports at each exchange rate. Let us suppose that the world price of oil is $25 per barrel and that Britain has no effect on this price when it changes its oil exports.

If we begin with an exchange rate of $2/£, the pound price of oil is $25 ÷ $2/£ = £12.5 per barrel. Figure 6.2*a* shows that at £12.5 per barrel, oil exports are zero, point *D*. That is, at £12.5 per barrel Britain's production of oil equals Britain's consumption of oil, so that the country is exactly self-sufficient. With zero oil exports, the quantity of pounds demanded to pay for Britain's oil exports is therefore also zero at $2/£. This is shown by point *D′* on the demand curve of pounds, $D_£$, in Figure 6.2*b*. If the exchange rate is $1.8/£, the pound price of oil is $25 ÷ $1.8/£ = £13.89, and oil exports are approximately 0.1 billion barrels per year, point *E* in Figure 6.2*a*. The value of oil exports and quantity of pounds demanded at $1.8/£ is therefore £13.89 × 0.1 billion = £1.389 billion. This is shown by point *E′* on $D_£$ in Figure 6.2*b*. Finally, at $1.50/£ the price of oil is $25 ÷ $1.5/£ = £16.67 per barrel,

Figure 6.2. Deriving the Demand for Pounds
A country's currency is demanded in the course of foreigners buying that country's exports. If we limit consideration to goods and services, the demand for a currency equals the value of exports. We find the currency demand curve by taking each possible exchange rate and finding the price of exports at that exchange rate. We then determine the quantity of exports at that price from the supply curve for exports and calculate the value of exports by multiplying the price by the quantity of exports. We then plot the value of exports against the exchange rate at which it occurs.

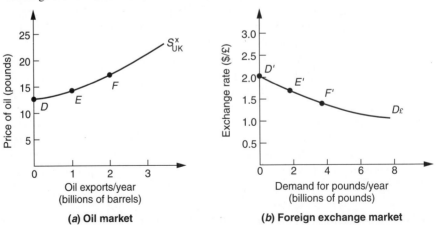

(*a*) **Oil market**   (*b*) **Foreign exchange market**

and exports are approximately 0.2 billion barrels, point *F* in Figure 6.2*a*. Therefore, the quantity of pounds demanded at \$1.5/£ is £16.67 × 0.2 billion = £3.33 billion per year, point *F′* in Figure 6.2*b*.

THE FACTORS AFFECTING EXCHANGE RATES

Terms of Trade and the Amount of Trade

If we plot the supply and demand curves for pounds in the same figure, as in Figure 6.3, we can find the exchange rate that equates the value of exports and imports, and hence that equates the supply of and demand for the country's currency resulting from these activities. We see that equality of supply and demand occurs at an exchange rate of approximately \$1.75/£.

It is clear from Figure 6.3 that, *ceteris paribus,* an exogenous increase in the value of exports at each exchange rate, which shifts the demand curve for pounds,

Figure 6.3. The Exchange Rate from Imports and Exports
The equilibrium exchange rate is that at which the quantity of currency supplied equals the quantity demanded. Factors other than the exchange rate which affect the value of imports and exports shift the currency supply and demand curves and thereby change the equilibrium exchange rate.

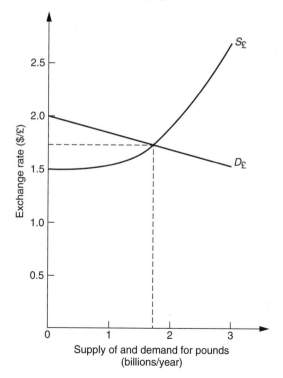

$D_£$, to the right, will, with the slopes of curves shown, result in an increase in the value of the pound. Such an increase in the value of exports could occur as a result of a higher world price of oil or from an increase in the quantity of oil exported at each oil price. It is also clear from the figure that, *ceteris paribus,* an exogenous increase in the value of imports at each exchange rate, which shifts the supply curve of pounds, $S_£$, to the right, will result in a decrease in the value of the pound. This could result from a higher world price of wheat or an increase in the quantity of wheat imported at each price.

The price of a country's exports relative to the price of its imports is called the country's terms of trade. A country's terms of trade are said to improve when the price of its exports increases relative to the price of its imports. Our description of Figure 6.3 makes it clear that the pound will appreciate in value as a result of an improvement of Britain's terms of trade. That is, the pound will appreciate if, *ceteris paribus,* oil prices increase more than wheat prices. The pound will also appreciate if the quantity of exports increases relative to the quantity of imports. This could happen, for example, if Britain steps up production and exports of oil at each oil price. It could also happen if Britain has a good wheat harvest and therefore imports less wheat at each exchange rate.

Inflation

Terms-of-trade effects concern export versus import prices, where the exports and imports are *different* products. Exchange rates are also influenced by inflation, which affects the competitiveness of one country's products versus the *same* or *similar* products from another country. In order to show the effects of inflation it is necessary to describe the derivation of the import demand and export supply curves. These curves were taken to be exogenous in Figures 6.1*a* and 6.2*a*. That is, we have not yet shown what is behind the import demand curve, D_{UK}^m, in Figure 6.1*a*, and the export supply curve, S_{UK}^x, in Figure 6.2*a*.

Deriving the Import Demand Curve

Figure 6.4*a* shows the demand for wheat in Britain, D_{UK}^w, and the quantity of wheat British farmers supply at each price, S_{UK}^w. If Britain can take the world price of wheat as given, whether Britain is an importer or exporter of wheat depends on the world price of wheat translated into pounds. For example, if the world price of wheat is equivalent to £1.5 per bushel, Britain produces 2.5 billion bushels per year and consumes 4 billion bushels per year, so that imports are 1.5 billion bushels per year. At £2.0 per bushel Britain is self-sufficient, producing and consuming 3.5 billion bushels per year, and at prices above £2.0 per bushel Britain is a wheat exporter.

If we consider only pound prices of wheat below £2 per bushel, where Britain is a wheat importer, we can plot the British demand curve for imports by selecting different pound prices and measuring the distance between D_{UK}^w and S_{UK}^w at each price. These distances, which are the quantities of wheat imported at each price, are plotted against the prices at which they occur. By doing this we obtain the British import demand curve D_{UK}^m shown in Figure 6.4*b*. This is the import demand curve that we took as our starting point in Figure 6.1*a*. As we saw earlier, using the curve D_{UK}^m and assuming that the world price of wheat is $3 per bushel, we can construct the supply curve of pounds, $S_£$, in Figure 6.1*b*.

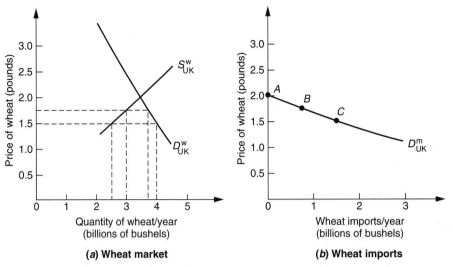

Figure 6.4. Deriving the Demand for Imports
The quantity of imports demanded at each price is the excess of the quantity of the product that is demanded over the quantity of the product produced in the country. That is, it is the horizontal distance between the country's demand curve for the product and its supply curve.

Deriving the Export Supply Curve

Curves D_{UK}^0 and S_{UK}^0 in Figure 6.5a show, respectively, British oil demand and supply at different oil prices. We can construct the export supply curve from D_{UK}^0 and S_{UK}^0 by considering different pound prices of oil and computing the excess of quantity supplied over quantity demanded at each price. For example, at £12.50 per barrel, oil consumption equals oil production, so that exports are zero. This is point D on the export supply curve, S_{UK}^x, shown in Figure 6.5b and Figure 6.2a. Proceeding in this way, we obtain the supply curve of exports, S_{UK}^x, that we merely assumed in Figure 6.2a. As we saw earlier, by assuming that the world price of oil is $25 per barrel and considering different exchange rates, we can derive the demand curve for pounds, $D_£$, in Figure 6.2b.

When we plot the supply and demand curves for pounds in the same figure, as in Figure 6.3, we find the exchange rate that equates the supply of and demand for pounds *before* inflation has occurred. Let us now consider what happens when there is inflation.

Inflation, Import Demand, and Export Supply

Let us assume that Britain experiences a 25 percent inflation. If all prices and wages in Britain increase 25 percent during a year, the British demand curves for wheat and oil at the end of the year will be 25 percent higher than at the beginning of the year. That is, they are shifted vertically upward by 25 percent. This is because with all prices and wages higher by the same amount, real incomes and relative prices are unchanged. Therefore, after the 25 percent inflation the same quantities of goods are purchased at prices 25 percent higher than before the inflation.

At the same time as the British demand curves for wheat and oil shift upward,

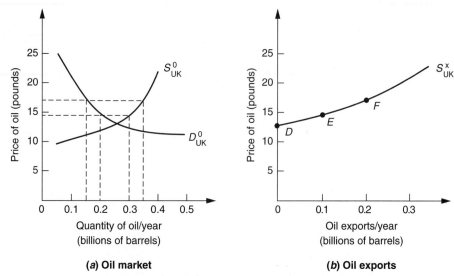

Figure 6.5. Deriving the Export Supply Curve
The quantity of exports supplied at each price is the excess of the quantity of the product that is supplied over the quantity demanded in the country. That is, it is the horizontal distance between the country's supply curve of the product and its demand curve.

so do the supply curves of wheat and oil. The easiest way of thinking about why this occurs is to note that the supply curves for competitive firms are their marginal cost curves. Indeed, the individual competitive firm's short-run supply curve is that firm's marginal cost curve, and the competitive industry's short-run supply curve is the horizontal sum of all existing firms' marginal cost curves. Long-run supply curves, which consider newly entering firms, also shift up by the rate of inflation because inflation also increases the marginal costs of new firms; if all wages and prices increase 25 percent, the marginal costs are 25 percent higher and therefore so are the supply curves. We can reach the same conclusion if we think of supply as being set to equate marginal cost and marginal revenue. At any given output the marginal cost is 25 percent higher after inflation, and therefore if the marginal revenue is also 25 percent higher from the demand curve shifting up 25 percent, there is no reason to change output; marginal cost remains equal to marginal revenue.

The left-hand diagrams in Figure 6.6 show the supply and demand curves for wheat and oil before and after 25 percent inflation. The supply and demand curves before inflation are identified by P_0, the price level at the beginning of the year, and those after inflation are identified by P_1, the price level at the end of the year.

The right-hand diagrams in Figure 6.6 show the demand for imports and the supply of exports before and after 25 percent inflation. The P_0 signifies the curve before inflation, and P_1 after inflation. We recall that the demand for imports and supply of exports are obtained by selecting different prices and calculating the differences between domestic supply and demand at each price. For example, before inflation, the demand for imports of wheat was zero at £2 per bushel. After inflation, it is zero at £2.50 per bushel. That is, the intercept of $D^m_{UK}(P_1)$ with the price axis is 25 percent higher than the intercept of $D^m_{UK}(P_0)$. Since the slopes of the supply and

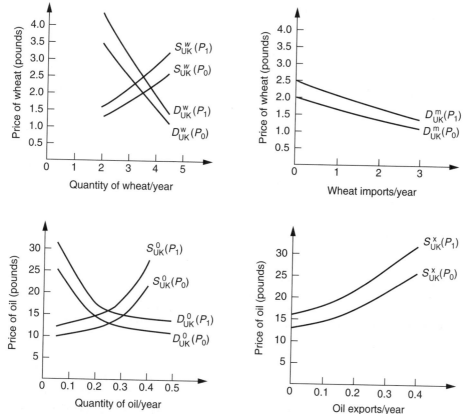

Figure 6.6. Inflation in Relation to Supply and Demand
Curves identified with P_0 represent the situation before inflation. Curves identified with P_1 represent the situation after inflation. We see that inflation in all prices and incomes shifts demand and supply curves vertically upward by the amount of inflation. Thus the demand curve for imports and supply curve of exports also shift vertically upward by the amount of inflation.

demand curves for wheat are the same before and after inflation, the slope of the demand curve for wheat imports is the same before and after inflation. Therefore, we find that $D_{UK}^m(P_1)$ is above $D_{UK}^m(P_0)$ by 25 percent, not only at the intercept with the price axis but at every other quantity of imports. Similarly, the supply curve of oil exports intercepts the price axis at £12.50 before inflation because this is where domestic oil supply equals demand, and after inflation the intercept is at a price 25 percent higher. Because the slopes of the supply and demand curves for oil are the same before and after inflation, the slope of the export supply curve is the same before and after inflation. Therefore, as in the case of the demand curve for imports, the supply curve of exports shifts upward 25 percent at every quantity.

We can employ Figure 6.6 to show how inflation affects currency supply and demand curves and hence exchange rates. There are different effects according to whether inflation occurs only in Britain or in Britain and elsewhere, and so we consider these situations in turn.

Inflation in Only One Country

Figure 6.7a shows the supply and demand curves for pounds that are implied by the demand curve for imports and supply curve of exports when inflation of 25 percent occurs in Britain but not in the United States. The curves labeled $S_£(P_0)$ and $D_£(P_0)$ are those existing before inflation and are the same supply and demand curves for pounds used in Figure 6.3. The curves labeled $S_£(P_1)$ and $D_£(P_1)$ are the supply and demand curves for pounds after 25 percent inflation in Britain but not in the United States. The derivation of $S_£(P_1)$ and $D_£(P_1)$ is based on the following reasoning.

Because inflation occurs only in Britain, we can take the U.S. dollar prices of wheat and oil as unchanged. Considering first the supply curve of pounds, we know from Figure 6.6 that the same quantity of wheat is imported after inflation as before inflation if the pound price of wheat is increased 25 percent; this follows immedi-

Figure 6.7. Inflation and Exchange Rates
Curves labeled with P_0 represent the situation before inflation. Curves labeled with P_1 represent the situation after inflation. With inflation in one country only (part *a*), the same quantity of exports is sold after a depreciation approximately equal to the country's rate of inflation. The same *quantity* sold at the higher prices means the *value* of exports is higher by the rate of inflation. This means the currency demand curve shifts down and to the right approximately in proportion to inflation. The same argument applies to the currency supply curve. Therefore, the exchange rate of the inflating country depreciates by approximately its rate of inflation as in part *a*, and the quantity of currency traded increases by the rate of inflation. When inflation also occurs in the other country (part *b*), the same *quantities* are imported and exported at the same exchange rates at the postinflation prices. Therefore, the *values* of imports and exports are higher by the rate of inflation at each exchange rate. That is, the currency supply and demand curves shift to the right in proportion to the rate of inflation, and the exchange rate is unaffected.

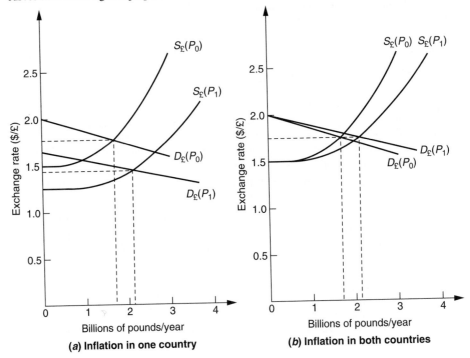

(*a*) Inflation in one country

(*b*) Inflation in both countries

ately from the fact that $D_{UK}^m(P_1)$ is 25 percent higher than $D_{UK}^m(P_0)$. When the same quantity of wheat is imported at a price that is 25 percent higher, the supply of pounds, which is the pound price of imports multiplied by the quantity of imports, is also 25 percent higher. The change in exchange rate that will achieve a 25 percent higher pound price and a corresponding 25 percent higher supply of pounds is a 20 percent depreciation of the pound. This follows because the dollar price of wheat is unchanged, and a 20 percent depreciation of the pound exactly offsets a 25 percent pound price increase.[6] That is, at an exchange rate that is 20 percent lower, the pound price of wheat is 25 percent higher and the quantity of imports is unchanged. Therefore, at an exchange rate that is 20 percent lower there is a 25 percent higher supply of pounds. This means that inflation of 25 percent shifts the supply curve for pounds downward by 20 percent and to the right by 25 percent, so that points on $S_£(P_1)$ in Figure 6.7a are 20 percent below and 25 percent to the right of corresponding points on $S_£(P_0)$.

The reasoning behind the effect of inflation on the demand for pounds is similar to the reasoning behind its effect on the supply of pounds described above. Figure 6.6 shows that the same quantity of oil is exported after inflation as before inflation if the pound price of oil increases by 25 percent; $S_{UK}^x(P_1)$ is 25 percent above $S_{UK}^x(P_0)$. Because the dollar price of oil is unchanged, to achieve a 25 percent higher pound oil price we need a 20 percent pound depreciation. Therefore, at a 20 percent lower exchange rate in Figure 6.7a we have a 25 percent higher pound price of oil and the same quantity of oil exports. This represents a 25 percent increase in the value of exports and the demand for pounds. Therefore, the effect of inflation is to shift each point on the demand curve for pounds downward by 20 percent and to the right by 25 percent; at a 20 percent lower exchange rate the demand for pounds is 25 percent higher after inflation than before.

Figure 6.7a shows the supply and demand curves for pounds shifted downward by 20 percent and to the right by 25 percent. If we compare the equilibrium where $S_£(P_1)$ intersects $D_£(P_1)$ with the equilibrium where $S_£(P_0)$ intersects $D_£(P_0)$, we see that the pound depreciates by 20 percent. That is, inflation in one country reduces the exchange rate of that country's currency by approximately the same percentage as the country's inflation. We also can see from comparing equilibria in Figure 6.7a that the quantity of pounds traded also increases by 25 percent. We should recall that in order to reach these conclusions we considered only exports and imports and assumed that *all* prices and wages in Britain increased by the same amount.

Inflation Also in Other Countries

The difference between having inflation only in Britain and having inflation in both Britain and the United States is that in the latter case we must allow for increases in the dollar prices of the imported and exported products. Let us assume U.S. inflation is also 25 percent, so that the dollar prices of wheat and oil increase to $3.75 per bushel and $31.25 per barrel.

---

[6]A 25 percent increase in price, for example, from £2 to £2.50, is offset by a 20 percent decrease in the exchange rate, for example, from $2/£ to $1.6/£. Specifically, wheat costs £2 × $2/£ = $4 per bushel before the changes, and £2.50 × $1.6/£ = $4 per bushel after the changes. For smaller values of inflation the required depreciation approaches the rate of inflation. For example, a 5 percent inflation is offset by a 4.76 percent depreciation.

Let us consider first the supply curve of pounds. We know from our earlier discussion and from Figure 6.6 that the quantity of wheat imports after inflation is the same as before inflation if the pound price of wheat increases by the amount of inflation, that is, 25 percent. When the dollar price of wheat increases from $3 per bushel to $3.75 per bushel, the pound price of wheat increases by 25 percent if the exchange rate is unchanged. That is, at the same exchange rate as before there is a 25 percent increase in the pound price of wheat and the same quantity of wheat imports. It follows that at the same exchange rate the supply of pounds is 25 percent higher after inflation than before inflation. This is due to an unchanged quantity of imports and a 25 percent higher price. That is, the supply curve of pounds is shifted 25 percent to the right at every exchange rate. This is shown in Figure 6.7b, in which $S_£(P_1)$ is at a 25 percent higher quantity of pounds at each exchange rate.

Considering the demand for pounds, we note that, as before, oil exports are the same after inflation as before inflation if the pound price of oil is 25 percent higher. This was seen in Figure 6.6. When the dollar price of oil increases 25 percent, from $25 per barrel to $31.25 per barrel, the pound price of oil increases 25 percent if the exchange rate is unchanged. That is, at the same exchange rate the pound price of oil is 25 percent higher and the quantity of oil exported is unchanged. This means that at the same exchange rate the quantity of pounds demanded to pay for oil is 25 percent higher after inflation than before. We discover that inflation in both Britain and the United States shifts $D_£$ to the right by the rate of inflation. That is, at each exchange rate in Figure 6.7b, $D_£(P_1)$, the demand for pounds after inflation, is at a 25 percent higher quantity of pounds than $D_£(P_0)$, the demand for pounds before inflation.

Comparing the two equilibria in Figure 6.7b, we see that when inflation occurs at the same rate in Britain and the United States, the exchange rate remains unchanged. This contrasts with the conclusion reached using Figure 6.7a, in which inflation in Britain alone causes the pound to depreciate by approximately the rate of inflation. More generally, the analysis above can be extended to show that a country's exchange rate depreciates by approximately the extent that the country's inflation exceeds that of other countries. Of course, this statement assumes that all other factors affecting exchange rates are unchanged. The conclusion, with the caveat that everything else is unchanged, is met again in the context of the purchasing-power parity (PPP) principle in Chapter 10, where we show that the effect of inflation on exchange rates we have obtained from supply and demand is also implied by commodity arbitrage.

We know from the description of the balance-of-payments account in Chapter 5 that there are many factors behind the supply and demand curves for a country's currency in addition to the terms of trade, inflation, and the other factors which affect the value of merchandise imports and exports. Let us consider how these other factors influence exchange rates by examining how they shift the supply and demand curves for pounds in Figure 6.3 on page 133.

Service Trade, Income Flows, and Transfers

Imports and exports of services, such as tourism, banking, consulting, engineering, and so on, respond to exchange rates in the same way as do imports and exports of merchandise. Therefore, the currency supply and demand curves derived from international trade in these services look like those in Figure 6.3 on page 133. The currency supply curve reflecting imports of services can be added to that reflecting imports of merchandise, and the currency demand curve reflecting exports of services can be added to that reflecting exports of merchandise. This has the effect of shifting both $S_£$ and $D_£$ in Figure 6.3 to the right. We can think of the currency supply and demand curves for imports and exports of services as being "horizontally added" to the currency supply and demand curves from imports and exports of merchandise. Horizontal addition involves the addition of quantities demanded and supplied at each price and the plotting of the resulting quantities against the prices at which they occur. With supply and demand curves for currencies from services sloping the same way as currency supply and demand curves from merchandise, the horizontally added curves slope the same direction as the component curves.

If exports of services exceed imports of services, then the currency demand curve, $D_£$, is shifted to the right more than the currency supply curve, $S_£$, from the inclusion of services. Therefore, the exchange rate is higher than in Figure 6.3. On the other hand, if imports of services exceed exports of services, then the currency supply curve is shifted to the right more than the demand curve. Therefore, the exchange rate is lower than in Figure 6.3.

The supply and demand for a currency from payments and receipts of interest, dividends, rents, and profits do not respond to exchange rates in the same manner as the currency supply and demand from imports and exports of merchandise or services. Income payments and receipts are largely determined by past investments and the rates of return on these investments. Therefore, we might consider income payments and receipts as being independent of exchange rates.[7] However, as in the case of services, we can simply add the value of income exports to the currency demand curve, and the value of income imports to the currency supply curve. If the values of income exports and imports are independent of the exchange rate, the addition of these items to the currency supply and demand curves involves simple parallel rightward shifts of the curves. It should be apparent that the higher income exports are relative to income imports, the higher is the exchange rate. It follows that, *ceteris paribus,* the more a country's residents have invested abroad in the past and the less they have borrowed, the higher is the country's exchange rate.

Transfers can easily be accommodated in the supply-and-demand model of exchange rates. We add the amount of transfers received from abroad to a currency's demand curve and the amount sent abroad to the supply curve. Clearly, *ceteris paribus,* net inflows of transfers tend to increase the value of a currency and net outflows tend to reduce it. Transfers depend on a country's need for help or its ability to help others. Transfers also depend on the number of residents sending funds to relatives abroad or receiving funds from relatives abroad.

Foreign Investment

Foreign investment in a country represents a demand for the country's currency when that investment occurs.[8] Therefore, foreign investment in a country, whether it

---

[7]Exchange rates do affect the domestic currency value of a given amount of foreign currency receipts or payments. However, this is an effect of translating foreign currency into domestic currency, and it is different from the effects of exchange rates on merchandise and services which involve an effect on competitiveness.

[8]In all future periods when interest or dividends are paid, or profits and rents are repatriated, there is a supply of the country's currency.

be direct investment, portfolio investment, or additions to bank deposits of nonresidents, shifts the demand curve for the country's currency to the right. Similarly, investment abroad by a country's residents represents a supply of the country's currency and shifts the currency supply curve to the right. Therefore, *ceteris paribus,* net inflows of investment tend to increase the foreign exchange rate of a country's currency, and net outflows tend to reduce it. The amount of investment flowing into or out of a country depends on rates of return in the country relative to rates of return elsewhere, as well as on relative risks. *Ceteris paribus,* increases in a country's interest rates or expected profits cause an increase in demand for that country's currency from increased foreign investment and cause a decrease in supply of that country's currency from a decrease in residents' investment abroad. Consequently, increases in interest rates or expected profits cause a currency to appreciate, and vice versa. Similarly, for given interest rates and expected profits, an expected appreciation of a country's currency increases the attractiveness of investments in that country and thereby causes the country's currency to appreciate. That is, expected future appreciation of a currency causes the currency to increase in value, just as is true for other assets.

All the conclusions we have reached have assumed that the supply curve of a currency slopes upward. It is time to show why this assumption may not be valid. In particular, it is time to see why the supply curve of a currency may slope downward, and what this implies for exchange rates. We shall focus on the implications for exchange rate stability which, as we have said, are particularly important in light of the volatility of exchange rates in recent years.

THE STABILITY OF EXCHANGE RATES

The Conditions Required for Instability

The supply curve for pounds, $S_£$, is derived from the British demand for imports. Figure 6.8*a* shows two demand curves for imports. The import demand curve labeled $D^m_{UK}(\eta_m > 1)$, where η_m stands for import price elasticity, is the same import demand curve drawn in Figure 6.1*a*. It is labeled with $\eta_m > 1$ in parentheses because it is an elastic curve. That is, when the price of imports falls, the quantity of imports increases by a greater percentage than the price declines; the demand elasticity exceeds unity. The currency supply curve derived from $D^m_{UK}(\eta_m > 1)$ is $S_£(\eta_m > 1)$. This is the same supply curve of pounds as in Figure 6.1*b*. The currency supply curve obtained from an elastic demand for imports is seen to slope upward.

Figure 6.8*a* also shows an inelastic demand curve for imports, $D^m_{UK}(\eta_m < 1)$. It is inelastic because a reduction in the price of imports causes a smaller percentage increase in the quantity of imports than the percentage reduction in price. We can derive the supply curve of pounds that is associated with the inelastic import demand curve by doing the same as before. That is, we consider a number of possible exchange rates, compute the price and quantity of imports at each of these exchange rates, and then plot the values of imports against the associated exchange rates; recall that it is the *value* of imports that is the *quantity* of currency supplied. Let us again assume that the given world price of wheat is $3 per bushel.

At an exchange rate of $1.5/£, the pound price of wheat is $3 ÷ $1.5/£ = £2.0 per bushel, and according to the inelastic demand curve $D^m_{UK}(\eta_m < 1)$, Britain imports 1.5 billion bushels at this price, point *A* in Figure 6.8*a*. The quantity of

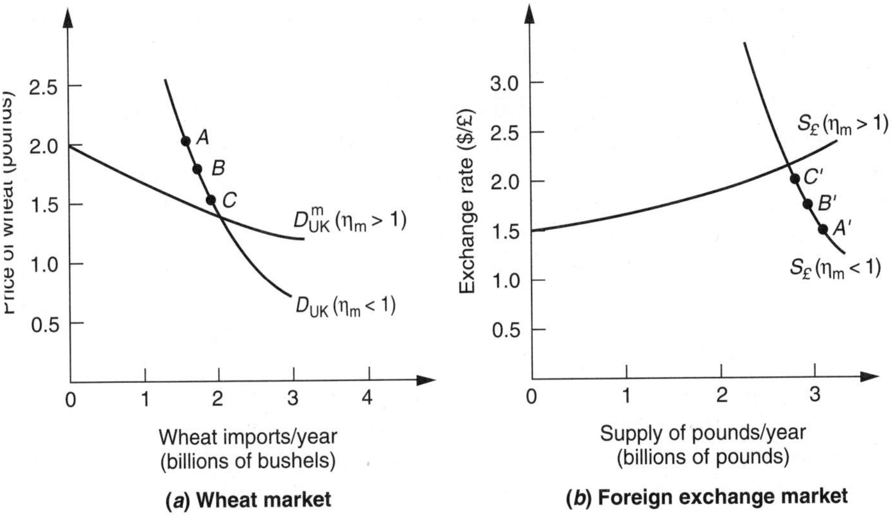

Figure 6.8. Currency Supply and Import Elasticity
When the demand for imports is elastic, that is, $\eta_m > 1$, the supply curve of the currency slopes upward. When the demand for imports is inelastic, that is, $\eta_m < 1$, the supply curve of the currency slopes downward. The downward slope occurs because depreciation raises import prices and reduces the quantity of imports, but the *value* of imports increases. This occurs when the percentage reduction in quantity imported is less than the percentage increase in the price of imports.

pounds supplied, which equals the value of imports, is therefore £3 billion (£2 per bushel × 1.5 billion bushels) at the exchange rate $1.5/£. This gives point *A´* in Figure 6.8*b*. At $1.7/£ wheat costs $3 ÷ $1.7/£ = £1.76 and Britain imports 1.6 billion bushels, point *B* in Figure 6.8*a*. Therefore, the quantity of pounds supplied at the exchange rate $1.7/£ is £2.82 billion (£1.76 per bushel × 1.6 billion bushels), point *B´* in Figure 6.8*b*. Similarly, at $2/£ wheat costs $3 ÷ $2/£ = £1.5 per bushel. At this price Britain imports 1.7 billion bushels, point *C* in Figure 6.8*a*. Therefore, the quantity of pounds supplied at the exchange rate $2/£ is £2.55 billion (£1.5 per bushel × 1.7 billion bushels). This gives point *C´* in Figure 6.8*b*. We find that when the demand for imports is inelastic, the supply curve of the country's currency slopes downward. The reason is that when demand is inelastic the amount spent on a product decreases with decreases in the price of the product. The price of imports decreases with increases in the foreign exchange value of the importer's currency. Therefore, when the demand for imports is inelastic: the higher is the exchange rate, the lower is the price of imports, the less is spent on imports, and so the lower is the quantity of the currency supplied. We discover that all we need for a downward-sloping currency supply curve is inelastic import demand. This could easily occur. For example, it is generally felt that when the price of oil falls due to an appreciation of a country's currency, the quantity of oil demanded and imported increases less than the percent decline in the price. Let us consider the consequences of an inelastic demand for imports and the associated downward-sloping currency supply curve for the stability of exchange rates.

Figure 6.9 shows two situations in which the currency supply curve slopes downward. In the situation depicted in Figure 6.9*a* the demand curve for pounds is steeper than the supply curve, but in Figure 6.9*b* the situation is the reverse. Let us consider the stability of the exchange rate in Figures 6.9*a* and *b* by allowing the exchange rate to deviate slightly from its equilibrium value $S^e(\$/£)$ where the supply and demand curves intersect. In particular, let us consider whether market forces are likely to push the exchange rate back to equilibrium.

In Figure 6.9*a* a small decline in the exchange rate below equilibrium will result in an excess supply of pounds: at rates below $S^e(\$/£)$ the quantity of pounds supplied exceeds the quantity demanded. This will push the value of the pound even lower, which will cause an even larger excess supply, and so on. Similarly, in Figure 6.9*a* a small increase in the exchange rate above equilibrium will result in an excess demand for pounds. This will push the value of the pound even higher, cause an even larger excess demand, and so on. We find that the equilibrium exchange rate in Figure 6.9*a* is unstable. Small shocks to exchange rates can result in substantial movements in exchange rates from equilibrium when the demand and supply curves for a currency have the configuration shown in Figure 6.9*a*.

Figure 6.9*b* has a downward-sloping supply curve of pounds just as does Figure 6.9*a,* but here the demand curve for pounds is flatter than the supply curve. In this case a small decline in the value of the pound below the equilibrium exchange rate $S^e(\$/£)$ causes an excess demand for pounds: at rates below $S^e(\$/£)$ the quantity of pounds demanded exceeds the quantity supplied. This pushes the exchange rate back to equilibrium. Similarly, a small increase in the exchange rate above the equilibrium causes an excess supply of pounds. This pushes the exchange rate back down to equilibrium. The equilibrium in Figure 6.9*b* is therefore stable.

Consideration of Figures 6.9*a* and *b* allows us to conclude that having a downward-sloping currency supply curve is necessary but not sufficient to cause an unstable foreign exchange market. A relatively flat or elastic currency demand curve

Figure 6.9. Stability of Foreign Exchange Markets
When the currency supply curve slopes downward, foreign exchange markets may be unstable. They are unstable if the currency demand curve is steeper than the supply curve, that is, the demand curve cuts the supply curve from above when going down the demand curve.

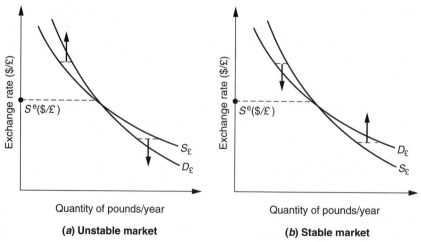

(*a*) Unstable market　　　　**(*b*) Stable market**

can offset the destabilizing nature of a downward-sloping supply curve. For an unstable market it is necessary to have a downward-sloping currency supply curve—which we recall requires inelastic demand for imports—*and* a relatively steep or inelastic currency demand curve. A sufficient condition for instability is that the supply curve slopes downward and the demand curve is steeper at equilibrium than the supply curve. A more precise statement of the condition for stability of the foreign exchange market is derived in Appendix 6.1. This condition is known as the **Marshall-Lerner condition** and is stated directly in terms of the import and export elasticities of demand, which are determinants of the slopes of the currency supply and demand curves.

Unstable Exchange Rates and the Balance of Trade

Because the possibility of unstable exchange rates is of considerable interest, we should not leave the matter until we have a solid intuitive understanding of why it can occur. Such an understanding can be obtained by examining how exchange rates affect the balance of trade.

A depreciation increases the price of imports in terms of domestic currency. This reduces the *quantity* of imports but does not necessarily reduce the *value* of imports. If import demand is inelastic, the higher price of imports more than offsets the lower quantity, so that the value of imports is higher. This means that if import demand is inelastic, a depreciation can worsen the balance of trade. (Recall that the balance of trade is the *value* of exports minus the *value* of imports.) However, even when more is spent on imports after a depreciation, the balance of trade is not *necessarily* worsened. This is because a depreciation makes exports cheaper in terms of *foreign* currency, and this increases the quantity exported. The value of exports unambiguously increases with the quantity of exports because exports are not made cheaper in *domestic* currency. Indeed, if anything, the stronger demand for exports can cause an increase in domestic-currency prices of exports. It follows that even if depreciation increases the value of imports, the balance of trade is worsened only if the value of exports increases less than the value of imports.

The preceding argument can be directly related to Figure 6.9. If import demand is inelastic, a depreciation of the pound, which is a movement down the vertical axis, causes an increase in the value of British imports and hence in the quantity of pounds supplied; the pound supply curve slopes downward. This on its own does not cause instability, for the same reason it does not necessarily worsen the balance of trade, namely, that the depreciation also increases the value of exports and hence the quantity of pounds demanded. The foreign exchange market is unstable only if the value of exports does not increase sufficiently to compensate for inelastic import demand, just as depreciation worsens the balance of trade only if the value of exports does not sufficiently increase to compensate for the increase in the value of imports.

SHORT-RUN VERSUS LONG-RUN TRADE ELASTICITIES AND THE J CURVE

A worsening of the balance of trade following a depreciation of a currency may be temporary. Similarly, instability in exchange rates may be only a short-run problem.

Because the consequences of the trade balance's worsening with depreciation and of exchange-rate instability are far more serious if they persist, it is well worthwhile considering why they may be temporary problems. Our consideration leads us to the J curve. The J curve has taken on such importance since the late 1980s that it has moved out of the textbooks and into the columns of the popular press.[9]

It takes time for people to adjust their preferences toward substitutes. Therefore, it is generally believed that demand is more inelastic in the short run than in the long run. This belief is particularly strong with regard to the elasticity of demand for imports, because the demand curve for imports is derived from the difference between the demand curve for a product in a country and the domestic supply curve of the product; with both supply and demand more inelastic in the short run than the long run, the difference between supply and demand is *a fortiori* more inelastic in the short run. That is, after a depreciation and consequent increase in import prices, a country's residents might continue to buy imports both because they have not adjusted their preferences toward domestically produced substitutes (an inelastic demand curve) and because the domestic substitutes have not yet been produced (an inelastic domestic supply curve). Only after producers begin to supply what was previously imported and after consumers decide to buy **import substitutes** can import demand fully decline after a depreciation. Similarly, exports expand from a depreciation only after suppliers are able to produce more for export and after foreign consumers switch to these products.

If import demand and export supply are more inelastic in the short run than the long run, we may find that a depreciation worsens the balance of trade in the short run but subsequently improves it. That is, the time path of changes in the balance of trade might look like that shown in Figure 6.10a.[10] The figure assumes that a depreciation occurs at time 0, and that because people temporarily spend more on imports and because exports do not sufficiently increase, the trade balance worsens immediately after the depreciation. Only later, when import and export elasticities increase, does the balance of trade turn around and eventually improve. Because of the shape of the time path followed by the trade balance in Figure 6.10a, the phenomenon of a worsening and subsequent improvement of the trade balance after a depreciation is known as the **J-curve effect.**

Figure 6.10b shows what might happen after an *appreciation* of the exchange rate if imports and exports are more inelastic in the short run than in the long run. The figure shows that after an appreciation at time 0, the decline in import prices could reduce spending on imports. If exports do not decrease as much as the value of imports declines, the balance of trade will improve, which is not what one would normally expect to follow an appreciation. However, over time, as import and export demand become more elastic, the quantity of imports increases more than the price declines, and/or exports decrease sufficiently for the balance of trade to worsen. In the case of an appreciation we find that the balance of trade follows the path of an inverted J. What we have shown is that the J curve occurs under the same conditions

[9]The J curve was also a topic of discussion in Britain after a 1967 sterling devaluation was followed by a worsening trade balance.

[10]For a further discussion of the time path see Michael H. Moffett, "The J-Curve Revisited: An Empirical Examination for the United States," *Journal of International Money and Finance,* September 1989, pp. 425–444, and David K. Backus, Patrick J. Kehoe, and Finn E. Kydland, "Dynamics of the Trade Balance and the Terms of Trade: The J-Curve?" *American Economic Review,* March 1994, pp. 84–103.

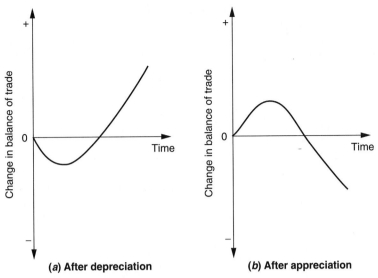

(a) After depreciation   **(b) After appreciation**

Figure 6.10. The J Curve
The J curve describes the balance of trade after a depreciation or appreciation.
The time path of the trade balance looks like a J if the elasticities of demand for
imports and supply of exports are smaller in the short run than the long run.

as instability of exchange rates in the short run but stability in the long run. When
imports and exports are sufficiently inelastic in the short run, we have both unstable
exchange rates and a temporary worsening/improvement of the balance of trade after
a currency depreciation/appreciation, and when the trade balance turns around, stability returns to foreign exchange markets.

Before leaving the question of the J curve and instability of exchange rates, we
should make it clear that foreign exchange markets can be stable even if imports and
exports are extremely inelastic. This is because there are numerous other reasons for
supplying or demanding a currency. For example, currency speculators might buy a
currency during the downward-sloping period of the J curve if they are confident the
balance of trade will eventually improve. This demand from speculators makes the
demand curve for a currency flatter than it would be if only considering the demand
for the currency by buyers of the country's exports.[11] On the other hand, the J-curve
effect, which relates to the balance of trade, is not obviated by currency speculators,
so we can have stable foreign exchange markets coexisting with a J curve.

SUMMARY

1. Flexible exchange rates are determined by supply and demand.
2. We can construct the supply curve of a currency from a country's demand curve for
   imports. We can construct the demand curve for a currency from the country's supply
   curve of exports.

---

[11]The question of whether speculators are likely to stabilize or destabilize exchange rates is addressed in
Chapter 9.

3. The effect of any item in the balance-of-payments account on the exchange rate can be determined by identifying how it shifts the currency supply or currency demand curve.

4. *Ceteris paribus,* an improvement in a country's terms of trade causes the country's currency to appreciate.

5. Inflation that is higher than in other countries causes a country's currency to depreciate. If inflation in different countries is equal, *ceteris paribus,* exchange rates do not change.

6. *Ceteris paribus,* the higher are service exports relative to service imports, the higher is the foreign exchange value of a country's currency.

7. A country's currency tends to appreciate with increases in interest rates and expected profits relative to those earned in other countries.

8. If import demand is inelastic the currency supply curve slopes downward. This is because depreciation raises the price of imports in domestic currency more than it reduces the quantity of imports. In this way depreciation increases the *value* of imports, meaning a downward-sloping supply curve of the currency. When the supply curve slopes downward the foreign exchange market may be unstable. Instability occurs when the currency demand curve is steeper than the downward-sloping supply curve.

9. Because import demand elasticities are smaller in the short run than in the long run, instability is more likely in the short run than the long run.

10. The same conditions that cause short-run instability and long-run stability result in a J curve. The J curve shows that a depreciation can temporarily worsen the balance of trade, while an appreciation can temporarily improve the balance of trade.

REVIEW QUESTIONS

1. Does currency supply depend on the quantity or the value of imports?
2. Under what condition does the value of imports vary in the opposite direction to the quantity of imports when exchange rates change?
3. Does currency demand depend on the quantity or the value of exports?
4. Why does the value of exports always vary in the same direction as the quantity of exports when exchange rates change?
5. Why does inflation shift up a country's supply curve of a product in proportion to inflation? Does the explanation have to do with the fact that a firm's supply curve of a good is the firm's marginal cost (MC) curve?
6. Why does inflation shift up a country's demand curve for a product in proportion to inflation? Does the explanation have to do with inflation raising all prices and incomes, leaving relative prices and real incomes unchanged?
7. How does a country's demand curve for imports relate to the country's demand curve for the good and its supply curve of the good?
8. Why can a downward-sloping currency supply curve destabilize exchange rates?
9. What is the J curve?
10. Does the J curve depend on short-run versus long-run elasticities of import demand?

ASSIGNMENT PROBLEMS

1. Assume that the foreign currency amount of interest and dividend earnings from abroad is fixed. Show how the horizontal addition of debt-service exports to a currency's demand curve will appear when consideration is given to the effect of exchange rates on the translated values of interest and dividend earnings.

2. Are debt-service imports as likely to be affected by exchange rates as are debt-service

exports? [*Hint:* It depends on the currency of denomination of debt-service earnings and payments.]

3. What is the slope of the currency supply curve when the demand for imports is unit-elastic, that is, equal to 1.0?
4. What is the intuitive explanation for the fact that a decrease in demand for a currency can cause it to appreciate if import and export demand are sufficiently inelastic?
5. How can speculators cause a stable foreign exchange market even when the economy is moving along the downward-sloping part of a J curve?
6. Why is the import demand curve likely to be more elastic in the long run than in the short run?
7. Why are exports likely to be more elastic in the long run than in the short run?
8. Does only the equilibrium exchange rate change with inflation, or is the quantity of currency traded also affected, and if so, why?

BIBLIOGRAPHY

ALEXANDER, SIDNEY S.: "The Effects of a Devaluation on the Trade Balance," IMF *Staff Papers,* April 1952, pp. 263–278. Reprinted in Richard E. Caves and Harry G. Johnson (eds.), *AEA Readings in International Economics,* Richard D. Irwin, Homewood, Ill., 1968.

HABERLER, GOTTFRIED: "The Market for Foreign Exchange and the Stability of the Balance of Payments: A Theoretical Analysis," *Kyklos,* Fasc. 3, 1949, pp. 193–218. Reprinted in Richard N. Cooper, (ed.), *International Finance,* Penguin, Baltimore, 1969.

HELLER, H. ROBERT: *International Monetary Economics,* Prentice-Hall, Englewood Cliffs, N.J., 1974, Chapter 6.

McKINNON, RONALD I.: *"Money in International Exchange: The Convertible Currency System,"* Oxford University Press, 1979.

MUNDELL, ROBERT A.: *International Economics,* Macmillan, New York, 1968, Chapter 1.

PIPPENGER, JOHN E.: *Fundamentals of International Finance,* Prentice-Hall, Englewood Cliffs, N.J., 1984, Chapter 5.

APPENDIX 6.1
The Condition for Stability in Foreign Exchange Markets

Let us consider the stability of $S(\$/£)$, assuming for simplicity that the only two countries in the world are the United States and the United Kingdom and that there are no capital flows. Under these assumptions, the quantity of pounds demanded is equal to the value of British exports. We can write this as $p_x \cdot Q_x(S \cdot p_x)$, where p_x is the pound price of British exports and $Q_x(S \cdot p_x)$ is the quantity of British exports. That is, the value of pounds demanded is the pound price of exports multiplied by the quantity of exports. [The term $(S \cdot p_x)$ has parentheses to signify that Q_x depends on $(S \cdot p_x)$, which is the *dollar* price of British exports; S is short for the spot rate, $S(\$/£)$. It is the dollar price that is relevant to the U.S. buyer of British exports.]

The quantity of pounds supplied is equal to the value of British imports. We can write this as $(p_m/S) \cdot Q_m(p_m/S)$, where p_m is the U.S. dollar price of British imports and $Q_m(p_m/S)$ is the quantity of British imports. That is, the value of pounds supplied is the pound price of imports (p_m/S) multiplied by the quantity of British imports, where the term in parentheses in $Q_m(p_m/S)$ signifies that the quantity of imports depends on p_m/S. [Recall that since S is the exchange rate $S(\$/£)$, dividing by S puts the dollar price of imports into British pounds. It is the pound price of British imports, p_m/S, that is relevant to the British buyer, and which hence determines the quantity of imports.]

We can write the excess demand for pounds, E, as

$$E = p_x \cdot Q_x(S \cdot p_x) - \frac{p_m}{S} \cdot Q_m\left(\frac{p_m}{S}\right) \tag{6A.1}$$

That is, the excess demand is the quantity of pounds demanded minus the quantity supplied. If we assume a perfectly elastic supply of exports and imports, then we can assume that p_x and p_m remain unchanged as the quantities of exports and imports vary with the exchange rate.[12] With this assumption we can differentiate equation (6A.1) to obtain

$$\frac{dE}{dS} = p_x \cdot \frac{dQ_x}{d(SP_x)} \cdot \frac{d(Sp_x)}{dS} - \frac{p_m}{S} \cdot \frac{dQ_m}{d(p_m/S)} \cdot \frac{d(p_m/S)}{dS} - Q_m \cdot \frac{d(p_m/S)}{dS}$$

or

$$\frac{dE}{dS} = p_x \cdot \frac{dQ_x}{d(Sp_x)} \cdot p_x + \frac{p_m}{S} \cdot \frac{dQ_m}{d(p_m/S)} \cdot \frac{p_m}{S^2} + \frac{p_m Q_m}{S^2} \tag{6A.2}$$

Multiplying and dividing the first two terms on the right-hand side of equation (6A.2) to form elasticities, we have

$$\frac{dE}{dS} = \left(\frac{Sp_x}{Q_x} \cdot \frac{dQ_x}{d(Sp_x)}\right) \cdot \frac{p_x Q_x}{S} + \left(\frac{p_m/S}{Q_m} \cdot \frac{dQ_m}{d(p_m/S)}\right) \cdot \frac{p_m Q_m}{S^2} + \frac{p_m Q_m}{S^2} \tag{6A.3}$$

[12]Stability conditions can be derived without assuming perfectly elastic supply of exports and imports, but only at the expense of considerable additional complexity. See Miltiades Chacholiades, *Principles of International Economics,* McGraw-Hill, New York, 1981, pp. 386–387, or Joan Robinson, "The Foreign Exchanges," in Joan Robinson, *Essays in the Theory of Employment,* Macmillan, London, 1939.

We can define the elasticity of demand for exports, η_x, and the elasticity of demand for imports, η_m, as follows:[13]

$$\eta_x = - \left(\frac{Sp_x}{Q_x} \cdot \frac{dQ_x}{dSp_x} \right) \quad \text{and} \quad \eta_m = - \left(\frac{p_m/S}{Q_m} \cdot \frac{dQ_m}{d(p_m/S)} \right)$$

We note that these elasticities are defined in terms of the currencies in which buyers are paying for their purchases, that is, exports from Britain are defined in terms of dollar prices, $S \cdot p_x$, and imports into Britain are defined in terms of pound prices p_m/S. Using these definitions in equation (6A.3) gives

$$\frac{dE}{dS} = -\eta_x \cdot \frac{p_x Q_x}{S} - \eta_m \cdot \frac{p_m Q_m}{S^2} + \frac{p_m Q_m}{S^2}$$

where we have defined the elasticities as positive. If the foreign exchange market started from a position of balance, then

$$p_x Q_x = \frac{p_m Q_m}{S}$$

That is, the pound value of British exports equals the pound value of British imports. This enables us to write

$$\frac{dE}{dS} = -\left(\eta_x + \eta_m - 1 \right) \cdot \frac{p_x Q_x}{S} \tag{6A.4}$$

The stability of the foreign exchange market requires that as the value of the pound goes up (S increases), the excess demand for pounds must fall (E falls). Similarly, it requires that as the pound falls in value (S goes down), the excess demand for pounds must rise (E goes up). This means that for stability, E and S must move in opposite directions ($dE/dS < 0$). That is, for stability:

$$\frac{dE}{dS} = -\left(\eta_x + \eta_m - 1 \right) \cdot \frac{p_x Q_x}{S} < 0 \tag{6A.5}$$

We know that $p_x Q_x/S$ is positive. Therefore, stability of the foreign exchange market requires that

$$\eta_x + \eta_m - 1 > 0$$

or

$$\eta_x + \eta_m > 1 \tag{6A.6}$$

We discover that for stability, the average elasticity of demand must exceed 0.5. For exchange-rate instability,

$$\eta_x + \eta_m < 1$$

When $\eta_x + \eta_m = 1$, the market is metastable, staying wherever it is. The condition (6A.6) is

---

[13]In this appendix we use the foreign elasticity of *demand* for exports, whereas in the main text we use the domestic elasticity of *supply* of exports. We can use the foreign elasticity of demand here because we are assuming only two countries. We could have assumed two countries in the text and then used the two elasticities of demand as we do here. However, the approach in the text is more general, because it uses the demand for the currency irrespective of who buys the country's exports.

generally known as the Marshall-Lerner condition, after Alfred Marshall and Abba Lerner, who independently discovered it.

Because demand elasticities are generally smaller in the short run than in the long run, foreign exchange markets might be unstable in the short run but eventually return to stability. However, if there are speculators who realize that stability occurs in the long run, the foreign exchange market may be stable in the short run even if the Marshall-Lerner condition does not hold.

CHAPTER 7

Modern Theories of Exchange Rates*

We first survey the plot, then draw the model. . . .
Then must we rate the cost of the erection;
Which if we find outweighs ability,
What do we then but draw anew the model. . . .

—WILLIAM SHAKESPEARE
Henry IV, Part 2
Act I, Scene iii

STOCK VERSUS FLOW THEORIES OF EXCHANGE RATES

The supply-and-demand view of exchange rates in the preceding chapter considers *flows* of currencies—amounts per period of time. An alternative way of viewing exchange-rate determination is in terms of the *stocks* of currencies relative to the willingness of people to hold these stocks. Several variants of stock-based theories of exchange rates have been developed in recent years, where these theories differ according to the time frame over which judgments are formed and according to the range of different assets considered. We begin with the simplest stock-based model, which considers only the stocks of different countries' monies versus the demands for these monies. This "monetary approach to exchange rates" is extended to the "asset approach" by considering how expectations about the future can affect exchange rates. This asset approach is followed by a more complete model which considers equilibrium in different countries' bond markets as well as their money markets. The chapter concludes with a discussion of models which extend the stock-based theories to explain exchange-rate volatility, where volatility takes the form of exchange rate "overshooting."

*This entire chapter can be omitted without loss of continuity. Although the chapter is self-contained and self-explanatory, the theories of exchange rates discussed are best understood by readers with an intermediate-level background in macroeconomics.

There are two essential components to the **monetary theory of exchange rates**.[1] The first relates the price levels in different countries to the countries' money supplies, and the second relates price levels to exchange rates.[2] The link between price levels and money supplies that is typically employed is a rearrangement of a demand equation for money. A specific version of the demand equation for money that has been used by John Bilson takes the form[3]

$$\frac{M_{US}}{P_{US}} = Q_{US}^{\alpha} e^{-\beta r_{US}} \tag{7.1}$$

$$\frac{M_{UK}}{P_{UK}} = Q_{UK}^{\alpha} e^{-\beta r_{UK}} \tag{7.2}$$

Here M_{US} and M_{UK} are, respectively, the U.S. and British money demands, P_{US} and P_{UK} are price levels, Q_{US} and Q_{UK} are real GNPs, r_{US} and r_{UK} are nominal interest rates, α and β are parameters that are assumed to be positive and the same for both countries, and e stands for exponential. The reason for the use of this specific money demand is the simplicity of the resulting equation for exchange rates which we shall derive.

The left-hand sides of equations (7.1) and (7.2) are the real money demands in the respective countries. (Division of any nominal variable by the price level converts it into a real variable. For example, dividing the nominal GNP, usually written as Y, by the price level gives the real GNP, usually writen as $Q = Y/P$.) The real quantity of money demanded is how much money, in terms of the ability to buy real goods and services, the public wants to hold. Equations (7.1) and (7.2) assume that the real quantity of money demanded increases with the real GNP. This is because the real GNP equals the real amount of goods and services people produce and buy, and the more people buy, the more money they need to hold for making purchases. The extent to which the real quantity of money demanded varies with the real GNP depends on α.

Equations (7.1) and (7.2) show that the quantity of money demanded in each country declines as that country's nominal interest rate increases. This is because the opportunity cost of holding money rather than buying bonds or some other interest-bearing asset is the nominal interest that would otherwise be earned.[4]

---

[1]The monetary theory of exchange rates is the flexible-exchange-rate form of the monetary approach to the balance of payments which pertains to fixed exchange rates. For a summary of the monetary approach to the balance of payments see Jacob A. Frenkel and Harry G. Johnson (eds.), *The Monetary Approach to the Balance of Payments,* Allen and Unwin, London, 1976, and Harry G. Johnson, "The Monetary Approach to the Balance of Payments: A Nontechnical Guide," *Journal of International Economics,* August 1977, pp. 251–268.
[2]The money supply is typically defined as currency held by the public plus all or some subset of deposits at financial institutions. The range of deposits included in the money supply depends on how broad a definition of money is being considered.
[3]John F. O. Bilson, "The Monetary Approach to Exchange Rates: Some Empirical Evidence," *Staff Papers,* International Monetary Fund, March 1978, pp. 48–75.
[4]Interest rates appear as exponents of e for no other reason than that this produces a convenient form of the exchange-rate equation. This becomes apparent as we proceed.

The assumption that the demand for money in each country depends on interest rates only in that country implicitly assumes that different countries' monies are not substitutable.[5] The alternative assumption, that different countries' monies are substitutable, would mean, for example, that the British view U.S. dollar holdings as satisfying their demand for money. In the extreme situation that different countries' monies are **perfectly substitutable**, changes in the money supply in any one country will not cause an excess supply of money because people in other countries will be prepared to hold the money. As we shall see, without an excess supply of money, there will be no depreciation in the exchange rate after an increase in the money supply as is predicted by the monetary approach.

The monetary approach to exchange rates assumes that people adjust their money holdings until the quantity of money demanded equals the quantity of money supplied. The way this occurs is as follows. If, for example, the supply of money exceeds the demand for money, the public attempts to spend the excess supply of money by buying goods and bonds. Of course, money does not disappear when it is spent, but rather ends up in somebody else's hands. However, the attempt to get rid of money does restore equilibrium between money supply and demand. This occurs because the buying of goods causes an increase in the price level, and the buying of bonds causes higher bond prices, which in turn mean lower interest rates. The higher price level and lower interest rates increase the nominal quantity of money demanded. The process continues until the demand for money has risen to match the supply. Similarly, an excess demand for money causes reductions in spending on goods and bonds, lower prices, higher interest rates, and a reduced quantity of money demanded. This continues until money demand has been reduced sufficiently to equal the money supply.

If the money demand equals the money supply, we can interpret M_{US} and M_{UK} as money supplies as well as money demands. If we rearrange equations (7.1) and (7.2) to put the money supplies on the right-hand sides, we have

$$P_{US} = M_{US}Q_{US}^{-\alpha}e^{-\beta r_{US}} \tag{7.3}$$

$$P_{UK} = M_{UK}Q_{UK}^{-\alpha}e^{-\beta r_{UK}} \tag{7.4}$$

Equations (7.3) and (7.4) show that price levels in the two countries vary in proportion with the countries' money supplies. Price levels also vary inversely with real GNPs, and in the same direction as nominal interest rates.[6]

According to the monetary theory of exchange rates, the ratio of prices in two different countries is closely related to the exchange rate between the two countries' currencies. In particular, in the context of the United States and the United Kingdom, the monetary theory assumes that

[5]The monetary approach also implicitly assumes that bonds from different countries *are* substitutable. This assumption is implicit in the exclusion of bond demand and supply equations, thereby implying bond markets clear whatever happens to bond supplies. Later we drop the assumption that different countries' bonds are substitutable. This is done when we consider the portfolio-balance approach to exchange rates.

[6]The conclusion that prices vary in proportion to the money supply is a conclusion of the quantity theory of money, and indeed, the real-demand-for-money equations are rearrangements of the quantity equation. The quantity equation is usually written as $MV = PQ$, where M, P, and Q are defined above, and V is the velocity of circulation of money. We could rewrite the quantity theory as $M/P = QV^{-1}$ and then make $V = e^{\beta r_{US}}$. This is directly comparable to our money demand equations when $\alpha = 1$.

$$S(\$/\pounds) = \frac{P_{\text{US}}}{P_{\text{UK}}} \tag{7.5}$$

where $S(\$/\pounds)$ is the exchange rate of dollars per pound. Equation (7.5) is known as the **purchasing-power parity (PPP) principle** and has the following rationale.[7]

Assume that there are no taxes or shipping costs and that the price of a representative good is \$10 in the United States and £6 in Britain. If the exchange were $S(\$/\pounds) = \$1.50/\pounds$ it would be possible to take \$9, purchase £6 on the foreign exchange market, buy one unit of the good in Britain, ship the good to the United States, and sell it for \$10. There would be an arbitrage profit of \$1, and as many people tried to exploit the opportunity, which requires buying pounds with dollars, they would bid up the dollar price of the pound until the arbitrage was no longer profitable.[8] Alternatively, if the exchange rate were \$1.75/£, it would be possible to take £5.71, buy \$10 on the foreign exchange market, use the \$10 to buy one unit of the good in the United States, ship the good to Britain, and sell it for £6. There would be an arbitrage profit of £0.29 (£6 − £5.71), which would encourage others to try to exploit the opportunity. This would involve buying dollars (selling pounds), which would push the dollar value of the pound below \$1.75/£. Only at \$1.67/£ does arbitrage become unprofitable. This is the exchange rate given by equation (7.5), since with $P_{\text{US}} = \$10$ and $P_{\text{UK}} = \pounds6$, we have

$$S(\$/\pounds) = \frac{P_{\text{US}}}{P_{\text{UK}}} = \frac{\$10}{\pounds6} = \$1.67/\pounds$$

Substituting equations (7.3) and (7.4) into equation (7.5), we find[9]

$$S(\$/\pounds) = \frac{M_{\text{US}}}{M_{\text{UK}}} \left(\frac{Q_{\text{UK}}}{Q_{\text{US}}} \right)^{\alpha} e^{\beta(r_{\text{US}} - r_{\text{UK}})} \tag{7.6}$$

Equation (7.6) captures the essential features of the monetary approach to exchange rates.

An examination of equation (7.6) shows that the first and most distinctive implication of the monetary approach is that the U.S. dollar value of the pound, $S(\$/\pounds)$, increases if the U.S. money supply increases more than the British money supply. The reason is that if M_{US} increases more than M_{UK}, U.S. prices increase more than British prices, so that according to the PPP principle, the dollar must fall vis-à-vis the pound.

The second prediction of the monetary approach characterized by equation (7.6) is that the value of the pound increases if British real GNP increases faster than U.S. real GNP. This occurs because a higher real GNP means a higher demand for money, which, for a given supply of money, means an excess demand for money. This causes reduced spending—both on goods and on bonds—and a lower price level. According to the PPP principle, a lower price level means an appreciation of

---

[7]The purchasing-power parity principle is discussed in Chapter 10.

[8]Alternatively, the arbitrage opportunity might be eliminated by changes in the pound and dollar prices of the good.

[9]Because only freely traded commodities lend themselves to the type of arbitrage we have described, it can be argued that instead of using the overall price levels in equation (7.5), we should use prices of traded goods. For the consequences of this see John F. O. Bilson, "Leading Indicators of Currency Devaluation," *Columbia Journal of World Business,* winter 1979, pp. 62–76.

the exchange rate, in this case of the pound vis-à-vis the dollar. The prediction that faster growth of real GNP causes currency appreciation runs counter to what the simple goods flow supply-and-demand view predicts. Supply-and-demand models such as that described in Chapter 6 predict that faster growth of real GNP means faster growth of imports, a consequent faster growth of the supply of a currency, and a depreciating exchange rate. Monetarists argue that simple goods flow supply-and-demand models overlook the link between the goods and money markets, that is, the link between GNP and the demand for money.

Another prediction of the monetary approach is that the higher are U.S. versus British interest rates, the higher is the U.S. dollar value of the pound. In terms of equation (7.6), the higher r_{US} is, the higher is $S(\$/£)$, because β is positive. A higher $S(\$/£)$ means a higher value of the pound and lower value of the dollar. It follows that an unexpected jump in nominal interest rates will cause a currency to depreciate. The reason for this prediction of the monetary approach is that the higher nominal interest rates are, the lower is the real quantity of money demanded, and consequently, the lower is the equilibrium real money supply. The real money supply is reduced to its lower equilibrium level by an increase in the price level.[10] The PPP condition, equation (7.5), requires that if the U.S. price level does increase because of higher U.S. interest rates, the U.S. dollar must lose value against the pound, that is, there must be more U.S. dollars per pound. Therefore, we reach the conclusion that the higher U.S. interest rates are relative to British interest rates, the lower is the value of the dollar. Flow theories of exchange rates such as that outlined in Chapter 6 suggest otherwise, predicting that higher U.S. interest rates will increase the demand for U.S. interest-bearing securities, thereby increasing the demand for dollars and the value of the dollar.[11]

A prediction of the monetary approach with which a large number of economists will agree concerns the effect of expected inflation. It is generally accepted that, *ceteris paribus,* higher expected inflation leads to higher nominal interest rates.[12] We have just seen that higher nominal interest rates cause a currency to depreciate. Therefore, the monetary approach predicts that higher expected inflation causes depreciation. Because higher expected inflation suggests a future depreciation via the PPP condition (higher future prices mean a lower future currency value), what the monetary approach tells us is that the effect occurs immediately rather than later, after the expected inflation has occurred. The idea that expected future events are reflected immediately in spot exchange rates is an important ingredient of the **asset approach to exchange rates** considered next.

---

[10]The price level increases because higher interest rates reduce money demand, thereby creating an excess supply of money. The excess supply of money causes extra spending, pushing up prices.

[11]The evidence supports the prediction of the flow theory in that appreciations (depreciations) of the dollar are empirically associated with increases (decreases) in U.S. nominal interest rates. See Brad Cornell and Alan C. Shapiro, "Interest Rates and Exchange Rates: Some New Empirical Results," *Journal of International Money and Finance,* December 1985, pp. 431–442, and Gikas A. Hardouvelis, "Economic News, Exchange Rates and Interest Rates," *Journal of International Money and Finance,* March 1988, pp. 23–35.

[12]For the theory behind expected inflation and interest rates see Maurice D. Levi and John H. Makin, "Anticipated Inflation and Interest Rates: Further Interpretation of Findings on the Fisher Equation," *American Economic Review,* December 1978, pp. 801–812. For the evidence, see Maurice D. Levi and John H. Makin, "Fisher, Phillips, Friedman and the Measured Impact of Inflation on Interest," *The Journal of Finance,* March 1979, pp. 35–52.

Exchange rates are relative prices of two assets: monies. The current value of an asset depends on what that asset is expected to be worth in the future. For example, the more valuable a stock is expected to be worth, the more it is worth now. Similarly, the more a currency is expected to be worth in the future, the more it *is* worth now. It follows that today's exchange rate depends on the expected future exchange rate. In turn, the expected future exchange rate depends on what is expected to happen to all the factors reflected in future balance-of-payments accounts.

The asset approach to exchange rates, which has been articulated most clearly by Michael Mussa, looks at the current spot exchange rate as a reflection of the market's best evaluation of what is likely to happen to the exchange rate in the future.[13] All relevant available information about the future is incorporated into the current spot rate. Because new information is random, and could as easily be good as bad for one currency versus the other, the path of the exchange rate should contain a random component. This random component fluctuates around the expected change in the exchange rate. The expected change can reflect the implications of PPP—with more rapid inflation implying depreciation—or any other influence on exchange rates reflected in the balance-of-payments accounts.

The asset approach holds implications for the effect of fiscal policy as well as monetary policy. For example, it predicts that high fiscal deficits can result in an immediate depreciation. This would happen if the fiscal deficit caused people to expect future expansion of the money supply as the government printed money to make interest payments on its growing debt. The higher future money supply implies higher future prices, and via the PPP principle, this implies a future depreciation. The future depreciation translates into an immediate depreciation via the asset approach.

The asset approach offers an explanation for departures from PPP. Because expectations about the future are relevant to the current exchange rate, there is no necessity for the spot exchange rate to ensure PPP at every moment. For example, if a country is expected to experience rapid inflation, poor trade performance, or something else leading to a depreciation, the current exchange rate of that country's currency is likely to be below its PPP value. However, because the expected future exchange rate could be based on a tendency for PPP to be restored, the asset approach is not inconsistent with PPP as a long-run tendency. Nor, therefore, is the asset approach necessarily inconsistent with the long-run implications of the monetary approach.

THE PORTFOLIO-BALANCE APPROACH TO EXCHANGE RATES

The monetary approach to exchange rates assumes that people want to hold their own country's currency but not the foreign country's currency. The **portfolio-**

---

[13]Michael Mussa, "A Model of Exchange Rate Dynamics," *Journal of Political Economy,* February 1982, pp. 74–104. This paper follows an earlier statement of the asset approach in Jacob A. Frenkel and Michael L. Mussa, "The Efficiency of Foreign Exchange Markets and Measures of Turbulence," *American Economic Review, Papers and Proceedings,* May 1980, pp. 374–381.

balance approach recognizes that people might want to hold both monies, although they might have a preference for one country's money, probably their own. The portfolio-balance approach makes the same argument for bonds. That is, it assumes that people in both countries demand domestic and foreign bonds or, more generally, that people prefer diversified portfolios of securities. However, the portfolio-balance model does not just have demand equations for different monies and bonds in each country, showing how these demands are related to incomes, interest rates, and so on. Rather, it recognizes that supplies and demands for monies and bonds must balance, that is, markets must clear.[14] (The fact that the approach is based on diversification of portfolios and a requirement that markets balance explains its name.)

In the monetary approach each country's bond market is assumed to clear, whatever happens to the supply of or demand for any country's bonds. This assumption is implicit in the absence of equations for bond supplies and demands, and in the absence of any conditions for the bond markets to clear; without there being conditions showing when the bond markets clear, by implication they always clear. It is possible to rationalize this assumption of the monetary approach if it is argued that one country's bonds are perfectly substitutable for another country's bonds. This is because then, if the supply of a country's bonds is increased, the extra bonds will be held by residents or foreigners substituting these for foreign bonds they currently hold. Changes in the supply of one country's bonds are of such insignificance in the global context that the global demand for bonds equals the global supply without any noticeable effect on interest rates or exchange rates.

When we add bond demand equations and equilibrium conditions for bond demands to equal bond supplies for each country's bonds, as we do in the portfolio-balance approach, the implications of changing bond supplies and demands are different from those in the monetary approach. In particular, we find effects of bond supplies and demands on exchange rates and interest rates.

In order to illustrate the consequences of bond supplies and demands for interest rates and exchange rates we can use the diagrammatic representation of the portfolio-balance theory in Figure 7.1. The figure shows the U.S. interest rate, r_{US}, on the vertical axis, and the exchange rate, $S(\$/£)$, on the horizontal axis, where a movement to the right along the horizontal axis is a depreciation of the dollar.

The curve labeled MM_1 represents all of the interest rate/exchange rate combinations consistent with initial equilibrium in the U.S. money market; along MM_1 the demand to hold U.S. money equals the U.S. money supply. MM_1 assumes a given, initial money supply. MM_1 slopes upward because a higher U.S. interest rate reduces the quantity of money that people demand; higher interest rates increase the opportunity cost of holding money. Because the supply of money is constant, a lower quantity of money demanded would represent an excess supply of money if nothing else were changed. However, by increasing $S(\$/£)$ as r_{US} increases, the value of Americans' holdings of British bonds and currency is increased; the pound values of British assets translate into more dollars. That is, a higher value of $S(\$/£)$ increases the wealth of Americans via their holdings of British bonds and currency.

---

[14]Therefore, the portfolio-balance model consists of demand and supply equations for money and bonds in all countries, as well as equations setting money and bond demands equal to supplies. We do not need to write down these equations in order to appreciate the essential features of the approach. See Pentti J. K. Kouri and Michael G. Porter, "International Capital Flows and Portfolio Equilibrium," *Journal of Political Economy*, May/June 1974, pp. 443–467.

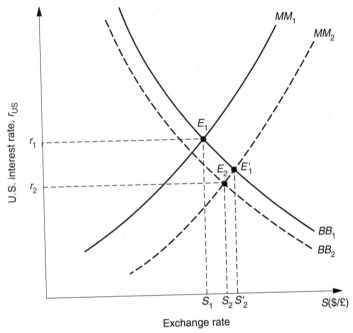

Figure 7.1. The Portfolio-Balance Theory: Effect of Open-Market Operations

MM_1 represents initial equilibrium in the U.S. money market. The line slopes up because higher r_{US} reduces money demand, while higher $S(\$/£)$ increases money demand via increasing wealth due to an increase in the dollar value of British bonds and currency. BB_1 represents initial equilibrium in the U.S. bond market. The line slopes down because lower r_{US} reduces demand for U.S. bonds versus British bonds, and a higher $S(\$/£)$ achieves this via making British bonds and currency more valuable. When the U.S. money supply increases via the Fed's buying of bonds, MM_1 shifts to the right to MM_2, and BB_1 shifts to the left to BB_2. Both movements reduce r_{US}; compare E_2 to E_1. Note that the bond supply reduction reduces the depreciation of the dollar; compare E_2 to E_1' where the latter is the equilibrium when the money supply is increased without the Fed buying bonds.

Higher wealth increases the demand for U.S. money; money is a component of wealth, and, *ceteris paribus*, money demand increases as wealth increases. The higher demand for U.S. money from a higher wealth associated with a higher $S(\$/£)$ offsets the lower quantity of U.S. money demanded from a higher r_{US}, so the demand for money can remain equal to the (constant) money supply. Therefore, the U.S. money market can remain in equilibrium if $S(\$/£)$ increases as r_{US} increases, meaning an upward-sloping line, MM_1.

The line BB_1 represents all of the interest rate/exchange rate combinations consistent with initial equilibrium in the U.S. bond market, which is where the demand to hold U.S. bonds equals the supply. The line slopes downward because, *ceteris paribus*, as r_{US} decreases, the fraction of wealth Americans want in U.S. bonds decreases. With U.S. bond supply given, equilibrium is maintained by having an increased value of $S(\$/£)$, which increases the U.S. dollar value of British bonds and currency; pounds translate into more dollars. This increases U.S. bond demand, offsetting the effect of lower r_{US}. A higher $S(\$/£)$ also achieves the desired *relative* reduction in U.S. bond holdings within portfolios; British bonds are worth more U.S. dollars. Therefore, we can maintain U.S. bond market equilibrium by having $S(\$/£)$ increase as r_{US} decreases, which means a downward-sloping line BB_1.

The diagrammatic framework in Figure 7.1 can show how the implications of the portfolio-balance theory differ from those of the monetary theory. Consider, for example, the effect of an increase in the U.S. money supply brought about by open-market operations.[15] The monetary approach summarized by equation (7.6) predicts, *ceteris paribus,* that an increase in M_{US} will cause a depreciation of the U.S. dollar by the same percentage as M_{US} increases. The portfolio-balance theory recognizes that in addition to the direct effect of the money supply, there is also an effect of the excess demand for bonds caused by the central bank's purchase of bonds; the supply of bonds available to the public is reduced.

In terms of Figure 7.1, the increase in M_{US} shifts the money market equilibrium line from MM_1 to MM_2. This follows because at a given r_{US} on the initial money market equilibrium line MM_1, there is an excess supply of money after the U.S. money supply has been increased. This excess supply can be reduced by a lower r_{US}, which increases the quantity of money demanded via a lower opportunity cost. This means a downward shift from MM_1 to MM_2; equilibrium occurs everywhere at lower r_{US}. The excess supply of money could also be reduced by an increase in $S(\$/£)$, which increases Americans' wealth; British bonds and currency are more valuable when translated into dollars. The higher American wealth increases Americans' demands for money. This means a rightward shift from MM_1 to MM_2. Whichever way we view the shift of MM—as downward or as rightward—the MM_1 curve has shifted to MM_2. The intersection of MM_2 with BB_1 is at a lower U.S. interest rate and a depreciated value of the dollar: compare E'_1 with E_1 in Figure 7.1. However, we have not yet accounted for the effect of the reduced supply of bonds brought about by the open-market operations used to increase the money supply.

Fewer U.S. bonds in the hands of Americans means an excess demand for U.S. bonds. This can be prevented if r_{US} is reduced or if $S(\$/£)$ is reduced. (A lower U.S. interest rate reduces the quantity of U.S. bonds demanded, helping match the reduced supply. Similarly, less of Americans' wealth in British bonds caused by a lower $S(\$/£)$ helps reduce the demand for U.S. bonds and achieve the preferred relative increase in U.S. versus British bond holdings.) Whether it be via r_{US} being reduced or via $S(\$/£)$ being reduced, the effect of the reduced supply of U.S. bonds is to shift BB_1 down and to the left to BB_2. With the shift of MM_1 to MM_2 and BB_1 to BB_2 we see what the portfolio-balance theory predicts. Specifically, an increase in the U.S. money supply causes less of a depreciation of the dollar when the bond supply is reduced, as it is with open-market operations, than when the bond supply is not reduced; compare E_2, where BB_2 intersects MM_2, with E'_1, which is the equilibrium with a constant bond supply.[16] That is, unlike the monetary approach, the

---

[15]In an open-market operation to expand the U.S. money supply, the Fed buys securities in the open market, paying by crediting sellers' accounts at the Fed. When spent, the sellers' deposits at the Fed become commercial bank reserves, permitting loans and thus an expansion of the money supply.

[16]In Figure 7.1 we assume that the effect of the shift in MM dominates the shift of BB so that the dollar depreciates.

portfolio-balance approach predicts that the effect of changes in money supplies on exchange rates depends on how money supplies are changed.

As a second example of the predictions of the monetary theory versus the prediction of the portfolio-balance theory, consider the effect of a higher U.S. real GNP. Equation (7.6) shows that the monetary theory predicts an appreciation of the U.S. dollar by proportion α. The effect of higher U.S. real GNP via the portfolio-balance theory is shown in Figure 7.2. The figure shows that MM_1 has shifted to MM_2. (The higher income increases the demand for money, which can be offset by a higher r_{US} or lower wealth. The latter is achieved by a reduction in $S(\$/£)$, making British bonds and currency less valuable in Americans' portfolios.) Higher income also increases Americans' savings and thereby Americans' demands for U.S. bonds relative to British bonds; U.S. bonds are preferred to British bonds. Balance with the fixed supply of U.S. bonds can be achieved via a lower r_{US}, shifting BB_1 down to BB_2, or via a lower $S(\$/£)$, shifting BB_1 left to BB_2. Figure 7.2 shows that the left-

Figure 7.2. Real Income Growth and the Portfolio-Balance Theory
Higher U.S. income increases the demand for money in the United States and shifts MM_1 to MM_2; money equilibrium can be maintained via higher r_{US}, reducing the quantity of money demanded, or via lower $S(\$/£)$, reducing wealth from a lower dollar value of British bonds and currency. Higher U.S. income also increases savings and the demand for U.S. versus British bonds. This causes BB_1 to shift left to BB_2; lower r_{US} and $S(\$/£)$ reduce the demand for U.S. bonds. The new equilibrium from income growth involves an appreciated dollar.

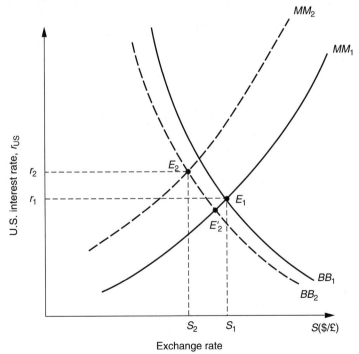

ward shift of MM_1 to MM_2 and of BB_1 to BB_2 both cause an appreciation of the U.S. dollar.[17] Qualitatively, this is the same conclusion reached by the monetary theory. However, in this case we see that the exchange-rate appreciation is the result of adjustments in both the money and bond markets and therefore is larger than the exchange-rate appreciation occurring only via the money market; compare E_2 with E'_2, where E_2 is the equilibrium with adjustments in the money *and* bond markets.

THEORIES OF EXCHANGE-RATE VOLATILITY

The Dornbusch Sticky-Price Theory[18]

In the monetary approach presented earlier, we implicitly assumed that the PPP condition holds for the overall price level; P_{US} and P_{UK} in equation (7.5) are the prices of baskets containing *all* goods and services. If this assumption about PPP is relaxed, the monetary approach can generate exchange-rate **overshooting,** which occurs when exchange rates go beyond their new equilibrium before returning to it.

Let us suppose that PPP holds for internationally traded goods but not for goods that are not traded internationally, such as land and services. Let us also suppose that prices of nontraded goods are "sticky," that is, they move slowly toward their new equilibrium after a disturbance.[19] In these circumstances, if the exchange rate falls in proportion to the percentage increase in a country's money supply, as suggested by the monetary approach, there remains an excess supply of money. [Traded-goods prices increase in proportion to the money supply because they move directly with the exchange rate as given by equation (7.6), but nontraded-goods prices increase only slowly. Therefore, the overall price level increases less than the money supply, leaving the demand for money lower than the supply.] Eventually, the excess supply of money is eliminated via rising nontraded-goods prices, but in the interim the excess supply of money causes increased spending on goods and bonds.

The theory of overshooting exchange rates concentrates on the effect of the increased spending on bonds, arguing that this causes higher bond prices and, consequently, lower interest rates. If a country's interest rates are lower than other countries', capital leaves the country until the country's currency is expected to appreciate by the extent to which its interest rates are below other countries'.[20] In order for the currency to be expected to appreciate, the exchange rate must overshoot, going

---

[17]In Figure 7.2 we assume the shift in *MM* dominates that of *BB* so that increases in income increase interest rates.

[18]More complete accounts of the Dornbusch sticky-price theory can be found in Rudiger Dornbusch, "Expectations and Exchange Rate Dynamics," *Journal of Political Economy,* December 1976, pp. 1161–1176, and in Rudiger Dornbusch, *Open Economy Macroeconomics,* 2d ed., Basic Books, New York, 1988.

[19]Any cause of price stickiness will generate overshooting. The assumption that it is nontraded-goods prices that cause stickiness of the overall price index is to provide a realistic rationale and help in exposition.

[20]This is because the return from investing in a country consists of two components: the interest rate, and the change in value of the country's currency between the time of the investment and the time of repatriation. Therefore, an expected appreciation of a country's currency compensates for lower interest rates in that country.

lower than its eventual equilibrium level. This means that prices of traded goods, which move with the exchange rate, increase by even more than the increase in the money supply, thereby augmenting the increase in the price index. This increases the demand for money, as does the low interest rate, helping to maintain equality of supply and demand for money in the short run.

In the long run, the prices of nontraded goods increase in proportion to the increase in the money supply; they increase slowly but do eventually catch up. This means that, in the long run, the exchange rate needs to depreciate only in the same proportion as the increase in the money supply. Therefore, after overshooting beyond the new (lower) long-run equilibrium level, the exchange rate appreciates back to its new equilibrium. This appreciation reduces traded-goods prices, so that in the end, prices of traded and nontraded goods have both increased in proportion to the money supply. Therefore, the overshooting is temporary, lasting only as long as nontraded-goods prices lag behind the increase in the money supply.

Figure 7.3 illustrates the overshooting we have described. The ray from the origin in the top right-hand quadrant shows the PPP principle for a given level of British prices. The line reflects the PPP condition, $P_{US} = S(\$/£) \cdot P_{UK}$. The upward-sloping line shows that for a given P_{UK}, higher U.S. prices are associated with a dollar depreciation of the same proportion; a higher $S(\$/£)$ is a dollar depreciation.

The downward-sloping line MM_1 in the top left-hand quadrant represents initial equilibrium in the U.S. money market for a given money supply. Higher prices increase the demand for money, and this is offset by an increase in the interest rate, which reduces the quantity of money demanded. The line FF_1 in the bottom left-hand quadrant represents initial equilibrium in the foreign exchange market. It shows a higher U.S. interest rate associated with a dollar appreciation. (A higher r_{US} attracts capital and improves the capital account. This is offset by a more expensive U.S. dollar, which worsens the current account.) FF_1 is drawn for the U.S. price level P_1.

Suppose that the U.S. money supply is initially such that for a given British price level, the U.S. is at point A on the PPP line, with price level P_1 and exchange rate S_1. Drawing a horizontal line from point A to point B on MM_1 shows the associated interest rate, r_1, where the U.S. money market is in equilibrium. Next, drawing a line from B on MM_1 down to C on the FF_1 line gives the spot rate S_1 on the vertical axis where the foreign exchange market is in equilibrium. The 45-degree line in the bottom right-hand quadrant allows us to trace the spot rate over to the horizontal axis, where we have S_1, the initial spot rate, consistent with the initial U.S. price level P_1; the 45-degree line simply allows us to transfer the vertical axis to the horizontal axis. Now let us consider what happens after an increase in the U.S. money supply.

An increase in the U.S. money supply shifts MM_1 to MM_2; to induce people to hold the extra money it is necessary to have a higher P_{US} or lower r_{US}. If prices are sticky at P_1, the new equilibrium interest rate is r_2, given off MM_2 at P_1. The line FF_1, which is drawn for price level P_1, shows the new spot rate S_2 associated with r_2. This spot rate is shown also on the horizontal axis; we transfer axes via the 45-degree line. With the current sticky price level P_1 and the spot rate S_2, we are at point D in the top-right quadrant, where point D is below the PPP line.

Eventually prices begin to increase. We can show that a new equilibrium is eventually attained at E. At E the price level is P_2, and the U.S. interest rate, given

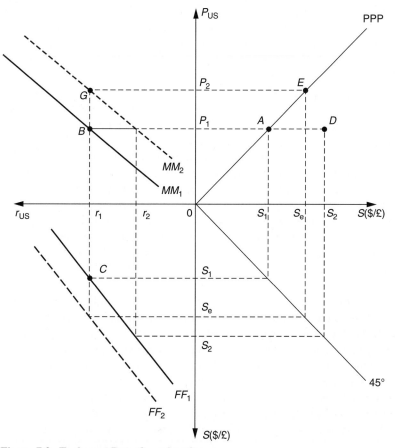

Figure 7.3. Exchange-Rate Overshooting
With the initial U.S. money supply the equilibrium price level is P_1 and the
exchange rate is S_1. An increase in the money supply shifts the money market
equilibrium line from MM_1 to MM_2, and at the sticky price P_1, r_{US} falls to r_2 and the
dollar depreciates from S_1 to S_2. As prices increase, the equilibrium P_{US} and $S(\$/£)$
move to E. At E the price level is P_2, and r_{US} returns to r_1. The higher price level
shifts FF_1 to FF_2; higher U.S. prices must be offset by a depreciated dollar. The
new exchange rate is S_e which is on the PPP line at price P_2.

off MM_2 at point G, is r_1. With prices higher at P_2 the foreign-exchange-market equilibrium line shifts from FF_1 to FF_2. [Higher prices would cause a current-account
deficit unless there was a dollar depreciation. Therefore, as the price level increases,
foreign-exchange-market equilibrium requires a higher value of $S(\$/£)$, which means
a downward shift from FF_1 to FF_2, where FF_2 is the foreign exchange market equilibrium line at U.S. price level P_2.] At r_1 and with FF_2 the spot rate is S_e. When S_e is
transferred to the horizontal axis via the 45-degree line, the value of S_e and P_2 coincide at E, the new equilibrium S and P with the higher U.S. money supply.

Figure 7.3 shows the spot rate going from S_1 to S_2 to S_e, an overshooting of the
eventual equilibrium S_e. The appreciation from S_2 to S_e occurs after the interest rate
has temporarily declined to r_2, with the expected appreciation of S compensating

for the lower r_{US}. As the appreciation ceases—as the equilibrium value S_e is attained—r_{US} moves to its initial level, r_1; there is no reason for the interest rate to change when the stock of money changes to a new level and then remains constant, because inflation should return to zero.

Varying Elasticities

As we saw in Chapter 6, if the demand for imports is inelastic in the short run, then depreciation can increase the value of imports; import prices increase by more than the quantity of imports declines, so that the value of imports increases. This means that the quantity of a country's currency supplied can increase with a depreciation. If the demand for the currency does not increase by as much as the supply because export demand is also very inelastic in the short run, a depreciation causes an excess supply of the currency. An excess supply means further depreciation. Therefore, while inelasticities persist there is depreciation, further excess supply, and so on. However, eventually, as elasticities of import demand and export supply increase, stability returns to exchange rates. Therefore, it is possible for exchange rates to overshoot.[21]

A particular variant of the varying-elasticities explanation of overshooting that has been advanced by Steven Magee is that previously agreed-upon export contracts make demand and supply elasticities effectively zero.[22] For example, if a stated quantity of wheat is purchased by Britain at a contracted U.S. dollar price, then a depreciation of the pound increases pound payments for wheat in proportion to the depreciation, causing an excess supply of pounds and further depreciation. What happens is that the British demand for imports has an elasticity of zero during the contract period. Only when the contract expires can the quantity purchased decline as a result of the higher pound price. In the interim, the exchange rate can overshoot.

Stock Adjustment and Flow Fluctuations

Overshooting of exchange rates can also be explained by arguments akin to those of the **accelerator model**.[23] Let us do this with the help of an example.

Suppose British investors save £10 billion each year and divide it evenly between British and U.S. investments. Suppose that they have accumulated £100 billion of investments in each country from their investments during previous years, but that suddenly, perhaps because of the election of a popular U.S. President or an unpopular British Prime Minister, British investors decide to increase their U.S. investments to 60 percent of their portfolios.

---

[21]Speculators may stabilize exchange rates if the pattern is predictable. Therefore, we do not necessarily observe overshooting from varying elasticities. This is not the case for the Dornbusch model, where speculators do not prevent overshooting. This is because in that model, interest rates move to nullify the benefit of currency speculation; interest rates are low on the currency that is expected to appreciate.

[22]Steven Magee, "Contracting and Spurious Deviations from Purchasing Power Parity," in Jacob A. Frenkel and Harry G. Johnson (eds.), *The Economics of Exchange Rates: Selected Readings,* Addison-Wesley, Reading, Mass., 1978.

[23]The accelerator model offers an explanation of the business cycle—an overshooting of the GNP—based on assuming the stock of capital is proportional to national income. Many students will be familiar with the accelerator model because it is covered in introductory economics courses.

After their portfolios have been adjusted, the British will purchase £6 billion of U.S. investment and therefore £6 billion of U.S. dollars per year to pay for this investment. However, in order to readjust their accumulated portfolios the British must purchase another £20 billion of U.S. investments and U.S. dollars; with £100 billion in each country, having 60 percent of the portfolio in U.S. assets requires having £120 billion of U.S. assets. If the readjustment of the accumulated portfolios occurs during one year, the path of the British demand for dollars goes from £5 billion before the adjustment to £26 billion during the readjustment, and then back to £6 billion per year. Therefore, the demand for dollars is abnormally high during the period in which accumulated portfolios are being readjusted, and this can cause the value of the U.S. dollar to overshoot. The basic reason is that accumulated portfolios are large relative to additions to portfolios, that is, stocks are large relative to flows.[24]

A reason why large shifts in desired portfolios might occur is that some forms of money do not pay interest. Normally, interest rates increase to make up for expected depreciations, so that investors do not switch assets because they anticipate a depreciation. Without interest being paid on money, this compensation is not possible. Consequently, large adjustments between different countries' monies can occur, causing large flow demands and exchange-rate overshooting.[25]

Other Theories of Overshooting

We have by no means exhausted the theories of overshooting. For example, Jeffery Frankel and Kenneth Froot have offered a theory of "speculative bubbles" in exchange rates, based on changes in the amount of attention portfolio managers pay to chartists, who extrapolate recent trends, and fundamentalists, who consider the fundamentals such as adherence of exchange rates to PPP.[26] Frankel and Froot argue that portfolio managers attach more weight to the predictions of the group that has been more accurate in the recent past. If chartists happen to be correct for a while, their predictions are followed, making their predictions correct, causing even greater attention to be paid to them, and so on. Because the chartists' predictions are self-reinforcing, it is only when exchange rates have become completely out of line with fundamentals that the chartists are likely to falter, making portfolio managers switch their attention to the advice of fundamentalists. When this shift in attention occurs, exchange rates move back from their disequilibrium levels. Eventually, even if just by chance, the chartists are likely to be more correct than the fundamentalists, again with self-realizing effects which cause another bout of overshooting exchanges rates.

---

[24]This explanation for exchange-rate overshooting has been advanced by Robert M. Dunn, Jr., *The Many Disappointments of Flexible Exchange Rates,* Essays in International Finance 154, Princeton University, December 1983.

[25]For variants of this explanation of volatility of exchange rates see Lance Girton and Donald Roper, "Theory and Implication of Currency Substitution," *Journal of Money, Credit, and Banking,* February 1981, pp. 12–30, and Ronald I. McKinnon, "Currency Substitution and Instability in the World Dollar Market," *American Economic Review,* June 1982, pp. 302–333.

[26]Jeffrey A. Frankel and Kenneth Froot, "The Dollar as an Irrational Speculative Bubble: A Tale of Fundamentalists and Chartists," National Bureau of Economic Research, Cambridge, Mass., 1986. For an earlier model of overshooting based on different market players see Richard G. Harris and Douglas D. Purvis, "Diverse Information and Market Efficiency in a Monetary Model of Exchange Rates," *Economic Journal,* December 1981, pp. 829–847.

The relatively difficult material presented in this chapter is not required for an understanding of anything that follows in this text, so readers who feel a little shaky on some matters need not delay moving ahead. The remaining two chapters of Part Two are concerned with the alternative ways the international financial system can and has been organized and with the problems facing the system today.

SUMMARY

1. Several theories of exchange rates have been advanced which are based on the stocks of countries' monies versus the demands to hold these monies.
2. The stock-based theories differ according to the assets they consider and whether they involve expectations of the future.
3. The monetary approach to exchange rates is based on links between money supplies and price levels and between price levels and exchange rates.
4. The monetary approach predicts that an exchange rate will depreciate by the excess of money growth in one country over another. It also predicts that faster growth of real GNP will cause appreciation and that higher interest rates and expected inflation will cause depreciation.
5. The asset approach to exchange rates suggests that the current exchange rate depends on the expected future exchange rate. Since the expected future rate can depend on expected inflation or anything appearing in the balance-of-payments account, the asset approach is consistent with other theories of exchange rates.
6. The portfolio-balance approach assumes different countries' bonds are not perfect substitutes. As a result, changes in preferences for bonds of one country over another, or changes in bond supplies, can affect exchange rates.
7. If prices are sticky, exchange rates may overshoot their equilibrium. Other explanations of exchange-rate overshooting include varying elasticities of import demand and export supply, and jumps in currency supplies or demands caused by portfolio readjustment.

REVIEW QUESTIONS

1. What are the two essential components of the monetary theory of exchange rates?
2. What does the monetary theory of exchange rates assume about the substitutability of different countries' monies and bonds?
3. What does the monetary theory of exchange rates imply for:
   a. Relatively rapid growth in a country's money supply?
   b. Relatively rapid growth in a country's national income?
   c. An increase in a country's interest rates versus interest rates in another country?
4. Does the asset approach to exchange rates consider expectations about future exchange rates?
5. What does the portfolio-balance approach to exchange rates assume about the substitutability of different countries' monies and bonds?
6. What is meant by exchange-rate overshooting?
7. What does the Dornbusch overshooting theory assume about the speed of adjustment of prices?
8. According to the Dornbusch overshooting theory, what happens to interest rates after exchange rates have overshot their eventual equilibrium?

1. Why does the monetary approach imply that higher expected inflation causes a currency to depreciate?
2. Suppose that

$$M_{US} = \$500 \quad \text{billion}$$

$$M_{Can} = \text{C}\$50 \quad \text{billion}$$

$$Q_{US} = \$7000 \quad \text{billion}$$

$$Q_{Can} = \text{C}\$600 \quad \text{billion}$$

$$\alpha = 1$$

$$\beta = 0$$

and that PPP holds. What exchange rate is implied by the monetary theory of exchange rates?
3. Assume in the previous question that all magnitudes are unchanged except that of the Canadian money supply, which increases from C$50 billion to C$55 billion. What happens to the implied exchange rate, and how does this compare to the proportional change in the Canadian money supply?
4. Assume that all data in question **2** are unchanged except the U.S. GNP, Q_{US}, which increases from $7000 billion to $7700 billion. What happens to the exchange rate, and how does this compare in magnitude to the change in U.S. GNP?
5. What does the asset approach imply about the ability to make money by speculating in foreign exchange?
6. How can the asset approach explain deviations from PPP based on current prices?
7. What are the principal differences and similarities between the monetary and portfolio-balance approaches to exchange rates?
8. What is the crucial assumption required for exchange-rate overshooting in the Dornbusch model? Do you think this assumption is valid?
9. Why does the foreign exchange equilibrium line *FF* move downward in Figure 7.3 when there is an increase in the U.S. price level?
10. How does the portfolio-balance approach differ in its predictions of the effect of a money supply expansion via open-market operations and a money supply expansion via a reduction in minimum reserve requirements? Use a figure such as Figure 7.1 to reach your conclusions.
11. Is the long-run equilibrium of Dornbusch's overshooting theory consistent with the monetary theory of exchange rates?
12. Why does the interest rate return to its initial level in the Dornbusch overshooting theory after an increase in the stock of money to a new level?

BIBLIOGRAPHY

BILSON, JOHN F. O.: "The Monetary Approach to the Exchange Rate: Some Empirical Evidence," *Staff Papers,* International Monetary Fund, March 1978, pp. 48–75.
CHEN, CHAU-NAN, CHING-CHONG LAI, and TIEN-WANG TSAUR: "The Loanable Funds Theory and the Dynamics of Exchange Rates: The Mundell Model Revisited," *Journal of International Money and Finance,* June 1988, pp. 221–229.

DOOLEY, MICHAEL P., and PETER ISARD: "The Portfolio Balance Model of Exchange Rates," *International Finance Discussion Papers,* Board of Governors of the Federal Reserve, no. 141, May 1979.

DORNBUSCH, RUDIGER: "Expectations and Exchange Rate Dynamics," *Journal of Political Economy,* December 1976, pp. 1161–1176.

————: *Open Economy Macroeconomics,* 2d ed., Basic Books, New York, 1988.

HOOPER, PETER, and JOHN MORTON: "Fluctuations in the Dollar: A Model of Nominal and Real Exchange Rate Determination," *Journal of International Money and Finance,* April 1982, pp. 39–56.

STULTZ, RENÉ M.: "Currency Preferences, Purchasing Power Risks and the Determination of Exchange Rates in an Optimizing Model," *Journal of Money, Credit and Banking,* August 1984, pp. 302–316.

"Why Exchange Rates Change," *The Economist,* Schools Brief, November 24, 1984, pp. 66–67.

CHAPTER 8

Alternative Systems of Exchange Rates

As science joins with technology to reduce man's ignorance and appease his wants at appalling speed, human institutions lag behind, the victim of memory, convention and obsolete education in man's life cycle. We see the consequences of this lag . . . at the nerve center of national sovereignties: international economic arrangements.

—ROBERT MUNDELL

When exchange rates are flexible, as they were assumed to be in Chapters 6 and 7, they are determined by the forces of private supply and demand. When exchange rates are fixed, they are determined by governments or government-controlled authorities such as central banks.[1] During the last century, several methods have been employed for fixing exchange rates. All these systems of fixed exchange rates involve mechanisms which automatically help correct deficits and surpluses in the balance of payments, a function performed by exchange rates themselves when they are flexible. One mechanism which has received particularly close attention is that involving prices. We shall explain the so-called **automatic price-adjustment mechanism** as we explain the different systems of fixed exchange rates. This is done because the differences in price-adjustment mechanisms help highlight the differences in alternative exchange-rate systems.[2]

THE CLASSICAL GOLD-STANDARD SYSTEM

The Gold Standard and Arbitrage

The essential feature of a **gold standard** is that each country stands ready to convert its paper money, or **fiat money,** into gold at a fixed price.[3] This fixing of the price of gold fixes exchange rates between paper monies. For example, if the U.S. Federal Reserve (the "Fed") agrees to buy and sell gold at $400 per ounce and the Bank of

---

[1]The exchange rate and trade systems in effect today are summarized in Appendix 8.1.

[2]Two other adjustment mechanisms, one involving national income and the other interest rates, are explained in Appendix 8.2.

[3]Fiat money is money whose face or stated value is greater than its intrinsic value. Its value comes from the edict, or fiat, that it must be accepted in discharge of financial obligations.

171

England agrees to buy and sell gold at £250 per ounce, the exchange rate between the pound and dollar in the form of paper currency or bank deposits will be $1.6/£ ($400 ÷ £250). If the exchange rate is not $1.6/£, the foreign exchange market will not balance because it will be used for converting one currency into the other, but not vice versa. For example, if the exchange rate in the foreign exchange market is $1.50/£, the market will be used for converting dollars into pounds but not for converting pounds into dollars. This is because it is cheaper for people converting pounds into dollars to buy gold from the Bank of England (one pound buys $\frac{1}{250}$ oz. of gold), ship the gold to the United States, and sell it to the Federal Reserve for dollars; for $\frac{1}{250}$ oz. the Fed pays $1.60 ($400/oz. $\times \frac{1}{250}$ oz.). This roundabout method gives more dollars per pound to those converting pounds into dollars than does the foreign exchange market, which gives only $1.50/£. On the other hand, if people converting dollars into pounds face an exchange rate of $1.50/£ on the foreign exchange market versus the $1.60/£ they would pay if they chose to buy, ship, and sell gold, they will convert dollars into pounds on the foreign exchange market: pounds are cheaper this way than via buying and selling gold.[4] Since people are converting dollars into pounds but not pounds into dollars at an exchange rate of $1.50/£, there is a demand for pounds on the foreign exchange market but no supply of pounds. This excess demand for pounds will increase the price of the pound on the foreign exchange market to $1.60/£. Similarly, if we begin with an exchange rate of $1.70/£, the foreign exchange market will be used by people converting pounds into dollars, but not by people converting dollars into pounds; the latter group will instead buy gold with dollars, ship the gold to Britain, and sell the gold for pounds. With people selling pounds and not buying pounds, the dollar value of the pound will fall until it reaches $1.60/£. Thus, if the price of gold is $400/oz. in the U.S. and £250/oz. in Britain, the equilibrium exchange rate on the foreign exchange market is $1.60/£.

We have based our argument on one-way arbitrage, that is, we have considered people who plan to exchange currencies and are looking for the cheaper of two methods: exchange via the foreign exchange market or exchange via buying, shipping, and selling gold. An alternative way of reaching the same conclusion is with round-trip arbitrage, which involves showing that if the exchange rate in our example is not $1.60/£, people can profit by buying gold, shipping the gold to the other country, selling the gold for the foreign currency, and then selling the foreign currency for domestic money. When there are no transaction costs, one-way arbitrage and round-trip arbitrage produce the same result. However, when it is costly to exchange currencies as well as to ship, buy, and sell gold, round-trip arbitrage implies too large a possible range in the exchange rate. Appendix 8.3 derives the possible range in exchange rates based on the correct, one-way arbitrage argument. The end points of the possible range are call **gold points.**

---

[4]Each pound requires selling $\frac{1}{250}$ oz. of gold to the Bank of England. To buy $\frac{1}{250}$ oz. of gold from the Federal Reserve costs $400 \times \frac{1}{250} = \$1.60$.

Price Adjustment under the Gold Standard

As we have mentioned, different exchange-rate systems involve different mechanisms for adjusting to imbalances in international payments and receipts, and one of the most discussed mechanisms involves the price level. The price-level adjustment mechanism under the gold standard is known as the **price-specie automatic adjustment mechanism,** where "specie" is just another word for precious metal. This mechanism was explained as early as 1752.[5] In order to explain the mechanism, let us continue to assume that gold is $400/oz. in the U.S. and £250/oz. in Britain and that the resulting exchange rate is $1.60/£. Let us also assume that Britain buys more goods and services from the United States than the United States buys from Britain, that is, Britain has a trade deficit with the United States. The price-specie adjustment mechanism explains how the British deficit and the U.S. surplus are corrected in the following manner.

With Britain buying more goods and services from the United States than the United States is buying from Britain, there is an excess supply of pounds; more pounds are supplied by residents of Britain than are demanded by residents of the United States. With flexible exchange rates this situation would reduce the value of the pound below $1.60/£, but with a gold standard in place such a reduction will not happen because nobody will sell pounds in the foreign exchange market for less than $1.60. Rather, as soon as the pound dips even slightly below $1.60, people will sell pounds to the Bank of England in return for gold, ship the gold to the United States, and sell the gold to the Federal Reserve for dollars. This gives people $1.60 for each pound. Therefore, the result of the British balance-of-payments deficit is the movement of gold from the Bank of England to the Federal Reserve.

An alternative way of reaching this conclusion is to assume that all international transactions are settled in gold, so that if Britain buys more goods and services from the United States than the United States buys from Britain, more gold leaves Britain than arrives in Britain, with the reverse being the case for the United States. Whatever way we view it, we have gold leaving the deficit country, Britain, and arriving in the surplus country, the United States.

The movement of gold from the deficit country, Britain, to the surplus country, the United States, has effects on both countries' money supplies. In standing ready to exchange gold for paper money at a fixed price, central banks have to make sure they have sufficient gold on hand for those occasions when many people wish to return paper money for gold. Prudent banking requires that a minimum ratio of gold reserves to paper money be held, and indeed, this used to be mandated in many countries, including the United States, where a gold reserve equal to 25 percent of circulating currency was required. The maintenance of a minimum reserve ratio means that as the Bank of England loses gold it is forced to reduce the amount of its paper money in circulation. At the same time, the increase in the Federal Reserve's gold reserves allows the Federal Reserve to put more paper money into circulation.

In the minds of the eighteenth-century classical economists who described the working of the gold standard, the fall in the money supply in the deficit country would cause a general fall in prices. At the same time, the increase in the money

---

[5]David Hume, "Of the Balance of Trade," in *Essays on Money,* Political Discourses, London, 1752, reprinted in Richard Cooper, *International Finance,* Penguin, Baltimore, 1969.

supply in the surplus country (in the simplified world we are describing, one country's deficit is the other country's surplus) would cause a general increase in prices. The link between the money supply and prices that the classical economists had in mind was the **quantity theory of money.** This theory predicts that prices change in proportion to changes in the money supply. With prices falling in the deficit country, Britain, and increasing in the surplus country, the United States, there is a decline in British prices versus U.S. prices. This makes British exports more competitive in the United States, helping them increase. At the same time, U.S. goods in Britain become less competitive than Britain's own import substitutes, so that British imports decline.[6] With British exports increasing and imports decreasing, Britain's deficit declines. Indeed, until the deficit has been completely eliminated there will be an excess supply of pounds, the sale of pounds to the Bank of England, the shipment of gold to the United States, a decrease in the British money supply, an increase in the U.S. money supply, increasing competitiveness of British products at home and abroad, and a continued reduction in the British deficit.

The price-specie adjustment mechanism works not only via changes in relative prices *between* countries but also via changes in relative prices *within* each country. In the deficit country, for example, the prices of nontraded goods will decline, but the prices of goods which enter international trade will remain unchanged. This is because prices of traded goods are determined by world supply and demand, not by the local money supply. The fall in the relative prices of nontraded goods in the deficit country will encourage local consumers to switch from traded goods to nontraded goods. At the same time, local producers will find it relatively more profitable to produce traded goods. The switch in consumer spending will free more exports, and the producers will produce more export items. These effects will be reinforced by developments in the surplus countries. The prices of nontraded goods there will rise in relation to the prices of traded goods, switching consumers toward traded goods and producers away from them. Altogether, we shall find more exports from deficit countries, fewer imports, and an improved balance of payments.[7]

Unfortunately for the effectiveness of the price-specie automatic adjustment mechanism of the gold standard, governments were often tempted to abandon the required reserve ratio between gold and paper money when the maintenance of that ratio ran counter to other objectives. If a deficit is not allowed to reduce the money supply because, for example, the government thinks the reduction will raise interest rates or unemployment to intolerable levels, the adjustment mechanism is lost. If, at the same time, the surplus countries with rising gold reserves do not allow their money supplies to grow from surpluses because of, for example, a fear of inflation, then both causes of a relative price-level adjustment are lost: we lose the lower prices in the deficit country and the higher prices elsewhere. The policy of not allowing a change in reserves to change the supply of money is known as **sterilization**, or **neutralization policy**. As goals of full employment became common in the

---

[6]However, we showed in Chapter 6 that, even if Britain buys a smaller *quantity* of imports from the United States because U.S. goods become more expensive, there could be an increase in the total *value* of imports. This would occur if the British demand for imports is inelastic.

[7]For an account of this and other fixed-exchange-rate adjustment systems, see Rudiger Dornbusch, *Open Economy Macroeconomics,* 2d ed. Basic Books, New York, 1988, or Leland Yeager, *International Money Relations: Theory, History, and Policy,* 2d ed., Harper & Row, New York 1976, Chapter 5.

twentieth century, many countries abandoned their efforts to maintain the required reserve ratio and focused on their local economic ills.

As a result of sterilization, the gold standard was not allowed to work. This is the most common criticism of the system. Not allowing the system to work does not mean that it *could not have* worked. However, some economists, most notably Robert Triffin, have said that it could not work.[8] Central to this view is the notion that prices are rigid downward (a feature of Keynesian economics) and that therefore deficits from gold outflows cannot be self-correcting via the automatic price-adjustment mechanism. Critics of the gold standard support this view with evidence on the parallel movement of prices in surplus and deficit countries, rather than the reverse movement implied by the gold standard.

It is true that without a decline in *absolute* prices, improving the balance of trade of deficit countries is more difficult. However, it is *relative* prices which are relevant (including those of nontraded versus traded goods *within* the country), and these prices could decline if surplus countries' prices rose to a greater extent than those of deficit countries. If, therefore, prices are flexible upward and surplus countries' prices rise faster than those of deficit countries, we still have an automatic price-adjustment mechanism, although it is weaker than the mechanism that might have existed if absolute prices could fall. The other common criticism of the gold standard—that gold flows were frequently sterilized—is a valid criticism, but it is as much a criticism of governments—for not allowing the gold standard to operate—as it is of the gold standard itself.

A number of twentieth-century economists and politicians have favored a return to the gold standard. What appeals to the proponents of this system is the discipline that the gold standard placed on the expansion of the money supply and the check that this therefore placed on the creeping evil of inflation.[9] The economists who prefer a return to the gold standard include Jacques Rueff and Michael Heilperin.[10] Politicians who have endorsed such a move include the late French president Charles de Gaulle and New York congressman Jack Kemp. A return to the gold standard, or some standard based on gold, would make exchange-rate forecasting a relatively straightforward task. The exchange rate in normal times would vary within the gold points, which are set by the buying or selling prices of gold at the central banks and by the cost of shipping gold from country to country. Larger changes in exchange rates would occur when countries changed the prices of their currencies in terms of gold, and this would be a reasonably predictable event. Countries that were running out of reserves would raise the price of gold, while countries that were gaining reserves might lower it.

[8]Robert Triffin, "The Myth and Realities of the So-called Gold Standard," *The Evolution of the International Monetary System: Historical Reappraisal and Future Perspective,* Princeton University Press, Princeton, N.J., 1964; reprinted in Richard Cooper, *International Finance,* Penguin, Baltimore, 1969.
[9]In the nineteenth century, rather than favoring the gold standard because it kept inflation under control, many opposed it on the grounds it was deflationary. As Exhibit 8.1 explains, the political debate over ending the gold standard and replacing it with a **bimetallic standard** was sufficiently intense to spawn the famous allegorical children's classic *The Wonderful Wizard of Oz.*
[10]See Jacques Rueff, "Gold Exchange Standard: A Danger to the West," *The Times* (London), June 27–29, 1961, reprinted in Herbert G. Grubel (ed.), *International Monetary Reform: Plans and Issues,* Stanford University Press, Palo Alto, Calif., 1963; and Michael Heilperin, "The Case for Going Back to Gold," *Fortune,* September 1962, also reprinted in Grubel, ibid.

THE BRETTON WOODS AND DOLLAR STANDARDS

The Mechanics of the Bretton Woods System

With a gold standard, exchange rates, or at least their ranges of potential variation, are determined indirectly via the conversion price of each currency vis-à-vis gold. When the gold standard came to an end with the depression of 1929–1933—after temporary abandonment in 1914—the exchange-rate system which eventually replaced it in 1944 offered an alternative method of determination of exchange rates. The system adopted in 1944 is called the **gold-exchange standard.** It is also called the **Bretton Woods system** after the town in New Hampshire at which its outlines were worked out. This alternative method of determining exchange rates allowed movement in exchange rates between **support points.** Support points were the exchange rates at which foreign central banks purchased or sold their currency for U.S. dollars to ensure that the exchange rate did not move beyond these points. In return for foreign central banks' fixing, or **pegging,** their currencies to the U.S. dollar, the United States fixed the price of the U.S. dollar to gold. Therefore, the gold-exchange standard involved:

1. An offer by the United States to exchange U.S. dollars for gold at an official price
2. Offers by other countries to exchange their currencies for dollars around an official, or **parity,** exchange rate

We shall deal with the history of the international financial system in the next chapter, but we can note that the ability to convert foreign *privately* held gold to dollars by the United States lasted until 1968, and the ability to convert foreign *officially* held gold lasted until 1971. With only the second part of the gold-exchange standard remaining in effect—that part involving the exchange of foreign currencies for dollars—the fixed exchange system from 1968 until the end of the Bretton Woods system in 1973 is best described as a **dollar standard.**

Under the gold-exchange standard and the dollar standard, countries which pegged their exchange rates to the U.S. dollar were required to keep the actual rate within 1 percent of the selected parity value. In order to ensure that the exchange rate vis-à-vis the dollar remained within the required 1 percent of official parity, it was necessary for central banks to intervene whenever free-market forces would have created an exchange rate that was outside the range. This intervention took the form of buying and selling the local currency for U.S. dollars at the upper and lower support points around official parity. The support points meant adding to or reducing central-bank official reserves whenever the uncontrolled exchange rate would have moved beyond the official limits. We can illustrate the way these fixed exchange standards operated by using a diagram.

Suppose that the Bank of England has decided, as it did from 1949 to 1967, to peg the value of the pound within 1 percent of a parity value of $2.80. The upper and lower support points that the bank must maintain are $2.8280/£ and $2.7720/£. These are shown on the vertical axis of Figure 8.1, which gives the spot price of pounds in terms of dollars. The horizontal axis gives the quantity of pounds, and so the diagram has the price and quantity axes familiar from the theory of supply and demand. We have added to the diagram conventionally sloping supply and demand curves for pounds drawn against the price of pounds (measured in dollars). We have drawn the initial private demand curve for pounds, $D_1(£)$, intersecting the private supply curve of pounds, $S(£)$, within the 1 percent range allowed under the gold-exchange and dollar standards.

Suppose that for some exogenous reason there is an increase in demand for British exports. This might, for example, be because of a general economic expansion outside of Britain, a change in taste toward British goods, or the discovery of oil in the North Sea. This will shift the private demand curve for pounds to the right, from $D_1(£)$ to $D_2(£)$, and the private demand for pounds will then intersect the private supply curve at an exchange rate above the allowed ceiling. In order to prevent

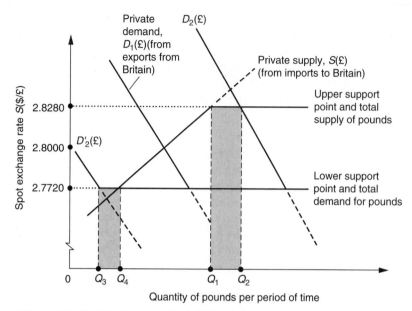

Figure 8.1. The Workings of the Gold-Exchange and Dollar Standards
The Bank of England stood ready to buy pounds at the lower support point and sell
pounds at the upper support point. This made the demand curve for pounds
perfectly elastic at the lower support point and the supply curve of pounds
perfectly elastic at the upper support point, ensuring that the exchange rate fell in
the allowable range.

this, the Bank of England must, according to the gold-exchange and dollar standards, intervene at the upper support point of \$2.8280/£ and supply, in exchange
for dollars, the pounds necessary to keep the rate from moving above this level. In
terms of Figure 8.1, the Bank of England will supply Q_1Q_2 pounds for dollars. This,
with the private supply of $0Q_1$ pounds and the demand curve of $D_2(£)$, would leave
the exchange rate at \$2.8280/£. Because the Bank of England will supply whatever
number of pounds is required at the upper support point, the total supply curve of
pounds becomes flat at this point, like the solidly drawn line in Figure 8.1. This is a
feature of the gold-exchange and dollar standards; the total supply curve of the local
currency—consisting of private and official supply—becomes perfectly elastic at
the upper support point.

While the Bank of England supplies Q_1Q_2 pounds in Figure 8.1, it will be buying Q_1Q_2 times 2.8280 of U.S. dollars, which is the shaded area above Q_1Q_2. The
amount Q_1Q_2 is the gain in the Bank of England's foreign exchange reserves (its
balance-of-payments surplus) valued in terms of pounds, and the shaded area above
Q_1Q_2 is the gain in foreign exchange reserves, valued in terms of dollars.

Suppose that instead of rising to $D_2(£)$, the demand for pounds falls to $D_2'(£)$ as
a result of, perhaps, a general slowdown in economic activity outside of Britain or a
decline in oil prices: Britain is an oil-exporting nation. According to private supply
and demand, the price of the pound will fall below the lower support point, and to
prevent this from happening, the Bank of England has to enter the market and purchase pounds. It will purchase Q_3Q_4 pounds with $2.7720 \times Q_3Q_4$ U.S. dollars. The

dollar amount is given by the shaded area above Q_3Q_4; it represents the decline in dollar reserves of the Bank of England. It is hence the deficit in the balance of payments, measured in U.S. dollars. Because the Bank of England must demand whatever number of pounds is not wanted by private buyers, the total demand for pounds that includes both private and official demand is horizontal at the lower support point, $2.7720/£. This is another feature of the gold-exchange and dollar standards: the total demand curve for local currencies becomes perfectly elastic at the lower support point.

Price Adjustment under the Gold-Exchange and Dollar Standards

To explain the price-level adjustment mechanism of the gold-exchange and dollar standards, we refer to the situation in Figure 8.2. Suppose that after starting with $S_1(£)$ and $D_1(£)$ and a privately determined exchange rate within the allowed range, there is an increase in private demand for pounds to $D_2(£)$. As before, the Bank of

Figure 8.2. The Price-Level Adjustment Mechanism of the Gold-Exchange and Dollar Standards

If the demand for pounds moves to $D_2(£)$ and the quantity of pounds demanded exceeds the quantity supplied at the upper support point, the Bank of England must sell pounds in exchange for dollars. *Ceteris paribus,* this increases the British money supply and prices. Higher prices make British exports decline, shifting the demand curve for pounds back toward $D_2'(£)$. Higher prices also increase imports into Britain, and the currency supply curve shifts from $S_1(£)$ toward $S_2(£)$. Shifts in currency demand and supply curves move equilibrium exchange rates toward their allowable limits.

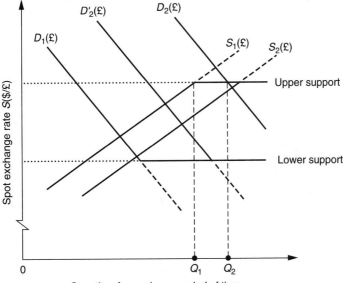

England will be required to supply Q_1Q_2 pounds. These pounds will increase the money supply in Britain; this occurs as the Bank of England sells pounds for dollars. If we again assume that prices vary with the money supply, the increase in the number of pounds in circulation will raise British prices. At each exchange rate on our vertical axis, this will lower the competitiveness of British goods. Exports will fall, assuming the demand for exports is elastic so that quantity declines more than export prices increase, and imports will increase. The decline in British exports will mean a lower demand for pounds. Therefore, the demand curve for pounds will move to the left. We assume that it moves to $D_2'(\pounds)$. The increase in British imports will mean a larger supply of pounds to the foreign exchange market, and so the private supply curve moves to the right. We move it to $S_2(\pounds)$. With the demand and supply curves at $D_2'(\pounds)$ and $S_2(\pounds)$, the privately determined exchange rate will return to the allowed range.

We find that intervention by a central bank affects the supply of money, local prices, and exports and imports and thus restores equilibrium between private supply and demand. Of course, if there is sterilization of the balance-of-payments surplus or deficit and the money supply is not allowed to change, the price-level adjustment mechanism will not work. Sterilization will result in a continued change in foreign exchange reserves and a need to eventually revise the parity exchange rate. This makes exchange-rate forecasting a potentially highly rewarding activity since the need to change the parity value becomes clearly apparent in foreign exchange reserve statistics. It is worthwhile to consider how exchange-rate forecasting can be done.

We have already noted that when exchange rates are determined on a gold standard, changes in exchange rates are likely to follow large changes in gold reserves. For example, a country that is losing reserves will eventually be forced to raise the price of gold in terms of its own currency. This means a fall in the foreign exchange value of the currency. To take an example, if Britain were losing gold and raised its gold price from £250 per ounce to £300 per ounce while the U.S. price remained fixed at $400 per ounce, the exchange rate would change from

$$S(\$/\pounds) = \frac{\$400/\text{ounce}}{\pounds250/\text{ounce}} = \$1.60/\pounds$$

to

$$S(\$/\pounds) = \frac{\$400/\text{ounce}}{\pounds300/\text{ounce}} = \$1.33/\pounds$$

This is a devaluation of the pound.

By keeping track of gold reserves, a speculator could see when a central bank was under pressure to raise the price of gold, that is, to devalue. The exact date would be difficult to predict, but actions based on such an assumption would be unlikely to result in losses. A country that is losing reserves might manage not to devalue, but it certainly would not revalue, that is, raise the value of its currency by reducing the official price of gold. This means that a speculator would discover either that he or she was correct and a devaluation did occur or that the exchange rate remained as before. Thus there is an opportunity for a one-way bet, and the worst that is likely to happen is that no speculative gain will be made. Indeed, widespread speculation that a devaluation will occur is likely to make it occur. Speculation against a currency causes the central bank to buy its own currency, reducing foreign exchange reserves, thereby making devaluation appear even more likely. For example, prior to the devaluations of the Mexican peso in 1980 and 1994–1995, speculators had decided that a peso devaluation was imminent. They therefore sold pesos, and the Mexican authorities were required to purchase them at the lower support point. The pesos were purchased with U.S. dollars, and hence the Mexican reserves were lowered. Eventually, reserves were so much reduced that the Mexican government was forced to devalue. The speculators' beliefs were vindicated. In a sense, their expectations were self-fulfilling.

The need to reduce the value of a currency in a country experiencing deficits and declining reserves depends on the ability of the central bank to borrow additional reserves. There are arrangements between central banks for exchanging currency reserves, and procedures for borrowing from international institutions such as the International Monetary Fund (which is discussed in the next chapter). The borrowing arrangements include **central-bank swaps**; for example, the U.S. government might make U.S. dollars available to the Bank of Canada when Canadian foreign exchange reserves are low. The Bank of Canada temporarily swaps these U.S. dollars for Canadian dollars. The swap is reversed later, according to the original agreement. Often the swap is reversed only after a number of years to allow the borrowing country to correct its balance of payments. Central banks also frequently borrow from private banks. The Bank of Canada, for example, borrowed heavily from both Canadian and U.S. commercial banks during early 1995 despite the fact that the exchange rate was supposed to be flexible. The ability of central banks to borrow from other central banks, from private banks, and from international institutions makes the forecasting of exchange rates more difficult; revisions of par values can be delayed many years.

Another factor adding to the difficulty of forecasting changes in "fixed" rates is the difference in the need to react to surpluses and deficits. Countries that are facing a deficit and losing reserves will eventually be forced into a devaluation because their reserves and ability to borrow will eventually be gone. On the other hand, the countries enjoying surpluses will be under no pressure to revalue their currencies and may instead allow reserves to keep growing. This represents one of the major problems with the gold-exchange and dollar standards, namely, that the responsibility for adjustment, whether this be via a change in the exchange rate or via an automatic change in money supplies and prices, falls on deficit countries more heavily than on surplus countries. This problem of asymmetric need for adjustment between deficit and surplus countries under the gold-exchange and dollar standards is one of the major differences between these fixed-exchange-rate systems and the European Monetary System.

THE EUROPEAN MONETARY SYSTEM (EMS)

The Structure of the EMS

At virtually the same time as the dollar standard collapsed, a new fixed-exchange-rate system emerged among the European Union (EU) countries. This new system began in 1972 as the **snake,** which was designed to keep the EU countries' exchange rates within a narrower band than had been adopted as part of a last-minute attempt to salvage the dollar standard. The snake involved maintaining exchange rates within $1\frac{1}{8}$ percent of either side of selected par values, compared to the $2\frac{1}{4}$ percent deviations allowed as part of a revision to the dollar standard in 1971. The snake got its name from the shape of the time path of EU exchange rates "wiggling" within the wider band allowed for other exchange rates. The snake, with some refinements including a widening of the band to $2\frac{1}{4}$ percent deviations, became the **Exchange Rate Mechanism (ERM)** of the **European Monetary System (EMS)** in 1979.

A central feature of the ERM was a **grid** that placed an upper and lower limit on the possible exchange rates between each pair of member currencies. The grid took the form of a matrix showing for each pair of currencies the par value as well as the highest and lowest permitted exchange rates, these being $2\frac{1}{4}$ percent above and below the par rates. That is, the matrix, which listed the currencies across the columns and down the rows, had three exchange rates in each element: the par value, an upper limit, and a lower limit. If an exchange rate was at either limit, *both* countries were supposed to intervene. For example, if the Belgian franc was at its lower support point vis-à-vis the German mark, the Belgian authorities were required to buy Belgian francs *and* the German authorities were also supposed to sell marks. The fact that the Germans were also supposed to sell marks made the ERM fundamentally different from the gold-exchange and dollar standards. As we have seen, under the gold-exchange and dollar standards, if, for example, the pound was at its lower support point, Britain was required to buy pounds with dollars, but the U.S. was not required to cooperate by selling dollars for pounds. Under the ERM, Germany was supposed to sell Deutschemarks if the Deutschemark was at its upper limit against the Belgian franc, whether or not Germany liked the implications of having the increasing money supply the sale of Deutschemarks brought about.

Partly because of the no-fault nature of the ERM, a **divergence indicator** was designed to identify if, for example, the Belgian franc was at its lower support point vis-à-vis the Deutschemark because of overly expansive Belgian monetary policy or overly restrictive Germany monetary policy. The divergence indicator was based on the value of the **European Currency Unit (ECU).**[11]

The ECU was an artificial unit defined as a weighted average of each of the EMS currencies. Each EMS country was required to maintain its exchange rate within a specified range of the ECU, as well as within a specific range vis-à-vis the other individual EMS currencies. This served to indicate which country was at fault when a currency approached a limit vis-à-vis another currency, because the country at fault would also be close to its limit vis-à-vis the ECU. For example, if it was inflationary Belgian policy that forced the Belgian franc down vis-à-vis the German mark, the Belgian franc was also likely to be low against other currencies, and hence against the ECU. The country that was at fault was required to take corrective action or explain to other EMS members why it should not. Only as a last resort were par values realigned, although this happened on several occasions.

The ECU served an additional role in denominating loans among the EMS

---

[11]The acronym of the European Currency Unit, ECU, or *écu,* is the name of a silver coin that once circulated in France.

countries. For example, if Belgium borrowed from Holland to defend its exchange rate vis-à-vis the Dutch guilder or against the ECU, the loan could be denominated in ECUs. Private loans could also be denominated in ECUs. This reduced foreign exchange risk to the borrower and lender because the value of the ECU was likely to be more stable than the value of individual currencies; the ECU was like a portfolio of currencies, and as such offered some diversification benefits. The ECU was also used to denominate loans made by the **European Monetary Co-operation Fund, or EMCF.** The EMCF made short-term and medium-term readjustment loans to EMS members out of a pool of funds at the **Bank for International Settlements (BIS)** located in Basle, Switzerland. These lending arrangements as well as other detailed aspects of the EMS are dealt with in Exhibit 8.2.

The EMS ran into trouble during 1992. Britain was in severe recession with unemployment rates higher than at any other time since the Great Depression of 1929–1933. Despite the recession, inflation had been relatively high, certainly vis-à-vis inflation in Germany during the several years prior to 1992. Italy was also experiencing recession and high inflation. These conditions in Britain and Italy occurred while Germany was experiencing its costly reunification. This required unprecedented offshore borrowing, and this in turn put German interest rates up; the need to attract capital meant German rates were above those in, for example, the United

---

EXHIBIT 8.2
Alphabet Soup: ERM, EMS, ECU, and All That

The European Monetary System was an attempt to improve upon Bretton Woods, keeping some of its features and adding new ones where necessary. The following article succinctly summarizes the important similarities and differences.

Like Bretton Woods, the EMS was based on a set of fixed parties called the Exchange Rate Mechanism (ERM). Each country was to establish a central parity of its currency in terms of ECU, the official unit of account. The ECU consisted of a basket containing a set number of units of each currency. As the value of currencies varied, the weights of each country in the basket would change. A parity grid of all bilateral rates could then be derived from the ratio of members' central rates. Again, like Bretton Woods, each currency was bounded by a set of margins of 2.25 percent on either side of parity, creating a total band of 4.5 percent (for Italy, and later the United Kingdom, when it joined the ERM in 1990, the margin was set at 6 percent on either side of parity). The monetary authorities of both the depreciating and appreciating countries were required to intervene when a currency hit one of the margins. Countries were also allowed, but not required, to undertake intramarginal intervention. The indicator of divergences, which measured each currency's average deviation from the central parity, was devised as a signal for the monetary authorities to take policy actions to strengthen or weaken their currencies. It was supposed to work symmetrically.

Intervention and adjustment was to be financed under a complicated set of arrangements. These arrangements were designed to overcome the weaknesses of the IMF during Bretton Woods. The very short-term financing facility (VSTF) was to provide credibility to the bilateral parties by ensuring unlimited financing for marginal intervention. It provided automatic unlimited lines of credit from the creditor to the debtor members. The short-term monetary support (STMS) was designed to provide short-term finance for temporary balance of payments disequilibrium. The medium-term financial assistance (MTFA) would provide longer-term support.

Unlike Bretton Woods, where members (other than the United States) could effectively decide to unilaterally alter their parities, changes in central parities were to be decided collectively. Finally, like Bretton Woods, members could (and did) impose capital controls.

Source: Michael D. Bordo, "The Gold Standard, Bretton Woods and Other Monetary Regimes: A Historical Appraisal," *Review,* Federal Reserve Bank of St. Louis, March/April 1993, p. 180.

States, a stark reversal of traditional interest rate differentials. The high German interest rates put upward pressure on the Deutschemark, forcing Britain and Italy to raise interest rates if they were to keep their exchange rates within the EMS limits. Doubting Britain and Italy would do this, speculators sold British pounds and Italian lire hoping to gain from eventual devaluation. Germany refused to make any major concession by lowering interest rates, eventually forcing Britain and Italy to withdraw from the EMS in September 1992.

The European currency crisis of 1992 was matched in the following summer by a run on the French franc that eventually brought about a collapse of the EMS in August 1993. Only Germany and Holland decided to keep their currencies closely linked. The others agreed to a 15 percent deviation on either side of EMS-agreed par values. With a 30 percent range of variation, in effect the EMS fixed-rate era was over. Nevertheless, the European Union ministers have continued to cling to the **Maastricht Agreement**, which commits the Union members to work to establish a **common currency.** A common currency would mean truly fixed rates, because with all European member countries using the same currency, exchange rates could never change.

Price Adjustment under the EMS

Our explanation of the price-level adjustment mechanism of the gold-exchange and dollar standards applies also to the EMS, with the one major difference that with the EMS, both countries' money supplies were influenced by official intervention. For example, if the Belgian franc was at its lower support point versus the Deutschemark, the Belgian money supply declined and the German money supply increased. *Ceteris paribus,* this reduced the Belgian price level and increased the German price level. This improved Belgium's trade in comparison with Germany's because of the lowering of Belgian prices versus German prices. Because prices in both countries contributed to the automatic adjustment—rather than just one country's prices contributing, as with the gold-exchange and dollar standards—the EMS price-adjustment mechanism was in principle relatively more effective. Furthermore, the requirement that both countries intervene helped overcome the problem of asymmetric needs for adjustment, a problem that detrimentally affected the functioning of the gold-exchange and dollar standards.

The EMS did allow for realignment of central values of the parity grid, and indeed there were several realignments. Forecasting when realignment would occur was made difficult by the cooperation built into the EMS in terms of joint foreign exchange market intervention, intercountry short-term lending, and loans from the EMCF. Nevertheless, as with the gold-exchange and dollar standards, it became evident to speculators when a currency needed to be realigned, not least because of the currency's value vis-à-vis the ECU. This meant that speculators could guess which way the realignment would go. Indeed, as we have explained, pressure from speculators eventually helped bring about the collapse of the EMS.

HYBRID SYSTEMS OF EXCHANGE RATES

Fixed and flexible exchange rates are only two alternatives defining the extremes of exchange-rate systems. In between these extremes are a number of other systems which have been practiced at various times.

Dirty Float

Central banks sometimes intervene in the foreign exchange markets even when they have declared that exchange rates are flexible. For example, Canada, which practiced floating exchange rates throughout the 1950s and has floated its currency since 1970, frequently intervenes (via the Bank of Canada) to "maintain order" in the foreign exchange markets. The Canadian central bank's policy is to try to prevent sharp changes in its exchange rate but to allow market forces to operate over the long run. The purpose of this policy is to reduce short-run exchange-rate uncertainty but to allow the exchange rate to reflect differential rates of inflation and other fundamental forces over the long run. The Bank of Canada combines foreign exchange market intervention with interest-rate policy to stabilize Canada's exchange rate. This model of a so-called dirty float is a compromise between fixed and flexible exchange rates, and it has been adopted by several other countries.

Wider Band

Another compromise between fixed and flexible exchange rates was tried for a very short while after December 1971, when the International Monetary Fund members decided at a meeting at the Smithsonian Institution in Washington, D.C., to allow the range of fluctuation of exchange rates to be $2\frac{1}{4}$ percent on either side of the official value. This gave a $4\frac{1}{2}$ percent total range of variation before the central bank would intervene, compared with the 2 percent range that existed from 1944 to 1971. The intention was to reduce the uncertainty about future exchange rates and at the same time allow more adjustment. The wider the band, the closer the system came to being a flexible-rate system.

The **wider band** was not tried by many of the major countries. Canada had opted for a floating rate before the Smithsonian meeting, and Britain and the other major European countries floated their currencies (some of which remained fixed to each other) shortly afterward.[12]

Crawling Peg

The **crawling peg** is an automatic system for revising the par, or central, value—the value around which the rate can fluctuate. This system can be combined with a wider band. The crawling peg requires the central bank to intervene whenever the exchange rate approaches a support point. However, the central value, around which the support points are set, is revised according to the average exchange rate over the previous weeks or months. If the rate tends to remain at or near, for example, the lower support point, the new central value will be revised downward. In this way the rate can drift up or down gradually, giving some degree of certainty without completely frustrating long-term fundamental trends.

Figure 8.3 illustrates a crawling peg. Starting at time t_0, intervention points are defined which are above and below a middle or par exchange rate. The intervention points are shown by parallel lines. If the actual exchange rate hovers at the lower end of its allowed range, then at the next setting of the intervention points the middle

---

[12]For more on the wider band see John Williamson, "Surveys in Applied Economics: International Liquidity," *Economic Journal,* September 1973, pp. 685–746.

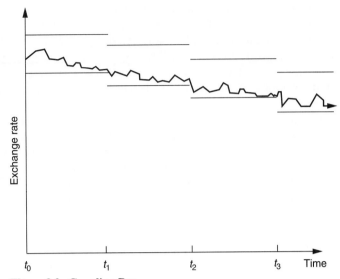

Figure 8.3. Crawling Peg
Under a crawling-peg system, the support points are periodically
revised according to a formula typically based on economic
fundamentals such as inflation differentials, or according to past
behavior of the exchange rate within its permissible band.

value is set at the average actual value during the previous period. If the actual
exchange rate moves to the lower end of the new allowable trading range, the intervention points are again lowered at the next setting of these points. In this way the
exchange rate can drift according to fundamental forces such as inflation rates, but
importers and exporters can be reasonably sure about exchange rates applying to
short-term foreign-currency receivables and payables.

An alternative way of readjusting the band within which a currency can trade is
according to recent rates of inflation. For example, the central value of the band vis-
à-vis the U.S. dollar could be changed by the country's inflation rate minus the U.S.
inflation rate. This keeps exchange rates moving directly according to economic
fundamentals over long periods of time, but keeps them predictable in the short
term. A crawling peg can also be based on balance-of-trade statistics or changes in
external debt. Most examples of crawling pegs have involved countries experiencing
very rapid inflation. Several South American countries have at some time tried a
crawling peg.

Mixed Fixed and Flexible Rates

Another compromise between fixed and flexible exchange rates that has been tried
is to have fixed exchange rates for some transactions, such as those on the current
account of the balance of payments, but to have flexible rates for other transactions,
such as those on the capital account. This division of systems would be motivated by
a desire not to exert influence over international trade but to maintain control over
capital flows. Such a dual exchange-rate system was practiced by Belgium, which

had a commercial exchange rate for imports and exports of goods and services and a financial exchange rate for trading in financial assets. The commercial exchange rate was fixed, and the financial exchange rate was flexible. Only authorized banks were permitted to trade in the commercial market, while the financial market was open to all participants. The two tiers of the foreign exchange market were separated by a prohibition on buying foreign exchange in one market and selling it in the other.

Britain operated with two exchange rates for more than a quarter century while functioning under the Exchange Control Act of 1947. This act was designed to restrict capital outflows and required those making foreign investments to buy foreign currency from a **currency pool.** Funds in the pool came only from sales of securities trading in a currency or from occasional authorized additions. As a result the size of the pool of each currency was determined by the value of investments when the pool was established, subsequent realized gains on the value of investments, and special authorized additions. Exchange rates for investment funds from the pool were flexible and usually traded at a premium over exchange rates for non-investment transactions. The exchange rates for other transactions were fixed over most of the years the currency-pool system was in effect.

Numerous other mixed exchange-rate systems have been tried, such as different exchange rates for imports versus exports, different exchange rates for different categories of imports, and so on, but these other systems are combinations of different fixed rates, not mixtures of fixed and flexible rates. Those interested in the other types of arrangements can consult *Exchange Arrangements and Restrictions,* shown in Appendix 8.1.

Cooperative Intervention in Disorderly Markets

After a period of considerable volatility in exchange rates, involving a substantial appreciation of the U.S. dollar from its 1980 level and an equally sharp fall after 1985, a new compromise exchange-rate system was agreed to at an economic summit held in Paris at the Louvre Museum in 1987. This agreement, which became known as the **Louvre Accord,** represented a shift from a completely flexible exchange-rate system to a dirty float in which the leading industrial powers would cooperate.

The Louvre Accord followed the **Plaza Agreement** of 1985—named after the Plaza Hotel in New York where it was worked out—in which the United States accepted the need to intervene in the foreign exchange markets during unstable times. The other leading industrial powers had recognized this need somewhat earlier but knew that intervention would not work without close cooperation, given the very large size of private speculative capital flows. The Plaza Agreement was later confirmed at the 1986 Tokyo economic summit and reconfirmed at other economic summits, most notably the 1987 meeting in Paris that resulted in the Louvre Accord. These meetings took place against a background of immense exchange-rate instability and resulted in a new compromise between completely flexible and completely fixed exchange rates. The meetings up to and including the 1986 Tokyo summit involved the United States, Japan, United Kingdom, West Germany, and France—the so-called **Group of Five**, or **G-5.** Subsequent meetings were expanded to include Canada—the U.S.'s largest trading partner—and Italy and thus became known as the **G-7 summits.** The system that emerged is not unlike Canada's approach of flexibility with intervention to achieve orderly markets, but because it involves cooperation, it is a little different from the Canadian dirty float.

The international financial system that emerged from the Louvre Accord can be characterized as a floating-exchange-rate system within **target zones** that are periodically revised but for which the intervention levels are not precisely specified. The acceptable ranges of fluctuation have to be deduced from official communiqués released after summit meetings, or from statements by senior officials of the nations involved. For example, it might be stated after a G-7 meeting that the leaders are satisfied with exchange rates in their recent trading range. Alternatively, after a substantial movement of exchange rates, the governor of a central bank or a treasury official might say he or she believes that the dollar is too low or too high and that if the markets do not adjust there could be intervention. Market participants react to these statements according to how credible they believe them to be and may, for example, buy currencies the authorities say are too cheap. This process of statements and market reaction can help reduce the need for intervention and has been described as "talking" exchange rates in the officially desired direction.

TARGET ZONES

The fixed-exchange-rate and compromise systems that have been described in this chapter can be characterized as involving, at least in part, a target zone for the exchange rate. For example, the zone in the gold-exchange standard was a 2 percent band around parity, in the EMS it was a $4\frac{1}{2}$ percent band, and so on. Having a credible target zone, which is one that private foreign-exchange-market participants believe is a government commitment, can help keep exchange rates *within* the declared zone—not at the outer limits—even if governments never actually intervene in the markets. Indeed, even if there is a less-than-total commitment to a declared target zone, the presence of the zone can be self-realizing. These conclusions have been reached in research by Paul Krugman.[13]

The stabilizing role of target zones can be described with the help of Figure 8.4. The actual exchange rate, taken as $S(\$/\pounds)$, is shown on the vertical axis, while economic fundamentals affecting exchange rates are shown on the horizontal axis. Krugman assumed the fundamentals to consist of factors outside the control of government which evolve randomly, plus a factor—Krugman uses the money supply—that is under government control. Indeed, Krugman assumed that by appropriate adjustments of the money supply the government could counter any realization of the random factors, keeping the combined effects of the fundamentals—random factors plus money supply—such that the exchange rate would remain within the target zone. Krugman further assumed that the money supply is changed only at the ceiling or floor of the target zone, and not in between. That is, exchange-rate intervention occurs only at the margins, with the money supply increasing at the ceiling, declin-

---

[13]See Paul R. Krugman, "Target Zones and Exchange Rate Dynamics," *Quarterly Journal of Economics,* August 1991, pp. 669–682, and the papers in Paul R. Krugman and Marcus Miller, eds., *Exchange Rate Targets and Currency Bands,* Cambridge University Press, New York, 1992. For a survey of target-band research, see Lars E. O. Svensson, "An Interpretation of Recent Research on Exchange Rate Target Zones," *Journal of Economic Perspectives,* fall 1992, pp. 119–144.

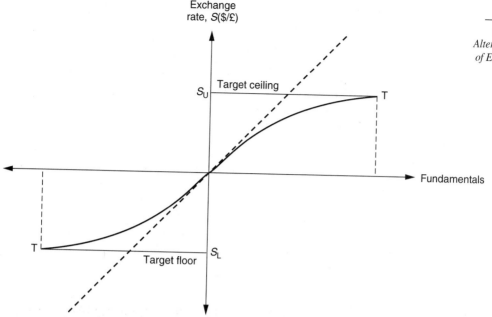

Figure 8.4. Target Zones for Exchange Rates
The horizontal axis measures fundamentals, which consist of random uncontrolled factors, and the money supply, which is changed only at the target-zone edges to keep exchange rates within the zone. Exchange rates depend on fundamentals plus expectations about the future exchange rate. To the right of the midpoint along the horizontal axis there is expected depreciation—the probability of $S(\$/£)$ being pushed down is higher than the probability of $S(\$/£)$ increasing—and to the left of the midpoint there is expected appreciation. The combined effect of fundamentals and expectations is curve TT. This is tangent to the lines at the zone edges, implying no effect of fundamentals on exchange rates at the edges of zones.

ing at the floor, and otherwise being constant. (An increase in money supply would cause inflation or lower interest rates pushing the currency down, while a decrease would achieve the reverse.)

The line showing the combined effect of the fundamentals on $S(\$/£)$ is the straight upward-sloping dashed line in Figure 8.4. This means that by adjusting the money supply as necessary at the margins—the target-zone ceiling and floor—so that the combined fundamentals are within the necessary limits, the exchange rate would remain within the target zone S_L to S_U.

Krugman realized that in addition to fundamentals, another factor affecting current exchange rates is expectations about changes in exchange rates in the future. That is, actual current exchange rates depend on current fundamentals plus exchange-rate expectations. Expectations of changes in the future exchange rate depend on how close the current exchange rate is to the intervention levels. Specifically, the closer the exchange rate is to the upper level, S_U, the more likely is intervention, in this case consisting of the Bank of England's increasing the money supply to keep the pound from exceeding S_U. Similarly, the closer is $S(\$/£)$ to S_L, the more likely is a reduction in the British money supply to keep $S(\$/£)$ from moving below S_L. This means that as the exchange rate approaches S_U, the probability of action to depreciate the pound makes the probability of depreciation exceed that of further appreciation. Therefore, there is an expected depreciation, where we use the term "expected" in the statistical sense: the probability-weighted outcomes that constitute the expected change in exchange rate are tilted toward a depreciation. As the exchange rate moves closer to S_L the reverse occurs, with the probability of official action to cause appreciation of the pound being relatively high. That is, to the right of the midpoint on the horizontal axis of Figure 8.4 there is expected depreciation of the pound in the statistical sense, and along the left there is expected appreciation. In addition, the further a point is to the right or left, the greater is the expected depreciation or appreciation.

We recall that the actual exchange rate is the result of fundamentals plus exchange-rate expectations. While *within* the target zone the fundamentals follow random patterns—intervention via money supply occurs only *at* the intervention points—the other component of exchange-rate determination, the expectation of change in the future exchange rate, pushes the rate to within the target zone. In terms of Figure 8.4, the effect of the nonrandom fundamentals on their own is for the exchange rate to follow the upward-sloping dashed line until the ceiling or floor is reached, and then to follow the horizontal lines at the ceiling or floor as the official intervention occurs. However, the other element of exchange-rate determination, namely, expectations about the future, works toward lowering current exchange rates to the right of the vertical axis in Figure 8.4 and toward raising exchange rates to the left of the vertical axis. The aggregate effect of the two forces is the elongated curve, *TT*. This curve, which is always flatter than the dashed line, makes it clear that via the prospect of intervention, the exchange rate follows a path *within* the target zone, even if the possible intervention does not occur. In some sense, stability is achieved, possibly without the government's doing anything other than *promising* to intervene if necessary.

There is a further conclusion derived from Krugman's model in addition to the "free stabilizing" conclusion we have just reached. The second conclusion is that at the edges of the target zone the exchange rate is insensitive to the fundamentals. This conclusion follows by first noting that at the target-zone edges the expected values of the total fundamentals are not continuous and random, as are the values of noncontrolled fundamentals, but rather the total fundamentals take "jumps." Specifically, at the moment the upper-edge S_U is reached there is an upward jump in money, causing an expected negative change in the fundamental. Similarly, the very moment S_L is reached there is a downward jump in the money supply, causing an expected positive change in the fundamental. (The noncontrolled fundamentals themselves *are* random.) While expected fundamentals themselves jump at the edges of the zone, the expected exchange rate cannot have jumps or there would be profit opportunities; jumps would allow one-way exchange-rate bets. It follows that if expectations of fundamentals jump at the target-zone edges but there is no corresponding jump in exchange rates at the target-zone edges, then at the edges the fundamentals cannot be affecting exchange rates. This means that *TT* is horizontal and tangent to the target-zone edges S_L and S_U; with *TT* horizontal, changes in the fundamentals have no effect on $S(\$/\£)$.

The preceding discussion assumes that intervention always occurs at the target-zone edges. While relaxation of the assumption that intervention *always* occurs does affect the preceding conclusions, there is still some stabilizing of exchange rates, even if intervention occurs only *sometimes*.[14]

---

[14]See Krugman and Miller, *op. cit.*

In this account of the many possible compromises between truly fixed and truly flexible exchange rates and the way they work, we have given a rather patchy history of international finance. In order to provide a more systematic overview, in the next chapter we present a chronology of international financial developments during the twentieth century. This chronology has been deferred so that we would be equipped with an understanding of the systems and events we describe. Our chronology should serve to give a historical perspective on the international financial system and to demonstrate that the international financial system is not static but is something that continues to evolve. Possible directions of this evolution are also sketched in the next chapter.

SUMMARY

1. A gold standard involves the open offer by central banks to exchange domestic paper money for gold at a fixed price. A deficit causes an outflow of gold. The reduction in gold reserves reduces the local money supply and puts downward pressure on prices in the deficit country. The fall in prices stimulates exports and lowers imports. In the surplus countries, the money supplies increase, raising prices in these countries. This causes a further reduction of relative prices in the deficit country. In addition, changes in relative prices *within* each country help eliminate a deficit or surplus.

2. The price-specie adjustment mechanism can be frustrated by a neutralization policy. This policy severs the link between gold flows and money supplies, so that the adjustment mechanism is lost.

3. Critics of the gold standard argue that prices in surplus and deficit countries showed parallel movement rather than the reverse movement implied by the gold standard. Downward price rigidity is responsible. However, an adjustment of relative prices will still occur if prices go up by more in surplus countries than in deficit countries. Another criticism of the gold standard is that governments did not allow it to work. This is as much a criticism of government as of the gold standard.

4. The gold-exchange standard required the United States to fix its exchange rate to gold, and other countries to fix to gold or to the U.S. dollar. This system operated from 1944 to 1968. From 1968 to 1973, the U.S. dollar was not fixed to gold, but most other currencies were still fixed to the dollar. This was called a dollar standard.

5. To maintain the fixed exchange rate in terms of the dollar, central banks must purchase or sell their local currency at the support points on either side of the parity value. If the free-market exchange rate would be above the upper support point, the central bank must sell its currency and purchase dollars. This raises official reserves and means a surplus in the balance of payments. It also raises the supply of money. At the lower support point, the central bank must purchase the local currency with dollars, which reduces official reserves and results in a deficit in the balance of payments. This lowers the money supply. Therefore, under fixed exchange rates, surpluses raise money supplies and deficits lower money supplies.

6. Because deficit countries which run out of foreign exchange reserves are eventually forced to devalue, it is possible to identify which currencies face devaluation. The need to revalue is less urgent than the need to devalue, making the timing of forecasts of revaluations more difficult.

7. The European Monetary System (EMS) was a fixed-exchange-rate system in which countries cooperated to maintain exchange rates. Exchange rates were fixed within limits set by a parity grid, which involved an upper and lower limit for each exchange rate. Exchange rates were also maintained within limits vis-à-vis the European Currency Unit. This helped identify which country was at fault for any difficulties in maintaining

exchange rates. With both deficit and surplus countries being supposed to intervene under the EMS, it was intended that the burden of adjustment would be shared.

8. Alternatives to fixed-rate systems and flexible-rate systems include a fixed rate with a wide band, a crawling peg, fixed rates for some transactions and flexible rates for others, and a dirty float with intervention to maintain orderly markets. These alternatives combine attributes of both fixed-rate systems and flexible-rate systems.

9. The credible announcement of target zones helps to keep exchange rates within the zones.

10. At the edges of target zones, fundamentals have no effect on exchange rates.

REVIEW QUESTIONS

1. What is the essential feature of the gold standard concerning the exchange of paper money into gold?
2. What are gold points?
3. What does the price-specie automatic adjustment mechanism assume about the connection between the gold reserves of a country and that country's trade balance?
4. What does the price-specie adjustment mechanism assume about the connection between the trade balance and a country's money supply?
5. How are the money supply and prices linked, according to the price-specie adjustment mechanism?
6. What is sterilization or neutralization policy as applied to the functioning of the gold standard?
7. What is meant by the "support points" in the Bretton Woods system?
8. What is the difference between the dollar standard and the Bretton Woods system?
9. If a country increases its official price of gold, does that constitute a devaluation or a revaluation of its currency?
10. Why might speculation be profitable in a gold-standard system?
11. What is a central-bank swap?
12. What exchange-rate system evolved from "the snake"?
13. What is the European Currency Unit?
14. To what type of exchange-rate system does the Maastricht Agreement commit participating European Union member countries?
15. What is a dirty float?
16. What is a crawling peg?
17. What was the Louvre Accord?
18. According to target-zone research, does the establishment of a target zone for exchange rates increase or decrease the range within which exchange rates typically fluctuate?

ASSIGNMENT PROBLEMS

1. Assume the following gold prices have been declared by the central banks:
   a. Bank of England £300
   b. Federal Reserve System $475
   c. Bank of France FFr2,500
   d. Bundesbank DM750
   e. Bank of Canada C$600
   Calculate all possible exchange rates between the currencies.
2. What assumptions have you made in question 1?
3. How can government objectives such as the maintenance of full employment hinder the functioning of the gold standard?

4. Why might historical patterns of prices show parallel movements between deficit and surplus countries? Could gold discoveries and common movements in national incomes cause this?

5. Use Figure 8.2 to show the effect of a fall in demand for British goods in terms of (a) the balance of payments measured in terms of pounds and (b) the balance of payments measured in terms of dollars. Show also the movements of curves that the deficit and associated contraction in the money supply will create in restoring equilibrium.

6. Why can speculators make profits with less risk under fixed rates? From whom do they make their profits?

7. Why do we observe deficits or surpluses under "flexible" rates? Does this tell us something about the management of the rates?

8. Do you think that the collapse of the Bretton Woods system would have been less likely had surplus countries expanded their economies to ease the burden of adjustment on the countries with deficits?

9. Why have central bankers frequently intervened in the foreign exchange market under a system of flexible exchange rates? If they have managed to smooth out fluctuations, have they made profits for their citizens?

10. Does a crawling-peg system lend itself to profitable speculation?

BIBLIOGRAPHY

BARRO, ROBERT J.: "Money and the Price Level Under the Gold Standard," *Economic Journal,* March 1979, pp. 13–33.

BELONGIA, MICHAEL T.: "Prospects for International Policy Coordination: Some Lessons for the EMS," *Review,* Federal Reserve Bank of St. Louis, July/August 1988, pp. 19–27.

BORDO, MICHAEL D.: "The Gold Standard, Bretton Woods, and Other Monetary Regimes: A Historical Appraisal," *Review,* Federal Reserve Bank of St. Louis, March/April 1993, pp. 123–187.

DORNBUSCH, RUDIGER: *Open Economy Macroeconomics,* 2d ed., Basic Books, New York, 1988.

HABERLER, GOTTFRIED: *Money in the International Economy,* Harvard University Press, Cambridge, Mass., 1965.

HUME, DAVID: "Of the Balance of Trade," in *Essays on Money,* Political Discourses, London, 1752.

KRUGMAN, PAUL R., and MARCUS MILLER (eds.): *Exchange Rate Targets and Currency Bands,* Cambridge University Press, New York, 1992.

MELTZER, ALLAN H: "U.S. Policy in the Bretton Woods Era," *Review,* Federal Reserve Bank of St. Louis, May/June 1991, pp. 54–83.

MILLS, TERENCE C., and GEOFFREY E. WOOD: "Does the Exchange Rate Regime Affect the Economy?" *Review,* Federal Reserve Bank of St. Louis, July/August 1993, pp. 3–20.

ROCKOFF, HUGH: "Some Evidence on the Real Price of Gold, Its Costs of Production, and Commodity Prices," in Michael D. Bordo and Anna J. Schwartz (eds.), *A Retrospective on the Classical Gold Standard, 1821–1931,* University of Chicago Press, Chicago, 1984, pp. 613–644.

————: "The Wizard of Oz as a Monetary Allegory," *Journal of Political Economy,* August 1990, pp. 739–760.

SOLOMON, ROBERT: *The International Monetary System, 1945–1981,* Harper & Row, New York, 1982.

SVENSSON, LARS E. O.: "An Interpretation of Recent Research on Exchange Rate Target Zones," *Journal of Economic Perspectives,* fall 1992, pp. 119–144.

APPENDIX 8.1
Summary of Exchange-Rate and Trade Practices of IMF Members, December 1992

	Afghanistan	Albania	Algeria	Angola	Antigua and Barbuda	Argentina	Armenia	Aruba	Australia	Austria	Azerbaijan	The Bahamas	Bahrain	Bangladesh	Barbados	Belarus	Belgium and Luxembourg	Belize	Benin	Bhutan	Bolivia	Botswana	Brazil	Bulgaria	Burkina Faso
A. Acceptance of Article Status																									
1. Article VIII status	–	–	–	–	●	●	–	●	●	●	–	●	●	–	–	–	●	●	–	–	●	–	–	–	–
2. Article XIV status	●	●	●	●	–	–	●	–	–	–	●	–	–	●	●	●	–	–	●	●	–	●	●	●	●
B. Exchange Arrangement																									
1. Exchange rate determined on the basis of:																									
(a) A peg to:																									
(i) the U.S. dollar	–	–	–	●	●	●	–	●	–	–	–	●	–	●	–	–	–	●	–	–	–	–	–	–	–
(ii) the pound sterling	–	–	–	–	–	–	–	–	–	–	–	–	–	–	–	–	–	–	–	–	–	–	–	–	–
(iii) the French franc	–	–	–	–	–	–	–	–	–	–	–	–	–	–	–	–	–	–	●	–	–	–	–	–	●
(iv) other currencies	–	–	–	–	–	–	●	–	–	–	–	–	–	–	–	–	–	–	–	●	–	–	–	–	–
(v) a composite of currencies	–	–	●	–	–	–	–	–	–	–	●	–	–	–	–	–	–	–	–	–	–	●	–	–	–
(b) Limited flexibility with respect to:																									
(i) single currency	–	–	–	–	–	–	–	–	–	●	–	–	–	–	–	–	–	–	–	–	–	–	–	–	–
(ii) cooperative arrangement	–	–	–	–	–	–	–	–	–	–	–	–	–	–	–	–	●	–	–	–	–	–	–	–	–
(c) More flexible arrangements:																									
(i) adjusted according to a set of indicators	–	–	–	–	–	–	–	–	–	–	–	–	–	–	–	–	–	–	–	–	–	–	–	–	–
(ii) other managed floating	–	–	–	–	–	–	–	–	–	–	–	–	–	–	–	–	–	–	–	–	–	–	–	–	–
(iii) independently floating	●	●	–	–	–	–	–	–	●	–	–	–	–	–	–	–	–	–	–	–	●	–	●	●	–
2. Separate exchange rate(s) for some or all capital transactions and/or some or all invisibles	●	–	–	●	–	–	–	–	–	–	●	–	–	–	–	●	–	–	–	–	●	–	●	–	–
3. More than one rate for imports	●	–	–	●	–	–	–	–	–	–	–	–	–	–	–	●	–	–	–	–	●	–	●	–	–
4. More than one rate for exports	●	–	–	●	–	–	–	–	–	–	–	–	–	–	–	●	–	–	–	–	●	–	●	–	–
5. Import rate(s) different from export rate(s)	●	–	–	●	–	–	–	–	–	–	–	–	–	–	–	–	–	–	–	–	●	–	●	–	–
C. Payments Arrears	–	●	–	●	–	●	–	–	–	–	–	–	–	–	–	–	–	–	–	–	●	–	–	●	●
D. Bilateral Payments Arrangements																									
1. With members	●	●	●	–	–	–	●	–	–	–	●	–	–	●	–	●	–	–	●	–	–	–	●	●	●
2. With nonmembers	●	●	–	●	–	–	–	–	–	–	–	–	–	–	●	–	–	–	–	–	–	–	–	●	–
E. Payments Restrictions																									
1. Restrictions on payments for current transactions	●	●	●	●	–	●	●	–	–	–	●	–	–	●	●	●	–	–	–	–	●	–	●	●	–
2. Restrictions on payments for capital transactions	●	●	●	●	–	●	●	●	–	–	●	–	–	●	●	–	–	●	●	–	●	–	●	●	●
F. Cost-Related Import Restrictions																									
1. Import surcharges	–	–	–	–	–	●	–	●	–	–	–	–	–	–	–	–	–	–	●	–	–	–	–	–	●
2. Advance import deposits	●	–	–	–	–	–	–	–	–	–	–	–	–	–	–	–	–	–	–	–	–	–	–	–	–
G. Surrender or Repatriation Requirement for Export Proceeds	●	●	●	●	–	●	●	●	–	–	●	–	●	●	●	●	–	●	●	●	●	●	–	●	●

	Burundi	Cambodia	Cameroon	Canada	Cape Verde	Central African Rep.	Chad	Chile	China	Colombia	Comoros	Congo	Costa Rica	Côte d'Ivoire	Croatia	Cyprus	Czech Republic	Denmark	Djibouti	Dominica	Dominican Republic	Ecuador	Egypt	El Salvador	Equatorial Guinea	Estonia	Ethiopia	Fiji	Finland	France	Gabon	The Gambia	Georgia	Germany	Ghana
	–	–	–	•	–	–	–	•	–	–	–	–	•	–	–	•	–	•	•	•	•	•	–	•	–	–	–	•	•	•	–	•	–	•	–
	•	•	•	–	•	•	•	–	•	•	•	•	–	•	•	–	•	–	–	–	–	–	•	–	•	•	•	–	–	–	•	–	•	–	•
	–	–	–	–	–	–	–	–	–	–	–	–	–	–	–	–	–	•	•	–	–	–	–	–	–	–	•	–	–	–	–	–	–	–	–
	–	–	•	–	•	•	–	–	–	•	•	–	•	–	–	–	–	–	–	–	–	–	–	–	•	–	–	–	–	–	•	–	–	–	–
	–	–	–	–	–	–	–	–	–	–	–	–	–	–	•	–	–	–	–	–	–	–	–	–	–	•	–	–	–	–	–	–	•	–	–
	•	–	–	–	•	–	–	–	–	–	–	–	–	–	–	•	•	–	–	–	–	–	–	–	–	–	•	–	–	–	–	–	–	–	–
	–	–	–	–	–	–	–	–	–	–	–	–	–	–	–	–	–	–	–	–	–	–	–	–	–	–	–	–	–	–	–	–	–	–	–
	–	–	–	–	–	–	–	–	–	–	–	–	–	–	–	–	–	•	–	–	–	–	–	–	–	–	–	–	–	•	–	–	–	•	–
	–	–	–	–	–	–	–	•	–	•	–	–	–	–	–	–	–	–	–	–	–	–	–	–	–	–	–	–	–	–	–	–	–	–	–
	–	•	–	–	–	–	–	•	–	–	–	–	–	–	–	–	–	–	–	–	–	•	•	–	–	–	–	–	–	–	–	–	–	–	–
	–	–	•	–	–	–	–	–	–	•	–	–	–	–	–	–	–	–	–	–	•	–	–	–	•	–	–	•	–	–	•	–	•	–	•
	–	•	–	–	–	–	–	•	•	–	–	–	–	–	–	–	•	–	–	–	–	•	•	–	–	–	–	–	–	–	–	–	•	–	•
	–	•	–	–	–	–	–	•	–	–	–	–	–	–	–	–	–	–	–	–	–	•	•	–	–	–	–	–	–	–	–	–	•	–	•
	–	•	–	–	–	–	–	•	•	–	–	–	–	–	–	–	–	–	–	–	–	•	•	–	–	–	–	–	–	–	–	–	•	–	•
	–	•	–	–	–	–	–	•	•	–	–	–	–	–	–	–	–	–	–	–	–	•	•	–	–	–	–	–	–	–	–	–	•	–	•
	–	–	•	–	•	•	•	–	–	•	•	•	•	•	–	–	–	•	•	•	•	–	•	•	•	–	•	–	–	–	•	–	–	–	–
	•	–	–	–	•	–	–	–	•	•	–	–	–	•	–	•	–	•	–	•	–	•	•	–	–	•	–	–	–	–	–	–	•	–	•
	–	–	–	–	–	–	–	–	•	•	–	–	–	–	–	–	–	–	–	•	–	•	–	–	–	–	–	–	–	–	–	–	–	–	•
	•	•	•	–	•	–	•	•	•	•	•	•	•	•	•	•	•	–	–	–	•	•	•	•	–	•	–	–	–	–	–	–	–	–	•
	•	•	•	–	•	•	•	•	•	•	•	•	•	•	•	•	•	–	–	•	•	–	•	•	•	•	•	•	–	•	•	–	•	–	•
	–	–	–	–	–	–	–	•	–	–	–	•	–	–	–	–	–	•	–	•	•	–	–	–	–	–	–	–	–	–	–	•	–	–
	–	–	–	–	–	–	–	–	•	–	–	–	–	–	–	–	–	–	–	•	•	•	–	–	–	–	–	–	–	–	–	–	–	–	–
	•	•	•	–	•	•	•	•	•	•	•	•	•	•	•	•	•	–	–	•	•	•	•	•	•	•	•	–	•	•	•	•	•	–	•

	Greece	Grenada	Guatemala	Guinea	Guinea-Bissau	Guyana	Haiti	Honduras	Hong Kong	Hungary	Iceland	India	Indonesia	Iran, Islamic Rep. of	Iraq	Ireland	Israel	Italy	Jamaica	Japan	Jordan	Kazakhstan	Kenya	Kiribati	Korea
A. Acceptance of Article Status																									
1. Article VIII status	●	–	●	–	–	●	●	●	●	–	●	–	●	–	–	●	–	●	●	●	–	–	–	●	●
2. Article XIV status	–	●	–	●	●	–	–	–	–	●	–	●	–	●	●	–	●	–	–	–	●	●	●	–	–
B. Exchange Arrangement																									
1. Exchange rate determined on the basis of:																									
(a) A peg to:																									
(i) the U.S. dollar	–	●	–	–	–	–	–	–	–	–	–	–	–	–	●	–	–	–	–	–	–	–	–	–	–
(ii) the pound sterling	–	–	–	–	–	–	–	–	–	–	–	–	–	–	–	–	–	–	–	–	–	–	–	–	–
(iii) the French franc	–	–	–	–	–	–	–	–	–	–	–	–	–	–	–	–	–	–	–	–	–	–	–	–	–
(iv) other currencies	–	–	–	–	–	–	–	–	–	–	–	–	–	–	–	–	–	–	–	–	–	●	–	●	–
(v) a composite of currencies	–	–	–	–	–	–	–	–	–	●	●	–	–	–	–	–	–	–	–	–	●	–	●	–	–
(b) Limited flexibility with respect to:																									
(i) single currency	–	–	–	–	–	–	–	–	–	–	–	–	–	–	–	–	–	–	–	–	–	–	–	–	–
(ii) cooperative arrangement	–	–	–	–	–	–	–	–	–	–	–	–	–	–	–	●	–	–	–	–	–	–	–	–	–
(c) More flexible arrangements:																									
(i) adjusted according to a set of indicators	–	–	–	–	–	–	–	–	–	–	–	–	–	–	–	–	–	–	–	–	–	–	–	–	–
(ii) other managed floating	●	–	–	●	●	–	–	–	●	–	–	–	●	–	–	–	–	–	–	–	–	–	–	–	●
(iii) independently floating	–	–	●	–	–	●	●	●	–	–	–	●	–	–	–	–	●	●	–	–	–	–	–	–	–
2. Separate exchange rate(s) for some or all capital transactions and/or some or all invisibles	–	●	●	–	–	●	–	●	–	●	–	–	–	●	–	–	–	–	–	–	●	●	–	–	–
3. More than one rate for imports	–	●	●	–	–	●	–	–	–	–	–	–	–	●	–	–	–	–	–	–	●	●	–	–	–
4. More than one rate for exports	–	–	●	–	–	●	–	–	–	–	–	–	–	●	–	–	–	–	–	–	●	●	–	–	–
5. Import rate(s) different from export rate(s)	–	●	●	–	–	●	–	–	–	–	–	–	–	●	–	–	–	–	–	–	●	●	–	–	–
C. Payments Arrears	–	●	●	●	●	–	●	●	–	–	–	–	–	●	–	–	–	–	–	–	●	–	●	–	–
D. Bilateral Payments Arrangements																									
1. With members	–	–	–	●	●	–	–	–	–	●	–	●	–	●	–	–	–	–	–	–	●	●	–	–	–
2. With nonmembers	–	–	–	●	–	–	–	–	–	–	–	–	–	●	–	–	–	–	–	–	–	●	–	–	–
E. Payments Restrictions																									
1. Restrictions on payments for current transactions	–	●	–	●	●	●	–	●	–	●	–	●	–	●	●	–	●	–	●	–	●	●	●	–	–
2. Restrictions on payments for capital transactions	●	●	–	●	●	●	●	●	–	●	●	●	–	●	●	–	●	●	●	–	●	●	●	–	●
F. Cost-Related Import Restrictions																									
1. Import surcharges	●	●	–	●	–	–	–	●	–	–	–	●	●	●	●	–	●	–	●	–	–	–	–	–	–
2. Advance import deposits	–	–	–	–	–	–	–	–	–	–	–	–	–	●	–	–	–	–	–	–	–	–	–	–	–
G. Surrender or Repatriation Requirement for Export Proceeds	●	●	●	●	●	●	●	●	●	–	●	●	●	–	●	●	●	●	●	–	–	●	●	●	–

Kuwait	Kyrgyzstan	Lao People's Dem. Rep.	Latvia	Lebanon	Lesotho	Liberia	Libyan Arab Jamahiriya	Lithuania	Madagascar	Malawi	Malaysia	Maldives	Mali	Malta	Marshall Islands	Mauritania	Mauritius	Mexico	Fed. States of Micronesia	Moldova	Mongolia	Morocco	Mozambique	Myanmar	Namibia	Nepal	Netherlands	Netherlands Antilles	New Zealand	Nicaragua	Niger	Nigeria	Norway	Oman
•	–	–	–	–	–	–	–	–	–	–	•	–	–	–	•	–	–	•	•	–	–	•	–	–	–	–	•	•	•	•	–	–	•	•
–	•	•	•	•	•	•	•	•	•	•	–	•	•	•	–	•	•	–	–	•	•	–	•	•	•	•	–	–	–	–	•	•	–	–
–	–	–	–	–	–	•	–	–	–	–	–	–	–	–	•	–	–	•	–	–	•	–	–	–	–	–	•	–	•	–	–	–	–	•
–	–	–	–	–	–	–	–	–	–	–	–	–	–	–	–	–	–	–	–	–	–	–	–	–	–	–	–	–	–	–	–	–	–	–
–	–	–	–	–	–	–	–	–	–	–	–	•	–	–	–	–	–	–	–	–	–	–	–	–	–	–	–	–	–	–	–	•	–	–
–	•	–	–	•	–	–	–	–	–	–	–	–	–	–	–	–	–	–	–	•	–	–	–	–	•	–	–	–	–	–	–	–	–	–
•	–	–	–	–	–	–	•	–	–	–	–	–	•	–	–	•	•	–	–	–	–	•	–	•	–	–	–	–	–	–	–	–	–	–
–	–	–	–	–	–	–	–	–	–	–	–	–	–	–	–	–	–	–	–	–	–	–	–	–	–	–	–	•	–	–	–	–	–	–
–	–	–	–	–	–	–	–	–	•	–	–	–	–	–	–	–	–	–	–	–	–	–	–	–	–	–	–	–	–	–	–	–	–	–
–	–	•	–	–	–	–	–	–	–	–	•	•	–	–	–	–	–	•	–	–	–	–	–	–	–	–	–	–	–	–	–	–	–	–
–	–	–	•	•	–	–	–	•	–	–	–	–	–	–	–	–	–	–	–	–	–	–	•	–	–	•	–	–	•	–	–	•	•	–
–	–	•	–	–	•	–	–	–	–	–	–	–	–	–	•	–	–	–	–	•	–	•	–	–	•	–	–	–	–	•	•	–	–	–
–	–	•	–	–	–	–	–	–	–	–	–	–	–	–	–	–	–	–	–	•	•	–	•	–	–	–	–	–	–	–	–	–	–	–
–	–	•	–	–	–	–	–	–	–	–	–	–	–	–	–	–	–	–	–	•	•	–	•	–	–	–	–	–	–	–	–	–	–	–
–	–	•	–	–	–	–	–	–	–	–	–	–	–	–	–	–	–	–	–	•	•	–	–	–	–	–	–	–	–	–	–	–	–	–
–	–	–	–	•	–	–	–	–	–	–	–	–	–	–	•	–	–	–	–	•	–	–	•	–	–	–	–	–	–	•	–	•	–	–
–	•	•	•	•	–	–	–	•	•	–	–	–	•	–	•	–	•	–	–	•	•	•	•	–	•	–	–	–	–	–	–	–	–	–
–	–	•	–	–	–	–	–	•	•	–	–	–	–	–	–	–	–	–	–	•	•	–	–	–	–	–	–	–	–	–	–	–	–	–
–	–	•	–	–	–	•	–	•	•	–	–	•	•	–	•	•	–	•	–	•	•	•	•	•	•	•	–	•	–	•	–	–	–	–
–	•	•	•	–	•	•	•	•	•	–	–	•	•	•	–	•	•	•	–	•	•	•	•	•	•	•	–	•	–	•	•	•	•	–
–	–	–	•	•	–	•	•	–	•	–	–	–	–	–	–	•	–	–	–	•	–	–	–	•	–	–	–	•	–	•	•	–	–	–
–	–	–	–	•	–	–	•	–	–	–	–	–	–	–	–	–	–	–	–	–	–	–	–	–	–	–	–	–	–	–	–	–	–	–
–	–	•	–	–	•	•	•	–	•	•	–	•	•	•	–	•	•	–	•	•	•	•	–	•	–	–	•	–	•	•	•	•	•	–

	Pakistan	Panama	Papua New Guinea	Paraguay	Peru	Philippines	Poland	Portugal	Qatar	Romania	Russian Federation	Rwanda	St. Kitts and Nevis	St. Lucia	St. Vincent and Grenadines	San Marino	Sao Tome and Principe	Saudi Arabia	Senegal	Seychelles	Sierra Leone	Singapore	Slovak Republic	Slovenia	Solomon Islands
A. Acceptance of Article Status																									
1. Article VIII status	–	●	●	–	●	–	–	●	●	–	–	–	●	●	●	●	–	●	–	●	–	●	–	–	●
2. Article XIV status	●	–	–	●	–	●	●	–	–	●	●	●	–	–	–	–	●	–	●	–	●	–	●	●	–
B. Exchange Arrangement																									
1. Exchange rate determined on the basis of:																									
(a) A peg to:																									
(i) the U.S. dollar	–	●	–	–	–	–	–	–	–	–	–	–	●	●	●	–	–	–	–	–	–	–	–	–	–
(ii) the pound sterling	–	–	–	–	–	–	–	–	–	–	–	–	–	–	–	–	–	–	–	–	–	–	–	–	–
(iii) the French franc	–	–	–	–	–	–	–	–	–	–	–	–	–	–	–	–	–	–	●	–	–	–	–	–	–
(iv) other currencies	–	–	–	–	–	–	–	–	–	–	–	–	–	–	–	●	–	–	–	–	–	–	–	–	–
(v) a composite of currencies	–	–	●	–	–	–	–	–	–	–	–	●	–	–	–	–	–	–	–	●	–	–	–	–	●
(b) Limited flexibility with respect to:																									
(i) single currency	–	–	–	–	–	–	–	–	●	–	–	–	–	–	–	–	–	●	–	–	–	–	–	–	–
(ii) cooperative arrangement	–	–	–	–	–	–	–	●	–	–	–	–	–	–	–	–	–	–	–	–	–	–	–	–	–
(c) More flexible arrangements:																									
(i) adjusted according to a set of indicators	–	–	–	–	–	–	–	–	–	–	–	–	–	–	–	–	–	–	–	–	–	–	–	–	–
(ii) other managed floating	●	–	–	–	–	–	●	–	–	–	–	–	–	–	–	–	●	–	–	–	–	–	●	●	–
(iii) independently floating	–	–	–	●	●	●	–	–	–	●	●	–	–	–	–	–	–	–	–	–	●	–	–	–	–
2. Separate exchange rate(s) for some or all capital transactions and/or some or all invisibles	–	–	–	–	–	●	–	–	–	●	●	–	–	–	–	–	–	–	–	–	–	–	–	–	–
3. More than one rate for imports	–	–	–	–	–	●	–	–	–	●	●	–	–	–	–	–	–	–	–	–	–	–	–	–	–
4. More than one rate for exports	–	–	–	–	–	●	–	–	–	●	●	–	–	–	–	–	–	–	–	–	–	–	–	–	–
5. Import rate(s) different from export rate(s)	–	–	–	–	–	●	–	–	–	●	●	–	–	–	–	–	–	–	–	–	–	–	–	–	–
C. Payments Arrears	–	●	–	●	●	–	●	–	–	●	–	–	–	–	–	–	●	–	–	–	●	–	–	–	–
D. Bilateral Payments Arrangements																									
1. With members	–	–	–	–	–	●	–	–	●	●	●	–	–	–	–	–	–	–	–	–	●	–	●	●	–
2. With nonmembers	–	–	–	–	–	–	–	–	–	●	●	–	–	–	–	–	–	–	–	–	–	–	●	–	–
E. Payments Restrictions																									
1. Restrictions on payments for current transactions	●	–	–	–	–	●	●	–	–	●	–	●	–	–	–	–	●	–	–	–	●	–	●	●	–
2. Restrictions on payments for capital transactions	●	–	●	●	●	●	●	●	–	●	●	●	●	●	●	–	●	–	●	–	●	–	●	●	●
F. Cost-Related Import Restrictions																									
1. Import surcharges	●	●	–	●	●	–	–	–	–	–	–	–	–	–	–	–	–	–	–	–	–	–	–	–	–
2. Advance import deposits	●	–	–	–	–	–	–	–	–	–	●	–	–	–	–	–	●	–	–	–	–	–	–	–	–
G. Surrender or Repatriation Requirement for Export Proceeds	●	–	●	●	–	–	●	●	–	●	●	●	●	●	●	●	●	–	●	–	●	–	●	●	●

Somalia	South Africa	Spain	Sri Lanka	Sudan	Suriname	Swaziland	Sweden	Switzerland	Syrian Arab Republic	Tanzania	Thailand	Togo	Tonga	Trinidad and Tobago	Tunisia	Turkey	Turkmenistan	Uganda	Ukraine	United Arab Emirates	United Kingdom	United States	Uruguay	Uzbekistan	Vanuatu	Venezuela	Viet Nam	Western Samoa	Republic of Yemen	Zaïre	Zambia	Zimbabwe
–	●	●	–	–	●	●	●	●	–	–	●	–	●	–	●	●	–	–	–	●	●	●	●	–	●	●	–	–	–	–	–	–
●	–	–	●	●	–	–	–	–	●	●	–	●	–	●	–	–	●	●	●	–	–	–	–	●	–	–	●	●	●	●	●	●
–	–	–	–	–	●	–	–	–	●	–	–	–	–	–	–	–	–	–	–	–	–	–	–	–	–	–	–	–	●	–	–	–
–	–	–	–	–	–	–	–	–	–	–	–	–	–	–	–	–	–	–	–	–	–	–	–	–	–	–	–	–	–	–	–	–
–	–	–	–	–	–	–	–	–	–	–	●	–	–	–	–	–	–	–	–	–	–	–	–	–	–	–	–	–	–	–	–	–
–	–	–	–	–	–	●	–	–	–	–	–	–	–	–	–	–	–	●	–	–	–	–	–	●	–	–	–	–	–	–	–	–
–	–	–	–	–	–	–	–	–	●	●	–	●	–	–	–	–	–	–	–	–	–	–	–	–	–	–	●	–	●	–	–	●
–	–	–	–	–	–	–	–	–	–	–	–	–	–	–	–	–	–	–	–	●	–	–	–	–	–	–	–	–	–	–	–	–
–	–	●	–	–	–	–	–	–	–	–	–	–	–	–	–	–	–	–	–	–	–	–	–	–	–	–	–	–	–	–	–	–
–	–	–	–	–	–	–	–	–	–	–	–	–	–	–	–	–	–	–	–	–	–	–	–	–	–	–	–	–	–	–	–	–
●	–	–	●	–	–	–	–	–	–	–	–	–	●	●	–	–	–	–	–	●	–	–	–	–	●	–	–	●	–	–	–	–
–	●	●	–	●	–	–	●	●	–	–	–	–	–	–	●	–	–	●	●	–	●	●	–	–	–	–	●	–	–	●	●	–
●	●	–	–	–	–	–	–	–	●	●	–	–	–	–	–	–	–	●	●	–	–	–	–	–	–	–	●	●	–	●	●	●
●	–	–	–	–	–	–	–	–	●	●	–	–	–	–	–	–	–	●	●	–	–	–	–	–	–	–	●	●	–	–	●	–
●	–	–	–	–	–	–	–	–	●	●	–	–	–	–	–	–	–	●	●	–	–	–	–	–	–	–	●	–	–	–	●	–
●	–	–	–	–	–	–	–	–	●	●	–	–	–	–	–	–	–	●	●	–	–	–	–	–	–	–	●	●	–	–	●	–
●	●	●	●	–	–	–	–	–	●	–	–	–	–	–	–	–	–	●	●	–	–	–	–	–	–	–	●	–	–	●	●	–
–	–	–	–	●	–	–	–	–	●	–	–	–	–	–	–	–	–	●	●	●	●	–	–	–	–	●	–	–	●	–	●	–
–	–	–	–	–	–	–	–	–	–	–	–	–	–	–	–	–	–	–	●	–	–	–	–	–	–	–	●	–	–	–	–	–
●	●	–	–	●	●	–	–	–	●	●	–	●	–	–	●	–	–	●	●	●	–	–	–	●	–	–	●	●	●	●	●	●
●	●	●	●	●	●	●	●	–	●	●	●	●	●	●	●	●	●	●	●	–	–	–	●	–	●	●	●	●	●	●	●	●
–	●	–	–	●	●	–	–	–	●	–	●	–	●	–	●	–	–	–	●	–	–	–	●	–	●	–	–	●	–	●	–	●
●	●	–	–	●	–	–	–	–	–	–	–	–	–	–	–	●	–	–	–	–	–	–	–	–	–	–	–	●	–	–	–	–
●	●	●	–	●	●	●	–	–	●	●	–	●	●	●	●	●	●	●	●	–	–	–	●	●	–	●	●	●	●	●	●	●

Source: Exchange Arrangements and Exchange Restrictions; Annual Report 1993, International Monetary Fund, Washington, D.C., 1993.

APPENDIX 8.2
Other Fixed-Exchange-Rate Automatic Adjustment Mechanisms

NATIONAL INCOME

The price-level adjustment mechanism requires flexibility of prices in order to operate. The macroeconomic revolution marked by the publication of *The General Theory of Employment, Interest and Money* by John Maynard Keynes, while focusing on a closed economy, spilled over into international finance and introduced an alternative adjustment mechanism that works if price flexibility does not exist.[15] This mechanism, popularized by the followers of Keynes, involves automatic adjustment via changes in national income. Like the price-level adjustment mechanism, the income adjustment mechanism operates on the current account. The most straightforward way of describing Keynesian adjustment is to employ a Keynesian income-expenditure model and show how variations in national income work to correct balance-of-payments surpluses and deficits.

A straightforward model which will reveal the important features of income adjustment consists of the following equations:

$$Y \equiv C + I_0 + \left(Ex_0 - Im \right) \tag{8A.1}$$

$$C = C_0 + cY \tag{8A.2}$$

$$Im = Im_0 + mY \tag{8A.3}$$

In these equations, Y is the national income, or GDP, C is aggregate consumption of goods and services, I_0 is the given amount of aggregate investment or capital formation, Ex_0 is the given amount of exports, and Im is imports.

The national-income accounting identity is given by equation (8A.1), where, because it is not relevant for our purposes, we have omitted government spending. The GDP, Y, is the total value of *domestically produced* goods and services. Because it is difficult for government statisticians to separate consumption and investment of domestic goods from consumption and investment of imported goods, especially when domestic goods have imported components, C and I refer to the *total* consumption and investment of goods and services. In addition, exports, Ex_0, include re-exports, that is, items from abroad that are resold after reprocessing or are used as inputs in exported products. Because Y refers to domestic production only, as the relevant output/income of a nation, and because C, I_0, and Ex_0 include imports, we must subtract imports, Im, to ensure the identity of (8A.1). This is the most convenient approach from the viewpoint of a national-income statistician, because records of imports exist with customs agents, and records of consumption and investment reveal total amounts and do not show imported components separated from domestic components.

Equation (8A.2) is the **consumption function**. The intercept, C_0, is the part that does not depend on income. The effect of national income on consumption is given by the **marginal propensity to consume,** c, which will be between zero and unity. Since C represents all consumption, it includes imports (Im), where the import equation itself is equation (8A.3). We assume that investment and exports are exogenous, or at least exogenous in relation to national income in the economy we are examining.

In order to discover how automatic adjustment via national income works, we can begin

---

[15]John Maynard Keynes, *The General Theory of Employment, Interest and Money,* Macmillan, London, 1936.

with an intuitive explanation. Suppose the balance of payments is initially in balance and that there is an exogenous increase in exports, Ex. This means an increase in national income via equation (8A.1), which itself indirectly further increases income via the extra induced consumption in equation (8A.2). The higher national income will increase imports via equation (8A.3). We find that the initial increase in exports that moved the balance of payments into surplus will induce an increase in imports, which will tend to offset the effect of exports. This is an automatic adjustment working via income. It is not apparent from our intuitive explanation that this adjustment, while tending to restore balance, will not be complete. In order to see this, we can employ our model.

If we substitute equations (8A.2) and (8A.3) into the national-income accounting identity, equation (8A.1), we obtain

$$Y = C_0 + cY + I_0 + Ex_0 - Im_0 - mY \tag{8A.4}$$

By gathering terms, we can write Y as a function of exogenous terms:

$$Y = \frac{1}{1 - c + m} \left(C_0 + I_0 + Ex_0 - Im_0 \right) \tag{8A.5}$$

The factor $1/(1 - c + m)$ is the **multiplier.** We can note that the larger the **marginal propensity to import,** m, the smaller will be the multiplier. The multiplier depends on the leakages from the circular flow of income, and by having imports, we add a leakage abroad, m, to the leakage into savings given by the marginal propensity to save, $1 - c$. The more leakages we have, the smaller the increase in income from any exogenous shock.

Let us allow exports to increase exogenously from Ex_0 to $Ex_0 + \Delta Ex$ and the corresponding increase in GDP to be from Y to $Y + \Delta Y$. We can therefore write

$$Y + \Delta Y = \frac{1}{1 - c + m} \left(C_0 + I_0 + Ex_0 + \Delta Ex - Im_0 \right) \tag{8A.6}$$

Subtracting each side of equation (8A.5) from equation (8A.6), we have

$$\Delta Y = \frac{1}{1 - c + m} \Delta Ex \tag{8A.7}$$

The value of ΔY in equation (8A.7) gives the effect on national income of an exogenous change in exports. To find the induced effect on imports of this change in national income, we can use ΔY from equation (8A.7) in the import equation (8A.3). Putting equation (8A.3) in terms of the new level of imports, $Im + \Delta Im$, after an increase in income to $Y + \Delta Y$, we have

$$Im + \Delta Im = Im_0 + m(Y + \Delta Y) \tag{8A.8}$$

Subtracting equation (8A.3) from equation (8A.8) on both sides gives

$$\Delta Im = m\Delta Y \tag{8A.9}$$

and substituting ΔY from equation (8A.7) in equation (8A.9) gives

$$\Delta Im = \frac{m}{1 - c + m} \Delta Ex \tag{8A.10}$$

Equation (8A.10) tells us that the automatic adjustment working via national income will raise imports by $m/(1 - c + m)$ times the initial increase in exports. The value of $m/(1 - c + m)$ is, however, below unity. This follows because the marginal propensity to consume is below unity, that is, $c < 1$, so that $1 - c > 0$. We hence have m divided by itself *plus* the positive number $1 - c$. When a number is divided by a total larger than itself, the result is below unity. For example, if $c = 0.8$ and $m = 0.2$, imports will increase by only half of any exogenous increase in exports. If $c = 0.4$ and $m = 0.2$, the offset is only a quarter. What we have is an adjustment process via national income that is not complete. While an exogenous change in exports will change imports in the same direction, imports will change by less than the initial change in exports, and so initial effects persist.

Income and income adjustment are relevant to the financial manager who is trying to forecast movements in exchange rates. If a country's national income is growing more rapidly than that of others *as a result of growth in exports,* then the country's foreign exchange reserves will increase, and eventually the currency will probably increase in value. Induced increases in imports resulting from export growth will only partially dampen the growth of reserves and the need to eventually revalue the currency. When a nation's income is growing from a growth in consumption (C_0), then foreign exchange reserves will shrink, and eventually the foreign exchange value of the currency will have to be reduced. The growth in income will raise imports but not exports, since exports are determined by the incomes of *other* nations.

There is an additional force, also working via changes in national income, that will help complete the automatic adjustment process. This force is induced changes in the money supply, which in turn affects interest rates, the rate of investment, national income, and imports. The process works as follows. If we start in balance and an exogenous increase in exports does not induce a sufficient rise in imports to offset the increase in exports, a trade surplus will remain. *Ceteris paribus,* under fixed exchange rates this will require the central bank to supply its currency to prevent its exchange rate from appreciating. This means an increase in the money supply. A money-supply increase tends to lower the interest rates. Lower interest rates stimulate investment, I, which will in turn both directly and indirectly work toward raising the national income, Y. Higher income will raise imports, Im, via equation (8A.3) and thereby help close the trade imbalance.

The force that we have just described involves a lowering of interest rates working via capital investment, income, imports, and the current account. In addition, interest rates have an effect on capital flows and the capital account.

INTEREST RATES

The automatic **interest-rate adjustment mechanism** relies on the effect of the balance of payments on the money supply. We have seen that if the effects are not sterilized, a balance-of-payments deficit will reduce the money supply and a surplus will increase it. With a gold standard this occurs because a deficit means a gold outflow and a shrinking money supply, and a surplus means a gold inflow and an increasing money supply. In the gold-exchange and dollar standards, and in the EMS, the money supply also declines after deficits and increases after surpluses. In these cases the money supply changes because of intervention in the foreign exchange market. A deficit requires the local monetary authority to purchase its currency to keep the value up. Thus money is withdrawn from circulation. Similarly, a surplus requires the central bank to sell its currency and hence increase the money supply. With this we can explain the interest-rate adjustment mechanism which works via the capital account.

The interest-rate adjustment mechanism via the capital account involves the following. If a deficit occurs, it will reduce the money supply and raise the interest rate.[16] The deficit means surpluses elsewhere; therefore, the money supplies of other countries will be rising,

---

[16]The interest rate will not increase as a result of a reduction in the money supply if there is a **liquidity trap,** which occurs if the demand for money is perfectly elastic. If they have ever existed, liquidity traps are probably limited to serious recessions and will not hinder the interest-rate adjustment process in normal times.

which will reduce their interest rates. For both reasons there is a rise in interest differentials in favor of the deficit country. This will make investment (in securities, and so on) in that country appear relatively more attractive. The resultant inflows on the capital account should improve the balance of payments, thereby correcting the original deficit.

Because capital flows are highly responsive to interest-rate differentials when capital can flow without restriction, the interest-rate adjustment mechanism working via the capital account is likely to be the most effective mechanism in the short run. However, it is necessary that adjustment eventually occur via prices or national income and the current account. This is because capital inflows must be serviced. That is, there will be payments of interest which will appear as a debit in the invisibles part of the current account as income imports. This means that in the future, the current-account deficit will increase.

APPENDIX 8.3
Gold Points

Gold points are the extreme values between which the exchange rate can vary in a gold-standard world. The width of the zone defined by the extreme values within which exchange rates can vary is determined by the cost of exchanging currencies in the foreign exchange market and the cost of shipping gold between central banks. The gold points arising from the gold standard allowed exchange rates to vary within a zone of 1 or 2 percent of the middle value. This idea of a zone was carried into the Bretton Woods system and the European Monetary System. We hence obtain a historical perspective by a study of gold-point determination.

Suppose that the U.S. Federal Reserve and the Bank of England both offer to exchange their paper money for gold at fixed prices. Let us define these prices as follows:

$$P_G^{US}(\text{ask}) = \text{Federal Reserve selling price of gold, in dollars}$$

$$P_G^{US}(\text{bid}) = \text{Federal Reserve buying price of gold, in dollars}$$

$$P_G^{UK}(\text{ask}) = \text{Bank of England selling price of gold, in pounds}$$

$$P_G^{UK}(\text{bid}) = \text{Bank of England buying price of gold, in pounds}$$

Let us also define c_G as the cost of shipping gold between the United States and Britain. We can think of c_G as the fraction of the total value of gold shipped between the United States and the United Kingdom that is paid for shipping the gold. For example, $c_G = 0.01$ if shipping costs are 1 percent of the value of the cargo. Finally, let us define the bid and ask exchange rates as in the text, namely:

$S(\$/\text{bid}£)$ is the number of dollars received from the sale of pounds in the foreign exchange market, and $S(\$/\text{ask}£)$ is the number of dollars paid to buy pounds in the foreign exchange market.

Consider first a person wanting to buy dollars with pounds. For each pound, that person will receive $S(\$/\text{bid}£)$ dollars in the foreign exchange market. Alternatively, he or she can use one-way arbitrage and buy gold from the Bank of England, ship the gold, and sell it to the U.S. Federal Reserve for dollars. The number of dollars received per pound this way is calculated as follows:

Each pound buys $1/P_G^{UK}(\text{ask})$ ounces of gold from the Bank of England. Shipping this to the United States involves a cost of c_G per ounce so that after shipping

$$\frac{1}{P_G^{UK}(\text{ask})} \cdot (1 - c_G) \quad \text{ounces}$$

arrive in the United States. This can be sold to the Federal Reserve for

$$\$ \, \frac{P_G^{US}(\text{bid})}{P_G^{UK}(\text{ask})} \cdot (1 - c_G) \tag{8A.11}$$

The value in equation (8A.11) is the number of dollars received for one pound via buying, shipping, and selling gold.

People buying dollars with pounds will use the foreign exchange market if they receive at least as many dollars for their pounds in that market as via one-way arbitrage. That is, for the exchange market to be used it is necessary that

$$S(\$/\text{bid}£) \geq \frac{P_G^{US}(\text{bid})}{P_G^{UK}(\text{ask})} \cdot (1 - c_G) \tag{8A.12}$$

The amount on the right-hand side of equation (8A.12) is the **lower gold point,** and it is the minimum exchange rate for dollars to pounds in the foreign exchange market in a gold-standard world.

A person who wants to buy pounds for dollars could do this via the foreign exchange market and pay $S(\$/\text{ask}£)$ for each pound or alternatively, could use one-way arbitrage and use dollars to buy gold from the Federal Reserve, ship the gold, and sell it to the Bank of England. If this person chooses to use one-way arbitrage, the number of dollars he or she will pay per pound is calculated as follows:

Each pound requires selling to the Bank of England $1/P_G^{UK}(\text{bid})$ ounces of gold. In order to have this amount of gold in Britain it is necessary to buy in the United States

$$\frac{1}{P_G^{UK}(\text{bid})} \cdot \frac{1}{(1 - c_G)} \quad \text{ounces} \tag{8A.13}$$

because only $(1 - c_G)$ of gold that is purchased remains after shipping costs. The amount that must be paid to the Federal Reserve for the amount of gold in equation (8A.13) is

$$\$ \frac{P_G^{US}(\text{ask})}{P_G^{UK}(\text{bid})} \cdot \frac{1}{(1 - c_G)} \tag{8A.14}$$

The value in equation (8A.14) is the number of dollars that must be paid for one pound via buying, shipping, and selling gold.

People buying pounds with dollars will use the foreign exchange market rather than one-way arbitrage if they pay no more dollars via the foreign exchange market than via one-way arbitrage, that is, if

$$S(\$/\text{ask}£) \leq \frac{P_G^{US}(\text{ask})}{P_G^{UK}(\text{bid})} \cdot \frac{1}{(1 - c_G)} \tag{8A.15}$$

The amount of the right-hand side of equation (8A.15) is the **upper gold point,** and it is the maximum exchange rate of dollars for pounds if the foreign exchange market is to be used. We find that when each central bank offers to buy and sell its currency for gold, a range of values will be established in the foreign exchange market within which the exchange rate can vary. The bid and ask exchange rates can vary between the limits of $S(\$/\text{bid}£)$ in (8A.12) and $S(\$/\text{ask}£)$ in (8A.15). No exchange-rate quotation can lie outside this range. That is, the exchange rate in the foreign exchange market must be in the range:

$$\frac{P_G^{US}(\text{bid})}{P_G^{UK}(\text{ask})} \cdot (1 - c_G) \leq S(\$/£) \leq \frac{P_G^{US}(\text{ask})}{P_G^{UK}(\text{bid})} \cdot \frac{1}{(1 - c_G)} \tag{8A.16}$$

where $S(\$/£)$ stands for the exchange rate, whether it be a bid rate or an ask rate. For example, if the gold prices of the central banks are

$$P_G^{US}(\text{ask}) = \$402$$

$$P_G^{US}(\text{bid}) = \$400$$

$$P_G^{UK}(\text{ask}) = £251$$

$$P_G^{UK}(\text{bid}) = £250$$

and $c = 0.01$, the exchange rate must be in the range

$$1.58 \leq S(\$/£) \leq 1.62$$

The ends of the range are the gold points; in this case the gold points are $1.58/£ and $1.62/£. We find that the gold points result from both the bid-ask spreads on gold prices and the cost of shipping gold between the two countries.

The International Financial System: Past, Present, and Future

The 1870–1914 gold standard could flourish in an age of creative *nationalism, when national self-interest was tempered by a decent respect for world order; gold was accepted as the anonymous monarch and sterling as the power behind the throne, the true international money.*
—ROBERT MUNDELL

In this chapter we follow a time line of the international financial system, from the latter half of the nineteenth century until today. This takes us on a journey through the four principal types of financial systems we have experienced: gold standard, Bretton Woods standard, flexible exchange rates, and cooperative intervention. After the historical tour, we extend the time line into the future by looking at the problems the international financial system faces and how these are likely to affect the evolution of international financial arrangements. We focus on the mounting debt of some key economic players, on the shifting of economic power from the industrial leaders of the twentieth century to a broader base of successful trading nations, and on the direction of the international financial system itself. By analyzing the pros and cons of fixed and flexible exchange rates we are forced to conclude that despite extensive experimentation with different international financial arrangements during this century, there is no obvious, dominant solution. Furthermore, we note that the speed of economic change is likely to place increasing pressure on whatever arrangements are employed.

THE PAST

The Classical Gold Standard, 1870–1914

For almost half a century before the First World War of 1914–1918, the international financial system ran according to the rules of the classical gold standard. The success of this system has been traced to the credible commitment represented by the unconditional guarantee to convert paper money for gold at a fixed price. As we have seen in the preceding chapter, such a commitment is the essential element of the classical gold standard. Few, if any, doubted the willingness of governments to

207

continue to exchange gold for fiat money, even after temporary suspensions during periods of war. Not only did participating countries such as the United States and France gain the confidence of others, but everybody could count on Britain to do whatever was necessary to underwrite the system.[1]

The criticality of credibility to the success of a rule-based system such as the gold standard has been cast in modern **game theory** terms, following the successful application of game theory to domestic monetary policy.[2] The key insight is that without rules and a credible commitment to maintain a stable price level, governments can be counted on to say they intend to fight inflation in order to induce people to lend to them at low interest rates, and then afterward to abandon that promise. The government-induced inflation, *if* unexpected, reduces the government's real borrowing costs; interest rates would not compensate for realized inflation. However, with rational expectations it is not possible for governments to play this game successfully. Lenders know that the government will misrepresent its intentions, pursuing inflationary policy despite its promises. This drives the economy to an inefficient equilibrium—one in which the public expects the government to **defect** (that is, to cheat) by inflating and the government knows that the public expects this and does indeed cheat. Therefore, interest rates are high to reflect the expected, and actual, inflation. This is a so-called **Nash equilibrium:** expectations are consistent and ultimately vindicated, and each "player" chooses the best available action given these expectations. All this follows if governments take no costly steps to gain credibility.

Knowing how the "game" unravels when there is nothing to constrain government behavior, it becomes optimal for the government to agree to a constraint on its behavior. The promise to convert fiat money for gold is just such a constraint and is a **signal** of its sincerity. In this way gold serves as a **nominal anchor**—a credible commitment to a stable value of fiat money. The public reasons that the government would not agree to a fixed price of gold—or a fixed price of currency versus the U.S. dollar under the Bretton Woods system—if it intended to defect. The government knows this and indeed, does not want to defect, instead preferring to keep inflation low even after it has borrowed. In this way the government keeps interest rates low; low inflationary expectations mean low interest rates.[3]

Flexible Rates and Controls, 1914–1944

The credibility that the gold standard brought to government policy was eroded somewhat by the First World War. As is usual in wartime, governments imposed

[1]See, for example, Alberto Giovannini, "Bretton Woods and Its Precursors: Rules versus Discretion in the History of International Monetary Regimes," in Michael D. Bordo and Barry Eichengreen, eds., *A Retrospective on the Bretton Woods System,* University of Chicago Press, Chicago, 1993, pp. 109–155, and Michael D. Bordo, "The Gold Standard, Bretton Woods and Other Monetary Regimes: A Historical Appraisal," in *Review,* Federal Reserve Bank of St. Louis, March/April 1993, pp. 123–199.
[2]See Finn E. Kydland and Edward C. Prescott, "Rules Rather than Discretion: The Inconsistency of Optimal Plans," *Journal of Political Economy,* June 1977, pp. 473–491, and Robert J. Barrow and David B. Gordon, "Rules, Discretion and Reputation in a Model of Monetary Policy," *Journal of Monetary Economics,* July 1983, pp. 101–121.
[3]See Michael D. Bordo and Finn E. Kydland, "The Gold Standard as a Rule," National Bureau of Economic Research, Working Paper No. 3367, May 1990, and G. de Kock and Vittorio U. Grilli, "Endogenous Exchange Rate Regime Switches," National Bureau of Economic Research, Working Paper No. 3066, August 1989.

209

CHAPTER 9
The International
Financial System:
Past, Present, and
Future

currency controls and abandoned the commitment to convert their paper currencies into gold. Immediately after the First World War ended in 1918, rather than return to gold, there was a period of flexible exchange rates that lasted until 1926, during which time many countries suffered from hyperinflation. The gold standard was eventually readopted in 1926 in an effort to bring inflation under control and to help cure a number of other economic ills, such as sweeping protectionism, competitive devaluation, and so on. However, for the gold standard to retain credibility, it is necessary that deficit countries allow the influence of deficits on their gold reserves to slow monetary growth. It is also necessary that surplus countries allow their increased gold reserves to liberalize their monetary policies. After the First World War, the burden of both types of adjustment was considered so great that there was reluctance to behave in this way. Many countries began to manipulate exchange rates for their own domestic objectives. For example, the French devalued the franc in 1926 to stimulate their economy, and the undervalued currency contributed to problems for Britain and the pound sterling. Then in 1928, the French government decided to accept only gold and no more foreign exchange. When in 1931 the French decided that they would not accept any more pounds sterling and also that they would exchange their existing sterling holdings for gold, there was little Britain could do other than make sterling inconvertible into gold. This they did in 1931. With the ability to exchange currencies for gold being the central feature of the gold standard, and with Britain having been the nucleus of the gold standard, this marked the end of the era. Indeed, when other countries found their holdings of pounds no longer convertible, they followed Britain. By 1934 only the U.S. dollar could be exchanged for gold.

Since a full recovery from the Great Depression of 1929–1933 did not take place until the onset of World War II, the conditions for a formal reorganization of the international financial order were not present. The Depression had provided an environment in which self-interested **beggar-thy-neighbor policies**—competitive devaluations and increased tariff protection—followed the model established earlier by France. Since no long-lasting effective devaluations were possible and the great interruption of world trade eliminated the gains from international trade, such an environment hindered global economic growth: all countries cannot simultaneously devalue by raising gold prices, with collective action doing nothing more than devaluing money by causing inflation. When the war replaced the Depression, no cooperation was possible. It was not until July 1944 that, with victory imminent in Europe, the representatives of the United States, Great Britain, and other allied powers met at the Mount Washington Hotel in Bretton Woods, New Hampshire, to hammer out a new international financial order to replace the failed gold standard.

Bretton Woods and the International Monetary Fund (IMF), 1944–1973

Of paramount importance to the representatives at the 1944 meeting in Bretton Woods was the prevention of another breakdown of the international financial order, such as the one which followed the peace after the First World War. From 1918 until well into the 1920s the world had witnessed a rise in protectionism on a grand scale to protect jobs for those returning from the war, competitive devaluations designed for the same effect, and massive hyperinflation as the inability to raise conventional taxes led to use of the hidden tax of inflation: inflation shifts buying power from the holders of money, whose holdings buy less, to the issuers of money, the central banks. A system was required that would keep countries from changing exchange rates to obtain a trading advantage and to limit inflationary policy. This meant that some sort of control on rate changes was needed, as well as a reserve base for deficit countries. The reserves were to be provided via an institution created for this purpose. The International Monetary Fund (IMF) was established to collect and allocate reserves in order to implement the **Articles of Agreement** signed in Bretton Woods.[4]

The Articles of Agreement required IMF member countries (of which there were 178 as of March 1994) to:

[4]Exhibit 9.1 describes the competing views that had to be resolved before agreement was reached.

1. Promote international monetary cooperation
2. Facilitate the growth of trade
3. Promote exchange-rate stability
4. Establish a system of multilateral payments
5. Create a reserve base

211

CHAPTER *9*
*The International
Financial System:
Past, Present, and
Future*

The reserves were contributed by the member countries according to a quota system (since then many times revised) based on the national income and importance of trade in different countries. Of the original contribution, 25 percent was in gold—the so-called **gold tranche** position—and the remaining 75 percent was in the country's own currency. A country was allowed to borrow up to its gold-tranche contribution without IMF approval and to borrow an additional 100 percent of its total contribution in four steps, each with additional stringent conditions established by the IMF. These conditions were designed to ensure that corrective macroeconomic policy actions would be taken.

The lending facilities have been expanded over the years. Standby arrangements were introduced in 1952, enabling a country to have funds appropriated ahead of the need so that currencies would be less open to attack during the IMF's deliberation of whether help would be made available. Other extensions of the IMF's lending ability took the form of:

1. The **Compensating Financing Facility,** introduced in 1963 to help countries with temporarily inadequate foreign exchange reserves as a result of events such as crop failures.
2. The **Extended Fund Facility** of 1974, providing loans for countries with structural difficulties that take longer to correct.
3. The **Trust Fund** from the 1976 **Kingston Agreement** to allow the sale of gold, which was no longer to have a formal role in the international financial system. The proceeds of gold sales are used for special development loans.
4. The **Supplementary Financing Facility,** also known as the **Witteveen Facility** after the then managing director of the IMF. This gives standby credits and replaced the 1974–1976 **Oil Facility,** which was established to help countries with temporary difficulties resulting from oil price increases.
5. The **Buffer Stock Facility,** which grants loans to enable countries to purchase crucial inventories.

These facilities were supplemented by the 1980 decision allowing the IMF to borrow in the private capital market when necessary and by the extension of borrowing authority in the 1990 **General Arrangements to Borrow**, which allows the IMF to lend to nonmembers. The scope of the IMF's power to lend was further expanded in 1993, when new facilities to assist in exchange-rate stabilization were made available.

As we have seen, the most important feature of the Bretton Woods agreement was the decision to have the U.S. dollar freely convertible into gold and to have the values of other currencies fixed in U.S. dollars. The exchange rates were to be maintained within 1 percent on either side of the official parity, with intervention required at the support points. This required the United States to maintain a reserve of gold, and other countries to maintain a reserve of U.S. dollars. Because the initially selected exchange rates could have been incorrect for balance-of-payments equilibrium, each country was allowed a revision of up to 10 percent within a year of the initial selection of the exchange rate. In this basic form the system survived until 1971.

The central place of the U.S. dollar was viewed by John Maynard Keynes as a potential weakness. Keynes preferred an international settlement system based on a new currency unit, the **Bancor.** However, the idea was rejected, and it was not until the 1960s that the inevitable collapse of the Bretton Woods arrangement was recognized by a Yale economist, Robert Triffin.[5] According to the **Triffin paradox,** in order for the stock of world reserves to grow along with world trade, the provider of reserves, the United States, had to run balance-of-payments deficits. These deficits were the means by which other countries could accumulate dollar reserves. Although the U.S. deficits were needed, the more they occurred, the more the holders of dollars doubted the ability of the United States to convert dollars into gold at the agreed price. This built-in paradox meant that the system was doomed.

Among the more skeptical holders of dollars was France, which began in 1962 to exchange dollars for gold despite the objection of the United States. Not only were the French doubtful about the future value of the dollar, but they also objected to the prominent role of the United States in the Bretton Woods system. Part of this distaste for a powerful United States was political, and part was based on the seigniorage gains that France believed accrued to the United States by virtue of the U.S. role as the world's banker. **Seigniorage** is the profit from "printing" money and depends on the ability to have people hold your currency or other assets at a noncompetitive yield. Every government which issues legal-tender currency can ensure that it is held by its own citizens, even if it offers no yield at all. For example, U.S. citizens will hold Federal Reserve notes and give up goods or services for them, even though the paper the notes are printed on costs very little to provide. The United States was in a special position because its role as the leading provider of foreign exchange reserves meant that it could ensure that foreign central banks as well as U.S. citizens would hold U.S. dollars. However, most reserves of foreign central banks were and are kept in securities such as treasury bills, which yield interest. If the interest that is paid on the reserve assets is a competitive yield, then the seigniorage gains to the United States from foreigners holding U.S. dollar assets is small. Indeed, with sufficient competition from (1) alternative reserves of different currencies and (2) alternative dollar investments in the United States, seigniorage gains would be competed away.[6] Nevertheless, the French continued to convert their dollar holdings into gold. This led other countries to worry about whether the United States would have sufficient gold to support the U.S. dollar after the French had finished selling their dollars: under a fractional reserve standard, gold reserves are only a fraction of dollars held.

By 1968, the run on gold was of such a scale that at a March meeting in Washington, D.C., a two-tier gold-pricing system was established. While the official U.S. price of gold was to remain at $35 per ounce, the private-market price of gold was to be allowed to find its own level.

---

[5]Robert Triffin, *Gold and the Dollar Crisis,* Yale University Press, New Haven, Conn., 1960.
[6]For an account and estimates of seigniorage gains, see the papers in Robert Mundell and Alexander Swoboda (eds.), *Monetary Problems of the International Economy,* University of Chicago Press, Chicago, 1969.

213

CHAPTER 9
*The International
Financial System:
Past, Present, and
Future*

After repeated financial crises, including a devaluation of the pound from $2.80/£ to $2.40/£ in 1967, some relief came in 1970 with the allocation of **Special Drawing Rights (SDRs).**[7] The SDRs are book entries that are credited to the accounts of IMF member countries according to their established quotas. They can be used to meet payments imbalances, and they provide a net addition to the stock of reserves without the need for any country to run deficits or mine gold. From 1970 to 1972, approximately $9.4 billion worth of the SDRs (or paper gold) was created, and there was no further allocation until January 1, 1979, when SDR 4 billion was created. Similar amounts were created on January 1, 1980, and on January 1, 1981, bringing the total to over SDR 20 billion. No allocations of SDRs have occurred since 1981. A country can draw on its SDRs as long as it maintains an average of more than 30 percent of its cumulative allocation, and a country is required to accept up to 3 times its total allocation. Interest is paid to those who hold SDRs and by those who draw down their SDRs, with the rate based on an average of money-market interest rates in the United States, the United Kingdom, Germany, Japan, and France.

The SDR was originally set equal in value to the gold content of a U.S. dollar in 1969, which was 0.888571 grams, or 1/35 oz. The value was later revised, first being based on a weighted basket of 16 currencies and subsequently being simplified to 5 currencies. The amount of each currency and the U.S. dollar equivalents are

Currency	Currency Amount	U.S.$ Equivalent
Deutschemark	0.4530	0.2659
French franc	0.0800	0.1324
Japanese yen	31.8000	0.3150
Pound sterling	0.0812	0.1189
U.S. dollar	0.5720	0.5720
		Total $1.4042 = SDR1

Source: IMF Treasurer's Department, August 16, 1993.

The currency basket and the weights are revised every 5 years according to the importance of each country in international trade. The value of the SDR is quoted daily.

If the SDR had arrived earlier, it might have prevented or postponed the collapse of the Bretton Woods system, but by 1971, the fall was imminent. After only two major revisions of exchange rates in the 1950s and 1960s—the floating of the Canadian dollar during the 1950s and the devaluation of sterling in 1967—events suddenly began to unfold rapidly. On August 15, 1971, the United States responded to a huge trade deficit by making the dollar inconvertible into gold. A 10 percent surcharge was placed on imports, and a program of wage and price controls was introduced. Many of the major currencies were allowed to float against the dollar, and by the end of 1971 most had appreciated, with the German mark and the Japanese yen both up 12 percent. The dollar had begun a decade of decline.

On August 15, 1971, the United States made it clear that it was no longer content to support a system based on the U.S. dollar. The costs of being a reserve-

---

[7]See Fritz Machlup, *Remaking the International Monetary System: The Rio Agreement and Beyond*, Johns Hopkins Press, Baltimore, 1968, for the background to the creation of SDRs.

currency country were perceived as having begun to exceed any benefits in terms of seigniorage. The 10 largest countries were called together for a meeting at the Smithsonian Institution in Washington, D.C. As a result of the **Smithsonian Agreement,** the United States raised the price of gold to $38 per ounce (that is, devalued the dollar). Each of the other countries in return revalued its currency by an amount of up to 10 percent. The band around the new official parity values was increased from 1 percent to 2¼ percent on either side, but several European Community countries kept their own exchange rates within a narrower range of each other while jointly allowing the 4½ percent band vis-à-vis the dollar. As we have seen, the "snake," as the European fixed-exchange-rate system was called, became, with some minor revisions, the Exchange Rate Mechanism (ERM) of the European Monetary System (EMS) in 1979.

The dollar devaluation was insufficient to restore stability to the system. U.S. inflation had become a serious problem (see Exhibit 9.2). By 1973 the dollar was under heavy selling pressure even at its devalued or depreciated rates, and in February 1973, the price of gold was raised 11 percent, from $38 to $42.22 per ounce. By the next month most major currencies were floating. This was the unsteady state of the international financial system as it approached the oil crisis of the fall of 1973.

The Flexible-Exchange-Rate Period, 1973–1985

The rapid increase in oil prices after the oil embargo worked to the advantage of the U.S. dollar. Since the United States was relatively self-sufficient in oil at that time, the U.S. dollar was able to weather the worst of the storm. The strength of the dollar allowed the United States to remove controls on capital outflows in January 1974. This opened the way for large-scale U.S. lending to companies and countries in need—and came just in time. The practice of paying for oil in U.S. dollars meant that the buyers needed dollars and that the sellers—principally the members of the Organization of Petroleum Exporting Countries (OPEC)—needed to invest their dollar earnings. And so the United States began to recycle petrodollars, taking them in from OPEC countries and then lending them to the oil buyers.

It was not until 1976, at a meeting in Jamaica, that the system that had begun to emerge in 1971 was approved, with ratification coming later, in April 1978. Flexible exchange rates, already extensively used, were deemed to be acceptable to the IMF members, and central banks were permitted to intervene and manage their floats to prevent undue volatility. Gold was officially demonetized, and half of the IMF's gold holdings was returned to the members. The other half was sold, and the proceeds were to be used to help poor nations. Individual countries were allowed to sell their gold holdings, and the IMF, the United States, and some other countries began sales. IMF sales were completed by May 1980.

The U.S. presidential election of 1980 and the subsequent adoption of **supply-side economics** by the Reagan administration was followed by a period of growing U.S. fiscal and balance-of-trade deficits. Nevertheless, the U.S. dollar experienced a substantial appreciation, further adding to the U.S. trade deficit. This took place against the backdrop of the worsening third-world debt crisis, which was aggravated by the high-flying dollar; since most of the debt was denominated in dollars, it was more expensive for the debtor nations, such as Brazil and Mexico, to acquire dollars to meet debt-service payments. Adding to the difficulties of the

Inflation is a hidden tax; it reduces the value of fixed face-value assets such as currency. The United States resorted to the inflation tax to fight the unpopular Vietnam War, knowing that more explicit taxes, such as those on sales or incomes, would not be received favorably by the American public. The inflation tax was applied via accelerated growth in the money supply. The resulting inflation was "shipped" via the Bretton Woods system in the following way: U.S. inflation with fixed exchange rates caused U.S. trade deficits and corresponding trade surpluses elsewhere. In order to prevent appreciation of exchange rates in the surplus countries, their central banks were forced to increase the supplies of their currencies. This caused inflation among the U.S. trading partners. The following explains how the inflation brought down the quarter-century-old Bretton Woods system after a brief period with a dollar standard (1971–1973).

After the establishment of the two-tier arrangement, the world monetary system was on a *de facto* dollar standard. The system became increasingly unstable until it collapsed with the closing of the gold window in August 1971. The collapse of a system beset by the fatal flaws of the gold exchange standard and the adjustable peg was triggered by an acceleration in world inflation, in large part the consequence of an earlier acceleration of inflation in the United States. Before 1968, the U.S. inflation rate was below that of the GNP weighted inflation rate of the Group of Seven countries excluding the United States. It began accelerating in 1964, with a pause in 1966–67. The increase in inflation in the United States and the rest of the world was closely related to an increase in money growth and in money growth relative to the growth of real output. . . .

The key transmission mechanism of inflation was the classical price specie *flow* mechanism augmented by capital flows. The Bretton Woods system collapsed because of the lagged effects of U.S. expansionary monetary policy. As the dollar reserves of Germany, Japan and other countries accumulated in the late 1960s and early 1970s, it became increasingly more difficult to sterilize them. This fostered domestic monetary expansion and inflation. In addition, world inflation was aggravated by expansionary monetary and fiscal policies in the rest of the Group of Seven countries, as their governments adopted full employment stabilization policies. The only alternative to importing U.S. inflation was to float—the route taken by all countries in 1973.

The U.S. decision to suspend gold convertibility ended a key aspect of the Bretton Woods system. The remaining part of the system—the adjustable peg—disappeared 19 months later.

The Bretton Woods system collapsed for three basic reasons. First, two major flaws undermined the system. One flaw was the gold exchange standard, which placed the United States under threat of a convertibility crisis. In reaction it pursued policies that in the end made adjustment more difficult.

The second flaw was the adjustable peg. Because the costs of discrete changes in parities were deemed high, in the face of growing capital mobility, the system evolved into a reluctant fixed exchange rate system without an effective adjustment mechanism. Finally, U.S. monetary policy was inappropriate for a key currency. After 1965, the United States, by inflating, followed an inappropriate policy for a key currency country. Though the acceleration of inflation was low by the standards of the following decade, when superimposed on the cumulation of low inflation since World War II, it was sufficient to trigger a speculative attack on the world's monetary gold stock in 1968, leading to the collapse of the Gold Pool. Once the regime had evolved into a *de facto* dollar standard, the obligation of the United States was to maintain price stability. Instead, it conducted an inflationary policy, which ultimately destroyed the system.

Source: Michael D. Bordo, "The Gold Standard, Bretton Woods and Other Monetary Regimes: A Historical Appraisal," *Review,* Federal Reserve Bank of St. Louis, March/April 1993, pp. 175–178.

debtor nations was a general disinflation that was particularly severe for the resource exports including oil, which were the source of much of their revenue. Furthermore, because they had to meet debt payments, the debtors could not reduce oil and other resource production as they would normally do at low prices. Indeed, some debtor nations had to increase production to make up for lower prices, and this put even more downward pressure on their export prices. That is, declining oil and other prices caused producers to produce more to meet debt payments, further lowering resource prices, thereby causing a further increase in output, and so on. While the third-world debt crisis which accompanied this resource deflation overlaps the period of flexible rates and the subsequent cooperative intervention period, it is worth singling out the debt-crisis years because the crisis helped transform international financial arrangements.

The Third-World Debt Crisis, 1982–1989

The Background

The high interest rates on loans to countries such as Brazil, Mexico, and Argentina, as well as the rapid economic growth these countries had enjoyed in the 1970s, led even some of the most conservative banks from industrialized countries to make substantial fractions of their loans to developing nations. For example, for the largest 15 U.S. banks, developing-country loans at the outset of 1982 amounted to 7.9 percent of their assets and 150 percent of their capital. This meant that default on all these loans would place the banks in technical insolvency. However, since many of the loans were made to governments or were guaranteed by governments—that is, they were so-called **sovereign loans**—few bankers seemed aware that defaults were possible. A commonly voiced opinion was that "countries don't go bankrupt, only companies go bankrupt." What was overlooked by the bankers in their complacency was that countries can go bankrupt *in terms of U.S. dollars,* and the vast majority of third-world debt was denominated in U.S. dollars. Clearly, if countries borrowed in their own currencies they could always repay debts; they have unlimited power to "print" their currencies. Of course, bankers would have been very wary of loans denominated in the borrowers' currencies, knowing that on repayment the currencies they received would probably have little value. It is worth noting that if the debtor nations had issued bonds rather than arranged bank loans, the inability to pay would have meant outright default, not **rescheduling.** For example, in a similar international debt crisis of the 1930s involving bonds, defaults occurred on the majority of foreign-issued U.S. dollar bonds.[8]

The debt crisis first became obvious when in August 1982, Mexico announced it could not meet scheduled repayments on its almost $100 billion of external debt. Within one year of that announcement, 47 debtor nations were negotiating with their creditors and international organizations such as the IMF and World Bank to reschedule payments. The negotiations involved possible changes in magnitude, maturity, and currency composition of debt. Talk of a "debtors' cartel" and default by debtors was matched against the threat of denial of future credits by the creditor banks and their governments. This was the background to the intense bargaining between debtors and creditors which stretched on throughout the 1980s. The creditors knew that debtors would repudiate if the value of repudiated debt exceeded the present value of the cost of repudiation in the form of denied access to future credit.[9]

---

[8]See Barry Eichengreen, "Resolving Debt Crises: An Historical Perspective," National Bureau of Economic Research, Working Paper No. 2555, April 1988.

[9]The problem of creditor-debtor bargaining clearly fits in the paradigm of noncooperative game theory, and indeed, the debt crisis spawned numerous papers in this vein. See, for example, Jonathan Eaton and Mark Gersovitz, "Debt with Potential Repudiation: Theoretical and Empirical Analysis," *Review of Economic Studies,* April 1981, pp. 289–309.

The Causes

217

CHAPTER 9
The International
Financial System:
Past, Present, and
Future

Numerous factors combined to make the crisis as severe as it was. Taking developments in no particular order, we can cite the following:

1. In the two years 1979 and 1980 there was a 27 percent decline in commodity prices, and a recession began in developing and developed nations alike. This meant that export revenues of debtor nations which depended on commodity exports were plunging, and yet it was from these export revenues that they had to service debts. The loans had been sought and granted based on an expectation of increasing commodity prices and export revenues, and yet the very opposite occurred.
2. The debts were denominated in U.S. dollars, and in 1980 the U.S. dollar began a spectacular climb that by 1985 had almost doubled its value against the other major currencies. Bankers and borrowers had not anticipated this surge in the dollar.
3. Interest rates experienced an unprecedented increase after a switch to anti-inflationary monetary policy in October 1979, with the U.S. prime rate topping 20 percent. This made the payment of interest difficult for many borrowers and the repayment of principal just about impossible.
4. A substantial component of borrowed funds had not been devoted to investment which would have generated income to help service debts. Rather, much of the debt had been used to subsidize consumption. Furthermore, it was difficult to remove these subsidies, and so borrowing continued. Many debtor nations were on a knife edge, risking riots or revolution if they reduced subsidies, but risking isolation from creditor nations if they maintained them. At the height of the debt crisis in the mid-1980s, visits by IMF officials to debtor nations to encourage reduced consumption-subsidization were frequently met with protests. In its efforts to force economic reorganization on debtors by making help contingent on a return to market forces, the IMF became a villain in the eyes of the poor in many developing nations.

The Fear

The principal fear of officials was the consequence of bank failures brought about by outright defaults. This fear was based on the view that losses would exceed the capital of many banks, so that effects would not be limited to bank shareholders. Rather, losses would spill over to depositors. There could be runs on banks if governments did not bail them out by purchasing bad debts. Bank bailouts were viewed by many as inflationary.[10] Many argued, therefore, that the consequences of the debt crisis would be financial panic and runaway inflation.

The Handling of the Crisis

The fact that the 1980s ended without widespread bank failures and financial chaos reflects the step-by-step rescheduling that has occurred, a long period of eco-

---

[10]This view is difficult to support if all that the governments did was prevent a collapse of their money supplies. In fact, failure of governments to prevent losses on deposits would almost certainly have been deflationary, as it was in the 1930s, and the maintenance of deposit levels, if done properly, should have been a neutral action.

nomic growth from 1982 to 1990, and a number of steps taken by international organizations and banks. Some of the more notable of the actions taken are listed below:

1. In 1982, the U.S. Treasury and Federal Reserve extended $1.7 billion of short-term credit to Mexico to help it maintain payments and participated with other developed-country governments to grant loans to Brazil and Argentina.

2. Between 1982 and 1984, the IMF and the World Bank made $12 billion of standby credits available to the six largest Latin American debtor nations on condition that they adopt austere economic policies. These policies included devaluations and elimination of subsidies and were designed to bring about the required structural changes to deal with the problems over the long run.

3. In 1983 and 1984, private creditor banks agreed among themselves and with their debtors to reschedule payments, stretching the repayment interval. This required considerable cooperation because each creditor bank had to resist trying to take its money first.

4. In 1985, U.S. Secretary of Treasury James Baker proposed $20 billion of additional private bank lending to the debtor nations and offered to arrange $9 billion of new loans from the World Bank and the Inter-American Development Bank. The **Baker Initiative** showed recognition that the economic interdependence among nations required that debtors be able to continue buying crucial imports.

5. In 1988, led by Citibank of New York, the most exposed creditor banks began to write off bad debts to third-world countries. This reduced the debt carried on their books toward more realistic levels and marked a recognition that the banks would accept the consequences of past mistakes.

6. In 1989 at the Paris G-7 meetings, Japan offered $65 billion over 5 years to needy nations. Some of the $65 billion was allocated to support the U.S. program to ease third-world debt.

7. Also in 1989, Mexico and a committee representing nearly 500 creditor banks agreed to the **Brady Plan,** named after U.S. Secretary of the Treasury Nicholas Brady. The plan allowed each creditor to chose one of three options: it could forgive 35 percent of the principal of old loans, reduce interest rates to 6.25 percent, or provide new loans.

The experience with the third-world debt crisis shows how financially and economically interdependent we have become. Nations have come to recognize that failure of other countries' banks will spill over to their own banks and that economic setbacks among their customers will hurt their own firms that supply these customers. Through regular economic summits among national leaders and through even more frequent contact among central bankers and other senior officials, countries have been cooperating. It has become recognized that the global good can no longer be achieved through independent, competitive action, and this view was undoubtedly part of the shift in thinking that prompted the Plaza Agreement in 1985.

Cooperative Intervention: The Plaza Agreement Era, 1985 and Beyond

Throughout the runup in the value of the dollar in the early 1980s, the U.S. administration repeatedly argued that the appreciating dollar was a sign of confidence in the U.S. economy and that the free market would take care of exchange rates if they were seriously out of line. However, many economists argued otherwise, saying that the soaring U.S. dollar was the result of an exploding U.S. fiscal deficit that was too large to be financed by bond sales to Americans. Instead, the fiscal deficit required borrowing from foreign savers such as those of Japan and Germany. Bond purchases by Japanese, German, and other foreign investors meant a demand for U.S. dollars when paying for the bonds, and this pushed up the dollar's value. Furthermore, many economists argued that because a flexible exchange rate results in a balanced balance of payments, the capital inflow and resulting capital-account surplus required a matching current-account deficit, and this in turn was achieved by an overvalued U.S. dollar.

As the U.S. capital inflows and current-account deficits rose in tandem, the U.S. response was to leave fiscal policy in place and instead push the dollar down by foreign-exchange-market intervention. The decision to take this tack was made at a meeting in the Plaza Hotel in New York in 1985. The Plaza Agreement marks a turning point in the fortunes of the U.S. dollar. During the following several years the U.S. dollar lost its earlier gains in value against the other leading currencies, and the decline was often very rapid. Despite this spectacular depreciation, the U.S. trade balance worsened further.

With the plight of the dollar grabbing newspaper headlines, attention became focused on how to prevent the dollar from falling further. Economic summits of the world's leaders were organized in which the volatility of exchange rates became a central issue. These summits culminated in the Louvre Accord reached in Paris in 1987, in which the G-7 industrial countries decided to cooperate on exchange-rate matters to achieve greater stability. This agreement marked a shift toward an orchestrated dirty float, or **managed float.** The reason for coordinating the management of the float was that the size of private capital flows had become so large that it had become difficult for the country whose currency was falling to muster sufficient exchange reserves to keep its exchange rate steady. However, since countries never run out of their own currencies, they can indefinitely prevent their exchange rates from increasing. Therefore, by agreeing to manage exchange rates cooperatively, it was felt that the authorities could keep them stable, even in the face of very heavy private speculation.

The agreement to intervene jointly in foreign exchange markets came in conjunction with an agreement for greater consultation and coordination of monetary and fiscal policy. This coordination was needed because, as indicated in Exhibit 9.2, when countries work to maintain exchange rates, inflation starting in one country can be shipped to the others. For example, there was fear that if the United States maintained its very expansionary monetary and fiscal policy, the U.S. dollar would drop, forcing other countries to buy dollars and hence sell their currencies, thereby increasing their money supplies. Japan, West Germany, and the other G-7 countries were afraid the U.S. fiscal deficit would eventually force the United States to expand its money supply, and therefore the agreement to cooperate with the United States was linked to U.S. efforts to reduce its deficit.

The system that emerged from the Louvre Accord, which has been reaffirmed in subsequent economic summits, is one that is based on flexible exchange rates but which enables the authorities to periodically let it be known what trading ranges of exchange rates they believe are appropriate. Intervention is used to try to maintain

219

CHAPTER 9
The International
Financial System:
Past, Present, and
Future

orderly markets within stated target zones. However, as we showed in Chapter 8, the threat of intervention helps provide stability because the closer are exchange rates to the limits of their target zones, the greater is the probability of official intervention. For example, the more the dollar drops toward the bottom end of the target zone, the greater is the probability of official dollar buying; this leads speculators to buy dollars before the intervention occurs, which helps keep the dollar within the target zone. Nevertheless, despite the prediction of target zones research that intervention would not have to occur, intervention has occurred on many occasions, including, for example, the extensive U.S. dollar buying during the summer of 1994 and spring 1995. Despite the foreign-exchange-market intervention, the dollar fell to postwar lows by April 1995, falling to just 80 Japanese yen. (In 1985, the dollar was worth more than 250 yen.) A further example of intervention that failed is the "peso crisis" of December 1994, when despite large purchases, the Mexican peso plunged almost 40 percent.

THE PRESENT

If anything is clear from our brief description of the history of the international financial system, it is that it evolves in response to the environment it serves. For example, the shift from the gold standard to the standard adopted at Bretton Woods came in response to the beggar-thy-neighbor and protectionist exchange-rate policies of the Depression and war. In reaction to these competitive devaluations, the system that was chosen was characterized by extreme rigidity of exchange rates. With the oil shock of the late 1960s and early 1970s, the rigidity of Bretton Woods could not provide the adjustment needed between oil-using and oil-producing nations, and so there followed after 1973 a period of exchange-rate flexibility. With the increasing financial and economic interdependence spawned by financial deregulation and the growth in trade, and with massive structural imbalances of trade and fiscal deficits, the unfettered flexibility of the 1970s and early 1980s was replaced by the more cooperative arrangements of the Plaza Agreement and the Louvre Accord. The obvious question with important implications for the future conduct of international business is, where do we go from here? Since the direction we take is again likely to be a response to current conditions, the answer requires that we identify the problems we face today. These include

1. Shifting global economic power
2. Growing trade imbalances associated with the shift in economic power
3. Increasing environmental concerns relating to international financial and trade flows
4. Need to select an appropriate degree of exchange-rate flexibility

Let us consider each matter, and how it might influence the future.

THE FUTURE

Shifting Global Economic Power

At the end of the Second World War, the United States was the dominant power of the free world, and it is therefore little surprise that the international financial system adopted at Bretton Woods in July 1944 was in large measure the U.S. plan. As would be predicted by an application of game theory, in situations involving an overwhelmingly dominant player, solutions invariably take shape according to the dominant player's preferences. The "golden rule" is that "he who has the gold makes the rules," and in 1944 the U.S. held the majority of the free world's official gold reserves, approximately 75 percent of the total.

The economic hegemony enjoyed by the United States at the end of the Second World War has been eroded by the phenomenal economic performance of South East Asian countries, most particularly Japan, the Peoples' Republic of China, and the "four tigers"—Hong Kong, Singapore, Taiwan, and South Korea—and also by the growing strength of an increasingly integrated Europe. This change in the balance of economic power can be seen clearly in Figure 9.1. What the figure reveals is that today there is a much more even sharing of economic power between the United States, Europe, and Japan. This means that we can no longer predict important economic changes, such as changes in the nature of the international financial system, simply by studying the preferences of any one country. In any situation involving three players who can form coalitions, outcomes are notoriously difficult to predict. [The G-7 can be thought of as three groups: North America (United States plus Canada), Europe (Germany, Britain, France, and Italy) and Japan.] Indeed, if we associate power with economic output, a country with 20 percent of the power, roughly Japan's share, has equal power to the other two players, the U.S. and

221

CHAPTER 9
The International
Financial System:
Past, Present, and
Future

Figure 9.1. The Changes in Economic Power
The U.S. GDP as a fraction of the combined GDPs of the United States, Europe, and Japan has diminished during the postwar period. The more even sharing of economic power makes it more difficult to predict changes in the international financial system. (*Source:* International Monetary Fund, *International Financial Statistics Yearbook,* 1993, plus *International Financial Statistics,* March 1994.)

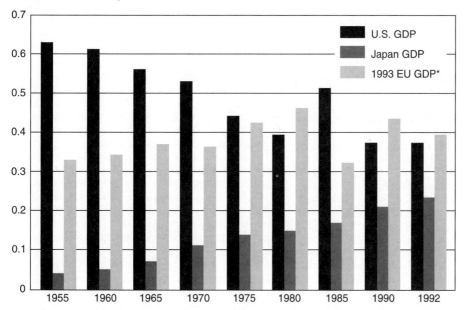

*All data for EU based on the 12 members as of December 31, 1993.

Europe, which each have 40 percent of the countries' combined outputs. Japan has equal power because by forming a coalition with either larger economic unit, the small country holds the balance of power. Indeed, each country holds the balance of power. So what can we say about the likely evolution of the international financial and economic system in the face of this changed economic reality?

One clear consequence of the new balance of power is a need for each party to consult with the others. No single power can take the chance of triggering actions by the other two. This recognition of the need to cooperate has manifested itself in the G-7 summits, in the cooperative exchange-rate intervention policy of the Plaza Agreement and the Louvre Accord, in the frequent meetings of leading central bankers under the aegis of the Bank for International Settlements (see Exhibit 9.3), in the renewed attention paid to tariff negotiations, and in numerous matters involving taxation, interest rates, and other policies. It seems likely that with increasing financial and economic interdependence, the evolving international financial system will involve even closer cooperation.

One of the consequences of the more even sharing of economic power is the

EXHIBIT 9.3
The Bank for International Settlements

The Bank for International Settlements (BIS) is the world's oldest international financial institution, having been in operation since 1930. The following account of the BIS from the Federal Reserve Bank of New York highlights the important functions the Bank performs.

The Bank for International Settlements is a "bank" for central banks.

Almost all European central banks as well as those of the United States, Canada, Japan, Australia and South Africa, participate in, or are closely associated with, the various activities of the BIS.

Based in Basle, Switzerland, the BIS assists central banks in the investment of monetary reserves; provides a forum for international monetary cooperation; acts as agent or trustee in carrying out international loan agreements; and conducts extensive economic research.

In managing central banks' funds, the BIS engages in traditional types of investment. Funds not required for lending to other central banks are placed in world financial markets. The main forms of investment include deposits with commercial banks and purchases of short-term negotiable paper, including U.S. Treasury bills. These operations currently constitute a major portion of the bank's business. . . .

In acting to further international cooperation, the BIS provides a forum for the governors of certain central banks including the Federal Reserve. Representatives of international institutions meet 10 times a year at the BIS for discussions on current monetary policy. Since several central banks of eastern European countries also are BIS members, the bank serves as a forum for contacts between East and West. . . .

In conducting banking operations, the BIS is required by its statutes to ensure conformity with the monetary policy of the central banks concerned.

The BIS has the legal form of a corporation as provided by its charter as an international organization originating from the 1930 Hague Agreement, and a board of directors is responsible for the bank's operations.

The board of directors is comprised of the governors of the central banks of Belgium, France, West Germany, Italy and the United Kingdom, as well as five representatives of finance, industry or commerce appointed one each by the governors of those five central banks. . . .

As an international organization the BIS performs several trustee and depository functions for official groups. For example, the BIS provides the secretariat for the Committee of Governors of the European Community central banks and for the board of governors of the European Monetary Cooperation Fund, as well as for their subcommittees and groups of experts, which prepare documents for the central bank governors.

Source: Bank for International Settlements, Fedpoints 22, Federal Reserve Bank of New York, undated.

potential emergence of three trading blocs of currencies, a dollar bloc based on the Americas, a yen bloc centered around Japanese trade, and a Deutschemark bloc centered on German trade in the European Union. As we indicated in Table 1.2 on page 5, there is ample evidence of increasing regionalism of trade with associated risks of increased protectionism. Indeed, the larger the regional trading blocs become, the greater is the danger of trade protectionism, both because the blocs believe there is less to lose from trade restrictions and because in larger trading areas more industrial constituencies are represented and such constituencies have an interest in keeping competition for their own products more restricted.

223

CHAPTER 9
The International
Financial System:
Past, Present, and
Future

Trade Imbalances

While there have always been imbalances of trade, there has been a growing concern since the mid 1980s that trade imbalances have become larger and more persistent. For example, Figure 9.2 shows the overall imbalances of trade for the United States and Japan. It shows continued growth in Japan's surplus and a continued high U.S. deficit. Even a very major appreciation of the Japanese yen from 1985 to 1995 has not reversed Japan's surplus. The U.S. deficit, while smaller than in the mid-1980s, persists despite a general depreciation of the dollar vis-à-vis the yen, Deutschemark, and several other major currencies.

Even when countries have overall balances in trade, bilateral surpluses and deficits are bound to exist. What happens is that surpluses a country enjoys with some nations are matched by deficits with other nations. For example, the United States might have a deficit with Japan and an offsetting surplus with Central and South America. Similarly, Japan's surplus with the United States could offset a

Figure 9.2. Trade Deficits and Surpluses of the United States and Japan, 1965–1992
(*Source: Direction of Trade,* International Monetary Fund, Washington, D.C., 1993.)

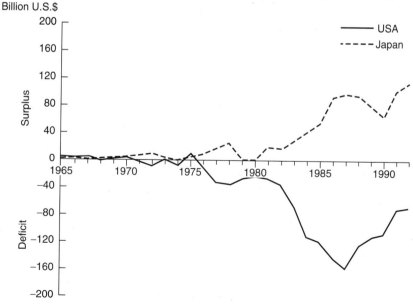

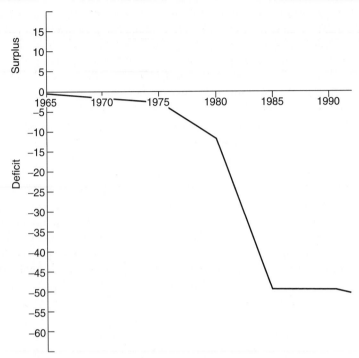

Figure 9.3. Bilateral Trade Deficit of United States with Japan
(*Source: International Financial Statistics Yearbook,* International
Monetary Fund, Washington, D.C., 1993.)

deficit with Central and South America. All countries could, at least in principle, have overall balanced trade. Despite the fact that this argument can mitigate anxiety about recent data on **bilateral trade**, substantial attention has been paid to a particular bilateral imbalance, that between the United States and Japan.[11] As Figure 9.3 shows, this imbalance has grown to approximately $50 billion by the early 1990s and has not shown signs of reversal. The imbalance has been an irritant in U.S.-Japan relations, culminating in the failure to take action after a "crisis" meeting in Washington, D.C., in February 1994. The danger is that even though bilateral imbalances are inevitable, if they are perceived to result from unfair trade practices they can prompt trade actions that interfere with the international flow of goods and services. We can expect increased bilateral bargaining outside of international trade organizations such as the World Trade Organization (WTO) if bilateral trade imbalances persist.

Environmental Damage and International Finance

While the natural environment and international finance might appear to be disconnected, the two matters come together around the actions of an important interna-

---

[11]For an account of this imbalance and its significance, or insignificance, see Alison Butler, "Trade Imbalances and Economic Theory: The Case for a U.S.-Japan Trade Deficit," *Review,* Federal Reserve Bank of St. Louis, March/April 1991, pp. 16–31.

tional financial institution, the **World Bank.** Also known as the **International Bank for Reconstruction and Development**, the World Bank has been assisting developing nations since its creation out of the Bretton Woods agreement in 1944. Today, World Bank loans total $24 billion per year. Despite several attempts to incorporate environmental considerations into World Bank lending policies, it has been argued that the bank has contributed to environmental and social damage on a massive scale. By funding dams that have flooded prime agricultural lands and ancient villages, and financing highways into forests that have provided access to miners and farmers who have plundered the rain forests, the Bank has been accused of assisting widespread global environmental destruction.[12] For example, in a 1993 internal review it was found that over 37 percent of recently evaluated projects did not even meet the Bank's own social and environmental performance goals.[13] With increasing concern over the environment we can expect mounting pressure on international institutions and national governments to have "greener" lending and/or trading practices. For example, embargoes could be placed on nonrenewable resources, just as they have been on ivory and endangered animals. While thus far action against countries has been limited mostly to public-interest organizations, the stage is set for wider action, some of which is likely to involve official agencies.

225

CHAPTER 9
The International
Financial System:
Past, Present, and
Future

Degree of Exchange-Rate Flexibility: Fixed versus Flexible Exchange Rates

During the last century the pendulum has swung back and forth between fixed and flexible exchange rates. Rather than end this chapter by speculating on the next experiment in international financial arrangements, let us list the pros and cons of flexible versus fixed exchange rates. The arguments we list seem bound to circulate continuously as debate continues over the "ideal" system. It should become clear from the arguments we present that either system has its weaknesses. The reader can reach his or her own judgment on whether we will move toward more or less exchange-rate flexibility from our current managed float (dirty float) system. First we present the arguments favoring flexible exchange rates.

Arguments Favoring Flexible Exchange Rates[14]

Better Adjustment

One of the most important arguments for flexible exchange rates is that they provide a less painful adjustment mechanism to trade imbalances than do fixed exchange rates. For example, an incipient deficit with flexible exchange rates will merely cause a decline in the foreign exchange value of the currency, rather than requiring a recession to reduce income or prices as fixed exchange rates would. We

---

[12]For a scathing attack on World Bank lending practices, see Bruce Rich, *Mortgaging the Earth,* Beacon Press, Boston, 1994.
[13]See Emily T. Smith, "Is the World Bank a World Menace?" *Business Week,* March 21, 1994.
[14]The classic case for flexible exchange rates has been made by Milton Friedman in "The Case for Flexible Exchange Rates," in *Essays in Positive Economics,* University of Chicago Press, Chicago, 1953, and by Egon Sohmen in *Flexible Exchange Rates: Theory and Controversy,* University of Chicago Press, Chicago, 1969.

should note, however, that the decline in the value of a nation's currency still cures a trade deficit by reducing real (price-level-adjusted) income and wages. A country's products can become more competitive either by a reduction of local currency prices or by a reduction in the foreign exchange value of its currency. For political and social reasons it may be impractical to reduce local-currency wages, so instead it may be necessary to reduce the international value of the currency.

We can see how a currency devaluation or depreciation reduces real wages in two ways. First, it means more expensive imports and domestically produced tradable goods, which raises the cost of living and thereby reduces the buying power of given local wages. Second, when the wages or incomes of the workers in different countries are ranked in terms of a common currency, the fall in the value of a currency will mean that wages and incomes in that country fall vis-à-vis those in other countries. It should hence be clear that a decline in the value of a currency via flexible exchange rates is an alternative to a relative decline in local-currency wages and prices to correct payments deficits. The preference for flexible exchange rates on the grounds of better adjustment is based on the potential for averting adverse worker reaction by only indirectly reducing real wages.

Better Confidence

It is claimed as a corollary to better adjustment that if flexible exchange rates prevent a country from having large persistent deficits, then there will be more confidence in the country and the international financial system. More confidence means fewer attempts by individuals or central banks to readjust currency portfolios and thus gives rise to calmer foreign exchange markets.

Better Liquidity

Flexible exchange rates do not require central banks to hold foreign exchange reserves since there is no need to intervene in the foreign exchange market. This means that the problem of having insufficient liquidity (international foreign exchange reserves) does not exist with truly flexible rates, and competitive devaluations aimed at securing a larger share of an inadequate total stock of reserves will not take place.

Gains from Freer Trade

When deficits occur with fixed exchange rates, tariffs and restrictions on the free flow of goods and capital invariably abound. If, by maintaining external balance, flexible rates avoid the need for these regulations, which are costly to enforce, then the gains from trade and international investment can be enjoyed.

Avoiding the So-called "Peso Problem"

During the 1980s, Mexico fought to keep the peso fixed to the U.S. dollar despite widespread opinion that it would eventually be forced to devalue. To discourage investors from withdrawing funds from Mexico to avoid losses when the devaluation eventually occurred, the Mexican government had to maintain high interest rates. These high rates were the indirect consequence of fixed exchange rates and stifled investment and job creation. Because of the situation in which it was identified, the problem of high interest rates due to delayed devaluation with fixed exchange rates became known as the **peso problem.**

Increased Independence of Policy

Maintaining a fixed exchange rate can force a country to follow the same economic policy as its major trading partners. For example, as we have seen, if the United States allows a rapid growth in the money supply, this will tend to push up U.S. prices and lower interest rates (in the short run), the former causing a deficit or deterioration in the current account and the latter causing a deficit or deterioration in the capital account. If, for example, the Canadian dollar were fixed to the U.S. dollar, the deficit in the United States would most likely mean a surplus in Canada. This would put upward pressure on the Canadian dollar, forcing the Bank of Canada to sell Canadian dollars and hence increase the Canadian money supply. In this case an increase in the U.S. money supply would cause an increase in the Canadian money supply. However, if exchange rates were flexible, all that would happen is that the value of the U.S. dollar would depreciate against the Canadian dollar.[15]

The advantage of flexible rates in allowing independent policy action has been put in a different way in the so-called **optimum-currency-area argument,** developed primarily by Robert Mundell and Ronald McKinnon.[16] A **currency area** is an area within which exchange rates *are* fixed. An optimum currency area is an area within which exchange rates *should be* fixed. We can explain what constitutes an optimum currency area by asking what would happen if the European Union (EU) achieved its declared goal under the Maastrict Treaty of creating a common currency, or alternatively, for the EU currencies to be truly fixed to each other. We can begin by asking what would happen if, as occurred in the late 1980s, Britain would suffer a fall in demand for its exports with resultant high unemployment while the remainder of the EU continued to grow.

Offsetting the fall in demand and easing the unemployment in Britain would require an expansion in the money supply. With a common currency throughout the EU, this would involve the risk of inflation in the economies with full employment. We see that Britain cannot have an independent monetary policy. If, however, Britain has its own currency, then the money supply can be expanded to take care of Britain's problem. Moreover, even if the discretionary policy action is not taken, having a separate currency with a flexible foreign exchange value means that this adjustment can be achieved automatically; the fall in demand for British exports would lower the external value of the pound, and the lower value would then stimulate export sales. In addition, a lower pound would encourage investors to build plants in Britain and take advantage of the cheap British wages vis-à-vis those in other countries.

The optimum-currency-area argument can be taken further. Why not have a separate currency with a flexible exchange rate for Wales, which is part of Britain?

---

[15]For more on the theory and evidence of the linkage between the U.S. and other countries' money supplies under fixed and flexible exchange rates see Richard G. Sheehan, "Does U.S. Money Growth Determine Money Growth in Other Nations?" *Review,* Federal Reserve Bank of St. Louis, January 1987, pp. 5–14. For an alternative view, see Edgar L. Feige and James M. Johannes, "Was the United States Responsible for Worldwide Inflation under the Regime of Fixed Exchange Rates?" *Kyklos,* 1982, pp. 263–277.

[16]See Robert Mundell, "A Theory of Optimum Currency Areas," *American Economic Review,* September 1961, pp. 657–665, and Ronald McKinnon, "Optimum Currency Areas," *American Economic Review,* September 1963, pp. 717–725. See also Harry Johnson and Alexander Swoboda (eds.), *Madrid Conference on Optimum Currency Areas,* Harvard University Press, Cambridge, Mass., 1973.

Then a fall in the demand for coal or steel, major products of Wales, would cause a fall in the value of this hypothetical Welsh currency, stimulating other industries to locate in Wales. A separate currency would also allow discretionary policies to solve the economic difficulties specific to the region. And if Wales, then why not Cardiff, a city in Wales, or even parts of Cardiff? Extending the argument to the United States, why shouldn't there be a separate northeastern dollar or a separate northwestern dollar? Then if, for example, there is a fall in the demand for the lumber of the northwest, the northwestern dollar can decline in value, and other industries would be encouraged to move to the northwest. But what limits this?

We can begin our answer by saying that there is no need to have a separate northwestern dollar if the people in the northwest can and are prepared to move to where opportunities are plentiful so that unemployment does not occur. We need a separate currency for areas from which factors of production cannot move or prefer not to move. Such an idea prompted Robert Mundell to argue that the optimum currency area is the **region.** A region is defined as an area within which factors of production are mobile and from which they are immobile. Mundell argued that if currency areas are smaller than existing countries, then there is considerable inconvenience in converting currencies, and there is exchange-rate risk in local business activity. This risk might be difficult to avoid with forward contracts and the other usual risk-reducing devices because the currency area is too small to support forward, futures, and options markets. That is, the optimum currency area, like so many other things, is limited by the size of the market. In addition, thin currency markets can experience monopolistic private speculation. Mundell therefore limited the optimum currency area to something larger than a nation. This makes the problem one of asking which countries should have a common currency, or alternatively, truly fixed exchange rates.

Another factor affecting the extent of an optimum currency area is the degree to which economic activity is correlated throughout the area. For example, if all of Europe followed the same business cycle, countries could have a common currency without having local problems from rigid exchange rates. Transfers between areas can also reduce the harmful effects of fixed exchange rates. Money can be paid to areas suffering from a high currency caused by strong demand elsewhere in the area.[17]

The notion that the minimum feasible size of a currency area is limited by the greater risk and inconvenience of smaller areas is closely related to one of the leading arguments against flexible exchange rates: that they cause uncertainty and inhibit international trade. Let us begin with this in our discussion of the negative side of the flexible-exchange-rate argument.

Arguments Against Flexible Exchange Rates

Flexible Rates Cause Uncertainty and Inhibit International Trade and Investment

It is claimed by proponents of fixed rates that if exporters and importers do not know the future exchange rate, they will stick to local markets. This means less

---

[17]Transfers between U.S. states have helped the United States maintain a common currency. See Jeffrey Sachs and Xavier Sala-i-Martin, "Fiscal Federalism and Optimum Currency Areas: Evidence for Europe from the United States," National Bureau of Economic Research, Paper No. 3855, 1991.

enjoyment of the advantages of international trade and of making overseas investments, and it is a burden on everyone. To counter this argument, a believer in a flexible system can say the following:

229

CHAPTER 9
The International
Financial System:
Past, Present, and
Future

1. Flexible rates do not necessarily fluctuate wildly, and fixed rates do change—often dramatically.[18] There have been numerous well-publicized occasions when so-called "fixed exchange rates" have been changed by as much as 25 percent. Many changes have taken place in the "fixed" value of British pounds, Deutschemarks, Israeli shekels, French francs, and Mexican pesos. In addition, there have been periods of relative stability of flexible exchange rates. For example, the Canadian dollar varied within a range of about 2 percent for a period of several years in the 1970s.
2. Even if flexible exchange rates are more volatile than fixed exchange rates, there are several inexpensive ways of avoiding or reducing uncertainty due to unexpected changes in them. For example, exporters can sell foreign-currency receivables forward, and importers can buy foreign-currency payables forward. Uncertainty can also be reduced with futures contracts, currency options, and swaps. Furthermore, the cost of these uncertainty-reducing techniques is typically small.[19]

Flexible Rates Cause Destabilizing Speculation

A highly controversial argument is that under flexible exchange rates, speculators will cause wide swings in the values in different currencies. These swings are the result of the movement of "hot money." This expression is used because of the lightning speed at which the money moves in response to news items. There are two counterarguments that can be made:

1. To be destabilizing, speculation will, in general, have to result in losses. The argument goes like this. To cause destabilization, a speculator must buy when the price is high to make it go higher and sell when it is low to make it go lower. In this way the variations in rates will be higher than they would otherwise be, as is illustrated in Figure 9.4. If the rate without speculation would have followed the path shown, then for speculation to make the rate vary by more than this, pounds must be purchased when $S(\$/£)$ is at A, making $S(\$/£)$ rise to A'; sold when $S(\$/£)$ is at B, making $S(\$/£)$ fall to B'; and so on. But this means buying high and selling low, which is a sure recipe for losses. If speculators are to make a profit, they must sell pounds when $S(\$/£)$ is at A, forcing $S(\$/£)$ toward A'', and buy pounds when $S(\$/£)$ is at B, forcing $S(\$/£)$ toward B''. In this way speculators will dampen variations in exchange rates and stabilize the market.[20]

[18]Occasionally, proponents of fixed exchange rates refer to flexible rates as "fluctuating exchange rates." There is no such thing as a *system* of fluctuating rates.

[19]There are, however, limits on the ability to hedge exchange-rate risk, especially when tendering on overseas contracts. Such matters are discussed in Chapter 15.

[20]It has been argued that if there is an imperfect signal that demand for a currency will be high in the next period, speculators may buy the currency even though they know the signal may not be correct. Then, if there is not another high-demand signal next period, speculators might sell their currency holdings, pushing the exchange rate lower than it would have gone. This can be destabilizing and, it is argued, may also be profitable. See Oliver D. Hart and David M. Kreps, "Price Destabilizing Speculation," *Journal of the Political Economy,* October 1986, pp. 927–952. For other special circumstances in which destabilizing speculation can be profitable see Robert M. Stern, *The Balance of Payments,* Aldine, Chicago, 1973.

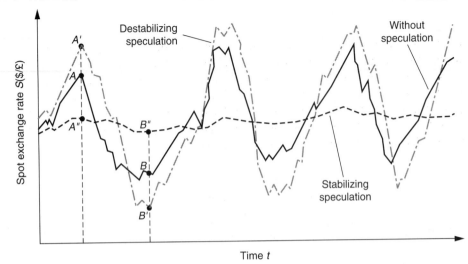

Figure 9.4. Stabilizing and Destabilizing Currency Speculation
Destabilizing speculation occurs if variations in exchange rates are larger than they would
otherwise be without speculation. Profitable speculation involving buying low and selling high
should, however, reduce variability.

2. Speculation with fixed exchange rates is destabilizing, and it can be profitable,
too. When a country is running out of foreign exchange reserves, its currency is
likely to be under selling pressure, with the exchange rate at its lower support
point. When speculators see this, they will sell the currency. Under fixed rates
the central bank will purchase the currency sold by the speculators at the lower
support price and use up foreign exchange reserves. This will make the shortage
of reserves even worse, causing other holders of the troubled currency to sell.
This will further lower foreign exchange reserves and eventually force the central bank to reset the rate at a lower level. This is highly destabilizing speculation. It is also profitable for the speculator.

With fixed exchange rates speculators know in which direction the rate will
move. For example, when the pound sterling was pegged to the Deutschemark
within the EMS during the early 1990s, a *re*valuation of the pound was exceedingly unlikely. By selling pounds the worst that could have happened was that the
rate would not have changed. And if it had changed, it would have been a pound
devaluation, and a speculator could have bought back the pounds later at a lower
price. And so fixed-rate speculation is destabilizing, and because it provides one-
way bets, may also be profitable for the speculators (and costly for central banks
and taxpayers.)

Flexible Rates Will Not Work for Open Economies

This is a valid argument that has been made by a number of economists, including Robert Mundell. The argument begins by noting that a depreciation or devaluation of currency will help the balance of trade if it reduces the relative prices of
locally produced goods and services. However, a depreciation or devaluation will

raise the prices of tradable goods. This will increase the cost of living, which will put upward pressure on wages. If, for example, a 1 percent depreciation or devaluation raises production costs by a full 1 percent, then if real wages are maintained, nominal wages must rise by the amount of depreciation or devaluation. If wages rise 1 percent when the currency falls by 1 percent, the effects are offsetting, and changes in exchange rates, whether in flexible or pegged values, will be ineffective. In such a case the country may as well fix the value of its currency to the currency of the country with which it trades most extensively.

231

CHAPTER 9
The International
Financial System:
Past, Present, and
Future

Flexible Rates Are Inflationary

Rigid adherence to the gold standard involved a constraint on monetary authorities. They had to keep their money supplies and inflation under control. It is claimed by proponents of fixed rates that the Bretton Woods and dollar standards also involved discipline, since inflation would eventually force devaluation. This, it is said, gave the central bank public support for strong action to keep inflation under control. On the other hand, according to this argument, flexible exchange rates allow inflation to occur without any eventual crisis. Therefore, there is less motivation for governments to combat inflation.

It has alternatively been argued that flexible exchange rates have an inherent inflationary bias because depreciations increase prices of traded goods but appreciations do not cause parallel reductions in prices. This argument is based on a **ratchet effect** that is avoided with fixed rates; with fixed rates there are fewer changes in exchange rates to be subject to a ratchet. However, the empirical evidence does not support the existence of a ratchet.[21] Economists who believe that prices are related to the money supply are not surprised. This is because they believe that higher and higher price levels resulting from fluctuations in exchange rates would cause an excess demand for money that would reduce spending unless the higher prices were **accommodated** by the central bank expanding the money supply in line with the higher prices.

Flexible Rates Are Unstable Because of Small Trade Elasticities

If import demand or export supply elasticities are small, the foreign exchange market may be unstable in the sense that small disturbances to exchange rates can grow into large disturbances.[22] Instability is possible because, for example, a depreciation can increase the value of imports by increasing import prices more than it decreases the quantity of imports. A depreciation can therefore increase the currency supply more than it increases the value of exports and currency demand. Consequently, a depreciation can cause an excess supply of currency, further depreciation, and so on. If this is the case, and other factors influencing currency supply and demand do not limit the movements in exchange rates once they begin, the government might wish to limit exchange-rate movements itself by fixing exchange rates. Of course, then the country must depend on the potentially painful price-level, income, and interest-rate adjustment mechanisms of fixed exchange rates.

---

[21]Morris Goldstein, "Downward Price Inflexibility, Ratchet Effect and the Inflationary Impact of Import Price Changes," *Staff Papers,* International Monetary Fund, November 1976, pp. 509–544.
[22]This was shown in Chapter 6.

Flexible Rates Can Cause Structural Unemployment

After the discovery and development of vast supplies of natural gas off the Dutch coast, the Dutch guilder appreciated substantially. This made traditional Dutch exports expensive, causing unemployment in these industries. The gas industry is far less labor-intensive than the traditional Dutch export industries, making it difficult for the displaced workers to find alternative employment. Because of the place where this problem was first identified it has become known as the **Dutch disease**.[23]

There are clearly valid arguments on both sides of the ledger for fixed and flexible exchange rates. Therefore, in the absence of any new, as-yet-untried dominant approach, we can expect the international financial system to respond to circumstances. Rising trade imbalances could push the system toward flexibility, whereas increased volatility from political events could push the system in the other direction. The compromise of the Louvre Accord in place since 1987 might continue to serve us well, but judging from the shifting systems of the twentieth century, further change seems almost inevitable.

SUMMARY

1. The classical gold standard was in effect for the half century before World War I and again from 1926 to 1931. The guarantees by governments to convert paper money to gold provided a credible commitment that inflationary policy would not be pursued.
2. The 1930s were marked by "beggar-thy-neighbor" policies of competitive devaluations. During World War II there were controls on currency convertibility.
3. The Bretton Woods system of 1944 was a response to the conditions between the wars. Exchange rates were fixed to gold or the U.S. dollar, and the International Monetary Fund, IMF, was established to administer the system.
4. The IMF still functions after having gone through many changes, but the Bretton Woods system ended in 1973, by which time many major countries had moved to flexible exchange rates. According to the Triffin paradox, the collapse of the gold-exchange standard was inevitable because growing reserves required continuing U.S. deficits, which reduced the acceptability of U.S. dollars as reserves. SDRs were an attempt to address the Triffin paradox.
5. Exchange rates were flexible from 1973 to 1985, with only infrequent interventions by central banks to maintain order. After September 1985 and the Plaza Agreement, action was taken to force down the dollar, and a dirty-float period began.
6. An agreement to coordinate foreign-exchange-market intervention and domestic economic policies was reached in Paris in 1987. Known as the Louvre Accord, this agreement marked a change to flexible exchange rates within imprecisely specified target zones.
7. The third-world debt crisis reached a head in the early 1980s, when several Latin American borrowers were unable to meet scheduled payments. The causes of the crisis included worsening terms of trade of debtor nations, a rapid appreciation of the U.S. dollar, high interest rates, and the use of debt for subsidizing consumption rather than for investment.

---

[23]It has been argued that Britain suffered from the Dutch disease, too. See K. Alec Chrystal, "Dutch Disease of Monetarist Medicine? The British Economy under Mrs. Thatcher," *Review,* Federal Reserve Bank of St. Louis, May 1984, pp. 27–37.

8. The much-feared bank failures due to the debt crisis did not occur, because international institutions and private banks cooperated to provide credits. This cooperation was necessary to prevent panic in an interdependent financial and economic environment.

9. The global balance of economic power has shifted from U.S. dominance to a more even distribution of power between Europe, Japan, and the United States. Stability requires cooperation among these economic powers, helped by periodic economic summit meetings.

10. Trade imbalances have widened and been persistent since the 1980s, raising the danger of protectionist policies.

11. Environmental consequences of trade in, for example, lumber from rain forests, and of large-scale projects financed by the World Bank have become—and are likely to remain—major issues in the functioning of the international financial system.

12. Arguments *for* flexible rates include better adjustment to payments imbalances, better confidence, more adequate foreign exchange reserves, and increased economic policy independence.

13. The case *against* flexible exchange rates includes the argument that they cause uncertainty and thereby inhibit international trade. Counterarguments are that fixed rates, as they have worked in practice, have also been uncertain and that forward, futures, and options contracts allow exporters and importers to avoid exchange rate risk at a low cost.

14. Another argument against flexible rates is that they allow destabilizing speculation. However, it is generally believed that destabilization requires that speculators incur losses, and in any case, speculation with fixed rates is destabilizing as well as profitable.

15. A valid argument against flexible rates is that they will not work for small economies because wages are likely to be forced up along with prices of imports, offsetting the effect of a depreciation. Other arguments are that flexible rates are inflationary and that international trade elasticities are too small for foreign exchange market stability.

16. An optimum currency area is an area within which exchange rates ought to be fixed. The optimum-currency-area argument provides an alternative viewpoint with regard to the debate on fixed versus flexible exchange rates. Having many small currency areas improves automatic adjustment and allows local monetary policy. However, it adds to uncertainty and introduces costs of exchanging currencies in local trade. The optimum currency area is the region, which is the area within which there is factor mobility. It is generally claimed that this area is at least as large as a country.

REVIEW QUESTIONS

1. What role did commitment play in the successful functioning of the gold standard?
2. What are the Articles of Agreement that helped shape the Bretton Woods system?
3. How did the International Monetary Fund, IMF, help implement the Bretton Woods system?
4. What is the Triffin paradox?
5. What is meant by "seigniorage"?
6. What are sovereign loans, and what error did some bankers make when considering the risk of such loans?
7. What factors contributed to the third-world debt crisis?
8. How has economic power shifted in recent years?
9. What type of bank is the Bank for International Settlements?
10. What type of bank is the International Bank for Reconstruction and Development, or World Bank?

11. What is the "peso problem"?

12. What is an optimum currency area?

13. What counterarguments can be made to the claim that flexible rates contribute to uncertainty and thereby inhibit trade?

14. What is the "Dutch disease"?

ASSIGNMENT PROBLEMS

1. How can government objectives such as the maintenance of low and steady interest rates be helped by agreeing to convert paper money into gold at a fixed price?

2. Why might the Articles of Agreement which were adopted at the Bretton Woods conference in 1944 be viewed as inconsistent with a system of flexible exchange rates?

3. In what ways did Bretton Woods require countries to sacrifice economic sovereignty for the public good?

4. Why can speculators make profits by observing changes in official foreign exchange reserves under fixed exchange rates?

5. Assume that you are going to poll the following groups:
   a. Central bankers
   b. Business executives
   c. Consumers
   How do you think each group would weigh the arguments for and against flexible rates? What does each group have to gain or lose from more flexibility?

6. When we observe deficits or surpluses under "flexible" rates, does this tell us something about what would have happened without central bank intervention?

7. Should Appalachia have its own currency? Should the members of the European Union have separate currencies?

8. Will *re*valuations or appreciations work for small, open economies? Why is there asymmetry in the effect of a revaluation and a devaluation?

9. Do you think that the collapse of the Bretton Woods system would have been less likely had countries been required under the agreement to coordinate their monetary and fiscal policies?

10. How would you go about trying to estimate the seigniorage gains to the United States? (*Hint:* They depend on the quantity of U.S. dollars held abroad, the competitive rate of interest that would be paid on these dollars, and the actual rate of interest paid.)

11. Why do you think some EC countries adopted "the snake"? Does your answer have to do with optimum currency areas?

12. Australia and New Zealand do extensive trading with each other. Should they have fixed exchange rates?

13. Do you think exchange rates should be fixed in the NAFTA?

14. What would be the costs and benefits of having different currencies for each U.S. state, with the exchange rates between these currencies being flexible?

15. Which argument for fixed exchange rates do you think would be most compelling for Fiji? [*Hint:* Fiji's major "export" is tourism, and most manufactured goods are imported.]

16. Do you think Americans might find it difficult to accept a relative decline in economic power? What problems might arise from this difficulty, and what form might these problems take?

BIBLIOGRAPHY

235

CHAPTER *9*
*The International
Financial System:
Past, Present, and
Future*

ALOGOSKOUFIS, GEORGE S.: "Monetary Accommodation, Exchange Rate Regimes and Inflation Persistence," *Economic Journal,* May 1992, pp. 461–480.

BORDO, MICHAEL D.: "The Gold Standard, Bretton Woods and Other Monetary Regimes: A Historical Appraisal," *Review,* Federal Reserve Bank of St. Louis, March/April 1993, pp. 123–199.

————, and BARRY EICHENGREEN (eds.): *A Retrospective on the Bretton Woods International Monetary System,* University of Chicago Press, Chicago, 1993.

BAYOUMI, TAMIN, and BARRY EICHENGREEN: "Shocking Aspects of European Monetary Unification," National Bureau of Economic Research, Working Paper No. 3949, January 1992.

BLACK, STANLEY W.: "International Monetary Institutions," *New Palgrove Dictionary of Economics,* MacMillan, London, 1987, pp. 665–673.

FELDSTEIN, MARTIN: "The Case Against EMU," *The Economist,* June 13, 1992, pp. 19–22.

FRIEDMAN, MILTON: "The Case for Flexibility Exchange Rates," in *Essays in Positive Economics,* University of Chicago Press, Chicago, 1953.

GIAVAZZI, FRANCESCO, and MARC PAGANO: "The Advantage of Tying One's Hands: EMS Discipline and Central Bank Credibility," *European Economic Review,* June 1988, pp. 1055–1075.

GRUBEL, HERBERT G.: *International Economics,* Richard D. Irwin, Homewood, Ill., 1977.

HELLER, H. ROBERT: *International Monetary Economics,* Prentice-Hall, Englewood Cliffs, N.J., 1974.

JOHNSON, HARRY G.: "The Case for Flexible Exchange Rates, 1969," in George N. Halm (ed.), *Approaches to Greater Flexibility of Exchange Rates: The Burgenstock Papers,* Princeton University Press, Princeton, N.J., 1970; reprinted in Robert E. Baldwin and J. David Richardson, *International Trade and Finance: Readings,* Little, Brown, Boston, 1974.

MCKINNON, RONALD I.: "Optimum Currency Areas," *American Economic Review,* September 1963, pp. 717–724.

————: "The Rules of the Game: International Money in Historical Perspective," *Journal of Economic Literature,* March 1993, pp. 1–44.

MUNDELL, ROBERT A.: *International Economics,* Macmillan, New York, 1968, Chapter 12.

SOHMEN, EGON: *Flexible Exchange Rates: Theory and Controversy,* rev. ed., University of Chicago Press, Chicago, 1969.

WILLETT, THOMAS D., and EDWARD TOWER: "The Concept of Optimum Currency Areas and the Choice Between Fixed and Flexible Exchange Rates," in George N. Halm (ed.), *Approaches to Greater Flexibility of Exchange Rates: The Burgenstock Papers,* Princeton University Press, Princeton, N.J., 1970.

YEAGER, LELAND B.: *International Monetary Relations: Theory, History and Policy,* 2d ed., Harper & Row, New York, 1976.

The Fundamental International Parity Conditions

Part Three explains the nature of, and limitations of, two fundamental international financial relationships that are manifestations of the so-called "law of one price." The first of these relationships occurs in the commodities markets, where the law of one price states that, when measured in a common currency, freely traded commodities should cost the same everywhere. An extension of this first relationship is the purchasing-power parity (PPP) principle. The second relationship occurs in the money markets, where the law of one price states that, when measured in a common currency, interest yields and borrowing costs should be the same everywhere. This relationship is known as the covered interest parity principle.

Chapter 10 begins by explaining the law of one price as it applies to an individual commodity such as gold or wheat. In this context the law of one price states that the dollar cost of each commodity should be equal everywhere. This means that when prices are measured in local currency, the ratio of, for example, the dollar price of wheat in the United States and the pound price of wheat in Britain should be the exchange rate of dollars

for pounds. If not, commodity arbitrage would occur. It is shown, however, that shipping costs, tariffs, and quotas can result in deviations from the law of one price.

Chapter 10 also explains the extension of the law of one price from an individual commodity to goods and services in general. The extension gives rise to the PPP principle, which states that the ratio of the dollar price of a *bundle* of goods and services in the United States to the pound price of the same *bundle* in Britain should be the exchange rate of the dollar for the pound.

When considered as a relationship over time rather than at a point in time, PPP becomes a link between changes in exchange rates and differences between inflation rates: currencies of countries with rapid inflation will depreciate vis-à-vis currencies of countries with slow inflation. Chapter 10 explains the nature of this link and why it might be—and indeed frequently is—broken. It is also shown that PPP in its relative or dynamic form over time can be derived by considering speculation as well as arbitrage.

In the context of the money market, which is

the market in which short-term securities are traded, the law of one price states that dollar rates of return and dollar costs of borrowing will be the same irrespective of the currency of denomination. If this were not so, there would be interest arbitrage. This involves borrowing in one currency and lending in another currency, with foreign exchange risk hedged on the forward exchange market. The effect of interest arbitrage is to make the currency of denomination irrelevant when a person invests or borrows. The relationship between interest rates and exchange rates for which it is irrelevant in which currency a person invests or borrows is called the covered interest-parity condition. This condition is explained in Chapter 11, along with the way that the forward exchange market can be used to eliminate exchange-rate risk and exposure when engaging in interest arbitrage.

The covered interest-parity condition is derived with the assumptions that there are no transaction costs, no political risks of investing abroad, no taxes which depend on the currency of investment or borrowing, and no concerns over the liquidity of investments. Chapter 11 describes the effects of dropping these assumptions which, as we shall see, have bearing on international financial management.

The Purchasing-Power Parity Principle

It would be too ridiculous to go about seriously to prove that wealth does not consist in money, or in gold and silver; but in what money purchases, and is valuable only for purchasing.

—ADAM SMITH

Of the many influences on exchange rates mentioned in Chapter 6, one factor is considered to be particularly important for explaining changes in exchange rates over the long run. That factor is inflation. In this chapter we examine the theory and the evidence for a long-run connection between inflation and exchange rates. This connection has become known as the **purchasing-power parity (PPP) principle,** which was briefly introduced in Chapter 7 in the context of modern theories of exchange rates. An entire chapter is devoted to the exploration of this principle because it plays an important role in foreign exchange risk and exposure and in many other topics covered in the remainder of this book.

The PPP principle, which was popularized by Gustav Cassell in the 1920s, is most easily explained if we begin by considering the connection between exchange rates and the local currency price of an individual commodity in different countries.[1] This connection between exchange rates and commodity prices is known as the **law of one price.**

THE LAW OF ONE PRICE

Virtually every opportunity for profit will catch the attention of an entrepreneur somewhere in the world. One type of opportunity that will rarely be missed is the chance to buy an item in one place and sell it in another for a profit. For example, if gold or copper was priced at a particular U.S. dollar price in London and the dollar price was simultaneously higher in New York, people would buy the metal in London and ship it to New York for sale. Of course, it takes time to ship physical commodities, and so at any precise moment, dollar prices might differ a little between

---

[1] See Gustav Cassell, *Money and Foreign Exchange after 1914,* Macmillan, London, 1923, and Gustav Cassell, "Abnormal Deviations in International Exchange," *Economic Journal,* December 1918, pp. 413–415.

markets. Transportation costs are also involved. But if there is enough of a price difference, people will begin to take advantage of it by buying commodities in the cheaper market and then shipping them to and selling them in the more expensive market.

People who buy in one market and sell in another are **commodity arbitragers.** Through their actions commodity arbitragers remove any profitable opportunities that may exist. They force up prices in low-cost countries and reduce prices where they are high. Normally, arbitragers cease their activities only when all profitable opportunities have been exhausted, which means that except for the costs of moving from place to place, including any tariffs that might be involved, prices of the same product in different markets are equal.[2]

In fact, prices of commodities should be the same in different countries even if there is no direct commodity arbitrage between countries themselves. This is because *outside* buyers will select the lowest price. For example, even if there was no arbitrage of wheat between Canada and the United States, the two countries' prices would need to be the same; otherwise, outside buyers would buy everything from the cheaper supplier and none from the more expensive supplier. In other words, shipping costs between Canada and the United States set only a maximum on the possible price difference between the countries; the actual price difference is generally smaller than this maximum. For example, if Canadian and U.S. ports used to export wheat are the same distance away from Chinese receiving ports so that shipping costs from the U.S. and Canada are the same, shipping costs *between* Canada and the United States will not result in different selling prices. Similarly, even when there are tariffs, if they apply equally to potential sources, they cannot cause price differences. In the terminology of Chapter 2, one-way arbitrage creates a tighter link between prices in different countries than does traditionally discussed two-way arbitrage.

When prices in different countries are expressed in the *same* currency, the outcome of commodity market arbitrage—that particular commodity prices are everywhere equal—is easily seen. For example, we observe, as in Table 10.1, that dollar prices of an ounce of gold in London, Paris, Frankfurt, Zurich, and New York are very similar. But what does it mean for arbitrage to ensure that prices are the same when they are in *different* foreign currencies? The answer follows from the **law of one price,** which states that in the absence of frictions such as shipping costs, tariffs, and so on, the price of a product when converted into a common currency such as the U.S. dollar, using the spot exchange rate, is the same in every country.[3] For example, because the dollar equivalent price of wheat in Britain is $S(\$/£) \cdot p_{UK}^{wheat}$, where p_{UK}^{wheat} is the pound price of wheat in Britain, the law of one price states that

$$p_{US}^{wheat} = S(\$/£) \cdot p_{UK}^{wheat} \tag{10.1}$$

When the law of one price does not hold, buying decisions help restore the equality. For example, if $p_{US}^{wheat} = \$4$ per bushel, $p_{UK}^{wheat} = £2.5$ per bushel, and $S(\$/£) = 1.70$, then the dollar equivalent price of wheat in Britain is $\$1.70/£ \times £2.5$ per bushel $= \$4.25$ per bushel. With the U.S. price of $\$4$ per bushel, wheat buyers will buy

[2]We exclude local sales taxes from the price.
[3]As we have just said, even in the *presence* of shipping costs and tariffs, the law of one price might still hold as a result of one-way arbitrage.

TABLE 10.1. Gold Prices in Different Centers
(Friday, April 29, 1994)

London:	Morning fixing	$375.75
	Afternoon fixing	$376.45
Paris:	Afternoon fixing	$375.84
Frankfurt:	Fixing	$376.65
Zurich:	Late afternoon bid	$376.50
New York:	Handy & Herman	$376.45
New York:	Engelhard	$377.74

Source: The New York Times, April 30, 1994 (© 1994 The New York Times Company; reprinted by permission).

from the United States and not from Britain, forcing up the U.S. price and forcing down the British price until they satisfy equation (10.1).

ABSOLUTE FORM OF THE PPP CONDITION

If equation (10.1) were to hold for each and every good and service, and we computed the cost of the same basket of goods and services in Britain and the United States, we would expect to find that

$$P_{US} = S(\$/£) \cdot P_{UK} \qquad (10.2)$$

Here, P_{US} and P_{UK} are the costs of the basket of goods and services in the United States in dollars and in Britain in pounds, respectively. Equation (10.2) is the **absolute form of the purchasing-power parity condition.** The condition in this form can be rearranged to give the spot exchange rate in terms of the relative costs of the basket in the two countries, namely,

$$S(\$/£) = \frac{P_{US}}{P_{UK}} \qquad (10.3)$$

For example, if the basket costs $1000 in the United States and £600 in Britain, the exchange rate according to equation (10.3) should be $1.67/£.

The PPP condition in the absolute form in equation (10.2) or (10.3) offers a very simple explanation for changes in exchange rates. However, it is difficult to test the validity of PPP in the form of equations (10.2) or (10.3), because different baskets of goods are used in different countries for computing price indexes. Different baskets are used because tastes and needs differ. For example, people in cold, northern countries consume more heating oil and less olive oil than do people in more temperate countries. This means that even if the law of one price holds for each individual good, price indexes, which depend on the weights attached to each good, will not conform to the law of one price. For example, if heating oil prices increased more than olive oil prices, the country with a bigger weight in its price index for heating oil would have more inflation than the olive-oil-consuming country, even though heating oil and olive oil prices increased the same amount in both countries. For this reason an alternative form of the PPP condition which is stated in terms of rates of inflation can be very useful. This form is called the **relative form of PPP.**

THE RELATIVE FORM OF PPP

In order to state PPP in its relative form let us define the following:

$\dot{S}(\$/£)$ is the percentage change in the spot exchange rate over a year, and $\dot{P}_{US}$ and $\dot{P}_{UK}$ are the percentage changes in the price levels in the United States and Britain over a year. That is, $\dot{P}_{US}$ and $\dot{P}_{UK}$ are the U.S. and British annual rates of inflation.

If the PPP condition holds in its absolute form at some moment in time, that is,

$$P_{US} = S(\$/£) \cdot P_{UK} \tag{10.2}$$

then at the end of 1 year, for PPP to continue to hold it is necessary that

$$P_{US}\left(1 + \dot{P}_{US}\right) = S(\$/£)\left[1 + \dot{S}(\$/£)\right] \cdot P_{UK}\left(1 + \dot{P}_{UK}\right) \tag{10.4}$$

The left-hand side of equation (10.4) is the price level in the United States after 1 year, written as the price level in the United States at the beginning of the year, multiplied by 1 plus the U.S. annual rate of inflation. Similarly, the right-hand side of equation (10.4) shows the spot exchange rate at the end of 1 year as the rate at the beginning of the year multiplied by 1 plus the rate of change in the spot exchange rate. This is multiplied by the price level in Britain after 1 year, written as the price level at the beginning of the year multiplied by 1 plus the British annual rate of inflation.

Taking the ratio of equation (10.4) to equation (10.2) by taking the ratios of the left-hand sides and of the right-hand sides gives by cancelation

$$\left(1 + \dot{P}_{US}\right) = \left[1 + \dot{S}(\$/£)\right] \cdot \left(1 + \dot{P}_{UK}\right) \tag{10.5}$$

Equation (10.5) can be rearranged into

$$1 + \dot{S}(\$/£) = \frac{1 + \dot{P}_{US}}{1 + \dot{P}_{UK}}$$

or

$$\dot{S}(\$/£) = \frac{1 + \dot{P}_{US}}{1 + \dot{P}_{UK}} - 1 \tag{10.6}$$

Alternatively, equation (10.6) can be written as

$$\dot{S}(\$/£) = \frac{\dot{P}_{US} - \dot{P}_{UK}}{1 + \dot{P}_{UK}} \tag{10.7}$$

Equation (10.7) is the PPP condition in its relative, or dynamic, form.

To take an example, if U.S. inflation is 5 percent ($\dot{P}_{US} = 0.05$) and British inflation is 10 percent ($\dot{P}_{UK} = 0.10$), then the dollar price of pounds should fall—that is, the pound should depreciate—at a rate of 4.5 percent, because

$$\dot{S}(\$/£) = \frac{\dot{P}_{US} - \dot{P}_{UK}}{1 + \dot{P}_{UK}} = \frac{0.05 - 0.10}{1.10} = -0.045, \text{ or } -4.5 \text{ percent}$$

If the reverse conditions hold, with the United States having 10 percent inflation versus 5 percent in Britain, then $\dot{S}(\$/£)$ is positive, and the pound appreciates in value against the dollar by 4.8 percent:

$$\dot{S}(\$/£) = \frac{0.10 - 0.05}{1.05} = 0.48, \text{ or } 4.8 \text{ percent}$$

Both values are close to the 5 percent obtained from taking an approximation of equation (10.7) and writing instead

$$\dot{S}(\$/£) = \dot{P}_{US} - \dot{P}_{UK} \tag{10.8}$$

What the PPP condition in this approximate form says is that the rate of change in the exchange rate is equal to the difference between the inflation rates.

Equation (10.8) is a good approximation of equation (10.7) when inflation is low. However, when inflation is high, equation (10.8) is a poor approximation of equation (10.7). For example, suppose we are interested in the rate of change in the number of U.S. dollars per British pound when British inflation is 25 percent and U.S. inflation is 5 percent. Equation (10.7), the exact PPP formula, implies that

$$\dot{S}(\$/£) = \frac{\dot{P}_{US} - \dot{P}_{UK}}{1 + \dot{P}_{UK}} = \frac{0.05 - 0.25}{1.25} = -0.16, \text{ or } -16 \text{ percent}$$

However, from the approximation based on equation (10.8)

$$\dot{S}(\$/£) = \dot{P}_{US} - \dot{P}_{UK} = 0.05 - 0.25 = -0.20, \text{ or } -20 \text{ percent}$$

Higher inflation makes the approximation even worse. For example, if British inflation was 50 percent and U.S. inflation 5 percent, then from the precise PPP condition in equation (10.7)

$$\dot{S}(\$/£) = \frac{\dot{P}_{US} - \dot{P}_{UK}}{1 + \dot{P}_{UK}} = \frac{0.05 - 0.50}{1.5} = -0.30, \text{ or } -30 \text{ percent}$$

However, from the approximation,

$$\dot{S}(\$/£) = \dot{P}_{US} - \dot{P}_{UK} = 0.05 - 0.50 = -0.45, \text{ or } -45 \text{ percent}$$

The approximation implies a depreciation of the pound that is much higher than the exact PPP condition.

The relative form of PPP in equation (10.7) and its approximation in equation (10.8) are not necessarily violated by sales taxes or shipping costs that make prices higher than their static-form PPP levels. For example, suppose that because of a British value-added tax (VAT) or because of higher shipping costs of principal commodity imports to Britain than to the United States, U.S. prices are consistently lower than British prices as given by equation (10.2) by the proportion τ. That is

$$P_{US} = S(\$/£) \cdot P_{UK}(1 - \tau) \tag{10.9}$$

Equation (10.9) means that for a given exchange rate and price level in Britain, U.S. prices are only $(1 - \tau)$ of the British level. If the same connection exists 1 year later after inflation has occurred and the exchange rate has changed, we have

$$P_{US}(1 + \dot{P}_{US}) = S(\$/£) \left[1 + \dot{S}(\$/£)\right] \cdot P_{UK}(1 + \dot{P}_{UK})(1 - \tau) \tag{10.10}$$

Taking the ratio of equation (10.10) to equation (10.9) gives

$$\left(1 + \dot{P}_{US}\right) = \left[1 + \dot{S}(\$/£)\right]\left(1 + \dot{P}_{UK}\right) \tag{10.11}$$

which is exactly the same as equation (10.5). It follows that equations (10.7) and (10.8) which follow from equation (10.5) are unaffected by τ. The relative form of PPP can hold even if the absolute form of PPP is (consistently) violated.

AN ALTERNATIVE DERIVATION OF PPP

The PPP condition, which we have derived from arbitrage considerations, can also be derived by considering the behavior of speculators.[4] In order to do this let us define the *expected* rates of change of the spot exchange rate and prices in the United States and Britain as follows:

$\dot{S}^*(\$/£)$ is the market's overall annual expected percentage change in the spot exchange rate, and $\dot{P}_{US}^*$ and $\dot{P}_{UK}^*$ are the market's annual expected rates of inflation in a common basket of commodities in the United States and Britain.

The expected return in terms of dollars from buying and holding the basket of commodities in the United States is $\dot{P}_{US}^*$, the U.S. expected rate of inflation in this basket of commodities.[5] The expected return *in terms of dollars* from buying and holding the same basket of commodities in Britain is $\dot{P}_{UK}^* + \dot{S}^*(\$/£)$. This is because there are two components to the expected *dollar* return from holding commodities in Britain, namely,

1. The expected change in commodity prices in British pounds
2. The expected change in the dollar value of the pound

If we ignore risk, then if markets are efficient, the expected returns to buying and holding the common basket of commodities in the two countries will be driven to equality and we therefore have

$$\dot{P}_{US}^* = \dot{P}_{UK}^* + \dot{S}^*(\$/£)$$

or

$$\dot{S}^*(\$/£) = \dot{P}_{US}^* - \dot{P}_{UK}^* \tag{10.12}$$

Equation (10.12) is the relative form of the PPP condition written in terms of expectations, and it is called the **efficient markets form** or **expectations form** of PPP. For expectations to be rational the expectations of variables should on average equal realized rates of change, so that there are no persistent biases.[6] That is, if

---

[4]This approach has been suggested by Richard Roll, "Violations of PPP and Their Implications for Efficient Commodity Markets," in Marshall Sarnat and George Szegö (eds.), *International Finance and Trade,* Ballinger, Cambridge, Mass., 1979. A further alternative approach to PPP, involving an internationally renown snack, is described in Exhibit 10.1.

[5]We do not include costs of storage because, although the presence of storage costs will reduce expected returns in the United States and Britain, if storage costs are similar in the two countries they will cancel.

[6]The lack of bias in expectations if expectations are rational is one of the conditions of rationality described by John F. Muth, "Rational Expectations and the Theory of Price Movements," *Econometrica,* July 1961, pp. 315–335.

EXHIBIT 10.1
Big MacCurrencies

It has been suggested by *The Economist* that rather than use price levels, we might view PPP exchange rates from prices of Big Macs®; each Big Mac is, in a sense, a basket of goods—bun, meat, labor, sauce. The Big Mac Index shows the strengths and weaknesses of PPP.

The Economist's Big Mac index was first launched in 1986 as a ready reckoner to whether currencies are at their "correct" exchange rate. . . .

The case for munching our way around the globe on Big Macs is based on the theory of purchasing-power par-

ity. This argues that the exchange rate between two currencies is in equilibrium when it equalises the prices of an identical basket of goods and services in both countries. Advocates of PPP argue that in the long run currencies tend to move towards their PPP.

Our basket is simply a Big Mac, one of the few products that is produced locally in a great many countries. Many of our readers ask why we do not simply derive our PPPs from different cover prices of *The Economist*. But because the magazine is not printed in every country, local prices would be distorted by transport and distribution costs.

The Big Mac PPP is the exchange rate that leaves

TABLE 10E.1. The Hamburger Standard

Country	Price* in Local Currency	Implied PPP** of the Dollar	Actual Exchange Rate 10 April 92	% Over (+) or Under (−) Valuation of Dollar
Argentina	Peso3.30	1.51	0.99	−34
Australia	A$2.54	1.16	1.31	+13
Belgium	BFr108	49.32	33.55	−32
Brazil	Cr3,800	1,735	2,153	+24
Britain	£1.74	0.79	0.57	−28
Canada	C$2.76	1.26	1.19	−6
China	Yuan6.30	2.88	5.44	+89
Denmark	DKr27.25	12.44	6.32	−49
France	FFr18.10	8.26	5.55	−33
Germany	DM4.50	2.05	1.64	−20
Holland	F15.35	2.44	1.84	−24
Hong Kong	HK$8.90	4.06	7.73	+91
Hungary	Forint133	60.73	79.70	+31
Ireland	I£1.45	0.66	0.61	−8
Italy	Lire4,100	1,872	1,233	−34
Japan	¥380	174	133	−24
Russia	Rouble58	26.48	98.95†	+273
Singapore	S$4.75	2.17	1.65	−24
S. Korea	Won2,300	1,050	778	−26
Spain	Pta315	144	102	−29
Sweden	SKr25.50	11.64	5.93	−49
United States††	$2.19	—	—	—
Venezuela	Bs 170	77.63	60.63	−22

*McDonald's® prices may vary locally.

**Purchasing-power parity; local price divided by dollar price.

†Market rate.

††New York, Chicago, San Francisco, and Atlanta.

Source: "Big MacCurrencies," *The Economist,* p. 81, April 18, 1992.

expectations are rational, then on average $\dot{S}^*(\$/£)$, $\dot{P}_{US}^*$, and $\dot{P}_{UK}^*$ should equal the actual rates of change in these variables, so that for equation (10.12) to hold, it is necessary that equation (10.8) also hold on average over a long period of time. We see that speculation, in conjunction with expectations being rational, means that the PPP condition in its relative form holds on average.

If PPP held in its relative form [Equation (10.8)], we would be able to explain short-run changes in exchange rates from short-run differences in inflation rates. If, instead, PPP held in its expectations form [Equation (10.12)], then by arguing that on average over a long interval of time the expected and actual change are equal, we would be able to explain long-run changes in exchange rates from long-run differences in inflation rates. Unfortunately, PPP does not fit the data very well. This is because, as we saw in Part Two, there are many factors other than commodity prices which influence exchange rates, and these other factors can dominate inflation, at least in the short run. However, rather than simply dismiss the PPP condition as an explanation of exchange rates, let us consider the evidence in more detail to see whether there are circumstances under which PPP gives useful predictions.

THE EMPIRICAL EVIDENCE ON PPP

A major problem in testing the validity of the PPP condition is the need to use accurate price indexes for the inflation rates for the countries being studied. Price indexes cover many items, and what is happening to relative prices within an index is not revealed.

In an effort to use as specific a set of prices as can be obtained and to avoid index-number problems, J. David Richardson employed data on prices of narrowly classified industrial items in the United States and Canada.[7] The classifications are as specific as "cement," "animal feeds," "bakery products," "chewing gum," and "fertilizers." That is, Richardson examined the law of one price rather than the PPP condition. Clearly, if the law of one price does not hold between the United States and Canada, there is not much hope for the PPP condition, especially between countries further apart and more different in the contents of price indexes than are the United States and Canada.

Richardson estimated an equation similar to that in equation (10.8) for several commodity groups, and found that it did not fit the data well in most commodity categories. Richardson's results suggest that even the law of one price is violated, at least in its relative form.

A possible explanation of Richardson's results on the law of one price is the differential pricing of the same object in different countries by multinational firms. Such differential pricing, with higher prices charged where demand is more inelastic, is predicted by the theory of discriminating monopoly. Firms with monopoly power may be able to prevent arbitragers from taking advantage of price differences by withholding supply from any outlets for the monopolists' products where there is cooperation with arbitragers.[8] This possibility is supported by the observation that where there is little or no opportunity for price discrimination, as in the case of commodity markets, the law of one price does appear to hold in the long run although not in the short run.[9]

Irving B. Kravis and Richard E. Lipsey extensively studied the relationship between inflation rates and exchange rates using different price indexes.[10] They used the GNP implicit deflator (which includes prices of all goods and services in the GNP), the consumer price index, and the producer price index. They also took care to distinguish between goods that enter into international trade (tradable goods) and those that do not (nontradable goods). They discovered, using these many prices and price indexes, that there were departures from purchasing-power parity. They concluded, "As a matter of general judgement we express our opinion that the results do not support the notion of a tightly integrated international price structure. The record . . . shows that price levels can move apart sharply without rapid correction through arbitrage."[11] They did find that PPP holds more closely for tradable goods than for nontradable goods, but the departures from PPP even over relatively long periods were substantial even for traded goods.

Hans Genberg concentrated on testing to see whether PPP holds more precisely when exchange rates are flexible rather than fixed.[12] The most important aspects of

[7]J. David Richardson, "Some Empirical Evidence on Commodity Arbitrage and the Law of One Price," *Journal of International Economics,* May 1978, pp. 341–351.

[8]Substantial evidence supports the discriminating-monopoly argument. See Peter Isard, "How Far Can We Push the 'Law of One Price'?" *American Economic Review,* December 1977, pp. 942–948.

[9]See Aris A. Protopapadakis and Hans R. Stoll, "The Law of One Price in International Commodity Markets: A Reformulation and Some Formal Tests," *Journal of International Money and Finance,* September 1986, pp. 335–360.

[10]Irving B. Kravis and Richard E. Lipsey, "Price Behavior in the Light of Balance of Payments Theories," *Journal of International Economics,* May 1978, pp. 193–246.

[11]*Ibid.,* p. 216.

[12]Hans Genberg, "Purchasing Power Parity under Fixed and Flexible Exchange Rates," *Journal of International Economics,* May 1978, pp. 247–267.

TABLE 10.2 Average Absolute Deviations from PPP, in Percent
(There are larger departures from PPP for the years 1957–1976, which include a period of flexible exchange rates. However, this could be because conditions were more volatile during the 1967–1976 period.)

	1957–1966	1957–1976
United States	1.2	3.8
United Kingdom	0.5	3.8
Austria	1.3	2.0
Belgium	1.4	2.1
Denmark	1.3	2.0
France	2.5	3.0
Germany	1.3	2.7
Italy	1.2	5.8
Netherlands	0.5	1.7
Norway	0.9	2.9
Sweden	0.7	1.4
Switzerland	0.7	5.8
Canada	2.0	3.3
Japan	1.9	3.8
Average	1.2	3.2

Source: Hans Genberg, "Purchasing Power Parity under Fixed and Flexible Exchange Rates," *Journal of International Economics,* North-Holland Publishing Company, May 1978, p. 260.

his conclusion can be seen by comparing the two columns in Table 10.2. The table gives the average deviations, in percentages, from an estimated PPP condition. The estimates show departures from PPP for each country with its combined trading partners. The importance of each partner is judged by the share of that partner in the country's export trade. The PPP condition is then statistically fitted between the country, for example, Belgium, and the weighted average of its trading partners. The table shows, for example, that for the United States from 1957 to 1976, the actual difference between the inflation rate in the United States and the inflation rate in its (weighted) trading partners differed from the exchange rate change by, on average, 3.8 percent per annum.

The second column of Table 10.2 includes the flexible-exchange-rate period which began in 1973. We find from the average deviations from PPP given at the bottom of the table that the addition of the flexible period makes the deviations increase. The implication is that there were greater violations during the flexible years, 1973 to 1976.[13]

Niels Thygesen has summarized the results of a study by the Commission of the European Communities, which set out to discover how long it takes for inflation

[13]Genberg also discovered that most of the departures from PPP resulted from movements in exchange rates rather than from changes in price levels. This supports Richardson's conclusion. See also Mario Blejer and Hans Genberg, "Permanent and Transitory Shocks to Exchange Rates: Measurement and Implications for Purchasing Power Parity," unpublished manuscript, International Monetary Fund, 1981.

rates to restore PPP after exchange rates have been artificially changed by the government to gain competitiveness for exports.[14] The idea is that a devaluation should raise the rate of inflation until PPP is restored. This could come about via higher import prices and consequent wage demands setting off reactions elsewhere in the economy. Using economic models of Britain and Italy, the study concluded that it took 5 to 6 years for inflation differentials to restore the PPP condition. However, Thygesen also observed that 75 percent of the return to PPP was achieved within 2 years.

Another study that examined how long it takes for PPP to be restored after being disturbed is that of John Hodgson and Patricia Phelps.[15] They used a statistical model that allows lags and discovered that differential inflation rates precede the change in exchange rates with a lag of up to 18 months. A similar conclusion was reached by William Folks, Jr., and Stanley Stansell.[16] Their purpose was to forecast changes in exchange rates, and they discovered that exchange rates do adjust to relative inflation rates, but with a long lag.

A conclusion different from that of Hodgson and Phelps and of Folks and Stansell was reached by Richard Rogalski and Joseph Vinso.[17] They chose a flexible-exchange-rate period, 1920 to 1924, and studied relative inflation for six countries.[18] Rogalski and Vinso concluded that there is no lag. This, they claim, is what would be expected in an efficient market, because relative inflation rates are publicly available information and should therefore be reflected in market prices such as exchange rates. This question of efficiency in the spot exchange rate has been tackled by Jacob Frenkel and Michael Mussa, who argue that even if we do observe departures from PPP, this does not imply that foreign exchange markets are inefficient. Exchange rates, they show, move like stock and bond prices. Indeed, Frenkel and Mussa find average monthly variations in exchange rates to be more pronounced than the variation of stock prices.[19]

As we have mentioned, a possible reason for departures from PPP is the use of different weights in different countries' baskets of goods. This possibility is considered in the careful work of Irving Kravis, Zoltan Kenessey, Alan Heston, and Robert Summers.[20] To overcome the problem of different weights they recalculated foreign inflation using U.S. weights for all countries' price indexes, rather than own-country weights. They also separated data according to whether the items were

---

[14]Niels Thygesen, "Inflation and Exchange Rates: Evidence and Policy Guidelines for the European Community," *Journal of International Economics,* May 1978, pp. 301–317.

[15]John A. Hodgson and Patricia Phelps, "The Distributed Impact of Price-Level Variation on Floating Exchange Rates," *Review of Economics and Statistics,* February 1975, pp. 58–64.

[16]William R. Folks, Jr., and Stanley R. Stansell, "The Use of Discriminant Analysis in Forecasting Exchange Rate Movements," *Journal of International Business Studies,* spring 1975, pp. 33–50.

[17]Richard J. Rogalski and Joseph D. Vinso, "Price Level Variations as Predictors of Flexible Exchange Rates," *Journal of International Business Studies,* spring 1977, pp. 71–81.

[18]This period was also studied by Jacob A. Frenkel, not because exchange rates were flexible but because the inflationary experience was so extreme. See Jacob A. Frenkel, "Purchasing Power Parity: Doctrinal Perspective and Evidence from the 1920's," *Journal of International Economics,* May 1978, pp. 169–191.

[19]Jacob Frenkel and Michael Mussa, "Efficiency of Foreign Exchange Markets and Measures of Turbulence," National Bureau of Economic Research, Working Paper 476, Cambridge, Mass., 1981.

[20]Irving Kravis *et al., A System of International Comparisons of Gross Product and Purchasing Power,* Johns Hopkins University, Baltimore, 1975.

traded or nontraded. Far stronger support for the PPP condition was found in the common-weight inflation data, especially for the traded goods. However, since the usefulness of PPP for explaining exchange rates hinges largely on its applying to broad baskets of goods and using available price indexes based on local consumption patterns, we are left to conclude that PPP provides a limited description of exchange-rate levels and changes.

Our conclusion to the survey of empirical evidence, that PPP violations occur, should come as little surprise. Those who travel extensively often observe that purchasing-power parity does not occur. There are countries that travelers view as expensive and others that are viewed as cheap. For example, in the 1990s Switzerland and Japan are generally viewed as expensive, while India is viewed as relatively cheap. This indicates, without any formal empirical evidence, that there are departures from PPP, at least in the absolute, or static, form. There are two major reasons we can offer as to why this occurs.

REASONS FOR DEPARTURES FROM PPP

Restrictions on Movement of Goods

The possibility of two-way arbitrage allows prices to differ between markets by up to the cost of transportation. For example, if it costs $0.50 per bushel to ship wheat between the United States and Canada, the price difference must exceed $0.50 in either direction before two-way arbitrage occurs. This means a possible deviation from the absolute form of purchasing-power parity for wheat that spans $1.00. In reality, however, competitive pressures for similar prices to buyers in other countries will keep prices in a narrower range than would result from two-way arbitrage between Canada and the United States. This is the one-way arbitrage referred to earlier.

Import tariffs can also cause PPP violations. If one country has, for example, a 15 percent import tariff, prices within the country will have to move more than 15 percent above those in the other before it pays to ship and cover the tariffs that are involved. The effect of tariffs is different from the effect of transportation costs. Tariffs do not have a symmetric effect. As a result of tariffs, prices can move higher only in the country which has the import tariffs.

Whether it be transportation costs or tariffs that must be paid, they explain departures from PPP only in its absolute, or static, form. As indicated earlier in the derivation of Equation (10.11), when the maximum price difference from shipping costs and import tariffs has been reached, the PPP principle in its relative or dynamic form should explain movements through time that push against the maximum price difference. For example, suppose that prices at existing exchange rates are already 25 percent higher in one country because of import tariffs and high transportation costs. If that country has an inflation rate that is 10 percent higher than the inflation rate in another country, its exchange rate will have to fall, on the average, by 10 percent to prevent commodity arbitrage.

Quotas, which are limits on the amounts of different commodities that can be imported, generally mean that price differences can become quite sizable, because commodity arbitragers are limited in their ability to narrow the gaps. Therefore, quotas provide a reason for persistent departures from PPP.

Price Indexes and Nontraded Outputs

We have already observed in describing the work of Irving Kravis and Richard E. Lipsey that many of the items that are included in the commonly used price indexes do not enter into international trade. We cannot, therefore, invoke the notion of commodity arbitrage to create an equivalent of Equation (10.1) for these items. Most difficult to arbitrage between countries are immovable items such as land and buildings; highly perishable commodities such as fresh milk, vegetables, eggs, and some fruits; and also services such as hotel accommodations and repairs. These "untraded" items can allow departures from PPP to persist when we measure inflation from conventional market-bundle price indexes.

To some extent, a tendency toward parity even in untraded items can be maintained by the movement of the buyers instead of the movement of the items themselves. For example, factories and office complexes can be located where land and rent are cheap. Vacationers can travel to places where holidays are less expensive. The movement of *buyers* tends to keep prices in different countries in line with each other.

The relative prices of traded versus nontraded outputs will not differ greatly between countries if *producers* within each country can move into the production of the nontraded outputs when their prices are very high. Consequently, if comparative advantages do not differ significantly between nations (that is, the nations have similar relative efficiencies in producing different goods), the relative prices of traded versus nontraded items will be kept similar between countries by the prospective movement of domestic producers. But if the prices of traded goods satisfy PPP, then so will the prices of nontraded items if they move with the prices of traded goods. However, we do require that the producers can move between traded and nontraded goods, which is frequently very difficult. And even when producers can move, the price adjustment can take a very long time, during which departures from PPP can persist.[21]

Statistical Problems of Evaluating PPP

It has been suggested that the difficulty finding empirical support for PPP may be due to the statistical procedures that have been used.[22] We can indicate the problems with the statistical procedures by examining the bases for judging empirical support for PPP.

Most tests of PPP are based on estimates of a regression equation that in the context of the dollar-pound exchange rate can be written

$$\dot{S}(\$/\pounds) = \beta_0 + \beta_1 (\dot{P}_{US} - \dot{P}_{UK}) + \mu \qquad (10.13)$$

[21]Mario Blejer and Ayre Hillman have provided a formal model with the costs of commodity arbitrage allowing temporary departures from PPP. See their article "A Proposition on Short-Run Departures from the Law of One Price: Unanticipated Inflation, Relative Price Dispersion, and Commodity Arbitrage," *European Economic Review*, January 1982, pp. 51–60.

[22]The statistical problems have been surveyed by John Pippenger in "Arbitrage and Efficient Markets Interpretations of Purchasing Power Parity: Theory and Evidence," *Economic Review*, Federal Reserve Bank of San Francisco, winter 1986, pp. 31–48. See also Sandra Betton, Maurice D. Levi, and Raman Uppal, "Index-Induced Errors and Purchasing Power Parity: Bounding the Possible Bias," *Journal of International Financial Markets, Institutions and Money*, 1995.

where μ is the *ex ante* regression error. It is argued that if PPP is valid, then in estimates of equation (10.13), β_0 should be close to zero, β_1 should be close to 1.0, and the *ex post* regression errors should be small.[23] This is because in such a case the regression equation reduces to equation (10.8). The statistical problems that can result in incorrect rejection of PPP are:

1. *Errors in measuring the inflation differential $\dot{P}_{US} - \dot{P}_{UK}$*. It is a characteristic of the regression methodology that errors in the measurement of explanatory variables bias regression coefficients toward zero.[24] This means that if the inflation differential is poorly measured because different baskets are used in each country, then we could find the estimated β_1 to be smaller than 1.0 even if the true β_1 is exactly equal to 1.0.
2. *Simultaneous determination of the variables $\dot{S}(\$/£)$ and $\dot{P}_{US} - \dot{P}_{UK}$*. It is another characteristic of the regression methodology that if the direction of causation goes from inflation to exchange rates and vice versa, then failure to use simultaneous-equation methods biases coefficients such as β_1, again usually toward zero.[25] In the case of PPP, causation does go both ways because changes in exchange rates affect inflation and inflation affects exchange rates.

Researchers who have tried to overcome the statistical problems and who have considered inflation versus exchange rates over long time periods have tended to support PPP. For example, by considering only the long-term trends which remain after removing "noise" in the data, Mark Rush and Steven Husted have shown that PPP holds for the U.S. dollar versus other currencies.[26] The Rush and Husted results indirectly support the view that departures from PPP are due to poor measurement of inflation: long-term trends should reduce or remove the unsystematic errors in calculating inflation because the errors should average out and become relatively less important as the interval of measurement increases. Further support for the view that data errors are responsible for rejection of PPP is provided by Craig Hakkio, who reduced the possible problem of poor inflation measurement by considering many countries concurrently over many periods.[27] This reduces the role of measurement errors by reducing the role of any one variable containing unsystematic errors. Hakkio is unable to reject PPP.

Further indication that errors in the inflation variable may be responsible for poor support for PPP is found in tests using **cointegration techniques,** which involve studying the differences between two variables versus the variables themselves. The basic intuition behind the cointegration method is that if two economic variables move together, then differences between them should be more stable than

[23]Small errors mean that the equation fits well. The "goodness of fit" measure that is usually used is the R^2 statistic, which gives the fraction of the variation in the dependent variable, $\dot{S}(\$/£)$, that is explained by the explanatory variable(s), in this case, $\dot{P}_{US} - \dot{P}_{UK}$.

[24]See Maurice D. Levi, "Errors in the Variables Bias in the Presence of Correctly Measured Variables," *Econometrica,* September 1973, pp. 985–986, and Maurice D. Levi, "Measurement Errors and Bounded OLS Estimates," *Journal of Econometrics,* September 1977, pp. 165–171.

[25]This bias exists if common factors affect $\dot{P}_{US} - \dot{P}_{UK}$ *and* $\dot{S}(\$/£)$. See Maurice D. Levi, "World-Wide Effects and Import Elasticities," *Journal of International Economics,* May 1976, pp. 203–214.

[26]See Mark Rush and Steven Husted, "Purchasing Power Parity in the Long Run" *Canadian Journal of Economics,* February 1985, pp. 137–145.

[27]Craig S. Hakkio, "A Re-examination of Purchasing Power Parity: A Multi-Country and Multi-Period Study," *Journal of International Economics,* November 1984, pp. 265–277. See also Yoonbai Kim, "Purchasing Power Parity in the Long-Run: A Cointegration Approach," *Journal of Money, Credit and Banking,* November 1990, pp. 491–503.

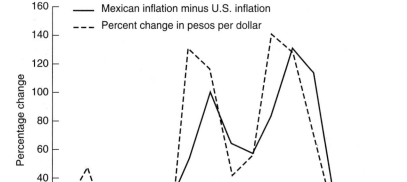

Figure 10.1. U.S.-Mexican Inflation and the Peso-Dollar Exchange Rate
The dotted line plots the percentage change in the spot rate of pesos per dollar, while the solid line shows Mexican inflation minus U.S. inflation. The ups and down of these series show that while the two series are different, they move closely enough together to provide casual support for PPP. (*Source: International Financial Statistics*, International Monetary Fund, Washington, D.C., 1992.)

the original series. This means that if the spot exchange rate and the inflation differential do move together according to long-run PPP, then even though the two series may temporarily move apart, they must move back eventually through their cointegration. The cointegrating coefficient, which is the equivalent to β_1 in equation (10.13), should equal unity if PPP holds.

Yoonbai Kim has applied cointegration methods to the PPP relationship of the U.S. dollar versus the currencies of Britain, France, Italy, Japan, and Canada.[28] He used annual data and found support for PPP using both consumer price indexes and wholesale price indexes in all cases except for Canada. Robert McNown and Myles Wallace have also applied cointegration techniques, focusing on the situation for countries with very high inflation rates.[29] This is a potentially fruitful context because the extreme values of changes in exchange rates and inflation differentials should minimize statistical problems such as the use of imperfect indexes. McNown and Wallace studied Israel, Argentina, Brazil, and Chile, all of which have had periods of very high inflation as well as periods of modest inflation. The estimates of cointegration coefficients were not significantly different from unity as hypothesized according to long-run PPP.

Casual support for PPP involving a country which has had periods of high inflation is provided by a simple plot of the spot rate between the Mexican peso and the U.S. dollar versus the inflation differential between these countries. This is shown in Figure 10.1. While the time paths of the two series do not track each other exactly from year to year, the overall correspondence is quite clear.

[28]See Yoonbai Kim, *ibid.*
[29]See Robert McNown and Myles S. Wallace, "National Price Levels, Purchasing Power Parity and Cointegration: A Test of Four High Inflation Economies," *Journal of International Money and Finance,* December 1989, pp. 533–546.

SUMMARY

1. The law of one price states that a commodity will have the same price in terms of a common currency in every country. The law follows from commodity arbitrage, which involves buying in the cheapest country if prices are different.
2. It follows from the law of one price that the dollar price of a commodity in the United States equals the pound price of the commodity in Britain multiplied by the spot exchange rate of dollars per British pound. Deviations from this relationship can be caused by shipping costs and import tariffs.
3. The principle of purchasing-power parity (PPP) is the extension of the law of one price to prices of a basket of goods. In its absolute form, PPP says that the dollar price of a basket of goods in the United States is the pound price of the basket in Britain, multiplied by the exchange rate of dollars per pound.
4. In its relative form, PPP says that the rate of change of the exchange rate is approximately equal to the difference between inflation rates.
5. Speculation and efficient markets also produce the relative form of the PPP condition in terms of expected values.
6. Empirical support for the PPP condition is weak, although there is some evidence it may hold in the long run.
7. The reasons the law of one price and PPP do not hold include transportation costs, tariffs, quotas, and the fact that there are goods and services that are nontradable. PPP may not hold even if the law of one price holds for every item because of different weights for different items in different countries' price indexes.
8. The fact that empirical evidence does not support PPP may be due to statistical difficulties.

REVIEW QUESTIONS

1. What is the law of one price?
2. How does the law of one price relate to purchasing-power parity?
3. Explain what a commodity arbitrager does.
4. Write down the absolute form of PPP and interpret it.
5. Write down the relative form of PPP and interpret it.
6. Write down the efficient-markets (or expectations) form of PPP and interpret it.
7. Why might the efficient-markets (or expectations) form hold exactly even though the relative form of PPP does not?
8. What statistical problems are associated with empirical tests of PPP?

ASSIGNMENT PROBLEMS

1. Why might the law of one price hold even in the presence of import tariffs?
2. Assume that the prices of a standard basket of goods and services in different countries are as follows:

United States	$400
Canada	C$550
United Kingdom	£280
Japan	¥60,000

   a. What are the implied PPP exchange rates?

   b. How would the presence of a high sales tax in Britain, such as the value-added tax (VAT), influence your guess of where the actual value of S($/£) would be vis-à-vis the PPP value of S($/£)?

3. Why might there be departures from PPP even if the law of one price holds for every commodity?

4. **a.** Assume $\dot{P}_{Mex} = 50$ percent and $\dot{P}_{US} = 2$ percent. Calculate $\dot{S}(Ps/\$)$ and $\dot{S}(\$/Ps)$ according to the precise and approximate dynamic-form PPP conditions.

   b. Assume that Mexican inflation increases to 100 percent, while U.S. inflation remains at 2 percent. Calculate $\dot{S}(Ps/\$)$ and $\dot{S}(\$/Ps)$ according to the precise and approximate PPP conditions.

   c. How does the error in the approximate condition depend on whether you are measuring $\dot{S}(\$/Ps)$ or $\dot{S}(Ps/\$)$?

   d. How would a constant-percentage sales tax in Mexico affect your answers above?

5. If speculators are risk-averse, could this affect the accuracy of the link between the expected change in the exchange rate and the difference between expected inflation rates?

6. Is the accuracy of the approximate relative-form PPP condition negatively affected by the level of inflation?

7. Why might the relative form of PPP hold even though the absolute form does not?

8. Assume inflation in Italy is 15 percent and in Germany, 2 percent. What is the percent change in the exchange rate of Italian lire per Deutschemark, and Deutschemark per Italian lire, and why do these two percent changes differ?

9. What is required for price discrimination between markets to cause departures from the law of one price?

10. What is the relevance of "goodness of fit," such as the R^2 statistic, for judging the accuracy of PPP?

11. What is one-way versus two-way arbitrage in the context of PPP, and how do the implications of the two types of arbitrage differ?

12. Specialization, which has accompanied freer trade, has caused countries to produce larger amounts of each of a narrower range of products, trading these for the wider range of products that people consume. How might this have affected PPP?

13. What characteristics of a Big Mac® led *The Economist* to choose it as a basis for the magazine's alternative PPP exchange rate measure? Can you suggest any other items which might be used?

14. Several possibilities, both theoretical and empirical, have been raised to explain the apparent failure of PPP. List and explain at least three of these. Comment on the validity of the explanations.

15. Does empirical evidence suggest PPP may be more likely to hold in the short run or the long run? Can you suggest an explanation for why this might be true?

BIBLIOGRAPHY

BALASSA, BELA: "The Purchasing-Power Parity Doctrine: A Re-Appraisal," *Journal of Political Economy,* December 1964, pp. 584–596; reprinted in Richard N. Cooper (ed.), *International Finance: Selected Readings,* Penguin Books, Middlesex, U.K., 1969.

DORNBUSCH, RUDIGER, and DWIGHT JAFFEE: "Purchasing Power Parity and Exchange Rate Problems: Introduction" and the papers included in "Purchasing Power Parity: A Symposium," *Journal of International Economics,* May 1978, pp. 157–351.

GAILLOT, HENRY J.: "Purchasing Power Parity as an Explanation of Long-Term Changes in Exchange Rates," *Journal of Money, Credit and Banking,* August 1970, pp. 348–357.

HAKKIO, CRAIG: "A Re-examination of Purchasing Power Parity: A Multi-Country and Multi-period Study," *Journal of International Economics,* November 1984, pp. 265–277.

HUANG, ROGER: "Expectations of Exchange Rates and Differential Inflation Rates: Further Evidence on Purchasing Power Parity in Efficient Markets," *Journal of Finance,* March 1987, pp. 69–79.

———: "Risk and Parity in Purchasing Power," *Journal of Money, Credit and Banking,* August 1990, pp. 338–356.

KIM, YOONBAI: "Purchasing Power Parity in the Long Run: A Cointegration Approach," *Journal of Money, Credit and Banking,* November 1990, pp. 491–503.

LEE, MOON H.: *Purchasing Power Parity,* Marcel-Dekker, New York, 1976.

MANZUR, MEHER: "An International Comparison of Prices and Exchange Rates: A New Test of Purchasing Power Parity," *Journal of International Money and Finance,* March 1990, pp. 75–91.

MCNOWN, ROBERT, and MYLES S. WALLACE: "National Price Levels, Purchasing Power Parity, and Cointegration: A Test of Four High Inflation Economies," *Journal of International Money and Finance,* December 1989, pp. 533–546.

MEESE, RICHARD, "Currency Fluctuations in the Post-Bretton Woods Era," *Journal of Economic Perspectives,* winter 1990, pp. 117–134.

OFFICER, LAWRENCE H.: "The Purchasing Power Theory of Exchange Rates: A Review Article," *Staff Papers,* International Monetary Fund, March 1976, pp. 1–60.

PIPPENGER, JOHN: "Arbitrage and Efficient Market Interpretations of Purchasing Power Parity: Theory and Evidence," *Economic Review,* Federal Reserve Bank of San Francisco, winter 1986, pp. 31–48.

ROLL, RICHARD: "Violations of PPP and Their Implications for Efficient Commodity Markets," in Marshall Sarnat and George Szegö (eds.), *International Finance and Trade,* Ballinger, Cambridge, Mass., 1979.

RUSH, MARK, and STEVEN L. HUSTED: "Purchasing Power Parity in the Long Run," *Canadian Journal of Economics,* February 1985, pp. 137–145.

SHAPIRO, ALAN C.: "What Does Purchasing Power Parity Mean?" *Journal of International Money and Finance,* December 1983, pp. 295–318.

VINER, JACOB: *Studies in the Theory of International Trade,* Harper & Row, New York, 1937.

CHAPTER 11

Interest Parity

International finance is the art of borrowing on the strength of what you already owe.

—Evan Esar

The purchasing-power parity condition, the subject of the previous chapter, applies to goods and services markets. There is an important parallel condition that applies to financial markets, the **covered interest parity condition.** It states that when steps have been taken to avoid foreign exchange risk, costs of borrowing and rates of return on financial investments will be equal irrespective of the currency of investment or the currency borrowed.

In this chapter we derive the covered interest parity condition and show its connection to the purchasing-power parity principle. We also consider the "frictions" that must be absent for the covered interest parity condition to hold. The frictions that must be absent include restrictions on the movement of capital, transaction costs, and taxes. These frictions play an analogous role to the frictions that must be absent for PPP to hold, namely, restrictions on the movement of goods, transportation costs, and tariffs.

Our approach to deriving the covered interest parity condition begins by explaining how to make short-term investment and borrowing decisions in the international context. We then show how shopping around for the highest investment yield or lowest borrowing cost pushes yields and costs in different currencies towards equality, thereby resulting in the covered interest parity condition. Our focus is on investment yields and borrowing costs in different *currencies,* and not different *countries,* because as we shall see, securities are often denominated in different currencies within a single country. For most purposes in this book the *currency* of denomination is more important than the *country* in which a security is issued. Currency of denomination introduces foreign exchange risk while country of issue introduces political risk, and for most countries and time periods, foreign exchange risk is a far larger concern than political risk.

As we proceed, and indeed for the remainder of the book, it will be useful at a number of points to develop concepts by referring to a specific example. For this purpose, we shall consider a manufacturing company that makes denim clothing, primarily jeans. The company is called Aviva Corporation. Aviva is headquartered in the United States but has sales, and purchases its denim, in many different coun-

257

tries. For this chapter, the important characteristic about Aviva is that it has uneven cash flows; therefore, on some occasions it has surplus funds to invest, and on other occasions it needs to borrow.

Short-term borrowing and investment take place in the **money market.** This is the market in which short-term securities such as treasury bills and commercial paper are traded. Because there are actively traded forward contracts with relatively short-term money-market maturities, the money market deserves special treatment. Forward contracts allow money-market borrowers and investors to avoid foreign exchange risk and exposure. Foreign exchange risk and exposure are discussed in some detail in Chapter 12. For the time being we note that it is the result of uncertainty in asset or liability values, or in income flows, due to unexpected changes in exchange rates.[1] Let us start by asking in which currency Aviva should invest.

THE INVESTMENT AND BORROWING CRITERIA

Determining the Currency of Investment

Suppose that a firm like Aviva Corporation has some funds to place in the money market for 3 months. Perhaps it has received a major payment but can wait before paying for a large investment in new equipment. The firm could place these funds in securities denominated in its own domestic currency at an interest rate that can be discovered simply by calling around for the going rates on, for example, locally traded commercial paper or treasury bills. Alternatively, it could invest in foreign currency-denominated securities. Should it buy money-market securities denominated in domestic or in foreign currency?

Many countries have money markets in which financial securities denominated in the countries' own currencies are actively traded. For example, there is a well-developed market in Canadian dollar securities in Canada, of Deutschemark securities in Germany, and of lire securities in Italy. Furthermore, in the large international financial centers such as London and New York, there are active markets in securities denominated in a variety of different major currencies. For example, in London there are active markets in U.S. dollar securities, Japanese yen securities, Deutschemark securities, Swiss franc securities, and other currency-denominated instruments, as well, of course, as securities denominated in British pounds. By glancing at quoted interest rates it might sometimes seem possible to obtain higher yields on some foreign currency-denominated securities than on others. However, realized yields on foreign-currency securities depend on what happens to exchange rates as well as on interest rates. If, for example, the value of the foreign currency in which Aviva's investments are denominated happens to fall unexpectedly before maturity, then there will be a foreign exchange loss when the investments are converted back into dollars. As we shall see, the existence of the forward exchange market allows us to compute yields which include the effects of exchange rates. However, we shall also see that when the forward market is used to remove foreign

[1]Risk can exist even if values of assets, liabilities, or income flows are not uncertain. Risk also exists if there is uncertainty in the prices of what people buy, so-called **inflation risk,** due to uncertainty in the buying power of given amounts of money.

exchange exposure, yield differences on different currency-denominated securities are likely to be very, very small.

Let us see how an exchange-risk-free investment decision is made. We will select for our example Aviva's choice between alternative 3-month rather than full-year securities to make clear the need to keep exchange-rate movements and interest rates in comparable annualized terms.

Aviva knows that if it puts its funds in a U.S. dollar investment such as a bank deposit for 3 months, each dollar will provide

$$\$\left(1 + \frac{r_\$}{4}\right)$$

where $r_\$$ is the annualized U.S. dollar interest rate, and division by 4 gives the 3-month return.[2] The interest rate is in decimal form, so an 8 percent rate would be expressed as $r_\$ = 0.08$.

Suppose that Aviva considers investing in a pound-denominated bank deposit and that the spot dollar/sterling exchange rate, in the conventional U.S. terms of quotation, is $S(\$/£)$. The exchange rate $S(\$/£)$ gives the number of dollars per pound sterling, and so for $1 Aviva will obtain $1/S(\$/£)$ in British pounds, assuming that there are no transaction costs. If the annualized interest rate on 3-month British pound bank deposits is $r_£$, then for every dollar invested, Aviva will receive after 3 months the number of pounds that was invested (the principal), $1/S(\$/£)$, plus the 3-month interest on this, which is the principal times $r_£/4$. That is, Aviva will receive

$$£ \, \frac{1}{S(\$/£)}\left(1 + \frac{r_£}{4}\right) \tag{11.1}$$

For example, if $S(\$/£) = 1.4780$ and $r_£ = 0.0644$, then each dollar invested in pound-denominated bank deposits will provide after 3 months:

$$£ \, \frac{1}{1.4780}\left(1 + \frac{0.0644}{4}\right) = £0.6875$$

This certain number of pounds represents an uncertain number of dollars, but a forward contract can offer a complete hedge and guarantee the number of dollars that will finally be received.

If, at the time of buying the 3-month pound-denominated deposit, Aviva sells forward the amount of pounds to be received at maturity, that is, the amount in equation (11.1), or £0.6875 in our example, then the number of dollars that will be obtained is set by the forward contract. After 3 months, Aviva delivers the British pounds and receives the number of dollars stated in the forward contract. If, for example, the 3-month forward rate at the time of investment is $F_{1/4}(\$/£)$, then we multiply the amount in equation (11.1) by this exchange rate to find the number of dollars received for each original dollar invested in the pound deposit. We obtain

$$\$ \, \frac{F_{1/4}(\$/£)}{S(\$/£)}\left(1 + \frac{r_£}{4}\right) \tag{11.2}$$

[2]Later, we allow for compound interest in computing returns. However, division by 4 is expositionally more convenient than taking the fourth root to find the 3-month return, and because we do the same for U.S. dollar and for other interest rates, the simplification does not affect our conclusions.

For example, if $F_{1/4}(\$/\pounds) = 1.4725$, then the number of pounds from equation (11.1), £0.6875, will provide $\$1.4725/\pounds \times \pounds0.6875 = \$1.0123$ when sold forward for dollars. This is the number of dollars received after 3 months, or $1/4$ year, for each original dollar in the pound-denominated bank deposit. This implies an annual rate of return of approximately

$$4\left(\frac{1.0123 - 1.0000}{1.0000}\right) = 0.0493, \text{ or } 4.93 \text{ percent}$$

It is important to remember that the number of dollars given in equation (11.2) is a certain amount and is known at the time of investment. The purchase of the spot pounds, the investment in the pound-denominated deposit, and the forward sale of pounds all take place at the same time, and so there is no doubt about the number of dollars that will be received. If the spot exchange rate changes before the deposit matures, that will make no difference. The exchange rate to be used is already set in the forward contract, which is part of the swap of dollars for pounds. (Recall from Chapter 3 that a swap is any exchange of currencies that is reversed, in this case dollars into pounds and back to dollars, a "swap-in" pounds.) In terms of our example, it is guaranteed that $1.0123 will be received.

It is now a simple matter to express the rule for deciding the currency in which to invest. The investor should choose a 3-month U.S. dollar deposit, rather than a pound deposit, whenever[3]

$$\left(1 + \frac{r_\$}{4}\right) > \frac{F_{1/4}(\$/\pounds)}{S(\$/\pounds)}\left(1 + \frac{r_\pounds}{4}\right)$$

The investor should select the pound deposit rather than the U.S. dollar deposit whenever the reverse inequality holds, that is

$$\left(1 + \frac{r_\$}{4}\right) < \frac{F_{1/4}(\$/\pounds)}{S(\$/\pounds)}\left(1 + \frac{r_\pounds}{4}\right)$$

Only if

$$\left(1 + \frac{r_\$}{4}\right) = \frac{F_{1/4}(\$/\pounds)}{S(\$/\pounds)}\left(1 + \frac{r_\pounds}{4}\right) \tag{11.3}$$

should the investor be indifferent, since the same amount will be received from a dollar invested in securities denominated in either currency.[4]

We can convert equation (11.3) into a more meaningful equality if we subtract $(1 + r_\pounds/4)$ from both sides:

---

[3]When exchange rates are in European terms, the forward and spot rates must be inverted, and subsequent deduction gives results which are more difficult to interpret. This is left as an exercise at the end of the chapter.

[4]In more general terms, equation (11.3) can be written as

$$\frac{F}{S} = \frac{1+r}{1+r_f}$$

where the form of the exchange-rate quotation and the annualization are assumed to be understood. The term r_f is the foreign-currency interest rate.

$$\left(1 + \frac{r_\$}{4}\right) - \left(1 + \frac{r_£}{4}\right) = \frac{F_{1/4}(\$/£)}{S(\$/£)}\left(1 + \frac{r_£}{4}\right) - \left(1 + \frac{r_£}{4}\right)$$

With cancelation and rearrangement we obtain

$$r_\$ = r_£ + 4\left(\frac{F_{1/4}(\$/£) - S(\$/£)}{S(\$/£)}\right)\left(1 + \frac{r_£}{4}\right) \tag{11.4}$$

We interpret this equation below, but before we do, we can note that part of the second right-hand term in equation (11.4) involves the multiplication of two small numbers, the forward pound premium and $r_£/4$. This product is very small. For example, if the forward premium is 5 percent and British interest rates are 8 percent per annum, the cross-product term from equation (11.4) will be 0.001 (0.05×0.02), or only one-tenth of 1 percent. In order to interpret equation (11.4), we might therefore temporarily drop the term formed from this product (which means dropping the $r_£/4$) and write it as

$$r_\$ = r_£ + 4\left(\frac{F_{1/4}(\$/£) - S(\$/£)}{S(\$/£)}\right) \tag{11.5}$$

The first term on the right of equation (11.5) is the annualized pound interest rate. The second right-hand term is the annualized (because of the 4) forward premium on pounds. Therefore, we can interpret equation (11.5) as saying that investors should be indifferent between home- and foreign-currency denominated securities if the home-currency interest rate equals the foreign-currency rate plus the annualized forward exchange premium/discount on the foreign currency. Investors should invest in the home currency when the domestic-currency interest rate exceeds the sum of the foreign-currency rate plus the forward exchange premium/discount and invest abroad when the domestic currency rate is less than this sum. We discover that a mere comparison of interest rates is not sufficient for making investment choices. In order to determine in which currency-denominated securities to invest, we must add the foreign-currency interest rate to the forward premium or discount. Using the terminology of Chapter 3, we must add the foreign-currency interest rate to the cost of the spot-forward swap of dollars into pounds, where this swap is put in annualized terms.

The difference between equation (11.4) and equation (11.5) is that in equation (11.4) we include the forward exchange premium on the principal invested in pound securities *and* the forward exchange premium on the interest earned. In the approximate form, equation (11.5), we consider the forward premium earned on the principal but not the premium on the interest.

An Example: Comparing Investments

Suppose Aviva Corporation faces the exchange-rate and interest rate situation shown in Table 11.1 and has $10 million to invest for 3 months. Into which currency should it place its funds?

The yield on pound-denominated deposits when the proceeds are sold forward, called the **covered,** or **hedged,** yield, can be calculated from

$$r_£ + 4\left(\frac{F_{1/4}(\$/£) - S(\$/£)}{S(\$/£)}\right)\left(1 + \frac{r_£}{4}\right)$$

TABLE 11.1. Exchange Rates and Interest Rates on Different Currency-Denominated 3-Month Bank Deposits

	U.S. Dollar	British Pound	Italian Lire	Swiss Franc	Japanese Yen
Interest rate*	4.4375%	5.1250%	7.4300%	3.9375%	2.125%
Spot rate (U.S. equivalent)	1.0	$1.5140/£	Lit1582.80/$ ($0.00063179/Lit)	SFr 1.4065/$ ($0.710985/SFr)	¥104.02/$ ($0.0096135/¥)
Forward rate† (U.S. equivalent)	1.0	$1.5121/£	Lit1594.50/$ ($0.00062716/Lit)	SFr 1.4052/$ ($0.711642/SFr)	¥103.40/$ ($0.0096712/¥)
Covered yield	4.4375%	4.6167%	4.4404%	4.3112%	4.5385%

*Interest rates in London on 3-month time deposits.
†3-month forward rate.
Source: Harris Bank, May 20, 1994.

where the first element is the pound interest rate and the second element is the premium/discount on the pound vis-à-vis the dollar, including the premium/discount on both the principal and interest. Substituting the values in Table 11.1:

$$\text{British pound covered yield} = 0.051250 + 4\left(\frac{1.5121 - 1.5140}{1.5140}\right)\left(1 + \frac{0.051250}{4}\right)$$

$$= 0.046167, \text{ or } 4.6167 \text{ percent}$$

This yield, which involves no foreign exchange risk because the pounds are sold forward, is slightly higher than the yield on U.S. dollar deposits.

For the covered yields on the Italian lire, Swiss franc, and Japanese yen hedged against the U.S. dollar it is necessary to use the exchange rates in U.S. dollar terms shown in parentheses below the European-terms quotations. For example, for the covered yield on Swiss franc deposits we compute

$$\text{Swiss franc covered yield} = 0.039375 + 4\left(\frac{0.711642 - 0.710985}{0.710985}\right)\left(1 + \frac{0.039375}{4}\right)$$

$$= 0.043112, \text{ or } 4.3112 \text{ percent}$$

The *covered* yields in Table 11.1 are much closer in value than the yields in the local currencies. An inspection of the spot versus forward exchange rates shows why. The British pound and Italian lire, the two currencies with higher interest rates than the U.S. dollar rate, are both at a forward discount. The discounts offset the higher foreign currency interest rates. On the other hand, the Swiss franc and Japanese yen, the currencies with lower interest rates than on the U.S. dollar, are both at a forward premium. The premiums make up for the lower interest rates.

If Aviva were to invest its $10 million for 3 months in the British pound deposits, covered in the forward market, it would receive back

$$\$10,000,000\left(1 + \frac{0.046167}{4}\right) = \$10,115,415$$

However, if Aviva had chosen U.S. dollar deposits it would have received back

$$\$10,000,000\left(1 + \frac{0.044375}{4}\right) = \$10,109,375$$

The difference between the two paybacks is $6040. This is Aviva's reward for doing its homework and finding the covered yield on different currency-denominated investments.

Determining the Currency in Which to Borrow

Imagine that Aviva Corporation needs to borrow for 3 months. If the annualized interest rate for domestic-currency borrowing is $r_\$$, then the required repayment after 3 months is the principal plus interest, or

$$\$\left(1 + \frac{r_\$}{4}\right) \tag{11.6}$$

for each dollar borrowed. However, if Aviva considers a pound-denominated loan, and if the going spot exchange rate is $S(\$/£)$, then borrowing $1 means borrowing $1/S(\$/£)$ in pounds. For example, at the exchange rate $S(\$/£) = 1.5140$, borrowing $1 means borrowing £0.6605. If the annualized interest rate is $r_£$, then for each dollar borrowed via pounds, Aviva must repay after 3 months

$$£\frac{1}{S(\$/£)}\left(1 + \frac{r_£}{4}\right) \tag{11.7}$$

For example, if $r_£ = 0.06$ (the 3-month *annualized* borrowing rate), Aviva must repay £0.6704 (£0.6605 × 1.015). Without a forward exchange contract the number of dollars this would represent when Aviva repays its pound debt is uncertain. However, with a forward exchange contract the risk is eliminated.

Suppose that Aviva buys forward the amount of pounds in equation (11.7) at $F_{1/4}(\$/£)$. When the debt is repaid, Aviva will receive the required number of pounds on the forward contract for which it must pay

$$\$\frac{F_{1/4}(\$/£)}{S(\$/£)}\left(1 + \frac{r_£}{4}\right) \tag{11.8}$$

For example, if $F_{1/4}(\$/£) = 1.5121$, then repaying £0.6704 involves paying $1.0137 ($1.5121/£ × £0.6704). On the other hand, if Aviva borrowed dollars for 3 months at $r_\$ = 0.05$, or 5 percent per annum, it would have to repay $1.0125 on each dollar. In general, a firm should borrow pounds via a swap whenever the amount in equation (11.8) is less than that in equation (11.6), that is, when

$$\left(1 + \frac{r_\$}{4}\right) > \frac{F_{1/4}(\$/£)}{S(\$/£)}\left(1 + \frac{r_£}{4}\right)$$

A firm should borrow dollars when the reverse inequality holds. In our particular example of $r_\$ = 0.05$, $r_£ = 0.06$, $S(\$/£) = 1.5140$, and $F_{1/4}(\$/£) = 1.5121$, Aviva should borrow in dollars: the amount to be repaid is lower from a dollar loan than from a pound loan. The borrowing decision criterion is seen to be the same as the investment criterion with, of course, the inequality reversed.

Borrowing and Investing for Arbitrage Profit

Imagine a firm that can borrow its own currency and/or a foreign currency, as can a large corporation or bank. Suppose that it can borrow dollars for 3 months at an annualized interest rate of $r_\$$. Thus, for each dollar it borrows, it must repay $1 + r_\$/4$ dollars. The firm can take each borrowed dollar and buy $1/S(\$/£)$ pounds. If these pounds are invested for 3 months at $r_£$ per annum, and if the resulting receipts are sold forward, the firm will receive

$$\$ \frac{F_{1/4}(\$/£)}{S(\$/£)} \left(1 + \frac{r_£}{4}\right)$$

Note that the company has begun with no funds of its own, and has taken no risk. Borrowing in dollars and simultaneously investing in pounds will result in a profit if the number of dollars received from the hedged pound investment exceeds the repayment on the dollar loan, that is, if

$$\left(1 + \frac{r_\$}{4}\right) < \frac{F_{1/4}(\$/£)}{S(\$/£)} \left(1 + \frac{r_£}{4}\right)$$

The reverse activity, borrowing in pounds and investing in dollars, will be profitable if the reverse inequality holds. As long as either inequality holds, it pays to borrow in one currency and lend, or invest, in the other. Borrowing and investing in this way with exchange-rate risk hedged in the forward market is known as **covered interest arbitrage.**

It should be no surprise that the potential for covered interest arbitrage helps guarantee that little opportunity for profit remains, and that investors and borrowers will be relatively indifferent with regard to choosing a currency. This is clear, for example, from the similarity of covered yields in Table 11.1.

THE COVERED INTEREST PARITY CONDITION

Mathematical Statement of Interest Parity

We have determined that 3-month investors and borrowers would be indifferent between the dollar and pound if

$$\left(1 + \frac{r_\$}{4}\right) = \frac{F_{1/4}(\$/£)}{S(\$/£)} \left(1 + \frac{r_£}{4}\right) \tag{11.9}$$

More precisely, if we allow for compound interest, as we should for long-term investing and borrowing, investors and borrowers will be indifferent between the dollar and pound for investing and borrowing when

$$\left(1 + r_\$\right)^n = \frac{F_n(\$/£)}{S(\$/£)} \left(1 + r_£\right)^n \tag{11.10}$$

When equation (11.10) holds, no covered interest arbitrage is profitable. Equation (11.10) is the covered interest parity condition. When this condition holds, there is no advantage to covered borrowing or investing in any particular currency or from covered interest arbitrage.

The covered interest parity condition is the financial-market equivalent of the law of one price from the commodity market and follows from financial-market efficiency. The market forces leading to covered interest parity, as well as the factors which might result in small deviations from the parity condition, can be illustrated graphically.

Market Forces Resulting in Covered Interest Parity: A Graphical Presentation

We can represent covered interest parity by using the framework of Figure 11.1. The annualized 3-month forward premium on the pound—on the principal plus interest—is drawn on the vertical axis, and the annualized interest advantage of the dollar versus the pound is drawn along the horizontal axis. The section above the origin represents a pound forward premium, and the section below the origin represents a pound forward discount. To the right of the origin there is a dollar interest advantage, and to the left there is a dollar interest disadvantage.

Covered interest parity, as expressed in equation (11.4), can be written as

$$r_\$ - r_\pounds = 4\left(\frac{F_{1/4}(\$/\pounds) - S(\$/\pounds)}{S(\$/\pounds)}\right)\left(1 + \frac{r_\pounds}{4}\right) \qquad (11.11)$$

FIGURE 11.1. The Covered Interest Parity Diagram
The diagonal is the line of covered interest parity. On that line, investors and borrowers are indifferent between dollar and pound investing/borrowing. Above and to the left of the line there is an incentive to invest in pounds and borrow dollars. Below and to the right of the line there is an incentive to invest in dollars and borrow pounds. In situations off the interest parity line, forces are at work pushing us back toward it.

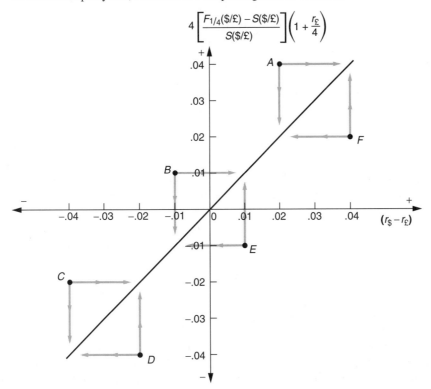

If the same scale is used on the two axes in Figure 11.1, this parity condition is represented by a 45-degree line. This line traces the points where the two sides of our equation are indeed equal.

Suppose that instead of having equality, as in equation (11.11), we have the following inequality:

$$r_\$ - r_£ < 4\left(\frac{F_{1/4}(\$/£) - S(\$/£)}{S(\$/£)}\right)\left(1 + \frac{r_£}{4}\right) \tag{11.12}$$

This condition means, for example, that any pound forward premium more than compensates for any dollar interest advantage. Thus:

1. Covered investment in pounds yields more than in dollars.
2. Borrowing in dollars is cheaper than covered borrowing in pounds.

It also means that it is profitable for an interest arbitrager to borrow dollars and make a covered investment in pounds. Because this act of covered interest arbitrage involves borrowing in the cheaper currency *and* investing in the higher-yielding currency, we can concentrate on interest arbitrage rather than separately considering borrowing or investment.

The incentive in inequality (11.12) to borrow dollars and make a covered investment in pounds means an incentive to:

1. Borrow dollars, perhaps by issuing and selling a security—and thus tend to increase $r_\$$
2. Buy spot pounds with the borrowed dollars—and thus increase $S(\$/£)$
3. Buy a pound security—and thus reduce $r_£$
4. Sell the pound proceeds forward for U.S. dollars—and thus reduce $F_{1/4}(\$/£)$

Inequality (11.12) can be represented in Figure 11.1 by points such as A, B, and C that are above and to the left of the 45-degree line. The character of these points is summarized in Table 11.2. At point B, for example, dollar interest rates are lower than pound rates, and at the same time the dollar is at a forward discount. For both reasons there is an advantage to covered borrowing dollars and investing in pounds. The **covered margin**, or advantage of doing this, is the interest differential plus the forward pound premium—on principal plus interest—for a total of 2 percent. In terms of inequality (11.12), the inequality holds because the left-hand side is negative (−0.01) and the right-hand side is positive (+0.01). The covered interest arbitrage, in each of the four steps we have distinguished, will tend to restore covered

TABLE 11.2. Points off the Interest Parity Line*

	Point					
	A	B	C	D	E	F
Interest differential	+.02	−.01	−.04	−.02	+.01	+.04
Forward premium†	−.04	−.01	+.02	+.04	+.01	−.02
Covered margin	−.02	−.02	−.02	+.02	+.02	+.02

*Dollar advantage = +; dollar disadvantage = −.
†Forward premium (+) or discount (−) on the U.S. dollar.

interest parity by pushing the situation at B back toward the parity line. The same thing will occur at every other point off the interest parity line, and we should show why.

Consider the situation at point A, where there is an incentive to borrow dollars and invest in pounds, covered. The borrowing in dollars to profit from the arbitrage opportunity will put upward pressure on dollar interest rates. If the borrowing is through selling dollar money-market instruments, efforts to sell them will reduce their prices. For given coupons or maturity values, this will raise their yields. Thus, we will find $r_\$$ increasing. The increase in $r_\$$ can be represented in Figure 11.1 as a force pushing to the right of A, toward the interest parity line.

The second step in covered interest arbitrage requires the spot sale of U.S. dollars for British pounds. This will help bid up the spot price of the pound; that is, $S(\$/£)$ will increase. For any given $F_{1/4}(\$/£)$, this will lower the value of

$$\frac{F_{1/4}(\$/£) - S(\$/£)}{S(\$/£)}$$

This is shown in Figure 11.1 by an arrow pointing downward from A, toward the interest parity line.

The pounds that were purchased will be used to invest in pound securities. If there are enough pound-security buyers, the price of the pound securities will increase, and therefore the pound yield will decrease, that is, $r_£$ will fall. This means an increase in $(r_\$ - r_£)$, which is shown by an arrow pointing to the right from A. Again, the movement is back toward the covered interest parity line.

Covering the funds moved abroad, which involves the forward sale of pounds, will lower $F_{1/4}(\$/£)$. For any given value of $S(\$/£)$, there will be a lower value of $[F_{1/4}(\$/£) - S(\$/£)]/S(\$/£)$. Thus, there is a second force that will also push downward from A toward the parity line. We can observe, of course, that since all four steps of arbitrage occur simultaneously, all the forces shown by the arrows occur simultaneously.

Points B and C in Figure 11.1, like point A, indicate profitable opportunities for covered borrowing in dollars and investment in pounds, and so there will be changes in interest and exchange rates also at these two points as shown by the arrows. For example, at point C the dollar-interest rate is 4 percent lower than the pound rate, and there is a 2 percent annual forward discount on pounds. This will encourage covered arbitrage flows toward pound investments. As before, there will be borrowing in dollars, and hence an increase in $r_\$$; spot purchases of pounds, which will raise $S(\$/£)$; investment in pound securities, which will lower $r_£$; and forward sales of pounds, which will lower $F_{1/4}(\$/£)$. All these changes are forces back to the interest parity line. Indeed, at any point above the interest parity line the forces shown by the arrows emanating from A, B, and C in Figure 11.1 are at work. We find that if we are off the covered interest parity line and above it, market forces force us back down toward the line.

Below the interest parity line, forces push us back up. At points such as D, E, and F, covered-interest arbitragers will wish to borrow in pounds and invest in dollars. For example, at point E, dollar interest rates are 1 percent higher than pound rates, *and* the dollar is at a 1 percent forward premium. Thus, dollar investments have a 2 percent advantage. This will cause arbitragers to sell pound securities, lowering their prices and raising $r_£$. This is shown in Figure 11.1 by an arrow that points to the left. The arbitragers then sell pounds for dollars, lowering $S(\$/£)$ and thereby increasing $[F_{1/4}(\$/£) - S(\$/£)]/S(\$/£)$, causing a movement upward, toward the line. They also purchase dollar securities, lowering $r_\$$ and causing a second movement toward the left. Hedging by buying pounds forward for dollars increases $F_{1/4}(\$/£)$ and thereby raises the forward premium on sterling, $[F_{1/4}(\$/£) - S(\$/£)]/S(\$/£)$. This means that again there will be movement toward the line, since the forward premium is the primary component on the vertical axis.

We find that above the covered interest parity line, flows of funds from dollars to pounds push us back toward it, and below the line, flows of funds from pounds to dollars also push us back toward it. The amount of adjustment in interest rates vis-à-vis spot and/or forward exchange rates depends on the "thinness" of the markets. The spot exchange market and the securities markets are generally more active than the forward market. It is likely, therefore, that a large part of the adjustment toward covered interest parity will occur in the forward exchange rate. As a result, the actual paths followed from points such as *A* or *E* back toward the parity line will lie closer to the vertical arrows than to the horizontal ones. We can therefore think of the forward premium as being determined by the interest differential, rather than vice versa.[5]

COMBINING PPP AND INTEREST PARITY

The Uncovered Interest Parity Condition

Equation (11.10) is the condition for hedged or covered interest parity because it involves the use of the forward market. It can be argued that a very similar *unhedged* interest parity condition should also hold. This follows because, as we explained in Chapter 3 and shall confirm later, speculation will make the forward exchange rate approximately equal to the expected future spot rate. That is, if we define $S_n^*(\$/£)$ as in Chapter 3, namely,

$S_n^*(\$/£)$ is the expected spot exchange rate between the dollar and the pound in *n* years time,

then it follows that to a close approximation

$$S_n^*(\$/£) = F_n(\$/£) \tag{11.13}$$

Recall that the reason equation (11.13) holds is that if

$$S_n^*(\$/£) > F_n(\$/£)$$

speculators will buy pounds *n* years forward; they can buy pounds forward for less than they expect to be able to sell them. This will force up the forward rate, $F_n(\$/£)$, until it is no longer less than the expected future spot rate. Similarly, if

$$S_n^*(\$/£) < F_n(\$/£)$$

---

[5]Indeed, foreign exchange traders and brokers frequently compute forward premiums from interest differentials.

speculators will sell pounds *n* years forward; they can sell forward pounds for more than they expect to be able to buy them when they honor their forward contract. Selling pounds forward pushes the forward rate down until it is no longer more than the expected future spot rate. Only when equation (11.13) holds is the forward rate in equilibrium in the sense that speculative pressures are not forcing the forward rate higher or lower.

Substituting equation (11.13) into equation (11.10) allows us to say that, to a close approximation, **uncovered interest parity** should hold in the form

$$\left(1 + r_\$\right)^n = \frac{S_n^*(\$/£)}{S(\$/£)}\left(1 + r_£\right)^n \tag{11.14}$$

This is only an approximate condition because *uncovered* interest parity involves risk: we assume $S_n^*(\$/£) = F_n(\$/£)$, and as we shall see in Chapter 16, this assumption is invalid if there is a risk premium in the forward market.

Equation (11.14) can be put in a different form by noting that by definition

$$S_n^*(\$/£) \equiv S(\$/£)\left(1 + \dot{S}^*\right)^n \tag{11.15}$$

where $\dot{S}^*$ is the average annual expected rate of change of the spot exchange rate. Substituting equation (11.15) into equation (11.14) gives

$$\left(1 + r_\$\right)^n = \left(1 + \dot{S}^*\right)^n\left(1 + r_£\right)^n \tag{11.16}$$

Taking the *n*th root of both sides gives

$$1 + r_\$ = 1 + \dot{S}^* + r_£ + \dot{S}^* \cdot r_£ \tag{11.17}$$

Assuming $\dot{S}^*$ and $r_£$ are small compared to 1, the "interaction term" $\dot{S}^* \cdot r_£$ will be very small, allowing us to write to a close approximation

$$r_\$ - r_£ = \dot{S}^* \tag{11.18}$$

That is, the interest differential should approximately equal the expected rate of change of the spot exchange rate.

The Expectations Form of PPP

We recall from Chapter 10 that the expected dollar return from holding commodities in the United States is $\dot{P}_{US}^*$, that is, the expected U.S. rate of inflation. Similarly, we recall that the expected dollar return from holding commodities in Britain is $\dot{P}_{UK}^* + \dot{S}^*$ because there are expected changes both in the pound prices of commodities and in the dollar value of the pound. We have seen that if we ignore risk, the rates of return from holding commodities in the two countries will be driven to equality by speculators until[6]

$$\dot{P}_{US}^* - \dot{P}_{UK}^* = \dot{S}^* \tag{10.12}$$

where $\dot{S}^*$ is the expected rate of change of the spot rate, $S(\$/£)$. Equation (10.12) from Chapter 10 is the PPP condition in terms of expectations.

---

[6]As before, we assume no holding costs, or that holding costs are equal in the two countries.

The Interrelationship of the Parity Conditions

If we take the PPP condition in its expectations form in equation (10.12) and compare it with the uncovered interest parity condition in equation (11.18), we note a clear similarity. We have

$$\dot{P}_{US}^* - \dot{P}_{UK}^* = \dot{S}^* \tag{10.12}$$

$$r_\$ - r_£ = \dot{S}^* \tag{11.18}$$

The right-hand sides of these two equations are equal. It follows that the left-hand sides must likewise be equal. This means that

$$r_\$ - r_£ = \dot{P}_{US}^* - \dot{P}_{UK}^* \tag{11.19}$$

By rearranging, we have

$$r_\$ - \dot{P}_{US}^* = r_£ - \dot{P}_{UK}^* \tag{11.20}$$

The two sides of this equation are the two currencies' interest rates less the expected rates of inflation in the associated two countries. The interest rate minus expected inflation is the **real interest rate,** popularized principally by Irving Fisher.[7] As a result, equation (11.20) is called the **Fisher-open condition.**[8] The Fisher-open condition is the condition that the real rates of interest are equal in different countries. From purchasing-power parity and uncovered interest parity we have been able to derive an equality between real returns in different countries.[9]

The equality of real interest rates can be considered as having an independent existence, one that does not have to be derived from PPP and interest parity. It follows from investors allocating their funds to where real returns are highest. Investing according to the highest real yield will tend to reduce returns in the countries with high returns where funds are sent, because of the greater supply of funds. It will also tend to increase returns in countries from which the funds are taken, because of the reduced supply of funds. The flow of funds will continue until the real returns in different countries are equalized.[10]

If we write the uncovered interest parity, expected purchasing-power parity, and Fisher-open conditions all together, that is,

[7]See Irving Fisher, *The Theory of Interest,* A. M. Kelley, New York, 1965.

[8]Generally, economists refer to equation (11.18), not equation (11.20), as the Fisher-open condition. However, since Fisher spoke of real interest rates as actual rates minus the expected inflation rate, equation (11.20) would be more appropriately referred to by his name. Equation (11.18) should perhaps be called the "interest-open" condition, where "open" means "open economy."

[9]We state this in terms of countries rather than currencies because inflation refers to countries. Of course, returns within countries are in the countries' currencies.

[10]The relationship between security yields in different countries can be extremely complex because of taxes, regulations, currency risks, citizens' tastes, and so on. The problem has been tackled by F. L. A. Grauer, R. H. Litzenberger, and R. E. Stehle, "Sharing Rules and Equilibrium in an International Capital Market under Uncertainty," *Journal of Financial Economics,* June 1976, pp. 233–256, and Fischer Black, "International Capital Market Equilibrium with Investment Barriers," *Journal of Financial Economics,* December 1974, pp. 337–352. Few data exist on real rates in different countries. See, however, Robert Z. Aliber, "Real Interest Rates in a Multicurrency World," unpublished paper, University of Chicago.

$$\text{interest parity}: \quad r_\$ - r_\pounds = \dot{S}^*(\$/\pounds)$$

$$\text{PPP}: \quad \dot{P}^*_{US} - \dot{P}^*_{UK} = \dot{S}^*(\$/\pounds)$$

$$\text{Fisher-open}: \quad r_\$ - \dot{P}^*_{US} = r_\pounds - \dot{P}^*_{UK}$$

we find that we can derive any one from the other two. This is left as an end-of-chapter problem for the reader. The conditions are shown in Figure 11.2. Each side of the triangle in Figure 11.2 represents a condition. The figure helps clarify why satisfying any two conditions implies that the remaining condition is satisfied.

Because each of the three parity conditions along the sides of Figure 11.2 can be derived from the other two, any one condition must be correct if the other two are correct. For example, if we believe real returns are equal and that interest parity holds precisely, we are implicitly accepting that PPP in its expectations form also holds precisely.

WHY COVERED INTEREST DIFFERENCES PERSIST

In reality, interest parity holds very closely, but it does not hold precisely. This is apparent from, for example, the covered interest differentials in Table 11.1 on page 262. The failure to achieve exact covered interest parity could occur because in actual financial markets there are:

1. Transaction costs
2. Political risks
3. Potential tax advantages to foreign exchange gains versus interest earnings
4. Liquidity differences between foreign securities and domestic securities

FIGURE 11.2. The Interdependence of Exchange Rates, Interest Rates, and Inflation Rates
Interest parity, purchasing-power parity, and the Fisher-open condition are related. Any one of these conditions can be derived from the other two.

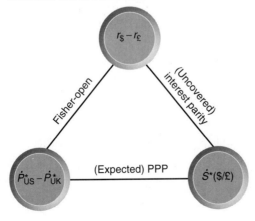

Here, we explain how these factors contribute to departures from interest parity. Later, in Chapter 17, we show that these same factors also influence cash management.

Transaction Costs and Interest Parity

The cost of transacting in foreign exchange is reflected in the bid-ask spread in exchange rates. The bid-ask spread represents the cost of two foreign exchange transactions, a purchase and a sale of foreign currency. That is, if a person buys and then immediately sells a foreign currency, the cost of these two transactions is the difference between the buying and selling prices of the currency, which is the bid-ask spread. Covered investment or borrowing involve two foreign exchange transaction costs—one on the spot market and the other on the forward market. These two transaction costs discourage foreign-currency-denominated investment and borrowing. Interest arbitrage also involves two foreign exchange transaction costs, since the borrowed currency is sold spot and then bought forward. However, there are additional transaction costs of interest arbitrage due to interest-rate spreads. This is because the borrowing interest rate is likely to exceed the investment interest rate.[11]

It might seem that the extra cost of investing in foreign-currency-denominated securities vis-à-vis domestic-currency securities would require covered foreign-currency yields to be higher than domestic-currency yields before investors would choose the foreign-currency alternative; investors need to find it worthwhile to incur the extra transaction costs for a foreign-currency security. Similarly, it might seem that borrowing costs in foreign currency would have to be lower than borrowing costs in domestic currency before borrowers choose the foreign-currency alternative; borrowers face extra costs when borrowing via the foreign-currency swap. In other words, it might seem that there could be deviations from interest parity by up to the extra transaction costs of investing or borrowing in foreign currency before the benefits of the foreign alternative are sufficient to compensate for the added costs. In terms of Figure 11.1, it would appear that transaction costs could allow the situation to be slightly off the interest parity line; the apparent advantages to foreign-currency investment/borrowing at points just off the line should not trigger foreign borrowing/investing because the benefits are insufficient to compensate for the costs. Indeed, because the cost of covered interest arbitrage includes the borrowing-investing interest rate spread as well as foreign exchange transaction costs, it might appear that deviations from interest parity could be relatively large before being sufficient to compensate for the transaction costs of covered interest arbitrage.

Despite the preceding, which would suggest that deviations from interest parity could result from transaction costs, it has generally become recognized that transaction costs do not contribute to deviations from interest parity. A major reason for this recognition is the realization that one-way interest arbitrage circumvents transaction costs in foreign exchange and securities markets. We can explain the nature of one-way interest arbitrage and how it influences the interest parity condition by contrasting one-way arbitrage and **round-trip arbitrage.** In order to do this, we

---

[11]The borrowing-investment spread can be considered as a transaction cost in the same way that we consider the bid-ask spread on currencies a transaction cost, namely, it is the cost of borrowing and then immediately investing the borrowed funds.

need to be explicit about foreign exchange and borrowing-lending transaction costs. Using the same notation as in Chapter 2 for transaction costs on spot exchange, let us use the following definitions:

> $S(\$/\text{ask}\pounds)$ and $F_n(\$/\text{ask}\pounds)$ are respectively the spot and n-year forward exchange rates for buying pounds with dollars, and $S(\$/\text{bid}\pounds)$ and $F_n(\$/\text{bid}\pounds)$ are respectively the spot and forward exchange rates when selling pounds for dollars, $r_\$^I$ and $r_\pounds^I$ are the interest rates earned on investments in the two currencies, and $r_\$^B$ and $r_\pounds^B$ are the interest rates on borrowing in the two currencies.

This notation is used in Figure 11.3 to show the difference between one-way and round-trip arbitrage and the implications of this distinction for covered interest parity.

Part a of Figure 11.3 illustrates round-trip covered interest arbitrage. The four corners of the diagram show current dollars ($\$_0$), current pounds, ($\pounds_0$), future dollars ($\$_n$), and future pounds ($\pounds_n$). The arrows drawn between the corners of the figure show the interest rates or exchange rates when going between the corners in the directions of the arrows. For example, when going from $\$_0$ to $\pounds_0$, as shown by the downward-pointing arrow in the left-hand panel of Figure 11.3a, the transaction occurs at the spot exchange rate, $S(\$/\text{ask}\pounds)$. Similarly, when going from $\$_n$ to $\$_0$, as shown by the horizontal leftward-pointing arrow in the left-hand panel of Figure 11.3a, this involves borrowing dollars and so occurs at the dollar-borrowing rate, $r_\$^B$.

The left-hand diagram in Figure 11.3a shows the round-trip arbitrage involving borrowing in dollars and investing in pounds. To understand the nature of this arbitrage we begin at corner $\$_n$. The top leftward-pointing arrow from $\$_n$ shows the interest rate on dollar borrowing which gives immediate dollars, $\$_0$, in return for paying dollars back in the future, $\$_n$. The left downward-pointing arrow shows the spot exchange rate at which the borrowed dollars are exchanged into pounds; the pounds must be purchased, so the spot rate is the ask rate for pounds, $S(\$/\text{ask}\pounds)$. The bottom rightward-pointing arrow shows the interest rate earned on the pound-denominated investment which converts today's pounds, $\pounds_0$, into future pounds, $\pounds_n$. Finally, the right upward-sloping arrow shows the forward exchange rate at which the dollars needed for repaying the dollar loan are purchased with pounds, $F_n(\$/\text{bid}\pounds)$. The counterclockwise journey in this left-hand diagram in Figure 11.3a from $\$_n$ and back to $\$_n$ is seen to involve foreign exchange transaction costs—the ask on spot pounds $S(\$/\text{ask}\pounds)$ versus bid on forward pounds $F_n(\$/\text{bid}\pounds)$, and therefore a bid-ask spread—and also to involve borrowing-investment transaction costs—the borrowing rate on dollars, $r_\$^B$, versus the investment rate on pounds, $r_\pounds^I$. That is, round-trip arbitrage is expensive in terms of facing costs in the currency and security markets.

The right-hand diagram in Figure 11.3a illustrates the alternative direction of round-trip arbitrage, with borrowing of pounds and investment in dollars. Starting at $\pounds_n$, pounds are borrowed at $r_\pounds^B$ giving the borrower current pounds $\pounds_0$. These are sold spot for dollars at $S(\$/\text{bid}\pounds)$ and the dollars are invested at $r_\$^I$. The pound-denominated loan is covered by buying forward pounds at the forward ask rate for pounds, $F_n(\$/\text{ask}\pounds)$. As with the left-hand figure in Figure 11.3a, we see that the pound-borrowing–dollar-investment arbitrage also involves a transaction cost spread in the foreign exchange market—spot bid versus forward ask on pounds—and also in the securities market—pound borrowing rate versus the dollar investment rate.

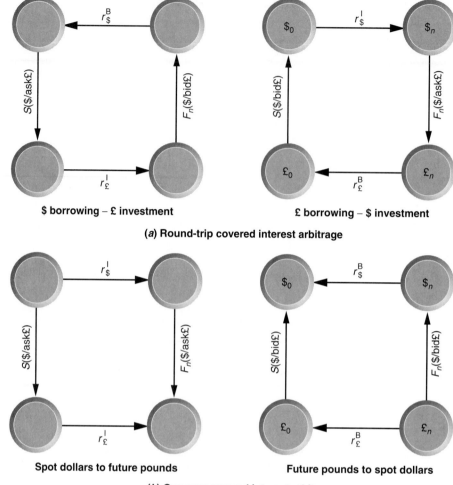

(a) Round-trip covered interest arbitrage

(b) One-way covered interest arbitrage

FIGURE 11.3. One-way and Round-trip Interest Arbitrage
Round-trip interest arbitrage, illustrated in *(a)*, involves going along all four sides of the diagram at the interest rates and exchange rates that are shown. The presence of four transaction costs allows for large deviations from interest parity. One-way interest arbitrage, illustrated in *(b)*, involves comparing two alternative ways of going from one corner to another corner that is diagonally opposite. Either route involves two transaction costs, but since these are for the same types of transactions, they do not cause deviations from interest parity.

If the maximum possible sizes of deviations from covered interest parity due to transaction costs were determined only by round-trip covered interest arbitrage, the deviations could be considerable. This is because for round-trip interest arbitrage to be profitable it is necessary to overcome the transaction costs in the foreign exchange markets and the borrowing-lending spread on interest rates. Let us attach some numbers to see the size of deviations that might result. We shall use transactions costs faced by the lowest-cost arbitragers, such as large commercial banks, since it is they who are likely to act first and preclude others from profiting from interest arbitrage.

Let us assume a potential interest arbitrager can borrow for 1 year at $\frac{1}{4}$ percent above his or her investment rate, and can borrow a sufficient amount to reduce the spot and forward transaction costs both to only $\frac{1}{10}$ of 1 percent. In this situation, it is necessary that the interest parity deviation calculated using interest rates and exchange rates that exclude transaction costs would have to exceed approximately $\frac{1}{2}$ of 1 percent for profitable arbitrage. This is because it is necessary to earn $\frac{1}{4}$ of 1 percent to cover the borrowing-investment spread, and another $\frac{1}{5}$ of 1 percent to cover the two transaction costs, those for the spot and forward exchange transactions, both of which are $\frac{1}{10}$ of 1 percent. This is illustrated in Figure 11.4. We can

FIGURE 11.4. Interest Parity in the Presence of Transaction Costs, Political Risk, or Liquidity Premiums
Interest parity might not hold exactly because of transaction costs, political risk, and liquidity preference. This means interest rates and exchange rates may not plot on the interest parity line. Rather, they may be somewhere within a band around the line; only outside this band are the covered yield differences enough to overcome the costs or risk of covered interest arbitrage. However, the band is narrow because there are some participants for whom the costs and risk of arbitrage are unimportant or irrelevant. For example, transaction costs are irrelevant for one-way arbitragers.

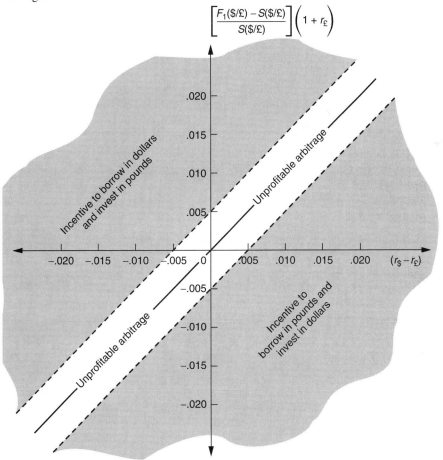

interpret the interest rates on the horizontal axis as the midpoints between the borrowing and lending rates, and the exchange rates on the vertical axis as the midpoints between the bid and ask rates.

We show a band around the interest parity line within which round-trip interest arbitrage is unprofitable. This band has a width of approximately $1/2$ percent on either side of the interest parity line, as is seen, for example, along the horizontal axis around the origin. The band reflects the fact that arbitrage must cover the $1/2$ percent lost in transaction costs. Above and to the left of the band it is profitable to borrow in dollars and make covered investments in pounds, and to the right of the band it is profitable to do the reverse.[12] Let us next consider the implication of *one-way* arbitrage.

One-way arbitrage can come in various forms. However, we need to consider only the form which involves the lowest transaction cost, because it is this arbitrage that will determine the maximum deviation from interest parity; just as the *arbitrager* with the lowest cost of interest arbitrage drives interest rates and exchange rates to levels closest to the interest-parity line, so it is that the *form* of one-way arbitrage that faces the lowest transaction cost drives us closest to the parity line.

Let us consider first the one-way interest arbitrage illustrated by the left-hand diagram in part *b* of Figure 11.3. This shows an arbitrager holding dollars ($\$_0$) who wants pounds in the future ($\pounds_n$).[13] The arbitrager has two choices. The dollars can be sold for pounds immediately and invested in pound-denominated securities until the pounds are needed, or the dollars can be invested in dollar securities and forward pounds can be purchased. The first of these choices is illustrated by the downward-pointing arrow on the left of the diagram from $\$_0$ to $\pounds_0$ and the rightward-pointing arrow along the bottom from $\pounds_0$ to $\pounds_n$. The second choice is illustrated by the rightward-pointing arrow on the top from $\$_0$ to $\$_n$ and the downward-pointing arrow on the right from $\$_n$ to $\pounds_n$. We note that both routes take the arbitrager from today's dollars, $\$_0$, to future pounds, $\pounds_n$. The choice is to pick the route providing the pounds at lower cost.

If the choice that is made is to invest in dollar securities and buy pounds forward, each pound purchased will cost $\$F_n(\$/\text{ask}\pounds)$. In order to have this many dollars in n years requires investing today at $r_\$^1$:

$$\$ \frac{F_n(\$/\text{ask}\pounds)}{\left(1 + r_\$^1\right)^n} \qquad (11.21)$$

---

[12]If interest rates were for 3 months rather than 1 year, the band would be considerably wider. Even if the borrowing-lending spread remained at $1/4$ of 1 percent and the foreign exchange transaction costs remained at $1/10$ of 1 percent, the band would be more than 1 full percent on either side of the interest parity line. The reason is that the costs of buying spot and selling forward are incurred within a 3-month period, and when annualized, are effectively 4 times larger. With $1/5$ of a percent lost in 3 months, it is necessary for the interest arbitrage to generate $4/5$ of a percent to cover foreign exchange costs, plus $1/4$ of a percent to cover the borrowing-lending spread. If we were dealing with 1-month or shorter arbitrage, the potential deviations from interest parity would be even larger.

[13]The use of the term "arbitrager" in this context stretches the usual meaning of the term, because we have assumed that dollars are already held and that there is already a need for pounds in the future. Without engaging in excessive semantics we can note that the essence of what our "arbitrager" is doing is judging which of two ways of going from current dollars to future pounds is the cheaper. This choice of the preferred route is the same type of choice met in deriving cross exchange rates in Chapter 2. The term "arbitrage" comes from "arbitrate," which means "choose." However, a reader who still objects to the term "arbitrager" can substitute his or her own term; the conclusion is the same whatever word we use.

This is the cost per pound using the dollar-investment, forward-pound route from $\$_0$ to $\pounds_n$. If the other choice is made, that is, to buy pounds immediately and invest in pound-denominated securities for n years, the number of pounds that must be purchased immediately for each pound to be obtained in n years is

$$\pounds \frac{1}{\left(1 + r_\pounds^I\right)^n} \tag{11.22}$$

The cost of this number of pounds at the spot price of pounds, $S(\$/\text{ask}\pounds)$, is:

$$\$ \frac{S(\$/\text{ask}\pounds)}{\left(1 + r_\pounds^I\right)^n} \tag{11.23}$$

In the same way that we saw that there are forces pushing interest rates and exchange rates to the interest parity line, there are forces making the amounts in equations (11.21) and (11.23) equal to each other. For example, if equation (11.23) gave a lower cost per pound than equation (11.21), there would be spot purchases of pounds and funds invested in pound-denominated securities. These actions would increase $S(\$/\text{ask}\pounds)$ and reduce $r_\pounds^I$. At the same time, the lack of forward pound purchases would reduce $F_n(\$/\text{ask}\pounds)$, and the unwillingness to invest in dollar securities would increase $r_\$^I$. The choice between alternatives would therefore drive them to the same cost, that is,

$$\frac{F_n(\$/\text{ask}\pounds)}{\left(1 + r_\$^I\right)^n} = \frac{S(\$/\text{ask}\pounds)}{\left(1 + r_\pounds^I\right)^n} \tag{11.24}$$

We can rewrite (11.24) as

$$\left(1 + r_\$^I\right)^n = \frac{F_n(\$/\text{ask}\pounds)}{S(\$/\text{ask}\pounds)}\left(1 + r_\pounds^I\right)^n \tag{11.25}$$

If the sizes of transaction costs in the spot and forward foreign exchange markets were the same, then equation (11.25) is essentially the same as equation (11.10). This is because we have investment interest rates on both sides of the equation, and we have ask exchange rates for forward and spot transactions.[14] This means that if spot and forward transaction costs were equal, the choice we have described would drive us all the way to the interest parity line like that from equation (11.10), even though there are transaction costs. The reason this happens is that either method of going from $\$_0$ to $\pounds_n$ requires buying pounds, the only difference being whether they are purchased on the spot or the forward market. Therefore, transaction costs will be paid whatever the choice. Similarly, investment interest rates are earned if the choice is to buy pounds spot or forward, the only difference being in which currency the interest is earned.

Another form of one-way interest arbitrage is illustrated by the lower right-hand diagram in Figure 11.3b. The choice in this case is between two ways of going from $\pounds_n$ to $\$_0$. (A U.S. exporter who is to receive pounds and needs to borrow dollars

[14]That is, because both exchange rates are ask rates, the exchange rates in the numerator and denominator of equation (11.25) are both on the high side of bid-ask spread. To the extent that transaction costs in the spot and forward markets are equal, they cancel. Similarly, because the interest rates on the two sides of equation (11.25) are investment rates, they are both on the low side of the borrowing-lending spread. The cost component again cancels.

would be interested in going from £$_n$ to $\$_0$.) The two ways of going from the £$_n$ to $\$_0$ involve either going from £$_n$ to £$_0$ by borrowing pounds, and then from £$_0$ to $\$_0$ via the spot market, or going from £$_n$ to $\$_n$ via the forward market, and from $\$_n$ to $\$_0$ by borrowing dollars.

If the route that is taken from £$_n$ to $\$_0$ is to borrow pounds and sell them spot for dollars, the number of pounds that can be borrowed today for each pound to be repaid in n years is

$$£ \, \frac{1}{\left(1 + r_£^B\right)^n}$$

This number of pounds, when sold spot for dollars, provides

$$\$ \, \frac{S(\$/\text{bid}£)}{\left(1 + r_£^B\right)^n} \tag{11.26}$$

The alternative route of selling pounds forward and borrowing dollars means receiving in the future for each pound sold

$$\$F_n(\$/\text{bid}£)$$

The number of dollars that can be borrowed today and repaid with these pounds is

$$\$ \, \frac{F_n(\$/\text{bid}£)}{\left(1 + r_\$^B\right)^n} \tag{11.27}$$

The dollar amounts in equations (11.26) and (11.27) show the dollars available today, $\$_0$, for each pound in the future, £$_n$. The choice between the alternative ways of obtaining dollars will drive exchange rates and interest rates to the point that

$$\frac{S(\$/\text{bid}£)}{\left(1 + r_£^B\right)^n} = \frac{F_n(\$/\text{bid}£)}{\left(1 + r_\$^B\right)^n}$$

that is,

$$\left(1 + r_\$^B\right)^n = \frac{F_n(\$/\text{bid}£)}{S(\$/\text{bid}£)} \left(1 + r_£^B\right)^n \tag{11.28}$$

Again, if forward and spot transaction costs are equal, this is an exact interest parity line; we have borrowing interest rates on both sides, and both exchange rates are bid rates.

In fact, forward exchange transaction costs are slightly higher than spot costs, and so equation (11.25) and equation (11.28) might differ a little from the interest parity line drawn without transaction costs. However, the departures will be much smaller than those obtained from consideration of round-trip interest arbitrage.[15] This is because round-trip interest arbitrage involves the borrowing-investment interest-rate spread and the foreign exchange transaction costs of buying spot and

[15]In fact, even if there are transaction cost differences between spot and forward exchange, when all one-way arbitrages are considered simultaneously with a requirement that there is both supply and demand in every market, interest parity holds exactly. This is shown in Maurice D. Levi, "Non-Reversed Investment and Borrowing, Transaction Costs and Covered Interest Parity," *International Review of Economics and Finance,* vol. 1, no. 2, 1992, pp. 107–119.

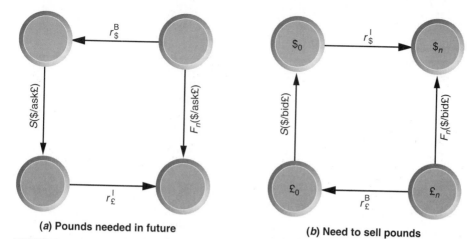

(a) Pounds needed in future   **(b) Need to sell pounds**

FIGURE 11.5. A More Roundabout One-way Arbitrage
We can reduce the band around the interest parity line by considering whether to use the
forward market or the spot market plus money markets. This choice, however, involves one
transaction versus three transactions and is likely to leave larger deviations from interest parity
than other, more similar one-way arbitrage choices.

selling forward, or of buying forward and selling spot. On the other hand, one-way
arbitrage does not involve interest-rate spreads, and foreign exchange transaction
costs are faced whatever the choice.

The one-way arbitrage we have described produces the interest parity line
because we have established situations where the arbitrager has in any case to
buy/sell foreign exchange and to invest/borrow. An alternative one-way arbitrage
is a choice between buying/selling forward on the one hand, and buying/selling spot
and using the money markets on the other hand.[16] For example, an arbitrager could
buy pounds forward or, alternatively, could borrow dollars, buy pounds spot, and
invest the pounds. Either way the arbitrager receives pounds in the future and has to
deliver dollars. This is illustrated in Figure 11.5a, where the arbitrager can go from
$\$_n$ to $£_n$ via the forward market (the downward-pointing arrow on the right-hand
side), or by borrowing dollars (the upper leftward-pointing arrow), buying pounds
spot with the borrowed dollars (the left-hand downward-pointing arrow), and investing in pounds (the lower rightward-pointing arrow). This one-way arbitrage does
make foreign exchange transaction costs irrelevant, or at least less relevant, because
it involves ask rates in either case. However, it does not avoid the borrowing-
investing spread. It does not, therefore, take us as close to the interest parity line as
the type of one-way arbitrage we considered. We reach the same conclusion if we
consider the reverse forward exchange, going from $£_n$ to $\$_n$, versus the alternative of
borrowing pounds, using these to buy dollars spot, and investing the dollars. This is
illustrated in Figure 11.5b; it again gives a line further from the interest parity line
than the one-way arbitrage we described.

An alternative way of concluding that the deviations from interest parity as a

[16]This is the more usual one-way arbitrage considered in explaining why transaction costs are not important. For example, see Alan V. Deardorff, "One-Way Arbitrage and Its Implications for the Foreign
Exchange Markets," *Journal of Political Economy,* April 1975, pp. 351–364.

result of transaction costs are small is to consider the choice faced by third-country borrowers and investors. For example, if Japanese or German investors and borrowers are looking for the best currency to invest or borrow, they will drive the situation between dollars and pounds to the interest parity line. This is because the Japanese or Germans pay foreign exchange costs whatever the currency of their investment or borrowing, and compare investment rates in the two currencies or borrowing rates in the two currencies.[17] For this reason, or because of the presence of one-way arbitrage, we can expect deviations from interest parity to be too small for round-trip arbitrage to ever occur. We conclude that transaction costs are probably not a cause of deviations from interest parity.[18]

Political Risk and Interest Parity

When securities which are denominated in different *currencies* trade in different *countries,* deviations from interest parity can result from **political risk.** Political risk involves the uncertainty that while funds are invested in a foreign country, they may be frozen, become inconvertible into other currencies, or be confiscated. Even if such extremes do not occur, investors might find themselves facing new or increased taxes in the foreign country. Usually, the investment that involves the least political risk is at home; if funds are invested abroad, to the risk of tax or other changes at home is added the risk of changes in another political jurisdiction. However, it is possible that for investors in some countries, it is politically less risky to send funds abroad. This will be true if investors thereby avoid politically risky possibilities at home. For example, people in some volatile countries have invested in Switzerland and the United States for political safety. In these circumstances, a foreign investment might be made even at a covered interest disadvantage. In general, however, we expect investors to require a premium from a foreign investment versus a domestic investment.

In diagrammatic terms, political risk creates a band like that shown in Figure 11.4; only in the area beyond some particular covered differential is there an incentive to invest abroad.[19] The political risk band does not have to be of equal width on the two sides of the interest parity line if one country is viewed as riskier than the other. For example, Canadian yields are generally a little higher than U.S. yields, even after allowance for forward hedging. This can be attributed to the fact that U.S. investors generally view Canada as being politically more risky than Canadians view the United States as being, thereby causing a larger political-risk premium on Canadian securities than on U.S. securities.

It is important to remember that political risk relates to the country, not the currency, of investment. For example, there is no political risk involved in the devia-

[17]This assumes that cross exchange rates of pounds for yen or pounds for marks do not have a larger bid-ask spread than direct yen-dollar or mark-dollar exchange rates. When cross-exchange-rate spreads are larger, dollar investments and borrowing will be favored.
[18]The arguments we have given for transaction costs to be a minor or irrelevant reason for deviation from interest parity can be supplemented by an argument advanced by Kevin Clinton involving the trading of swaps. See Kevin Clinton, "Transaction Costs and Covered Interest Arbitrage: Theory and Evidence," *Journal of Political Economy,* April 1988, pp. 358–370.
[19]Of course, political risk does not create a band via the *borrowing* decision. Borrowers have to pay back their loans whatever happens in the country from which they borrowed.

tions from covered interest parity in Table 11.1 because the yields are on bank deposits in London. That is, there are no political differences between the instruments in Table 11.1, but rather only differences in the currencies of denomination. Indeed, by comparing yield differences when there are no political differences, as on bank deposits (covered) in a given country, with yield differences when there are political differences, as on treasury bills (covered) in different countries, it is possible to estimate the importance of political risk. The extra spread when political risk is faced versus when it is not faced is a measure of the political risk premium.[20]

Even when covered yields are on instruments which trade in different countries, third-country investors might force interest rates and exchange rates onto the interest parity line. For example, if Japanese investors view the United States and Britain as equally risky politically from their perspective, then they will drive the interest rates and exchange rates for the United States and Britain onto the interest parity line. This is true even if investors in, for example, the United States and Britain perceive foreign investment as riskier than investment at home. Of course, if conditions are driven onto the interest parity line, this will encourage U.S. and British investors to keep funds at home, because neither is receiving compensation for the perceived risk of investing in the other country.

Taxes and Interest Parity

If taxes are the same on domestic and on foreign investment and borrowing, then the existence of taxes will make no difference in our investment and borrowing criteria or the interest parity line; taxes will cancel out when yield comparisons are made. However, if tax rates depend on the currency or country in which funds are invested or borrowed, the interest parity condition will be affected. There are two ways in which taxes could conceivably affect the parity condition. One way involves withholding taxes, and the other involves differences between the tax rate on income and that on capital gains. Let us consider these in turn.

Withholding Taxes

One might think that a potential cause of higher taxes on foreign earnings than on domestic earnings, and hence of a band around the interest parity line, is the **foreign-resident withholding tax.** A withholding tax is a tax applied to foreigners at the source of their earnings. For example, when a Canadian resident earns $100 in the United States, the payer of that $100 is required to withhold and remit 15 percent of the earnings to the U.S. Internal Revenue Service. Similarly, the earnings of U.S. residents in Canada are subject to a withholding tax. Withholding taxes, however, are unlikely to offer a reason for a band around the covered interest parity line.

As long as the rate of withholding is less than or equal to the tax rate that would be applied to the earnings at home, domestic **withholding tax credits** will offset the tax withheld. For example, suppose that a resident of the United States pays the equivalent of $15 on $100 of interest or dividends earned in Canada, and the total tax payable on the $100 when declared in the United States is $25. The Internal Revenue Service will grant the U.S. resident a $15 credit on taxes paid to the taxing

---

[20]See Robert Z. Aliber, "The Interest Parity Theorem: A Reinterpretation," *Journal of Political Economy,* November/December 1973, pp. 1451–1459.

authority in Canada. Only an additional $10 will be payable in the United States. The investor ends up paying a total of $25, which is the same as he or she would have paid on $100 earned at home. Complete or full withholding tax credit leaves no incentive to choose domestic securities rather than foreign securities. Only if withholding tax credits are less than the amounts withheld will there be a reason to keep money at home.[21] This means that the interest parity condition is in general not affected, and we have no band around the parity line as a result of withholding taxes.

Capital Gains versus Income Taxes*

Taxes can affect the investment and borrowing criteria and the interest parity condition if investors pay different effective tax rates on foreign exchange earnings than on interest earnings. This can be the tax situation of investors who only infrequently buy or sell foreign exchange, because such investors can obtain capital-account treatment of their foreign exchange gains or losses; gains and losses are normally given capital-account treatment if they are not part of the "normal conduct of business."[22] If the tax rate on capital gains is lower than that on ordinary income, this affects the slope of the interest parity line. Let us see how, by considering a U.S. investor who pays a lower effective tax rate on capital gains than on interest income.[23]

Let us write the U.S. investor's tax rate on capital gains as τ_k and the U.S. tax rate on income as τ_y, and let us assume that for this particular investor, $\tau_y > \tau_k$. Since all interest earnings are considered to be income, after paying taxes and ignoring transaction costs the U.S. investor will receive from each dollar invested in dollar-denominated securities for 1 year

$$1 + \left(1 - \tau_y\right)r_\$ \tag{11.29}$$

That is, the investor will lose a fraction τ_y of the interest earned. If he or she instead invests in pound securities, then before taxes the U.S. dollar receipts will be

$$\frac{F_1(\$/\pounds)}{S(\$/\pounds)}\left(1 + r_\pounds\right) = \left(\frac{F_1(\$/\pounds) - S(\$/\pounds)}{S(\$/\pounds)}\right)\left(1 + r_\pounds\right) + \left(1 + r_\pounds\right)$$

We have expanded the total return into the earnings from exchange rates—the first term on the right-hand side—and the principal plus interest. After taxes, if capital gains taxes are paid even on hedged foreign exchange earnings, the investor will receive only $1 - \tau_y$ of the interest and $1 - \tau_k$ of any gain from a forward premium, that is,

---

*Sections marked with an asterisk can be omitted on first reading without loss of continuity.

[21]Even when full credit is obtained, interest earnings are lost on the funds withheld in comparison with what might have been earned if taxes had been paid at home at the end of the tax period. This should, however, be a relatively small consideration, except when interest rates are very high.

[22]Even where the tax rate on realized capital gains is the same as on ordinary income, the *effective* tax rate on capital gains is lower if capital gains can be deferred, or if there are capital losses against which the capital gains can be taken. In many countries the *actual* tax rate on capital gains is lower than that on ordinary income.

[23]For the conditions for capital-account treatment of foreign exchange earnings, see Martin Kupferman and Maurice Levi, "Taxation and the International Money Market Investment Decision," *Financial Analysts Journal,* July/August 1978, pp. 61–64.

$$1 + \left(1 - \tau_y\right)r_\pounds + \left(1 - \tau_k\right)\left(\frac{F_1(\$/\pounds) - S(\$/\pounds)}{S(\$/\pounds)}\right)\left(1 + r_\pounds\right) \qquad (11.30)$$

We have used the income tax rate τ_y on $r_\pounds$, since all interest, whatever the currency or country of source, is subject to that rate.

We can show the effect of taxes in terms of the graphical presentation of interest parity if we proceed the same way as we did when we included transaction costs. The U.S. investor for whom we have assumed $\tau_y > \tau_k$ will be indifferent between investing in dollar or pound securities if the amounts in equations (11.29) and (11.30) are equal, which requires that

$$r_\$ - r_\pounds = \frac{1 - \tau_k}{1 - \tau_y}\left(\frac{F_1(\$/\pounds) - S(\$/\pounds)}{S(\$/\pounds)}\right)\left(1 + r_\pounds\right) \qquad (11.31)$$

In comparing equation (11.31) with the equation for the interest parity line in Figure 11.1 drawn for 1-year investments, which is

$$r_\$ - r_\pounds = \left(\frac{F_1(\$/\pounds) - S(\$/\pounds)}{S(\$/\pounds)}\right)\left(1 + r_\pounds\right)$$

we see that differential taxes on income versus capital gains/losses adds the ratio $(1 - \tau_k)/(1 - \tau_y)$ to the front of the forward premium/discount term. When the capital gains tax rate is lower than the income tax rate,

$$\frac{1 - \tau_k}{1 - \tau_y} > 1$$

For example, if $\tau_k = 0.10$ and $\tau_y = 0.25$, then

$$\frac{1 - \tau_k}{1 - \tau_y} = 1.20$$

This means that the line of indifference for investors who face lower taxes on foreign exchange earnings than on interest income is flatter than a 45-degree interest parity line like that in Figure 11.1; each percent change in $\left(\frac{F_1(\$/\pounds) - S(\$/\pounds)}{S(\$/\pounds)}\right)\left(1 + r_\pounds\right)$ on the vertical axis of Figure 11.1 (drawn for 1-year investments) is associated with more than a 1 percent change in $(r_\$ - r_\pounds)$ on the horizontal axis.

While some investors may enjoy a lower tax rate on foreign exchange than on interest earnings, banks and other major players do not; such investors, for whom international investment is a normal business, pay the same tax on interest and foreign exchange earnings. For this reason we can expect interest rates and exchange rates to remain on or close to the 45-degree interest parity line; banks will take positions which move the situation toward the line. This implies that those investors who *do* pay lower taxes on foreign exchange earnings than on interest income may find valuable **tax arbitrage** opportunities. For example, suppose interest rates and exchange rates are such that interest parity holds precisely on a before-tax basis with:

$$r_\$ = 12 \text{ percent}$$

$$r_\pounds = 8 \text{ percent}$$

$$\left(\frac{F_1(\$/£) - S(\$/£)}{S(\$/£)}\right)(1 + r_£) = 4 \text{ percent}$$

For a U.S. investor for whom $\tau_y = 0.25$ and $\tau_k = 0.10$, U.S. dollar investments yield $(1 - \tau_y)r_\$ = 9$ percent after tax, while pound investments yield after tax:

$$\left(1 - \tau_y\right)r_£ + \left(1 - \tau_k\right)\left(\frac{F_1(\$/£) - S(\$/£)}{S(\$/£)}\right)(1 + r_£) = 9.6 \text{ percent}$$

The pound investment will be preferred on an after-tax basis even though interest parity holds exactly on a before-tax basis. More generally, if covered interest parity holds on a before-tax basis, investors with favorable capital gains treatment will prefer investments denominated in currencies trading at a forward premium. It is a natural extension of our argument to show that in the same tax situation, borrowers will prefer to denominate borrowing in currencies at a forward discount.[24]

Liquidity Differences and Interest Parity

The liquidity of an asset can be judged by how quickly and cheaply it can be converted into cash. For example, when a *domestic*-currency-denominated asset such as a 90-day security is sold before maturity after only 50 days, domestic security selling transaction costs must be paid that would not have been incurred had the security been held to maturity. If, however, a covered *foreign*-currency 90-day investment is sold after only 50 days, more than security selling costs are faced. This should be explained carefully.

The brokerage costs for selling a foreign-currency-denominated security are likely to be similar to those for selling a domestic-currency security. However, transaction costs are faced when investors convert the foreign exchange from the hedged foreign-currency security on the spot market. These costs would have not been faced had the security been held to maturity and the proceeds converted according to the original forward contract. Further, when a security is sold prior to maturity and the funds are converted into domestic currency, there is still the matter of honoring the original forward contract to sell the foreign exchange at the maturity of the foreign-currency investment. If a cash manager wants to avoid the foreign exchange risk that would be faced by leaving the original forward contract in effect, the manager must cover his or her position. In our example, if there is a 90-day forward contract and the funds are converted into domestic currency after only 50 days, the investor should buy a new forward exchange contract of 40 days maturity. This purchase of forward foreign exchange will offset the sale of foreign exchange that was part of the original covered investment. At the conclusion of the full 90-day period, the foreign exchange that was originally sold forward will be obtained from that bought forward 40 days previously.

The extra spot and forward exchange transaction costs from the premature sale of a foreign-currency investment require an initial covered advantage of foreign investment to make the initial investment worthwhile. **Liquidity preference** is

[24]This is because the high interest rates they pay are tax-deductible. For more on taxes and interest parity see Maurice Levi, "Taxation and 'Abnormal' International Capital Flows," *Journal of Political Economy,* June 1977, pp. 635–646.

hence another reason for a band around the parity line. The amount of extra required return and hence the potential width of the band due to liquidity preference depend on the likelihood that the funds will be needed early and on whether these funds can be borrowed by using the original covered investment to secure the loan. Since the required extra return depends on the *likelihood* that the funds will be needed, it is clear that this liquidity consideration is different from the transaction-costs consideration discussed earlier, which involved *known* amounts of transaction costs. Liquidity does relate to transaction costs, but these are *expected* costs. Clearly, if it is known that funds will not be required, or if it is known that the foreign investment can be used as the guarantee or security for borrowing funds, no foreign yield premium is required. The more uncertainty there is concerning future needs and alternative sources of short-term financing, the higher are the premiums that should be required before venturing into foreign-currency securities. This will mean wider bands around the interest parity line.[25]

As in the case of transaction costs and political risk, the choice by third-country (outside) investors as to which currency-denominated securities to invest in should be symmetrical. That is, if there is the same probability of needing to liquidate investments from either currency and the same transaction costs if liquidation occurs, liquidity preference in the presence of third-country investors should not cause deviations from interest parity.

Effect of the Reasons for Interest Disparity on Investment and Borrowing Decisions

Each investor or borrower must evaluate yields and borrowing costs from his or her own perspective. This means using exchange rates that include transaction costs and appropriate tax rates, and then comparing yield or borrowing-cost differences with the difference the investor or borrower believes is necessary to compensate for the risk or illiquidity that is faced. What we have argued suggests that except for banks, transaction costs are likely to work toward keeping investing and borrowing in the home currency. Withholding taxes are likely to matter only if withholding rates are higher than domestic tax rates, but differential taxes on interest income versus capital gains could induce investors with favorable capital gains treatment to place funds in currencies that trade at a forward premium. As for political risk, this will create yield and cost differences that are not exploitable for those facing the political risk, although the differences may be exploitable by others.[26] A similar conclusion applies to liquidity preference. That is, to the extent that interest parity does not hold because foreign investments are less liquid, those investors for whom liquidity is not relevant can enjoy a higher yield. We can see that it can pay to shop around when investing or borrowing, but it all depends on the specific circumstances of the investor or borrower.

[25]It might be felt that movements in security values because of changes in market interest rates also affect the liquidity of domestic investment versus foreign investment. Although the reason is not obvious, this view is not, in general, correct, because relative interest-rate movements should be offset by exchange-rate movements, which are all related according to the interest parity condition.
[26]Those who can exploit differences are third-country investors for whom the political risks are similar, and borrowers for whom political risks are irrelevant. Borrowers will tend to borrow in the low-risk countries because covered interest costs there can remain lower than elsewhere.

SUMMARY

1. Forward exchange markets allow short-term investors and borrowers to avoid foreign exchange risk.

2. An investor should be indifferent with respect to investing in domestic or foreign currency when the domestic-currency interest rate equals the foreign-currency rate plus the annualized forward exchange premium or discount on the foreign currency. The investor should invest in domestic currency when the domestic-currency interest rate exceeds the foreign-currency rate plus the forward premium/discount on the foreign currency, and vice versa.

3. A borrower should borrow in foreign currency when the domestic-currency interest rate exceeds the foreign-currency rate plus the forward foreign exchange premium or discount, and borrow in domestic currency when the domestic-currency interest rate is lower than the foreign-currency interest rate plus the forward foreign exchange premium or discount.

4. Covered interest arbitrage involves borrowing in one currency to invest in another, with foreign exchange risk hedged. It is profitable when there are differences between covered borrowing costs and investment yields.

5. The interest parity condition states that there will be no advantage to borrowing or lending in one currency rather than another. Forces set up by interest arbitragers will move the money and foreign exchange markets toward covered interest parity.

6. The uncovered interest parity condition and the PPP condition in terms of expected inflation can be used to derive the equality of real rates of return between countries. This latter relationship is the Fisher-open condition, which has an independent rationale.

7. If round-trip arbitrage were the only force moving exchange rates and interest rates toward interest parity, the deviations could be relatively large. This is because it would be necessary to be compensated in the covered-interest differential for foreign exchange transaction costs and borrowing-lending spreads on interest rates.

8. One-way interest arbitrage involves choosing between alternative ways of going from current dollars/pounds to future pounds/dollars. Because the choices involve the same transaction costs whichever route is taken, one-way arbitrage should drive markets very close to covered interest parity.

9. Third-country investors or borrowers who face the same transaction costs whichever currency of denomination they choose for borrowing or investment should also drive markets very close to covered interest parity.

10. Political risks can also cause deviations from interest parity between countries and allow a band around the interest-parity line, because investors from each country need compensation for the greater risk of investing in the other country. However, if investors outside the two countries view the countries as equally risky politically, they will drive markets to interest parity.

11. Withholding taxes do not normally affect the interest parity condition.

12. For those who face differential taxes on income versus capital gains, the relevant interest parity line has a different slope than the conventional interest parity line. However, since banks pay the same tax on interest and foreign exchange gains, significant interest disparity should not result from differential taxes.

13. Covered foreign-currency investments are less liquid than domestic-currency investments because extra foreign exchange transaction costs are met on liquidating covered foreign-currency securities. The liquidity relates to expected rather than actual transaction costs.

14. Each investor or borrower must evaluate opportunities from his or her own perspective of transaction costs, taxes, political risks, and liquidity concerns. Shopping around can be advantageous.

1. What is the money market?
2. How does a forward-covered investment avoid exchange-rate risk?
3. According to covered interest parity, if the British pound is at a forward premium vis-à-vis the U.S. dollar, what do we know about pound-versus-dollar interest rates?
4. What is covered interest arbitrage?
5. Does the covered interest parity condition arise from different perspectives? Name them.
6. If the covered yield on pound-denominated securities were to become temporarily higher than on dollar securities, what would happen to interest rates and the spot and forward exchange rates?
7. What is uncovered interest parity?
8. What is the Fisher-open condition?
9. What conditions together imply the Fisher-open condition?
10. What is round-trip interest arbitrage?
11. Can transaction costs affect interest parity?
12. Does political risk affect covered yields on different currency-denominated deposits at London banks?
13. Does political risk affect covered yields on U.S. government bills versus Canadian government bills?
14. What is a withholding tax credit?
15. Do low rates of withholding tax affect covered interest parity?
16. What is liquidity preference, and can it affect covered interest parity if people can borrow without penalty against covered foreign-currency assets?

ASSIGNMENT PROBLEMS

1. Derive the criteria for making covered money-market investment and borrowing decisions when the exchange rates are given in European terms. Derive the equivalent of equation (11.4).
2. You have been given the following information:

$r_\$$	$r_£$	$S(\$/£)$	$F_{1/4}(\$/£)$
5%	6%	1.5000 -10	1.4985 - 97

   where $r_\$$ = annual interest on 3-month U.S. dollar commercial paper

   $r_£$ = annual interest on 3-month British pound commercial paper

   $S(\$/£)$ = number of dollars per pound, spot

   $F_{1/4}(\$/£)$ = number of dollars per pound, 3-months forward

   On the basis of the precise criteria:
   a. In which commercial paper would you invest?
   b. In which currency would you borrow?
   c. How would you arbitrage?
   d. What is the profit from interest arbitrage per dollar borrowed?
3. a. Use the data in question 2 and the precise formula on the right-hand side of equation (11.4) to compute the covered yield on investment in pounds. Repeat this using the approximate formula on the right-hand side of equation (11.5).

b. Compare the error between the precise formula and the approximate formula in **a** above with the error in the situation where $r_\$ = 15$ percent, $r_£ = 16$ percent, and $S(\$/£)$ and $F_{1/4}(\$/£)$ are as above.

c. Should we be more careful to avoid the use of the "interest plus premium or minus discount" approximation in equation (11.5) at higher or at lower interest rates?

d. If the interest rates and the forward rate in question **2** are for 12 months, is the difference between equation (11.4) and equation (11.5) greater than when we are dealing with 3-month rates?

4. Derive the equivalent of Table 11.1 where all covered yields are against pounds rather than dollars. This will require computing appropriate cross spot and forward rates.

5. Draw a figure like Figure 11.1 to show what interest arbitrage will do to the interest-rate differentials and the forward premiums at points A to F in the table below. If all the adjustment to the interest parity occurs in the forward exchange rate, what will $F_{1/12}(\$/£)$ be after interest parity has been restored?

	A	B	C	D	E	F
$S(\$/£)$	1.6200	1.6200	1.6200	1.6200	1.6200	1.6200
$F_{1/12}(\$/£)$	1.6220	1.6150	1.6220	1.6150	1.6180	1.6120
$r_\$(1$ month), %	8.00	8.00	8.00	8.00	8.00	8.00
$r_£(1$ month), %	10.00	9.00	8.00	7.00	6.00	5.00

6. Write down the expectations form of PPP, the uncovered interest parity condition, and the Fisher-open condition. Derive each one from the other two.

7. Assuming that there are a large number of third-country borrowers and investors, do you think that political risk will cause larger deviations from interest parity than are caused by transaction costs?

8. If banks are as happy to advance loans that are secured by domestic-currency money-market investments as they are to advance loans secured by similar foreign-currency covered money-market investments, will firms prefer domestic-currency investments on the grounds of liquidity?

9. How does the importance of liquidity relate to the probability that cash will be needed?

10. Use the framework of Figure 11.4 to show how the band of unprofitable arbitrage when one-way arbitrage occurs compares to the band when only round-trip arbitrage occurs.

11. Why might a borrower want to borrow in a currency that is at a forward discount if that borrower faces a higher tax rate on interest income than on capital gains?

12. Why does the Fisher-open condition relate to countries rather than currencies?

13. In general, are transactions costs higher in spot or forward markets? Does this hold any implications for whether interest parity will hold exactly?

14. What role does the rest of the world play in determining whether covered interest rate parity will hold between any two currency-denominated securities?

15. Suppose that real interest rates are equal for all countries in the world. Does this imply anything for the relationship between covered interest rate parity and the PPP condition?

BIBLIOGRAPHY

ALIBER, ROBERT Z., and CLYDE P. STICKNEY: "Accounting Measures of Foreign Exchange Exposure: The Long and Short of It," *The Accounting Review,* January 1975, pp. 44–57.

BAHMANI-OSKOOEE, MOHSEN, and SATYA P. DAS: "Transaction Costs and the Interest Parity Theorem," *Journal of Political Economy,* August 1985, pp. 793–799.

BLENMAN, LLOYD P., and JANET S. THATCHER: "Arbitrage Opportunities in Currency and Credit Markets: New Evidence," *International Journal of Finance,* no. 3, 1995.

———: "Arbitrage Heterogeneity, Investor Horizon and Arbitrage Opportunities: An Empirical Investigation," *Financial Review,* vol. 30, 1995.

BRANSON, WILLIAM H.: "The Minimum Covered Interest Needed for International Arbitrage Activity," *Journal of Political Economy,* December 1969, pp. 1029–1034.

CLINTON, KEVIN: "Transaction Costs and Covered Interest Arbitrage: Theory and Evidence," *Journal of Political Economy,* April 1988, pp. 358–370.

DEARDORFF, ALAN V.: "One-Way Arbitrage and Its Implications for the Foreign Exchange Markets," *Journal of Political Economy,* April 1979, pp. 351–364.

FRENKEL, JACOB A., and RICHARD M. LEVICH: "Covered Interest Arbitrage: Unexploited Profits?" *Journal of Political Economy,* April 1975, pp. 325–338.

GIDDY, IAN H.: "An Integrated Theory of Exchange Rate Equilibrium," *Journal of Financial and Quantitative Analysis,* December 1976, pp. 883–892.

HUANG, ROGER D.: "Expectations of Exchange Rates and Differential Inflation Rates: Further Evidence on Purchasing Power Parity in Efficient Markets," *Journal of Finance,* March 1987, pp. 69–79.

KUBARYCH, ROGER M.: *Foreign Exchange Markets in the United States,* Federal Reserve Bank of New York, New York, 1978.

LEVI, MAURICE D.: "Taxation and 'Abnormal' International Capital Flows," *Journal of Political Economy,* June 1977, pp. 635–646.

———: "Non-Reversed Investment and Borrowing, Transaction Costs, and Covered Interest Parity," *International Review of Economics and Finance,* vol. 1, no. 2, 1992, pp. 107–119.

———: "Spot versus Forward Speculation and Hedging: A Diagrammatic Exposition," *Journal of International Money and Finance,* April 1984, pp. 105–110.

LLEWELLYN, DAVID T.: *International Financial Integration: The Limits of Sovereignty,* Macmillan, London, 1980.

OFFICER, LAWRENCE H., and THOMAS D. WILLET: "The Covered-Arbitrage Schedule: A Critical Survey of Recent Developments," *Journal of Money, Credit and Banking,* May 1970, pp. 247–257.

WOODWARD, ROBERT S.: "Some New Evidence on the Profitability of One-Way versus Round-Trip Arbitrage," *Journal of Money, Credit and Banking,* November 1988, pp. 645–652.

Managing Foreign Exchange Risk and Exposure

Until this point our concern has been with the nature of markets in which currencies and currency derivatives trade and with the international financial environment of multinational business. The focus of the remainder of the book is with managerial issues, such as using international financial markets to deal with the special opportunities and risks of international trade and investment. We shall see on numerous occasions on this journey through international managerial finance that an understanding of the financial markets and environment are essential elements of financial decision making. The chapters in Part Four begin our journey with a discussion of the objectives of international financial management and how to achieve these objectives. The focus is on operating issues, from the measurement of foreign exchange risk and exposure, to the methods and potential for success of currency speculation.

The opening chapter of Part Four, Chapter 12, takes us directly to the meaning of foreign exchange exposure. It is shown that exposure is a measure of the sensitivity of changes in domestic-currency values of assets, liabilities, or operating incomes to unanticipated changes in exchange rates. We show that surprisingly, domestic as well as foreign financial instruments and incomes can face foreign exchange exposure, and that under special circumstances, foreign financial instruments or incomes may *not* be exposed. The chapter also explains foreign exchange risk, a matter which is often confused with exposure. Exchange-rate risk is shown to relate to the *variability* of domestic-currency values of assets, liabilities, and incomes, whereas exposure is the *amount at risk.* This makes risk and exposure conceptually and even dimensionally different: the two concepts have different units of measurement.

Chapter 13 provides a brief introduction to international accounting principles and how these influence the measurement of exposure in financial statements—accounting exposure—versus true, underlying exposure—real exposure. While it is real exposure that should really matter to the owners of a multinational firm, values that show up in financial statements cannot be ignored when, for example, taxes are based on operating incomes as expressed in a company's "reporting currency."

291

Chapter 14 is devoted to the effect of exchange rates on sales and operating profitability, so-called "operating exposure." Use is made of the microeconomic theory of the firm, which emphasizes marginal cost and marginal revenue. It is shown that the amount of operating exposure depends on such factors as elasticity of demand and flexibility of production. The chapter ends with a consideration of situations in which exchange rates have different effects on firms in the short run versus the long run. This distinction between the short run and the long run for firms is analogous to the distinction between the short run and the long run for the economy as a whole, which was discussed in Chapter 6 in conjunction with the J curve.

With exposure and risk defined and explained in Chapters 12, 13, and 14, in Chapter 15 we shift attention to the management of exposure and risk. We begin by asking whether managers should hedge foreign exchange risk and exposure or whether they should leave this to shareholders. Alternative means of dealing with risk and exposure are contrasted and compared using the building blocks of payoff profiles. This approach is sometimes called financial engineering.

The opposite of hedging is speculation, which involves purposefully taking exposed positions in foreign exchange. Chapter 16 begins by describing the methods that exist for currency speculation. This leads naturally into a discussion of market efficiency, because as we shall show, speculation cannot be persistently successful if foreign exchange markets are efficient. Chapter 16 ends with a discussion of the successes and failures of attempts to forecast exchange rates. This discussion appears alongside the discussions of speculation and market efficiency because, as we shall see, an ability to forecast exchange rates and profit from such forecasts is closely related to market efficiency and the expected returns from speculation.

CHAPTER 12

Foreign Exchange Exposure
and Risk

If you want the fruit you have to go out on a limb.

—ANCIENT SAYING

Even though foreign exchange risk and exposure have been central issues of international financial management for many years, a considerable degree of confusion remains about their nature and measurement. For example, it is not uncommon to hear the term "foreign exchange exposure" used interchangeably with the term "foreign exchange risk" when in fact they are conceptually completely different. (Foreign exchange risk is related to the variability of domestic-currency values of assets, liabilities, or operating incomes due to unanticipated changes in exchange rates, whereas foreign exchange exposure is what *is* at risk.) This chapter is devoted to clarifying the nature and measurement of risk and exposure, as well as to explaining the factors contributing to them. Subsequent chapters deal with the management of risk and exposure.

THE NATURE OF EXCHANGE-RATE RISK AND EXPOSURE

Definition of Foreign Exchange Exposure

Foreign exchange exposure can be defined in the following way:

> Foreign exchange exposure is the sensitivity of changes in the real domestic-currency value of assets, liabilities, or operating incomes to unanticipated changes in exchange rates.[1]

Several features of this definition are worth noting.

---

[1]Exposure is defined this way in Michael Adler and Bernard Dumas. "Exposure to Currency Risk: Definition and Measurement," *Financial Management,* summer 1984, pp. 41–50. See also Christine R. Hekman, "Measuring Foreign Exchange Exposure: A Practical Theory and Its Application," *Financial Analysts Journal,* September/October 1983, pp. 59–65; and Lars Oxelheim and Clas G. Wihlborg, *Macroeconomic Uncertainty: International Risks and Opportunities for the Corporation,* Wiley, New York, 1987.

First, we notice that exposure is a measure of the *sensitivity* of domestic currency values. That is, it is a description of the *extent* or *degree* to which the home-currency value of something is changed by exchange rate changes. Second, we notice that it is concerned with *real domestic-currency values.* By this we mean, for example, that from a U.S. perspective exposure is the sensitivity of changes in real—that is, inflation-adjusted—U.S. dollar values of assets, liabilities, and operating incomes, to changes in exchange rates. Third, we notice that exposure can exist on assets and liabilities, or on the operating incomes of firms. Since the values of assets and liabilities are so much at a particular moment in time, and the values of operating incomes are so much per period of time, we see that exposure exists on stocks and flows. Fourth, we notice that we have not qualified the list of exposed items by describing them as being *foreign* assets, and so on. This is because, as we shall see, unanticipated changes in exchange rates can affect domestic as well as foreign assets, liabilities, and operating incomes. Finally, we notice that the definition refers only to *unanticipated* changes in exchange rates. This is because markets compensate for changes in exchange rates that are anticipated. Consequently, it is only to the extent that exchange rates change by more or less than had been expected that there will be gains or losses on assets, liabilities, or operating incomes.

Exposure as a Regression Slope

We can further clarify the definition of foreign exchange exposure at the same time as we describe how it can be calculated by considering Figures 12.1*a* and *b*. The horizontal axis in both figures shows unexpected changes in exchange rates, $\Delta S^u(\$/\pounds)$, with these being positive to the right of the origin and negative to the left of the origin. Positive values of $\Delta S^u(\$/\pounds)$ are unanticipated appreciations of the pound, and negative values are unanticipated depreciations of the pound. The vertical axis of each figure shows the changes in the real values of assets, liabilities, or operating incomes, in terms of a **reference currency,** which for a U.S. firm is the U.S. dollar. We can interpret ΔV as the change in the real value of particular individual assets, liabilities, or operating incomes or as the change in the real value of a collection of assets, liabilities, or operating incomes. As we have said, ΔV is in real terms, and so it is adjusted for U.S. inflation.[2]

When there is an unanticipated change in an exchange rate, there will be an accompanying change in the dollar value of, for example, a foreign-currency bank account, real-estate investment, stock, bond, or loan. Of course, factors other than exchange rates may also influence the dollar values of these items, and so we cannot always predict with certainty how dollar values will change with any particular unanticipated change in exchange rates. However, there is often a tendency for values to change in more or less predictable ways. When there is such a tendency we say that there is a **systematic relationship** between the dollar value of the item and the exchange rate. This systematic relationship is particularly strong when foreign-currency values are fixed. For example, when the pound unexpectedly jumps from $1.50/£ to $1.70/£, the U.S. dollar value of a £1 million bank deposit changes from

---

[2]Of course, inflation itself is unknown and contributes to uncertainty. However, because of the difficulty of dealing with inflation, in much of what follows we ignore the level of inflation as well as uncertainty about inflation.

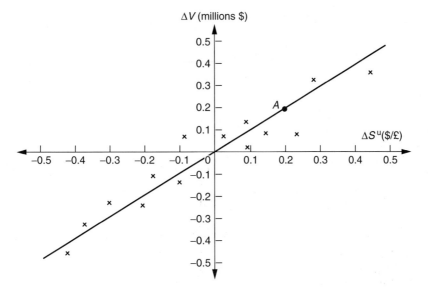

(a) Exposure line for "foreign" assets

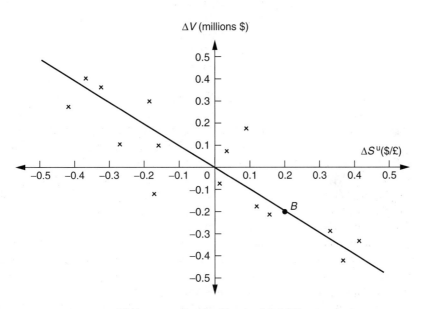

(b) Exposure line for "foreign" liabilities

FIGURE 12.1. Exposure as the Slope of a Regression Line
Each unanticipated change in the exchange rate will be associated with a change in the dollar
value of an asset, liability, or operating income. The unanticipated change in the exchange rate
can be plotted against the associated change in dollar value. Because other factors also affect
values, the same $\Delta S^u(\$/\pounds)$ will not always be associated with the same ΔV. However, there may
be a systematic relationship between $\Delta S^u(\$/\pounds)$ and ΔV. For example, unanticipated pound
appreciations may typically be associated with higher dollar values of pound-denominated
assets and lower dollar values of pound-denominated liabilities, the former implying an upward-
sloping scatter and the latter a downward-sloping scatter.

$1.5 million to $1.7 million, and this change in dollar value can be accurately known. We can then plot a ΔV of $200,000 against a ΔS^u of $0.2/£ in Figure 12.1*a*. This is shown by point *A* in the upper right-hand quadrant. Similarly, an unexpected drop in the pound would be associated with an accurately known lower U.S. dollar value of the bank deposit, giving rise to a point in the lower left-hand quadrant. With the pound value of the bank deposit unchanged by changes in exchange rates, all points sit exactly on the **exposure line,** which for the bank deposit is upward-sloping.

If we consider a pound-denominated bank loan instead of a bank deposit, the effect of unanticipated changes in exchange rates is again accurately known. However, in this case there is a downward-sloping relationship between ΔV and ΔS^u. For example, an unanticipated jump in the pound from $1.50/£ to $1.70/£ results in a $200,000 loss on a £1 million bank loan, because this is the extra dollar amount of the liability. This gives point *B* in the lower right-hand quadrant of Figure 12.1*b*. Similarly, an unanticipated depreciation of the pound gives a point in the upper left-hand quadrant.

It should be emphasized that the U.S. dollar value of many other assets or liabilities would not be as predictably affected by changes in exchange rates as the pound-denominated bank account or loan just considered. For example, the pound values of British real estate or equity investments might well change at the same time as the exchange rate changes. Furthermore, the changes in the pound values of the real estate, equities, and so on may not always be the same when there is a given change in the exchange rate. This means that a given value of ΔS^u could be associated with different possible values of ΔV. It should also be emphasized that, as we shall see, domestic assets and liabilities, as well as the operating incomes of domestic firms, may also change with changes in exchange rates and therefore may also be exposed to exchange rates.

Exposure is measured by the sensitivity of the *systematic* relationship between ΔS^u and ΔV, where, as we have said, by "systematic" we mean the tendency for ΔV to change in a more or less predictable way with respect to ΔS^u. That is, by "systematic relationship" we mean the way ΔS^u and ΔV are *on average* related to each other. Of course, because the actual ΔV associated with a given ΔS^u is not always the same, the equation which describes the relationship between ΔV and ΔS^u must allow for random errors. Such an equation is a **regression equation,** which, for exposure to the dollar-pound exchange rate for which $\Delta S^u = \Delta S^u(\$/£)$, takes the form

$$\Delta V = \beta \Delta S^u(\$/£) + \mu \tag{12.1}$$

Here β is the **regression coefficient** describing the systematic relation between ΔV and $\Delta S^u(\$/£)$. That is, β describes the tendency for ΔV and $\Delta S^u(\$/£)$ to be related. The term μ is the random error in the relationship, and is called the **regression error.** The role of μ is to allow the value of ΔV to be less than perfectly predictable for a given $\Delta S^u(\$/£)$.[3]

The item of most interest in equation (12.1) is β. This is because β describes the sensitivity of the systematic relation between unanticipated changes in exchange rates, $\Delta S^u(\$/£)$, and changes in the values of assets and so on, ΔV. That is, β is the

---

[3]If V is increasing over time from, for example, inflation, we can add a constant to the right-hand side of equation (12.1). For simplicity, we suppress the constant.

sensitivity measure we have called foreign exchange exposure.[4] Because β is the slope of the line described by equation (12.1) we can redefine exposure as follows:

> Foreign exchange exposure is the slope of the regression equation which relates changes in the real domestic currency value of assets, liabilities, or operating incomes to unanticipated changes in exchange rates.

Let us consider how we might estimate β.

Estimating Exposure

As we have seen, we can plot the values of ΔV and associated ΔS^u's on a graph such as Figure 12.1. Of course, to do this we would have to know how much of the actual changes in exchange rates was unanticipated and also be able to measure the changes in the real dollar values of assets, and so on. However, this may not be as difficult as one might think. In particular, the unanticipated changes in exchange rates may be judged from looking back at forward exchange rates, which are predictions of future spot exchange rates, and subtracting the forward rates from the actual exchange rates.[5] Similarly, dollar values of assets and liabilities may be apparent in stock and bond prices.[6] After we have plotted the values of the ΔV's and associated ΔS^u's, we can fit a line to the scatter of points.

Of course, if the values of ΔV are affected only by the values of ΔS^u, as in the examples of the British pound bank deposit and bank loan, the observed ΔV's and ΔS^u's would all sit exactly along a line. Then, exposure is deduced from joining the points and measuring the slope of the resulting line. However, for other assets, liabilities, incomes, and payments, there is noise in the relation, so the points describing ΔV's and associated ΔS^u's will look like the scatters in Figure 12.1a and b. When this happens we must use statistical procedures to fit the line and find the systematic relationship through the scatter of points. Once we have fitted a line to the scatter of observations on ΔV's and associated ΔS^u's, we have estimates of the regression coefficient. Our estimate of exposure is the estimated value of β. However, before we consider questions such as how accurate this estimate is and how closely ΔV is related to ΔS^u, we should consider the units of measurement of exposure, β. We shall find that exposure is measured in units that make good sense.

Units of Measurement of Exposure

If ΔV is measured in U.S. dollars, as it will be if we are measuring exposure from a U.S. perspective, and if ΔS^u is measured in dollars per pound, then exposure, that is,

---

[4]This means that exposure can be defined in the terms used to define the slope coefficient of a regression. Those readers with a background in statistics will realize that this means that by definition the exposure is $cov(\Delta V, \Delta S^u)/var(\Delta S^u)$. This definition, and some of the implications of writing exposure in this way, are explored in Appendix 12.1. See also Adler and Dumas, *op. cit.,* and Oxelheim and Wihlborg, *op. cit.*

[5]The reason why forward rates can be considered to proxy for expected future spot rates was explained in Chapter 3.

[6]The effects on operating incomes are likely to be much more difficult to measure. This is discussed in Chapter 14.

β, must be measured in pounds. This is because in terms of units of measurement, equation (12.1) involves $\$ = \beta(\$/£)$, so that $\beta = \$ \div (\$/£) = £$.

The fact that exposure is measured in units of the foreign currency is most appropriate, as can be seen by reconsidering our examples involving pound-denominated bank deposits and loans. In the case of bank deposits, when the exchange rate unexpectedly changes from $\$1.50/£$ to $\$1.70/£$, a £1 million bank deposit is worth $\$200,000$ more. That is, assuming $\mu = 0$ in equation (12.1),

$$\$200,000 = \beta \cdot \$0.20/£$$

or

$$\beta = \$200,000 \div \$0.20/£ = £1,000,000$$

We find that exposure is £1 million. This is the amount that is at risk to unanticipated changes in exchange rates. In a similar way, exposure on a £1 million bank loan is calculated from the fact that a loss of $\$200,000$ is made when $\Delta S^u = \$0.20/£$, so that

$$-\$200,000 = \beta \cdot \$0.20/£$$

or

$$\beta = \$200,000 \div \$0.20/£ = -£1,000,000$$

In the case of the slope being negative we say the item has a **short exposure,** whereas when the slope is positive we say the item has a **long exposure.** However, because *a priori* we do not know whether ΔS^u will be positive or negative, we sometimes drop the negative sign and say the exposure is, for example, £1 million, whether the exposure is on a bank deposit or bank loan.

In the case of bank deposits and loans the pound amounts are unchanged as the exchange rate changes. However, what do we do if, at the same time as exchange rates change, there is a change in the pound value of an asset or liability? Or what do we do if there are many exchange rates changing at the same time? It is in these situations that the definition of exposure in terms of slope coefficients of a regression line comes to the fore. Indeed, when we consider these more complex situations, we find out why even assets, liabilities, and operating incomes that appear to be entirely domestic may in fact be exposed to exchange rates and subject to exchange-rate risk.

Exposure When Local-Currency Values Vary with Unanticipated Changes in Exchange Rates

Suppose a piece of British real estate has a market value of £1 million when the exchange rate is $\$1.80/£$. Let us suppose that inflation subsequently occurs and is reflected both in the value of the real estate and in the exchange rate. In particular, let us suppose the inflation causes the pound to depreciate to $\$1.60/£$, and the property value to increase to £1.125 million. In this case the dollar value of the real estate before inflation has occurred is

$$\$1.80/£ \times £1 \text{ million} = \$1.8 \text{ million}$$

and after the inflation has occurred it is

$$\$1.60/£ \times £1.125 \text{ million} = \$1.8 \text{ million}$$

We see that with the assumed numbers there is no change in the dollar value of the British real estate.

In terms of equation (12.1), if all the assumed change in exchange rate is unanticipated, what we have is $\Delta V = 0$ and $\Delta S^u = -\$0.20/£$, so that

$$0 = \beta(-\$0.20/£) + \mu \qquad (12.2)$$

If μ is zero, then the only way equation (12.2) can hold is if $\beta = 0$. That is, if the pound value of the British real estate and the exchange rate of the pound change systematically as in the example, the real estate is not exposed. The reason is that the change in the exchange rate exactly compensates for the change in the pound value of the real estate.

Of course, we have constructed a special case in this example, and on selecting different numbers we would have found the real estate to be exposed to unanticipated changes in exchange rates. For example, if the real estate systematically increased in value from £1 million to £1.0625 million with the depreciation of the exchange rate from \$1.80/£ to \$1.60/£, then

$$\Delta V = (\$1.60/£ \times £1.0625 \text{ million}) - (\$1.80/£ \times £1.00 \text{ million})$$

$$= -\$0.10 \text{ million}$$

Assuming μ is zero, the exposure given by equation (12.1) is β from

$$-\$0.10 \text{ million} = \beta \cdot (-\$0.20/£)$$

i.e.,

$$\beta = £500,000$$

That is, if this outcome occurred systematically, then the exposure on the British real estate would be only half its market value. Similarly, if the value of the real estate happened to decrease systematically from £1 million to £0.9375 million with the same change in the exchange rate, then

$$\Delta V = (\$1.60/£ \times £0.9375 \text{ million}) - (\$1.80/£ \times £1.00 \text{ million})$$

$$= -\$0.3 \text{ million}$$

and the exposure is given by

$$-\$0.3 \text{ million} = \beta \cdot (-\$0.20/£)$$

i.e.,

$$\beta = £1.50 \text{ million}$$

That is, the exposure on the £1 million British real estate is 50 percent larger than the value of the real estate itself.

Exposure against Numerous Exchange Rates

When many different exchange rates can affect ΔV, as when ΔV is the value of a firm that holds assets and liabilities in many countries and currencies or earns incomes in many countries and currencies, we can use an extension of equation (12.1) to estimate exposure. For example if ΔV could conceivably be influenced by the exchange rates of the dollar versus the British pound, German mark, Japanese yen, French franc, and so on, we can use the **multiple regression equation**

$$\Delta V = \beta_1 \Delta S^u(\$/£) + \beta_2 \Delta S^u(\$/DM)$$

$$+\beta_3 \Delta S^u(\$/¥) + \beta_4 \Delta S^u(\$/SFr) + \mu \qquad (12.3)$$

Each slope coefficient gives exposure to the associated foreign currency. For example, β_2 gives the sensitivity of ΔV to unanticipated changes in the U.S. dollar value of the German mark. As in the case of exposure to only one exchange rate, the coefficients are all measured in units of the foreign currency. For example, if ΔV is a U.S. dollar amount, and we are measuring exposure to the dollar-mark exchange rate assuming all other ΔS^u's to be zero, then in terms of measurement units

$$\$ = \beta_2 \cdot (\$/DM)$$

and since the dollar signs cancel:

$$\beta_2 = DM$$

That is, exposure to $\Delta S^u(\$/DM)$ is a Deutschemark amount.

When we are not thinking in terms of regression coefficients but rather of exposure as a sensitivity, we can define exposure to an individual currency as follows:

> Exposure to an individual currency is the sensitivity of the real home-currency value of an asset, liability, or operating income to unanticipated changes in the foreign exchange value of that currency, assuming unanticipated changes in all other exchange rates are zero.

Exposure to an individual currency is analogous to a partial derivative, in this case of ΔV with respect to a particular ΔS^u.

Exposure on "Domestic" Assets, Liabilities, and Operating Incomes

It might seem that from a U.S. perspective, such items as U.S. treasury bills and bonds, U.S. corporate stocks and bonds, and operating incomes from businesses in the United States are not exposed to exchange rates. After all, we do not have to multiply foreign-currency values of such items by an uncertain exchange rate in order to compute their U.S. dollar values. The reality is, however, that all these items may well be exposed to exchange rates. This is because their U.S. dollar values may be systematically affected by exchange rates, even though we do not have to do any translation into dollar terms. Let us see why exposure might exist by considering first the case of U.S. bonds.

Suppose that when the U.S. dollar falls vis-à-vis other leading currencies, the Federal Reserve typically tries to reduce the dollar's depreciation by increasing interest rates. Such a policy is known as **leaning against the wind**, and there is substantial evidence that it is practiced.[7] When interest rates increase, the market values of bonds decline. If the relationship between exchange rates and interest rates is systematic, the U.S. holders of U.S. bonds are exposed to exchange rates. This is the case because they lose when the dollar unexpectedly depreciates, and they gain when it appreciates.

Our definition of exposure in terms of the slope of a regression line confirms that U.S. holders of U.S. bonds are indeed exposed if the Federal Reserve systematically leans against the wind. This is because in such a case when, for example, $\Delta S^u(\$/£)$ is large and positive—a depreciation of the dollar—ΔV is typically large and negative. Therefore, there is a negative association between $\Delta S^u(\$/£)$ and ΔV. This produces a negative slope β in equation (12.1). Furthermore, the larger the impact of an unanticipated dollar depreciation on U.S. interest rates and bond prices, the greater is the exposure. Similarly, if U.S. stock prices systematically decline as U.S. interest rates increase, then the Federal Reserve's policy of leaning against the wind will expose U.S. stocks too. That is, a depreciating dollar will mean lower stock prices. This means that from a non-U.S. perspective, U.S. stocks are exposed more than their market value. This follows because the combined effect of a depreciating dollar and a declining dollar value of U.S. stocks is a more substantial decline in the foreign-currency values of U.S. stocks than in exchange rates.

While stock prices in general might decline when the U.S. dollar unexpectedly depreciates, some stocks may benefit from the dollar depreciation. In particular, stocks of U.S. export-oriented firms might increase in value because the cheaper dollar makes the firms more competitive in foreign markets. Indeed, since a dollar depreciation makes imports to the United States more expensive, some U.S. firms which sell exclusively in the U.S. market, but which compete against imports, may also gain from a depreciation. If the extra profitability of the U.S. export-oriented and import-competing firms shows up in higher stock prices, then these stocks are exposed. In this case there is a positive association between ΔV and ΔS^u.[8]

Estimation Difficulties

Unfortunately, the calculation of exposure is not as straightforward as our definition might suggest. This is because exposure changes over time. Consequently, we cannot collect values of ΔV and relevant ΔS^u's over a period of time and fit an equation like equation (12.3).[9] Instead, it is necessary to employ other techniques such as

[7]For example, see Bruno Solnik, "Using Financial Prices to Test Exchange Rate Models: A Note," *Journal of Finance,* March 1987, pp. 141–149. Solnik shows that exchange rates and interest rates are negatively related, which suggests that central banks increase interest rates when their currencies are depreciating.

[8]As we mentioned earlier, because the effects on operating incomes show up in the future, the exposure of export-oriented and import-competing firms is different from the exposure on assets and liabilities, which shows up as gains or losses only at the time changes in exchange rates occur. Of course, market values of publicly traded export-oriented and import-competing firms should change immediately, converting operating exposure into asset exposure.

[9]See Maurice D. Levi, "Exchange Rates and the Valuation of Firms," and Yakov Amihud, "Exchange Rates and the Valuation of Equity Shares," both in Yakov Amihud and Richard M. Levich (eds.), *Exchange Rates and Corporate Performance,* New York University, New York, 1994.

an analysis of possible scenarios. This involves the generation of values of ΔV which might occur for different ΔS^u's. For example, possible values of ΔV and $\Delta S^u(\$/\pounds)$ might be generated for different rates of inflation. A regression line can then be fitted to the generated data. As might be surmised, this is a rather lengthy process.

Definition of Foreign Exchange Risk

Michael Adler and Bernard Dumas define foreign exchange risk in terms of the variance of unanticipated changes in exchange rates.[10] That is, they define exchange-rate risk in terms of the unpredictability of exchange rates as reflected by the variance of ΔS^u, that is, var(ΔS^u).

While Adler and Dumas's definition makes it clear that unpredictability is paramount in the measurement of exchange-rate risk, this author prefers a different focus on variability. The definition of **exchange-rate risk** we shall use is as follows:

> Foreign exchange risk is measured by the variance of the domestic-currency value of an asset, liability, or operating income that is attributable to unanticipated changes in exchange rates.

The principal difference between the definition used in this book and that of Adler and Dumas is that the definition used here focuses on the unpredictability of values of assets, liabilities, or operating incomes due to uncertainty in exchange rates, not on the uncertainty of exchange rates themselves. This difference in definitions can have important consequences. For example, according to our definition, an asset is not subject to exchange-rate risk if its value does not depend on exchange rates, even though exchange rates might be extremely volatile. According to our definition, volatility in exchange rates is responsible for exchange-rate risk only if it translates into volatility in real dollar values of assets, liabilities, or operating incomes. This makes exchange-rate risk dependent on exposure as well as on var(ΔS^u). Let us see why this is so by reconsidering the regression equation (12.1).

Equation (12.1) makes it clear that changes in the values of assets, liabilities, or operating incomes depend both on exchange rates and on other factors, with the effect of the non-exchange-rate factors captured by the term μ. We can isolate the effect of exchange rates from the effect of other factors if we define the variable

$$\Delta \hat{V} = \beta \Delta S^u(\$/\pounds) \tag{12.4}$$

$\Delta \hat{V}$ is the change in value of an asset, liability, or operating income *that is due to unanticipated changes in the exchange rate.* That is, we have partitioned the total change in value, ΔV, into that due to changes in exchange rates, $\Delta \hat{V}$, and that due to other influences, μ; this follows by relating equation (12.4) to equation (12.1), giving

$$\Delta V \equiv \Delta \hat{V} + \mu \tag{12.5}$$

With ΔV so partitioned, we can explain how our definition of exchange-rate risk relates to exchange-rate exposure and to the definition of risk due to Adler and Dumas.

---

[10]Michael Adler and Bernard Dumas, *op. cit.* We might note that because the probabilities of outcomes are not known, it would be more appropriate to refer to exchange-rate *uncertainty* rather than *risk*. However, because it has become customary to use the term "risk," we also use this term.

Our definition of exchange-rate risk as the variance of the values of assets, liabilities, or operating incomes due to unanticipated changes in exchange rates is a definition in terms of $\text{var}(\Delta\hat{V})$, where $\Delta\hat{V}$ is as defined in equation (12.4). Applying standard statistical procedures to equation (12.4), we have

$$\text{var}(\Delta\hat{V}) = \beta^2\,\text{var}(\Delta S^u) \qquad (12.6)$$

Equation (12.6) shows that risk as we have defined it depends on foreign exchange exposure. This is because β appears on the right-hand side of equation (12.6). However, exchange-rate risk also depends directly on $\text{var}(\Delta S^u)$, the variance of unanticipated changes in exchange rates, which is the risk measure used by Adler and Dumas.

Equation (12.6) makes it clear that exchange-rate risk requires both exposure and unpredictability of exchange rates. Exposure on its own does not mean exchange-rate risk if exchange rates are perfectly predictable. Similarly, unpredictability of exchange rates does not mean exchange-rate risk for items that are not exposed. Equation (12.6) shows that exchange-rate risk is proportional to exposure squared, and proportional to the variance of unanticipated changes in exchange rates.

EXPOSURE, RISK, AND THE PARITY RELATIONSHIPS

With exchange-rate risk and exposure now defined and compared, we can consider whether and how risk and exposure on particular items are related to PPP and interest parity. This will allow us to clarify several features of risk and exposure that we have alluded to, but not so far systematically explored.

Exposure, Risk, and Interest Parity

Covered interest parity can be summarized in the dollar-pound context by equation (11.10):

$$\left(1 + r_\$\right)^n = \frac{F_n(\$/\pounds)}{S(\$/\pounds)}\left(1 + r_\pounds\right)^n \qquad (11.10)$$

The right-hand side of equation (11.10) gives the hedged dollar receipts to an investor on a covered n-year British pound interest-bearing security. Clearly, if the pound security is hedged and held to maturity, unanticipated changes in exchange rates can have no effect on the dollar value of the security. That is, the hedged pound security is not exposed and faces no foreign exchange risk. Indeed, this is why the return equals that on U.S. securities. However, the lack of exposure and risk on the pound security is only because the security is combined with a forward contract, and because both the security and forward contract are held to maturity.

When a foreign-currency-denominated security is not hedged with a forward contract or may be sold before maturity, the security is exposed and subject to exchange-rate risk, irrespective of interest parity. Indeed, the presence or absence of interest parity has no bearing on the amount of exchange-rate risk or exposure. While interest parity does suggest that *anticipated* changes in exchange rates are

TABLE 12.1. PPP and Real-Asset Values

Time	£ value, millions	$S($/£)$	$ value, millions
0	1.000	1.80	1.80
1	1.125	1.60	1.80
2	1.286	1.40	1.80
3	1.500	1.20	1.80
4	1.800	1.00	1.80

compensated for in interest differentials, there is no compensation for *unanticipated* changes in exchange rates.[11] With no implication of interest parity for a systematic effect of $\Delta S^u($/£)$ on the value of pound-denominated interest-bearing securities, there is no implication for exposure.[12]

Interest parity also has no implication for exchange-rate risk, which we have measured by

$$\text{var}(\Delta \hat{V}) = \beta^2 \text{var}(\Delta S^u) \qquad (12.6)$$

This is because it has no implications for the exposure β or for the variability of unanticipated changes in exchange rates, $\text{var}(\Delta S^u)$.

Exposure, Risk, and Purchasing-Power Parity

Whereas there are no implications of interest parity for exposure and risk, the situation is quite different for purchasing-power parity. In the case of PPP there are implications for exposure and risk on real assets such as real estate and equities, the prices of which can systematically vary with exchange rates.[13] There are also implications of PPP for exposure and risk on the operating incomes of export-oriented, import-competing, and import-using firms. It is useful to consider the implications of PPP for real assets—called fixed assets by accountants—separately from those for operating incomes.

PPP and Real-Asset Exposure

We can explore the implications of PPP for risk and exposure of **real** (or **fixed**) **assets** such as real estate and equities by referring to the example involving British real estate discussed earlier in this chapter. The essential features of the example are summarized in the top two rows of Table 12.1. The table shows a British real-estate investment that has a value of £1 million at time 0 when the exchange rate is

---

[11]As we saw in Chapter 11, the interest differential is closely related to the *anticipated* change in the spot rate.

[12]Of course, while interest parity does not imply anything about a systematic relationship between $\Delta S^u($/£)$ and the value of pound-denominated securities, this does not mean there is no systematic relationship between $\Delta S^u($/£)$ and the value of pound-denominated securities. For example, if the Bank of England systematically leans against the wind, British security prices will decline as $\Delta S^u($/£)$ decreases.

[13]Assets without a fixed face value, such as real estate and equities, are sometimes referred to as **non-contractual assets,** while assets with a fixed face value, such as bills and bonds, are referred to as **contractual assets.** A bank loan or corporate bond is a **contractual liability** to the borrower.

$1.80/£, and has a value of £1.125 million one period later when the exchange rate is $1.60/£. As the table shows, these numbers imply that the dollar value of the real estate is unchanged and equal to $1.8 million despite the change in exchange rate. We pointed out earlier that if this situation systematically occurred the real-estate investment would not be exposed. What we did not point out earlier is what might cause the numbers to behave as they do in Table 12.1, causing an exposure of zero.

We recall from Chapter 10 that in its relative form PPP can be written as

$$\dot{S}(\$/£) = \frac{\dot{P}_{US} - \dot{P}_{UK}}{1 + \dot{P}_{UK}} \tag{10.7}$$

where the dots over variables mean rates of change. The numbers in Table 12.1 would occur if British real-estate prices followed the overall British rate of inflation, and this rate were 12.5 percent while the U.S. inflation was zero. In such a case we have from equation (10.7)

$$\dot{S}(\$/£) = \frac{0.0 - 0.125}{1.125} = -0.1111$$

This rate of change of the exchange rate would mean that if at time 0 the exchange rate was $1.80/£, then at time 1 it would be 11.11 percent lower than at time 0. That is, if PPP is to hold, the exchange rate at time 1 must be

$$(\$1.80/£) \cdot (1 - 0.1111) = \$1.60/£$$

We can see that the numbers in Table 12.1 would occur if PPP held precisely in an *ex post* sense, and if the pound value of the British real estate precisely followed the British rate of inflation. In such a situation there is zero *exposure*. There is also no foreign exchange *risk* if PPP always holds *ex post*. That is so because the dollar value of the asset is the same whatever happens to the exchange rate; any change in exchange rate is precisely offset by the change in the pound value of the asset.[14]

In reality, two empirical facts force us to reconsider the absence of exposure and risk on real assets such as real estate:

1. As we saw in Chapter 10, PPP does not hold.
2. Any individual real-estate investment, or even real estate in general, will not usually change in value by the overall rate of inflation.

Let us consider the implications of each of these facts.

If the deviations from PPP are random in the sense that exchange rates are sometimes higher and sometimes lower than their PPP values, but on average equal their PPP values, then the exposure is still zero, just as if PPP always held. In the event that PPP holds exactly, ΔV is always zero. This gives an exposure of zero. In the event that deviations from PPP occur, but are random with a zero mean, ΔV is sometimes positive and sometimes negative. However, if the average value of ΔV is zero, exposure is again zero.

If PPP holds only on average, the variations in the domestic-currency values of

---

[14]Exhibit 12.1 shows that offsets between asset values and exchange rates may depend on the length of investors' horizons.

If currencies depreciate when asset prices denominated in those currencies increase, exposure is less than the value of the foreign assets; the movements in exchange rates and asset prices are offsetting when translating values into a different currency. When there is no connection between asset prices and exchange rates, as with bank deposits, exposure equals the value of foreign assets. Finally, when currencies and asset prices move in the same direction, with currency appreciation accompanying increasing asset values and vice versa, exposure *exceeds* the value of the foreign assets. As the following explains, the size of exposure appears to depend on the length of the horizon that is studied. Specifically, it appears that an offsetting of exchange rates and asset values resulting in exposure of less than the asset values occurs in the short run, but the reverse occurs in the longer run.

Exposure to changes in exchange rates represents a major risk for international investors. During the 1980s, it became common practice for investors to hedge currency risk as fully as possible by methods including the purchase of futures contracts. But for many investors, this simple and seemingly sensible hedging strategy actually may increase exchange rate risk rather than reducing it, according to NBER Research Associate Kenneth Froot.

In *Currency Hedging Over Long Horizons (NBER Working Paper No. 4355),* Froot examines the variability of returns to British residents on U.S. stock and bond investments during the period between 1802 and 1990. Where short-term investments are concerned, currency hedging greatly affects British investors' returns. Over a one-year period, Froot finds, the earnings from unhedged U.S. stock portfolios, expressed in British pounds of constant value, are 13 percent more variable than the earnings from fully

hedged portfolios. Unhedged portfolios of U.S. bonds show 56 percent more variance than hedged portfolios for British investors.

But as the time horizon lengthens, the value of hedging drops sharply. After three years, Froot reports, fully hedged U.S. stock portfolios show *greater* variability than unhedged portfolios when their returns are expressed in real pounds. The same is true for bond portfolios at horizons of about seven years.

The length of the investor's time horizon is important where exchange rate hedging is concerned, Froot contends, because while short-term currency fluctuations are random, over the longer term, currencies move toward purchasing power parity: the level at which amounts of similar value have similar buying power in each country. That movement creates a "natural" exchange rate hedge for physical assets, such as factories and equipment, and for common stocks. If the value of the currency declines, the local-currency value of such assets will rise over the long term to keep their international value stable.

The value of bonds, however, depends much more heavily on each country's inflation and interest rates, as well as on the real exchange rate. Convergence toward purchasing power parity therefore will have less effect in reducing the variability of foreign bond investors' returns, which is why currency hedging may be more useful.

Multinational corporations' currency hedging strategies, Froot concludes, should be based on the nature of the investment and the duration of the anticipated exposure. If, for example, a company borrows in one currency to build a plant in a country with another currency, then hedging may be unnecessary, as the physical assets will be naturally hedged as exchange rates move toward purchasing power parity. . . ."

Source: "The Value of Exchange Rate Hedging Depends on Your Horizon," *The NBER Digest,* October 1993, pp. 3–4.

assets or liabilities will, *ceteris paribus,* be higher than if PPP always holds exactly. This is because the deviations from PPP will contribute to variations in the values of assets and liabilities. That is, if PPP holds on average, var(ΔV) will be higher, *ceteris paribus,* than if PPP holds at all times. However, the variations in ΔV due to departures from PPP are not attributable to changes in exchange rates. Rather, they are due to other factors affecting ΔV, which themselves contribute to deviations from PPP. That is, while random deviations from PPP contribute to var(ΔV), the total variance in ΔV, they do not affect var($\Delta \hat{V}$), the variance in ΔV due to unanticipated changes in exchange rates. This conforms with what we would conclude from equation (12.6), namely, that when there is no exposure, so that $\beta = 0$, there is no exchange-rate risk, irrespective of whether $\beta = 0$ because PPP always holds, or whether it is because PPP holds only on average.

The second fact we mentioned is that individual asset prices do not in general change at a country's overall rate of inflation. As with random PPP violations, this does not change exposure if, on average, individual asset prices move at the rate of inflation; there is no change in the systematic relationship between ΔS^u and ΔV. What is affected by individual asset prices moving differently than overall inflation is the total amount of risk. Added to the risk caused by PPP deviations is a **relative-price risk.** This risk is not, however, due to exchange-rate changes, and so, while it adds to total risk, it does not add to exchange-rate risk.

PPP and Operating Exposure

As we have mentioned, there are implications of PPP for the exposure of operating incomes of export-oriented, import-competing, and import-using firms. This type of exposure is called **operating exposure,** and the risk is called **operating risk.** In particular, operating exposure is the sensitivity of operating income to unanticipated changes in exchange rates. Similarly, operating risk is the variance of operating income directly attributable to unanticipated changes in exchange rates.

Operating risk and exposure involve the effects of exchange rates on the current and future profitability of firms. We should be careful to distinguish operating risk and exposure from the effects of exchange rates on the dollar values of foreign-currency accounts receivable and payable. Accounts receivable and payable are fixed-face-value, short-term assets and liabilities, and have risk and exposure like those of foreign-currency bank accounts and loans. On the other hand, operating incomes do not have fixed face values. Indeed, as we shall see, operating exposure depends on such factors as the elasticity of demand for imports or exports, the fraction of input prices that depend on exchange rates, the flexibility of production to respond to exchange-rate-induced changes in demand, and the reference currency for computing operating incomes.[15]

We can show how different operating risk and exposure are from risk and exposure on assets and liabilities, as well as show the relevance of PPP for operating risk and exposure, by considering the case of a U.S. exporter selling to Britain. Let us consider under what conditions the profit or operating income of the exporter is systematically affected by exchange rates.

Let us denote the dollar profits of the U.S. exporting firm by π; then from the definition of profits as revenue minus costs we can write

$$\pi = S(\$/\pounds)p_{UK}q - C_{US}q$$

or

$$\pi = \left[S(\$/\pounds)p_{UK} - C_{US}\right]q \qquad (12.7)$$

Here p_{UK} is the pound price of the U.S. firm's export good in Britain, and C_{US} is the (constant) per-unit U.S. dollar production cost of the export. The product, $S(\$/\pounds)p_{UK}$, is the export sales price of the company's product in dollars, and so the difference

---

[15]These and other factors influencing operating risk and exposure are explained in Chapter 14. The complexities of operating risk and exposure, as well as the distinction between accounts-receivable exposure versus operating exposure, are covered in Exhibit 12.2, which considers the situation facing American Airlines.

EXHIBIT 12.2
Flying High: Risk and Exposure at American Airlines

In a study involving the regression method for determining foreign exchange risk and exposure facing American Airlines, John Bilson discussed the numerous ways that exchange rates can affect an airline. As the following excerpt explains, the routes through which exchange rates work are many and varied.

Foreign exchange exposure is of increasing importance in the airline industry as the large carriers expand into foreign markets. Net foreign currency cash flows at American Airlines (AMR) have grown from $119 million in 1986 to $393 million in 1990. International revenue has grown from 19.3 percent of the system total in 1986 to an estimated 26.7 percent in 1990. While the bulk of this expansion has been in the European market, service to the Far East is expected to grow rapidly in the near future. It is consequently important to know how the profitability of the airline will be influenced by the inevitable fluctuations in the price of foreign currencies against the dollar.

There are two primary sources of currency exposure. The largest source arises from the timing lag between the sale of a ticket in a foreign currency and the receipt of the revenue in dollars. This delay averages 15 to 45 days in the major markets. After a ticket is sold in a foreign currency, a delay will occur before AMR receives the revenue (denominated in foreign currency) from the sale. If the foreign currency should depreciate between the time the ticket is sold and the time the revenues are repatriated, a loss will be recognized on the transaction. Since AMR has positive excess cash flows in its foreign markets, this analysis suggests that AMR is net long in foreign currencies and that hedge activities should involve short positions in foreign currencies.

The second source of exposure results from the impact of exchange rates on anticipated future cash flows. Since it is impractical to reset ticket prices at short intervals, a depreciation of a foreign currency will reduce the dollar value of future cash flows if the foreign currency price and the load factors are stable. This consideration also suggests that AMR is naturally net long in the foreign currencies where it is operationally involved.

If this approach is correct, an appreciation of foreign currencies should be associated with increased profitability and a rise in the value of AMR stock. However, the effect of the exchange rate on the profitability of an airline is considerably more complex than its effect on cash flows and contemporaneous load factors. For the American consumer of international air travel services, appreciation in foreign currencies increases the total costs of international travel. While the airline ticket cost, which is denominated in dollars, is typically not affected immediately, all other travel costs should increase in proportion to the change in the exchange rate. It is therefore reasonable to assume that American overseas travel will be adversely affected by the appreciation of foreign currencies. It is true that a depreciation of the dollar should make travel to the United States by foreigners less expensive, but if foreign travellers have a preference for their national airline, U.S. carriers could still be adversely affected. This effect would not be immediately apparent in load factors since international travel typically is planned in advance. However, if the market efficiently forecasts anticipated future revenues, the decline in profitability should be immediately reflected in the stock price.

Movements in exchange rates also reflect underlying economic conditions. The prospect of a recession in the United States will decrease the demand for the U.S. currency and lead to a depreciation of the dollar. Since airline travel is cyclical, anticipated future revenue from both domestic and international travel is likely to decline with prospective recession. While this decline is unlikely to be reflected in current revenues, it should be reflected in the stock price. Finally, the exchange rate could also have an indirect effect on energy prices. When the dollar depreciates, U.S. energy prices have to rise in order to maintain parity with world prices. If the industry cannot offset the cost increases with higher prices, anticipated future profitability will be adversely affected.

Source: John F. O. Bilson, "Managing Economic Exposure to Foreign Exchange Risk: A Case Study of American Airlines," in Yakov Amihud and Richard M. Levich (eds.), *Exchange Rates and Corporate Performance,* New York University Salomon Center, New York, 1994, pp. 221–246.

---

between $S(\$/£)p_{UK}$ and C_{US} is the dollar profit ("markup") per unit sold. By multiplying this difference by the total quantity of sales, q, we get the U.S. exporter's total profit in dollar terms, or π.

In order to see the conditions under which changes in exchange rates will raise or lower a U.S. exporter's profits, we will write the annual rates of change in exchange rates and profits as $\dot{S}$ and $\dot{\pi}$. As before, the dot over a variable signifies a rate of change. Let us assume that the market selling price of the company's product in the United Kingdom grows at the British general rate of inflation, which we have written as $\dot{P}_{UK}$. Let us also assume that the production cost of the product, which is made in the United States, grows at the general rate of inflation in the United States, $\dot{P}_{US}$. For the given output level q, we can write the U.S. exporter's profit at the end of the year as follows:

$$\pi(1 + \dot{\pi}) = \left[S(\$/\pounds)p_{UK}(1 + \dot{S})(1 + \dot{P}_{UK}) - C_{US}(1 + \dot{P}_{US})\right]q \qquad (12.8)$$

Equation (12.8) is obtained from equation (12.7) merely by replacing π with $\pi(1 + \dot{\pi})$, $S(\$/\pounds)$ with $S(\$/\pounds)(1 + \dot{S})$, and so on.

Subtracting equation (12.7) from equation (12.8) gives

$$\dot{\pi} = \left\{S(\$/\pounds)p_{UK}\left[\dot{S}(1 + \dot{P}_{UK}) + \dot{P}_{UK}\right] - C_{US}\dot{P}_{US}\right\}q/\pi$$

Profits will grow after, for example, a depreciation or devaluation of the dollar (when $\dot{S}$ is positive) if $\dot{\pi} > 0$, that is, if

$$S(\$/\pounds)p_{UK}\left[\dot{S}(1 + \dot{P}_{UK}) + \dot{P}_{UK}\right] - C_{US}\dot{P}_{US} > 0$$

If the devaluation or depreciation takes place when the profits are zero [$S(\$/\pounds)p_{UK} = C_{US}$], we can rewrite this as

$$S(\$/\pounds)p_{UK}\left[\dot{S}(1 + \dot{P}_{UK}) + \dot{P}_{UK} - \dot{P}_{US}\right] > 0$$

Since $S(\$/\pounds)$ and p_{UK} are positive, a devaluation or depreciation of the dollar will raise a U.S. exporter's profits if $[\dot{S}(1 + \dot{P}_{UK}) + \dot{P}_{UK} - \dot{P}_{US}] > 0$, that is, if

$$\dot{S} > \frac{\dot{P}_{US} - \dot{P}_{UK}}{1 + \dot{P}_{UK}} \qquad (12.9)$$

Similarly, a devaluation or depreciation will reduce profits if

$$\dot{S} < \frac{\dot{P}_{US} - \dot{P}_{UK}}{1 + \dot{P}_{UK}} \qquad (12.10)$$

Comparison of the inequalities (12.9) and (12.10) with the relative form of PPP in equation (10.7) on page 242 shows that for effects on profits to occur, that is, for there to be operating exposure, it is necessary to have *ex post* violations of PPP. The intuitive explanation of this is that for the U.S. exporter's product to gain in competitiveness in Britain from a dollar depreciation, it is necessary for the product's price to fall vis-à-vis prices of competing British goods. This requires that the depreciation exceed the extent to which U.S. prices are increasing faster than British prices. For example, if U.S. prices are increasing by 8 percent and British prices are increasing by 6 percent, it is necessary for the dollar depreciation to exceed 2 percent for the U.S. exporter's competitiveness to be improved by a depreciation.

Consideration of the inequalities (12.9) and (12.10) tells us that if PPP always held, and the assumptions we made in deriving these equations are correct, there is no operating risk or exposure. Similarly, as with assets and liabilities, if PPP is violated, but deviations from PPP are as likely to be positive as be negative and on average are equal to zero, there is still no exposure. In terms of Figure 12.1, in this situation we have a scatter of observations around the horizontal axis with, for example, positive ΔS^u's associated with some positive ΔV's and some negative ΔV's, depending on whether PPP is violated positively or negatively. However, the *systematic* relationship between ΔV and ΔS^u is zero, just as it is when all observations are along the horizontal axis. Again, as with assets and liabilities, random deviations from PPP add to the total operating risk but do not add to exchange-rate risk, which is the variation in operating income due to unanticipated changes in exchange rates. That is, when PPP holds only as a long-run tendency, the firm faces greater risk than when PPP always holds exactly, but this added risk is due to the factors causing the deviations from PPP, not to the exchange rate.

In the course of deriving the inequalities (12.9) and (12.10) we assumed that the market selling price of the U.S. exporter's product in Britain grows at the overall British rate of inflation and that the cost of production grows at the overall U.S. rate of inflation. If these assumptions are invalid at every moment but are valid on average, there is still no exposure, provided of course that PPP holds, at least on average.[16] However, violation of the assumptions does add a relative price risk to any risk from random deviations from PPP. This conclusion is very similar to that reached for real assets.

While operating risk and exposure and real-asset risk and exposure relate similarly to PPP, these two types of risk and exposure are completely different in nature. Indeed, gains and losses from operating risk and exposure have a different dimension to those from real-asset exposure and from exposure on any type of asset or liability. Operating gains and losses have the dimension of flows, with profit changes occurring by so much *per month* or *per year,* that is, over a period of time. On the other hand, asset and liability gains or losses have the dimension of stocks, occurring at the moment of the change in exchange rates.

SUMMARY

1. From a U.S. perspective, foreign exchange exposure is the sensitivity of the real U.S. dollar value of assets, liabilities, or operating incomes with respect to unanticipated changes in exchange rates.
2. Exposure can be measured by the slope coefficient(s) in a regression equation relating the real change in the dollar value of assets, liabilities, or operating incomes to unanticipated changes in exchange rates.
3. There is exposure only if there is a systematic relationship between dollar values of assets, liabilities, or operating incomes, ΔV, and unanticipated changes in exchange rates, ΔS^u. That is, for exposure to exist, dollar values must on average change in a particular way vis-à-vis unanticipated changes in exchange rates.
4. Exposure on, for example, a British pound-denominated bank account is measured in pounds.
5. Normally there is noise in the relationship between domestic-currency values and unanticipated changes in exchange rates. However, the size of exposure of, for example, a pound-denominated bond is still the face value of the bond if the noise is random and on average equal to zero.

---

[16]By the assumptions being valid "on average" we mean that there is no systematic difference between the rate of change of the product's price and British inflation, and no systematic difference between the rate of change in production costs and U.S. inflation.

6. When exposures exist against numerous currencies, they can be measured from the slope coefficients in a multiple regression.

7. Domestic-currency-denominated assets can be exposed to exchange rates if, for example, unanticipated depreciations of the country's currency cause its central bank to increase interest rates.

8. Foreign exchange risk is measured by the variance of the domestic-currency value of an asset, liability, or operating income that is due to unanticipated changes in exchange rates.

9. Foreign exchange risk is positively related to both exposure and the variance of unanticipated changes in exchange rates.

10. When a foreign-currency-denominated security is not hedged with a forward exchange contract, it is exposed and subject to exchange-rate risk, irrespective of whether interest parity holds.

11. If individual asset values do not always change by the overall rate of inflation for a country but on average change at the rate of inflation, exposure is still zero if PPP holds on average. With random departures from PPP there is an added source of risk, but this is part of the total risk, not the foreign exchange risk.

12. The sensitivity of operating income to changes in exchange rates is called operating exposure, and the variance of operating income due to unanticipated changes in exchange rates is called operating risk.

13. If PPP always holds exactly and market prices and production costs always move in line with overall inflation, there is no exchange-rate exposure or exchange-rate risk. If PPP holds only on average and prices and production costs move on average at the overall rate of inflation, there is still no exchange-rate exposure or risk, but there is greater risk.

REVIEW QUESTIONS

1. What is foreign exchange exposure?
2. Why does exposure relate to *un*expected rather than expected changes in exchange rates?
3. What is a reference currency?
4. What is meant by a "systematic relationship"?
5. What variables go on the axes of an exposure line? How do these variables relate to those used for drawing payoff profiles?
6. What are the units of measurement of exposure to a particular exchange rate, for example, Deutschemarks per U.S. dollar?
7. How does the sign associated with exposure—positive versus negative—relate to whether exposure is "long" or "short"?
8. What is foreign exchange risk?
9. Can an unexposed asset face foreign exchange risk?
10. Can a domestic-currency-denominated asset face foreign exchange risk?
11. How does foreign exchange exposure on real assets relate to the PPP condition?
12. How does operating exposure relate to the PPP condition?

ASSIGNMENT PROBLEMS

1. In what sense is the sign of the slope coefficient which measures exposure relevant, and in what sense is it irrelevant?
2. How can exposure exceed the face value of a foreign-currency-denominated asset or liability?

3. If the Bank of Canada "leans against the wind," which means increasing interest rates when the Canadian dollar depreciates and lowering interest rates when the Canadian dollar appreciates, what would this mean for the exposure of:
   a. Canadian residents holding the Canadian government's Canadian-dollar-denominated bonds?
   b. U.S. residents holding Canadian bonds?
   Relate your answer to question 2 above.
4. How does PPP relate to:
   a. Exposure on real (or fixed) assets?
   b. Operating exposure?
5. Would it make sense to add a firm's exposures in different currencies at the spot exchange rate to obtain a measure of the firm's aggregate exposure, and if not, why not?
6. What is the problem in using the variance of exchange rates as a measure of foreign exchange risk?
7. If a company has used its currency of debt denomination and/or forward contracts to make its exposure zero, what would *measured* exposure be from the β of a regression line if in calculating β, the debt and/or forward contracts were omitted from the regression equation?
8. Would the distinction between real and actual changes in exchange rates be important if inflation and interest rates were everywhere the same and were also small?
9. By studying the stock price of a U.S.-based publicly traded company you have noticed that when the dollar drops against various currencies the company's value on the stock exchange increases. By averaging the link between exchange rates and the company's value you have determined the size of the change in each exchange rate that increases the value of the company by $1 million:

$$\Delta S^u(\text{DM}/\$) = 0.1$$

$$\Delta S^u(\yen/\$) = 5$$

$$\Delta S^u(\text{SFr}/\$) = 0.05$$

$$\Delta S^u(\text{C}\$/\$) = 0.04$$

What is the company's exposure to the various currencies?
10. Redo the analysis in this chapter of the effect of exchange-rate changes on an exporter by allowing the quantity sold, q, to change with the exchange rate instead of holding it constant. Use calculus to make the problem easier, and note that p_{UK} and q should be at profit-maximization levels in every period. [This is a very difficult question.]

BIBLIOGRAPHY

ADLER, MICHAEL, and BERNARD DUMAS: "Exposure to Currency Risk: Definition and Measurement," *Financial Management,* summer 1984, pp. 41–50.

FLOOD, EUGENE, JR., and DONALD R. LESSARD: "On the Measurement of Operating Exposure to Exchange Rates: A Conceptual Approach," *Financial Management,* spring 1986, pp. 25–37.

GARNER, C. KENT, and ALAN C. SHAPIRO: "A Practical Method of Assessing Foreign Exchange Risk," *Midland Corporate Finance Journal,* fall 1984, pp. 6–17.

HEKMAN, CHRISTINE R.: "Measuring Foreign Exchange Exposure: A Practical Theory and its Application," *Financial Analysts Journal,* September/October 1983, pp. 59–65.

HODDER, JAMES E., "Exposure to Exchange-Rate Movements," *Journal of International Economics,* November 1982, pp. 375–386.

JORION, PHILIPPE: "The Exchange Rate Exposure of U.S. Multinationals," unpublished manuscript, Columbia University, February 1986.

KHOO, ANDREW: "Estimation of Foreign Exchange Exposure: An Application to Mining Companies in Australia," *Journal of International Money and Finance,* June 1994, pp. 342–363.

KORSVOLD, PAUL E.: "Managing Strategic Foreign Exchange Exposure of Real Assets," presented at European Finance Association meetings, Madrid, September 1987.

LESSARD, DONALD R., and DAVID SHARP: "Measuring the Performance of Operations Subject to Fluctuating Exchange Rates," *Midland Corporate Finance Journal,* fall 1984, pp. 18–30.

LEVI, MAURICE D.: "Exchange Rates and the Valuation of Firms," in Yakov Amihud and Richard M. Levich (eds.), *Exchange Rates and Corporate Performance,* New York University, New York, 1994, pp. 32–48.

———— and JOSEPH ZECHNER: "Foreign Exchange Risk and Exposure," in Robert Z. Aliber (ed.), *Handbook of International Financial Management,* Richard Irwin-Dow Jones, New York, 1989.

NOBES, CHRISTOPHER: *International Guide to Interpreting Company Accounts: Overcoming Disparities in National Accounting Procedures,* Financial Times Management Reports, London, 1994.

OXELHEIM, LARS, and CLAS G. WIHLBORG: *Macroeconomic Uncertainty: International Risks and Opportunities for the Corporation,* Wiley, New York, 1987.

SHAPIRO, ALAN C.: "Defining Exchange Risk," *The Journal of Business,* January 1977, pp. 37–39.

————: "What Does Purchasing Power Parity Mean?" *Journal of International Money and Finance,* December 1983, pp. 295–318.

SOLNIK, BRUNO: "International Parity Conditions and Exchange Risk," *Journal of Banking and Finance,* August 1978, pp. 281–293.

APPENDIX 12.1
The Statistical Measurement of Exchange-rate Risk and Exposure

In this appendix we explore a little further the statistical dimensions of risk and exposure. This is done both to clarify the nature of risk and exposure and to provide a simple way of judging how important foreign exchange risk is relative to other risks that a company faces.

In the main part of the chapter we defined exposure as the slope, β, of the regression equation

$$\Delta V = \beta \Delta S^u(\$/\pounds) + \mu \tag{12.1}$$

The slope coefficient β can be written as

$$\beta = \frac{\text{cov}(\Delta V, \Delta S^u)}{\text{var}(\Delta S^u)} \tag{12A.1}$$

where cov(ΔV, ΔS^u) is the covariance between ΔV and ΔS^u, and var(ΔS^u) is the variance of unanticipated changes in exchange rates. The definition of the regression coefficient makes it clear that when ΔV does not covary systematically with ΔS^u, the exposure is zero. This is the conclusion we reached in the example giving rise to equation (12.2), in which the value of British real estate in U.S. dollars is unaffected by the exchange rate. It is also clear from the definition of the regression coefficient that the more ΔV changes systematically with ΔS^u, the greater is the exposure.

While exposure is defined in terms of the slope coefficient, risk was defined as var($\Delta \hat{V}$), where

$$\Delta \hat{V} = \beta \Delta S^u(\$/\pounds) \tag{12.4}$$

That is, exchange-rate risk is judged by the variance of the change in the dollar value of an asset, liability, or operating income, due only to unanticipated changes in exchange rates. The remainder of the total risk faced by a company is the result of other influences, which are captured by the term μ in equation (12.1). That is, total risk is judged by var(ΔV), where ΔV is given in equation (12.1).

The connection between total risk and exchange-rate risk can be shown by noting that because

$$\Delta V \equiv \Delta \hat{V} + \mu \tag{12.5}$$

then

$$\text{var}(\Delta V) = \text{var}(\Delta \hat{V}) + \text{var}(\mu) + 2\,\text{cov}(\Delta \hat{V}, \mu) \tag{12A.2}$$

Using the definition of $\Delta \hat{V}$ in equation (12.4), cov($\Delta \hat{V}$, μ) can be written as

$$\text{cov}(\Delta \hat{V}, \mu) = \beta\,\text{cov}(\Delta S^u, \mu) \tag{12A.3}$$

It is an assumption of regression analysis that explanatory variables such as ΔS^u are not correlated with the error term, so that cov(ΔS^u, μ) = 0. If this assumption is valid, then from equation (12A.3) cov($\Delta \hat{V}$, μ) = 0, and so equation (12A.2) becomes

$$\text{var}(\Delta V) = \text{var}(\Delta \hat{V}) + \text{var}(\mu) \tag{12A.4}$$

We can see from equation (12A.4) that the total risk of an asset, liability, or operating income consists of its exchange rate risk, var(($\Delta \hat{V}$), and the risk due to non-exchange-rate factors, var(μ).

The relative importance of exchange-rate risk can be judged by the size of var($\Delta\hat{V}$), the variance of value due to exchange rates, relative to var(ΔV), the total variance due to exchange-rate and non-exchange-rate factors. The ratio

$$\frac{\text{var}\left(\Delta\hat{V}\right)}{\text{var}\left(\Delta V\right)}$$

plays an important role in statistics and econometrics, where it is known as R^2.

The R^2 statistic, which is an output of just about every available regression package, gives the fraction of overall variance of a dependent variable such as ΔV that is explained by the explanatory variables. If we limit the explanatory variables to exchange rates, then the resulting R^2 gives the fraction of total variance due to exchange rates. It is clear that R^2 is bounded by zero and 1.0. When $R^2 = 0$ exchange rates contribute none of the total risk, and when $R^2 = 1$ they are responsible for all the risk.

We can conclude that if exposure can be assumed to be nearly constant over time, a firm can estimate the historical relationship between changes in its share price and relevant ΔS^u's. Management should be interested in both the resulting estimates of regression coefficients and the R^2 statistic. If the regression coefficients are insignificantly different from zero, the firm is not exposed. If in addition $R^2 = 0$, none of the risk the firm faces is due to exchange rates. On the other hand, if there are regression coefficients that differ from zero, the firm might consider paying attention to exposure. The amount of attention paid to managing exposure relative to managing the other risks faced by the firm should depend on R^2 in a regression containing only exchange rates.

CHAPTER 13

Accounting Exposure versus Real Exposure*

There is no such source of error as the pursuit of absolute truth.
—Samuel Butler

The definitions of foreign exchange exposure and risk in the preceding chapter relate to the true *economic* effects of exchange rates, and indeed, exposure and risk as we have defined them are often called **economic exposure** and **economic risk.** While we are principally concerned with the economic measures which we have described, the effects of exchange rates that appear in financial statements rarely if ever correspond with the economic measures. The effect of exchange rates which appears in financial statements is called **accounting exposure.** In this chapter we trace through the ways different accounting principles measure the effects of exchange rates, and how these measures compare to what we refer to as **real changes in exchange rates,** where by "real changes" we mean true economic effects of exchange rates. We begin with an outline of accounting principles used to record international transactions.

ACCOUNTING PRINCIPLES

It is necessary to have rules for converting values of foreign assets, liabilities, payments, and receipts into domestic currency in order to include them in consolidated financial statements in a firm's **domestic reporting currency.** (The domestic reporting currency is usually that of the country where the head office is located.) Different countries use different conversion rules, and so it is difficult to provide generally valid guidelines in this book. However, by focusing on the accounting principles of one country, the United States, many of the common issues and problems can be addressed. Acceptable rules for preparing financial statements in the United States are provided by the Financial Accounting Standards Board.

The principal concern about accounting standards involves the effect of the rules governing the choice of exchange rates for the gains or losses on assets and liabilities appearing in income statements. While there is also concern with the effect

*This entire chapter can be omitted without loss of continuity.

of exchange rates on operating income and expenses, this concern is less with the role of accounting rules and more with how exchange rates affect sales, costs, and profits from ongoing operation.[1] The income statement, which is also called the profit and loss statement, typically attracts more attention than a firm's balance sheet because taxes are based on income, and as we shall claim, it is usually assumed that shareholders can see through the veil of accounting rules that affect balance-sheet values. Our focus in this chapter reflects the primary concern about accounting standards by considering how they affect the gains and losses on assets and liabilities appearing in income statements.

It will help the reader's understanding of how U.S. international accounting principles affect gains and losses on assets and liabilities if we take time here to distinguish between **translation risk** and **translation exposure** on the one hand, and **transaction risk** and **transaction exposure** on the other. From a U.S. perspective, translation risk is the uncertainty of real U.S. dollar asset or liability values *appearing in financial statements,* where this uncertainty is due to unanticipated changes in exchange rates. Similarly, translation exposure is the sensitivity of changes in real U.S. dollar asset or liability values *appearing in financial statements,* with respect to unanticipated changes in exchange rates. On the other hand, transaction risk is the uncertainty of realized U.S. dollar asset or liability values *when the assets or liabilities are liquidated,* due to unanticipated changes in exchange rates. Similarly, transaction exposure is the sensitivity of changes in realized U.S. dollar values of assets or liabilities *when the assets or liabilities are liquidated,* with respect to unanticipated changes in exchange rates.[2]

Until 1982, the United States used an accounting standard generally known as **FAS 8.** Under FAS 8 a company was required to show all foreign exchange translation gains or losses (those from converting foreign assets or liabilities into dollar amounts) in the current-period income statement. Different treatment was given to current operating receipts and expenditures and financial assets/liabilities on the one hand, and to fixed (or real) assets on the other hand. This was referred to as a **temporal distinction,** and the rules were as follows:[3]

1. Revenues and expenses from foreign entities (overseas operations) were translated at the average exchange rate prevailing during the period, except for assets valued on a historical basis such as depreciation. These assets were translated at historical exchange rates. Financial assets and liabilities were translated at the average exchange rate during the period.
2. Other assets, primarily fixed assets, were translated at historical exchange rates. Historical costs were used in terms of local (foreign) currency.[4]

---

[1] The impact of exchange rates on operations, called operating exposure, is the topic of the next chapter, Chapter 14, while the management of operating exposure is discussed in Chapter 15.

[2] The distinction between translation and transaction exposure is discussed in Exhibit 13.1.

[3] See *Statement of Financial Accounting Standards, No. 8,* Financial Accounting Standards Board, Stamford, Conn., October 1975. The accounting system which replaced the FAS 8 system is described in *Statement of Financial Accounting Standards, No. 52—Foreign Currency Translation,* Financial Accounting Standards Board, Stamford, Conn., December 1981.

[4] Fixed assets include buildings, equipment, and other items for which prices tend to reflect inflation. While economists refer to fixed assets as "real assets," we use the term preferred by accountants in this chapter to reduce confusion between *real* assets and *real* changes in exchange rates.

EXHIBIT 13.1
Translating Accountants' and Economists' Languages

The excerpt below emphasizes the distinction between translation and transaction exposure according to whether conversion of currencies has occurred. It also makes clear why the need to consolidate worldwide income causes translation exposure.

TRANSACTION EXPOSURE

Transaction exposure occurs when one currency must be exchanged for another, and when a change in foreign exchange rates occurs between the time a transaction is executed and the time it is settled. Take the case of ABC Corporation, a U.S.-based multinational with extensive operations in Europe. Suppose ABC's UK subsidiary sells product to a German company. The customer wishes to transact in Deutsche Marks. The sale is made on May 1, 1990 on 30-day terms. ABC-UK receives DM on June 1 and converts to British pounds. If the £/DM exchange rate changes in May, ABC-UK receives more or fewer pounds than anticipated at the time of the transaction. The risk here thus involves uncertainty about a specific identifiable cash flow; it is referred to as "transaction" exposure because it involves an actual gain or loss due to conversion of one currency into another.

TRANSLATION EXPOSURE

Translation exposure arises in multinational firms from the requirement that U.S. companies (and those foreign firms following U.S. accounting practices) produce consolidated financial statements. Subsidiaries of multinational companies operating in different countries typically transact in local currencies. Local currency is also normally the unit of account for accounting, performance measurement, and taxation at the local level; and thus the operating financial statements of subsidiaries are generally denominated in local currencies.

Periodically (often quarterly but at least annually), however, these subsidiary statements must be summed into consolidated statements for the entire multinational enterprise and denominated in the home currency. In ABC's case, this means consolidating statements denominated in a wide variety of currencies around the globe and expressing them in U.S. dollar equivalents. To provide a measure of ABC's worldwide performance in the home currency, operating results and asset values denominated in foreign currencies must be *translated* into dollar equivalents.

Although there is a restatement of values into a different currency, there is no actual *conversion* of one currency into another.

Source: John J. Pringle, "Managing Foreign Exchange Exposure," *Journal of Applied Corporate Finance,* winter 1991, pp. 73–82. Emphasis in original.

What FAS 8 therefore required was that if local-currency values were measured at current cost, they were to be translated at current exchange rates, and if they were measured at historical cost, they were to be translated at historical exchange rates.

The fact that FAS 8 required that all translation adjustments appear in the income statement made income appear highly volatile and caused numerous corporate treasurers to take permanently hedged positions. The procedure which has replaced FAS 8 is called **FAS 52,** and this involves two principal changes:

1. The **functional currency** is selected for each subsidiary. This is the primary currency of the subsidiary. For example, a British subsidiary of a U.S. parent firm will declare that the pound is its functional currency. Any foreign-currency income of the subsidiary (for example, marks or francs earned by the British subsidiary) is translated into the functional currency according to the FAS 8 rules. After this, all amounts are translated from the functional currency into dollars at the current exchange rate.

2. Translation gains and losses are disclosed and accumulated in a separate account showing shareholders' equity. Only when foreign assets or liabilities are liqui-

EXHIBIT 13.2
From Historical to Current Rates: The Rationale for a Change in Approach

U.S. international accounting rules went through a major revision in 1982. The following excerpt explains these revisions, their rationale, and the reasons it was decided to separate foreign exchange translation gains or losses from income.

WHAT EXCHANGE RATE SHOULD BE USED IN MAKING THE TRANSLATION?

This issue has been the center of a longstanding controversy among accountants and financial officers. Should it be the *current* exchange rate at the time the translation is done? Or should it be the *historical* rate at the time the asset or liability went on the books? It can make a big difference, especially in the case of long-lived items such as fixed assets.

Financial Accounting Standard #8, promulgated in the U.S. in 1975, mandated the so-called *temporal* method, which uses the rate at the time the asset or liability was booked. This meant different rates for different items.

FAS #8 was widely criticized and gave way to FAS #52 in 1982, which mandates the *current rate* method. Under the current rate method, all assets and liabilities are translated at the current exchange rate at the time of the translation; equity accounts are translated at historical rates; and income statement items are converted at a weighted average rate for the period.*

Translation *exposure* thus arises because changes in

exchange rates change the dollar equivalents of foreign currencies. A profit of FF (French Franc) 10 million in ABC-France would translate into USD (U.S. dollar) 1,960,784 at an exchange rate of FF 5.1 per USD. But if the dollar strengthens to FF 6.0 per USD, the same FF 10 million falls to USD 1,666,667. An asset worth FF 25 million translates into USD 4.902 million at an exchange rate of FF 5.1 per USD, but into only USD 4.167 million at 6.0. In short, the USD representation of the asset's value depends on the exchange rate.

And so it should. The shareholders of the parent company ABC Corporation are ultimately interested in results expressed in dollar terms. And, for this reason, ABC Corporation's profits and market value are vulnerable to shifts in the FF/USD exchange rate. There is no impact on the subsidiary's financial statements in FF terms; the impact in only in the dollar equivalents. Note also that in this case there is no conversion of French francs into actual dollars; we have merely expressed or translated FF into U.S. dollar equivalents.

Source: John J. Pringle, "Managing Foreign Exchange Exposure," *Journal of Applied Corporate Finance,* winter 1991, pp. 73–82. Emphasis in original.

_____

*FAS #52 was promulgated in 1982 and made mandatory for U.S. companies in 1983. It required the selection of a "functional currency" for foreign subsidiaries, defined as the currency of the "primary economic environment." If the U.S. dollar were selected as the functional currency, the translation rules were identical to those of FAS #8. If the local currency were chosen, FAS #52 permitted

two important changes: (1) it mandated the current rate method in place of the temporal method, thus permitting the use of the current forex (foreign exchange) rate for translating fixed assets: and (2) it allowed firms to separate transactions and translation exposures, and to charge translation gains and losses to a special equity account rather than running them through the profit and loss (P & L) statement, as had been required under FAS #8. Transaction gains and losses continued to go through the P & L as before.

---

dated do they become transaction gains or losses and appear in the income statement.[5]

The rule on using current exchange rates on all items is relaxed when there is extremely high inflation in the country whose currency is being translated. Extremely high inflation means a cumulative amount of over 100 percent during the preceding 3 years. If this condition is met, the temporal distinction used in FAS 8 still applies. This means that in circumstances of extreme inflation, current

_____

[5]See Exhibit 13.2 for more on the rules and rationale for the exchange rates used to compute gains or losses on assets and liabilities, and on where these gains or losses should appear.

exchange rates are used for current-cost items such as financial assets and liabilities, and historical rates are used for historical-cost items.

The best way to illustrate the effects of these accounting procedures is to take examples. However, before we consider these examples it is useful to define the concept of real changes in exchange rates. This is because our examples show not only the implications of U.S. accounting principles for translation and transaction gains and losses but also the extent to which the accounts accurately reflect what has really happened to exchange rates.

REAL CHANGES IN EXCHANGE RATES

Definition of the Real Change in Exchange Rates

We can define the real change in exchange rates in this way:

> The real change in exchange rates is the change that produces a difference between the overall rate of return on domestic versus foreign assets/liabilities or in the profitability of export-oriented, import-using, or import-competing firms.

As we proceed, we shall see that in order for real changes in exchange rates to occur there must be *ex post* departures from interest parity or PPP. As we have seen, PPP departures are also necessary for there to be exchange-rate exposure on real assets and operating incomes. However, this is as far as the analogy goes. The real change in exchange rates is a measure of how much *a particular change in exchange rates* has affected domestic versus foreign returns or profitability. On the other hand, exchange-rate exposure is a measure of the sensitivity of asset or liability values or operating incomes to *exchange-rate values that could occur*. Therefore, while the sources of exchange-rate exposure and of real changes in exchange rates are similar, they are measures of very different phenomena.[6]

Financial Assets and Liabilities and Real Changes in Exchange Rates

Suppose that Aviva Corporation, which we introduced in Chapter 11, has invested in British bonds. Let us assume that these are long-term bonds. Clearly, a depreciation of the British pound will decrease the dollar value of these financial securities when they are translated (that is, converted into dollars) at the new exchange rate. But would we want to consider Aviva as being worse off by holding pound-denominated bonds rather than dollar-denominated bonds? Alternatively, would an appreciation of the pound make Aviva better off?

A depreciation of a currency that is compensated for in terms of higher interest yields on financial assets should not be considered a real depreciation from the point of view of these assets. For example, if the pound fell in value against the dollar by 10 percent but British interest rates were 10 percent higher than those in the United States, the firm would be no worse off from British than from U.S. investments.

---

[6]Indeed, the units of measurement are different. We measure real changes in exchange rates in percent, whereas exchange-rate exposure has the dimension of units of a particular currency.

According to our definition of a real change in exchange rates, that is, a change which affects the rate of return on foreign versus domestic assets, we might therefore define the real change for financial assets held for a year as follows:

$$\text{Real change in } (\$/£) = \frac{S_1(\$/£) - S(\$/£)}{S(\$/£)} - \left(r_\$ - r_£\right)$$

$S_1(\$/£)$ is the actual spot rate at year end, and $r_\$$ and $r_£$ refer to interest earnings during that year. The definition consists of the actual proportional decrease in the value of the pound—assuming $S_1(\$/£) < S(\$/£)$—adjusted for the extent to which higher pound versus dollar interest rates have compensated for this decrease.

Because translation losses or gains are made on the interest earned on pound bonds as well as on the principal, a more precise definition is

$$\text{Real change in } (\$/£) = \frac{S_1(\$/£) - S(\$/£)}{S(\$/£)}\left(1 + r_£\right) - \left(r_\$ - r_£\right) \qquad (13.1)$$

The real change of $/£ shown in equation (13.1) is equal to the *ex post* deviation from unhedged interest parity, which can be seen as follows.

Each dollar a U.S. investor invests in pound bonds will buy $1/S(\$/£)$ of British pounds, which will pay back after 1 year

$$£ \; \frac{1}{S(\$/£)} \left(1 + r_£\right)$$

If the British investment is not hedged by selling the pounds forward, the pounds will be sold at the following year's spot rate, $S_1(\$/£)$, giving

$$\$ \; \frac{S_1(\$/£)}{S(\$/£)} \left(1 + r_£\right)$$

The return from the unhedged British security is therefore this amount minus the original dollar invested, that is

$$\frac{S_1(\$/£)}{S(\$/£)} \left(1 + r_£\right) - 1$$

The difference between this return and the U.S. dollar return, which is the *ex post* deviation from unhedged interest parity, is

$$\frac{S_1(\$/£)}{S(\$/£)} \left(1 + r_£\right) - \left(1 + r_\$\right)$$

By subtracting and adding $1 + r_£$ this can be written as

$$\frac{S_1(\$/£) - S(\$/£)}{S(\$/£)} \left(1 + r_£\right) + \left(1 + r_£\right) - \left(1 + r_\$\right)$$

or

$$\frac{S_1(\$/£) - S(\$/£)}{S(\$/£)} \left(1 + r_£\right) - \left(r_\$ - r_£\right) \qquad (13.2)$$

Comparison of equation (13.2) with equation (13.1) shows that a real change in the exchange rate for financial securities occurs when there is an *ex post* departure from uncovered interest parity.

Financial Assets and Liabilities and Financial Accounts: Learning by Example

In order to describe how U.S. international accounting principles show translation gains or losses on financial assets and liabilities, and to compare the accounting treatment with the definition of the real change in exchange rates, suppose that in the previous year Aviva placed $1 million in a U.S. dollar long-term bond yielding 12 percent ($r_\$ = 0.12$) and $1 million in a pound long-term bond yielding 20 percent ($r_£ = 0.20$). Suppose that last year the spot rate was $S(\$/£) = 2.0$ and that during the year the pound depreciates to $S_1(\$/£) = 1.8$.

The actual pound depreciation is 10 percent. However, higher pound versus dollar interest rates make up for some of this. The real depreciation of the pound given by equation (13.1) is

$$\text{Real change in } (\$/£) = \frac{1.8 - 2.0}{2.0}(1.20) - (0.12 - 0.20) = -0.04$$

The negative value means a real depreciation of the pound of 4 percent, which is a real appreciation of the dollar. The 10 percent decline in the value of the pound is not fully compensated by the higher pound interest rate.

In terms of the financial accounts, after placing $1 million in the dollar bond for 1 year, there will be $120,000 in interest appearing in the income statement, and if interest rates and hence dollar bond prices do not change, there is no change in the value of financial assets. Therefore, total earnings on the dollar bond are $120,000. How does this compare to the pound bond?

Placing $1 million in a pound bond at the initial exchange rate $S(\$/£) = 2.0$ means investing £500,000. At $r_£ = 0.20$, this will earn £100,000. At the exchange rate of $1.8/£ at the end of the year, the £100,000 will be translated into $180,000 of income. This is shown as interest earnings in the top row of Table 13.1.

The £500,000 pound bond is worth only $900,000 at the exchange rate of $1.8/£ at the end of the year. Since the initial value of the bond was $1 million, there is a translation loss of $100,000. Under FAS 8 this would have appeared in the income account, but with the FAS 52 accounting procedure it will appear separately under shareholder equity as shown in the top row of Table 13.1. We see that under the

TABLE 13.1. Earnings on Domestic versus Foreign Financial Assets

Realized Spot Rate	Interest Earnings	Declared Income, FAS 52	Shareholder Equity, FAS 52	Overall Income	Real Gain/Loss on Pound Bond
$S_1(\$/£) = 1.8000$	+$180,000	+$180,000	−$100,000	+$80,000	−$40,000
$S_1(\$/£) = 1.8667$	+$186,667	+$186,667	−$66,667	+$120,000	0
$S_1(\$/£) = 1.9000$	+$190,000	+$190,000	−$50,000	+$140,000	+$20,000

FAS 52 system, there is a declared income of $180,000 if the translation loss is not realized, that is, if the bond is not sold, and a $100,000 loss in the shareholder-equity account. Combining the shareholder-equity account with the declared income, we have an overall income on the pound bond of $180,000 − $100,000 = +$80,000. Compared with the $120,000 that would have been earned on the dollar bond, this involves a relative loss of $40,000, which is 4 percent of the original investment. The real depreciation or devaluation of 4 percent found from the FAS 52 procedure agrees with what we found in the definition, equation 13.1. But we note that we must include shareholder-equity effects if we are to make the correct judgment of the real change in the exchange rate with FAS 52.

If the exchange rate after a year of investment had moved to $S_1(\$/£) = 1.8667$, then the real change in the exchange rate would have been zero, since the definition, equation (13.1), tells us that

$$\frac{1.8667 - 2.0}{2.0}(1.20) - (0.12 - 0.20) = 0.0$$

This result occurs because the end-of-year exchange rate of $1.8667/£ is the rate that produces *ex post* unhedged interest parity.[7]

In terms of the entries in the financial accounts, $1 million invested in the pound bond at $S(\$/£) = 2.0$ is £500,000, which as before earns £100,000. At $S_1(\$/£) = 1.8667$, the £100,000 of interest is worth $186,667. The translation loss on the financial asset at the realized exchange rate, after correcting for rounding error, is $66,667 [($1.8667/£ × £500,000) − $1,000,000]. Using FAS 52, this gives total earnings of $120,000 ($186,667 − $66,667) if we are careful to aggregate the interest earnings from the income account and the foreign exchange loss given in the separate shareholder-equity account. We obtain the same recorded earnings on both bonds, $120,000. This corresponds with the conclusion from equation (13.1) of no real change in the exchange rate.

If the pound falls in actual value by only 5 percent to $S_1(\$/£) = 1.9$, then the £100,000 in earnings from the pound bond will be worth $1.9/£ × £100,000 = $190,000, and the translation loss will be $50,000 [($1.9 × 500,000)−$1,000,000]. The total recorded earnings are therefore $140,000 ($190,000 − $50,000) if we are careful to include all earnings. This is $20,000 more than the earnings from the dollar bond, or a 2 percent extra return. Even though the pound has fallen in value, the overcompensation in the British interest rate is a real gain from the British bond of 2 percent. This will be found as the real change in the exchange rate from the definition, equation (13.1), but we again note that in order for the accounts to give the correct result, they must be integrated so that shareholder-equity effects are added to interest income earned.

Judging the borrowing decision, which means judging financial liabilities, is the reverse of judging the investment decision, and we must reverse the interpretation of equation (13.1). When borrowing is unhedged, real borrowing costs are the

---

[7]With $r_£ = 0.20$, $r_s = 0.12$, and $S(\$/£) = 2.0$ we can rearrange the unhedged interest parity condition

$$S_1(\$/£) = S(\$/£)\frac{1 + r_s}{1 + r_£}$$

to find $S_1(\$/£) = 1.8667$.

same on foreign and domestic currency as long as the depreciation in the value of the foreign currency is compensated for by higher interest payments. There is an *ex post* real gain from borrowing foreign instead of domestic currency if the realized depreciation of the foreign currency is more than the extra interest rate that is paid on the foreign-currency borrowing. There is a loss from borrowing foreign rather than domestic currency if the realized depreciation of the foreign currency is less than the extra interest paid. These effects can be found in financial statements using FAS 52, provided we integrate the shareholder-equity account with the income statement.

Fixed Assets and Real Changes in Exchange Rates

If fixed-asset prices have risen at the rate $\dot{P}_{US}$ and the real rate of return (in the form of, for example, rental income or dividends on the assets) has been ρ_{US}, then the overall rate of return on each dollar of fixed assets held at home is[8]

$$\rho_{US} + \dot{P}_{US} \tag{13.3}$$

Each dollar placed in British fixed assets that rose with inflation at $\dot{P}_{UK}$ with a rent or dividend rate of ρ_{UK} will produce, when translated at the new realized exchange rate $S_1(\$/£)$, dollar receipts of

$$\$ \frac{S_1(\$/£)}{S(\$/£)} \left(1 + \rho_{UK} + \dot{P}_{UK}\right) \tag{13.4}$$

This is because the original dollar will purchase $£[1/S(\$/£)]$ of British fixed assets, on which there is a rental or dividend of ρ_{UK} and inflation of $\dot{P}_{UK}$, and which is translated back into dollars at $S_1(\$/£)$. The rate of return on each dollar invested in the British fixed asset is therefore

$$\frac{S_1(\$/£)}{S(\$/£)} \left(1 + \rho_{UK} + \dot{P}_{UK}\right) - 1 \tag{13.5}$$

According to our definition of the real change in the exchange rate as the change causing a difference between the overall return on domestic versus foreign investments, from expression (13.5) minus expression (13.3) we have

$$\text{Real change in } (\$/£) = \left(\frac{S_1(\$/£)}{S(\$/£)} \left(1 + \rho_{UK} + \dot{P}_{UK}\right) - 1\right) - \left(\rho_{US} + \dot{P}_{US}\right) \tag{13.6}$$

By adding and subtracting $\dot{P}_{UK}$ this can be written as

$$\text{Real change in } (\$/£) = \frac{S_1(\$/£)}{S(\$/£)} \left(1 + \dot{P}_{UK}\right) - \left(1 + \dot{P}_{UK}\right) + \dot{P}_{UK}$$

$$+ \frac{S_1(\$/£)}{S(\$/£)} \rho_{UK} - \rho_{US} - \dot{P}_{US}$$

---

[8] We use the subscripts US and UK rather than $ and £ because fixed assets are specific to a *country*, not a *currency*. For simplicity we refer to U.S. and British inflation, $\dot{P}_{US}$ and $\dot{P}_{UK}$, even though we are dealing with asset prices, not with overall price levels. We do this because "fixed assets" is a big category, making it inappropriate to refer to the law of one price. Thinking of $\dot{P}_{US}$ and $\dot{P}_{UK}$ as inflation allows us to reach conclusions in terms of PPP which can be related to other parts of the book.

which by combining terms gives

$$\text{Real change in }(\$/\pounds) = \frac{S_1(\$/\pounds) - S(\$/\pounds)}{S(\$/\pounds)}\left(1 + \dot{P}_{UK}\right) - \left(\dot{P}_{US} - \dot{P}_{UK}\right)$$

$$-\left(\rho_{US} - \frac{S_1(\$/\pounds)}{S(\$/\pounds)}\rho_{UK}\right) \qquad (13.7)$$

Examination of equation (13.7) shows that if rental or dividend yields in the United States and Britain are equal when we include the translation gain/loss in the British yield, that is, if $\rho_{US} = [S_1(\$/\pounds) \, / \, S(\$/\pounds)] \, \rho_{UK}$, then equation (13.7) becomes

$$\text{Real change in }(\$/\pounds) = \dot{S} \cdot \left(1 + \dot{P}_{UK}\right) - \left(\dot{P}_{US} - \dot{P}_{UK}\right) \qquad (13.8)$$

where $\dot{S} = [S_1(\$/\pounds) - S(\$/\pounds)]/S(\$/\pounds)$ is the proportional change in the exchange rate. A comparison of equation (13.8) with the relative form of PPP in equation (10.7) on page 242 shows that real changes in exchange rates on fixed assets require *ex post* deviations from PPP.[9] We recall that this conclusion also applies to real changes in exchange rates for the profitability of export-oriented, import-using, or import-competing firms; as we saw in our discussion of operating exposure in Chapter 12, a change in profitability requires *ex post* departures from PPP.

Fixed Assets and Financial Accounts: Learning by Example

When we examine the financial accounts in order to judge the performance of domestic versus foreign fixed investments, we are up against even more problems than we face with financial assets and liabilities. With financial assets and liabilities we can obtain the correct judgment as long as we are sure to include both the income and the separate shareholder-equity effects within total earnings. With fixed assets this is not sufficient. Indeed, by including shareholder-equity effects as they are measured with the FAS 52 accounting procedure, we might distort the picture even more than by leaving these effects out of the calculations. These points are by no means obvious, so we will show them by taking an example.

Suppose that in the previous year, $1 million was invested in U.S. fixed assets that provided a 5 percent real rate of return and $1 million was invested in British fixed assets that provided a 5.5556 percent real rate of return. Suppose that over the previous year, inflation in the United States was 10 percent and inflation in Britain was 16 percent, with fixed-asset prices and general prices moving at the same rates. Suppose that in the previous year the exchange rate was $2.0/£ and that by the end of the year it was $1.8/£. We have

$$\rho_{US} = 0.0500 \qquad \rho_{UK} = 0.05556 \qquad \dot{P}_{US} = 0.10 \qquad \dot{P}_{UK} = 0.16$$

$$S(\$/\pounds) = 2.0 \quad \text{and} \quad S_1(\$/\pounds) = 1.8$$

What we want to know from the example is what we will find in a company's accounts.

---

[9]Alternatively, if we think of a specific type of fixed asset so that $\dot{P}_{US}$ and $\dot{P}_{UK}$ refer to specific prices, we can conclude that real changes in exchange rates require deviations from the law of one price rather than deviations from PPP.

TABLE 13.2. Earnings on Foreign Fixed Assets

Realized Spot Rate	Rental or Profit Income	Translation Gain		Income plus Declared Translation Gain		Income plus Actual Translation Gain	
		FAS 52	Correct Method	FAS 52	Correct Method	FAS 52	Correct Method
$S_1(\$/\pounds) = 1.8000$	+$50,000	−$100,000	+$44,000	+$50,000	+$94,000	−$50,000	+$94,000

The actual pound depreciation or devaluation is 10 percent. However, the higher inflation in asset values in Britain has made up for some of this. The real pound depreciation (dollar appreciation) against which to judge the measured accounting effects is calculated with equation (13.7), which gives

$$\text{Real change in } (\$/\pounds) = \frac{1.8 - 2.0}{2.0}(1.16) - (-0.06) - \left(0.05 - \frac{1.8}{2.0}0.05556\right)$$

$$= -0.056, \text{ or } -5.6 \text{ percent}$$

Since the change is negative, we call it a real pound depreciation. It is smaller than the actual depreciation because the actual change in the exchange rate has been partially compensated by higher rates of return and higher inflation in the market value of British fixed assets. But what will the financial accounts show?

In terms of the financial accounts, the $1 million in the U.S. fixed assets earned a return of $\rho_{US} \times \$1,000,000 = \$50,000$. In addition, the 10 percent inflation in the United States raised the dollar value of the fixed assets by $100,000, which is a "gain" to the company even if it does not show in accounts until it is realized. Therefore, the total earnings on the U.S. fixed asset is $150,000. How does this compare to the British asset?

The $1 million sent to Britain at $S(\$/\pounds) = 2.0$ had an initial value of £500,000. At $\rho_{UK} = 0.05556$, the £500,000 earned $\rho_{UK} \times \pounds500,000 = \pounds27,778$. When translated into U.S. dollars at the current exchange rate $S_1(\$/\pounds)$ as current earnings, this £27,778 becomes $1.8/\pounds \times \pounds27,778 = \$50,000$ in the income statement. The $50,000 is shown as the first item in Table 13.2. Translation gains and losses—those resulting from converting foreign-asset values into units of domestic currency—require more careful treatment than real returns.

With FAS 52, the values of fixed assets are translated at current exchange rates, but historical costs are used for the value of the assets in the local currency. The current exchange rate is $S_1(\$/\pounds) = 1.8$ and the historical cost is £500,000, so the value is recorded as $900,000. There is a translation loss of $100,000 from the original $1 million value of the British fixed asset. This is excluded from current income and goes only into the separate shareholder-equity account, so the declared income is only the $50,000 of earnings.[10] However, if exchange rates do not return to the previous levels before the British fixed asset is sold, the $100,000 will appear as

---

[10]Our treatment is valid for countries which do not suffer from extreme inflation and for which the straightforward forms of FAS 52 rules apply. Countries with extreme inflation (over 100 percent cumulative inflation in three years) continue to use the temporal distinction of FAS 8.

income when it becomes a transaction loss, showing a loss of −$50,000 ($50,000 − $100,000).

The economically correct method for handling foreign fixed assets uses the current exchange rate and the current market value of assets. This is different from the current FAS 52 procedure and the older FAS 8 procedure. We note that by the year end, the initial £500,000 invested in the British fixed asset has increased with 16 percent inflation to £580,000. At the current exchange rate of $S_1(\$/£) = 1.8$, this translates into $1,044,000 on the income statement, so there is a translation gain of $44,000 ($1,044,000 − $1,000,000). If this is included as income, the total earnings from Britain are $50,000 + $44,000 = $94,000, compared with the total return from U.S. fixed assets of $150,000. The relative loss from the change in exchange rates is −$56,000 ($94,000 − $150,000), which is 5.6 percent of the original investment, the same as the percentage change in exchange rate computed with equation (13.7). This correct result is in contrast with the outcome of FAS 52. When the shareholder-equity effect is included in FAS 52 and the total return from the British fixed asset is compared with the return from the U.S. asset, we have a relative loss on the British asset of −$200,000 (−$50,000 − $150,000), implying a real change in exchange rate of −20 percent, far larger than the −5.6 percent obtained in equation (13.7). We do not obtain the correct picture from the FAS 52 procedure.

The Relevance of Translation Exposure

FAS 8 rules were frequently criticized because by bringing translation gains and losses into income statements, corporate taxes were affected. While many were willing to accept *transaction* gains and losses as part of income—as they were under FAS 8 rules and continue to be under FAS 52—*translation* gains or losses were another matter. In order to prevent volatile income from FAS 8 translation rules it was common for firms to hedge their accounting exposure. Some economists believed this hedging to be unnecessary because, on average, gains and losses from fluctuating exchange rates average out to zero. Therefore, provided that corporate tax rates are not progressive, the long-run situation should not be affected by what appeared in income statements from year to year. These economists also believed that actual and potential shareholders would be able to see through the veil of accounting rules to the true economic effects. Therefore, they believed that if a firm decided to hedge, it should hedge against exposure as measured by β in equation (12.1) on page 296, rather than hedge accounting exposure. However, as we shall see in Chapter 15, there are arguments that suggest that firms should not bother to hedge their exposure *whatever way it is measured*.

SUMMARY

1. Accounting exposure concerns the effect that exchange rates have on values appearing in financial statements.
2. Translation risk and exposure have to do with how asset and liability values appear when translated into a firm's domestic reporting currency for inclusion in financial accounts. Transaction risk and exposure have to do with asset or liability values when the assets or liabilities are liquidated.

3. The real change in exchange rates is the change that produces a difference between the overall rate of return on domestic versus foreign assets/liabilities, or a change in the profitability of export-oriented, import-using, or import-competing firms.
4. There are no real changes in exchange rates on financial assets and liabilities if uncovered interest parity always holds *ex post*.
5. There are no real changes in exchange rates for fixed assets if PPP always holds *ex post*.
6. The FAS 52 procedure values assets using historical costs and current exchange rates but puts translation gains or losses in a separate account.
7. FAS 52 produces correct measures of real changes in exchange rates for financial assets if shareholder-equity effects are included as part of income.
8. FAS 52 produces incorrect measures of real changes in exchange rates for fixed assets.

REVIEW QUESTIONS

1. What is accounting exposure?
2. What are translation risk and translation exposure?
3. What are transaction risk and transaction exposure?
4. What is the nature of the temporal distinction under FAS 52 when inflation is high?
5. What is meant by a "real change in exchange rates"?
6. What is the relationship between *ex post* departures from uncovered interest parity and real changes in exchange rates for financial assets?
7. What items in the financial statements must be combined in order for accounting exposure on financial assets to reflect the real change in exchange rates?
8. What is the relationship between *ex post* departures from PPP and real changes in exchange rates for fixed assets?
9. How well do financial statements reflect real changes in exchange rates in terms of their effect on fixed assets?
10. If the choice could be made between current exchange rates and current costs, and historical exchange rates and historical costs, what would you select in order to accurately reflect real changes in exchange rates in financial statements?

ASSIGNMENT PROBLEMS

1. Suppose you had invested $500,000 for 6 months in the United States and in Italy, and interest rates and exchange rates are as follows:

r_{US}	r_{IT}	$S(\$/\text{Lit})$	$S_{1/2}(\$/\text{Lit})$
15%	28%	0.0010	0.0009

$S(\$/\text{Lit})$ is the exchange rate when the investment was made, and $S_{1/2}(\$/\text{Lit})$ is the actual rate 6 months later. Was foreign investment a good idea?

2. Using the information in question **1**, what values will appear in the income account and the shareholder-equity account with the FAS 52 accounting procedure?

3. Suppose you had invested $1 million in U.S. fixed assets and in Italian fixed assets under the following conditions:

$\dot{P}_{US}$	$\dot{P}_{IT}$	$\dot{P}_{US}$	$\dot{P}_{IT}$	$S(\$/\text{Lit})$	$S_1(\$/\text{Lit})$
2%	4%	10%	25%	0.00100	0.00085

Assume that fixed-asset prices in local currency have kept pace with prices in general.

a. Which investment yielded higher returns over the year?

b. What will appear in the income statement and the shareholder-equity account under the FAS 52 procedure?

c. What should appear as income?

d. Why does your answer to **b** (where income and shareholder equity are aggregated) disagree with your answer to **c**?

4. The text provides an analysis of the real change in exchange rates for financial assets. Redo the analysis, this time for financial liabilities. Describe how a declining value of a currency of denomination of liabilities retires debt.

5. If capital moves around the world so that *expected* rates of return on fixed assets are the same, are overseas investors exposed to exchange rates?

6. Why do the FAS 52 rules for translating assets in very high inflation countries—inflation exceeding 100 percent in the previous three years—use a temporal distinction? (The temporal distinction involves translating current-cost items at current exchange rates and historical-cost items at historical exchange rates.)

7. To what extent do you think that the difficulty of verifying declared current costs of fixed assets has limited the use of current-cost/current-exchange-rate reporting in financial statements?

8. FAS 8 rules, which caused exchange-rate effects to show directly in financial statements, caused managers to cover foreign exchange exposure very actively. Do you agree with the action managers took?

BIBLIOGRAPHY

ADLER, MICHAEL, and BERNARD DUMAS: "Should Exposure Management Depend on Translation Accounting Methods?" *Economoney,* June 1981, pp. 132–138.

CARSBERG, BRYAN: "FAS #52—Measuring the Performance of Foreign Operations," *Midland Corporate Finance Journal,* summer 1983, pp. 48–55.

EVANS, THOMAS G., and THIMOTHY S. DOUPNIK: *Determining the Functional Currency Under Statement* 52, Financial Accounting Standards Board, Stamford, Conn., 1986.

GARLICKI, T. DESSA, FRANK J. FABOZZI, and ROBERT FONFEDER: "The Impact of Earnings Under FAS 52 on Equity Returns," *Financial Management,* autumn 1987, pp. 36–44.

HOSKIN, ROBERT E.: "The Effects of the FAS-52 Translation Mandate on Financial Measures of Corporate Success," unpublished manuscript, Fuqua School of Business, February 1985.

HOUSTON, CAROL O.: "Translation Exposure Hedging Post SFAS No. 52," *Journal of International Financial Management and Accounting,* summer/autumn 1990, pp. 145–170.

MILLER, MARTIN A.: *Comprehensive GAAP Guide,* Harcourt Brace Jovanovich, New York, 1989.

PRINGLE, JOHN J.: "Managing Foreign Exchange Exposure," *Journal of Applied Corporate Finance,* winter 1991, pp. 73–82.

——— and ROBERT A. CONNOLLY, "The Nature and Causes of Foreign Currency Exposure," *Journal of Applied Corporate Finance,* fall 1993, pp. 61–72.

ROSENFELD, PAUL: "Accounting for Foreign Operations," *Journal of Accountancy,* August 1987, pp. 103–112.

SHAPIRO, ALAN C., *Statement of Financial Accounting Standards No. 52—Foreign Currency Translation,* Financial Accounting Standards Board, Stamford, Conn., December 1981.

WYMAN, HAROLD E.: "Analysis of Gains and Losses from Foreign Monetary Items: An Application of Purchasing Power Parity Concepts," *The Accounting Review,* July 1976, pp. 545–558.

CHAPTER 14

Operating Exposure

International companies now know that what happens to the currencies in which they tot up the costs, revenues and assets affects their results as much as their success in making and selling products.

—*The Economist,* April 4, 1987

This chapter explains the implications of exchange rates for the cash flows of exporting and importing firms and is hence concerned with operating exposure. For example, it describes the effects of exchange rates on an exporter's product price and sales (which affect cash inflows) as well as on production costs (which affect cash outflows). It explains how the elasticity of demand and the nature of production influence the extent to which profits are affected by exchange rates. We discover, for example, how the effects of changes in exchange rates depend on such things as the time span considered and the degree of competition from other firms.

We reach the important conclusion in this chapter that even if a company has hedged its foreign exchange receivables and payables and has no foreign assets or liabilities, there is still an important element of foreign exchange exposure. This is the operating exposure which occurs because future profits from operations depend on exchange rates. The techniques used for hedging assets and liabilities are not designed to eliminate operating exposure. Indeed, because operating exposure is so difficult to eliminate, it has been called **residual foreign exchange exposure.** We shall discover that the extent of operating, or residual, exposure depends on such factors as the elasticity of demand for the product, production-cost conditions, the currency relevant for income measurement, and whether inputs are traded internationally.

Before beginning, we should point out that some firms face operating exposure without even dealing in foreign exchange. For example, restaurants in U.S. resorts that are visited by foreign tourists gain or lose customers according to the exchange rate. This happens despite the fact that they are generally paid in U.S. dollars and they pay for food, labor, rent, and interest in U.S. dollars. Similarly, industries which compete with imported goods face operating exposure. For example, U.S. firms that supply beef to U.S. supermarkets and that never see foreign exchange can find competition from foreign beef suppliers—in Canada and Latin America—more fierce when the U.S. dollar gains against other currencies, lowering prices of the non-U.S. product.

Since the links in the economic chain of interdependence are many, industries that provide supplies to U.S. resort hotels, U.S. beef producers, or other industries more directly involved in international trade will find themselves affected by changes in exchange rates. It should therefore be apparent that operating exposure makes the required perspective of management extremely broad. It should also be apparent that operating exposure is difficult to avoid with the exposure-reducing techniques we have met so far. But let us begin by examining what influences the extent of operating exposure.

THE EXPORTER

Competitive Markets in the Short Run

The most straightforward situation of operating exposure involves an exporter selling in a perfectly competitive market, which by definition is a market where any one firm can sell all it wishes without affecting the market price. To put this in context, let us suppose that before a devaluation of the U.S. dollar, Aviva Corporation was able to sell in Britain all the jeans that it wished to produce at a dollar-equivalent price of $p_1^\$$ a pair. The dollar sign denotes that the price is in terms of Aviva's home currency. After a devaluation, Aviva Corporation will be able to sell all the jeans it wishes to produce at a higher price, $p_2^\$$. This is because with the U.S. dollar cheaper to foreigners, Aviva can charge a higher U.S. dollar price and yet leave the foreign exchange price unchanged.

We can go further and say precisely how much higher the new price, $p_2^\$$, will be after a devaluation. To determine this, we define $p_1^\pounds$ as the pound price of Aviva's jeans in Britain before the devaluation and $S(\$/\pounds)$ as the predevaluation exchange rate. We can write the pound price of jeans sold in Britain as

$$p_1^\pounds = \frac{1}{S(\$/\pounds)} \cdot p_1^\$ \tag{14.1}$$

This equation merely defines the relationship between the price charged in Britain in pounds and the price in dollars. If Aviva is operating in a competitive market, there are many other firms—at home, in Britain, and around the world—that are prepared to supply similar jeans. There is no reason for the foreign suppliers to change their pound prices just because the United States has experienced a depreciation/devaluation. (Henceforth, by "devaluation" we mean either devaluation, which occurs with fixed exchange rates, or depreciation, which occurs with flexible exchange rates. Similarly, "revaluation" refers either to revaluation, which happens with fixed rates, or appreciation, which happens with flexible rates.)

After a devaluation to an exchange rate of $S'(\$/\pounds)$, the pound and dollar prices are related as follows:

$$p_2^\pounds = \frac{1}{S'(\$/\pounds)} \cdot p_2^\$$$

If the price of jeans in Britain is changing in line with the British inflation rate, $\dot{P}_{UK}$, and we can write $p_2^\pounds = p_1^\pounds(1 + \dot{P}_{UK})$, then

$$p_1^\pounds\left(1 + \dot{P}_{UK}\right) = \frac{1}{S'(\$/\pounds)} \cdot p_2^\$ \tag{14.2}$$

That is, after the foreign exchange value of the dollar falls to $S'(\$/£)$, the price that Aviva charges in Britain will move in line with the prices of other jeans suppliers. Prices of these other suppliers are assumed to change at the rate of British inflation. Equation (14.2) follows because Aviva can sell all it wishes at the price charged by other suppliers, and there is therefore no advantage to lowering its price after a devaluation.

Taking the ratios of equation (14.1) and equation (14.2), we have

$$1 + \dot{P}_{UK} = \frac{S(\$/£)}{S'(\$/£)} \cdot \frac{p_2^\$}{p_1^\$}$$

or

$$\frac{p_2^\$}{p_1^\$} = \frac{S'(\$/£)}{S(\$/£)} \left(1 + \dot{P}_{UK}\right)$$

This tells us that after a devaluation of the dollar and an increase in the price of foreign exchange to $S'(\$/£)$, the U.S. dollar price of jeans in Britain will rise by the combined rate of devaluation and British inflation. This is true no matter what the rate of inflation is in the United States. For example, if the dollar falls in value by 5 percent and Britain has 10 percent inflation affecting jeans (and other) prices, the dollar price that Aviva charges will go up 15 percent. Of course, the rate of inflation in the United States will determine production-cost increases and the extent to which the 15 percent gain in the dollar price of the product represents an increase in profitability.

The predevaluation and postdevaluation prices, $p_1^\$$ and $p_2^\$ = [S'(\$/£)/S(\$/£)](1 + \dot{P}_{UK})p_1^\$$, are shown in Figure 14.1, where the price axes are drawn in home-currency (\$) units. To keep the diagrams straightforward, we take the U.S. inflation to be zero so that the marginal cost curve, MC, does not shift. Since the firm is perfectly competitive, the demand curve is a horizontal line at the relevant price. Further, since additional units can be sold at a constant price, the horizontal demand curve is also the marginal revenue (MR) curve. The marginal cost, MC, is assumed to increase as output increases.

In Figure 14.1, before the devaluation, our firm, Aviva Corporation, would have produced and sold X_1 units per period by seeking its optimum output where marginal revenue MR_1 equals marginal cost MC. This is the point of maximum profit. If output is less than X_1, MR > MC, and profit is increased by producing more and adding more revenue than costs. At an output greater than X_1, we have MC > MR, and profit is increased by producing less and thereby reducing costs by more than revenue.

If we are dealing with a situation without U.S. inflation, where all inputs such as the denim cloth are nontradable, we can expect—at least in the short run—that MC will remain as it was before the devaluation. Tradable inputs will probably become more expensive after the devaluation, raising production costs and hence MC, but when inputs are all nontradable there is no immediate reason for marginal costs to increase.

It is the *tradability* of inputs that determines whether a devaluation increases input costs, not whether inputs are *imported*. After a devaluation, domestically produced inputs which could be sold abroad increase in price: the opportunity cost of

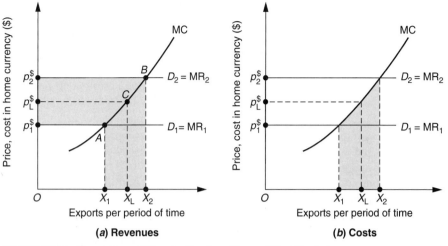

FIGURE 14.1. Exporter and Devaluation in a Competitive Market
A depreciation or devaluation raises the price an exporter can charge in terms of his or her own currency. In the perfectly competitive situation the price rises by the percentage of devaluation/depreciation plus the percentage of inflation in the United Kingdom. This raises profit-maximizing output, sales revenues, and the total cost of production. In the long run, new firms and the expansion of older firms reduce selling prices, output, and profits to original levels. If the country's exporters are a small part of the overall market, some benefits will remain.

selling them at home is higher. Of course, by definition, imported inputs are tradable and therefore cost more after a devaluation. However, so does, for example, domestically produced oil, because it is tradable: *ceteris paribus,* U.S. consumers pay more for Texas oil after a fall in the foreign exchange value of the dollar. Even U.S.-produced manufactured goods should cost more dollars after a dollar devaluation if the goods could also be sold overseas.

With the price and hence marginal revenue of jeans in dollar terms rising to $p_2^\$ = [S'(\$/£)/S(\$/£)](1 + \dot{P}_{UK})p_1^\$$ after the devaluation and the marginal cost remaining unchanged, Aviva will want to raise its production to X_2 per period. This is the new profit-maximizing output, where $MR_2 = MC$. We find that a higher price in dollars and a higher level of sales have resulted from the devaluation.

Part *a* of Figure 14.1 shows how revenues in units of domestic currency have increased because the price is higher and the quantity sold is greater. Revenues will increase by the shaded area in part *a*. There is an unambiguous increase in cash inflows in terms of home currency after a devaluation. A simple reversal of interpretation in the diagram to determine the effects of a *revaluation* would similarly show that there would be an unambiguous decrease in cash inflows for an exporter when they are measured in terms of the home currency.

In the short run, with no U.S. inflation and per-unit costs of production unaffected by the devaluation, the total production cost will rise by only the cost of producing the additional quantity that is sold. Since MC is the cost of producing each additional item, the area under MC between X_1 and X_2 will be the additional cost incurred in providing the extra goods sold. Hence, the total manufacturing cost will rise by the shaded area in part *b* of Figure 14.1. We can see that with revenues rising by the shaded area in part *a* and costs rising by the shaded area in part *b*, profits, which rise by the difference between revenues and costs, will rise by the area $p_2^\$ BAp_1^\$$ in part *a*. After a devaluation, the increase in cash outflows for production costs will always be less than the increase in cash inflows from export revenues.

What are the factors affecting the amount by which total profits will increase? We note that with $p_2^\$$ exceeding $p_1^\$$ by the U.K. inflation and the percentage of the devaluation, the increase in nominal profits—even if output remains at X_1—will be equal to the sum of the U.K. inflation rate and the percentage of the devaluation multiplied by the original revenues. For example, with a 10 percent devaluation and 5 percent U.K. inflation, $p_2^\$$ exceeds $p_1^\$$ by 15 percent, and so if initial revenues were $1000, nominal profits will rise by at least $150. With output increasing, profits will rise by an even bigger percentage. This is clear from part *a* of Figure 14.1 by comparing the size of the extra profit, area $p_2^\$ BAp_1^\$$, with the original revenues given by the unshaded rectangle, $Op_1^\$ AX_1$.

We notice also from Figure 14.1 that the flatter MC is, the greater is the increase in profit. That is, production flexibility increases the gain from a devaluation. This is what one would expect, namely, that firms that are able to increase production gain more after devaluation than firms that are producing at capacity. The reader is urged to draw Figure 14.1*a* with MC curves of different slopes and show that changes in profits are larger with a flatter curve. In redrawing Figure 14.1, allow all MC curves to pass through point *A*.

Long-Run Effects: Tradable Inputs

Since the accurate forecasting of cash flows is an important job for the financial manager, we should not limit our discussion to the immediate effects of devaluation on flows of revenues and production costs. When we are dealing with a firm in perfect competition with others, as we are here, it is important to appreciate that any increase in profits that will accompany devaluation will probably be temporary. A perfectly competitive market, by definition, involves the free entry of new firms. The additional profit that might be available after a real devaluation (that is, one that does not just make up for differences in inflation) will serve as an incentive for new firms to get involved and existing firms to expand. This can bring the rate of profit back to its predevaluation level. Therefore, it is possible that only in the interim will the higher-than-normal profits be made. Hence, if Aviva is operating in a perfectly competitive market, management might not be too excited after falls in the exchange value of the dollar, even if they are real. Let us show these conclusions graphically.

The immediate higher profits after devaluation will induce firms in purely domestic endeavors to move into the export sector until the "last" firm to enter can reap a profit equal to the best it could achieve in some alternative endeavor. Competition from new firms might tend to move the price that the original firms such as Aviva can gain for their product back toward $p_1^\$$. As a result, we would move back toward the predevaluation situation of price $p_1^\$$ and output X_1 with original cash flows. Extra profits will last only as long as it takes new firms to get involved. This will depend largely on the nature of the product.

We might want to note that if the devaluing country produces only a small fraction of the world's output of a particular good, then the free entry of firms *within* the country may have little effect when cutting into the extra profit from devaluation. This is true because many new firms might enter the industry within the devaluing country without significantly affecting the world price. Prices might move back very little from $p_2^\$$, perhaps only to $p_L^\$$ in Figure 14.1. Output would be X_L. Profits would remain abnormally high and be given by area $p_L^\$ CAp_1^\$$. Furthermore, industry-level profits are higher from the profits of newly entering firms.

There is another route that is possible through rising costs that can also limit the period of obtaining extra profit after a real devaluation and hence limit the postdevaluation celebrations of an exporter. This involves the eventual reduction in the *real* devaluation via the inflation that the *actual* devaluation itself sets up. This will work in all market settings, not only in competitive markets, and so we will consider the effect separately. The effect will come about even if none of the inputs used by the firm under consideration are tradable, in which case there is no immediate increase in the firm's costs. Cost increases may nevertheless take place eventually.

Tradable consumer goods prices tend to rise after a depreciation or devaluation. To the extent that tradable products figure in the cost-of-living index, a devaluation increases the cost of living and thereby reduces the buying power of wages. If efforts to maintain real or price-adjusted wages result in wage increases to compensate for the higher cost of living, then the firm's production costs will rise. That is, the firm's production costs can increase because of indirect effects of devaluation-induced price increases on wages even if there are no direct effects on input prices. Figure 14.2 describes the effect of higher wages caused by the devaluation.

FIGURE 14.2. Exporter and Devaluation in a Competitive Market: Effect of Cost Increases

A devaluation raises input costs and the costs of production. This means a reduction in the extent of the real devaluation. Profit-maximizing output and profits return toward original levels. However, as long as some real devaluation remains, there are extra sales and profits.

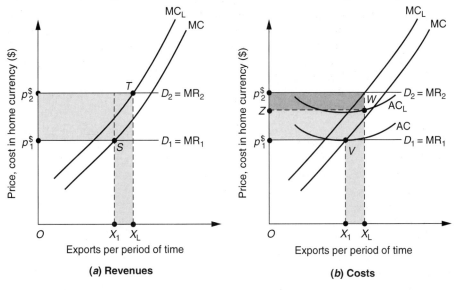

(a) Revenues   (b) Costs

In part *a* of Figure 14.2, we show the marginal cost of production rising from MC to MC_L. Every unit is shown to cost more to produce as money wages rise. We can think of MC moving up by the U.S. inflation rate, and so we have

$$\frac{MC_L}{MC} = 1 + \dot{P}_{US}$$

at each output level. In order to retain an effective (or real) devaluation, we draw a smaller vertical shift in MC than in the demand curve, which, as we have already stated, shifts by

$$\frac{p_2^\$}{p_1^\$} = \frac{S'(\$/£)}{S(\$/£)}\left(1 + \dot{P}_{UK}\right)$$

Indeed, the real extent of the devaluation is the difference between the proportional shift in the price line, $D = MR$, and the proportional shift in the MC curve, since from the equations above this is

$$\frac{p_2^\$}{p_1^\$} - \frac{MC_L}{MC} = \frac{S'(\$/£)}{S(\$/£)}\left(1 + \dot{P}_{UK}\right) - \left(1 + \dot{P}_{US}\right)$$

$$= \frac{S'(\$/£) - S(\$/£)}{S(\$/£)}\left(1 + \dot{P}_{UK}\right) - \left(\dot{P}_{US} - \dot{P}_{UK}\right)$$

$$= \dot{S}(\$/£)\left(1 + \dot{P}_{UK}\right) - \left(\dot{P}_{US} - \dot{P}_{UK}\right) \qquad (14.3)$$

For small values of $\dot{P}_{UK}$, equation (14.3) is approximately

$$\frac{p_2^\$}{p_1^\$} - \frac{MC_L}{MC} = \dot{S}(\$/£) - \left(\dot{P}_{US} - \dot{P}_{UK}\right) \qquad (14.4)$$

The amount on the right-hand side of equation (14.4) is the real change in exchange rate for an operating firm and is equal to the extent that there are departures from PPP. Specifically, if $\dot{S}\,(\$/£) > (\dot{P}_{US} - \dot{P}_{UK})$ there is a real devaluation of the dollar—the number of dollars per pound increases more than the extent to which the United States has higher inflation. In this case the dollar prices of U.S. exporters increase more than their costs. That is, from equation (14.4), if $\dot{S}\,(\$/£) > (\dot{P}_{US} - \dot{P}_{UK})$ then $p_2^\$/p_1^\$ > MC_L/MC$. Similarly, if $\dot{S}\,(\$/£) < (\dot{P}_{US} - \dot{P}_{UK})$ there is a real revaluation of the dollar.

If a real devaluation increases the dollar price to $p_2^\$$ and via devaluation-induced inflation increases costs to MC_L and AC_L, total revenues increase from $Op_1^\$SX_1$ to $Op_2^\$TX_L$. Total cost is average cost, AC, multiplied by the output, which before the devaluation was $Op_1^\$VX_1$. After the devaluation, at the output X_L, the total cost is area $OZWX_L$. This cost exceeds the predevaluation cost by the lightly shaded area in part *b* of Figure 14.2. Since revenues rise by the shaded area in part *a*, or the entire shaded area in part *b*, and costs rise by the lightly shaded area in part *b*, profits rise by the difference, the darkly shaded area in part *b*.[1]

---

[1]To simplify the argument, we have drawn area $Op_1^\$SX_1$ so that it is equal to area $Op_1^\$VX_1$. This means that before the devaluation, revenues equal costs, and profits are zero. Any profit after the devaluation is a result of the devaluation itself. We have also simplified the argument by ignoring the long-run envelope of AC curves and by assuming all costs are variable costs.

In the long run, the dampening effect on profits from the competition-induced price reduction shown in part *a* of Figure 14.1 must be added to the profit reduction from higher costs. Both effects contribute to a smaller profit increase from devaluation.

The effect of having tradable inputs is, diagrammatically, precisely the same as the effect of wage pressure from devaluation-induced inflation that we have just discussed. Consequently, Figure 14.2 also describes the effect of having tradable inputs. A devaluation makes tradable inputs immediately more expensive to our exporting firm. As a result, MC and AC both shift upward to the extent that tradable inputs figure in production. We know that this vertical shift will be less than the shift in the selling price when at least some inputs are nontradable. As before, the shift is given in Figure 14.2 by the MC_L and AC_L curves, and the output increase is smaller than it would be without tradable inputs. Output increases to X_L, where MC_L cuts D_2. Profits rise by the darkly shaded area in part *b* of Figure 14.2.

The difference between the effect of tradable inputs and of wage increases from devaluation-induced inflation is only in the immediateness of effect, with tradable input prices probably rising much more quickly than with the link through wages. We should remember, however, that tradable input and wage effects can work together in the long run. From this point on, we shall consider only the short run. We shall see that this can become complicated enough.

Imperfect Competition

There are a large number of imperfect-market settings, but in general an imperfectly competitive firm can still sell some of its product if it raises the price. This is the case when perfect substitutes are not available, and it occurs frequently, since products of different firms generally have different characteristics.

To examine a firm like Aviva in an imperfect-market setting, we allow for some inelasticity in demand; that is, we draw a conventional downward-sloping demand curve. When, as before, the home currency is on the vertical axis, what is the effect on the demand curve of a devaluation? We shall see that it will move vertically upward, just as in a competitive market. Indeed, the argument will differ little from the one we used in the discussion of competitive markets.

Let us consider any particular sales volume on demand curve D_1 in Figure 14.3, for example, X_1. Now when the demand curve is at the predevaluation level, D_1, a volume X_1 can be sold at the domestic-currency price $p_1^\$$. With the exchange rate $S(\$/£)$, this means a foreign-currency price of $p_1^£ = [1/S(\$/£)]p_1^\$$ *at this output* of X_1.

After the devaluation, the same quantity—that is, X_1—will be sold abroad if the foreign-currency price is raised in line with prices of other suppliers to $p_2^£ = p_1^£(1 + \dot{P}_{UK})$. It is the foreign-currency price that always matters, and if Aviva keeps its pound prices in line with prices charged by other producers in the British market (which are assumed to rise at the U.K. inflation rate), it will remain competitive. This is because the British do not look at the price tag of a pair of U.S.-made jeans on sale in Britain in terms of the U.S. dollar. Rather, they consider the number of British pounds that must be paid for the jeans, just as a U.S. car buyer considers the dollar price of an imported car. It is the monetary unit of the country where the product is sold that influences the buyer's purchase decision. But at the devalued exchange rate of $S'(\$/£)$, the new pound price of $p_2^£ = (1 + \dot{P}_{UK})p_1^£$ means a dollar price of

FIGURE 14.3. Devaluation and the Demand Curve
For each sales level, the price that can be charged after the
devaluation with sales unchanged rises by the percentage
of the devaluation. This means that the demand curve
shifts vertically by the percentage of the devaluation (plus
any foreign inflation).

$$p_2^\$ = S'(\$/£)p_2^£ = S'(\$/£)\left(1 + \dot{P}_{UK}\right)p_1^£ \tag{14.5}$$

In other words, if, when the exchange rate changes from $S(\$/£)$ to $S'(\$/£)$, the dollar
price changes from $p_1^\$$ to $p_2^\$$, as in equation (14.5), then sales will remain unchanged
at X_1. In terms of Figure 14.3, we are saying that before the devaluation at price $p_1^\$$,
we will sell X_1 abroad and hence be at point A. After the devaluation, we will sell the
same amount, X_1, abroad only if the dollar price is $p_2^\$ = S'(\$/£)(1 + \dot{P}_{UK})p_1^£$. Therefore
we obtain point B. We find that the demand curve after the devaluation is moved
upward to $p_2^\$ = [S'(\$/£)/S(\$/£)](1 + \dot{P}_{UK})p_1^\$$; that is, the vertical shift is equal to the
devaluation plus the U.K. inflation.

We can now take another sales volume, say X_2, and follow precisely the same
argument. Each and every point on the new demand curve, D_2, will be vertically
above the old demand curve, D_1, in proportion to the devaluation and the U.K. infla-
tion.

We should think of vertical movements of demand rather than a "rightward
shift" along the lines that "more is sold for the same dollar price after a devalua-
tion." Although this is true, it does not tell us how much, whereas our argument in
the text makes it clear that the vertical shift is in exactly the same proportion as the
change in the exchange rate and U.K. inflation. Of course, we notice that since the
vertical shift is always in the same *proportion* as the change in the exchange rate
and the U.K. inflation, the *absolute* shift is less at lower prices on the demand curve.
This is shown in Figure 14.3, with demand curve D_2 closer to D_1 at lower prices.

Part *a* of Figure 14.4 shows the vertical shift in the demand curve (D_1 to D_2)
from a U.S. dollar devaluation, along with the corresponding shift in the MR curve.
We have assumed that the costs are constant in part *b* by drawing a flat MC. It

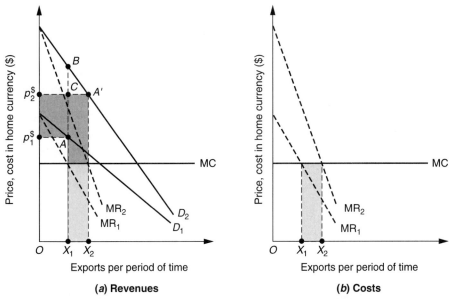

FIGURE 14.4. **Exporter and Devaluation in an Imperfectly Competitive Market**
In an imperfectly competitive market the home-currency price of exports will increase by a
smaller percentage than the devaluation. Sales will increase by a smaller fraction than in the
case of perfect competition.

would complicate matters only a little to allow for increasing costs by also considering AC curves. Rising costs would tend to reduce the effects of devaluation on
profits, but they would not eliminate these positive effects.

We see from Figure 14.4 that before the devaluation, the firm will produce X_1
per period, which is where $MC = MR_1$, and it will be able to sell this output at the
price $p_1^\$$. After the devaluation, the firm will produce X_2 per period and sell this at
the price $p_2^\$$. The increase in revenue from $Op_1^\$ AX_1$ to $Op_2^\$ A'X_2$ is represented by
the total shaded area in part *a* of Figure 14.4. An important point to realize is that
with a downward-sloping curve, the price increase from $p_1^\$$ to $p_2^\$$ is less than the
vertical shift in the demand curve ($AC < AB$). We discover that export prices when
stated in the domestic currency rise *less than* the combined percentage of the deval-
uation and the U.K. inflation. This is different from the case of perfect competition,
where we found the product price rising by an amount *equal* to the devaluation and
the U.K. inflation.

With output rising from X_1 to X_2, and with each unit costing the manufacturer an
amount given by the height of the MC curve, the total cost increases by the lightly
shaded area in part *b* of Figure 14.4 (shown also in part *a*). Profits increase by the
difference between the change in total revenue, given by the total shaded area in
part *a*, and the change in total cost, given by the lightly shaded area. The change in
profits is therefore represented by the darkly shaded area in part *a*, which is the dif-
ference between the total shaded area and the lightly shaded area.

The extent to which prices will rise, output will increase, and profits will be
affected depends on the slope (elasticity) of the demand curve and the slope of the
MC curve, which we have made horizontal so that profits can be easily computed.

The reader might note that if the firm is up against a rigid constraint in raising output, then MC can be vertical, and a devaluation will leave output and sales unchanged, with domestic-currency prices rising by the full percentage of devaluation and U.K. inflation—just as in the case of perfect competition. It has been observed, for example, that auto exporters have raised their home-currency prices in proportion to any devaluation; that is, they have left foreign prices unchanged. This has been attributed to their inability to raise output in the short run. Why lower your foreign-currency selling price if you cannot satisfy any extra demand that this might create? The slopes of the demand and cost curves are thus vital parameters for effective financial planning in an exporting firm. The demand sensitivity of the firm should be estimated, and the degree of capacity utilization should be measured to determine the response that the production side should make to real changes in exchange rates.

Analysis in Foreign-Currency Units

So far we have measured the vertical axes in our diagrams in units of the domestic currency, which we have taken as the U.S. dollar. By drawing our diagrams in terms of home-currency units, we have been able to examine the effects of exchange-rate changes when these effects are measured in the same units. Our revenue, cost, and profit changes that result from devaluations or revaluations are therefore U.S. dollar amounts; in general, they are the amounts that are relevant for U.S. firms. Some firms that are operating within a country, however, will be concerned with revenues, costs, and profits in some particular foreign-currency unit. For example, a British firm with a manufacturing operation in the United States may not be directly concerned with whether devaluation of the U.S. dollar raises its U.S. dollar earnings. Since the dollar is less valuable, the higher U.S. dollar earnings might bring fewer pounds than before the devaluation, or so it might seem. Similarly, a U.S. firm with a subsidiary in, for example, Canada, may not be thrilled if a depreciation of the Canadian dollar raises the Canadian-dollar earnings of its subsidiary. These higher earnings might, it might seem, be worth less in U.S. dollars. However, as we shall show, these possibilities need not concern parent firms.

Interest in the effects of a devaluation or revaluation, when measured in foreign-currency units, should not be limited to firms with subsidiaries abroad. Any firm that denominates borrowing in some foreign currency—even if it enjoys only one location—will care about the effect of exchange-rate changes on its operating revenues, measured in units of the currency of its debt. For example, a U.S. firm that has borrowed in British pounds will care very much about its trading revenues as measured in pounds after an exchange-rate change. This is because the firm has payables in British pounds. Similarly, Canadian firms that borrow in U.S. dollars care about their U.S. dollar revenues, since they are required to service U.S. dollar debts. For these reasons, we should consider the effects of exchange-rate changes on revenues, costs, and profits when measured in units of foreign currency. We will limit our discussion to an imperfect market; the competitive case, with a flat demand curve and an upward-sloping MC, is extremely similar and is left as an exercise for the reader.

As we said, the price that is relevant to a buyer is the price he or she has to pay in terms of his or her own currency. When the price of Aviva jeans in Britain remains unchanged in terms of British pounds but changes in terms of U.S. dollars, there is no reason for sales in Britain to change. It follows that when there is, for example, a devaluation of the U.S. dollar, there is no reason for the demand curve for Aviva's jeans to shift if it is drawn against the pound price. At the same pound price as before, the same monthly volume of jeans will be sold. The demand curve in Figure 14.5, and hence also the MR curve, is the same before and after the devaluation.

The effect of changes in exchange rates on the cost curves is different from the effect on the demand curve. When our diagrams are drawn in units of foreign currency and there is an exchange-rate change, the cost curves will move vertically in proportion to the exchange rate. Why is this so?

If it costs, say, $MC_1^\$$ to produce an extra pair of Aviva's jeans and no inputs are tradable, then after a devaluation the production cost should still be $MC_1^\$$ if the devaluation has not induced general inflation. However, before the devaluation, with an exchange rate of $S(\$/\pounds)$, the cost in units of foreign exchange was

$$MC_1^\pounds = \frac{1}{S(\$/\pounds)} \cdot MC_1^\$$$

After the devaluation to $S'(\$/\pounds)$, with the dollar cost the same, the foreign exchange cost becomes

FIGURE 14.5. Exporter and Devaluation in an Imperfectly Competitive Market: Foreign-Currency Units

The relevant price for demanders is the price denominated in the buyers' currency. When we measure the vertical axis in the buyers' currency, the demand and MR curves are unaffected by changes in exchange rates. If production costs are unchanged in the producers' currency, a devaluation of that currency will lower costs denominated in the buyers' currency. The export price will decline in the buyers' currency after a devaluation, and the quantity of exports will increase.

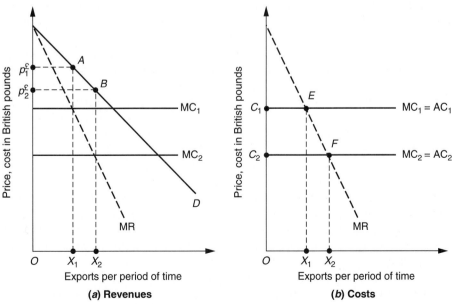

(a) Revenues

(b) Costs

$$MC_2^£ = \frac{1}{S'(\$/£)} \cdot MC_1^\$$$

By simply taking ratios, we get

$$\frac{MC_2^£}{MC_1^£} = \frac{S(\$/£)}{S'(\$/£)}$$

That is, the MCs, in terms of British pounds, change in proportion to the exchange rate. Since a devaluation of the dollar means that $S'(\$/£) > S(\$/£)$, the MC, in terms of British pounds, falls as the dollar is devalued. In Figure 14.5, this is shown with MC moving downward from MC_1 to MC_2. Since we have drawn Figure 14.5 with a constant MC, we know that MC = AC, and so the AC curve moves downward with the devaluation of the dollar when the vertical axis is in British pounds.

With profit maximization requiring that MC = MR, we see from Figure 14.5 that a devaluation of the U.S. dollar increases Aviva's profit-maximizing output from X_1 to X_2. With the demand curve remaining at D, the pound price falls from $p_1^£$ to $p_2^£$. We see that even with the demand curve unshifted by a devaluation, the devaluation lowers the foreign exchange price of exports and raises the quantity sold.[2] With lower prices and higher sales, what has happened to total revenue in terms of the British pound?

The answer clearly depends on whether sales have risen by a larger or smaller proportion than the reduction in price. If the increase in sales is greater than the price reduction, revenue will be higher. Such a situation requires that the elasticity of demand exceed unity, that is, it is elastic, which we know to be the case by making a straightforward observation. Since MC is positive, and the firm produces where MR = MC, MR must also be positive. But with MR positive, an extra unit of sales, even though it requires a fall in price, must raise total revenue. We know, therefore, that pound revenue must rise, with area $Op_2^£BX_2$ necessarily greater than area $Op_1^£AX_1$.

Part *b* of Figure 14.5 gives the required curves for considering the effect of a devaluation on total cost. Since total cost is given by AC multiplied by the output, whether total cost has increased depends on the slope of MR. Total cost has changed from area OC_1EX_1 to area OC_2FX_2. Has total cost increased, and if so, by how much? Well, continuing at this point without the help of mathematics is difficult. Mathematics helps us show that for profitable firms total cost, in terms of pounds, increases after the dollar is devalued, but by a smaller amount than the increase in total revenue. In terms of pounds, profit is therefore increased. This, along with the other results we have reached, is demonstrated in the appendix of this chapter.

THE IMPORTER

It is generally presumed that importers lose from a devaluation and gain from revaluation. This presumption is correct, with the exact magnitude of effect of exchange rates depending on such factors as the degree of competition and which currency we use for our analysis. The amount of change in cash flows is important information for the financial manager of an importing firm, whether the firm is importing

[2]By referring back to the equivalent home-currency diagram, Figure 14.4, the reader will see that while the pound price *falls,* devaluation *raises* the export price in terms of dollars (from $p_1^\$$ to $p_2^\$$).

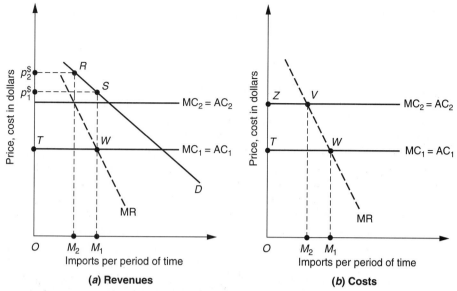

FIGURE 14.6. The Importer and a Devaluation

If the importer's buying costs are unchanged from a devaluation in terms of the foreign supplier's currency, cost curves will move up by the percentage of devaluation when measured against the importer's currency. Demand curves will not be affected if they are drawn against the demander's currency. Only the amount demanded—a move along the curve—will be affected rather than the position of the curve. A devaluation will raise import prices and lower sales. The importer's profit declines.

finished goods for sale at home or some of the inputs used in producing its local output. If the goods are finished goods for sale, determining the effects of changes in real exchange rates requires that the financial manager know the elasticity of the market demand for the product. The financial manager must also decide on the relevant currency for measurement. We will begin by measuring in dollar amounts.

Analysis in Home-Currency Units

Let us again consider Aviva Corporation and assume that it has decided to import finished jeans that are manufactured in Britain for sale in the United States. The most straightforward case is one in which Aviva can import whatever quantity of jeans it wishes at the same pound cost per pair. Being able to buy jeans at a constant cost means that we have the horizontal cost curve $MC_1 = AC_1$ shown in parts *a* and *b* of Figure 14.6. We can think of the constant cost per pair as being a constant pound cost that is faced whatever the exchange rate, translated at the predevaluation exchange rate.[3]

Assume that Aviva faces market demand conditions that are less than perfectly

---

[3]The cost curve for jeans will be flat if shipping and production costs in Britain are constant. The cost curve will also be flat if Aviva is one of many buyers of these imported jeans. Every buyer, if sufficiently small, will be able to obtain whatever quantity it wants at the going price. This will mean that no buyer has any monopsony power. In fact, however, an assumption of constant costs is not necessary and only aids in computing total costs and profits.

elastic in selling the imported British jeans in the U.S. market. This requires that there be not many other *sellers* of the same jeans. This could very easily be the case in practice if, for example, Aviva is licensed as the sole importer of these particular jeans in the United States.[4] This situation is very common. Many of the products produced in foreign countries are sold in each market by licensed firms or sales subsidiaries with exclusive rights to distribute a product.

The demand curve is shown along with the associated MR and cost curves in Figure 14.6. Before the devaluation, Aviva Corporation will import and sell M_1 pairs of jeans per period, which is the profit-maximizing quantity where $MR = MC_1$. The jeans will be sold at the price $p_1^\$$ per pair, giving a total revenue in dollars of area $Op_1^\$SM_1$ in Figure 14.6a. The cost of the jeans, $MC_1 = AC_1$ per unit, gives a total cost of $OTWM_1$ dollars in Figure 14.6b. The initial profit is the difference between total revenue and total cost, which is area $Tp_1^\$SW$ in Figure 14.6a.

After a devaluation of the dollar to $S'(\$/£)$, there is no reason for the British-pound production cost to be affected. With the British-pound cost unchanged, the new dollar cost must increase in proportion to the exchange value of the British pound against the dollar. The cost curves in parts *a* and *b* of Figure 14.6 shift vertically upward by the percentage of the dollar devaluation.[5] The importer will reduce the amount imported and sold to M_2 per period, where $MR = MC_2$, and will sell this new amount, with the demand curve D, at the price $p_2^\$$. We see that the effect of a dollar devaluation is to reduce imports and quantity sold and raise prices.

The effect on revenues, costs, and profits of the importer is less obvious from Figure 14.6 than the effect on quantities and prices. Revenues have changed from $Op_1^\$SM_1$ dollars to $Op_2^\$RM_2$ dollars. However, we know from the straightforward observation made for the exporter that as a result of a dollar devaluation, revenues have fallen for the importer. All profit-maximizing firms sell at a point where the demand curve for their product is elastic. This is because they choose to be where $MR = MC$, and since MC must be positive, MR is positive—that is, revenues are increased by additional sales, even though higher sales require lower prices. With the importer on an elastic part of his or her demand curve, the percentage reduction in the quantity sold must exceed the percentage increase in price—that is, revenues are reduced by a devaluation.

To determine the effect of a devaluation on profits, we must determine the effect on costs and compare this with the effect on revenues. This is not easily done with the diagrammatic analysis of Figure 14.6. However, as the mathematics in the appendix reveals, a devaluation also reduces the total costs of the imports; that is, area $OZVM_2$ is less than area $OTWM_1$. The appendix also reveals that provided we begin with positive profits, the reduction in costs is smaller than the reduction in revenues, and so the dollar profits of the importer fall from a devaluation. The effects of a devaluation in terms of British pounds are more easily obtained from a digrammatic analysis than are the effects in terms of dollars.

[4]If the import were freely available to any importer or potential importer, any one firm would face a flat demand curve for the good at the going price. This perfect competition would put the demand curve at the level of the cost curve, and so no profit would be made above the normal return on the capital and enterprise involved.
[5]If we wish to allow for inflation in Britain, the vertical shift in MC can include this.

Analysis in Foreign-Currency Units

The effects of a dollar devaluation in terms of British pounds are shown in Figure 14.7. With the cost of the jeans to Aviva Corporation at $MC^£$ and the demand curve at D_1, Aviva will import and sell M_1 pairs of jeans per period at the price $p_1^£$ per pair. The volume and the price were obtained by choosing the profit-maximizing position, where $MC^£ = MR_1$.

Now, if the British-pound cost of the import does not change from a dollar devaluation, then $MC^£ = AC^£$ will remain in its original position. The quantity of items our importer can sell, however, will depend on the dollar price charged. At any level of sales—for example, M_1—the same quantity will be sold after the devaluation only if the dollar price remains unchanged. This must mean a lower British pound price (lower by the percentage of the devaluation). In terms of British pounds, the demand curve of the American buyers of Aviva's imported jeans must shift vertically downward by the percentage of the dollar devaluation. This is shown as a move from D_1 to D_2, with the associated MR curves moving from MR_1 to MR_2 in Figure 14.7.

Figure 14.7 tells us that a devaluation will reduce the profit-maximizing amount of imports from M_1 to M_2 (the same reduction as in Figure 14.6) and result in a lower British pound price for the jeans (which, nevertheless, is a higher dollar price, as is seen in Figure 14.6). With both the quantity and price falling, the British pound revenue must fall by the total shaded area in part *a* of Figure 14.7.

With the British pound cost of the jeans unaffected by a devaluation, but with a smaller amount imported, the total cost is reduced by the shaded area in part *b* of

FIGURE 14.7. Importer and Devaluation in Foreign-Currency Units
A devaluation shifts the demand curve downward by the percent of devaluation when the curve is drawn against the producer's, not the consumer's, currency. If the producer's cost is unaffected by a devaluation, total revenue, total cost, and profit are all reduced by a devaluation.

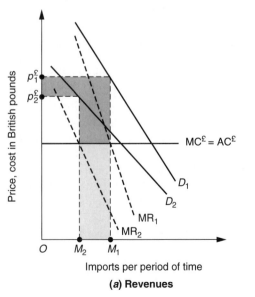

(a) Revenues

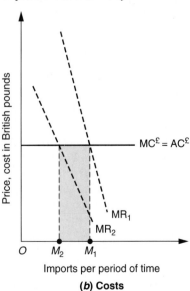

(b) Costs

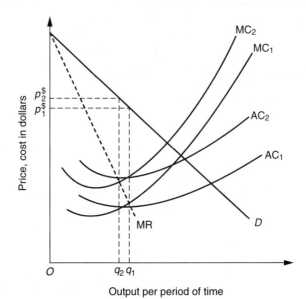

FIGURE 14.8. Importer of Inputs and Devaluation
When inputs are imported, a devaluation will raise
production costs. Higher production costs will lower the
output of goods sold domestically and raise prices.

Figure 14.7. Profits fall by the difference between the reduction in British pound revenues and the reduction in British pound costs. This fall in profits is shown by the darkly shaded area in part *a* of Figure 14.7. We conclude that an importer's pound profits are reduced from a devaluation of the importer's currency. This should be no surprise because we saw previously that dollar profits are reduced, and with fewer pounds per dollar after the devaluation, pound profits must be reduced *a fortiori*.

Tradable Inputs

Suppose that instead of importing finished jeans, Aviva is importing the denim cloth or perhaps cut denim that is ready for final manufacture in the United States. When a firm imports unfinished goods or other inputs for production, a devaluation of the domestic currency will raise production costs at each level of output.[6]

When a firm is engaged in production, marginal costs and average costs are likely to rise with output. The effect of a dollar devaluation will be to shift the rising cost curves upward, as shown in Figure 14.8. The amount by which costs increase depends on the importance of imported inputs and on whether alternative sources of inputs are available and can be substituted. As Figure 14.8 shows, the effect of the dollar devaluation is to raise the product price and reduce the quantity manufactured and sold.

---

[6]The same consequence follows from the use of any tradable input, whether the input is imported or domestically produced.

Before we add to our discussion the complications of forward hedging and the invoicing of exports or imports in different currencies, we shall summarize what we have learned:

1. Even with no foreign assets or liabilities or foreign currency payables or receivables, changes in exchange rates will affect operations. This is called operating or residual exposure and is very difficult to avoid.
2. Devaluations raise export prices in home-currency terms and at the same time raise export sales. Therefore, home-currency revenue is increased by devaluations. The reverse is true for revaluations.
3. Devaluations raise an exporter's profits. The gains are reduced by using tradable inputs and may be in any case removed in the long run by free entry of new firms or by general inflation brought about by a devaluation.
4. Foreign-owned companies or companies with foreign-currency debts care about receipts and payments in units of foreign currency. A devaluation lowers prices in foreign currency units (while raising prices in units of the devalued currency) and raises an exporter's sales. Total revenues increase because the percentage sales increase exceeds the price reduction. This follows because firms sell where demand is elastic. Production costs also increase, but it can be shown mathematically that if profits are being made, an exporter's total revenues will rise more than total costs, and so profits will increase.
5. Import prices rise in units of the devalued currency and fall in units of foreign currency. The quantity of imports will fall from a devaluation. The importer's sales revenues will fall in terms of the devalued currency because price increases are smaller than quantity reductions. Total costs also fall, but if profits are being made, not by as much as total revenues. The profits of importers therefore decline from a devaluation. This is true whether we measure in terms of the local currency or in terms of foreign currency.

EFFECT OF CURRENCY OF INVOICING AND FORWARD HEDGING

In our discussion of operating exposure we have so far allowed the quantity sold and the price the exporter receives or the importer pays to vary immediately as the exchange rate changes. However, these variations in quantity and price do not always occur immediately. Often, quantities and prices are fixed for a period into the future in sales or purchase contracts. This temporarily postpones the effects of operating exposure, causes a translation/transaction exposure to be faced in addition to the operating exposure, and results in conclusions that are potentially different from those reached earlier. For example, exporters can lose from devaluations and importers can gain—the reverse of the normal effects.

The effect of changes in exchange rates depends on whether sales and inputs are covered by existing contracts, and on which currency is used in the contracts. We will consider the following cases for exporters:

1. A fixed volume of exports has been promised for future delivery at prices fixed in dollars (or in pounds, which have been sold on the forward market), but inputs are subject to inflation or are at pound-contracted prices. This situation involves what is in effect a translation or transaction exposure on payables and the removal of this exposure on export revenues.
2. A fixed volume of exports has been promised for delivery at prices stated in pounds sterling, and the pounds have *not* been sold on the forward market. This situation involves a translation or transaction exposure on receivables.

We should note that what we shall be discussing involves the precontracting of prices and/or quantities. So far in this chapter we have taken price determination, production, and settlement as being contemporaneous. Clearly, there is then no transaction or translation exposure on receivables or payables, even though exchange rates do change profitability and therefore do leave some operating exposure. When we have the precontracting of prices and quantities, we have translation or transaction exposure and posponed operating exposure. Since this occurs frequently, we will sketch the potential consequences.

The Exporter with Exposed Inputs

Dollar Accounting

Assume that Aviva Corporation has fixed the dollar receipts from exports of a fixed number of pairs of jeans. As we shall explain in the next chapter, dollar receipts can be fixed either by invoicing the jeans in dollars or by invoicing in the buyer's currency and selling the foreign currency forward for a known, fixed number of dollars. With dollar receipts per pair of jeans and the quantity supplied fixed, total dollar revenues are fixed.

While total dollar revenues will not change from a devaluation, total costs could increase. This increase could stem from general inflation induced by rising tradable-goods prices, or it could occur because some inputs are tradable or are imported and priced in pounds. (As we shall see in the next chapter, it is possible to fix dollar costs of pound-priced inputs by buying the pounds forward. It is more difficult to hedge against inflation.) Let us take input prices to be fixed in pounds which are not bought forward. This means facing a payables exposure on pounds, and the situation shown in Figure 14.9.

The total revenue from sales is represented by area $Op_1^\$SX_1$. However, costs could increase to $OHJX_1$. If Aviva's profits were minimal before the devaluation, the devaluation will result in losses equal to the area $p_1^\$HJS$. We can see that a U.S. exporter might lose from a devaluation.[7] Of course, the loss is temporary and exists only while sales revenues are fixed and while more is paid for inputs.

If production costs as well as revenues from sales are fixed by buying forward foreign exchange for imported inputs and arranging a period of fixed dollar wages, then, of course, both costs and revenues will be unaffected by exchange rates while the various agreements are in effect. The exporting firm can therefore avoid temporary losses from a devaluation when foreign exchange is sold forward or invoicing is

---

[7]Aviva would prefer to reduce output and sales to the level where MC_L cuts $p_1^\$$. Losses would be reduced a little if this were done, but with an agreement to deliver X_1, it might not be possible.

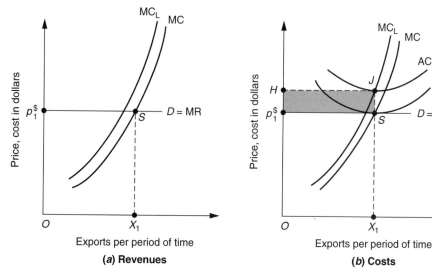

FIGURE 14.9. Exporter with Payables Exposure: Dollar Accounting
If a fixed number of goods are sold at a fixed dollar price, revenues will be unchanged after devaluations. We can think of operating exposure on revenues as being postponed. If a devaluation raises input costs, total costs will rise. This is because of transaction exposure if the prices of imported inputs are denominated in pounds. The higher input costs could reduce profits, and so exporters can temporarily lose from a devaluation.

in dollars by trying also to fix dollar input costs, including wages, for the same period.

We should note that the temporary decline in profits from a devaluation as a result of paying more for inputs is analogous to the temporary worsening of the balance of payments which in Chapter 16 was called the J-curve effect. The balance of payments can temporarily worsen because the value of imports may increase in dollars, and this may offset extra revenues from exports. Our analysis in this chapter shows for an individual firm the J curve that is usually shown for the economy. The J curve for the firm or the economy is shown in Figure 14.10. The figure shows that if a devaluation takes place at time t_0, profits could temporarily fall or the balance of payments could temporarily worsen, but eventually the economic effects of the devaluation will begin to improve both profits and the balance of payments.

Pound Accounting

With the prices of jeans fixed in dollars from selling export proceeds forward or from dollar invoicing, a dollar devaluation means that these contracted dollars represent fewer pounds. Production costs which are in dollars will also represent fewer pounds, but as long as the devaluation causes inflation, or some inputs are tradable and become more expensive, total revenues will fall more than total costs. Thus profits will decline or losses will increase. We find that exporters might lose not only in dollar terms but also in pound terms. This is no surprise, since lower profits in dollars are certainly lower profits in pounds after a dollar devaluation, because there are fewer pounds for each dollar.

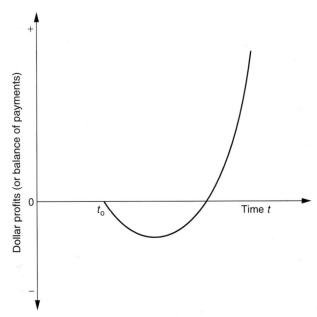

FIGURE 14.10. The J Curve
When prices of inputs increase, a devaluation can lower the profits of firms just as it can worsen the balance of payments of nations. The negative effects are temporary, and eventually the beneficial effects of a devaluation will begin to dominate.

The Exporter with Receivables Exposure

We have considered the case where the exporter's dollar receipts are temporarily fixed, either by selling foreign-currency-invoiced receivables forward or by invoicing in dollars. This temporarily eliminated operating exposure on revenues but left transaction exposure on payables. We can now consider what will happen when export prices are precontracted in the foreign currency, but the foreign currency is not sold forward. This postpones the operating exposure and causes a transaction exposure on receivables.

It is relatively easy to compute the effect of Aviva's having precontracted to supply jeans to Britain at a fixed pound-per-pair price when the pounds have not been sold forward. A dollar devaluation would make these pounds more valuable by the percentage of devaluation—a gain on pound receivables—but postpone the effect of operating exposure. Production costs might also rise because of tradable inputs or wage pressure from devaluation-induced inflation, but this effect is likely to be smaller than the effect on revenues, and so dollar profits will rise. This gain on receivables in pounds for jeans that have already been sold will be followed by gains on jeans not yet sold, resulting from the operating exposure described earlier.

The Importer

If Aviva agrees to purchase a given quantity of jeans at a dollar invoice price, or at a pound price when the pounds are bought forward, there is no immediate effect of a dollar devaluation in dollar terms. Aviva's costs are in dollars and are unaffected by exchange rates, as are Aviva's revenues. Only after the period during which dollar prices were fixed will a devaluation have the operating-exposure effect described earlier in this chapter. A revaluation of the dollar will also leave costs, revenues, and profits unaffected in dollar terms. We have a case where there is no translation or transaction exposure and where the effects of operating exposure have been postponed.

If Aviva agrees to purchase a given quantity of imports at pound prices, there is a fixed payable in pounds and hence payables transaction exposure. A dollar devaluation will increase the dollar value of this payable. For a given total revenue in dollars received on the contracted quantity, we have a reduction in dollar profits via losses on payables. The losses on payables will be followed by the importer's losses from operating exposure; recall that devaluations lower operating incomes of importers.

A Reminder: Importance of Lags

If sales, delivery, and payment could all occur simultaneously, there would be no need to worry about the contract currency or the presence of forward agreements. There would be no receivables or payables in trade, and the only effects of changes in exchange rates would be those from the operating exposure described earlier in this chapter. The currency used for sales invoicing and forward market covering are important only when price agreements and payments are separated in time. This, however, frequently happens to be the case. We then have the combined effects of translation/transaction exposure and operating exposure.

An Example: Aviva's Different Exposures

Suppose that Aviva has contracted to sell 100 pairs of jeans per year to Britain at $24 per pair and to buy 200 yards of denim from Britain in this same period for £2 per yard. Suppose that 2 yards of denim are required per pair and that the labor cost for each pair is $8.

Suppose that at the time of contracting the exchange rate is $S(\$/\pounds) = 1.5$ and that the dollar is then devalued to $S(\$/\pounds) = 2.0$. Suppose also that the elasticity of demand for Aviva jeans in Britain is −2 and that after the contract expires Aviva raises the price of jeans to $25 per pair.[8]

1. What are the gains/losses from the devaluation on the jeans sold and on the denim bought at the precontracted prices? (That is, what are the gains/losses from transaction exposure on payables and receivables?)
2. What are the gains/losses from the extra competitiveness of Aviva's jeans, that is, from operating exposure?

Assume that Aviva can buy all the denim it wishes at £2 per yard and that wages are not increased after the devaluation.

---

[8]Firms do not generally know the elasticity of demand for their products. An alternative practical approach taken by a European chemicals subsidiary of a U.S.-based multinational is described in Exhibit 14.1.

EXHIBIT 14.1
A Practical Solution to Estimating Operating Exposure

Rather than knowing elasticities of demand, firms have an idea of the extent to which the quantity demanded is sensitive to price changes. The following excerpt explains how one firm gains an idea of the price sensitivity of demand for its products and takes steps based on what it finds.

One company that manages economic exposure explicitly is the European chemicals subsidiary of a U.S.-based multinational. As an executive of the company commented, "Although a lot of people talk about economic exposure, we wanted to actually measure it and do something about it."

This company's system begins with a projection of cash flows for each of eight major geographical regions for one year ahead. The next step is to determine the sensitivity of the revenues of each product group and each major element of cost to forex (foreign exchange) movements. Because it is based in the U.S., the company is most concerned about movements against the dollar.

To measure this sensitivity, an analysis is made by taking a representative sample of products from each product group and interviewing the product marketing manager in each case. Questions concern the general characteristics of the market, who the competitors were, how pricing was determined, and what factors had the largest impact. Based on these interviews, a rating is assigned to each product

group signifying the extent to which the product price is sensitive to movements in the U.S. dollar. . . .

The product rating in a sense is a measure of the company's ability to pass on changes in exchange rates to customers. If a product is completely dollar-sensitive, forex changes can be passed on immediately; if completely insensitive, changes cannot be passed on. . . .

A similar analysis is done for costs. Each major cost component is given a rating using the same scale used for revenues. Feedstocks, for example, which consist of petroleum derivatives, are viewed as completely dollar-sensitive. Electric power was entirely local, while fuel and gas was entirely dollar-sensitive. Locally-sourced inputs such as labor and services were judged to be completely dollar-sensitive. . . .

Projected cash flows are then transformed into "economic" cash flows by multiplying them by the product ratings. . . . This procedure is repeated for revenues and costs for each of the company's European subsidiaries and then aggregated to obtain an estimate of total exposed and non-exposed cash flows for the company overall for the year ahead. The results provide the company with a measure of its effective exposure in each currency relative to the U.S. dollar.

Source: John J. Pringle, "Managing Foreign Exchange Exposure,"
Journal of Applied Corporate Finance, winter 1991, pp. 73–82.

Effect of Transaction Exposure

Before the devaluation:

$$\text{Expected total revenue/year} = 100 \text{ pairs} \times \$24/\text{pair} = \$2400$$

$$\text{Expected total cost/year} = 100 \text{ pairs} \times 2\text{yd/pair} \times £2/\text{yd} \times \$1.5/£$$

$$+ 100 \text{ pairs} \times \$8/\text{pair}$$

$$= \$1400$$

$$\therefore \quad \text{Expected profit} = \$2400 - \$1400 = \$1000/\text{year}$$

After the devaluation:

$$\text{Total revenue} = 100 \text{ pairs} \times \$24/\text{pair} = \$2400$$

$$\text{Total cost} = 100 \text{ pairs} \times 2\text{yd/pair} \times £2/\text{yd} \times \$2/£$$

$$+ 100 \text{ pairs} \times \$8/\text{pair}$$

$$= \$1600$$

$$\therefore \quad \text{Expected profit} = \$2400 - \$1600 = \$800/\text{year}$$

We find that the exporter's profit on contracted quantities and prices of jeans supplied and denim purchased is *reduced* by $200 per year because of the transaction exposure.

Effect of Operating Exposure

Before the devaluation:

$$\text{Expected profit} = \$1000/\text{year} \qquad \text{(as we just showed)}$$

After the contract expires: When the dollar price of jeans rises from $24 per pair to $25 per pair, the pound price falls from $24 ÷ $1.5/£ = £16 to $25 ÷ $2/£ = £12.5. This is a 21.875 percent price reduction. With a demand elasticity of –2, it will result in sales increasing by 43.75 percent to 143 pairs per year. It follows that after the contract expires

$$\text{Expected revenue} = 143 \text{ pairs} \times \$25/\text{pair} = \$3575$$

$$\text{Expected cost} = 143 \text{ pairs} \times 2\text{yd/pair} \times £2/\text{yard} \times \$2.0/£$$

$$+ 143 \text{ pairs} \times \$8/\text{pair}$$

$$= \$2288$$

$$\text{Expected profit} = \$3575 - \$2288 = \$1287/\text{year}$$

We find that the exporter's profit is increased by $287 ($1287 – $1000) per year from the devaluation because of operating exposure.

In this specific example the firm is likely to feel happy about the devaluation because in the long run it will come out ahead. It should be clear, however, that temporary setbacks from transaction exposure on payables can be serious.

SUMMARY

1. An exporting firm in a competitive market will experience a temporary increase in sales revenues and production costs after a real devaluation/depreciation of its currency. Revenues will rise by more than costs, and so profits will increase.
2. The higher temporary profit for a competitive firm will encourage new firms to get involved. This may limit the period of extra profit for any particular preexisting firm.
3. Higher input costs associated with a devaluation can also limit profit improvements. Increases in input costs can result from the effect of a devaluation on wages via a general inflationary impact or from the use of tradable inputs.
4. The home-currency price of an exporter's product will rise by the percentage of the devaluation and the foreign inflation rate when the product is sold in a competitive market.
5. An exporting firm in an imperfectly competitive market will experience an increase in total revenues and costs after a devaluation when amounts are measured in the firm's home currency. Revenues will rise by more than the increase in costs, and so profits will increase. The higher profits can persist if they are not offset by higher input costs. Revenues, costs, and profits that are measured in terms of foreign exchange will also increase from a devaluation.
6. The price of the goods sold by an exporter will, after a devaluation of the home currency, rise in terms of the home currency but fall in terms of the amount of foreign exchange. This happens because the home-currency price rises by a smaller percentage than the devaluation.

7. A devaluation raises the prices of imports in terms of the devalued currency and reduces the quantity that is imported and sold. Revenues and total costs in terms of dollars will fall, and so will the importer's profit. A revaluation lowers input prices and raises an importer's dollar revenues, total costs, and profits.

8. A devaluation lowers the prices of imports when these prices are measured in the foreign currency.

9. A dollar devaluation lowers an importer's revenue, costs, and profits in terms of the foreign currency. A revaluation will raise them.

10. When an arrangement exists to export to a foreign buyer a stated quantity at a price fixed in the home currency (or in foreign exchange that is sold forward), a devaluation can temporarily hurt the exporter. This is true in both dollar and foreign-currency units.

11. If prices in an export sales agreement are stated as foreign-currency amounts and these are not sold forward, a devaluation will raise the dollar revenues, costs, and profits of a U.S. exporter via both transaction and operating exposure.

12. An importer buying an agreed-upon quantity at an agreed-upon price in dollars (or with foreign exchange proceeds bought forward) will experience no change in dollar revenues, costs, or profits after a devaluation. An importer buying an agreed-upon quantity at prices invoiced in foreign exchange will experience unchanged dollar revenues, increased dollar costs, and reduced profits.

REVIEW QUESTIONS

1. What is meant by "operating exposure"?
2. What is a tradable input?
3. Are all imported inputs "tradable"?
4. In what way does an exporter's operating exposure depend on the elasticity of demand facing the exporter?
5. How does an exporter's operating exposure depend on the flexibility of production?
6. How does free entry in an industry affect operating exposure in the short run versus the long run?
7. How does the importance of tradable versus nontradable inputs affect an exporter's exposure?
8. How is exposure of a perfectly competitive exporter affected if the exporter's country produces only a tiny part of the world supply of the product the exporter sells?
9. Does the demand curve for an imperfectly competitive firm's product shift after a devaluation if the demand curve is drawn against the currency of the buyer, and if so how?
10. Does the exporter's demand curve shift after a devaluation when the curve is drawn against the exporter's home currency, and if so, in what way?
11. Why might an exporter care about the effect of a change in an exchange rate on the exporter's revenue, cost, and profit measured in terms of the currency of the *buyer* of the exporter's product?
12. How does the effect of a revaluation on an importer's domestic-currency price depend on the elasticity of demand for the product that is imported?
13. How does the effect of a devaluation on an importer's domestic-currency price compare to the size of the devaluation?
14. What happens to the quantity imported after a devaluation of the importer's currency?
15. What happens to an importer's total revenue after a devaluation of the importer's currency?

1. Rank the following export industries according to the amount of increase in sales volume you would expect to result from a fall in the value of the U.S. dollar.
   a. Wheat farming
   b. Automobile production
   c. Foreign travel to the United States
   d. Computer hardware
   Use diagrams in your answers.

2. Rank the industries in question **1** according to the effects of a devaluation/depreciation on profits. You may assume that there are different amounts of tradable inputs, different elasticities of demand, and so on.

3. Do you think that the United States is a sufficiently large importer of products in general so that the effect of a dollar depreciation would be eliminated by pressure on nominal wages from tradable-goods price increases? How about Canada, Fiji, or Iceland?

4. Assume that the elasticity of demand for Aviva's jeans is –2. Assume that production costs are constant and that there is a 10 percent dollar depreciation.
   a. By how much will the quantity sold increase?
   b. By how much will dollar revenues increase?
   c. By how much will foreign exchange revenues increase?
   d. By how much will costs increase?
   e. By how much will profits increase?

5. As in question **4**, assume that Aviva's jeans face an elasticity of demand of –2 with constant costs, and assume also approximately half the total cost is accounted for by denim cloth, which is imported. To an approximation, what will this mean for your answers in question **4?**

6. Redraw Figure 14.2 to show the *short-run effect* of a dollar *revaluation* on the profits of a U.S. exporter who sells in a competitive market.

7. Redraw Figure 14.2 to show the *long-run effects* of a dollar *revaluation* on the profits of a competitive U.S. exporter.

8. Redraw Figure 14.4 to show the effect of a *revaluation* of the dollar on a U.S. exporter in an imperfectly competitive market.

9. Redraw Figure 14.2 to show the effect of devaluation-induced cost increases when amounts are measured in foreign currency.

10. Why does a devaluation simultaneously raise export prices as measured in home currency and lower them as measured in foreign currency?

11. Redraw Figure 14.6 and Figure 14.7 to show the effect of a *revaluation* on revenues, costs, and profits.

12. Reconcile a rising domestic-currency price and a falling foreign-currency price for an imported good after a devaluation of the domestic currency. Why does this mean that the domestic-currency price rises by less than the percentage of devaluation?

13. What would the availability of very close substitutes for an import mean for the elasticity of demand of the firm that exports our imports? Who will bear the burden of devaluation in this case?

14. The "maquiladoras" are manufacturing companies located on the Mexican side of the U.S.-Mexican border, including many U.S. firms assembling goods for sale in the United States. What factors influence the size of operating exposure of these maquiladoras for their U.S. owners?

15. Under NAFTA, the operations of many firms are likely to be more integrated across North America's borders with, for example, manufacturers sourcing parts from U.S., Canadian, and Mexican factories. How might such integration influence operating exposure of a firm that integrates production but also sells its products throughout North America?

BODNAR, GORDON M., and WILLIAM M. GENTRY: "Exchange Rate Exposure and Industry Characteristics: Evidence from Canada, Japan and the U.S.A.," *Journal of International Money and Finance,* February 1993, pp. 29–45.

CEGLOWSKI, JANET: "Dollar Depreciation and U.S. Industry Performance," *Journal of International Money and Finance,* June 1989, pp. 233–251.

DUFEY, GUNTER: "Corporate Finance and Exchange Rate Changes," *Financial Management,* summer 1977, pp. 23–33.

FLOOD, EUGENE, JR.: "The Effect of Exchange Rate Changes on the Competitive Firm's Pricing and Output," unpublished, Massachusetts Institute of Technology, December 1981.

HEKMAN, CHRISTINE R.: "Measuring Foreign Exchange Exposure: A Practical Theory and Its Applications," *Financial Analysts Journal,* September/October 1983, pp. 59–65.

HUNG, WANSING, YOONBAI KIM, and KERICHI OHNO: "Pricing Exports: A Cross-Country Study," *Journal of International Money and Finance,* February 1993, pp. 3–28.

KALTER, ELLIOT R. J.: "The Effect of Exchange Rate Changes upon International Price Discrimination," International Finance Discussion Paper 122, Board of Governors of the Federal Reserve, Washington, D.C.

MARSTON, RICHARD: "Pricing to Market in Japanese Manufacturing," National Bureau of Economic Research, Working Paper Number 2905, 1989.

SHAPIRO, ALAN C.: "Exchange Rate Changes, Inflation and the Value of the Multinational Corporation," *Journal of Finance,* May 1975, pp. 485–502.

SUNDARAM, ANANT K., and VEENA MISHRA: "Exchange Rate Pass Through and Economic Exposure: A Review," Dartmouth College, working paper, October 1989.

APPENDIX 14.1
Exchange Rates and the Exporter and Importer—A Mathematical Treatment

---

THE EXPORTER

Consider the situation of a U.S. firm that exports to the British market. We shall present the effects of a change in the value of the dollar, first in terms of dollar amounts and then in terms of British pounds.

Effects in Terms of Home Currency (Dollars)

The total dollar revenue, TR, of our U.S. firm from selling its entire output in Britain can be written as

$$\text{TR} = Sp^{\pounds}q \tag{14A.1}$$

where S is the number of dollars per British pound, $p^{\pounds}$ is the sales price in British pounds in Britain, and q is the number of units sold. The total cost of production for the quantity q, if each unit costs the same, can be written in U.S. dollars as

$$\text{TC} = cq \tag{14A.2}$$

where c is the cost per unit in home currency.

A profit-maximizing firm will always equate marginal revenue and marginal cost in determining the amount to sell or, equivalently, in determining what price to charge. That is, it sets

$$\frac{d\text{TR}}{dq} = \frac{d\text{TC}}{dq}$$

By taking equation (14A.1) and equation (14A.2) and differentiating, using the fact that $dS/dq = 0$, since changes in the production of our firm could have no effect on the exchange rate, we have

$$Sp^{\pounds} + Sq\frac{dp^{\pounds}}{dq} = Sp^{\pounds}\left(1 + \frac{q}{p^{\pounds}}\frac{dp^{\pounds}}{dq}\right) = c \tag{14A.3}$$

The definition of elasticity of demand is that it is the percentage change in quantity, dq/q, divided by the percentage change in the price the buyer pays, $dp^{\pounds}/p^{\pounds}$. Writing η for the absolute value of the elasticity (since the elasticity is otherwise negative) allows us to write equation (14A.3) as

$$Sp^{\pounds}\left(1 - \frac{1}{\eta}\right) = c \tag{14A.4}$$

so that

$$p^{\pounds} = \frac{c}{S(1 - 1/\eta)} \tag{14A.5}$$

Equation (14A.5) tells our U.S. firm how to set its price abroad in pounds according to the cost of production, the prevailing exchange rate, and the elasticity of demand. We recall that firms with some control over price will always sell at a point where $\eta > 1$, that is, where MR is positive. This follows because the firm produces and sells where MR = MC, and we know that extra units always have positive costs (that is, MC > 0), so MR must also be positive. The relationship (14A.5) consequently makes sense only when $\eta > 1$.

If we differentiate equation (14A.5) with respect to S, since η and c are constants, we obtain

$$\frac{dp^£}{dS} = -\frac{c}{S^2(1 - 1/\eta)} = -\frac{p^£}{S} \qquad (14A.6)$$

Since we know that $p^£$ and S are both positive, we know that $dp^£/dS < 0$. This negative derivative means that a devaluation of the dollar (an increase in S, the price of a British pound) will lower the profit-maximizing British pound price that a U.S. firm exporting to Britain should charge. This is seen in the text from Figure 14.5.

To determine what changes in the exchange rate do to U.S. dollar revenues, we can find dTR/dS. We have

$$\frac{dTR}{dS} = p^£q + Sp^£ \frac{dq}{dp^£} \frac{dp^£}{dS} + Sq \frac{dp^£}{dS} = p^£q + Sq(1 - \eta)\frac{dp^£}{dS} \qquad (14A.7)$$

Now, equation (14A.6) gives us $dp^£/dS$, which when used in equation (14A.7) gives

$$\frac{dTR}{dS} = p^£q - Sq(1 - \eta)\frac{p^£}{S} = \eta p^£q \qquad (14A.8)$$

This expression tells us that $dTR/dS > 0$, since every term is positive. This means that a devaluation of the dollar (an increase in S) will increase the U.S. dollar revenues of our firm from sales to Britain. In general, a devaluation of a firm's own currency will raise the total revenue in domestic-currency units from sales abroad. This is consistent with the finding in part a of Figure 14.1, part a in Figure 14.2, and part a of Figure 14.4 in the text.

To determine the effect of exchange rates on profits arising from trade, we must first examine the effect on costs, dTC/dS. Since c is constant,

$$\frac{dTC}{dS} = c\frac{dq}{dS} = c\frac{dq}{dp^£} \frac{dp^£}{dS} = -c\frac{dq}{dp^£} \frac{p^£}{S} \qquad (14A.9)$$

In equation (14A.9) we use $dp^£/dS$ from equation (14A.6). By using $\eta = -(dq/dp^£)p^£/q$ we have

$$\frac{dTC}{dS} = \frac{\eta cq}{S} \qquad (14A.10)$$

Again, since the terms in equation (14A.10) are all positive, $dTC/dS > 0$, and we know that a devaluation of the dollar (an increase in S) will raise the dollar cost of production. This is consistent with the finding in part b of Figure 14.2 and part b of Figure 14.4 in the text.

We have learned that a devaluation of the dollar will raise dollar revenues and dollar costs. The impact on profits will depend on which has risen more. Since dollar profits, ϕ, are given by

$$\phi = TR - TC$$

so that

$$\frac{d\phi}{dS} = \frac{dTR}{dS} - \frac{dTC}{dS}$$

we get

$$\frac{d\phi}{dS} = \eta p^{\pounds} q - \frac{cq\eta}{S} = \eta q \left(p^{\pounds} - \frac{c}{S} \right)$$

where the factor in parentheses is the "markup" per unit in pounds. Since this is positive if profits were originally made, a devaluation of the dollar unambiguously raises dollar profits.

Effects in Terms of Foreign Currency (British Pounds)

In terms of British pounds, we can write

$$\text{TR}^{\pounds} = p^{\pounds} q \qquad \text{and} \qquad \text{TC}^{\pounds} = cq/S$$

Equating MR and MC, that is, equating $d\,\text{TR}^{\pounds}/dq$ and $d\,\text{TC}^{\pounds}/dq$, again gives, as in equation (14A.5),

$$p^{\pounds} = \frac{c}{S(1 - 1/\eta)}$$

and therefore, as in equation (14A.6),

$$\frac{dp^{\pounds}}{dS} = -\frac{c}{S^2(1 - 1/\eta)} = -\frac{p^{\pounds}}{S}$$

Now,

$$\frac{d\text{TR}^{\pounds}}{dS} = p^{\pounds}\frac{dq}{dS} + q\frac{dp^{\pounds}}{dS} = q(1 - \eta)\frac{dp^{\pounds}}{dS}$$

and so using $dp^{\pounds}/dS$ from equation (14A.6) allows us to write

$$\frac{d\text{TR}^{\pounds}}{dS} = \frac{cq\eta}{S^2} \tag{14A.11}$$

Since the terms in (14A.11) are positive, $d\,\text{TR}^{\pounds}/dS$ is unambiguously positive, so that a devaluation of the dollar will raise revenues in terms of British pounds. This is what we concluded in the text from Figure 14.5 and the added knowledge that demand must be elastic at chosen outputs of firms. Also,

$$\frac{d\text{TC}^{\pounds}}{dS} = c\frac{d(q/S)}{dS} = \frac{c}{S}\frac{dq}{dS} - \frac{cq}{S^2}$$

But

$$\frac{dq}{dS} = \frac{dq}{dp^{\pounds}}\frac{dp^{\pounds}}{dS} = -\frac{dq}{dp^{\pounds}}\frac{p^{\pounds}}{S} = \frac{q\eta}{S}$$

Therefore,

$$\frac{d\text{TC}^{\pounds}}{dS} = \frac{cq\eta}{S^2} - \frac{cq}{S^2} = \frac{c(\eta - 1)q}{S^2} \tag{14A.12}$$

Since equation (14A.12) is clearly positive, a devaluation of the dollar will raise production costs in terms of British pounds, even though this was not clear from part *b* of Figure 14.5 in the text. The effect on British-pound profits is given by

$$\frac{d\phi^£}{dS} = \frac{d\mathrm{TR}^£}{dS} - \frac{d\mathrm{TC}^£}{dS} = \frac{cq\eta}{S^2} - \frac{c(\eta-1)q}{S^2} = \frac{cq}{S^2} > 0$$

We discover that the British-pound value of profits for a U.S. firm selling in Britain will increase from a devaluation of the U.S. dollar.

THE IMPORTER

Effects in Terms of Home Currency (Dollars)

The total dollar revenue, TR, for a U.S. importer is

$$\mathrm{TR} = p^\$ q \qquad (14\mathrm{A}.13)$$

and the total cost, if each unit costs the same, is

$$\mathrm{TC} = Sc^£ q \qquad (14\mathrm{A}.14)$$

where $p^\$$ is the dollar sales price, q is the quantity imported and sold, $c^£$ is the fixed cost of the import in pounds, and S is the number of dollars per pound.

A profit-maximizing importer equates marginal revenue and marginal cost to determine the quantity to import and sell. By differentiating equation (14A.13) and equation (14A.14), we have

$$\mathrm{MR} = \frac{d\mathrm{TR}}{dq} = p^\$ + \frac{dp^\$}{dq} = p^\$\left(1 - \frac{1}{\eta}\right)$$

where η is the absolute value of $(p^\$/q)\,dq/dp^\$$, and

$$\mathrm{MC} = \frac{d\mathrm{TC}}{dq} = Sc^£$$

Equating MR and MC gives

$$p^\$ = \frac{Sc^£}{1 - 1/\eta} \qquad (14\mathrm{A}.15)$$

and so, since $c^£$ is fixed,

$$\frac{dp^\$}{dS} = \frac{c^£}{1 - 1/\eta} = \frac{p^\$}{S} > 0 \qquad (14\mathrm{A}.16)$$

That is, a dollar devaluation (an increase in S) will raise the dollar price of the good that is sold. We note that since firms always choose the elastic part of demand, our results make sense only when $\eta > 1$.

To determine the effect of exchange rates on U.S.-dollar revenues, we need $d\,\mathrm{TR}/dS$. We have

$$\frac{d\mathrm{TR}}{dS} = p^\$\frac{dq}{dS} + q\frac{dp^\$}{dS} = q(1-\eta)\frac{dp^\$}{dS}$$

which, when we use equation (14A.16), gives

$$\frac{d\mathrm{TR}}{dS} = \frac{p^\$ q}{S}(1-\eta) < 0 \qquad (14\mathrm{A}.17)$$

since $\eta > 1$ for any profit-maximizing firm. We learn that a devaluation of the dollar (an increase in S) must reduce U.S. dollar revenues, since the derivative is negative with $\eta > 1$. This is what we found in part a of Figure 14.6.

The effect of exchange rates on U.S. dollar costs is given by $d\,TC/dS$. Since $c^£$ is constant,

$$\frac{d\,TC}{dS} = c^£ q + Sc^£ \frac{dq}{dS} = c^£ q + Sc^£ \frac{dq}{dp^\$} \frac{dp^\$}{dS}$$

which, when we use equation (14A.16), gives

$$\frac{d\,TC}{dS} = c^£ q - c^£ q\eta = c^£ q(1 - \eta) < 0 \qquad (14A.18)$$

since $\eta > 1$. We learn that a devaluation reduces dollar costs (expenditures on imports), which is what we claimed but were unable to demonstrate directly in part b of Figure 14.6.

With revenues and costs in dollar terms both falling for our importer from a devaluation, the effects on profits will depend upon which falls by a larger amount. We learn, from equation (14A.17) and equation (14A.18), that

$$\frac{d\phi}{dS} = \frac{d\,TR}{dS} - \frac{d\,TC}{dS} = q(1 - \eta)\left(\frac{p^\$}{S} - c^£\right)$$

If the imported good is sold at a profit, then $p^\$/S$, which is the selling price in the United States in pounds, must exceed $c^£$, the cost in pounds; that is, $(p^\$/S) - c^£ > 0$. Since $1 - \eta < 0$ (because $\eta > 1$ for a profit maximizer), we can conclude that $d\phi/dS < 0$, that is, that the dollar profits of an importer are reduced from a dollar devaluation or depreciation. This was claimed but not proved in the text. Similarly, dollar profits rise from a dollar revaluation or appreciation. Of course, it is important that there be an initial profit. If there are initial losses—that is, if $(p^\$/S) - c^£ < 0$—profits will increase from a depreciation and decrease from an appreciation.

Effects in Terms of Foreign Currency (British Pounds)

In terms of British pounds, we can write $TR^£ = p^\$ q/S$, where as before, $p^\$$ is the dollar price of the imported good, which is what is relevant to the buyer. We can also write $TC^£ = c^£ q$, where $c^£$ is the constant pound cost of the import. Equating MR and MC, that is, $d\,TR^£/dq$ and $d\,TC^£/dq$, again gives

$$p^\$ = \frac{Sc^£}{1 - 1/\eta} \qquad (14A.19)$$

and therefore

$$\frac{dp^\$}{dS} = \frac{c^£}{1 - 1/\eta} = \frac{p^\$}{S} \qquad (14A.20)$$

We know that

$$\frac{d\,TR^£}{dS} = \frac{Sd(p^\$ q)/dS - p^\$ q}{S^2} = \frac{p^\$ q(1 - \eta)}{S^2} - \frac{p^\$ q}{S^2}$$

when we use the result of equation (14A.17). This gives

$$\frac{d\,TR^£}{dS} = -\frac{p^\$ q\eta}{S^2} < 0 \qquad (14A.21)$$

We can see that a devaluation of the dollar will unambiguously reduce British pound revenues. This is inevitable, since dollar revenues are known to fall, as we have shown, and since there are also fewer pounds to the dollar after a devaluation. The effect of exchange rates on British pound costs is

$$\frac{dTC^{\pounds}}{dS} = c^{\pounds}\frac{dq}{dp^{\$}}\frac{dp^{\$}}{dS} = -\frac{c^{\pounds}q\eta}{S} < 0 \qquad (14A.22)$$

where we use $dp^{\$}/dS$ from equation (14A.20). We see that like the British-pound value of revenues, the British-pound value of the total costs of the imports must fall after a devaluation.

The effect of exchange rates on profits is as follows:

$$\frac{d\phi^{\pounds}}{dS} = \frac{dTR}{dS} - \frac{dTC}{dS} = -\frac{p^{\$}q\eta}{S^{2}} + \frac{c^{\pounds}q\eta}{S} = \frac{q\eta}{S}\left(c^{\pounds} - \frac{p^{\$}}{S}\right)$$

That is, if the imported item is sold at a profit, so that, just as before, $(p^{\$}/S) - c^{\pounds} > 0$, we know that $d\phi/dS < 0$. In other words, a profitable importer loses in pounds from a devaluation. Since we have already learned that dollar profits are reduced by a devaluation, and since we know that there are fewer pounds per dollar after a devaluation, the lower pound profit from a devaluation should come as no surprise, and nor should the gains from a revaluation.

CHAPTER 15

Hedging Risk and Exposure

A good hedge keeps dogs off the yard.

—*Chicago Fed Letter,* November 1989

With the various forms of foreign exchange risk and exposure now defined, we can turn our attention to how they can be managed. However, before we proceed we must answer the question of whether corporate managers should incur the costs of hedging their exposure, or whether this should be left to shareholders. The choice between corporate-level and shareholder-level exposure is important because the preferred exposure of shareholders might differ from that of company managers. Indeed, shareholders may have to undo hedging by managers, thereby incurring hedging transaction costs twice. After dealing with the question of who should hedge, we consider a variety of means of hedging, employing the technique of **financial engineering** to contrast and compare the consequences of different hedging vehicles.

WHETHER TO HEDGE: MANAGERIAL HEDGING VERSUS SHAREHOLDER HEDGING

It is usually argued that the objective of management is to maximize the wealth of the company's shareholders. However, even though hedging reduces or even eliminates exchange-rate risk, and lower risk is valued by shareholders, it does not pay for a firm to hedge exchange-rate risk if shareholders can reduce this risk themselves for the same or lower cost; shareholders will not value risk reduction they can achieve as or more effectively themselves. This is particularly relevant because shareholders may be residents of different countries and have different risk perspectives.[1] However, several arguments have been advanced which suggest that managers rather than shareholders should hedge foreign exchange exposure. These arguments include:

---

[1]If PPP holds, the residence of shareholders should not matter provided tastes are similar; with PPP the same bundle of goods should cost the same in different countries.

1. A stable before-tax corporate income results in a higher average after-tax income than a volatile income of the same average value if corporate tax rates are progressive. This is because with progressive tax rates more taxes are paid in high-income periods than are saved in low-income periods.[2]

2. It may be difficult for shareholders to determine the amount of exposure in each currency that exists at any particular moment. Furthermore, even if the overall exposure is known, the share of this facing an individual shareholder may be so small that forward or swap hedging by the shareholder is impractical.[3]

3. Marketing of a company's product may be helped by a stable corporate income if buyers want assurance that the company will stay in business to service its product and supply parts.

4. Corporate employees may be frightened away by volatile corporate earnings, which might suggest less job security. Alternatively, those that accept employment might demand higher salaries to compensate for the employment uncertainty.

5. Bankruptcy costs constitute a higher reduction in corporate value when earnings are more volatile. It may be that suppliers of capital will demand higher returns to cover the expected bankruptcy costs.

6. Loan repayments can sometimes be triggered when earnings fall below a stated low level.

7. Managers may need to know the profit centers within a company in order to properly allocate marketing and R & D budgets. Leaving hedging to shareholders reduces the quality of information available to managers, because incomes of different divisions of the company can be a mixture of foreign exchange gains and losses and of operating income.[4]

8. There are hedging techniques involving selecting the currency of invoicing and buying inputs in markets or currencies of exports that are available to the firm but not to its shareholders.[5]

Let us assume that for one or more of these reasons it is the firm that should hedge. Before evaluating the techniques that are available for this purpose, let us give the problem a context by considering the hedging decision of importers and exporters, dealing first with the source of their risk and exposure.

---

[2]This and some of the other reasons given here for why managers rather than shareholders should hedge can be found in René Stulz and Clifford W. Smith, "The Determinants of Firms' Hedging Policies," *Journal of Financial and Quantitative Analysis,* December 1985, pp. 391–405, and Alan C. Shapiro, "Currency Risk and Relative Price Risk," *Journal of Financial and Quantitative Analysis,* December 1984, pp. 365–373.

[3]This impracticality is manifest in the large bid-ask spreads on small swap and forward transactions: a shareholder whose share of exposure is $100 might face a bid-ask spread that is 50 times that of the company whose exposure is, say, over $1 million, if the shareholder can find cover at all. We should note, however, that shareholders have ways of hedging other than using forward contracts and swaps. For example, they can hold a portfolio of shares in import- and export-oriented companies. If shareholders can select an alternative to the swap or forward markets, higher spreads are not a reason for firms rather than their shareholders to hedge.

[4]Of course, firms can calculate the profitability of different divisions "as if" they had hedged. However, this requires maintaining a lot of data on foreign-currency inflows and outflows as well as on forward exchange rates.

[5]Some of the reasons for corporate-level hedging given here, as well as further reasons, are mentioned in Exhibit 15.1, which discusses how the pharmaceutical giant, Merck & Co. Inc., views hedging.

EXHIBIT 15.1
To Hedge or Not to Hedge: Merck's Motives

The pharmaceutical giant, Merck & Co. Inc., does business in over 100 countries through approximately 70 subsidiaries. Because the company has 40 percent of total assets overseas and also has an important non-U.S. marketing presence, Merck's management has carefully considered whether it should hedge its foreign exchange exposure. The following excerpt from an article by the Treasurer and an Assistant Treasurer at Merck reinforces some of the reasons for hedging stated in the text. The article also adds some other reasons which are specific to technologically driven industries, such as the need for a steady income when committing to long-term R & D.

Over the long term, foreign exchange rate movements have been—and are likely to continue to be—a problem of volatility in year-to-year earnings rather than one of irreversible losses. . . . The question of whether or not to hedge exchange risk thus becomes a question of the company's own risk profile with respect to interim volatility in earnings and cash flows.

The desirability of reducing earnings volatility due to exchange can be examined from both external and internal perspectives.

EXTERNAL CONCERNS

These center on the perspective of capital markets, and accordingly involve matters such as share price, investor clientele effects, and maintenance of dividend policy. Although exchange fluctuations clearly can have material effects on reported accounting earnings, it is not clear that exchange-related fluctuations in earnings have significant effects on stock price. Our own analysis. . . .suggests only a modest correlation in recent years between exchange gains and losses and share price movements, a slight relationship in the strong dollar period—the scenario of greatest concern to us. . . .

With respect to investor clientele, exchange would seem to have mixed effects. To the extent that some investors—especially overseas investors—see Merck's stock as an opportunity for speculating on a weak dollar, hedging would be contrary to investors' interests. But, for investors seeking a "pure play" on the stocks of ethical drug companies, significant exchange risk could be undesirable. Thus, given this potential conflict of motives among investors, and recognizing our inability to ascertain the preferences of all of Merck's investor clienteles (potential as well as current), we concluded that it would be inappropriate to give too much weight to any specific type of investor.

On the issue of dividend policy, we came to a somewhat different conclusion. Maintaining Merck's dividend, while probably not the most important determinant of our share price, is nevertheless viewed by management as an important means of expressing our confidence in the company's prospective earnings growth. It is our way of reassuring investors that we expect our large investment in future research (funded primarily by retained earnings) to provide requisite returns. And, although both Merck and the industry in general were able to maintain dividend rates during the strong dollar period, we were concerned about the company's ability to maintain a policy of dividend *growth* during a future dollar strengthening. Because Merck's (and other pharmaceutical companies') dividend growth rates did indeed decline during the strong dollar 1981–1985 period, the effect of future dollar strengthening on company cash flows could well constrain future dividend growth. So, in considering whether to hedge our income against future exchange movements, we chose to give some weight to the desirability of maintaining growth in the dividend.

In general, then, we concluded that although our exchange hedging policy should consider capital market perspectives (especially dividend policy), it should not be dictated by them. The direct effect of exchange fluctuations on shareholder value, if any, is unclear; and it thus seemed a better course to concentrate on the objective of maximizing long-term cash flows and to focus on the potential effect of exchange rate movements on our ability to meet our internal objectives. Such actions, needless to say, are ultimately intended to maximize returns for our stockholders.

INTERNAL CONCERNS

From the perspective of management, the key factors that would support hedging against exchange volatility are the following two: (1) the large proportion of the company's overseas earnings and cash flows; and (2) the potential effect of cash flow volatility on our ability to execute our strategic plan—particularly, to make the investments in R & D that furnish the basis for future growth. The pharmaceutical industry has a very long planning horizon, one which reflects the complexity of the research involved as well as the lengthy process of product registration. It often takes more than 10 years between the discovery of a product and its market launch. In the current competitive environment, success in the industry requires a continuous, long-term commitment to a *steadily increasing* level of research funding.

Given the cost of research and the subsequent challenges of achieving positive returns, companies such as Merck require foreign sales in addition to U.S. sales to gen-

HEDGING OF RECEIVABLES AND PAYABLES

The Source of Risk and Exposure for Importers and Exporters

Importing and exporting firms can face significant exposure because of settlement delays when their trade is denominated in a foreign currency. An importer, for example, does not normally receive a product immediately after ordering it. Often, the product must first be produced, and this takes time. After production is completed, the goods must be shipped, and this again takes time. And after delivery, it is customary for the vending firm to grant the importer a short period of trade credit. As a result of all these delays the importer may not be required to pay until 6 months, a year, or even a couple of years after the order has been placed. Yet the price of a product is generally agreed on at the time of ordering.

As we explained in the preceding chapter, if an importer agrees on a price that is stated in the vendor's currency, the importer faces exposure on the account payable if steps are not taken to hedge it. Alternatively, if the price that is agreed upon is stated in the importer's currency, the exporter faces exposure on the account receivable if nothing is done to hedge it.[6] The exposure is due both to the delay between agreeing on the price and settling the transaction and to the settlement price being in terms of a foreign currency. However, the exposure can be hedged in various ways. Let us begin by considering hedging via the forward market.

Hedging via the Forward Market

Suppose that Aviva Corporation has placed an order with a British denim-cloth manufacturer for £1 million of fabric to be delivered in 2 months. Suppose also that

---

[6]Exposure exists if the import or export price is stated in any currency other than that of the importer or exporter. The frequent practice of stating prices in a major international currency such as the U.S. dollar means the importer and exporter can both face exposure if neither is an American firm.

the terms of agreement allow for 1-month trade credit after delivery, so that the sterling payment is due in 3 months.

One alternative open to Aviva is to buy £1 million forward for delivery on the settlement date. This will eliminate all uncertainty about the dollar cost of the denim. However, before Aviva can decide if forward hedging is a good idea, it must consider the cost. This can then be compared with the benefit of making the dollar cost certain. Let us therefore consider the cost and benefit of forward hedging.[7]

The Cost of Forward Hedging

If a firm does not hedge, there will be a gain or loss vis-à-vis hedging. However, this gain or loss is known only *ex post*. The relevant cost in deciding whether to hedge is not this *ex post* actual cost, but rather the *expected* cost. The expected cost of forward hedging is equal to the known cost of foreign currency if it is bought forward, minus the expected cost of the foreign currency if it is bought spot. That is, in the context of our example, the expected cost of buying pounds 3 months forward versus waiting and buying the pounds at the unknown future spot rate is

$$\text{Expected cost of hedging £ payables} \equiv F_{1/4}(\$/\text{ask£}) - S^*_{1/4}(\$/\text{ask£})$$

where $S^*_{1/4}(\$/\text{ask£})$ is the expected future spot cost of buying pounds in 3 months' time.[8]

As we showed in Chapter 3, *if speculators are risk-neutral and there are no transaction costs,* speculators will buy pounds forward when

$$F_{1/4}(\$/£) < S^*_{1/4}(\$/£) \tag{15.1}$$

This is because there is an expected gain from selling the pounds in the future at a higher spot price than will be paid when taking delivery of the pounds under the forward contract. Similarly, if

$$F_{1/4}(\$/£) > S^*_{1/4}(\$/£) \tag{15.2}$$

risk-neutral speculators will sell pounds forward and expect to gain by buying pounds spot when it is time to deliver the pounds on the forward contract. With speculation occurring whenever inequality (15.1) or (15.2) holds, and with this speculation forcing the forward rate toward the expected future spot rate, risk-neutral speculation and zero transaction costs ensure that

$$F_{1/4}(\$/£) = S^*_{1/4}(\$/£) \tag{15.3}$$

as was shown in Chapter 3. That is, with risk-neutral speculation and zero transaction costs the expected cost of hedging is zero.[9]

It is clear that for there to be an expected cost of hedging, one or both of the assumptions made in arriving at equation (15.3) must be invalid. These assumptions were:

---

[7]Exhibit 15.2 describes the choice between hedging and nonhedging alternatives.

[8]If we were instead to consider the expected cost of hedging pound receivables, the expected cost of hedging would be $F_{1/4}(\$/\text{bid£}) - S^*_{1/4}(\$/\text{bid£})$.

[9]This has given rise to the view that forward hedging is a "free lunch." See André F. Perold and Evan C. Shulman, "The Free Lunch in Currency Hedging: Implications for Policy and Performance Standards," *Financial Analysts Journal,* May/June 1988, pp. 45–50.

EXHIBIT 15.2
Different Corporate Choices over Hedging

As the following excerpt from *The Economist* indicates, there are different ways to face hedging, and some of the world's largest companies have made different choices. The excerpt focuses on hedging decisions of importers and exporters.

Currency volatility saddles exporters and importers with short-term trading risks—exchange rates may move against them between doing a deal and getting paid. They know, once a foreign deal is done, what their exposure—and hence their risk—in a currency will be. There are three things they can then do about it.

First, do nothing. They risk a real loss if exchange rates move against them. Second, hedge all exposure fully: they risk an opportunity loss (i.e., the money they could have made by doing nothing) if rates move in their favour. Or, third, try to predict the future exchange rate by hedging selectively. How do they choose?

Doing nothing might be sensible if exchange rates bobbed around only a little, averaging-out over a shortish period, and if small losses were excused by patient shareholders. It is the cheapest strategy. The company treasurer can devote his expensive time to cash management and raising funds as cheaply as possible. Doing nothing evidently involves risk, but it cannot strictly be called speculation—any more than never carrying an umbrella is speculating on the weather. It is more a faith in things working out on average.

Things don't work out that way in today's currency markets. Exchange rates go through long-term swings which do not relate to economic reality as perceived by importers and exporters. The long-term "overvaluation" of the dollar took Sir Freddie Laker, founder of the now-bust Laker Airways, by surprise in 1982. He left his dollar borrowings unhedged, the rising dollar pushed his sterling interest costs sky-high and contributed to his bankruptcy.

Some have better reasons for never hedging. BP receives 75% of its revenue in dollar-related currencies, but is a British company, with mainly British shareholders. It spent a long time deciding whether to hedge. Perhaps those shareholders expected exposure to the dollar—the currency of the oil trade. But it eventually decided in 1985 that they would wish it to stabilise BP's sterling earnings.

Others may have enviable natural hedges. Mr. Michael Harvey, group treasurer of Royal Dutch/Shell Group, is comforted by the tendency of petrol prices in oil-importing countries to offset exchange rates swings. Travel companies can pass risk onto compliant holiday makers by raising the prices given in their brochures if exchange rates move against them. They give no handouts if rates move the other way. . . .

Covering forward 100% does not, alas, insulate a company from the effects of the foreign exchange market, nor does it leave the treasurer indifferent to currency movements. If a sterling-based firm sells its dollar receipts three months forward, this merely delays by three months the impact on its sterling revenues of any change in the dollar-sterling rate. And in place of the risk of real loss the company can suffer an opportunity cost.

For Courtaulds' treasurer, "opportunity cost is acceptable, real loss isn't." This is an accountant's view—a real loss shows up in accounts, an opportunity loss doesn't. But the latter could become real in time, if a lucky, unhedged competitor cuts prices and steals business. Where full cover wins over not hedging is that it fixes an exporter's price list in his own currency for some time into the future and so lets him determine the required production costs and the achievable profits.

Jaguar provides an example. The British car manufacturer sells over half its cars in America. This produces an annual net flow of dollars to Jaguar of about $700m. By selling this entire flow forward for sterling Jaguar can, with certainty, print a price list in America, valid for one year, that is both competitive and consistent with its British costs of production. The exercise may well tell it that it must work at getting those British costs down, before the next American price list is printed, or raise its dollar prices.

Source: "Companies and Currencies: Payment by Lottery," *The Economist,* April 4, 1987, p. 81. © The Economist Newspaper Group, Inc. Reprinted with permission. Further reproduction prohibited.

1. Speculators are risk-neutral.
2. There are no transaction costs.

As it turns out, only the transaction-cost assumption is relevant for the existence of an expected net cost of hedging. Let us see why.

If speculators are risk-averse, they may not buy forward when the inequality (15.1) holds or sell forward when (15.2) holds. This is because with risk aversion, speculators will require an expected return for taking risk. This expected return is equal to the difference between $F_{1/4}(\$/£)$ and $S^*_{1/4}(\$/£)$. That is, risk aversion may result in a **risk premium** in the forward exchange rate; the risk premium is equal to the expected cost of hedging, assuming zero transaction costs.

Of course, there is no reason *a priori* why the need for a risk premium would result in inequality (15.2) holding rather than (15.1). The situation that prevails depends on how the forward market is imbalanced without any speculation occurring. For example, if forward purchases and sales of pounds from the combined hedging activities of importers, exporters, borrowers, investors, and interest arbitragers result in a net excess demand for forward pounds, then speculators will have to be drawn in to be sellers of forward pounds; otherwise, the forward exchange market will not be in equilibrium. In this case speculators will need an expected return from selling pounds, causing inequality (15.2) to be an equilibrium situation; with speculators selling pounds forward for more than the expected future spot value of the pound, speculators collect a forward risk premium.[10] However, the presence of such a risk premium is irrelevant for the hedging decision, for the following reason.

If there is an expected cost of hedging when buying pounds forward because $F_{1/4}(\$/£) > S^*_{1/4}(\$/£)$, the risk premium earned by the speculators who sell pounds forward must be appropriate for the risk they take; otherwise, more speculators would enter the market to sell pounds forward. If the hedgers who *buy* pounds forward have the same risk concerns as the speculators who *sell* them pounds forward, the hedgers receive a benefit that equals the expected cost. That is, the risk premium is paid by hedgers when buying pounds forward because this reduces risk to the hedger, just as it adds to the risk of the speculator. This means that if a company's shareholders are typical in their attitude toward the pound, the risk premium paid to buy (or sell) pounds forward comes with an offsetting benefit. That is, the presence of the forward risk premium is irrelevant in deciding whether to use the forward market.

Transaction Costs in Forward versus Spot Exchange Markets

Whereas the presence of a risk premium is irrelevant to the forward-hedging decision, this is not the case for transaction costs, because transaction costs constitute an expected cost of hedging. This cost arises because the bid-ask spreads on forward exchange are larger than that on spot exchange.[11] This means that even if in the absence of transaction costs

---

[10]The nature of the forward-market equilibrium, with speculators earning a premium for taking up imbalances in the forward market from the activities of hedgers, is described in Maurice Levi, "Spot versus Forward Speculation and Hedging: A Diagrammatic Exposition," *Journal of International Money and Finance,* April 1984, pp. 105–109.

[11]It can be argued that the bid-ask spread is larger on forward than on spot transactions because forward trading is riskier than spot trading, thereby basing the risk-premium and transaction-cost arguments both on the same source. However, in principle we might distinguish two types of risk. One risk is that faced by speculators who maintain open positions over time, the open positions being needed to balance the aggregate supply of, and demand for, forward exchange. (The mirror image of the imbalance of forward contracts absorbed by speculators consists of the net holdings of forward contracts by hedgers.) The other type of risk is that of banks accepting orders for forward purchases/sales, and trying

$$F_{1/4}(\$/£) = S^*_{1/4}(\$/£) \tag{15.3}$$

(that is, there is no risk premium), it would still be the case that

$$F_{1/4}(\$/\text{ask}£) > S^*_{1/4}(\$/\text{ask}£)$$

That is, transaction costs make the forward price of pounds higher than the expected future spot price. At the same time, we would expect transaction costs to result in

$$F_{1/4}(\$/\text{bid}£) < S^*_{1/4}(\$/\text{bid}£)$$

That is, the number of dollars received from selling pounds forward will be less than the expected number of dollars to be received from waiting and selling the pounds spot.

While the larger spread on forward than on spot transactions does mean an expected cost of forward hedging, this expected cost is small. There are two reasons for this. First, the transaction cost of (for example) buying pounds forward versus waiting and buying them spot is only the *difference* between the two transaction costs; a transaction cost is paid to buy the pounds whatever method is employed. Second, this difference between forward and spot transaction costs is small, because banks that buy and sell forward can readily hedge their positions. That is, the bid-ask spread on forward exchange is not due to the risk of changes in exchange rates over the maturity of the forward contract. Rather, it is due to the risk of changes in exchange rates *while covering a position the bank has taken*. This risk is higher in forward than in spot markets because forward markets are thinner.[12] However, the market for short maturity contracts is almost as deep as the spot market, and so the spreads on forward contracts used for hedging importers' and exporters' receivables and payables are only slightly higher than those on spot transactions.

The Benefit of Forward Hedging

What we have found is that the possibility of a risk premium on forward contracts is irrelevant because the expected cost of hedging is matched by a benefit, and that transaction costs constitute only a small cost of hedging via forward exchange. That is, there is an expected cost of buying or selling forward rather than waiting and buying or selling spot, but it is a very small cost. But how about the *benefit* of buying or selling forward? As we have explained, there are several benefits of forward hedging which are enjoyed if management hedges.[13] For example, forward hedging reduces taxes if tax rates are progressive, reduces expected bankruptcy costs, has marketing and hiring benefits, and can improve information on

---

to remain balanced at each moment in time. The former risk will cause what we have called a risk premium, while the latter will cause a larger bid-ask spread on forward than on spot transactions. Of course, both risks are related to uncertainty in exchange rates, and they differ only in the period of time over which the risk is faced.

[12]This was mentioned in Chapter 3.

[13]Of course, if shareholders (or management) hedge they reduce risk, but we cannot count this as a benefit to compare with the transaction cost of forward hedging, because, as we have just explained, the value of the benefit of reduced risk exactly equals the size of the risk premium in the forward rate that is paid for hedging. That is, we cannot count risk reduction as a benefit to shareholders or managers unless we also count the risk premium as an equal cost.

TABLE 15.1. Dollar Payments on £1-Million Accounts Payable Using Different Hedging Techniques

	Dollar Payment, Millions				
Technique	Rate* = 1.3	1.4	1.5	1.6	1.7 $/£
Unhedged	1.3	1.4	1.5	1.6	1.7
Forward £ purchase @$1.5/£	1.5	1.5	1.5	1.5	1.5
Futures £ purchase @$1.5/£	1.5±	1.5±	1.5±	1.5±	1.5±
$1.50/£ call option @$0.06/£	1.36	1.46	1.56	1.56	1.56
$1.40/£ call option @$0.12/£	1.42	1.52	1.52	1.52	1.52
$1.60/£ call option @$0.02/£	1.32	1.42	1.52	1.62	1.62

*Realized future spot exchange rates.

profit centers. These benefits accrue because hedging reduces the volatility of receipts and payments. Let us show how forward hedging reduces volatility within the context of our example of Aviva having agreed to pay £1 million in 3 months.

If Aviva does not hedge its £1 million account payable in 3 months, the dollar cost of the pounds will depend on the realized spot exchange rate at the time of settlement. The possible payments resulting from remaining unhedged are shown in the top line of Table 15.1. If instead of being unhedged Aviva decides to buy forward at $1.50/£, the cost of the pounds is $1.5 million, regardless of what happens to the spot rate by the time of settlement. This is shown on the second line of Table 15.1. Comparing the certain payment of $1.5 million via the forward contract with the uncertain payment if Aviva waits and buys pounds spot, we see that *ex post* it is sometimes better to hedge, and sometimes better not to hedge. However, since the gains from hedging versus not hedging equal the losses from hedging versus not hedging, on average the cost of the pounds is the same.[14] Let us make this our base case against which to compare alternative ways of hedging. Let us consider next hedging via the currency futures market.

Hedging via the Futures Market

If Aviva decides to hedge its pound payables exposure in the futures market and buys £1 million of futures contracts, it is necessary to post a margin. If subsequent to buying the futures contracts the price of these contracts declines, it is necessary to add to the margin account.[15] Alternatively, if the futures price increases, the margin account is credited by the amount gained. This addition or subtraction to the margin account is done on a daily basis and is called marking to market, as we said in Chapter 4. What marking to market means is that if, for example, the pound increases in value more than had been anticipated in the original pricing of the futures contract, at the maturity of the contract the margin account will include the

[14]The average of $1.3 million, $1.4 million, $1.5 million, $1.6 million, and $1.7 million, with equal probabilities of all outcomes, equals $1.5 million. Of course, this outcome is the result of assuming a zero expected hedging cost in determining the forward rate.

[15]As we mentioned in Chapter 4, it is necessary to supplement the margin only if it falls below the maintenance level.

value of the unanticipated increase in the value of the pounds represented by the futures contracts, as well as the original margin.

The gain that is made by buying pound futures contracts rather than waiting to buy spot pounds is the amount in or taken from the margin account minus what was originally placed in the account. This gain can be put towards buying the pounds on the spot market. As we saw in Chapter 4, the net result of paying the higher-than-anticipated spot rate for the pounds, and the compensation of the gain from the futures contracts, is to end up paying approximately the same for the pounds as if a forward rather than futures contract had been purchased. For example, if, in the pricing of the futures contracts for £1 million that Aviva purchased, the expected future spot exchange rate had implicitly been $1.5/£, and it turns out at the maturity date of the futures contracts that the actual spot rate is $1.7/£, then Aviva will find it has gained about $200,000 in its margin account. Aviva will, of course, have to pay $1.7 million for the £1 million pounds it needs, rather than $1.5 million that would have been paid with a forward contract. However, after the compensating gain in the margin account Aviva will be paying only approximately $1.5 million, the same as if the pounds had been purchased on the forward market. On the other hand, if the expected future spot rate had been $1.5/£, but the actual spot rate ended up at $1.3/£, Aviva would find it had contributed $200,000 to its margin account. Aviva would then buy the required £1 million for $1.3 million at the going spot rate, making the total cost of pounds $1.5 million. We find that whatever happens to the spot rate, Aviva pays approximately $1.5 million for its £1 million. The difference between using the forward and futures markets is that in the forward market all the payment is made at the end, whereas with the futures market some of the payment or compensation for the payment is made before the pounds are eventually bought at the spot rate.

As we explained in Chapter 4, because interest rates vary over time, it is possible that the amount in the margin account at the maturity of the futures contract, or the amount paid into the account and lost, does not bring the eventual price of the £1 million to exactly $1.5 million. For example, if interest rates are low when the margin account has a large amount in it and high when the margin account goes below the maintenance level, it could be that slightly more than $1.5 million is paid for the pounds. Alternatively, varying interest rates could make the eventual cost of the pounds slightly less than $1.5 million. This is the marking-to-market risk of futures contracts discussed in Chapter 4. Because of this risk, in Table 15.1 we write the cost of the £1 million when using the futures market as $1.5 ± million.

Hedging via the Options Market

If Aviva buys call options on pounds at a strike price of $1.50/£, the options will be exercised if the spot rate for the pound ends up above $1.50/£. The options to buy pounds will not be exercised if the spot rate for the pound is below $1.50/£, because it will be cheaper to buy the pounds at the spot rate; the option has no value. Table 15.1 shows the result of buying £1 million of $1.50/£ strike-price call options if the option premium, that is, the option price, is $0.06/£. At this option premium the cost of the option for £1 million is £1 million × $0.06/£ = $60,000. Let us examine the entries in Table 15.1 for the $1.50/£ call option to see how the entries are obtained.

If the realized spot rate at the time of payment is $1.30/£, then the $1.50/£ strike-price call option will not be exercised, and the pounds will be bought spot for

$1.3 million. However, $60,000 has been paid for the option, so we can think of the pounds as having a total cost of $1.36 million, as shown in Table 15.1.[16] Similarly, if the spot rate ends up at $1.40/£, the total cost of the pounds including the option premium is $1.46 million. If the spot rate is the same as the strike rate, both $1.50/£, then Aviva will be as well off to exercise as to buy spot, and in either case the total cost of pounds is $1.56 million. If the spot rate ends up at $1.60/£ or $1.70/£, Aviva will exercise and pay the call rate of $1.50/£, bringing the total cost of pounds to $1.56 million.

It is clear from examining Table 15.1 that the benefit of buying a call option on the pound when there is a pound payable is that it puts a ceiling on the amount that is paid for the pounds but allows the option buyer to benefit if the exchange rate ends up below the strike rate. It can similarly be demonstrated that if a firm has a receivable in pounds it can buy a put option and ensure that a minimum number of dollars is received for the pounds, and yet the firm can still benefit if the dollar value of the pound ends up higher than the strike rate.

Let us suppose that instead of buying a call option at a strike price of $1.50/£, Aviva buys one at a strike price of $1.40/£, which, if the spot rate at the time of buying the option is above $1.40/£, is an in-the-money option. Table 15.1 shows the effect of buying this option if it costs $0.12/£.

Aviva will not exercise the $1.40/£ call option if the eventually realized spot rate is $1.30/£. Instead, it will buy the pounds spot for $1.3 million. Adding the $0.12/£ × £1 million = $120,000 price of the option gives a total cost of £1 million, equal to $1.42 million. At a realized spot rate of $1.40/£ Aviva will be indifferent between exercising or buying spot. Either way the pounds will cost $1.52 million, including the cost of the option. At any spot rate above $1.40/£, the $1.40/£ call option will be exercised, and whatever the spot rate happens to be, the cost of the pounds is $1.40 million. When we include the amount paid for the option, this brings the cost to $1.52 million.

If Aviva chooses a $1.60/£ call option—which, if the spot rate of the pound at the time it is purchased is below this value, is an out-of-the-money option—and if the option premium is $0.02/£, then the effect is as shown on the bottom line of Table 15.1. These values are obtained in a similar fashion to those for the other options, recognizing that the option is exercised only when the spot rate ends up above $1.60/£.

A comparison of the effects of the different-strike-price options and of these versus forwards and futures can be made by looking along each row in Table 15.1. We can see that with the exposure of a payable in pounds, the out-of-the-money option (that with a strike price of $1.60/£) turns out to have been best if the pound ends up at a low value, but the in-the-money option (that with a strike price of $1.40/£) is best if the pound ends up at a high value. The at-the-money option is somewhere in between. All options are better than forwards and futures if the pound ends up very low, but options are worse if the pound ends up high. If the pound ends up at its expected value, $1.50/£, having used forwards or futures is *ex post* a little cheaper than having used options: the option time value is avoided.

---

[16]Our description is directly applicable to options on spot exchange, such as those trading on the Philadelphia Stock Exchange. For simplicity we exclude the opportunity cost of forgone interest on the payment for the option contract.

Hedging via Borrowing and Lending: Swaps

In the discussion of interest parity in Chapter 11 we pointed out that it is possible to use borrowing, investing, and the spot exchange market to achieve the same result as would be obtained by using the forward market. For example, Aviva can hedge its import of £1 million of denim fabric with payment due in 3 months by borrowing dollars, buying pounds spot with the dollars, and investing the pounds for 3 months in a pound-denominated security. If this is done, then in 3 months Aviva owes a known number of dollars on its dollar loan and receives a known number of pounds, just as with a forward contract. Let us consider the cost of hedging via borrowing and lending so that we can compare it with the cost of the forward market. We will use the notation introduced in Chapter 11 and will be careful to distinguish between borrowing and lending interest rates and between bid and ask exchange rates.

For every £1 Aviva wants in n years' time, where $n = \frac{1}{4}$ in our particular example, the company must purchase

$$£ \frac{1}{\left(1 + r_£^I\right)^n} \tag{15.4}$$

on the spot market. Here $r_£^I$ is the interest rate the pounds will earn—the pound investment rate—in the chosen pound-denominated security. For example, if $r_£^I = 0.12$, then if Aviva buys £970,874 immediately and invests it at 12 percent, it will receive £1 million in 3 months. The dollar cost of the spot pounds in (15.4) is

$$\$S(\$/\text{ask}£) \cdot \frac{1}{\left(1 + r_£^I\right)^n} \tag{15.5}$$

where $S(\$/\text{ask}£)$ is the cost of buying pounds spot from the bank. If the number of dollars in (15.5) has to be borrowed, then in n years Aviva will have to pay for each pound it receives

$$\$S(\$/\text{ask}£) \cdot \frac{\left(1 + r_\$^B\right)^n}{\left(1 + r_£^I\right)^n} \tag{15.6}$$

where $r_\$^B$ is Aviva's U.S. dollar borrowing rate.[17]

We should recall that this hedging technique involves:

1. Borrowing, if necessary, in home currency
2. Buying the foreign exchange on the spot market
3. Investing the foreign exchange
4. Repaying the domestic currency debt

Clearly, if the value in (15.6) is the same as the forward exchange rate for buying the pounds n years ahead, $F_n(\$/\text{ask}£)$, then Aviva will be indifferent to the choices of buying forward and going through this borrowing-investment hedging procedure. Indifference between these two hedging methods therefore requires that

---

[17]If Aviva does not have to borrow, but already has the dollars, we use Aviva's opportunity cost of dollars, $r_\$^I$, in place of $r_\$^B$.

$$S(\$/\text{ask}£) \frac{\left(1 + r_\$^B\right)^n}{\left(1 + r_£^I\right)^n} = F_n(\$/\text{ask}£) \qquad (15.7)$$

or

$$\left(1 + r_\$^B\right)^n = \frac{F_n(\$/\text{ask}£)}{S(\$/\text{ask}£)}\left(1 + r_£^I\right)^n \qquad (15.8)$$

Equation (15.8) is one of the forms of the interest parity condition. We find that when interest parity holds, an importer should not care whether he or she hedges by buying forward or by borrowing domestic currency and investing in the needed foreign currency. However, we note that since equation (15.7) involves a borrowing-investment spread—$r_\$^B$ versus $r_£^I$—interest parity may not hold exactly in this form. Specifically, because, *ceteris paribus*, $r_\$^B$ is high relative to $r_£^I$ as a result of borrowing rates exceeding lending rates, we expect the forward cost $F_n(\$/\text{ask}£)$ to be smaller than $S(\$/\text{ask}£) \dfrac{\left(1 + r_\$^B\right)^n}{\left(1 + r_£^I\right)^n}$. This would favor the use of forwards versus a swap.

Borrowing and investing can also be used by an exporter to hedge foreign exchange exposure. The exporter does the reverse of the importer. For example, if Aviva is to receive foreign currency for its jeans, it can sell it forward. Alternatively, it can:

1. Borrow in the foreign currency that is to be received
2. Sell the borrowed foreign currency spot for dollars
3. Invest or otherwise employ the dollars at home
4. Repay the foreign currency debt with its export earnings

Since the foreign currency debt will be repaid with the foreign exchange proceeds on its exports, Aviva will not have any foreign exchange exposure or risk. The amount borrowed should be such that the amount needed to repay the debt is equal to the export revenues that are to be received. If, for example, payment is due in n years, Aviva should borrow

$$£\frac{1}{\left(1 + r_£^B\right)^n}$$

for each pound it is due to receive; this will leave Aviva owing £1 in n years. This number of pounds will be exchanged for

$$\$S(\$/\text{bid}£) \cdot \frac{1}{\left(1 + r_£^B\right)^n}$$

where we use the bid rate on pounds because the borrowed pounds are sold forward. When invested in U.S. dollar securities this will provide

$$\$S(\$/\text{bid}£) \frac{\left(1 + r_\$^I\right)^n}{\left(1 + r_£^B\right)^n} \qquad (15.9)$$

at the time that payment for the jeans is received. The alternative is to sell the foreign pound receipts on the forward market at $F_n(\$/\text{bid}£)$. Clearly, an exporter will be indifferent between (1) using the forward market and (2) borrowing domestic currency and investing in foreign currency when

$$S(\$/\text{bid}£) \frac{\left(1 + r_\$^l\right)^n}{\left(1 + r_£^B\right)^n} = F_n(\$/\text{bid}£) \tag{15.10}$$

or

$$\left(1 + r_\$^l\right)^n = \frac{F_n(\$/\text{bid}£)}{S(\$/\text{bid}£)} \left(1 + r_£^B\right)^n \tag{15.11}$$

Equation (15.11) is another form of interest parity. Again, we conclude that if interest parity holds in this form, exporters receiving pounds are indifferent between selling them forward and using a swap. However, as before we note that, *ceteris paribus,* with $r_£^B$ high relative to $r_\$^l$ from the borrowing-investment spread, the left-hand side of Equation (15.10) is likely to be low vis-à-vis $F_n(\$/\text{bid}£)$.[18] Thus, more dollars are received from selling the pounds forward than using the swap.

Hedging via Currency of Invoicing

While it is usually a simple matter to arrange hedging via forwards, futures, options, or swaps, we should not overlook an obvious way for importers or exporters to avoid exposure, namely, by invoicing trade in their own currency.[19] For example, if Aviva can negotiate the price of its imported denim cloth in terms of U.S. dollars, it need not face any foreign exchange risk or exposure on its imports. Indeed, in general, when business convention or the power that a firm holds in negotiating its purchases and sales results in agreement on prices in terms of the home currency, the firm that trades abroad will face no more risk and exposure than the firm with strictly domestic interests. However, even when trade can be denominated in the importer's or exporter's local currency, only part of the risk and exposure is resolved. For example, an American exporter who charges for his or her products in U.S. dollars will still find the level of sales dependent on the exchange rate, and hence faces operating exposure and risk. This is because the quantity of exports depends on the price the foreign buyer must pay, and this is determined by the rate of exchange between the dollar and the buyer's currency. Therefore, even when all trade is in local currency, some foreign exchange exposure—operating exposure—will remain.

Of course, only one side of an international deal can be hedged by stating the price in the importer's or exporter's currency. If the importer has his or her way, the exporter will face the exchange risk and exposure, and vice versa.

When there is international bidding for a contract, it may be wise for the company calling for bids to allow the bidders to state prices in their own currencies. For

[18]For more on how borrowing-investment spreads and currency transaction costs affect costs of alternative hedging techniques, see Maurice D. Levi, "International Financing: Currency of Issue and Management of Foreign Exposure," *World Congress Proceedings,* 14th World Congress of Accountants, Washington, D.C., October 1992, pp. 13A.1–13A.12.

[19]The fact that this method has been overlooked became clear from a survey of firms conducted by Business International. See "Altering the Currency of Billing: A Neglected Technique for Exposure Management," *Money Report,* Business International, January 2, 1981, pp. 1–2.

example, if Aviva invites bids to supply it with denim cloth, Aviva may be better off allowing the bids to come in stated in pounds, marks, and so on, rather than insisting on dollar bids. The reason is that the bidders cannot easily hedge, because they do not know if their bids will succeed. (They can use options, but options contracts from options exchanges are contingent on future spot exchange rates rather than the success of bids, and so are not ideally suited for the purpose.) When all the foreign-currency-priced bids are in, Aviva can convert them into dollars at the going forward exchange rates, choose the cheapest, and then buy the appropriate foreign currency at the time it announces the successful bidder. This is a case of asymmetric information, where the buyer can hedge and the seller cannot, and where the seller may therefore add a risk premium to the bid. When the *seller* is inviting bids, as when equipment or a company is up for sale, the seller knows more than the buyer, and so bidding should be in the buyer's currency.

So far we have considered situations in which all of the exposure is faced by the importer or the exporter. However, another way of hedging, at least partially, is to mix the currencies of trade.

Hedging via Mixed-Currency Invoicing

If the British mill were to invoice its denim at £1 million, Aviva would face the exchange exposure. If instead Aviva agreed to pay, for example, $1.5 million, then it would be the British mill that accepted the exposure. In between these two extreme positions is the possibility of setting the price at, for example, £500,000 plus $750,000. That is, payment could be stated partly in each currency. If this were done and the exchange rate between dollars and pounds varied, Aviva's exposure would involve only half of the funds payable—those that are payable in pounds. Similarly, the British mill would face exposure on only the dollar component of its receivables.

The mixing of currencies in denominating sales contracts can go further than a simple sharing between the units of currency of the importer and exporter. It is possible, for example, to express a commercial agreement in terms of a **composite currency unit**—a unit that is formed from many different currencies. A prominent composite unit, which was mentioned in Chapter 9, is the Special Drawing Right, or SDR. This unit is constructed by taking a weighted average of five of the major world currencies. Another officially maintained currency unit, which was mentioned in Chapter 8, is the European Currency Unit (ECU), which consists of an average of the exchange rates of the European Union countries. Besides the official SDR and ECU units, there are private **currency baskets,** or **cocktails,** which are also designed to move smoothly. They are formed by various weighted averages of a number of different currencies.

The composite currency units will reduce risk and exposure because they offer some diversification benefits. However, they cannot eliminate risk and exposure as can a forward contract, and they themselves can be difficult to hedge forward. It is perhaps because of this that cocktails and baskets are not as common in denominating trade, where forward, futures, options, and swaps are frequently available, as they are in denominating long-term debt, where these other hedging techniques are not as readily available.

A large fraction of the world's trade is, by convention and for convenience, conducted in U.S. dollars. This is an advantage for American importers and exporters in that it helps them avoid exchange-rate exposure. However, when the U.S. dollar is used in an agreement between two non-American parties, *both* parties experience exposure. This situation occurs often. For example, a Japanese firm may purchase Canadian raw materials at a price denominated in U.S. dollars. Often both parties can hedge, for example, by engaging in forward exchange contracts. The Japanese importer can buy and the Canadian exporter can sell the U.S. dollars forward against their own currencies. In the case of some of the smaller countries where foreign business is often expressed in dollar terms, there may not be regular forward, futures, options, or swap markets in the country's currency. However, the denomination of trade in U.S. dollars might still be seen as a way of reducing exposure and risk if the firms have offsetting business in the dollar, or view the dollar as less volatile in value than the currency of either party involved in the trade.

Hedging via Selection of Supplying Country: Sourcing

A firm that can invoice its inputs in the same currency as it sells its goods can offset foreign-currency payables against receivables. This type of hedging practice is called **sourcing.** For example, Aviva Corporation might buy its denim cloth in the currencies in which it sells its jeans. If about one-half of the wholesale value of jeans is the value of the material, then on each pair of jeans the firm has only about one-half of the foreign exchange exposure of the jeans themselves. Aviva could buy the denim in the various currencies in rough proportion to the volume of sales in those currencies.

The risk-reducing technique of buying inputs in the currencies in which outputs are sold has a clear disadvantage: Aviva should buy its denim where the material is cheapest, and it should not pay more for its cloth just to avoid foreign exchange exposure. However, after an input source has been chosen at the best price, there will be some automatic hedging occurring in that currency. For example, if Aviva settles on buying its denim in Britain because the cloth is cheapest there, the total value of the jeans that it sells in that market should be netted against its denim purchases.

Now that we have explained the different techniques that are available for hedging exposure, we can consider their different consequences. This can be done most easily by examining payoff profiles, which, as we saw in Chapters 3 and 4, show graphically the rewards and/or costs of selecting different methods of hedging.

FINANCIAL ENGINEERING: PAYOFF PROFILES OF DIFFERENT HEDGING TECHNIQUES

Forward Profile

As before, let us assume the expected future spot rate is $1.50/£. Then the difference between the realized spot rate and this expected rate is the unanticipated change in the exchange rate, which we have previously written as ΔS^u.

When the expected spot rate for 3 months ahead is $1.50/£, and the spot rate indeed turns out to be $1.50/£, if Aviva has bought pounds forward at $1.50/£, the forward contract has a value of zero. Let us write this as $\Delta V = 0$, where we can think of ΔV as the gain or loss by having purchased the forward contract. If instead of $1.50/£, the realized spot rate happens to be $1.70/£ so that $\Delta S^u = \$0.2/£$, Aviva's forward contract to buy £1 million at $1.50/£ is worth $\$0.2/£ \times £1$ million $= \$0.2$ million. Then we can write ΔV as $0.2 million. Alternatively, if for example, the realized spot rate is $1.30/£ so that $\Delta S^u = -\$0.2/£$, then Aviva's $1.50/£ contract has a negative value of $-\$0.2/£ \times £1$ million $= -\$0.2$ million, because forward contracts, unlike options, must be honored. These and other values of ΔV are shown against the unanticipated changes in spot rates that bring them about in the first column of Table 15.2.

The values of ΔV and ΔS^u for the £1-million forward contract at $1.50/£ are plotted against each other in the left-hand panel of Figure 15.1a. We find an upward-sloping line because the forward contract has positive value when the pound experiences unanticipated appreciation ($\Delta S^u > 0$) and negative value when the pound experiences unanticipated depreciation ($\Delta S^u < 0$).

The middle panel of Figure 15.1a shows the underlying exposure for the £1-million account payable. The exposure is represented by a line with negative slope, showing a loss if the pound unexpectedly appreciates and a gain if the pound unexpectedly depreciates.

The right-hand panel of Figure 15.1a shows the effect of hedging pound payables with a forward purchase of pounds. The figure is obtained by adding the two ΔV's from the left-hand and middle panels at each ΔS^u. We find that the combination of a forward purchase of pounds and the underlying payables exposure produces a line with a zero slope. That is, the forward contract eliminates exposure on the account payable. Figure 15.1 is an example of how to use payoff profiles to see the effect of different hedging techniques. The approach of adding profiles is sometimes called financial engineering.

Futures Profiles

Table 15.2 shows the gains or losses on futures contracts to purchase £1 million at different unanticipated changes in the exchange rate. We see, for example, that if the future spot rate had been expected to be $1.50/£, but the realized rate turns out to be $1.30/£, that is, $\Delta S^u(\$/£) = -0.2$, then by buying £1 million via pound futures Aviva will find that it has lost approximately $0.2 million. This $0.2 million will have

TABLE 15.2. Payoffs from Different Hedging Techniques

	ΔV, millions of $				
$\Delta S^u(\$/£)$	Forward Contract	Futures Contract	At-the-money Option	In-the-money Option	Out-of-the-money Option
−0.2	−0.2	−0.2±	−0.06	−0.12	−0.02
−0.1	−0.1	−0.1±	−0.06	−0.12	−0.02
0	0.0	0.0±	−0.06	−0.02	−0.02
0.1	0.1	0.1±	0.04	0.08	−0.02
0.2	0.2	0.2±	0.14	0.18	0.08

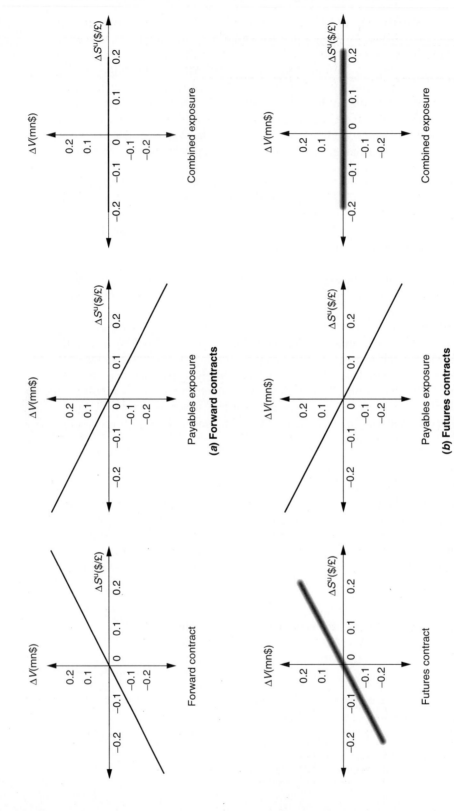

FIGURE 15.1. Payoff Profiles, Payables Exposure, and Resulting Exposure with Forward and Futures Contracts

When there is exposure on foreign-currency payables, as in the middle figures of parts *a* and *b*, the exposure can be hedged by buying the foreign currency forward or by buying a futures contract. The payoff profiles on the forward and futures contracts are shown in the left-hand figures of *a* and *b*. When the exposure profiles are combined, as in the right-hand figures of *a* and *b*, we can visualize the effects of hedging. The forward contract removes all exposure and risk, while the futures contract leaves marking-to-market risk.

been moved through Aviva's margin account. We note that the expected loss on futures contracts is the same as the loss from buying pounds forward. However, in the case of futures we add ± to the amount lost because the actual ΔV is unknown due to volatility of interest rates. Other values of ΔS^u also give rise to the same expected ΔV's on futures contracts as on forward contracts, but the actual ΔV's are uncertain for futures contracts, due to marking-to-market risk.

The values of ΔV and ΔS^u for the purchase of £1 million of futures contracts are plotted against each other in the left-hand panel of Figure 15.1b. We show a broadened line because of marking-to-market risk. The middle panel of the figure shows the underlying exposure on the £1-million account payable. When the two panels are combined by adding the ΔV's at each ΔS^u we obtain the right-hand panel. We see that the resulting combined exposure line has zero slope, thereby signifying elimination of exposure, but we see there is still risk.

Options Profiles

The middle column of Table 15.2 shows the values of an option to buy £1 million at a strike price of $1.50/£ for different realized spot exchange rates.[20] As before, we assume the option premium is $0.06/£, so that the option costs Aviva $60,000. Table 15.2 shows that if the realized spot rate is $1.30/£, $1.40/£, or $1.50/£, the option is not exercised, and so by buying the option Aviva loses $0.06 million. At a realized spot rate of $1.60/£ the option is worth $0.10 million, which, after subtracting the $0.06 million cost of the option, is a gain of $0.04 million. Similarly, at a spot rate of $1.70/£ the option is worth $0.20 million, or $0.14 million after considering its cost. These values of ΔV are plotted against the associated ΔS^u's, assuming the expected spot exchange rate is $1.50/£, in the left-hand panel of Figure 15.2a.

The middle panel of Figure 15.2a again shows the underlying exposure of £1 million of payables, and the right-hand panel shows the effect of combining the option and the underlying exposure. As before, this involves adding the ΔV's at each ΔS^u. We find that hedging with the pound call option allows Aviva to gain when the pound ends up somewhat cheaper than expected, because unlike the forward or futures contracts, the option does not have to be exercised if this occurs. However, this benefit comes at the expense of being worse off than by buying pounds forward when the pound ends up above or at its expected value. This is the same conclusion that we reached earlier, but the payoff profile gives us a straightforward way of seeing this, and of comparing the outcomes from different hedging techniques.[21]

The effects of using in-the-money and out-of-the-money call options to hedge an underlying short pound exposure, assuming the spot rate is $1.50/£, are described in Figure 15.2b and c. These graphs are based on the values in Table 15.2, which were obtained in the same fashion as the values for the at-the-money option. We see from the payoff profiles that both options allow the hedger to benefit if the

[20]This is an at-the-money option if the spot rate at the time the option is purchased is $1.50/£.
[21]For other examples of payoff profiles for hedging strategies see "Why Do We Need Financial Engineering?" *Euromoney,* September 1988, pp. 190–199. Another excellent introduction to the ways different instruments can be "clipped together" to form different payoff profiles is Charles W. Smithson, "A LEGO Approach to Financial Engineering: An Introduction to Forwards, Futures, Swaps, and Options," *Midland Corporate Finance Journal,* winter 1987, pp. 16–28.

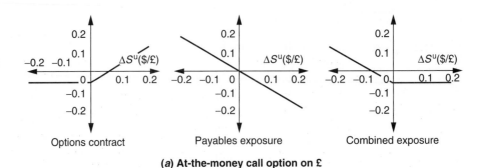

(a) At-the-money call option on £

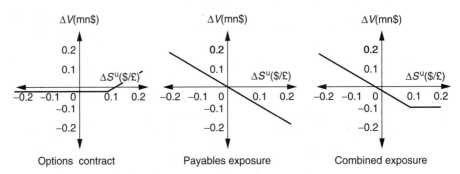

(b) In-the-money call option on £

(c) Out-of-the-money call option on £

FIGURE 15.2. Payoff Profiles from Option Hedges
The center figures in *a*, *b*, and *c* show the exposure line for a foreign currency payable. The left-hand figures in a, *a*, *b*, and *c* show the payoff profiles for call options on the foreign currency. In *a* the option is at-the-money, in *b* the option is in-the-money, and in *c* the option is out-of-the money. By combining the profiles for the underlying exposure and the different options the hedges can be visually compared.

pound is lower than was expected. However, the gain is less for the in-the-money option, because this is more expensive. On the other hand, if the pound unexpectedly appreciates, the in-the-money option is exercised at a lower price of the pound and so there is a benefit that offsets the higher price of the option. The choice between options with different strike prices depends on whether the hedger wants to insure only against very bad outcomes for a cheap option premium (by using an out-of-the money option) or against anything other than very good outcomes (by using an in-the-money option).

The payoff profile for swaps is exactly the same as for forward contracts, because, as with forward contracts, payment or receipt of dollars occurs in the future at the time the pounds are received or paid. For example, the borrowing of dollars combined with the spot purchase and investment of pounds produces an upward-sloping payoff profile like that in the left-hand panel of Figure 15.1*a*, which when combined with the underlying exposure on pound payables leaves Aviva with zero exposure.

Hedging via denominating trade in domestic currency eliminates the underlying exposure, giving a flat exposure profile. Mixed-currency invoicing and buying inputs in the currency of exports reduce the slope of the exposure line but leave some risk.

Hedging Risk and Exposure

SUMMARY

1. There are several reasons why hedging should be performed by the firm rather than its shareholders. These include progressive corporate taxes, scale economies in hedging transactions, marketing and employment benefits, lower expected bankruptcy costs, and better internal information.

2. An importer or exporter faces exposure and risk because of delay between agreeing on a foreign-currency price and settling the transaction.

3. The expected cost of hedging is the difference between the forward exchange rate and the expected future spot rate.

4. The decision to use forward hedging does not depend on there being a forward risk premium. However, if the bid-ask spread on forward transactions exceeds that on spot transactions, there is an expected cost of forward hedging.

5. The bid-ask spread on short-maturity forward transactions does not substantially exceed that on spot transactions, so that the expected cost of forward hedging is small. Because there are several benefits of forward hedging, it generally pays to use the forward market.

6. Futures-market hedging achieves essentially the same result as forward hedging. However, with futures the foreign exchange is bought or sold at the spot rate at maturity, and the balance of receipts from selling a foreign currency or cost of buying a foreign currency is reflected in the margin account. Because interest rates vary, the exact receipt or payment with futures is uncertain.

7. Foreign-currency accounts payable can be hedged by buying a call option on the foreign currency, and accounts receivable can be hedged by buying a put option on the foreign currency. Options set a limit on the worst that can happen from unfavorable exchange-rate movements without preventing enjoyment of gains from favorable exchange-rate movements.

8. An importer can hedge with a swap by borrowing in the home currency, buying the foreign-currency spot, and investing in the foreign currency. Exporters can hedge with a swap by borrowing in the foreign currency, buying the home-currency spot, and investing in the home currency.

9. Foreign exchange exposure can be eliminated by invoicing in domestic currency. Exposure can be reduced by invoicing in a mixture of currencies or by buying inputs in the currency of exports.

10. Payoff profiles provide a graphical comparison of the consequence of using different hedging techniques.

REVIEW QUESTIONS

1. How is the manager-versus-shareholder hedging choice influenced by progressive corporate income tax?
2. How is the manager-versus-shareholder hedging choice influenced by economies of scale when buying or selling forward exchange?
3. Are there informational gains to managers if they hedge foreign exchange exposure? How might the information be obtained without hedging?
4. What types of products might sell better when firms hedge foreign exchange exposure?
5. Why might expected bankruptcy costs be higher for firms that do not hedge than for those that do?
6. How does the expected cost of hedging forward relate to spot versus forward exchange-rate spreads?
7. Would a typical hedger be willing to pay a risk premium in order to hedge by buying foreign currency forward?
8. How does the risk of hedging via futures compare to that of hedging via forward exchange?
9. What type of swap would an American importer of Japanese-yen-invoiced products use?
10. Can importers and exporters simultaneously hedge by selecting the currency of invoicing, and are there any compromise invoicing strategies?
11. What is a composite currency unit?
12. Name two composite currency units.
13. What is meant by "sourcing"? Should this be used as a method of hedging foreign exchange exposure?
14. Why do you think financial engineering has been refered to as a "LEGO® approach" to financial decision making?

ASSIGNMENT PROBLEMS

1. In what sense are the forward risk premium and the bid-ask spread on forward contracts both related to risk? Does the fact that the bid-ask spread is always positive and yet the forward risk premium can be positive or negative suggest that the nature of the risk behind them is different?
2. Suppose that you were importing small electric transformers, that delivery from all suppliers would take approximately 6 months, and that you faced the situation shown in the table below:

	United States	Canada	Great Britain	France	Germany
Local cost	$20,000	Can$22,000	£10,000	Fr82,000	DM38,000
$S(\$/j)$	1	0.84	2.00	0.20	0.50
$S^*_{1/2}(\$/j)$	1	0.82	2.05	0.19	0.52
$F_{1/2}(\$/j)$	1	0.83	2.02	0.21	0.54

   a. Where would you buy if you decided on forward hedging?
   b. Where would you buy if you decided on being unhedged?
   c. If you knew that your own expected future spot rates were also the market's expected spot rates, could you deduce from the table if there is a forward risk premium?

3. Why might managers' motivations to hedge against foreign exchange exposure differ from those of company shareholders?

4. It has been said that expected bankruptcy costs can help explain the use of equity versus debt in corporate financial structure, even though interest but not dividends are tax-deductible. Can bankruptcy costs also explain hedging practices that on average reduce expected earnings?

5. If a currency can be sold forward for more than the currency's expected future value because of a risk premium on the currency, do the sellers of that currency enjoy a "free lunch"?

6. Why is the cost of forward hedging half of the difference between the forward and spot bid-ask spreads?

7. Assume that you are importing German transformers and that you face the following:

$r_\$^B$	12%
r_{DM}^I	8%
$S(\$/askDM)$	0.5000
$F_{1/2}(\$/askDM)$	0.5100

   a. How would you hedge? Would you buy Deutschemarks forward or would you borrow, buy spot, and invest in Deutschemarks for 6 months?

   b. Would it make any difference in your choice of hedging technique if you already had dollars that were earning 10 percent?

8. Suppose that as the money manager of a U.S. firm you faced the following situation:

$r_\$^B$	9.0%
$r_\$^I$	8.0%
$r_{C\$}^B$	10.5%
$r_{C\$}^I$	9.5%
$S(C\$/ask\$)$	1.2400
$S(C\$/bid\$)$	1.2350
$F_1(C\$/ask\$)$	1.2600
$F_1(C\$/bid\$)$	1.2550

Here, $r_\$^B$ and $r_\$^I$ are the 1-year interest rates at which you can, respectively, borrow and invest in the United States, and $r_{C\$}^B$ and $r_{C\$}^I$ are the 1-year borrowing and investing interest rates in Canada.

   a. If you had funds to invest for 1 year, in which country would you invest?

   b. If you wished to borrow for 1 year, in which country would you borrow?

   c. What is it that induces you to borrow and invest in the same country?

   d. If you needed Canadian dollars to pay for Canadian goods in 1 year and were not holding U.S. dollars, would you buy forward or use a swap?

   e. If you needed Canadian dollars to pay for Canadian goods in 1 year and already had some U.S. dollars, would you buy forward or use a swap?

BIBLIOGRAPHY

Euromoney: "Why Do We Need Financial Engineering?" *Euromoney*, September 1988, pp. 190–199.

Khoury, Sarkis J., and K. Hung Chan: "Hedging Foreign Exchange Risk: Selecting the Optimal Tool," *Midland Corporate Finance Journal*, winter 1988, pp. 40–52.

Levi, Maurice: "Spot versus Forward Speculation and Hedging: A Diagrammatic Exposition," *Journal of International Money and Finance*, April 1984, pp. 105–109.

PEROLD, ANDRÉ F., and EVAN C. SHULMAN: "The Free Lunch in Currency Hedging: Implications for Investment Policy and Performance Standards," *Financial Analysts Journal,* May/June 1988, pp. 45–50.

SMITHSON, CHARLES W.: "A LEGO Approach to Financial Engineering: An Introduction to Forwards, Futures, Swaps, and Options," *Midland Corporate Finance Journal,* winter 1987, pp. 16–28.

STULZ, RENÉ, and CLIFFORD W. SMITH: "The Determinants of Firms' Hedging Policies," *Journal of Financial and Quantitative Analysis,* December 1985, pp. 391–405.

Speculation, Market Efficiency, and Forecasting

The proportion of (monthly or quarterly) exchange rate changes that current models can explain is essentially zero.

—RICHARD MEESE

The three matters discussed in this chapter, namely, speculation in foreign exchange, the efficiency of foreign exchange markets, and the ability to forecast exchange rates, are very closely related. For example, if speculators can earn average returns that are abnormally high, then markets must not be efficient, and speculators must be able to forecast exchange rates better than the market. Because of the closeness of connections between the issues, this chapter deals first with speculation, then with market efficiency, and finally with forecasting. After explaining the vehicles of foreign exchange speculation, the evidence on market efficiency is examined. The chapter then turns to the record on exchange-rate forecasting, including a comparison of chartist versus fundamental forecasting techniques. The record of chartists versus fundamentalists is linked back to market inefficiency, specifically to the ability to earn from speculation using relatively simple trading rules.

It should be mentioned at the outset that opinions differ widely on the matters discussed in this chapter, and by no means do all researchers agree that abnormal speculative returns and market inefficiencies have been detected. Nevertheless, despite a traditional predisposition among finance researchers against finding abnormal returns to speculation, market inefficiencies, and chartist-forecasting success, when it comes to foreign exchange markets, traditional notions face a challenge.

SPECULATION

When many think of speculators in the foreign exchange market, they have an image of fabulously rich, overweight men in vested suits moving massive amounts of money and providing themselves with handsome profits. The phrase "the gnomes of Zurich" was coined by a former British Chancellor of the Exchequer when his country faced what he perceived as an outright attack on its currency by those ever-hungry and apparently heartless manipulators. In spite of the images we might have, it can be argued, as we did in Chapter 8, that speculators play a useful role in stabilizing exchange rates. However, our initial purpose here is not to discuss the merits of speculation but rather to simply describe the different ways to speculate. As we shall see, these are the same as the different ways to hedge, namely, via forwards, futures, options, and swaps.

Speculating via the Forward Market

Speculating without Transaction Costs

If we write a speculator's expected spot exchange rate in n years as $S_n^*(\$/\pounds)$, then, as we have indicated, if the speculator is risk-neutral and we ignore transaction costs, he or she will want to buy pounds n years forward if[1]

$$F_n(\$/\pounds) < S_n^*(\$/\pounds)$$

On the other hand, the risk-neutral speculator will want to sell pounds n years forward if

$$F_n(\$/\pounds) > S_n^*(\$/\pounds)$$

However, if the speculator is averse to risk, he or she will not buy or sell forward unless the expected return is sufficient for the systematic risk that is taken. This risk depends on the covariances of the exchange rate with other assets and liabilities. To the extent that exchange-rate risk is not diversifiable, there is a risk premium in the forward rate. This can cause the forward rate to differ from the market's expected future spot rate.

Speculating with Transaction Costs

When there are transaction costs in the spot and the forward foreign exchange market, a risk-neutral speculator will buy pounds n years forward when

$$F_n(\$/ask\pounds) < S_n^*(\$/bid\pounds) \tag{16.1}$$

That is, the speculator will buy forward if the *buying* price of the forward pound is less than his or her expected future spot *selling* price of the pound. For example, if the speculator can buy pounds 1 year forward for $F_1(\$/ask\pounds) = 1.5500$ and the speculator thinks that in 1 year the spot rate at which the pounds can be sold will be $S_1^*(\$/bid\pounds) = \$1.5580/\pounds$, then the speculator will buy pounds forward in the hope of selling them at a profit. The expected profit is $S_1^*(\$/bid\pounds) - F_1(\$/ask\pounds) = \$0.008$ per pound purchased, or $8000 per £1,000,000. Clearly, the expected movement of the exchange rate has to be sufficient to cover two transaction costs, one being half the forward spread and the other being half the spot spread. Similarly, the risk-neutral speculator will sell pounds n years forward if

$$F_n(\$/bid\pounds) > S_n^*(\$/ask\pounds) \tag{16.2}$$

For example, if the speculator can sell pounds 1 year forward for $F_1(\$/bid\pounds) = 1.5480$ and the speculator thinks the spot rate for buying pounds will be $S_1^*(\$/ask\pounds) = \$1.5420$, then the speculator will sell forward in the hope of being able to buy the pounds spot when making delivery on the forward contract at a lower price. The

---

[1]We should distinguish the *individual speculator's* expected future spot rate from the *market's* expected future spot rate. In this section of this chapter, expected future spot rates are those of the individual speculator.

Speculation, Market Efficiency, and Forecasting

The proportion of (monthly or quarterly) exchange rate changes that current models can explain is essentially zero.

—RICHARD MEESE

The three matters discussed in this chapter, namely, speculation in foreign exchange, the efficiency of foreign exchange markets, and the ability to forecast exchange rates, are very closely related. For example, if speculators can earn average returns that are abnormally high, then markets must not be efficient, and speculators must be able to forecast exchange rates better than the market. Because of the closeness of connections between the issues, this chapter deals first with speculation, then with market efficiency, and finally with forecasting. After explaining the vehicles of foreign exchange speculation, the evidence on market efficiency is examined. The chapter then turns to the record on exchange-rate forecasting, including a comparison of chartist versus fundamental forecasting techniques. The record of chartists versus fundamentalists is linked back to market inefficiency, specifically to the ability to earn from speculation using relatively simple trading rules.

It should be mentioned at the outset that opinions differ widely on the matters discussed in this chapter, and by no means do all researchers agree that abnormal speculative returns and market inefficiencies have been detected. Nevertheless, despite a traditional predisposition among finance researchers against finding abnormal returns to speculation, market inefficiencies, and chartist-forecasting success, when it comes to foreign exchange markets, traditional notions face a challenge.

SPECULATION

When many think of speculators in the foreign exchange market, they have an image of fabulously rich, overweight men in vested suits moving massive amounts of money and providing themselves with handsome profits. The phrase "the gnomes of Zurich" was coined by a former British Chancellor of the Exchequer when his country faced what he perceived as an outright attack on its currency by those everhungry and apparently heartless manipulators. In spite of the images we might have, it can be argued, as we did in Chapter 8, that speculators play a useful role in stabilizing exchange rates. However, our initial purpose here is not to discuss the merits of speculation but rather to simply describe the different ways to speculate. As we shall see, these are the same as the different ways to hedge, namely, via forwards, futures, options, and swaps.

Speculating via the Forward Market

Speculating without Transaction Costs

If we write a speculator's expected spot exchange rate in n years as $S_n^*(\$/£)$, then, as we have indicated, if the speculator is risk-neutral and we ignore transaction costs, he or she will want to buy pounds n years forward if[1]

$$F_n(\$/£) < S_n^*(\$/£)$$

On the other hand, the risk-neutral speculator will want to sell pounds n years forward if

$$F_n(\$/£) > S_n^*(\$/£)$$

However, if the speculator is averse to risk, he or she will not buy or sell forward unless the expected return is sufficient for the systematic risk that is taken. This risk depends on the covariances of the exchange rate with other assets and liabilities. To the extent that exchange-rate risk is not diversifiable, there is a risk premium in the forward rate. This can cause the forward rate to differ from the market's expected future spot rate.

Speculating with Transaction Costs

When there are transaction costs in the spot and the forward foreign exchange market, a risk-neutral speculator will buy pounds n years forward when

$$F_n(\$/\text{ask}£) < S_n^*(\$/\text{bid}£) \qquad (16.1)$$

That is, the speculator will buy forward if the *buying* price of the forward pound is less than his or her expected future spot *selling* price of the pound. For example, if the speculator can buy pounds 1 year forward for $F_1(\$/\text{ask}£) = 1.5500$ and the speculator thinks that in 1 year the spot rate at which the pounds can be sold will be $S_1^*(\$/\text{bid}£) = \$1.5580/£$, then the speculator will buy pounds forward in the hope of selling them at a profit. The expected profit is $S_1^*(\$/\text{bid}£) - F_1(\$/\text{ask}£) = \$0.008$ per pound purchased, or $8000 per £1,000,000. Clearly, the expected movement of the exchange rate has to be sufficient to cover two transaction costs, one being half the forward spread and the other being half the spot spread. Similarly, the risk-neutral speculator will sell pounds n years forward if

$$F_n(\$/\text{bid}£) > S_n^*(\$/\text{ask}£) \qquad (16.2)$$

For example, if the speculator can sell pounds 1 year forward for $F_1(\$/\text{bid}£) = 1.5480$ and the speculator thinks the spot rate for buying pounds will be $S_1^*(\$/\text{ask}£) = \$1.5420$, then the speculator will sell forward in the hope of being able to buy the pounds spot when making delivery on the forward contract at a lower price. The

---

[1]We should distinguish the *individual speculator's* expected future spot rate from the *market's* expected future spot rate. In this section of this chapter, expected future spot rates are those of the individual speculator.

expected profit is $S_1^*(\$/\text{bid}£) - F_1(\$/\text{ask}£) = \$0.006$ per pound sold forward, or $6000 per £1,000,000. The remarks about risk premiums that were made in the context of zero transaction costs also apply when transaction costs exist.

Speculating via the Futures Market

The decision criteria for the futures market are, not surprisingly, essentially the same as those for the forward market: the risk-neutral speculator buys pound futures if he or she believes the future spot price for selling pounds will exceed the current futures buying rate, that is, if inequality (16.1) holds. The risk-neutral speculator sells pound futures when the reverse is the case, that is, if inequality (16.2) holds. However, there are two small differences between the decision to buy or sell futures and the decision to buy or sell forward, namely:

1. Because of marking-to-market risk on futures, if speculators are risk-averse they might want a larger gap between the ask (bid) futures price and the expected future bid (ask) spot price to compensate for the extra risk. That is, there is risk from unanticipated changes both in the spot exchange rate, as there is on forwards, and in the interest rate, which adds marking-to-market risk.
2. Futures contracts are rarely held to their maturity, and the speculator may therefore be comparing today's futures price with an expected futures exchange rate for a date prior to the futures contract's maturity.

Speculating via the Options Market

A speculator buys an option if the expected payoff exceeds the cost of the option by enough to compensate for the risk of the option and for the opportunity cost of money paid for the option. Of course, the value of an option varies with the underlying asset price which can move the option into or out of the money at different times during its maturity and by different amounts. Furthermore, each of the different possible extents of being in or out of the money occurs with a different probability. This means that to calculate the expected payoff the different possible outcomes must be weighted by the probabilities of these outcomes.

Clearly, a speculator will buy an option if he or she values the option at more than its market price. This may occur if the speculator believes that the option will be in the money with a higher probability than the market in general believes. For example, a speculator may buy a call option on the pound with a strike price of $1.60/£ if he or she believes that the probability of the pound moving above $1.60/£ is higher than the probability attached to this eventuality by the market in general. Similarly, a speculator may buy a put option at $1.40/£ if he or she believes that the probability of the pound moving below this rate is higher than the probability attached to this eventuality by the market.

A speculator who is prepared to accept the possibility of large losses can also sell, or write, currency options. As we saw in Chapter 4, if the speculator writes a call option on the pound, he or she gives the buyer the right to buy the pound at the strike price, and if the speculator writes a put option, he or she gives the buyer the right to sell the pound at the strike price. Option writing provides an expected return on the risk taken. That is, the expected payout is less than the premium received for the option. Option writing is a risky speculative strategy unless, as usually is the case, the speculator creates offsetting exposure by using other options, forwards, swaps or futures or by holding the currencies against which call options are written.

Speculating via Borrowing and Lending: Swaps

We saw in Chapter 11 that by borrowing dollars, buying pounds spot, and investing in pound-denominated securities it is possible to achieve essentially the same objective as buying pounds forward. That is, at maturity, dollars are paid on the loan and pounds are received from the investment.

For each pound a speculator wants to have in n years, he or she must invest in pounds today

$$£\ \frac{1}{\left(1 + r_£^I\right)^n}$$

where $r_£^I$ is the per annum pound return. The dollar cost of buying this number of pounds on the spot market so as to have £1 in n years is

$$\$\ \frac{S(\$/\text{ask}£)}{\left(1 + r_£^I\right)^n}$$

If the speculator borrows dollars to do this at $r_\$^B$, the number of dollars that must be repaid on the loan is

$$\$S(\$/\text{ask}£) \cdot \frac{\left(1 + r_\$^B\right)^n}{\left(1 + r_£^I\right)^n} \tag{16.3}$$

In summary, the amount in expression (16.3) is the dollar amount to be paid in n years in order for the speculator to receive £1 in n years.

A risk-neutral speculator would use the swap to speculate in favor of the pound if

$$S(\$/\text{ask}£) \cdot \frac{\left(1 + r_\$^B\right)^n}{\left(1 + r_£^I\right)^n} < S_n^*(\$/\text{bid}£) \tag{16.4}$$

where $S_n^*(\$/\text{bid}£)$ is the number of dollars the speculator expects to be able to sell pounds for in n years time. That is, the speculator will borrow U.S. dollars, buy pounds spot, and invest in pound-denominated securities if he or she thinks the pounds to be received can be sold spot in n years for more dollars than must be repaid on the dollar loan used to buy the pounds.[2]

Speculating via Not Hedging Trade

While it might not seem like speculation, when a firm has a foreign-currency receivable or payable and does *not* hedge this by one of the procedures we have described, that firm is speculating: by not hedging an exposure the firm accepts the exposure,

[2]The criterion for speculating against the pound by borrowing pounds, buying dollars spot, and investing in dollar-denominated securities is left as an exercise for the reader.

just as it does when there is no underlying exposure and the firm uses one of the techniques for speculating that we have described. For example, a U.S. importer that receives an invoice in pounds and does nothing to hedge the exposure is speculating against the pound: the importer is short pounds. This should seem obvious after what we have said in Chapter 12, because it should be clear that speculation is synonymous with having an exposure line with nonzero slope. Yet despite the obvious fact that not hedging foreign-currency receivables or payables means speculating, it is remarkable how many firms, when asked if they use the forward, futures, options, or swap markets to hedge their trade, say, "Oh, no! We don't speculate!" As we have seen, in fact they are unwittingly speculating by not using these markets to hedge exposure.

Speculating on Exchange-Rate Volatility

It is possible to speculate on the possibility that the exchange rate will change by an unexpectedly large amount in *either* direction. That is, it is possible to speculate on the exchange rate being volatile, rather than on it moving in a particular direction. One way to speculate on volatility is to simultaneously buy a call option and a put option at the same strike price. Then, if the value of the foreign currency increases substantially, the call can be exercised for a profit, while the loss on the put is limited to the price paid for it. Likewise, if the value of the foreign currency decreases substantially, the put can be exercised. Such a speculative strategy is called a **straddle.**

MARKET EFFICIENCY

Foreign exchange speculation is worthwhile only if foreign exchange markets are inefficient. This is because in an inefficient market, by definition, there are abnormal returns from using information when taking positions in foreign exchange.[3] An abnormal return is equal to the actual return minus the return that would be expected, given the level of risk, if all available information concerning the asset had been utilized in determining the asset's price. Since it is necessary to specify the expected return when evaluating whether markets are efficient, tests of market efficiency are really joint tests of the model used to generate the expected returns and of market efficiency.

Efficiency can take on different meanings according to what we include in the set of information that is assumed to be available to decision makers. If information on only historical prices or returns on the particular asset is included, we are testing for **weak-form efficiency.** With all publicly known information included, we are testing for **semi-strong-form efficiency,** and with all information, including that available to insiders, we are testing for **strong-form efficiency.** Because of central-bank involvement in foreign exchange markets, exchange rates could well prove to be influenced by an important "insider" and that insider's information.

An important aspect of efficiency in the international context concerns the for-

---

[3]On the concept of market efficiency see Stephen F. LeRoy, "Efficient Capital Markets and Martingales," *Journal of Economic Literature,* December 1989, pp. 1583–1621.

eign exchange market's ability to form forecasts of spot exchange rates. As we have seen earlier in this chapter and in preceding chapters, if speculators are risk-neutral and we ignore transaction costs, speculators buy and sell forward until

$$F_n(\$/£) = S_n^*(\$/£)$$

that is, until the forward rate equals the market's expected future spot rate. Two questions arise in this context:

1. Do forward rates tend to equal the market's expected future spot rates, or do they systematically err?
2. Is all relevant information used by the market in determining the forward rate as a predictor of future spot rates, or are there factors overlooked by the market which would be helpful in making predictions?

The first of these questions relates to possible **forward bias** in forward exchange rates, and the second relates to market efficiency.

It is possible to construct a joint test of possible bias in the forward rate and of market efficiency by running a regression on data for forward exchange rates and eventually realized spot exchange rates. Specifically, for any value of n we choose, it is possible to estimate the equation:[4]

$$S_n(\$/£) = \beta_0 + \beta_1 F_n(\$/£) + \beta_2 Z + \mu \qquad (16.5)$$

In equation (16.5), $S_n(\$/£)$ is the realized spot rate for the maturity date of the forward contract, $F_n(\$/£)$ is the forward rate, Z represents any information that may be relevant for exchange rates, and μ is the regression error. Values of $F_n(\$/£)$, the realized spot rates $S_n(\$/£)$, and Z exist for each point in time during the period over which the regression equation is estimated. The variable or variables that Z represents depend on the form of market efficiency for which we are testing. If Z consists only of past values of the dollar-pound exchange rate—spot or forward—available to the market when forming expectations, the test is of weak-form efficiency; if Z consists of all publicly available information the test is of semi-strong-form efficiency; and if Z also includes information available only to central bankers and other insiders, the test is of strong-form efficiency.

The principal interest in equation (16.5) is with the estimated values of β_0, β_1, and β_2. β_0 is a constant (or intercept) term. β_1 and β_2 represent the partial impacts of $F_n(\$/£)$ and Z, respectively, that is, the impacts of each variable where the other variable is assumed constant.

Let us first consider β_2, the coefficient on potentially relevant information other than that already impounded in the forward rate. If relevant information were not incorporated in the forward rate by the market, the market would be inefficient. In this case, the estimate of β_2 would be significantly different from zero. Equation (16.5) can be estimated using a variety of alternative variables representing Z. If it is not possible to find any variables Z for which the null hypothesis that $\beta_2 = 0$ is rejected, then we can retain the null hypothesis that the market is efficient: an absence of statistically significant variables means that no relevant matters were

---

[4]We show the regression equation in the context of the dollar-pound exchange rate, but it is naturally extendable to other exchange rates.

ignored by the market in forming its expectation of future spot rates as incorporated in forward rates.[5] That is, whether or not we can reject the null hypothesis that $\beta_2 = 0$ is a test of efficiency.

It can be argued that under the null hypothesis that $\beta_2 = 0$, it is possible to estimate equation (16.5) *without* including Z. This is because if β_2 is indeed zero, then omission of Z should have no effect on the outcome of the regression in terms of other coefficient estimates, the extent to which forward rates predict future spot rates, and so on. Judging whether Z can be omitted requires studying the behavior of the actual regression errors, that is, those based on the actual coefficient estimates for β_0 and β_1. The behavior of the errors through time—called **serial correlation,** or **autocorrelation**—suggests whether relevant variables were omitted. If relevant variables were left out when estimating equation (16.5) excluding Z, that is, when estimating

$$S_n(\$/£) = \beta_0 + \beta_1 F_n(\$/£) + \mu$$

then measured regression errors are likely to exhibit patterns over time. The patterns arise because omitted relevant variables usually move through time with patterns; if the omitted variables exhibit patterns through time, their omission creates a pattern in regression errors. For example, forward rates may underestimate spot rates period after period if we ignore a relevant variable. There are statistical summaries which indicate whether significant serial correlation of errors is present. One such measure is the **Durbin-Watson statistic,** or **D-W.** Values of D-W close to 2 mean the null hypothesis of zero serial correlation cannot be rejected.

Before considering the evidence on whether $\beta_2 = 0$, let us see how β_0 and β_1 are related to the possible presence of bias in forward exchange rates. The joint null hypothesis concerning the presence of forward-rate bias is whether $\beta_0 = 0$ and $\beta_1 = 1$. This is because in this situation, from equation (16.5) and continuing to assume that $\beta_2 = 0$,

$$S_n(\$/£) = F_n(\$/£) + \mu \tag{16.6}$$

If the regression errors, μ, average zero, then equation (16.6) says that on average, forward rates correctly predict realized spot rates. On the other hand, if, for example, $\beta_0 = \alpha \neq 0$, then even if $\beta_1 = 1$ and $\beta_2 = 0$

$$S_n(\$/£) = \alpha + F_n(\$/£)$$

This means the forward rate is a biased predictor of the future realized spot rate. For example, if $\alpha > 0$, then on average the forward price of the pound, $F_n(\$/£)$, is less than the realized spot value of the pound. Therefore, buying the pound forward, which means selling dollars forward, earns a speculator a positive return on average. This is a risk premium being earned by the purchaser of pounds, a premium earned for going long on pounds. On the other hand, if $\alpha < 0$ there is a premium for going short on pounds—or long on the dollar.

---

[5]If a 95 percent confidence interval is used for determining whether a coefficient is significantly different from zero, then by design, 1 in 20 variables chosen will be significant just by chance. It is necessary to check whether variables help prediction outside the estimation period and to do other diagnostic tests of whether statistically significant variables really do matter.

The empirical evidence suggests that there are risk premiums in forward rates and these premiums vary over time.[6] However, it appears that risk premiums are very small. For example, Jeffrey Frankel has considered the change in risk premium that would occur if there were an increase in the supply of dollar assets of 1 percent of global assets. Theory suggests that in order to induce people to hold the extra dollar assets the market would have to provide a bigger forward premium on dollars: people need to be rewarded more to hold extra dollars. Frankel estimates that such a 1 percent increase in dollar assets would change the risk premium by 2.4 basis points, that is, by less than 1/40th of one percent.[7] Moreover, the evidence for there being a significant risk premium at all was thrown into question by further research by Jeffrey Frankel and his coresearcher Kenneth Froot.[8] Indeed, even some of those who originally identified a risk premium subsequently obtained evidence that casts some doubt on the model used to find it.[9]

Results of one particular joint test of the hypotheses that $\beta_0 = 0$; $\beta_1 = 1$, which implies a zero risk premium in forward rates, and $\beta_2 = 0$, which implies market efficiency, are shown in Table 16.1. The table gives the results from estimating equation (16.5) under the null hypothesis that $Z = 0$. Results are shown for the dollar-pound rate as well as for the dollar-Deutschemark and dollar-yen rates. The estimates cover the period 1978–1987 and are reported in a comprehensive and insightful survey of foreign exchange market efficiency by Douglas Pearce.[10] The values in parentheses below the coefficient estimates for β_0 and β_1 are *t*-statistics, which allow us to see

[6]A by no means exhaustive list of papers reaching this conclusion includes Richard T. Baillie, Robert E. Lippens, and Patrick C. McMahon, "Testing Rational Expectations and Efficiency in the Foreign Exchange Market," *Econometrica,* May 1983, pp. 553–563; Eugene F. Fama, "Forward and Spot Exchange Rates," *Journal of Monetary Economics,* November 1984, pp. 320–338; Lars P. Hansen and Robert J. Hodrick, "Forward Exchange Rates as Optimal Predictors of Future Spot Rates: An Economic Analysis," *Journal of Political Economy,* October 1980, pp. 829–853; David A. Hsieh, "Tests of Rational Expectations and No Risk Premium in Forward Exchange Markets," *Journal of International Economics,* August 1984, pp. 173–184; Rodney L. Jacobs, "The Effect of Errors in the Variables on Tests for a Risk Premium in Forward Exchange Rates," *Journal of Finance,* June 1982, pp. 667–677; Robert A. Korajczck, "The Pricing of Forward Contracts for Foreign Exchange," *Journal of Political Economy,* April 1985, pp. 346–368; and Christian C. P. Wolff, "Forward Foreign Exchange Rates, Expected Spot Rates and Premia: A Signal-Extraction Approach," *Journal of Finance,* June 1987, pp. 395–406.
[7]See Jeffrey A. Frankel, "In Search of the Exchange Risk Premium: A Six-Currency Test Assuming Mean-Variance Optimization," *Journal of International Money and Finance,* December 1982, pp. 255–274.
[8]Jeffrey A. Frankel and Kenneth A. Froot, "Using Survey Data to Test Some Standard Propositions Regarding Exchange Rate Expectations," *American Economic Review,* March 1987, pp. 133–153.
[9]Robert J. Hodrick and Sanjay Srivastava, "An Investigation of Risk and Return in Forward Foreign Exchange," *Journal of International Money and Finance,* April 1984, pp. 5–29. Other research that does not support the notion of a risk premium includes Bradford Cornell, "Spot Rates, Forward Rates and Exchange Market Efficiency," *Journal of Financial Economics,* August 1977, pp. 55–65; David L. Kaserman, "The Forward Exchange Rate: Its Determination and Behavior as a Predictor of the Future Spot Rate," *Proceedings of the American Statistical Association,* 1973, pp. 417–422; David Longworth, "Testing the Efficiency of the Canadian-U.S. Exchange Market under the Assumption of No Risk Premium," *Journal of Finance,* March 1982, pp. 43–49; and Alan C. Stockman, "Risk, Information and Forward Exchange Rates," in Jacob A. Frenkel and Harry G. Johnson (eds.), *The Economics of Exchange Rates: Selected Studies,* Addison-Wesley, Boston, 1978, pp. 159–178.
[10]Douglas K. Pearce, "Information, Expectations, and Foreign Exchange Market Efficiency," in Thomas Grennes (ed.), *International Financial Markets and Agricultural Trade,* Westview Press, Boulder, Colo., 1989, pp. 214–260.

TABLE 16.1. Test of Unbiasedness of Forward Rates as Predictors of Future Spot Rates, Monthly Data, 1978–1987

Rate	Coefficients/Statistics $S(i/\$) = \beta_0 + \beta_1 F_{1/12}(i/\$) + \mu,\ i = DM, ¥, £$			
	β_0	β_1	R^2	D-W
(DM/$)	0.013	0.988	0.962	1.71
	(0.867)	(0.667)		
(¥/$)	0.028	0.995	0.926	1.59
	(0.197)	(0.192)		
(£/$)	−0.002	0.993	0.974	1.57
	(−0.222)	(0.467)		

t-statistics in parentheses below coefficients, based on $\beta_0 = 0$, $\beta_1 = 1$.
Source: Douglas K. Pearce, "Information, Expectations, and Foreign Exchange Market Efficiency," in Thomas Grennes (ed.), *International Financial Markets and Agricultural Trade,* Westview Press, Boulder, Colo., 1989, pp. 214–260.

whether the point estimates are statistically significantly different from zero, for β_0, and from 1.0, for β_1; these are the values implied by the null hypothesis that there is no bias in forward rates. We see from the numbers in parentheses below the coefficient estimates that β_0 is insignificantly different from 0 and β_1 is insignificantly different from 1.0; the *t*-statistics, which are substantially below 2.0, allow us to retain the null hypothesis of no bias. In addition, the Durbin-Watson statistic is close to 2.0, indicating that relevant variables were not overlooked in forming expectations. Unfortunately, however, we can have only limited confidence in these results because the test statistics are based on the assumption that the process generating the data is **stationary,** which means that the underlying model, including any forward risk premium, is the same over time. Analysis of the data suggest strongly that the process is not stationary.[11]

There is an alternative means of testing for efficiency of foreign exchange markets. This second method also tests whether forecasts of future spot exchange rates are **rational;** by "rational" forecasts we mean forecasts that are on average correct and which do not reveal persistent errors.[12] This test replaces the forward rate, $F_n(\$/£)$, in equation (16.5) with the expected future spot rate as given in surveys of opinions of important market participants. That is, we estimate not equation (16.5), but

$$S_n(\$/£) = \gamma_0 + \gamma_1 S_n^*(\$/£) + \gamma_2 Z + \mu \tag{16.7}$$

In this case we can still judge market efficiency by whether γ_2 is significantly different from zero for any variable(s) Z. Furthermore, we can interpret a γ_0 that is

---

[11]See Richard A. Meese and Kenneth J. Singleton, "On Unit Roots and the Empirical Modelling of Exchange Rates," *Journal of Finance,* September 1982, pp. 1029–1035.
[12]The concept of rationality was also used in the context of the expectations form of PPP in Chapter 10, where we argued that rational people are as likely to overestimate as to underestimate and do not make persistent mistakes.

insignificantly different from zero and a γ_1 that is insignificantly different from 1.0 as implying rational forecasts, because under these joint conditions the market's forecasts are on average correct. Furthermore, if forecasts are rational, then prediction errors in forecasts should not be related between successive time periods.[13]

The evidence from the estimation of equation (16.7) is not supportive of market efficiency. Specifically, other variables *do* appear to help forecast future spot rates; in the regression, γ_2 is significantly different from zero for some variables, Z. This is the conclusion of, for example, Peter Liu and G. S. Maddala, and Stefano Cavaglia, Willem Verschoor, and Christian Wolff.[14] However, on the matter of rationality of expectations, the same researchers reach different conclusions. Rationality is supported by Liu and Maddala but rejected by Cavaglia, Verschoor, and Wolff, who find consistent biases in experts' forecasts.[15]

EXCHANGE-RATE FORECASTING

Model Success and Failure

A further, indirect way of testing foreign exchange market efficiency and whether speculation offers excess expected returns is to examine the forecasting performance of exchange-rate models. If markets are efficient so that exchange rates reflect all available information, it should not be possible to make abnormal returns from speculating by following the models' predictions; exchange rates should reflect the models' predictions, with the market behaving as if it "knew" the forecasts implied by the models.

In a frequently cited paper, Richard Meese and Kenneth Rogoff compared the forecasting performance of a number of exchange-rate models.[16] The models generally predicted well during the period of time over which they were estimated. That is, when using the estimated equations and the known values of the explanatory variables, these models predicted exchange rates that were generally close to actual exchange rates. However, when predicting *outside* the estimation period, the models did a poorer job than a naive forecast that future spot rates equal current spot rates.[17] This is despite the fact that the out-of-sample forecasts—those made outside the estimation period—were made using actual, realized values of explanatory variables. (In practice, forecasting would be based on forecast values of explanatory variables, adding to the forecast error.)

[13]As we said earlier, this can be judged by the Durbin-Watson statistic, given the assumption that the process generating the data is stationary.
[14]See Peter C. Liu and G. S. Maddala, "Rationality of Survey Data and Tests for Market Efficiency in the Foreign Exchange Markets," *Journal of International Money and Finance,* August, 1992, pp. 366–381, and Stefano Cavaglia, Willem F. C. Verschoor, and Christian C. P. Wolff, "Further Evidence on Exchange Rate Expectations," *Journal of International Money and Finance,* February 1993, pp. 78–98. See also Frankel and Froot, *op. cit.*
[15]Cavaglia, Verschoor, and Wolff, *op. cit.*
[16]Richard A. Meese and Kenneth Rogoff, "Empirical Exchange Rate Models of the Seventies: Do They Fit Out of Sample?" *Journal of International Economics,* February 1983, pp. 3–24.
[17]Support for this conclusion with fixed regression coefficients, but of reasonable forecasting ability when coefficients are allowed to change, can be found in Garry J. Schinasi and P.A.V.B. Swamy, "The Out-of-Sample Forecasting Performance of Exchange Rate Models When Coefficients Are Allowed to Change," *Journal of International Money and Finance,* September 1989, pp. 375–390.

TABLE 16.2. Correlation Coefficients between the Yen-Dollar Spot Rate and Various Possible Spot-Rate Predictors, 1974–1987

	Variable				
	$S(¥/\$)$	$(r_\$ - r_¥)$	P_{US}/P_{JP}	M_{US}/M_{JP}	Y_{US}/Y_{JP}
$S(¥/\$)$	1.00				
$(r_\$ - r_¥)$	−0.50	1.00			
P_{US}/P_{JP}	−0.59	0.63	1.00		
M_{US}/M_{JP}	−0.46	−0.08	0.72	1.00	
Y_{US}/Y_{JP}	0.30	−0.26	−0.88	−0.57	1.00

Source: Richard Meese, "Currency Fluctuations in the Post-Bretton Woods Era," *Journal of Economic Perspectives,* winter 1990, p. 120.

A comparison of the forecasting performances of the major macroeconomic models developed since the 1970s has been made by Mark Taylor and Robert Flood.[18] Models considered included the monetary theory of exchange rates, the sticky-price overshooting model, the portfolio-balance model, and the asset approach, all of which are discussed in Chapter 7. The authors used data for 21 industrialized countries for which exchange rates were flexible. Their results confirm those of Meese and Rogoff for forecasts of up to one year, namely, that macroeconomic fundamentals provide a poor prediction of movements in exchange rates. However, as we might expect, Taylor and Flood do find that macroeconomic fundamentals have considerably more explanatory power over longer forecasting horizons.

Because forward rates offer free estimates of future spot rates, the test of efficiency we normally make is whether a model's predictions outperform the forward exchange rate, not whether the model's predictions outperform naive forecasts that future spot rates will equal current spot rates. Surprisingly, however, it has been shown that the current spot rate is a better predictor of the future spot rate than is the forward rate. Therefore, if the models do worse than predicting future spot rates from current spot rates, they do *a fortiori* worse than predicting future spot rates from forward rates.[19]

The lack of success of forecasting models is reflected in the low correlations between the variables which would normally be associated with exchange rates. Indeed, many of the correlations are opposite to what one would normally expect. The low and sometimes surprising correlations are indicated in Tables 16.2 and 16.3. Table 16.2 shows the correlations between the level of the Japanese-yen–U.S.-dollar exchange rate, $S(¥/\$)$, and several variables which would be expected to be related to the exchange rate.[20] These variables include the U.S.-Japanese interest

---

[18]Mark Taylor and Robert P. Flood, "Exchange Rate Economics: What's Wrong with the Conventional Macro Approach?" conference paper in *Microstructure of Foreign Exchange Markets,* sponsored by National Bureau of Economic Research, the Centre for Economic Policy Research (London), and the Bank of Italy, July 1994.

[19]See Thomas C. Chiang, "Empirical Analysis of the Predictors of Future Spot Rates," *The Journal of Financial Research,* summer 1986, pp. 153–162.

[20]The correlations are provided by Richard Meese, "Currency Fluctuations in the Post-Bretton Woods Era," *Journal of Economic Perspectives,* winter 1990, pp. 117–134. All data are in logarithms, except interest rates, and cover the period January 1974–July 1987, which is the post-Bretton Woods floating era, before the Louvre Accord.

**TABLE 16.3. Correlation Coefficients between the Deutschemark-Dollar
Spot Rate and Various Possible Spot-Rate Predictors, 1974–1987**

	Variable				
	S(DM/\$)	$(r_\$ - r_{DM})$	P_{US}/P_{GY}	M_{US}/M_{GY}	Y_{US}/Y_{GY}
S(DM/\$)	1.00				
$(r_\$ - r_{DM})$	−0.20	1.00			
P_{US}/P_{GY}	−0.04	0.42	1.00		
M_{US}/M_{GY}	0.37	−0.25	0.50	1.00	
Y_{US}/Y_{GY}	0.04	0.51	0.80	0.45	1.00

Source: Richard Meese, "Currency Fluctuations in the Post-Bretton Woods Era," *Journal of Economic Perspectives,* winter 1990, p. 120.

rate differential, $r_\$ - r_¥$; U.S. versus Japanese prices, P_{US}/P_{JP}; U.S. versus Japanese narrowly defined money supplies, M_{US}/M_{JP}; and U.S. versus Japanese industrial production, Y_{US}/Y_{JP}. Table 16.3 shows the correlations for the equivalent variables for the United States versus Germany.

The first feature of these tables that is noticeable is the low level of some of the correlations. As Meese himself concludes, the correlations "suggest that it may be challenging to explain exchange rate fluctuations in the post-Bretton Woods era with macroeconomic fundamentals."[21] The second thing we notice is that the signs of some of the correlations are the opposite of what we would expect. For example, relatively rapid U.S. money supply growth causes the dollar to appreciate vis-à-vis the Deutschemark, the opposite of the prediction of the monetary theory of exchange rates; the positive correlation in Table 16.3 suggests that as M_{US}/M_{GY} goes up, S(DM/\$) also goes up, which means a dollar appreciation.[22] The negative correlations between the interest differentials and exchange rates are also quite curious: relatively higher U.S. interest rates are associated with a dollar depreciation in both tables.

News and Exchange Rates

When events occur that are relevant for spot exchange rates but which were widely expected to occur, these events should have no impact on exchange rates. Therefore, in regressions of such expected events on exchange rates, regression coefficients should be zero; when the explanatory variables change as expected, the spot exchange rate should not change. The situation is different for unexpected events, which are frequently referred to as "news" or "surprises." Examples of surprises are interest rate changes that were not anticipated, money supply growth that differed from expectations, and so on. These surprise events are the ones that should affect exchange rates. The low correlations and statistical insignificance of macroeconomic variables that have been found could be due to using the actual values of the vari-

[21]Meese, *ibid.,* p. 120.
[22]However, we should be careful interpreting simple correlations when the explanatory variables are correlated. For example, exchange-rate–money correlations could reflect effects of money working indirectly on exchange rates through interest rates and other variables.

ables instead of only the surprise components: in general, a large part of actual values, especially in the *levels* of variables, should be expected.

Basing his approach on the preceding argument, Jacob Frenkel examined how exchange rates respond to surprises in the interest rate differential.[23] Specifically, he estimated the following regression, stated in dollar-pound form but estimated also for the Deutschemark and French franc:

$$S_n(\$/£) = \beta_0 + \beta_1 F_n(\$/£) + \beta_2\left[\left(i_\$ - i_£\right) - \left(i_\$ - i_£\right)^*\right] + \mu \qquad (16.8)$$

where $(i_\$ - i_£)$ is the actual interest differential, and $(i_\$ - i_£)^*$ is the expected interest rate differential. The surprise is therefore $[(i_\$ - i_£) - (i_\$ - i_£)^*]$. Expectations are based on past interest rates and on forward exchange premiums/discounts. Frenkel finds a statistically significant β_2, suggesting that "news" in the form of unexpected interest differentials does relate to exchange rates. However, the nonstationary nature of the spot rate limits confidence in the findings. Following Frenkel, Sebastian Edwards includes news on money supply and national income as well as on interest rates and finds, as expected, that unexpectedly rapid money growth leads to depreciation.[24] On the other hand, using **vector auto regression**—a technique which bases expectations on the best-fitted relationship found from a long list of potential factors—Christian Wolff finds no effect of news.[25]

The role of surprises has also been investigated using the so-called **event study** methodology, in which specific news events are related to subsequent changes in exchange rates. This allows implications to be drawn about the possibility of predicting exchange rates—we can see if exchange rates respond to certain variables—as well as on market efficiency. (In an efficient market, prices respond immediately, not with a lag.) Craig Hakkio and Douglas Pearce find that during 1979–1982, when the U.S. Federal Reserve was trying to achieve target growth rates of the money supply, after money-supply growth rates were discovered to be higher than expected the dollar would appreciate.[26] Each appreciation was completed within 20 minutes of the release of the money-supply statistics. This is consistent with an efficient market and with the market's view that excessive money growth will be curbed in the future, forcing interest rates and hence the dollar higher. (The curbing of money growth in the future is necessary to keep the longer-term money growth within the target range. The slower money growth raises interest rates, and higher interest rates increase the demand for the currency and hence its price.) The dollar did not respond to *expected* changes in the money supply, just as we would predict. While some

[23]Jacob A. Frenkel, "Flexible Exchange Rates, Prices, and the Role of 'News': Lessons from the 1970s," *Journal of Political Economy,* August 1981, pp. 665–705. See also the summaries of Frenkel's study in Douglas K. Pearce, "Information, Expectations, and Foreign Exchange Market Efficiency," in Thomas Grennes (ed.), *International Financial Markets and Agricultural Trade,* Westview Press, Boulder, Colo., 1989, p. 241, and Mack Ott and Paul T. W. M. Veugelers, "Forward Exchange Rates in Efficient Markets: The Effects of News and Changes in Monetary Policy Regimes," *Review,* Federal Reserve Bank of St. Louis, June/July 1986, pp. 5–15.

[24]Sebastian Edwards, "Exchange Rates and 'News': A Multi-Currency Approach," *Journal of International Money and Finance,* December 1982, pp. 211–224.

[25]Christian C. P. Wolff, "Exchange Rates, Innovations and Forecasting," *Journal of International Money and Finance,* March 1988, pp 49–61.

[26]Craig S. Hakkio and Douglas K. Pearce, "The Reaction of Exchange Rates to Economic News," *Economic Inquiry,* October 1985, pp. 621–636. See also G. A. Hardouvelis, "Economic News, Exchange Rates and Interest Rates," *Journal of International Money and Finance,* March 1988, pp. 23–25.

effect of surprises in money growth persisted after the money-supply targeting period ended in 1982—perhaps because the market believed the Fed had not entirely given up money targeting—the effect did eventually disappear. This is consistent with the view that after the market had concluded that the Fed had finished targeting the money supply, surprises in money growth had no implication for future money supply, and hence no implication for interest rates or exchange rates. Similar studies of the effects of announcements of trade-balance statistics on exchange rates show similar results; trade-balance surprises have effects which depend on how markets expect governments to respond.[27]

Rather than separating variables into expected and unexpected components, Martin Evans and James Lothian have separated variables into **transitory** (temporary) and **permanent** components.[28] Normally, it would be expected that transitory shocks would play a small role in variations in exchange rates. However, contrary to expectations, Evans and Lothian have shown a significant role for transitory shocks.

Changing Regimes

As we explained when describing the effects of money-supply surprises on exchange rates, the nature of government economic policy plays an important role. In particular, we showed that if the Fed is attempting to keep the money-supply growth rate within a stated target range, surprise increases in the money supply should cause a dollar appreciation: the Fed would respond to excessive money growth by restricting the growth of money in the future, thereby increasing interest rates and, in turn, the dollar. On the other hand, if instead of targeting the money supply the Fed were to target interest rates, which means trying to keep interest rates at a given level, then a surprise increase in the money supply would have a different effect. Specifically, a surprisingly large money-supply growth would imply future inflation. This would tend to push up interest rates, a tendency that the Fed would try to offset by increasing the money supply even further. The resulting inflation would eventually cause a dollar depreciation.[29]

In reality, market participants do not hold a given view of the policy **regime** that is in effect. Rather, there is a **probability distribution** about the policy regime that is behind government action. The probability distribution could take the form of some investors believing that it is one policy that the government is following, while other investors think it is a different policy. Alternatively, the probability distribution could take the form of *all* investors attaching common probabilities to particu-

---

[27]See Ken Hogan, Michael Melvin, and Dan J. Roberts, "Trade Balance News and Exchange Rates: Is There a Policy Signal?," *Journal of International Money and Finance,* supplement, March 1991, pp. S90–S99; Raj Aggarwal and David C. Schirm, "Balance of Trade Announcements and Asset Prices: Influence on Equity Prices, Exchange Rates and Interest Rates," *Journal of International Money and Finance,* February 1992, pp. 80–95; and Keivan Deravi, Philip Gregorowicz, and Charles E. Hegji, "Balance of Trade Announcements and Movements in Exchange Rates," *Southern Economic Journal,* October 1988, pp. 279–287.

[28]Martin D. D. Evans and James R. Lothian, "The Response of Exchange Rates to Permanent and Transitory Shocks Under Floating Exchange Rates," *Journal of International Money and Finance,* December 1993, pp. 563–586.

[29]See Martin Eichenbaum and Charles Evans, "Some Empirical Evidence on the Effects of Monetary Policy Shocks on Exchange Rates," National Bureau of Economic Research, Working Paper No. 4271, 1993.

lar regimes being behind government actions. Whatever the nature of the probability distribution we have in mind, beliefs about the underlying policy regime that is in effect change slowly, and this has important implications for market efficiency. Let us explain this in terms of the peso problem, which is one of the earliest contexts in which the issue of perceived regime changes was raised.[30]

When the Mexican peso was under heavy selling pressure in 1982, beliefs in the willingness of the authorities to maintain the exchange rate started to shift. More and more individuals began to think the Mexican government would let the peso drop, and/or each participant began to reduce his or her estimate of the probability the authorities would continue to prop up the peso. This shifting of beliefs took place gradually over a period of time. However, empirical tests of market efficiency assume that a *given* regime is in effect. Estimating models which assume a given regime is in effect when in fact beliefs are shifting gradually over time produces sequentially related (repeated) prediction errors. These sequentially related errors could be interpreted as a market inefficiency: in an efficient market people do not make sequentially related (repeated) errors. However, instead of market inefficiency, the errors could represent shifting regime beliefs. Unless researchers can model the evolution of beliefs about the underlying policy regime, it is not possible to disentangle the alternate hypotheses of market inefficiency versus regime shifting and reach a definitive conclusion.[31] In other words, researchers may conclude that foreign exchange markets ignore relevant information because they consistently over- or underestimate future exchange rates, when in fact the model the researcher is using is the cause of the persistent errors: the model is the same in all periods, when in reality it should allow for a gradual change in beliefs over time.

The Record of Forecasting Services

Closely related to the question of market efficiency is the success of exchange-rate forecasting services. Do they give their users a better idea of where exchange rates are going than can be obtained by looking at other generally available sources of information? The answer appears to be that forecasting services have different levels of success but in general do a poor job. Let us consider the evidence.

Stephen Goodman performed a number of statistical tests on a large group of forecasting services.[32] He classified the services according to the techniques they employ. He separated those that use econometric (that is, statistical) techniques from those that use subjective evaluations and those that use technical decision rules. The econometric approach involves estimation of the relation between exchange rates and interest rates, inflation differentials, and other explanatory variables. The mod-

---

[30]See William S. Krasker, "The 'Peso Problem' in Testing the Efficiency of the Forward Market," *Journal of Monetary Economics,* April 1980, pp. 269–276.

[31]On regime switching see Richard G. Harris and Douglas D. Purvis, "Incomplete Information and the Equilibrium Determination of the Forward Exchange Rate," *Journal of International Money and Finance,* December 1982, pp. 241–253; René Stulz, "An Equilibrium Model of Exchange Rate Determination and Asset Pricing with Nontraded Goods and Imperfect Information," *Journal of Political Economy,* October 1987, pp. 1024–1040; and Karen K. Lewis, "The Persistence of the 'Peso Problem' when Policy is Noisy," *Journal of International Money and Finance,* March 1988, pp. 5–21.

[32]See Stephen H. Goodman, "No Better than the Toss of a Coin," *Euromoney,* December 1978, pp. 75–85.

els described earlier would fit in this category. The technical rules are generally based on relating future exchange rates to past exchange rates. The subjective approach is what you would think it is—forecasting by personal opinion. Goodman compared predictions made by the forecasting services with what eventually occurred. He examined the accuracy of predictions made between January and June in 1978.

Table 16.4 summarizes the results for the econometric forecasts in predicting trends and in predicting actual spot exchange rates ("point estimates"). The first column in the top half of the table on predicting trends shows how often the forward rate was on the correct side of the realized spot rate. Because speculators move the forward rate toward the expected future spot rate, the forward rate provides a benchmark against which to judge whether the forecasting services provide information in addition to what is readily available without charge. We see that except in the case of the French franc, the forward rate is in the correct direction more than 50 percent of the time. On the other hand, the remainder of the top half of Table 16.4 shows that many forecasters are correct about trends less than 50 percent of the time. This suggests that the predictive accuracy of forecasting services is weak. The bottom half of Table 16.4 compares the point estimate predictions of the forecasting services with the forward rate "predictions." The table shows that predicted levels of spot rates are frequently further away from the realized rates than forecasts based simply on forward rates.

Table 16.5 and Table 16.6 show the results of an additional test that Goodman performed. In order to compare forecasting success, Goodman computed the rates of return from following the advice of the different services. The rates of return from following the advice of the econometric-based services are given in Table 16.5. The performance of the advisory services can be compared with the strategy of just buying currencies and holding them, a practice which offered gains on every currency other than the Canadian dollar, because the U.S. dollar dropped against most currencies during the period. The econometric forecasters had a poor record. However, the technically oriented services, whose performances are summarized in Table 16.6, did a good job. Before adjustments for transaction costs or risk, the total returns from buying and selling according to their advice show an average yield of almost 8 percent. This means that if the advice of these services had been followed with the maintenance of a 5 percent margin, the return on the margin after adjusting for transaction costs would have been 145 percent. However, there would also have been periods of losses, and a follower of the advice might not have survived to enjoy the profit available to those currency speculators who did survive. Stated differently, we do not know whether the return of 145 percent is sufficient for the risk that is involved.

Richard Levich has also examined the performance of the advisory services, but his conclusions are rather different from the conclusions of Stephen Goodman.[33] While Levich also found the subjective and technical forecasts to be more accurate than econometric forecasts in the short run, he found the opposite for forecasts of a

[33]Richard Levich, "Analyzing the Accuracy of Foreign Exchange Advisory Services: Theory and Evidence," in Richard Levich and Clas Wihlberg (eds.), *Exchange Risk and Exposure: Current Developments in International Financial Management*, D.C. Heath, Lexington, Mass., 1980. See also Richard J. Sweeney, "Beating the Foreign Exchange Market," *Journal of Finance*, March 1986, pp. 163–182.

TABLE 16.4. The Performance of Econometric-oriented Services

EVALUATION OF ECONOMETRIC-ORIENTED SERVICES: ACCURACY IN PREDICTING TRENDS
(SHARE OF FORECASTS FOR WHICH THE EXCHANGE RATE MOVED IN THE INDICATED DIRECTION IN THE SUBSEQUENT 3-MONTH PERIOD)

Currency	Forward Rate	Berkeley Consulting Group	DRI	Forex Research	Predex	Service 5	Service 6	Arithmetic Average (Services Only)
Canadian dollar	62	83	53*	n.a.	30	31	n.a.	49
French franc	37	63	43*	30	73	27	25*	44
Deutschemark	67	57	77*	60	73	45	63	63
Yen	54	50	67*	67	47	37	n.a.	54
Swiss franc	80	n.a.	n.a.	n.a.	47	n.a.	10	29
Sterling	50	60	63*	60	43	37	29*	49
Arithmetic average	58	63	61	54	52	35	32	50

EVALUATION OF ECONOMETRIC-ORIENTED SERVICES: ACCURACY OF POINT ESTIMATES OF FUTURE SPOT RATES
(SHARE OF FORECASTS IN WHICH THE PREDICTED RATE WAS CLOSER TO THE SPOT RATE THAN WAS THE COMPARABLE FORWARD RATE)

Currency	Berkeley Consulting Group	DRI	Forex Research	Predex	Service 5	Service 6	Arithmetic Average (Services Only)
Canadian dollar	60	27*	n.a.	13	37	n.a.	34
French franc	57	33*	48	40	38	57*	46
Deutschemark	24	63*	57	41	33	53	45
Yen	37	60*	62	30	20	n.a.	42
Swiss franc	n.a.	n.a.	n.a.	30	n.a.	10	20
Sterling	70	33*	47	47	40	48*	48
Arithmetic average	50	43	54	34	34	42	43

*Based on part period data.
Source: Stephen Goodman, "No Better than the Toss of a Coin," *Euromoney*, December 1978, pp. 75–85.

TABLE 16.5. Speculative Return on Capital from Following the Advice of Econometric Services
(*In percentages*)

Currency		Buy and Hold	Berkeley Consulting Group	DRI	Forex Research	Predex	Service 5	Service 6	Arithmetic Average (Services Only)
Canadian dollar	Buy	(15.12)	2.52	(2.88)	n.a.	(4.96)	(0.60)	n.a.	(1.48)
	Sell		6.88	5.16*	n.a.	(2.08)	3.52	n.a.	3.37
	Total	(15.12)	4.40	1.64*	n.a.	(3.60)	0.28	n.a.	0.68
French franc	Buy	3.20	7.32	5.76*	2.40	7.20	3.24	10.08*	6.00
	Sell		2.28	(0.64)*	(3.16)	3.68	(2.68)	13.80*	(2.39)
	Total	3.20	4.20	1.40*	0.02	5.92	0.08	2.60*	2.37
Deutschemark	Buy	6.80	5.72	13.00*	6.52	7.56	16.08	10.84	9.95
	Sell		(13.92)	(1.96)*	(7.00)	(4.40)	(4.04)	(4.88)	(6.03)
	Total	6.80	(1.56)	5.80*	(1.60)	4.68	0.64	0.36	1.39
Yen	Buy	12.52	7.36	15.56*	12.92	21.08	4.80	n.a.	12.34
	Sell		(16.40)	(13.68)*	(8.92)	(9.56)	(15.76)	n.a.	(12.86)
	Total	12.52	(5.32)	3.88	6.16	(2.40)	(7.96)	n.a.	(1.13)
Swiss franc	Buy	9.64	n.a.	n.a.	n.a.	18.80	n.a.	n.a.	18.80
	Sell		n.a.	n.a.	n.a.	(6.12)	n.a.	n.a.	(6.12)
	Total	9.64	n.a.	n.a.	n.a.	0.52	n.a.	n.a.	0.52
Sterling	Buy	0.12	14.04	4.56	8.40	2.76	2.16	6.20*	6.35
	Sell		10.48	(12.40)*	4.68	2.44	1.12	(9.32)*	(0.50)
	Total	0.12	12.04	(2.24)*	6.04	2.60	1.52	(2.52)*	2.91
Arithmetic average	Total	2.86	2.75	2.10	2.66	1.29	(1.09)	0.15	1.12

*Based on part period data.
Parentheses indicate a negative.
The total is the return on all transactions, both buy and sell; it is equal to the weighted average of the return on buys and on sells, where the weights are the share of transactions which are buys and sells respectively.
Totals for arithmetic average column represent horizontal sums; arithmetic average for arithmetic average column represents vertical sum of totals.
Source: Stephen Goodman, "No Better than the Toss of a Coin," *Euromoney*, December 1978, pp. 75–85.

TABLE 16.6. Speculative Return on Capital from Following the Advice of Technical Services
(In percentages)

Currency		International Forecasting	Shearson Hayden, Stone	Waldner	Arithmetic Average
Canadian dollar	Buy	0.99	4.61	2.50	2.70
	Sell	4.60	5.19	6.22	5.34
	Total	5.59	9.80	8.72	8.04
Number of transactions/yr.		5	17	11	11
French franc	Buy	(2.42)	n.a.	3.82	0.70
	Sell	(3.66)	n.a.	0.53	(1.57)
	Total	(6.08)	n.a.	4.35	(0.87)
Number of transactions/yr.		5	n.a.	15	10
Deutschemark	Buy	10.49	8.78	7.53	8.93
	Sell	2.46	3.02	1.19	2.22
	Total	12.95	11.80	8.72	11.16
Number of transactions/yr.		5	25	13	14
Yen	Buy	12.42	10.95	11.78	11.72
	Sell	(1.73)	(1.63)	(1.52)	(1.63)
	Total	10.69	9.32	10.26	10.09
Number of transactions/yr.		5	21	12	13
Swiss franc	Buy	9.52	12.99	2.76	8.42
	Sell	2.07	3.11	(10.28)	(1.70)
	Total	11.60	16.10	(7.52)	6.73
Number of transactions/yr.		5	22	14	14
Sterling	Buy	6.70	2.62	9.24	6.19
	Sell	5.55	2.64	9.93	6.04
	Total	12.25	5.26	19.17	12.23
Number of transactions/yr.		4	24	12	13
Arithmetic average	Total	7.83	10.46	7.28	7.90
Number of transactions/yr.		5	22	13	13

Parentheses indicate a negative.
Total is the return on all transactions, both buy and sell.
Totals for arithmetic average column represent horizontal sums; arithmetic average for arithmetic average column represents vertical sum of totals.
Source: Stephen Goodman, "No Better than the Toss of a Coin," *Euromoney,* December 1978, pp. 75–85.

year (a period not checked by Goodman). Levich did find some gain from following the advice of the advisory services. Further evidence of success of professional forecasters over 1-year and 3-month horizons is described in Exhibit 16.1, while Exhibit 16.2 describes the success of a renown forecaster, George Soros. Unfortunately, as explained earlier, it is difficult to decide whether the return from following the forecasters is sufficient to compensate for the risk of taking positions based on these forecasts.

It has been said that an economist is a person with one foot in the freezer and the other in the oven who believes that on average things are just about O.K. The scepticism behind this comment reflects the view that averages can hide wide dispersions. Therefore, even if forecasters were able on average to predict exchange rates better than forward rates, we might still wonder how this average was formed. Were all forecasters successful, or were they widely different and successful only on average? Similarly, were some forecasters right year after year and others wrong year after year, or were the successful forecasters themselves difficult to predict? The summary below, which describes the research of Jeffrey Frankel and Menzie Chinn, tells us only of the success of forecasters, on average. We must still ask whether the risk, which would be present if it were different forecasters who were successful at different times or if individual forecasters made big errors and were correct only on average, is excessive for the returns earned.

Banks, multinationals, and anyone else who participates in international currency markets could use more accurate forecasts of foreign exchange rates. Yet predictions in this area have been notoriously bad. It often has been found that investors would do better to ignore current forecasts. Instead, they could view the exchange rate as an unpredictable random walk, just as likely to rise as to fall.

Now a new study by NBER Research Associate Jeffrey Frankel and Menzie Chinn finds that professional forecasts, under certain conditions, can help to predict changes in exchange rates. Frankel and Chinn examine the monthly predictions from an average of about 45 forecasters regarding the currencies of 25 developed and developing countries between February 1988 and February 1991. The data come from *Currency Forecasters' Digest.* Frankel and Chinn also examine monthly predictions for these currencies based on the value of their exchange rates in forward markets, where participants promise to exchange currencies in the future at a specified price.

In "Are Exchange Rate Expectations Biased? Tests for a Cross Section of 25 Currencies," Frankel and Chinn report that the prediction based on forward markets is wrong more often than not. Both the three-month-ahead predictions and the 12-month-ahead predictions of exchange rate shifts have the wrong sign more than half the time. The average of the professional forecasters when they look either three or 12 months ahead across the 25 currencies, on the other hand, is right more than half the time.

Source: "Forecasting Foreign Exchange Rates," *The NBER Digest,* National Bureau of Economic Research, November 1991.

Success of Different Forecasting Methods

A manifestation of the risk of following the advice of exchange-rate forecasters is that there is a large dispersion of opinion among them. This is evident directly from examination of the expressed opinions of forecasters and indirectly from the immense volume of transactions that occurs in foreign exchange markets. If all participants agreed on how exchange rates would evolve, transactions would occur only for commercial and investment reasons. Furthermore, transactions would largely involve nonfinancial firms—notably importers, exporters, borrowers, and investors—trading with financial firms—notably banks. However, analysis of foreign exchange transactions data collected biannually by the Federal Reserve Bank of New York shows that over 95 percent of foreign exchange changes hands between banks and other financial firms. That is, less than 5 percent of transactions involve a nonfinancial firm. In other words, banks and other financial establishments are trading between themselves, presumably because buyers believe a currency to be worth more than the sellers believe it to be worth.[34]

[34]If the value of a currency is judged in portfolio terms, diversification value would be behind trading as well as the expected change in the exchange rate. Therefore, it is possible that both buyer and seller

In 1992, with the British pound being pummelled by speculators, one individual was particularly closely associated with the huge losses incurred by the Bank of England as it tried to keep the pound within the European Exchange Rate Mechanism (ERM) band. His name is George Soros, and his story is told briefly below.

While Norman Lamont was dithering last autumn, unable to make up his mind whether to take the U.K. out of the European exchange rate mechanism, the Hungarian-born financier, George Soros, was clear that the pound was over-valued and needed to free itself from its constricting currency strait jacket. What is more, he was ready to gamble $10bn backing his judgement.

Mr. Soros was the one who read the economic runes correctly. With his now renowned sense of timing, he committed his Quantum Fund, based in the Netherlands Antilles, to selling sterling short up to this value (and, in fact, more). The Chancellor countered that he would spend up to $15bn defending his currency. But Mr. Soros's sales of sterling provided the momentum that put the pound into an uncontrollable spin. On Black Wednesday, 16 September 1992, Mr. Lamont was ignominiously forced to backtrack and bring sterling out of the ERM. Over the previous few days, the U.K. had lost around $10bn trying to shore up its currency, while Mr. Soros made a cool $1bn for the Quantum Fund out of his punt.

Today Mr. Lamont is out of his job, while the iconoclastic Mr. Soros is riding on the crest of a wave. One up for the hidden hand of the market? Or simply another dubious achievement for international speculators?

His gamble on sterling certainly put Mr. Soros on the world media map. Previously he was known to the general public only as the reclusive millionaire who in 1990 sacked his butler and his wife after a row involving the use of a £500 bottle of Château Lafite as cooking wine in a goulash. After Black Wednesday he became as a Thames Television documentary dubbed him, The Man Who Broke the Pound. . . .

Mr. Soros was born in Budapest in 1930. His father was a Hungarian-Jewish lawyer who survived internment as a prisoner of war in Siberia between 1917 and 1921. Similarly, George Soros, then known as Dzjehdzhe Shorosh, survived the Nazi occupation of Hungary during the Second World War. In 1947 he escaped the communist regime, coming first to Berne and then to London. Still only a teenager, he worked as a farm hand, house painter and railway porter before winning a place to study economics at the London School of Economics in 1949. There he met his intellectual mentor, the Austrian philosopher Karl Popper, whose theories on scientific method and whose book, *The Open Society and its Enemies,* deeply influenced the young fugitive from communism. . . .

Mr. Soros's break came in 1963 when he was hired by Arnhold and S. Bleichroader to advise American institutions on their European investments. He persuaded his employers to start up two offshore funds—the First Eagle Fund in 1967 and the Double Eagle Fund in 1969. By 1973, he wanted more of the action himself. With his then partner James Rogers, he took many of the Double Eagle investors and started up the Soros Fund (later the Quantum Fund) in Curaçao. By the end of the decade the fund was chalking up annual returns of over 100% and George Soros was up among the seriously rich.

Source: Andrew Lycett, "Soros: Midas or Machiavelli?" *Accountancy,* July 1993, pp. 36–40.

Jeffrey Frankel and Kenneth Froot have examined data for the British pound, German mark, Japanese yen, and Swiss franc and found that trading volume and dispersion of expectations were positively related in these four currencies.[35] They have also shown that the volatility of exchange rates is related to trading volume.

The connection between volatility of exchange rates and dispersion of expectations of forecasters can be related to one of the explanations of exchange overshooting discussed in Chapter 7. This explanation involves a choice between following the advice of technical forecasters—those basing views on past exchange rates—and following the advice of fundamentalist forecasters—those basing views

---

agree on the expected change in exchange rate but differ in terms of the value from diversification.

[35]Jeffrey A. Frankel and Kenneth A. Froot, "Chartists, Fundamentalists, and Trading in the Foreign Exchange Market," *American Economic Review, Papers and Proceedings,* May 1990, pp. 181–185.

TABLE 16.7. Connection between Past Changes in Exchange Rates and Median Forecasts of Future Rates, for Various Forecast Horizons

SOURCE OF DATA ON FORECASTS				
MMS International*		*The Economist†*		
1 week	4 weeks	3 months	6 months	12 months
0.13‡	0.08	−0.08‡	−0.17‡	−0.33‡
(4.32)	(1.60)	(−2.98)	(−4.98)	(−5.59)

t-statistics given in parentheses below coefficients.
*Period, October 1984–January 1988.
†Period, June 1981–August 1988.
‡Significant at 99 percent confidence level.
Source: Jeffrey A. Frankel and Kenneth A. Froot, "Chartists, Fundamentalists, and Trading in the Foreign Exchange Market," *American Economic Review, Papers and Proceedings,* May 1990, p. 184.

on economic fundamentals. The explanation of overshooting assumes a positive association between the success of forecasters and the numbers of market participants who follow the forecasters.[36] If the chartists who follow trends happen to be more correct than the fundamentalists, the chartists will gain followers, thereby reinforcing the trend. For example, when a currency is rising, the chartists who base beliefs on extrapolating the past will be correct, people will buy according to the chartists' recommendations, and therefore the chartists' forecasts will prove correct. This "positive feedback" can, according to the theory, cause exchange rates to move well beyond their values based on economic fundamentals. Eventually, however, the rates will be so inappropriate that the chartists' projections will prove wrong, and then followers of forecasters will switch to the fundamentalists' advice, reinforcing the opinion of the fundamentalists, causing more to follow the fundamentalists' advice, and so on.

Survey data from a variety of sources indicate a large and growing influence of chartist forecasting techniques, especially for very short horizons. For example, Table 16.7 shows the result of analysis of forecasts gathered by *MMS International* and *The Economist* for overlapping time periods.[37] The table shows the extent that a 1 percent increase in the value of the U.S. dollar in a 1-week period causes forecasters, as measured by the median (middle) forecast, to anticipate a further dollar appreciation. We see that for 1-week horizons a 1 percent dollar appreciation is associated with a median belief in a further 0.13 percent dollar appreciation. This drops to 0.08 percent at the 4-week horizon. The longer horizons forecasts using survey data from *The Economist* reveal reversions, with forecasters believing that past-week changes in exchange rates will be reversed. Indeed, the median forecast is for a third of past-week changes to be reversed within one year.

[36]See Jeffrey A. Frankel and Kenneth A. Froot, "The Dollar as an Irrational Speculative Bubble: A Tale of Fundamentalists and Chartists," National Bureau of Economic Research, Working Paper No. 959, January 1988.
[37]Jeffrey A. Frankel and Kenneth A. Froot, "Chartists, Fundamentalists, and Trading in the Foreign Exchange Market," *American Economic Review, Papers and Proceedings,* May 1990, pp. 181–185.

TABLE 16.8. Forecasting Methods of *Euromoney* Respondents

Year	Number Using Chartist Methods	Number Using Fundamentals	Number Using Both Methods
1978	3	19	0
1981	1	11	0
1983	8	1	1
1984	9	0	2
1985	15	5	3
1986	20	8	4
1987	16	6	5
1988	18	7	6

Source: Euromoney, August issues, as reported by Jeffrey A. Frankel, "Chartists, Fundamentalists, and Trading in the Foreign Exchange Market," National Bureau of Economic Researcher, *NBER Reporter,* 1991.

The overshooting role of chartists is indirectly supported by the forecasting techniques used by the services surveyed by *Euromoney.*[38] Table 16.8 shows the shift from economic fundamentals to chartist techniques in the period 1978–1988. The data also reveal, however, an increasingly large number of forecasting services using both methods. These conclusions are supported by a questionnaire survey conducted on behalf of the Bank of England in November 1988.[39] The questionnaire, which solicited the views of chief foreign exchange dealers based in London, revealed that more than 90 percent considered technical—that is, chartist—factors in making forecasts over one or more time horizons, with the dependence on technical views being more pronounced over shorter horizons. As with the evidence from *MMS International* versus *The Economist,* more attention is paid to fundamentalist analysis the longer the forecasting horizon.

The reliance on technical forecasts has been reinforced by the success of technical trading rules. These include rules based on past exchange rates, such as "Buy if the one-week moving average moves above the twelve-week moving average, and sell when the opposite occurs, holding balanced positions otherwise." A popular form of technical trading rule involves the use of a so-called **filter.** A filter rule might be to buy whenever a currency moves more than a given percentage above its lowest recent value, and to sell when it moves a given percentage above its highest recent value.[40]

The success of a variety of relatively simple rules has been reported by several researchers looking at different parts of the foreign exchange market. For example, Michael Dooley and Jeffrey Shafer, and also Dennis Logue, Richard Sweeney, and

[38]See Jeffrey A. Frankel, "Chartists, Fundamentalists, and Trading in the Foreign Exchange Market," National Bureau of Economic Research, Annual Research Conference, 1991.

[39]See Mark P. Taylor and Helen Allen, "The Use of Technical Analysis in the Foreign Exchange Market," *Journal of International Money and Finance,* June 1992, pp. 304–314.

[40]On forward market trading rules see Paul Boothe, "Estimating the Structure and Efficiency of the Canadian Foreign Exchange Market," unpublished Ph.D. dissertation, University of British Columbia, 1981, and on futures market rules see Richard M. Levich and Lee R. Thomas III, "The Significance of Technical Trading-Rule Profits in the Foreign Exchange Market: A Bootstrap Approach," *Journal of International Money and Finance,* October 1993, pp. 451–474.

Thomas Willett, found profits from trading in the spot market.[41] These profits persisted even after allowance for transaction costs, although it is not clear whether they are sufficient for the risk involved. Trading rules have also been found to be profitable when used in the forward market and, more recently, in the futures market. However, there is an indication that trading based on simple rules is becoming less profitable.[42] This is what one would expect as the rules become known and are followed by more speculators, because the profits are then competed away. Therefore, perhaps the inefficiencies found in the various studies discussed above are a matter of history, a mere artifact of foreign-exchange-market participants learning about the instruments in which they are trading. Alternatively, perhaps the inefficiencies are the result of predictability of central-bank intervention policies of the past, with central banks shifting to less predictable or to less activist behavior.

SUMMARY

1. In the absence of transaction costs, a risk-neutral forward speculator buys a foreign currency forward if the forward price of the currency is below the expected future spot price. A speculator sells forward if the forward price of the currency exceeds the expected future spot price.
2. With transaction costs, a risk-neutral speculator buys if the forward ask price of the foreign currency exceeds the expected future bid price and sells if the forward bid price exceeds the expected future ask price.
3. Futures speculation is similar to forward speculation except that the futures contract can be sold back to the exchange prior to maturity. There is also marking-to-market risk on currency futures.
4. A speculator buys a call on a foreign currency if the probability-weighted sum of possible payouts based on the speculator's opinion exceeds the price of the option by enough to compensate for the opportunity cost and risk involved.
5. Investment in favor of a foreign currency can be achieved by borrowing domestic currency, buying the foreign currency, and purchasing an investment instrument denominated in the foreign currency. This is equivalent to buying the foreign currency forward and is called a swap.
6. It is possible to speculate against a foreign currency by borrowing in that currency, converting into domestic currency, and investing in the domestic currency.
7. Not hedging trade is speculation.
8. Speculation offers abnormal returns if markets are inefficient. In an efficient foreign exchange market, relevant information is reflected in exchange rates. Weak-form efficiency occurs when relevant information on past exchange rates is reflected in current rates; semi-strong-form efficiency occurs when all publicly available information is reflected; and strong-form efficiency occurs when *all* information, public and private, is reflected.
9. A difference between the forward rate and the expected future spot rate is called for-

---

[41]See Michael Dooley and Jeffrey Shafer, "Analysis of Short-Run Exchange Rate Behavior: March 1973 to November 1981," in David Bigman and Teizo Taya (eds.), *Exchange Rates and Trade Instability,* Ballenger, Cambridge, Mass., 1983, pp. 43–49; Dennis Logue, Richard Sweeney, and Thomas Willett, "Speculative Behavior of Foreign Exchange Rates During the Current Float," *Journal of Business Research,* vol. 6, 1979, pp. 159–174; and Stephan Schulmeister, "Currency Speculation and Dollar Fluctuations," *Quarterly Review,* Banca Nationale del Lavoro, December 1988, pp. 343–365.
[42]See Levich and Thomas, *op. cit.*

ward bias. A joint test of forward bias and of foreign exchange market efficiency is to regress forward rates and other relevant information on realized spot exchange rates. The absence of forward bias is implied by a zero constant and a forward rate coefficient of unity. Efficiency is implied by zero coefficients on other included variables.

10. Efficiency can also be tested by examining the sequential errors in forward forecasts of realized spot exchange rates. Omitted information is likely to cause sequentially related (persistent) prediction errors.
11. Forward bias is the risk premium that forward market participants require to compensate them for taking positions in particular currencies. Others are willing to pay this compensation to avoid risk.
12. Exchange-rate forecasting models have not generally predicted well outside the estimation period. This is the case even when realized values of variables believed to influence exchange rates are used in the formation of predictions.
13. Correlations between exchange rates and variables believed to affect exchange rates are generally low and sometimes have signs that are the opposite of what we would expect.
14. While expected events should not cause exchange rates to change, surprise events should affect exchange rates. Evidence on the effect of surprises is mixed.
15. Slowly changing opinions among market participants about the underlying policy regime governing exchange rates can generate data that appears to support market inefficiency, when in fact it is caused by shifting beliefs. It is important that any model used to judge market efficiency be based on the regime beliefs that market participants hold, with the assumed beliefs revised as necessary.
16. Exchange-rate forecasting services have a generally poor record of outdoing the forward rate when predicting future spot exchange rates. This is what market efficiency would imply. However, some forecasts based on chartist techniques, which project according to past exchange rates, have allowed speculators to make profits. More emphasis seems to have been given to chartist forecasting techniques based on their success. This could cause exchange-rate volatility in the form of overshooting exchange rates.

REVIEW QUESTIONS

1. In what ways are speculation, market efficiency, and forecasting closely related matters?
2. Taking into account transaction costs, what does a speculator compare when deciding whether to go long in a particular foreign currency via a forward exchange contract?
3. Taking into account transaction costs, what does a speculator compare when deciding whether to go short in a particular foreign currency via a forward contract?
4. Are futures more or less liquid than forwards for a currency speculator?
5. What is the main advantage of options versus forwards or futures as an instrument of currency speculation?
6. What is required to go long in Deutschemarks vis-à-vis the U.S. dollar via a swap?
7. How would you short the Deutschemark via a swap?
8. Why is doing nothing when importing or exporting tantamount to speculation on exchange rates?
9. What is meant by weak-form, semi-strong-form, and strong-form market efficiency?
10. Are there any "insiders" in the foreign exchange markets?
11. What type of regression equation could you use to simultaneously test the efficiency of the foreign exchange market and the existence of forward bias?
12. Is it possible to test for the omission of important factors in the pricing of foreign currencies without any measures of these factors?
13. What is meant by "rational" forecasts?

14. Why would you normally compare the performance of a spot-exchange-rate forecasting model with forward exchange rates?
15. Is the correlation coefficient between the ratio of U.S. to Japanese prices, and the exchange rate of the Japanese yen per dollar, likely to be positive or negative?
16. Why might anticipated changes in variables appear statistically insignificant when related to exchange rates?
17. What is an event study and how could it be applied to learning about what influences exchange rates?
18. What problem is presented by "changing regimes" in a study of market efficiency?
19. What is involved in so-called "technical" forecasting?
20. What might you deduce about what has happened to different peoples' opinions on exchange rates from an increase in the volume of foreign exchange transactions?

ASSIGNMENT PROBLEMS

1. Why might a speculator prefer speculating on the futures market to speculating with forward contracts?
2. What is the advantage of speculating with options?
3. If foreign exchange markets were efficient, what would this imply about foreign exchange cash management?
4. Why might foreign exchange markets be efficient even if you can make a positive return from using forecasting techniques?
5. Why does forward bias depend on risk aversion?
6. How might you speculate on the exchange rate being *less* volatile than the market as a whole believes it to be?
7. Why can we test for market efficiency without including any variables which might influence exchange rates in our test?
8. How might low correlations of individual variables with exchange rates hide a strong relationship of many variables when included together?
9. What different interpretations can be given to the shifting of the probability distribution of beliefs?
10. Do huge profits by individual speculators such as George Soros necessarily imply market inefficiency?

BIBLIOGRAPHY

BOOTHE, PAUL, and DAVID LONGWORTH: "Foreign Exchange Market Efficiency Tests," *Journal of International Money and Finance,* June 1986, pp. 135–152.

CHEN, T. J., and K. C. JOHN WEI: "Risk Premiums in Foreign Exchange Markets: Theory and Evidence," *Advances in Financial Planning and Forecasting,* vol. 4, 1990, pp. 23–42.

CHIANG, THOMAS C.: "Empirical Analysis of the Predictors of Future Spot Rates," *The Journal of Financial Research,* summer 1986, pp. 153–162.

CHINN, MENZIE, and JEFFREY FRANKEL: "Patterns in Exchange Rate Forecasts for Twenty-five Currencies," *Journal of Money, Credit and Banking,* November 1994, pp. 759–770.

EVERETT, ROBERT M., ABRAHAM M. GEORGE, and ARYEH BLUMBERG: "Appraising Currency Strengths and Weaknesses: An Operational Model for Calculating Parity Exchange Rates," *Journal of International Business Studies,* fall 1980, pp. 80–91.

FRANKEL, JEFFREY A., and KENNETH A. FROOT: "Using Survey Data to Test Some Standard

Propositions Regarding Exchange Rate Expectations," *American Economic Review,* March 1987, pp. 133–153.

FROOT, KENNETH A., and RICHARD H. THALER: "Anomalies: Foreign Exchange," *Journal of Economic Perspectives,* summer 1990, pp. 179–192.

GOODMAN, STEPHEN H.: "No Better than the Toss of a Coin," *Euromoney,* December 1978, pp. 75–85.

HODRICK, ROBERT J.: *The Empirical Evidence on the Efficiency of Forward and Futures Foreign Exchange Markets,* Harwood Academic Publishers, New York, 1988.

———— and SANJAY SRIVATAVA: "An Investigation of Risk and Return in Forward Foreign Exchange," *Journal of International Money and Finance,* April 1984, pp. 5–29.

KOEDJIK, KEES G., and MACK OTT: "Risk Aversion, Efficient Markets and the Forward Exchange Rate," *Review,* Federal Reserve Bank of St. Louis, December 1987, pp. 5–8.

KOHERS, THEODOR: "Testing the Rate of Forecasting Consistency of Major Foreign Currency Futures," *International Trade Journal,* summer 1987, pp. 359–370.

KWOK, CHUCK C. Y., and LEROY D. BROOKS: "Examining Event Study Methodologies in Foreign Exchange Markets," *Journal of International Business Studies,* second quarter 1990, pp. 189–224.

LEVICH, RICHARD M.: "On the Efficiency of Markets for Foreign Exchange," in Rudiger Dornbusch and Jacob A. Frenkel (eds.), *International Economic Policy: Theory and Evidence,* Johns Hopkins University Press, Baltimore, 1979.

————: "Analyzing the Accuracy of Foreign Exchange Advisory Services: Theory and Evidence," in Richard Levich and Clas Wihlberg (eds.), *Exchange Risk and Exposure: Current Developments in International Financial Management,* D.C. Heath, Lexington, Mass., 1980.

———— and LEE R. THOMAS III: "The Significance of Technical Trading-Rule Profits in the Foreign Exchange Market: A Bootstrap Approach," *Journal of International Money and Finance,* October 1993, pp. 451–474.

LEWIS, KAREN K.: "Can Learning Affect Exchange Rate Behavior? The Case of the Dollar in the Early 1980s," *Journal of Monetary Economics,* vol. 23, 1989, pp. 79–100.

MEESE, RICHARD A., and KENNETH ROGOFF: "Empirical Exchange Rate Models of the Seventies: Do They Fit Out of Sample?" *Journal of International Economics,* February 1983, pp. 3–24.

————: "Currency Fluctuations in the Post-Bretton Woods Era," *The Journal of Economic Perspectives,* winter 1990, pp. 117–134.

PEARCE, DOUGLAS K.: "Information, Expectations, and Foreign Exchange Market Efficiency," in Thomas Grennes (ed.), *International Financial Markets and Agricultural Trade,* Westview, Boulder, Colo., 1989, pp. 214–260.

SWEENEY, RICHARD J.: "Beating the Foreign Exchange Market," *Journal of Finance,* March 1986, pp. 163–182.

TAYLOR, DEAN: "Official Intervention in the Foreign Exchange Market, or Bet against the Central Bank," *Journal of Political Economy,* April 1982, pp. 356–368.

PART FIVE

International Investment and Financing

If there is any individual factor which commands principal responsibility for the astonishingly rapid globalization of the world economy, that factor is surely international investment. While numerous measures of the phenomenal growth and scale of international investment were mentioned in Chapter 1, a few are worth restating. For example, in 1970, stock and bond transactions involving an American and a non-American were the equivalent of 3 percent of the U.S. GDP. By 1980 this value had become 9 percent, and by 1990 it had grown to 93 percent.* For Japan the equivalent numbers are 2 percent in 1975, 7 percent in 1980, and 119 percent in 1990. Overall global cross-border transactions in stocks grew at a compound rate of 28 percent per annum between 1980 and 1990. Direct foreign investment, which involves managerial control overseas through the extent of ownership, grew at 27 percent per annum in the second half of the 1980s. At that rate, the amount of new overseas investment occurring in 3 years exceeds the

cumulative foreign investment of all previous history! It is the factors behind and the consequences of these startling statistics that are the focus of Part Five of this book.

The first three chapters of Part Five consider the three categories of international capital flows appearing in the balance-of-payments accounts, namely, short-term investments (Chapter 17), portfolio investments (Chapter 18), and direct investments (Chapter 19). These categories are identified by balance-of-payments statisticians and presented separately in this book because they represent different degrees of liquidity, with short-term investments being the most liquid and direct investments the least liquid.

Chapter 17, which deals with short-term investments, begins with a discussion of the criterion for making short-term covered investments when there are costs of transacting in the foreign exchange markets. Since short-term investments are an important aspect of cash management, the chapter looks also at short-term borrowing decisions and a number of other aspects of the management of working capital in a multinational context.

*All statistics are from "Fear of Finance," in *World Economy,* a supplement in *The Economist,* September 19, 1992, pp. 1–6.

Chapter 18, which deals with portfolio investment, considers international aspects of stock and bond investment decisions, paying particularly close attention to the benefits of international portfolio diversification. It is shown that international diversification offers significant advantages over domestic diversification, despite uncertainty about exchange rates. A section is included on the international capital asset pricing model. This model is used to compare the implications of internationally segmented versus integrated capital markets. Chapter 18 ends with a discussion of bond investments, again with a focus on diversification issues.

Chapter 19 considers a capital-budgeting framework that management can employ when deciding whether or not to make foreign direct investments. We shall see that a number of problems are faced in evaluating foreign investments that are not present when evaluating domestic investments. These extra problems include the presence of exchange-rate and country risks, the need to consider taxes abroad as well as at home, the issue of which country's cost of capital to use as a discount rate, the problem posed by restrictions on repatriating income, and the frequent need to account for subsidized financing. The means for dealing with these difficulties are clarified by an extensive example.

Chapter 19 includes an appendix in which various topics in taxation are covered, some of which are relevant for the capital-budgeting procedure used for evaluating foreign direct investments. The appendix offers a general overview of taxation in the international context, covering such topics as valued-added tax—which is assuming increasing international importance—tax-reducing organizational stuctures, and withholding tax.

It is through direct foreign investment that some companies have grown into the giant multinational corporations (MNCs) whose names have entered every major language—Sony, IBM, Shell, Ford, Nestlé, Mitsubishi, Citibank, and so on. Chapter 20 examines various reasons for the growth in relative importance of MNCs, as well as the reasons for international business associations that have resulted in transnational alliances. The chapter also considers some special problems faced by multinational corporations and transnational alliances, including the need to set transfer prices of goods and services moving between divisions and the need to measure and monitor country risk. The difficulties in obtaining and using transfer prices are described, as are some methods of measuring country risk. Clarification is given of the differences between country risk and two narrower concepts, political risk and sovereign risk. Methods for reducing or eliminating country risk are described. Chapter 20 concludes with an account of the problems and benefits that have accompanied the growth of multinational corporations and transnational alliances. This involves a discussion of the power of these giant organizations to frustrate the economic policies of host governments, and of the transfer of technology and jobs that results from foreign direct investment.

The final chapter of Part Five, Chapter 21, deals with project financing. The issues addressed include the country of equity issue, foreign bonds versus Eurobonds, bank loans, government lending, and matters that relate to financial structure. Overall, we shall see in Part Five that there are important matters which are unique to the international arena, whether the issue concerns the uses or the sources of funds. We shall also see that substantial progress has been made in understanding many of the thornier multinational matters.

CHAPTER 17

Cash Management

Where credit is due, give credit. When credit is due, give cash.

—Evan Esar

For most corporations, both the inflow and the outflow of funds are frequently uncertain. It is therefore important for companies to maintain a certain degree of liquidity. The amount of liquidity, as well as the form it should take, constitute the topic of working-cash (or working-capital) management. Liquidity can take a number of forms, including coin and currency, bank deposits, overdraft facilities, and short-term readily marketable securities. These involve different degrees of opportunity cost in terms of forgone earnings available on less liquid investments. However, there are such highly liquid short-term securities in sophisticated money markets that virtually no funds have to remain completely idle. There are investments with maturities that extend no further than "overnight," or the next day, and there are overdraft facilities which allow firms to hold minimal cash balances. This makes part of the cash management problem similar to the problem of where to borrow and invest.

The objectives of effective working-capital management in an international environment are (1) to allocate short-term investments and cash-balance holdings between currencies and countries to maximize overall corporate returns and (2) to borrow in different money markets to achieve the minimum cost. These objectives are to be pursued under the conditions of maintaining required liquidity and minimizing any risks that might be incurred. The problem of having numerous currency and country choices for investing and borrowing, which is the extra dimension of international finance, is shared by firms with local markets and firms with international markets for their products. For example, a firm that produces and sells only within the United States will still have an incentive to earn the highest yield or borrow at the lowest cost, even if that means venturing to foreign money markets. There *are* additional problems faced by firms that have a multinational orientation of production and sales. These include the questions of local versus head-office management of working capital and how to minimize foreign exchange transaction costs, political risks, and taxes. These are the questions we address in this chapter. We will also describe some actual international cash management systems that have been devised.

Let us begin our discussion of cash management by considering whether a company should invest or borrow in domestic versus foreign currency, where any foreign exchange exposure and risk is hedged by using forward exchange contracts. While this choice was discussed in Chapter 11, we have not yet dealt with how to make the choice when there are transaction costs. After discussing the investment and borrowing criteria we turn to whether a company with receipts and payments in different countries and currencies should manage working capital locally or centrally. We shall see that there are a number of advantages to centralization of cash management, and only a few disadvantages.

INVESTMENT AND BORROWING CHOICES WITH TRANSACTION COSTS

Investment Criterion with Transaction Costs

An investment in pound-denominated securities by a holder of U.S. dollars requires a spot purchase of pounds. The pounds must be bought at the offer or ask rate, $S(\$/\text{ask}\pounds)$, so that \$1 will buy

$$\pounds \, \frac{1}{S(\$/\text{ask}\pounds)}$$

This initial investment will grow in n years at the investment return $r_\pounds^1$ to

$$\pounds \, \frac{1}{S(\$/\text{ask}\pounds)} \left(1 + r_\pounds^1\right)^n$$

This can be sold forward at the buying or bid rate on pounds, $F_n(\$/\text{bid}\pounds)$, giving a U.S. investor, after n years,

$$\$ \, \frac{F_n(\$/\text{bid}\pounds)}{S(\$/\text{ask}\pounds)} \left(1 + r_\pounds^1\right)^n$$

The proceeds from \$1 invested in dollar securities for n years are $\$(1 + r_\$^1)^n$. Therefore, the rule for a holder of U.S. dollars is to invest in pound securities when

$$\frac{F_n(\$/\text{bid}\pounds)}{S(\$/\text{ask}\pounds)} \left(1 + r_\pounds^1\right)^n > \left(1 + r_\$^1\right)^n \tag{17.1}$$

and to invest in dollar securities when the reverse inequality holds.

If we had ignored foreign exchange transaction costs, then instead of the condition (17.1) we would have written the criterion for investing in pound securities as

$$\frac{F_n(\$/\pounds)}{S(\$/\pounds)} \left(1 + r_\pounds^1\right)^n > \left(1 + r_\$^1\right)^n \tag{17.2}$$

In comparing the conditions (17.1) and (17.2) we can see that because transaction costs ensure that $F_n(\$/\text{bid}\pounds) < F_n(\$/\pounds)$ and $S(\$/\text{ask}\pounds) > S(\$/\pounds)$, where $F_n(\$/\pounds)$ and $S(\$/\pounds)$ are the middle exchange rates (that is, the rates halfway between the bid and ask rates), the condition for advantageous investment in pound securities is made less likely by transaction costs on foreign exchange. That is, the left-hand side of condition (17.1), which includes transaction costs, is smaller than the left-hand side of condition (17.2), which excludes transaction costs. However, because both interest rates are investment rates, transaction costs on securities represented by a borrowing-lending spread have no bearing on the decision and do not discourage foreign versus domestic-currency investment.

For example, suppose we have

$S(\$/\text{bid}£)$	$S(\$/\text{ask}£)$	$F_{1/2}(\$/\text{bid}£)$	$F_{1/2}(\$/\text{ask}£)$	$r_\$^I$	$r_£^I$
1.5800	1.5850	1.5600	1.5670	7%	10%

where $r_\$^I$ and $r_£^I$ are, respectively, the dollar and pound interest rates on 6-month securities, expressed on a full-year, or per annum, basis. Then, receipts from the dollar investment at the end of the 6 months on each dollar originally invested are

$$\$\left(1 + r_\$^I\right)^n = \$(1.07)^{1/2} = \$1.03441$$

If the investor does not bother to calculate the receipts from the pound security using the correct side of the spot and forward quotations but instead uses the midpoint values halfway between "bids" and "asks," that is, $S(\$/£) = 1.5825$ and $F_{1/2}(\$/£) = 1.5635$, then receipts from the hedged pound security are

$$\$\frac{F_{1/2}(\$/£)}{S(\$/£)}\left(1 + r_£^I\right)^{1/2} = \$\frac{1.5635}{1.5825}(1.10)^{1/2} = \$1.03622$$

This amount exceeds the $1.03441 from the dollar-denominated security, making the pound security the preferred choice. However, if the correct exchange rates are used, reflecting the fact that pound securities require *buying* pounds spot and *selling* pounds forward, then the proceeds from the pound security are calculated as

$$\$\frac{F_{1/2}(\$/\text{bid}£)}{S(\$/\text{ask}£)}\left(1 + r_£^I\right)^{1/2} = \$\frac{1.5600}{1.5850}(1.10)^{1/2} = \$1.03227$$

The dollar security with receipts of $1.03441 per dollar are seen to be higher. That is, the correct choice is the dollar security, a choice that would not be made without using the exchange rates which reflect the transaction costs. The example confirms that transaction costs on foreign exchange tend to favor the choice of domestic-currency investments.

Borrowing Criterion with Transaction Costs

When a borrower considers using a swap to raise U.S. dollars by borrowing pounds, the borrowed pounds must be sold at the pound selling rate, $S(\$/\text{bid}£)$. For each $1 the dollar borrower wants, he or she must therefore borrow

$$£\frac{1}{S(\$/\text{bid}£)}$$

The repayment on this number of borrowed pounds after n years at $r_£^B$ per annum is

$$£\frac{1}{S(\$/\text{bid}£)}\left(1 + r_£^B\right)^n$$

This number of pounds can be bought forward at the buying rate for pounds, $F_n(\$/\text{ask}£)$, so that the number of dollars paid in n years for borrowing \$1 today is

$$\$ \frac{F_n(\$/\text{ask}£)}{S(\$/\text{bid}£)} \left(1 + r_£^B\right)^n$$

Alternatively, if \$1 is borrowed for n years in U.S. dollars at $r_\$^B$ per annum, the repayment in n years is

$$\$\left(1 + r_\$^B\right)^n$$

The borrowing criterion that allows for foreign exchange transaction costs is that a borrower should obtain dollars by borrowing British pounds (that is, via a swap) whenever

$$\frac{F_n(\$/\text{ask}£)}{S(\$/\text{bid}£)} \left(1 + r_£^B\right)^n < \left(1 + r_\$^B\right)^n \qquad (17.3)$$

Because $F_n(\$/\text{ask}£) > F_n(\$/£)$ and $S(\$/\text{bid}£) < S(\$/£)$, condition (17.3) is more unlikely than the condition without transaction costs on foreign exchange, which is simply

$$\frac{F_n(\$/£)}{S(\$/£)} \left(1 + r_£^B\right)^n < \left(1 + r_\$^B\right)^n \qquad (17.4)$$

where $S(\$/£)$ and $F_n(\$/£)$ are midpoints between "bid" and "ask" exchange rates. For example, suppose a borrower who needs U.S. dollars for 6 months faces the following:

$S(\$/\text{bid}£)$	$S(\$/\text{ask}£)$	$F_{1/2}(\$/\text{bid}£)$	$F_{1/2}(\$/\text{ask}£)$	$r_\$^B$	$r_£^B$
1.5800	1.5850	1.5500	1.5570	8%	12%

where $r_\$^B$ and $r_£^B$ are the per annum 6-month borrowing rates in dollars and pounds, respectively. The dollar repayment after 6 months from dollar borrowing is

$$\$\left(1 + r_\$^B\right)^{1/2} = \$(1.08)^{1/2} = \$1.03923$$

If the borrower did not bother to calculate the cost of a "swap out" of pounds using the correct bid or ask exchange rates but instead used midpoint rates, that is, $S(\$/£) = 1.5825$ and $F_{1/2}(\$/£) = 1.5535$, the repayment per dollar borrowed would be computed from the left-hand side of condition (17.4) as

$$\$ \frac{F_n(\$/£)}{S(\$/£)} \left(1 + r_£^B\right)^n = \$ \frac{1.5535}{1.5825} (1.12)^{1/2} = \$1.03891$$

The borrower would choose the swap out of pounds because it requires a smaller repayment than directly borrowing dollars. However, if the borrower selected the proper bid and ask rates as in the left-hand side of condition (17.3), the repayment on the swap would be

$$\$ \frac{F_n(\$/\text{ask}£)}{S(\$/\text{bid}£)} \left(1 + r_£^B\right)^n = \$ \frac{1.5570}{1.5800} (1.12)^{1/2} = \$1.04289$$

This is larger than the repayment from borrowing dollars. We find that the incentive to venture into foreign-currency-denominated borrowing is reduced by the consideration of foreign exchange transaction costs, just as is the incentive to invest in foreign currency.

Unlike the situation with investment, where borrowing-lending spreads are irrelevant, in the case of borrowing, foreign-currency borrowing may be discouraged by borrowing-lending spreads. This is because *when foreign funds are raised abroad,* lenders may charge foreign borrowers more than they charge domestic borrowers because they consider loans to foreigners to be riskier. For example, the markup over the prime interest rate for dollars facing a U.S. borrower in the United States might be smaller than the markup over prime for the same U.S. borrower when raising pounds in Britain. This may be due to greater difficulty collecting on loans to foreigners, or to the difficulty of transferring information on creditworthiness of borrowers between countries. However, if the pounds can be raised in the United States, there should be no difference between dollar investment-borrowing spreads and pound investment-borrowing spreads.

Firms invest and borrow because sometimes they have net cash inflows and other times they have net cash outflows. While the investing and borrowing criteria that we have given provide a way of choosing between alternatives, they do not provide guidance on some of the complexities of multinational cash management. For example, how should a company respond when one subsidiary has surplus amounts of a currency while another subsidiary which operates independently needs to borrow the same currency? Should a company hedge all its foreign-currency investments and/or borrowing when it invests or borrows numerous different foreign currencies and thereby enjoys a degree of diversification? Good cash management in these and other situations requires some centralization of financial management and perhaps also of the funds themselves. As we shall see below, centralization has several advantages, but also some disadvantages when the funds as well as their management are centralized.

INTERNATIONAL DIMENSIONS OF CASH MANAGEMENT

Advantages of Centralized Cash Management

Netting

It is extremely common for multinational firms to have divisions in different countries, each having accounts receivable and accounts payable, as well as other sources of cash inflows and outflows, denominated in a number of currencies. If the divisions are left to manage their own cash, it can happen, for example, that one division is hedging a long pound position while at the same time another division is hedging a short pound position of the same maturity. This situation can be avoided by **netting,** which involves calculating the overall corporate position in each currency. This calculation requires some central coordination of cash management.

The benefit that is enjoyed from the ability to net cash inflows and outflows through centralized cash management comes in the form of reduced transaction costs. The amount that is saved depends on the extent that different divisions deal in the same currencies, and on the extent that different divisions have opposite positions in these currencies.[1] The benefit also depends on the length of the period over which it is feasible to engage in netting. This in turn depends on the ability to practice **leading and lagging.**

Leading and lagging involve the movement of cash inflows and outflows forward and backward in time so as to permit netting and achieve other goals.[2] For example, if Aviva has to pay £1 million for denim on June 10 and has received an order for £1 million of jeans from Britain, it might attempt to arrange payment for about the same date and thereby avoid exposure. If the payment for the jeans would normally have been after June 10 and the receivable is brought forward, this is called leading of the export. If the payment would have been before June 10 and is delayed, this is called lagging of the export. In a similar way imports can be led and lagged.

When dealing at arm's length, the opportunities for netting via leading and lagging are limited by the preferences of the other party. However, when transactions are between divisions of the same multinational, the scope for leading and lagging (for the purpose of netting and achieving other benefits such as deferring taxes) is considerable. Recognizing this, numerous governments regulate the length of credit and acceleration of settlement by putting limits on leading and lagging. The regulations vary greatly from country to country, and are subject to change, often with very little warning. If cash managers are to employ leading and lagging successfully, they must keep current with what is allowed.[3]

Currency Diversification

When cash management is centralized it is possible not only to net inflows and outflows in each separate currency, but also to consider whether the company's foreign exchange risk is sufficiently reduced via diversification that the company need not hedge all the individual positions. The diversification of exchange-rate risk results from the fact that exchange rates do not all move in perfect harmony. Consequently, a portfolio of inflows and outflows in different currencies will have a smaller variance of value than the sum of variances of the values of the individual currencies.[4] We can explain the nature of the diversification benefit by considering a straightforward example.

Suppose that in its foreign operations, Aviva buys its cloth in France and sells its finished garments in both France and Germany in the amounts shown below:

	Germany (DM)	France (Fr)
Denim purchase	0	8,000,000
Jeans sales	2,000,000	3,000,000

[1]Clearly, if all divisions are long in pounds, or all divisions are short in pounds, the transaction-cost advantage of centralized cash management exists only if there are economies of scale in transacting. Of course, there *are* in fact such economies of scale.

[2]Leading and lagging are practiced to defer income and thereby delay paying taxes and to create unhedged positions in order to speculate; cash managers may delay paying out currencies they expect to appreciate and accelerate paying out currencies they expect to depreciate. Leading and lagging are therefore used to hedge, speculate, and reduce taxes.

[3]The regulations governing leading and lagging are described each year by Business International in its *Money Report*. The large multinational accounting firms also publish the current regulations.

[4]For an account of the size of diversification benefits see Mark R. Eaker and Dwight Grant, "Cross-Hedging Foreign Currency Risk," working paper, University of North Carolina, August 1985.

The timing of payments for French denim and the timing of sales of jeans are the same. (Alternatively, we could think of the revenue from the export of jeans as receipts from foreign investments, and the payment for imports of cloth as repayment on a debt.)

One route open to Aviva is to sell forward DM2 million and, after netting its French-franc position, buy forward Fr5 million. Aviva would then be hedged against changes in exchange rates. An alternative, however, is to consider how the French franc and the German mark move vis-à-vis the dollar and hence between themselves. Let us suppose, simply to reveal the possibilities, that when the German mark appreciates vis-à-vis the dollar, generally the French franc does so also. In other words, let us suppose that the mark and the franc are highly positively correlated.

With net franc payables of Fr5 million, mark receivables of DM2 million, and spot exchange rates of, for example, $S(\$/DM) = 0.5$ and $S(\$/Fr) = 0.2$, the payables and receivables cancel out. The payable to France is $1 million at current rates, which is the same as the receivable from Germany. The risk is that exchange rates can change before payments are made and receipts are received. However, if the franc and the mark move together and the exchange rates become, for example, $S(\$/DM) = 0.55$ and $S(\$/Fr) = 0.22$, then payments to France will be $1,100,000, and receipts from Germany will also be $1,100,000. What will be lost in extra payments to France will be gained in extra revenue from Germany. We find in this case that Aviva is quite naturally unexposed if it can be sure that the currencies will always move together vis-à-vis the dollar.

In our example, we have, of course, selected very special circumstances and values for convenience. In general, however, there is safety in large numbers. If there are receivables in many different currencies, then when some go up in value, others will come down. There will be some canceling of gains and losses. Similarly, if there are many payables, they can also cancel. Moreover, as in our example, receivables and payables can offset each other if currency values move together. There are many possibilities that are not obvious, but it should be remembered that although some canceling of gains and losses might occur, some risk will remain. A firm should use forward contracts or some other form of hedging if it wishes to avoid all foreign exchange risk and exposure. However, a firm with a large variety of small volumes of payables and receivables (that is, small volumes in many different currencies) might consider that all the transaction costs involved in the alternative forms of hedging are not worthwhile in view of the natural hedging from diversification. The determination of whether the diversification has sufficiently reduced the risk can only be made properly when cash management is centralized.

Pooling

Pooling occurs when cash is held as well as managed in a central location. The advantage of pooling is that cash needs can be met wherever they occur without having to keep precautionary balances in each country. Uncertainties and delays in moving funds to where they are needed require that some balances be maintained everywhere, but with pooling, a given probability of having sufficient cash to meet liquidity needs can be achieved with smaller cash holdings than if holdings are decentralized. The reason pooling works is that cash surpluses and deficiencies in different locations do not move in a perfectly parallel fashion. As a result, the variance of total cash flows is smaller than the sum of the variances of flows for individual countries. For example, when there are large cash-balance outflows in Belgium, it is not likely that there will also be unusually large outflows in Britain, the United States, France, Holland, Germany, and so on. If a firm is to have sufficient amounts in each individual country, it must maintain a large cash reserve in each. However, if the total cash needs are pooled in, for example, the United States, then when the need in Belgium is unusually high, it can be met from the central pool because there will not normally be unusually high drains in other countries at the same time.

Security Availability and Efficiency of Collections

All of the advantages of centralized cash management that we have mentioned so far, which are all particular aspects of economies of scale, would accrue wherever centralization occurs. However, if the centralization occurs in a major international financial center such as London or New York, there are additional advantages in terms of a broader range of securities that are available and an ability to function in an efficient financial system.

It is useful for a firm to denominate as many payments and receipts as its counterparties will allow in units of a major currency and to have bills payable in a financial center. Contracts for payment due to the firm should stipulate not only the payment date and the currency in which payment is to be made, but also the branch or office at which the payment is due. Penalties for late payment can help ensure that payments are made on time. The speed of collection of payments can be increased by using post-office box numbers wherever they are available. Similarly, if a firm banks with a large-scale multinational bank, it can usually arrange for head-office accounts to be quickly credited, even if payment is made at a foreign branch of the bank.

Disadvantages of Centralized Cash Management

Unfortunately, it is rarely possible to hold all cash in a major international financial center. This is because there may be unpredictable delays in moving funds from the financial center to other countries. If an important payment is due, especially if it is to a foreign government for taxes or to a local supplier of a crucial input, excess cash balances should be held where they are needed, even if these mean opportunity costs in terms of higher interest earnings available elsewhere. When the cash needs in local currencies are known well ahead of time, arrangements can be made in advance for receiving the needed currency, but substantial allowances for potential delay should be made. When one is used to dealing in North America, Europe, and other developed areas, it is too easy to believe that banking is efficient everywhere, but the delays that can be faced in banks in, for example, the Middle East and Africa can be exceedingly long, uncertain, and costly.

In principle it is possible to centralize the *management* of working capital even if some funds do have to be held locally. However, complete centralization of management is difficult because local representation is often necessary for dealing with local clients and banks. Even if a multinational bank is used for accepting receipts and making payments, problems can arise that can only be dealt with on the spot. Therefore, the question a firm must answer is the degree of centralization of cash management that is appropriate, and in particular, which activities can be centralized and which should be decentralized.[5]

---

[5]Exhibit 17.1 explains how General Electric arrived at its decision about currency management centralization.

If interest parity always held exactly, the cash management problem would be simplified in that it would then not matter in which currency or country a firm borrowed or invested. However, as we explained in Chapter 11, there are factors which do allow limited departures from interest parity to occur, at least from the perspective of any one borrower or lender. Let us consider what each of the factors discussed earlier—transaction costs, political risk, liquidity preference, and taxes—implies for working-capital management. We shall see that each factor has slightly different implications.

Transaction Costs, Political Risk, Liquidity Preference, Taxes, and Cash Management

Transaction costs are a reason for keeping funds in the *currency* that is received if the funds might be needed later in the same currency. For example, if a firm receives 2 million won in payment for sales from its subsidiary in South Korea and needs approximately this quantity of won to meet a payment in a month or two, the funds should be left in Korean won if expected yields are not sufficiently higher in other currencies to cover two sets of transaction costs.

Political risk is a reason to keep funds in the company's home *country* rather than in the country in whose currency the funds are denominated. This is because the home jurisdiction is generally the most friendly one. The reduction in political risk that results from moving funds home must, of course, be balanced against the extra costs this entails when the funds are converted into domestic currency and therefore must later be converted back into the foreign currency. Between most developed countries, the transaction costs of temporarily moving funds home are likely to exceed the benefit from reduced political risk, and so cash balances should be maintained in the foreign countries. However, the political situation in some third-world countries might be considered sufficiently volatile that only minimal working balances should be maintained in those countries.

Liquidity considerations argue in favor of keeping funds in the currency in which they are *most likely* to be needed in the future. This might not be the currency in which the funds arrive or the company's home currency. The liquidity factor is hence different from transaction costs, which suggest that funds should be kept in the currency in which they arrive, and it is also different from political risk, which suggests that funds should be kept at home. We use the words "most likely" because it is the uncertainty of cash flows that is responsible for the need to maintain liquidity. If inflows and outflows were *perfectly* predictable, a firm could arrange the maturities of long-term securities so that each security would mature at the precise time the funds were needed. Complete certainty would do away with the so-called precautionary motive for holding money balances. However, even with uncertainty in the timing and amounts of cash inflows and outflows, extremely liquid money-market investments and overdraft facilities at banks have allowed firms to keep most of their funds in interest-bearing instruments.

Withholding taxes are a reason to avoid countries whose withholding rates exceed the investor's domestic tax rate, because in such a case it will not in general be possible to receive full withholding-tax credit. Lower taxes on foreign exchange gains than on interest income are a reason to invest in countries whose currencies are at a forward premium if the premium is treated as a capital gain. However, for firms that are heavily involved in dealing in many countries, foreign exchange gains and interest earnings are likely to face the same tax rates. There is therefore little need to favor any particular market. The factors affecting the location of working capital are summarized in Table 17.1.

TABLE 17.1. Factors Affecting Working-Capital Management

Factor	Implication
Absence of forward markets	Keep funds in the currency received if an anticipated future need exists.
Transaction costs	Keep funds in the currency received.
Political risk	Move funds to the domestic market.
Liquidity requirements	Keep funds in the currency most likely to be needed in the future.
Taxes	Avoid high withholding taxes and keep funds in appreciating currencies.

It will be illustrative to end our discussion of cash management by considering the cash management systems of two U.S. multinational corporations. These systems illustrate how netting can be done, and how centralized cash management through a **currency center** can be effected.

Navistar International

Navistar International was formed in a reorganization of International Harvester, the farm and transportation equipment manufacturer. The company has established a netting system that works as follows:[6]

The netting system is based at a currency clearing center, located in a finance company in Switzerland. Prior to clearing foreign exchange, the Swiss finance company had been responsible for transactions involving foreign currencies. The netting scheme works on a monthly cycle, as illustrated in Figure 17.1. By the 15th day of each month, all the participating subsidiaries have sent information to the currency clearing center on payables and receivables existing at that time in local currencies. The clearing center converts all amounts into dollar terms at the current spot exchange rate and sends information to those subsidiaries with net payables on how much they owe and to whom. These paying subsidiaries are responsible for informing the net receivers of funds and for obtaining and delivering the foreign exchange. Settlement is on the 25th of the month or the closest business day, and the funds are purchased 2 days in advance so that they are received on the designated day. Any difference between the exchange rate used by the Swiss center on the 15th and the rate prevailing for settlement on the 25th gives rise to foreign exchange gains or losses, and these are attributed to the subsidiary.

The original clearing system was for intracompany use and did not include outside firms. After a decade with this system, the company introduced a scheme for foreign exchange settlements for payments to outsiders. There are two different dates, the 10th and the 25th or the nearest business day, on which all foreign exchange is purchased by and transferred from the Swiss center. The payment needs are sent electronically to the center from the subsidiary more than 2 days before the settlement date, and the center nets the amounts of each currency so as to make the minimum number of foreign exchange transactions. The subsidiary which owes the foreign exchange settles with the clearing center by the appropriate settlement date. According to the company, netting can cut the total number of transactions with outsiders in half, saving the company transaction costs.

More flexibility is given to the cash management system by the use of interdivisional leading and lagging. If, for example, a subsidiary is a net payer, it may delay or lag payment for up to 2 months while compensating the net receiver at prevailing interest rates. Net receivers of funds may at their discretion make funds available to other subsidiaries at interest. In this way the need to resort to outside borrowing is reduced; the Swiss clearing center serves to bring different parties together. The netting with leading and lagging has allowed the company to eliminate intracompany floats and reduce by over 80 percent the amount that otherwise would have been transferred.

---

[6]See "Multilateral Netting System Cuts Costs, Provides Flexibility for International Harvester," *Money Report,* Business International, December 20, 1979.

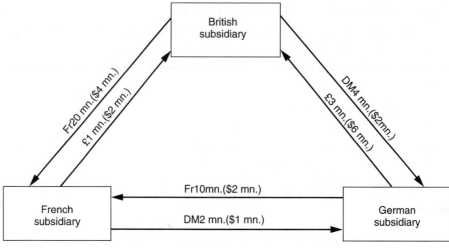

(*a*) **Receivables and payables reported to currency center before the 15th of month**

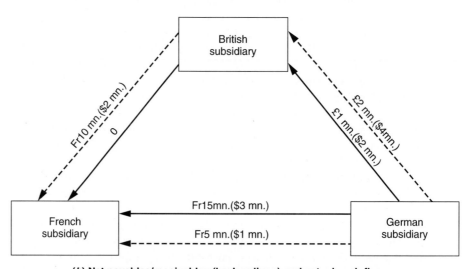

(*b*) **Net payables/receivables (broken lines) and actual cash flows (solid lines) made on the 25th of the month**

Figure 17.1. Example of Navistar International's Foreign Exchange Netting System
It is assumed that on the 15th of the month $S(DM/\$) = 2.0$, $S(£/\$) = 0.5$, and $S(Fr/\$) = 5.0$. Information on receivables and payables is provided for the Swiss currency center on or before the 15th of the month. The currency center converts the amounts of foreign exchange into dollars at the going exchange rate (as shown in part *a*) and evaluates the net amounts owed between subsidiaries (as shown by the broken lines in part *b*). Rather than having the German subsidiary pay the British subsidiary the equivalent of $4 million while the British subsidiary in turn pays the French subsidiary $2 million, the German subsidiary will be instructed to add $2 million onto what it pays the French subsidiary and to reduce what it pays the British subsidiary by this amount. The British and French subsidiaries will receive no instructions to pay anybody. The total number of transactions will be reduced from six to only two. Transaction costs will be faced on only $5 million worth of transactions.

Digital Equipment

Itself an advanced information-processing company, Digital Equipment centralizes its cash management in two currency centers.[7] The cash positions of European subsidiaries are monitored and managed from the European headquarters in Geneva. Cash management for other subsidiaries is handled by the company's principal headquarters, which is in Acton, Massachusetts. The subsidiaries and appropriate headquarters communicate electronically, and the movement of cash is facilitated by the use of a limited number of U.S. banks with offices in many countries. The cash management system works as shown in Figure 17.2.

Foreign exchange positions are established and adjusted on a weekly basis. Every Thursday, all subsidiaries send a report to the currency center at their headquarters. In their statements they give projected cash inflows and outflows in each foreign currency for the following week. They also give their bank-account positions. The foreign sales subsidiaries are generally net receivers of foreign exchange. On the following Monday the subsidiary borrows its anticipated net cash inflow via an overdraft facility and transfers the funds to the headquarter's account at the same bank. For example, if the British sales subsidiary expects net receipts of £10 million and has no bank balance, it will call its banks for the best exchange rate. If the most favorable rate for buying dollars is $S(\$/£) = 2.0$, it will transfer $20 million to the Geneva currency center by borrowing £10 million and converting it into dollars. The selected bank—the one which offered the best rate on dollars—will debit the British subsidiary's account in London by £10 million and, on the same day, credit the Geneva headquarter's account with $20 million. The British subsidiary will pay the £10 million debt due to the overdraft as the receipts come in.

In order to ensure that it is able to make the same-day transfers and obtain the overdrafts, Digital maintains close ties with a limited number of multinational U.S. banks. The subsidiaries obtain funds only via overdrafts; they do not use other means of borrowing funds. Subsidiaries that are net users of foreign exchange instead of net receivers use the reverse procedure. The subsidiary reports its need for cash to the appropriate headquarters on Thursday, and beginning on the following Monday it uses overdraft lines as payments are met. On the following Friday the subsidiary receives funds from the parent company to pay off the overdraft and make up for any unanticipated disbursements that have been made.

There are occasions when a subsidiary will receive more funds than it anticipated and transfers them to headquarters more than once a week. Alternatively, a subsidiary may face unprojected disbursements or late receipts. It will then use backup overdrafts. Similarly, if a subsidiary faces unusually large payments it will call its parent for extra funds. Digital uses post-office lock boxes in Canada and the United States in order to speed up the handling of receivables, and in Europe, Digital instructs customers to pay its bank directly rather than the local subsidiary itself.

---

[7]An excellent account of Digital Equipment's centralized cash management system can be found in "How Digital Equipment's Weekly Cash Cycle Mobilizes Idle Funds," *Money Report,* Business International, January 30, 1981. A similar system that uses a currency center in London is operated by RCA. The company adapted a system available from Citibank for large clients which keeps track of currency needs and netting. For a full account, see "Standard Netting System Remodelled to Suit RCA's Own Needs," *Money Report,* Business International, July 13, 1979. Chase Manhattan's system is known as Infocash, and the netting and information system available from the international financial advisory firm Business International is known as Xmis.

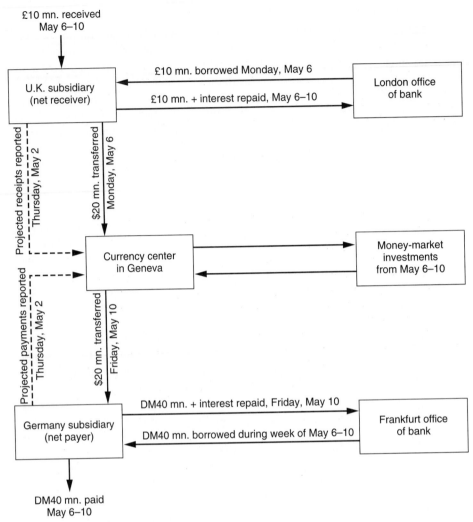

Figure 17.2. Digital Equipment's Weekly Cash Cycle

We assume that the U.K. subsidiary is a net receiver of pounds and that the German subsidiary is a net payer of German marks. Both subsidiaries send their cash-flow projections to the currency center on Thursday, May 2. On the following Monday the U.K. subsidiary borrows its expected cash receipts and then transfers the dollar equivalent to Geneva. [It is assumed that $S(\$/£) = 2.0$.] The debt is repaid in the currency of borrowing during the week of May 6–10. The German subsidiary borrows marks during the week of May 6–10 as its payments fall due. On Friday, May 10, the Geneva currency center transfers the dollar equivalent to the subsidiary. [It is assumed that $S(\$/DM) = 0.5$.] This is used to repay the overdraft on that day. During the week the currency center has $20 million to invest in the money market.

All investing or borrowing in currencies other than the U.S. dollar is hedged on the forward market to avoid foreign exchange risk.

Because the amount of cash handled by the two headquarters is so large, it can generally be invested more favorably than if each separate subsidiary placed it. Funds are invested in various money markets. The parent has the total amount of funds from its many subsidiaries to invest for a full week. A subsidiary will, however, repay the overdraft *during* the week. It follows that the interest costs on overdrafts are not as large as the interest earnings of the headquarters.

The major advantage of Digital Equipment's system is that there is no foreign exchange exposure for the subsidiary. This is because the payable on the overdraft is in the local currency, as is the receivable against which the funds have been borrowed. Local currency is paid out as it arrives. An additional advantage is that the currency centers handle large amounts of cash and can therefore get lower spreads when buying and selling foreign exchange. They can also take a broader perspective of investment and borrowing opportunities as well as enjoy the advantages of netting, currency diversification, pooling, and financial efficiency that we discussed earlier.

SUMMARY

1. The choice between domestic-currency and foreign-currency investment or borrowing should be based on spot and forward exchange-rate quotations which reflect transaction costs.
2. The need to buy/sell spot and then sell/buy forward for hedged foreign-currency investment/borrowing tends to favor the domestic-currency alternative.
3. Centralized cash management allows netting of long and short positions in each currency, where the positions are those of different divisions of a multinational firm. The scope for netting is enhanced by leading and lagging cash inflows and outflows.
4. Centralized cash management provides an ability to consider how exposure to numerous exchange rates provides diversification.
5. Centralization permits a broad view of investment and borrowing opportunities.
6. Centralized cash management reduces the precautionary cash needs via pooling; funds can be moved from the central location to where they are needed.
7. Complete centralization is limited by the need to maintain local funds and personnel for dealing with unpredictable delays in moving funds between countries and also dealing with local banks and clients.
8. The different reasons why interest parity may not hold have different implications for the management of working capital. In particular, transaction costs induce keeping funds in the currency in which cash arrives, political risk induces keeping funds at home, liquidity considerations induce holding currencies that are most likely to be needed, and taxes induce avoiding countries with very high withholding rates and holding appreciating currencies if facing favorable capital-gains treatment on foreign exchange gains.
9. Efficient cash management systems have been developed by several multinational corporations.

REVIEW QUESTIONS

1. What are the objectives of international cash management?
2. Why do transaction costs of spot and forward exchange reduce the incentive to invest in foreign-currency securities?
3. Why do transaction costs on spot and forward exchange reduce the incentive to borrow in a foreign currency?
4. What is meant by "netting"?
5. What is meant by "leading" and "lagging"?

6. What are the advantages of centralized cash management?

7. How can pooling provide benefits for international cash management?

8. How does liquidity preference affect international cash management decisions?

ASSIGNMENT PROBLEMS

1. Assume that you face the following money-market and exchange-rate quotations:

$r_\$$	$r_{C\$}$	$S(C\$/ask\$)$	$S(C\$/bid\$)$	$F_{1/2}(C\$/ask\$)$	$F_{1/2}(C\$/bid\$)$
4.20%	6.80%	1.3850	1.3830	1.4000	1.3960

  a. If $r_\$$ and $r_{C\$}$ are the 6-month borrowing rates on an annual basis facing a U.S. firm that wishes to borrow without incurring foreign exchange risk, should that firm borrow in U.S. dollars or in Canadian dollars?

  b. If $r_\$$ and $r_{C\$}$ are the rates available on 6 month U.S. and Canadian treasury bills on an annual basis, where should a U.S. firm wishing to invest place its funds?

2. Suppose that as the money manager of a U.S. firm you face the following situation:

$r_\$^B$	9.0%
$r_\$^I$	8.0%
$r_{C\$}^B$	10.5%
$r_{C\$}^I$	9.5%
$S(C\$/ask\$)$	1.2400
$S(C\$/bid\$)$	1.2350
$F_1(C\$/ask\$)$	1.2600
$F_1(C\$/bid\$)$	1.2550

Here $r_\$^B$ and $r_\$^I$ are the 1-year interest rates at which you can, respectively, borrow and invest in U.S. dollars, and $r_{C\$}^B$ and $r_{C\$}^I$ are the 1-year borrowing and investing interest rates in Canadian dollars.

  a. If you had funds to invest for 1 year, in which currency would you invest?

  b. If you wished to borrow for 1 year, in which currency would you borrow?

3. Suppose that you face the situation in question **2**, except that the effective tax rate on interest income is 50 percent and the effective tax rate on capital gains is 30 percent. In which currency-denominated securities would you wish to invest?

4. What is the connection between the size of the gain from netting and the nature of long and short positions of the different divisions of a multinational firm?

5. Which of the gains from centralization of cash management are related to foreign exchange transaction costs?

6. What are the differences and similarities between the gain from centralization of cash management via pooling and the gain via diversification of different currencies?

7. Will allowance for comovement between currencies allow a firm to eliminate foreign exchange risk or foreign exchange exposure?

8. Why might we suspect that any apparent covered interest arbitrage opportunity must be due to not considering transaction costs, political risk, taxes, or liquidity?

9. Why do multinational firms tend to use multinational banks rather than local banks in local markets?

10. Why do many governments restrict the maximum length of time over which firms can practise leading and lagging of accounts receivable and payable?

BUSINESS INTERNATIONAL: *Automated Global Financial Management,* Financial Executives Research Foundation, Morristown, N.J., 1988.

ESSAYYAD, MUSSA, and PAUL C. JORDAN: "An Adjusted-EOQ Model for International Cash Management," *Journal of Multinational Cash Management,* nos. 1/2, 1993, pp. 47–62.

SHAPIRO, ALAN C.: "Payments Netting in International Cash Management," *Journal of International Business Studies,* fall 1978, pp. 51–58.

SRINIVASAN, VENKAT, and YONG H. KIM: "Payments Netting in International Cash Management: A Network Optimization Approach," *Journal of International Business Studies,* summer 1986, pp. 1–20.

———, SUSAN E. MOELLER, and YONG H. KIM: "International Cash Management: State of the Art and Research Directions," *Advances in Financial Planning and Forecasting,* vol. 4, part B, 1990, pp. 161–194.

CHAPTER 18

Portfolio Investment

Economic forecasting houses . . . have successfully predicted fourteen of the last five recessions.

—DAVID FEHR

It should come as little surprise that just as the world as a whole is better off as a result of overseas investment, so can be an individual investor. As we explained in Chapter 1, the world as a whole benefits from international investment via (1) a better allocation of financial capital and (2) a smoother wealth or consumptive stream from the spreading of risk. Individual investors gain in these same ways. Stated in the vernacular of finance, diversified international investment offers investors higher expected returns and/or reduced risks vis-à-vis domestic investment. This chapter focuses on the sources and sizes of these gains from venturing overseas for **portfolio investment,** which is investment in bonds, and in equities where the investor's holding is too small to provide any effective control. (Direct investment, defined in Chapter 5 as investment for which the investor achieves some control, is discussed in Chapters 19 and 20.)

THE BENEFITS OF INTERNATIONAL PORTFOLIO INVESTMENT

Spreading Risk: Correlations between National Asset Markets

Because of risk aversion, investors will trade off lower expected return for lower risk. It is a well-established proposition in portfolio theory that whenever there is imperfect correlation between returns, risk is reduced by maintaining only a portion of wealth in any asset. More generally, by selecting a portfolio according to expected returns and correlations between returns, an investor can achieve minimum risk for a given expected portfolio return, or maximum expected return for a given risk. Furthermore, *ceteris paribus,* the lower the correlations between returns, the greater the benefits of portfolio diversification.[1]

---

[1]See Harry Markowitz, *Portfolio Selection: Efficient Diversification of Investments,* John Wiley & Sons, New York, 1959, and James Tobin, "Liquidity Preference as Behavior toward Risk," *Review of Economic Studies,* February 1958, pp. 65–86.

Within an economy there is some degree of independence of asset returns, and this provides some diversification opportunities for investors who do not venture abroad. However, there is a tendency for the various segments of an economy to feel jointly the influence of overall domestic activity, and for asset returns to respond jointly to prospects for domestic activity, and uncertainties about these prospects. This limits the independence of individual security returns and therefore also limits the gains to be made from diversification within only one country. Because of different industrial structures in different countries, and because different economies do not trace out exactly the same business cycles, there are reasons for smaller correlations of expected returns between investments in different countries than between investments within any one country. This means that foreign investments offer diversification benefits that cannot be enjoyed by investing only at home, and it also means that, for example, a U.S. investor might include British stocks in a portfolio even if they offer lower expected returns than U.S. stocks: the benefit of a risk reduction might more than compensate for lower expected returns.

Figure 18.1 graphically illustrates the degree of independence of foreign ver-

Figure 18.1. Correlations between U.S. and Other Countries' Stock Markets, U.S. Dollars, 1980–1990
The U.S. stock market is not very highly correlated with stock markets in other countries; correlation coefficients average about 0.5. These relatively low correlations mean a potential gain from holding an internationally diversified portfolio of stocks. (*Source:* Patrick Odier and Bruno Solnik, "Lessons for International Asset Allocation." Reprinted, with permission, from *Financial Analysts Journal,* March/April 1993. © 1993, Association for Investment Management and Research, Charlottesville, VA. All rights reserved.)

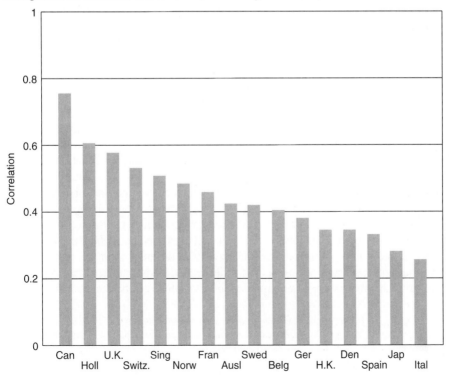

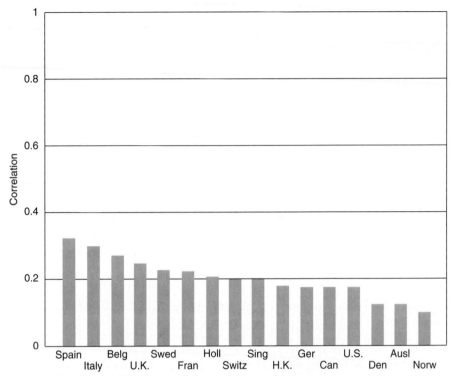

Figure 18.2. Correlations between Japanese and Other Countries' Stock Markets, Japanese Yen, 1980–1990
Japan's stock market follows a path which appears to be quite independent of the stock markets of other countries, with correlation coefficients averaging about 0.2. This situation suggests substantial potential benefits for Japanese investors holding an internationally diversified stock portfolio. (*Source:* Patrick Odier and Bruno Solnik, "Lessons for International Asset Allocation." Reprinted, with permission, from *Financial Analysts Journal,* March/April 1993. © 1993, Association for Investment Management and Research, Charlottesville, VA. All rights reserved.)

sus U.S. stock markets during the period 1980–1990, as reported by Patrick Odier and Bruno Solnik.[2] The correlations in the figure are based on U.S. dollar values of stock markets and have an average of about 0.5. This means a squared-correlation, called R^2, of 0.25. The R^2 statistic is an indicator of the extent to which two variables—in this case two countries' stock markets—respond jointly to common factors. Figure 18.1 suggests that different countries' stock markets have substantial idiosyncrasies of returns; with $R^2 = 0.25$, 75 percent of returns are due to factors specific to individual countries. In principle, the low correlations that are found could be the consequence either of different economic and political events in different countries or of different countries' stock-market indexes being formed from dissimilar mixes of industries. We shall show below that the latter explanation is not supported by the evidence.

[2]Patrick Odier and Bruno Solnik, "Lessons for International Asset Allocation," *Financial Analysts Journal,* March/April 1993, pp. 63–77. This excellent survey of international portfolio investment provides much useful data in addition to that cited in this chapter.

Figures 18.2 and 18.3 show, respectively, the correlation coefficients between the Japanese and non-Japanese markets and between the British and non-British markets. We see that it is not only the United States which has a major idiosyncratic element in its stock market. Indeed, for Japan in particular, the very low correlation coefficients—averaging less than 0.2—suggest that less than 4 percent of the factors behind the Japanese stock market are common to those affecting other stock markets. (The R^2 for Japan is approximately $0.2 \times 0.2 = 0.04$, or only 4 percent.)

Correlations between a larger number of stock markets, but for an earlier period than reflected in Figures 18.1, 18.2, and 18.3, are shown in Table 18.1 (the figures provide correlations for 1980–1990, while Table 18.1 is for 1973–1982). Despite the different time periods, the picture that emerges from the table is similar to that given by the figures, with, for example, U.S. market correlations high with Canada and low with Spain and Italy (compare the bottom line of Table 18.1 with the heights of bars in Figure 18.1). What the table provides beyond what is

Figure 18.3. Correlations between British and Other Countries' Stock Markets, British Pounds, 1980–1990

The British stock market is correlated with stock markets of other countries to about the same extent as is the U.S. stock market, with correlation coefficients averaging about or slightly below 0.5. As is the case for investors from the United States, Japan, and other countries, British investors, stand to benefit from international diversification. (*Source:* Patrick Odier and Bruno Solnik, "Lessons for International Asset Allocation." Reprinted, with permission, from *Financial Analysts Journal,* March/April 1993. © 1993, Association for Investment Management and Research, Charlottesville, VA. All rights reserved.)

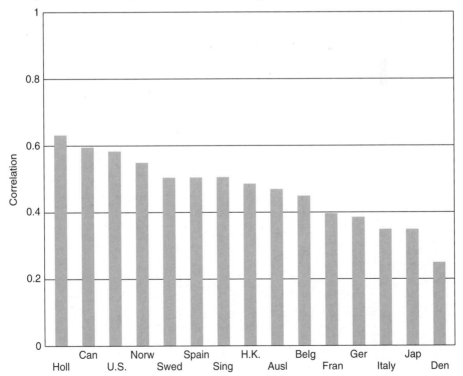

TABLE 18.1. Monthly U.S. Dollar Returns and Risks for National Stock Markets, 1973–1982

	Correlation Coefficient														Monthly Mean Return (%)	Risk (Stand. Dev.) (%)	Beta	Sharpe Ratio
	AUS	BEL	CAN	FR	GER	HK	ITAL	JAP	HOLL	SING	SPAIN	SWED	SWIT	U.K.				
Australia															0.63	7.97	1.25	0.027
Belgium	0.36														0.80	5.92	0.84	0.065
Canada	0.62	0.36													0.78	6.52	1.16	0.056
France	0.46	0.61	0.46												0.67	8.04	1.16	0.032
Germany	0.33	0.65	0.31	0.52											0.83	5.44	0.73	0.076
Hong Kong	0.34	0.36	0.27	0.30	0.33										1.10	14.54	1.52	0.047
Italy	0.29	0.36	0.28	0.39	0.28	0.21									0.27	8.47	0.74	0.017
Japan	0.34	0.43	0.29	0.40	0.49	0.45	0.37								0.85	5.77	0.78	0.075
Netherlands	0.43	0.69	0.53	0.59	0.70	0.45	0.30	0.44							1.01	5.80	1.06	0.102
Singapore	0.46	0.40	0.41	0.38	0.38	0.48	0.23	0.43	0.54						1.08	10.20	1.54	0.065
Spain	0.28	0.28	0.24	0.26	0.28	0.20	0.25	0.32	0.31	0.15					-0.46	6.12	0.45	-0.143
Sweden	0.30	0.44	0.28	0.29	0.42	0.24	0.16	0.35	0.46	0.34	0.23				1.18	5.89	0.66	0.130
Switzerland	0.48	0.72	0.46	0.60	0.75	0.38	0.38	0.46	0.78	0.53	0.25	0.52			0.77	6.01	1.00	0.059
United Kingdom	0.46	0.50	0.48	0.53	0.40	0.36	0.38	0.32	0.63	0.58	0.22	0.32	0.54		1.02	9.27	1.47	0.065
United States	0.53	0.37	0.68	0.41	0.32	0.24	0.16	0.27	0.58	0.48	0.15	0.36	0.49	0.46	0.57	4.84	1.03	0.032

Source: Cheol S. Eun and Bruce G. Resnick, "International Diversification under Estimation Risk: Actual *vs.* Potential Gains." Reprinted with the permission of Lexington Books, an imprint of the Free Press, a Division of Simon & Schuster Inc., from *Recent Developments in International Banking and Finance,* Volume I, by Sarkis Khoury and Alo Ghosh, editors.© 1987 by Lexington Books.

shown in the figures are mean returns, total country risks as measured by the standard deviations of returns, country "betas," and a measure of performance called the Sharpe ratio.

Mean returns are average monthly returns in U.S. dollars, while total risk is the standard deviation of these monthly returns. As we might expect, the high-return countries such as Hong Kong, Singapore, and the United Kingdom have accompanying high risks. Sweden offers the benefit of high return and low risk, which warns us not to forget that the data are *past* returns and risks and therefore not what one can *expect*. (While low risk means a low *expected* return, when the realized return exceeds the expected return, a low risk can be associated with a high actual return.) The betas (βs) are calculated using a world-market index and give the systematic (or nondiversifiable) risk of each country. They show that the high total risks of Hong Kong, Singapore, and Britain also mean high systematic risks—what remains if investors *do* diversify. The Sharpe ratio is a performance measure of mean excess return on a country's market vis-à-vis the risk-free rate—assumed to be 5 percent per annum—per unit of total risk. That is, the Sharpe ratio is calculated by taking one-twelfth of 5 percent away from the mean monthly return on the market and dividing the result by the standard deviation of returns. Not surprisingly, Sweden comes out on top by this measure: the market return vis-à-vis the risk-free return is high per unit of total risk.

Country-Specific Volatility versus Industrial Structure

As we have mentioned, two possible explanations for the generally low correlations between different countries' stock markets are (1) that the countries' economies and politics evolve differently and (2) that the countries have different industries in their stock-market indexes. In the latter case, the low correlations between overall stock-market indexes could occur even if firms in a given industry but in different countries have highly correlated stock values; high correlations *within* industries might be swamped by low correlations *between* industries. Evidence suggesting that the low correlations are not due to different industrial compositions of different countries' market indexes is shown in Tables 18.2 and 18.3.[3] The tables show correlation coefficients between monthly returns in U.S. dollars of major firms in given industries, but different countries. We see from Table 18.2 that correlations between automobile manufacturers in different countries are low. For example, Honda and GM have a correlation coefficient of only 0.23. Table 18.3 shows a similar pattern in the consumer electronics industry. With firms in given industries but different countries offering such different return experiences, international portfolio diversification offers significant potential.

---

[3]Steven Heston and K. Geert Rouwenhorst have examined industrial structure versus country-specific sources of low correlations between country indexes. By considering 12 European countries during the period 1978–1992, Heston and Rouwenhorst concluded that industrial structure plays very little role. Rather, low correlations between country indexes are almost exclusively due to country-specific factors. See Steven L. Heston and K. Geert Rouwenhorst, "Does Industrial Structure Explain the Benefits of International Diversification," *Journal of Financial Economics,* August 1994, pp. 3–27.

TABLE 18.2. Correlations between U.S. Dollar Monthly Returns in Automobile Manufacturing, 1986–1991

	GM	Ford	Chrysler	Fiat	Volks	Peugot	Honda	Nissan
GM	1.0000							
Ford	0.8020	1.0000						
Chrysler	0.6829	0.6150	1.0000					
Fiat	0.4909	0.3541	0.3393	1.0000				
Volkswagen	0.4016	0.3350	0.2604	0.6177	1.0000			
Peugot	0.4517	0.4105	0.2994	0.5166	0.6347	1.0000		
Honda	0.2321	0.2195	0.1635	0.4162	0.1755	0.2503	1.0000	
Nissan	0.2980	0.2505	0.3722	0.3908	0.1974	0.2837	0.5957	1.0000

Source: Tania Zouikin, "Is International Investing Losing Its Lustre?" *Canadian Investment Review,* winter 1992, p. 18.

TABLE 18.3. Correlations between U.S. Dollar Monthly Returns in the Consumer Electronics Industry, 1986–1991

	GE	Zenith	Phillips	Siemens	Matsushita	Sony
GE	1.0000					
Zenith	0.4816	1.0000				
Phillips	0.4295	0.3931	1.0000			
Siemens	0.4938	0.5389	0.5389	1.0000		
Matsushita	0.2562	0.1915	0.1885	0.1657	1.0000	
Sony	0.2035	0.1389	0.1108	0.2062	0.8286	1.0000

Source: Tania Zouikin, "Is International Investing Losing Its Lustre?" *Canadian Investment Review,* winter 1992, p. 18.

The Size of the Gain from International Diversification

Gain from Stock Diversification

An indication of the size of the gain from including foreign stocks in a portfolio has been provided by the research of Bruno Solnik.[4] Solnik computed the risk of portfolios of *n* securities for different values of *n* in terms of the volatility of these portfolios. As expected, it was found that volatility declines as more stocks are added. Moreover, Solnik discovered that an international portfolio of stocks has about half as much risk as a portfolio of the same size containing only U.S. stocks. This result is shown in Figure 18.4. We see that the risk of U.S. portfolios of over 20 stocks is approximately 25 percent of the risk of a typical security, whereas the risk of a well-diversified international portfolio is only about 12 percent of that of a typical security. When Solnik considered countries having far smaller stock markets, he found that the gains from international diversification were, not surprisingly, much larger than for the United States; in smaller countries there is less opportunity to diversify within the country than in larger countries. The gain from diversification through holding equities of different countries turns out to greatly exceed the gain through holding different equities within a single country.

[4]Bruno H. Solnik, "Why Not Diversify Internationally Rather than Domestically?" *Financial Analysts Journal,* July/August 1974, pp. 48–54.

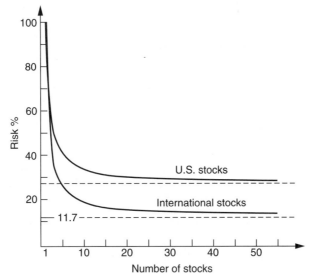

Figure 18.4. The Size of the Gain from International Diversification
For any given number of stocks, an internationally diversified portfolio typically has less than half the risk of a domestically diversified portfolio. (*Source:* Bruno H. Solnik, "Why Not Diversify Internationally Rather than Domestically?" Reprinted, with permission, from *Financial Analysts Journal,* July/August 1974. © 1974, The Financial Analysts Federation, Charlottesville, VA. All rights reserved.)

Risk from Exchange Rates

While there are gains from international diversification because of the independence between foreign and domestic stock returns, there is a possibility of added risk from unanticipated changes in exchange rates when foreign stocks are held. Therefore, it is important to consider whether the gains from imperfect correlations between stock returns more than compensate for the risk introduced by exchange rates. The extent to which holding foreign stocks increases risk from unanticipated changes in exchange rates depends on both the volatility of exchange rates and on the way exchange rates and stock returns are themselves related. The added risk from exchange rates also depends on whether stocks from only one foreign country or from a number of different foreign countries are added to a portfolio of domestic stocks.

The potential for exchange rates to add risk can be judged by comparing the volatility of stock values measured in local currencies to the volatility of stock values measured in U.S. dollars; U.S. dollar values involve converting foreign-currency values into dollars at the spot exchange rate, with variations in the spot rate providing an added source of volatility. The difference between these two volatilities—local-currency value versus U.S. dollar value—is an indication of the volatility contributed to the U.S. dollar value by variations in exchange rates.[5] Figure 18.5

[5]As we shall see, exchange rates contribute to volatility both via the variance of exchange rates and via the

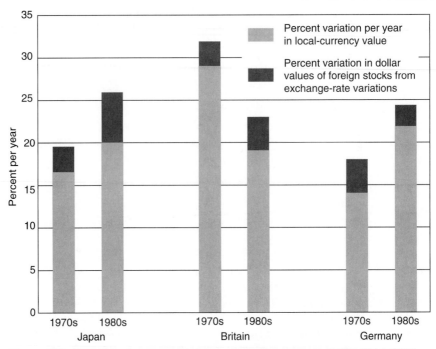

Figure 18.5. Local-Market versus Exchange-Rate Components of Volatility of U.S. Dollar Values of Non-U.S. Stocks, 1970s and 1980s

Most of the variation in the U.S. dollar value of non-U.S. stocks is the result of volatility in the local-currency value of the stocks, rather than in exchange rates. Typically, exchange rates contribute 10 to 15 percent of the U.S. dollar value variation of foreign stock markets. (*Source:* Patrick Odier and Bruno Solnik, "Lessons for International Asset Allocation." Reprinted, with permission, from *Financial Analysts Journal,* March/April, 1993. © 1993, Association for Investment Management and Research, Charlottesville, VA. All rights reserved.

graphically illustrates the volatility from the currency and local stock-market value components for Japanese, British, and German stocks. While exchange rates contribute risk, the exchange-rate element is seen to be the smaller of the two risk-contributing factors.

Evidence on exchange-rate risk from investing in one foreign country and in a group of foreign countries has also been provided by Cheol Eun and Bruce Resnick.[6] Eun and Resnick decompose the volatility of returns on foreign stocks into the volatility of stock returns in terms of local currency, the volatility of exchange rates, and the comovement of stock returns in local currency and exchange rates. That is, they separate the two sources of volatility from exchange

---

covariance of exchange rates with local-currency values of stocks. The measure we use combines these two sources of volatility from exchange rates. So, implicitly, do the results of Bruno H. Solnik's work, summarized in Figure 18.4; Solnik's portfolio returns and risks involve the use of U.S. dollar values.

[6]Cheol S. Eun and Bruce G. Resnick, "Exchange Rate Uncertainty, Forward Contracts and International Portfolio Selection," *Journal of Finance,* March 1988, pp. 197–215.

rates, namely, the volatility of exchange rates themselves and the volatility from covariance of exchange rates with local-currency stock returns. Specifically, they write the expected dollar rate of return to a U.S. holder of, for example, British stocks as

$$\text{Expected dollar return on British stocks} = \dot{S}^* + r_{\text{UK}}^* \qquad (18.1)$$

Here, r_{UK}^* is the expected return in terms of pounds, which consists of the expected dividend return plus the expected change in market value in pounds. This allows Eun and Resnick to write the variance of the dollar return on British stocks as

$$\text{Var(\$ return on British stocks)} = \text{var}(\dot{S}) + \text{var}(r_{\text{UK}}) + 2\text{cov}(\dot{S}, r_{\text{UK}}) \qquad (18.2)$$

This expression shows that the variance of the U.S. dollar rate of return on British stocks can be decomposed into the variance of the dollar-pound exchange rate, the variance of the return on British stocks valued in pounds, and the covariance between the exchange rate and the pound return on British stocks.

Table 18.4 shows the percentage composition of the U.S. dollar return from holding the stock-market indexes of six foreign countries, when each market is held on its own. The first column gives var($\dot{S}$) as a percentage of the variance of the dollar return from each foreign market, the second column gives var(r) as a percentage of the variance of the dollar return, and the final column gives 2 times the covariance between the exchange rate and associated local return as a percent of dollar return. We see that on its own the volatility in the exchange rate can contribute anything from less than 5 percent to over 50 percent of the volatility of dollar returns. We can also see that the covariance between exchange rates and local-currency returns contributes to the variance of U.S. dollar returns. That is, movements in exchange rates are reinforced by movements in local stock markets. For example, on average, when the pound is declining, so is the British stock-market index. This means that exchange rates add to the volatility both directly in being volatile themselves, and indirectly by being positively related to local stock-market returns.

The situation for a portfolio of stocks from different countries is essentially the same as that for stocks from an individual country. This is shown in Table 18.5. The table shows the composition of the U.S. dollar returns from holding an equally

TABLE 18.4. Composition of U.S. Dollar Weekly Returns on Individual Foreign Stock Markets, 1980–1985

Country	*Percentage of Variance in U.S. Dollar Returns from*		
	Exchange Rate	Local Return	2 × Covariance
Canada	4.26	84.91	10.83
France	29.66	61.79	8.55
Germany	38.92	41.51	19.57
Japan	31.85	47.65	20.50
Switzerland	55.17	30.01	14.81
U.K.	32.35	51.23	16.52

Source: Cheol S. Eun and Bruce G. Resnick, "Exchange Rate Uncertainty, Forward Contracts, and International Portfolio Selection," *Journal of Finance,* March 1988, pp. 197–215.

TABLE 18.5. Composition of Weekly U.S. Dollar Return on an Equally Weighted Portfolio of Seven Countries' Stock Markets, 1980–1985

Percentage of Variance in U.S. Dollar Return from		
Exchange Rate	Local Return	$2 \times$ Covariance
32.20	42.88	24.92

Source: Cheol S. Eun and Bruce G. Resnick, "Exchange Rate Uncertainty, Forward Contracts, and International Portfolio Selection," *Journal of Finance,* March 1988, pp. 197–215.

weighted portfolio of the stock markets of seven countries: the United States and the six countries in Table 18.4. The contribution of exchange-rate volatility is due both to the volatility of each exchange rate, and to the covariance between exchange rates. Similarly, the contribution of volatility of local returns is due both to the volatility of each stock market, and to the covariance among stock markets. Finally, the contribution of the covariance is due to the covariance between each exchange rate and each market return. We see from the table that the exchange rate contributes a substantial fraction of the volatility of dollar returns via the direct effect of the exchange-rate volatility itself, and via the indirect effect of positive covariance between exchange rates and local market returns. It would not appear that diversification among currencies has a substantial effect in reducing the *proportion* of risk attributable to changes in exchange rates.

With volatility directly or indirectly resulting from unanticipated changes in exchange rates, it is important to confirm whether this cancels the benefits from international diversification attributable to the presence of some independence between stock-market returns in different countries. The answer is no. One reason is that it is possible to diversify internationally without adding exchange-rate exposure—by hedging in the forward market, by borrowing in the foreign currencies, or by using futures or currency options. The hedges would have to be based on the exposure in each currency, as given by regression coefficients according to Chapter 12.[7] A second reason international diversification is beneficial despite exchange-rate variability is that, even without hedging, the variance of the dollar return on an internationally diversified portfolio of stocks remains lower than the variance of the expected dollar return on holding the domestic stock market. This has been shown by Bruno Solnik, who compared the variance of returns on portfolios of U.S. stocks with the variance of returns on internationally diversified portfolios, both when not hedging exchange-rate exposure and when hedging on the forward market.[8]

[7]It was explained in Chapter 12 that the exposure on a foreign stock depends on how the stock price covaries with the exchange rate, and consequently the exposure is not simply the market value of the stock. The appropriate hedge would have to take this into account. We should note that while exposure at any moment can be eliminated by hedging, it is not feasible to eliminate exposure. This is because the market value of foreign stocks varies, so that the hedge will not always be the correct amount, unless, of course, the hedge is changed continuously.

[8]Solnik, *op. cit.* Solnik's hedges on the international portfolios are not the optimal hedges as given by regression coefficients, but rather are equal to the values of the foreign stocks at the time of investment. Consequently, Solnik's results, if anything, understate the benefits of hedged international diversification.

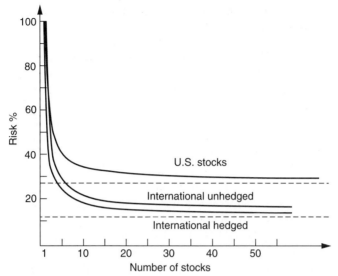

Figure 18.6. The Advantages of International Diversification with and without Exchange Risk

There are further gains from risk reduction through international diversification if forward markets are used to hedge exchange-rate risk. (*Source:* Bruno H. Solnik, "Why Not Diversify Internationally Rather than Domestically?" Reprinted with permission from *Financial Analysts Journal,* July/August 1974. © 1974, The Financial Analysts Federation, Charlottesville, VA. All rights reserved.)

Different-sized portfolios of U.S. stocks and internationally diversified stocks were compared, with the results shown in Figure 18.6. This figure reveals that even though there is exchange-rate risk—given by the gap between the hedged and unhedged curves—it is still better to diversify internationally than to hold only U.S. stocks. It is clear that the gain from having independence of returns due to holding securities of different countries in a portfolio more than offsets any exchange-rate risk that this implies, even when not hedging. And of course, when hedged, the benefits from international portfolio diversification are even greater.

Many researchers other than Eun and Resnick, and Solnik, have studied the gains from international diversification, and while all agree on the existence of gains, they differ substantially in the estimated size of these gains.[9] One major reason the estimates of gains are different is that some of the studies use past returns over different sample periods to form efficient, internationally diversified portfolios, rather than using the distribution of future returns as is called for by the the-

[9]Earlier, frequently referenced research showing the size of gains from international diversification includes Donald Lessard, "World, Country, and Industry Relationships in Equity Returns: Implications for Risk Reduction through International Diversification," *Financial Analysts Journal,* January/February 1976, pp. 2–8, and Haim Levy and Marshall Sarnat, "International Diversification of Investment Portfolios," *American Economic Review,* September 1970, pp. 668–675.

ory.[10] The problem introduced by using past returns and covariances for forming efficient diversified portfolios is that if, for example, the past return in Belgium was very high during the estimation period, Belgian stocks will be heavily weighted in the internationally diversified portfolio.[11] This is the case even though it may have been just by chance that Belgian stocks did so well. It is then little surprise that the internationally diversified portfolio with its abnormally high proportion of high-return Belgian stocks outperforms the domestic portfolio when applied to past data. The problem is that there is an upward bias in the estimated benefits of international diversification due to basing international portfolios on past returns rather than the distribution of future returns. This bias can be verified by taking the internationally diversified portfolio that is formed using past-return data during a given interval of time and seeing how it performs out of sample, that is, over other intervals. The results of this type of test suggest that the benefits of international diversification have indeed been overestimated in many studies.[12]

In an attempt to partially overcome the problem of using past returns to construct portfolios for judging the gain from international diversification, Phillippe Jorion used statistical procedures which "shrink" past returns in different countries toward the mean return for all countries combined.[13] This means, for example, that if the observed past return for Belgium happened to have been very high, a realistic investor is assumed to expect a future return less than the past return, and somewhere between the past return for Belgium and the past average return for all countries combined. The results from Jorion's study show that the gains from international diversification in earlier studies have been greatly overstated. His conclusions are supported by the fact that the portfolios he constructed outperform portfolios based on unadjusted past returns when their returns are compared with out-of-sample data. Nevertheless, Jorion shows there is still some gain from international portfolio diversification.

INTERNATIONAL CAPITAL ASSET PRICING

The central international financial question concerning the pricing of assets, and hence their expected rates of return, is whether they are determined in an integrated, international capital market or in local, segmented markets. If assets are priced in an internationally **integrated capital market,** expected yields on assets will be in accordance with the risks of the assets when they are held in an efficient, internationally diversified portfolio, such as the world-market portfolio. This means that while in such a situation it is better to diversify internationally than not to, the expected yields on assets will merely compensate for their systematic risk when this is measured with

[10]An **efficient portfolio** is one which is constructed to have maximum expected return for a given volatility, or minimum volatility for a given expected return. The studies by Solnik and by Eun and Resnick are not based on efficient portfolios and consequently are not subject to the problems we are about to describe.
[11]Belgian stocks will receive high weighting if their return is high relative to the risk they contribute to the international portfolio. The risk is a function of the covariance between Belgian and other returns.
[12]See Phillippe Jorion, "International Diversification with Estimation Risk," *Journal of Business,* July 1985, pp. 259–278.
[13]Jorion, *op. cit.*

respect to the internationally diversified world portfolio. That is, with internationally integrated capital markets the expected returns on foreign stocks will be appropriate for the risk of these stocks in an internationally diversified portfolio. There will be no "free lunches" from foreign stocks due to higher expected returns for their risk. On the other hand, if assets are priced in **segmented capital markets,** their returns will be in accordance with the systematic risk of their domestic market. This means that if an investor happens to have an ability to circumvent whatever it is that causes markets to be segmented, this investor will be able to enjoy special benefits from international diversification. It is consequently important for us to consider whether assets are priced in internationally integrated or in segmented capital markets. However before doing this it is useful to review the theory of asset pricing in a domestic context, because if we do not understand the issues in the simpler domestic context, we cannot understand the international dimensions of asset pricing.

The Domestic Capital Asset Pricing Model, CAPM

The domestic variant of the **capital asset pricing model (CAPM),** familiar from the so-called "beta analysis" used in security selection, can be written as follows:[14]

$$r_j^* = r_f + \beta\left(r_m^* - r_f\right) \tag{18.3}$$

where

$$\beta = \frac{\text{cov}\left(r_j, r_m\right)}{\text{var}\left(r_m\right)} \tag{18.4}$$

and where

r_j^* = equilibrium or required expected return on security or portfolio j

r_f = risk-free rate of interest

r_m^* = expected return on the market portfolio m

$\text{cov}\left(r_j, r_m\right)$ = covariance between security or portfolio j and the market m

$\text{var}\left(r_m\right)$ = variance of the market portfolio

The essential point of the CAPM is that a security or portfolio offers an equilibrium expected return, r_j^*, equal to the risk-free interest rate plus a risk premium. The risk premium, $\beta(r_m^* - r_f)$, is linearly related to the risk that the asset or portfolio contributes to the market as a whole, $\text{cov}(r_j, r_m)/\text{var}(r_m)$. This is the risk which cannot be diversified away, the **systematic risk.** If a security compensated for more than systematic risk it would be a bargain, and investors would buy it and combine it with other securities, causing the risk it contributes to be small relative to its contribution to the expected return. The buying of the security would raise its market price and thereby lower its expected return until the security was no longer a bargain, even within a diversified portfolio.

[14]See William Sharpe, "Capital Asset Pricing: A Theory of Market Equilibrium under Conditions of Risk," *Journal of Finance,* September 1964, pp. 424–447. The model is explained in many finance textbooks and is only stated here.

The International Capital Asset Pricing Model, ICAPM

With the domestic variant of the CAPM explained, we can clarify the conclusion stated earlier about internationally integrated versus segmented markets. If assets are priced in internationally integrated capital markets, expected yields are given by

$$r_j^* = r_f + \beta^w\left(r_w^* - r_f\right) \tag{18.5}$$

where

$$\beta^w = \frac{\text{cov}\left(r_j, r_w\right)}{\text{var}\left(r_w\right)} \tag{18.6}$$

and where r_w^* = world-market expected return. Unfortunately, it is difficult in practice to apply the **international CAPM, or ICAPM,** because this requires being able to define a world risk-free interest rate, making assumptions about preferences of investors from different countries who face different real returns according to the basket of goods they purchase, as well as dealing with several other thorny problems.[15]

If the international CAPM as summarized in equations (18.5) and (18.6) is valid, then investors do not receive abnormal returns from investing in foreign assets; returns appropriately compensate for the systematic risk of assets in an internationally diversified portfolio.[16] On the other hand, if assets are priced in segmented capital markets, then if it were possible for a particular investor or firm to overcome the reasons for market segmentation, perhaps by getting around capital flow regulations, such an investor could enjoy abnormal returns. (Later we shall explain that U.S. multinational corporations appear to be in this situation, investing where ordinary U.S. investors cannot.)

Segmentation versus Integration of Capital Markets: A Graphical View

The implications of integrated versus segmented capital markets can be viewed graphically in terms of the risk-return framework that is used frequently in the domestic context to describe diversification benefits. Figure 18.7 shows expected returns on the vertical axis, and total risk, given by the standard error σ of expected returns, on the horizontal axis. The upward-sloping part of the curve, or **envelope,** gives the best combinations of expected returns and risk that can be achieved with different portfolios; combinations along the upward-sloping part of the envelope are those of efficient portfolios. As before, r_f is the risk-free interest rate, and r_m^* is the expected return on the market portfolio. Again as before, the interpretation of r_f and

[15]Notable attempts to determine the conditions required for the international CAPM, and the implications if these conditions are satisfied, include those of Bruno Solnik, "An Equilibrium Model of the International Capital Market," *Journal of Economics Theory,* August 1974, pp. 500–524, and Michael Adler and Bernard Dumas, "International Portfolio Choice and Corporation Finance: A Synthesis," *Journal of Finance,* June 1983, pp. 925–984. For a summary of empirical applications and new test results see Bruno Solnik, "The World Price of Foreign Exchange Risk," working paper, H.E.C. School of Management, Paris, July 1993.

[16]Indeed, by not investing internationally, investors face more risk than is necessary.

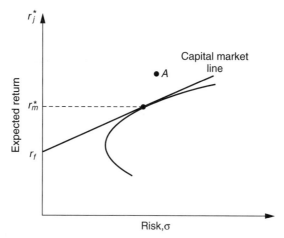

**Figure 18.7. The Relationship between Expected
Return and Total Risk**
If assets are priced in segmented markets, it may be
possible for an investor to enjoy a combination of
expected return and risk above the capital market line for
a *particular country* if the investor can overcome the
causes of segmentation and diversify internationally. If
assets are priced in internationally integrated capital
markets, then by not diversifying internationally an
investor will be accepting higher risk and/or lower return
than necessary.

r_m^* depends on whether we are considering integrated or segmented capital markets.
We note that r_m^* is the tangency point on a straight line drawn between the risk-free
rate and the envelope of efficient portfolios' risks and returns. This line is the **capital market line,** which gives the expected returns and risks of combinations of the
risk-free asset and the market portfolio. It is a well-known proposition in finance
that an investor cannot do better than select such a combination and therefore be
somewhere on the capital market line.

   If capital markets are internationally integrated, then we can interpret r_f in Figure 18.7 as the risk-free rate, and r_m^* as the expected world-market return, r_w^*.[17] That
is, with integrated capital markets the international CAPM is an extension of the
domestic CAPM where we reinterpret r_m^* as the expected world-market return, r_w^*.
Indeed, if the capital market is integrated, by not holding the world-market portfolio
the investor will be below the capital market line in Figure 18.7; the investor could
reduce risk and increase expected return by holding the world portfolio. On the other
hand, if capital markets are segmented so that we can interpret r_m^* as the domestic
market expected return, then by overcoming the obstacles to foreign investment an

---

[17]As we have mentioned, in practice, defining r_f and r_w^* is far from easy. The risk-free rate r_f requires
forming a portfolio of different treasury bills plus forward exchange contracts to remove exchange-rate
risk, and the expected world-market return r_w^* and world β require complex calculations and numerous
assumptions.

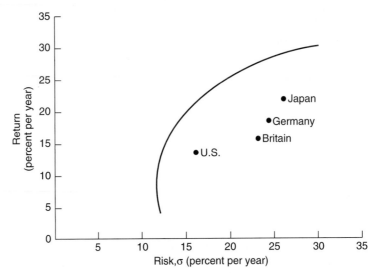

Figure 18.8. Efficiency Frontier of Global Stocks, U.S. Dollar, 1980–1990
The efficiency frontier shows the highest return for a given risk and/or the lowest risk for a given return by optimally combining the stock markets of different countries. The returns and risks of the individual countries' markets are seen to be below the efficiency frontier. This indicates the size of potential gains from international diversification if capital markets are integrated. For example, an internationally efficient allocation with the same risk as the U.S. market offers approximately 8 percent more return per annum than the U.S. market. (*Source:* Patrick Odier and Bruno Solnik, "Lessons for International Asset Allocation." Reprinted, with permission, from *Financial Analysts Journal,* March/April 1993. © 1993, Association for Investment Management and Research, Charlottesville, VA. All rights reserved.

investor might be able to create a risk-return portfolio that is above the domestic capital market line. For example, the investor might be able to reach a point such as *A* and enjoy gains from international diversification, since these are not priced by the market.

The Potential Gain from Integration of Capital Markets

The extent to which integration of world financial markets could empirically make a difference to the opportunities facing investors in terms of the risk-return profile is indicated in Figure 18.8. The figure shows a constructed efficiency frontier, with risk and return in U.S. dollars, from combining the stock-market indexes of different countries.[18] We see, for example, that an internationally efficient allocation of assets with the same risk as the U.S. market—16.2 percent per annum—provides a return almost 8 percent higher than the U.S. market return: 21 percent versus 13.3 percent per annum. The potential gains for the riskier but higher-return stock markets of

[18]See Odier and Solnik, *op. cit.*

Britain, Germany, and Japan are also indicated. The performance of the internationally diversified portfolio could be further enhanced by periodically revising the asset allocation—the figure uses fixed allocations—and by hedging the risk from exchange rates, but even without such refinements the diversification benefits are substantial. But are capital markets integrated so as to offer such benefits, or are they segmented?

(continuing)

The Evidence on Market Segmentation

The most immediately obvious evidence that markets are segmented is in the nature of portfolios held by typical investors. For example, despite the rapid *rate* of expansion of U.S. overseas portfolio investment in recent years, the level of foreign investment is still low. For example, between 1980 and 1993, U.S. investments in foreign equities grew from approximately 2 percent to 8 percent of Americans' portfolios. Given that non-U.S. investments represent substantially more than half of the world market portfolio, the holding of only 8 percent of typical portfolios in foreign stocks is a very clear indication that Americans have a **home-country bias,** not fully availing themselves of international diversification opportunities.[19] While European and Japanese investors do venture abroad to a greater extent than Americans, they too hold fewer foreign securities than are represented in the world portfolio.

Segmentation of capital markets can occur for a variety of different reasons.[20] The most obvious cause of segmentation is the presence of legal barriers to foreign investment. These barriers can take the form of outright restrictions on investing abroad, or they can involve higher rates of tax on income from foreign investment than on income from domestic investment. However, even if the majority of investors are subject to legal barriers, assets could still in principle be priced according to integrated markets. This is because some investors, such as giant multinational firms with operations in numerous countries, might be able to circumvent the legal barriers.

A slightly less obvious form of market segmentation occurs as a result of so-called **indirect barriers.**[21] Indirect barriers include the difficulty of finding and interpreting information about foreign securities and reluctance to deal with foreigners. As is true for legal barriers, those who can overcome the indirect barriers through, for example, access to better information or freedom from xenophobia might be able to enjoy abnormal returns by diversifying internationally. That is, those who can overcome the barriers might achieve a risk-return combination such as that at *A* in Figure 18.7.

[19]For discussion of the extent of international diversification and possible explanations of why a home-country bias occurs, see Raman Uppal, "The Economic Determinants of the Home Country Bias in Investors' Portfolios: A Survey," *Journal of International Financial Management and Accounting,* 4, 1992, pp. 171–189, and "A General Equilibrium Model of International Portfolio Choice," *The Journal of Finance,* June 1993, pp. 529–553. For the extent of turnover in foreign stocks, which has been very rapid, see Linda L. Tesar and Ingrid M. Werners, "Home Bias and High Turnover," *Journal of International Money and Finance,* forthcoming 1995.
[20]See Debra A. Glassman and Leigh A. Riddick, "Why Empirical International Portfolio Models Fail: Evidence that Model Misspecification Creates Home Asset Bias," working paper, University of Washington School of Business Administration, 1993.
[21]Phillipe Jorion and Eduardo Schwartz, "Integration vs. Segmentation in the Canadian Stock Market," *Journal of Finance,* July 1986, pp. 603–616.

When we interpret market segmentation in the more general terms of having different expected returns or risks according to where an investor lives, it becomes clear that as well as arising from legal and indirect barriers, segmentation can arise because prices of what investors consume relative to the returns they earn change differently in different countries.[22] In such a case the buying power of returns would depend on where investors live. It turns out, however, that this cause of segmentation requires that PPP does not hold. This is because, for example, if PPP holds and investors in one country, say Canada, happen to earn a lower nominal return than investors elsewhere because of an appreciation of the Canadian dollar, then the lower nominal return to Canadians is compensated for by lower inflation in Canada; an appreciation of the Canadian dollar is associated with lower prices in Canada.[23] It follows that if PPP holds, securities will be priced according to equation (18.5), in which the market return is the global-market return, provided of course there are no legal or indirect causes of segmentation.

When PPP does not hold, there is exchange-rate risk, and markets are segmented with different real rates of return for investors according to where they live; the changes in exchange rates will not be exactly offset by changes in prices. The effect of having exchange-rate risk for the asset pricing relationship in equation (18.5) is to make the international CAPM more complex than a mere reinterpretation of the domestic CAPM.[24]

Evidence on whether securities are priced in an integrated or a segmented capital market has been provided by Phillippe Jorion and Eduardo Schwartz,[25] They began by noting that integration means expected returns depend only on international factors, and in particular on the systematic risk of securities vis-à-vis the world market. That is, if markets are completely integrated, the r_j^{*}'s of different securities should depend only on their β's calculated vis-à-vis the world market return. On the other hand, if markets are completely segmented, expected returns will depend on only domestic factors, and in particular the β's vis-à-vis the domestic market return. By isolating the international and domestic β's Jorion and Schwartz were able to show that domestic factors are relevant for expected returns on Canadian securities, suggesting some degree of market segmentation.[26]

Jorion and Schwartz also separated out interlisted Canadian stocks—those trad-

---

[22]For an excellent account of this interpretation of segmentation see Michael Adler and Bernard Dumas, "International Portfolio Choice and Corporation Finance: A Synthesis," *Journal of Finance,* June 1983, pp. 925–984.

[23]The appreciation of the Canadian dollar means that to Canadians, there is a depreciation of the U.S. dollar, the pound, the yen, and so on. This would reduce the return on foreign securities to Canadians but would also reduce the prices of products that Canadians buy.

[24]For accounts of the international CAPM in the presence of exchange-rate risk due to deviations from PPP see Piet Serçu, "A Generalization of the International Asset Pricing Model," *Revue Française de Finance,* June 1980, pp. 91–135, and René Stulz, "A Model of International Asset Pricing," *Journal of Financial Economics,* December 1981, pp. 383–406. See also the excellent survey in Adler and Dumas (1983), *op. cit.*

[25]Jorion and Schwartz, *op. cit.*

[26]It has been argued that, if investors in the different countries care about different measures of inflation, so that PPP cannot hold, then the pricing of domestic factors does not necessarily mean markets are segmented. See Mustafa N. Gultekin, N. Bulent Gultekin, and Alessandro Penati, "Capital Controls and International Capital Markets Segmentation: The Evidence from the Japanese and American Stock Markets," paper presented to European Finance Association Meetings, Madrid, 1987.

ing simultaneously on both U.S. and Canadian stock exchanges—and found the same result, namely, that returns are related to systematic risk vis-à-vis the Canadian market. This suggests that the segmentation is not attributable to reporting of information on Canadian stocks, because Canadian companies with shares trading on U.S. exchanges must report information similar to that reported by U.S. companies.

Limited further support for segmentation based on an examination of interlisted stocks has been provided by Gordon Alexander, Cheol Eun, and S. Janakiramanan.[27] They begin by stating that if markets are segmented, the listing of a security abroad should reduce the security's expected rate of return. This should come about as a result of a jump in the stock price at the time the market learns of the additional listing. They find evidence consistent with a lower expected return after overseas listing for their sample of non-Canadian firms. However, they do not detect the implied jumps in stock prices and find insignificant effects for Canadian firms.

An alternative, although even more indirect, way of testing whether markets are integrated or segmented is to see whether securities of companies that can overcome segmentation have returns more related to systematic risk vis-à-vis the international than vis-à-vis the domestic market. For example, if U.S. multinational corporations can invest in countries where private U.S. citizens cannot, then the returns on U.S. multinationals' securities should be more closely related to their β's vis-à-vis the international market than vis-à-vis the U.S. market, whereas returns on other U.S. securities should not. Indeed, the extent to which the U.S. multinationals' securities are priced according to international or domestic risk should depend on their international orientation, judged, for example, by the fraction of sales made overseas. One test of this was performed by Tamir Agmon and Donald Lessard, who found some weak indication that multinationals can achieve something investors cannot achieve themselves.[28] However, it has been pointed out that the U.S. market index itself contains companies which earn a substantial fraction of their earnings overseas, so that the β's of securities vis-à-vis the U.S. market are not really measuring systematic risks vis-à-vis the domestic market. That is, the r_m^* for the U.S. market includes a substantial amount of the effect of international returns, so that studies comparing the use of r_m^* for an international index and a U.S. index understate the role of internationalization of investment by U.S. multinationals. When U.S. stock indexes are constructed in a way that removes the international returns in them, the results show a more significant benefit from the ability of multinational corporations to invest overseas.[29] This suggests that markets are segmented for the ordinary U.S. investor.

[27]Gordon J. Alexander, Cheol S. Eun, and S. Janakiramanan, "International Listings and Stock Returns: Some Empirical Evidence," *Journal of Financial and Quantitative Analysis,* June 1988, pp. 135–151.
[28]Tamir Agmon and Donald R. Lessard, "Investor Recognition of Corporate International Diversification," *Journal of Finance,* September 1977, pp. 1049–1056. The results of Agmon and Lessard disagree with those of Bertrand Jacquillat and Bruno Solnik, "Multinationals Are Poor Tools for Diversification," *Journal of Portfolio Management,* winter 1978, pp. 8–12; H. L. Brewer, "Investor Benefits from Corporate International Diversification," *Journal of Financial and Quantitative Analysis,* March 1981, pp. 113–126; and A. J. Senschak and W. L. Beedles, "Is Indirect International Diversification Desirable?" *Journal of Portfolio Management,* winter 1980, pp. 49–57.
[29]See John S. Hughes, Dennis E. Logue, and Richard J. Sweeney, "Corporate International Diversification and Market Assigned Measures of Risk and Diversification," *Journal of Financial and Quantitative Analysis,* November 1975, pp. 627–637.

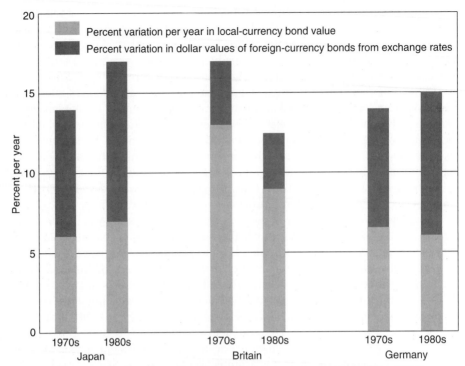

Figure 18.9. Local-Market versus Exchange-Rate Components of Volatility of Dollar Values of Non-U.S. Dollar Bonds, 1970s and 1980s
In the case of foreign-currency bonds valued in U.S. dollars, a substantial proportion of the volatility is the result of variation in exchange rates. This contrasts with stocks, for which volatility stems largely from variations in local-currency values of stock markets. (*Source:* Patrick Odier and Bruno Solnik, "Lessons for International Asset Allocation." Reprinted, with permission, from *Financial Analysts Journal,* March/April 1993. © 1993, Association for Investment Management and Research, Charlottesville, VA. All rights reserved.

BONDS AND INTERNATIONAL PORTFOLIO DIVERSIFICATION

When considering international investment in bonds, issues arise that are similar to those we have already discussed concerning stocks, including the extent to which foreign bonds, unhedged, introduce exchange-rate risk, and the extent to which bonds further allow investors to improve the risk-return opportunity set. The issue of the currency risk associated with individual countries' bonds is addressed in Figure 18.9. As with stocks, the construction of the figure involves calculating the volatility of the local-currency asset price and the volatility of the asset price converted into U.S. dollars. The difference between the two volatilities is introduced by exchange rates, with the exchange-rate volatility being of interest to an investor concerned with U.S. dollar magnitudes.[30]

---

[30]The data are from Odier and Solnik, *op. cit.*

Comparison of Figure 18.9 with the comparable figure for stocks, Figure 18.5 on page 442, shows that the contribution of exchange rates to the riskiness of bonds is much larger than it is for stocks. Some difference in this regard would be expected

Comparison of Figure 18.9 with the comparable figure for stocks, Figure 18.5 on page 442, shows that the contribution of exchange rates to the riskiness of bonds is much larger than it is for stocks. Some difference in this regard would be expected from the PPP principle. Specifically, if expected income streams and hence stock prices kept pace with inflation, then higher inflation in a country would increase stock prices at the same time as it caused depreciation of the currency: the inflation increases prices, including those of assets, but causes a depreciation. In such a situation the effect of inflation in the local-currency asset price is offset by the depreciation when the asset price is measured in terms of U.S. dollars. Stated differently, the local-currency asset price and the currency value are negatively correlated, at least to the extent that PPP holds. This reduces volatility measured in U.S. dollars. Of course, factors other than PPP are at work affecting the correlation, so any reduction in stock-price volatility in dollars is against the background of these other factors. In the case of bonds, the opposite could be occurring to the situation for stocks. Currency depreciation could lead to government action to increase interest rates in an attempt to prop up the currency, a practice we have called "leaning against the wind." Higher interest rates reduce bond prices in local currency, so that depreciation of the currency is associated with a decline in the local-currency value of bonds. In this case, unlike the case with stocks discussed previously, the local-currency asset value and exchange-rate movements are reinforcing, making variations in U.S. dollar bond values higher; a positive correlation between the local-currency asset value and the exchange rate adds to volatility. While other factors may be at work, what we have said does provide a rationale for the differences apparent from comparing Figure 18.9 and Figure 18.5.

The empirical importance of international portfolio diversification of bonds is addressed in Figure 18.10.[31] The figure shows two efficiency frontiers, one for an optimally internationally diversified portfolio of stocks only and the other for stocks plus bonds. The frontier that results when bonds are included in the portfolio shows reduced risk for given returns. This reduction in risk does not, of course, occur at high rates of return, because to achieve such returns it is necessary to hold only stocks. At lower expected returns the advantage of including bonds is substantial, with, for example, a volatility reduction from 12 percent to 8 percent at a 10 percent rate of return. The position of the combined stock and bond efficiency frontiers in Figure 18.10 makes the gain from international portfolio diversification very evident.

SETTLEMENTS OF INTERNATIONAL PORTFOLIO INVESTMENTS

When an investor acquires a stock or bond in an overseas market, the settlement and exchange of assets involve more than one regulatory environment. The mechanics of such multi-country exchange and settlement are handled by **global custodians.** Custodians provide the services of holding securities and making payments. For further fees, they also handle foreign exchange transactions, collect dividends,

---

[31]See Odier and Solnik, *op. cit.*

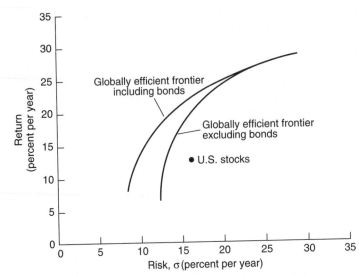

Figure 18.10. Contribution of Bonds to the Globally Efficient Frontier, U.S. Dollars, 1980–1990
Including bonds as well as stocks in an internationally diversified portfolio provides an opportunity to reduce risk for a given return vis-à-vis a stock-only portfolio. The benefit from holding bonds comes despite the relatively high exchange-rate risk on bonds. (*Source:* Patrick Odier and Bruno Solnik, "Lessons for International Asset Allocation." Reprinted, with permission, from *Financial Analysts Journal,* March/April 1993. © 1993, Association for Investment Management and Research, Charlottesville, VA. All rights reserved.

handle proxies, forward relevant corporate information to asset owners, and arrange to reclaim withholding taxes.[32] The custodians are typically large multinational banks, some of which handle over $100 billion in assets. While some countries such as the United States and Canada have so integrated their settlement procedures that the border does not represent much of a barrier, in situations where language and regulatory differences exist, settlement can be complex. For example, changes in exchange rates as well as asset prices make the timing of transactions related to settlement extremely important. In essence, by overcoming such complexities custodians help to integrate markets. However, they have clearly not yet made markets a seamless whole, or we would not observe so much evidence supporting market segmentation.

[32]For an account of the growing role of global custodians see "Global Custody: Speeding the Paperchase," special supplement to *Euromoney,* March 1989; Keith Martin, "The Changing Role of the Global Custodian," *Benefits and Pensions Monitor,* May/June 1994, pp. 12–15; and Jodi G. Scarlata, "Institutional Developments in the Globalization of Securities and Futures Markets," *Review,* Federal Reserve Bank of St. Louis, January/February 1992, pp. 17–30. For an alternative procedure for dealing with overseas portfolio investments, see the discussion of American Depository Receipts in Chapter 21.

1. If different countries' economic performances are not perfectly synchronized or if there are other differences between nations such as in the types of industries they have, there are benefits from international diversification of portfolios beyond those from diversification within a single country. Therefore, investments in foreign countries might be made even if they offered lower expected returns than some domestic investments; the diversification benefits might more than compensate for lower expected returns.

2. The evidence shows considerable independence between different countries' stock returns, suggesting large gains from international diversification. Portfolios that are internationally diversified do indeed prove to have lower volatility than portfolios of domestic stocks of the same size.

3. Stocks of companies in different countries but in the same industry are not highly correlated. This indicates that stock-market indexes have low correlations because of idiosyncratic economic circumstances, not because the indexes of different countries' markets have different compositions of industries.

4. Even if internationally diversified portfolios are not hedged against exchange-rate risk, they show lower volatility than do domestically diversified portfolios. This is despite the fact that exchange rates are an important component of overall volatility of foreign stocks, both directly and indirectly (via their covariance with local market returns).

5. Many early studies of the gains from international diversification overstated the gains because they constructed portfolios on the basis of past actual returns rather than expected future returns.

6. If assets are priced in internationally integrated capital markets, their returns are appropriate for their risk when combined with the world-market portfolio. Thus, by not diversifying internationally, an investor is accepting more risk than is necessary for a given expected return, or lower expected return than is necessary for a given risk.

7. If capital markets are segmented, those who can invest abroad can enjoy abnormal returns for the risk taken. This is because assets are priced only to compensate for the risk in internationally *un*diversified portfolios.

8. Evidence indicates that there is some segmentation of capital markets.

9. Multinational corporations' shares appear to be priced according to their systematic risk vis-à-vis an internationally diversified portfolio. Investors appear to value the ability of multinationals to invest abroad, overcoming the barriers which the investors themselves face on making overseas investments.

10. Exchange rates add substantially more to the volatility of foreign bonds than they do to the volatility of foreign stocks. This could be explained by the policy of "leaning against the wind," whereby central banks increase interest rates, thereby lowering bond prices, when their currencies are depreciating.

11. Despite the exchange-rate risk on bonds, the inclusion of bonds in an internationally diversified portfolio lowers risk and raises return vis-à-vis a stock-only diversified portfolio.

12. Global custodians help handle the exchange and settlement of foreign securities. In this way they help to integrate capital markets.

REVIEW QUESTIONS

1. What types of investments are included in international portfolio investment?

2. Why are the correlation coefficients between different countries' stock markets and stocks relevant for the potential benefit from international portfolio diversification?

3. How could different compositions of stock-market indexes reduce the correlation between returns on different countries' markets?

4. What are the different components of volatility from investment in stocks of an individual foreign country?

5. What do we mean by "integrated capital markets"?

6. What assumptions must be made to apply the international capital asset pricing model to an explanation of the pricing of securities?

7. How would you characterize the gains from international portfolio diversification?

8. What is meant by "home-country bias"?

9. How can the level of information cause international capital market segmentation?

10. How would you interpret the conclusion that returns are more closely related to systematic risk in the domestic market than to systematic risk in the international market?

11. How might multinational firms offer a vehicle for overcoming segmented capital markets?

12. What does a global custodian do?

ASSIGNMENT PROBLEMS

1. Why are the benefits from international diversification overstated if efficient portfolios are calculated on the basis of past returns?

2. Why are there gains from international diversification without hedging exchange-rate risk even though exchange rates contribute a substantial *proportion* of overall risk?

3. Could we judge whether markets are segmented or integrated by examining rules governing the international flow of capital?

4. Why does the calculation of the risk-free rate for the ICAPM involve the use of forward contracts?

5. What possible reasons exist for the segmentation of capital markets?

6. Why might an investor who is able to diversify globally benefit if for most other investors markets are segmented?

7. How might we calculate the importance of currency risk to the total risk on:
   a. An individual foreign stock?
   b. A portfolio of foreign stocks?

8. Could multinationals provide a vehicle for overcoming market segmentation?

9. How is the expected equilibrium return on bonds likely to vary with the covariance between the local-currency market value of bonds and the exchange rate?

10. What impact might global custodians have on capital markets if they do their job cheaply and effectively?

BIBLIOGRAPHY

ADLER, MICHAEL, and BERNARD DUMAS: "Optimal International Acquisitions," *Journal of Finance,* March 1975, pp. 1–19.

———: "International Portfolio Choice and Corporation Finance: A Synthesis," *Journal of Finance,* June 1983, pp. 925–984.

AGMON, TAMIR, and DONALD R. LESSARD: "Investor Recognition of Corporate International Diversification," *Journal of Finance,* September 1977, pp. 1049–1055.

COHEN, KALMAN, WALTER NESS, ROBERT SCHWARTZ, DAVID WHITCOMB, and HITOSHI OKUDA: "The Determinants of Common Stock Returns Volatility: An International Comparison," *Journal of Finance,* May 1976, pp. 733–740.

EUN, CHEOL S., and BRUCE G. RESNICK: "Exchange Rate Uncertainty, Forward Contracts, and International Portfolio Selection," *Journal of Finance,* March 1988, pp. 197–215.

FRANKEL, JEFFERY A.: "The Diversifiability of Exchange Risk," *Journal of International Economics,* August 1979, pp. 379–393.

GRAUER, FREDERICK L., ROBERT H. LITZENBERGER, and RICHARD E. STEHLE: "Sharing Rules and Equilibrium in an International Capital Market under Uncertainty," *Journal of Financial Economics,* June 1976, pp. 223–256.

HUGHES, JOHN S., DENNIS E. LOGUE, and RICHARD J. SWEENEY: "Corporate International Diversification and Market Assigned Measures of Risk and Diversification," *Journal of Financial and Quantitative Analysis,* November 1975, pp. 627–637.

JORION, PHILLIPPE: "International Diversification with Estimation Risk," *Journal of Business,* July 1985, pp. 259–278.

———, and EDUARDO SCHWARTZ: "Integration vs. Segmentation in the Canadian Stock Market," *Journal of Finance,* July 1986, pp. 603–614.

LESSARD, DONALD R.: "World, Country, and Industry Relationships in Equity Returns: Implications for Risk Reduction through International Diversification," *Financial Analysts Journal,* January/February 1976, pp. 2–8.

LEVY, HAIM, and MARSHALL SARNAT: "International Diversification of Investment Portfolios," *American Economic Review,* September 1970, pp. 668–675.

ODIER, PATRICK, and BRUNO SOLNIK: "Lessons for International Asset Allocation," *Financial Analysts Journal,* March/April 1993, pp. 63–77.

SERÇU, PIET: "A Generalization of the International Asset Pricing Model," *Revue Française de Finance,* June 1980, pp. 91–135.

SOLNIK, BRUNO H.: "Why Not Diversify Internationally Rather than Domestically?" *Financial Analysts Journal,* July/August 1974, pp. 48–54.

———: "An Equilibrium Model of International Capital Market," *Journal of Economic Theory,* August 1974, pp. 500–524.

———: "International Arbitrage Pricing Theory," *Journal of Finance,* May 1983, pp. 449–457.

SCARLATA, JODI G.: "Institutional Developments in the Globalization of Securities and Futures Markets," *Review,* Federal Reserve Bank of St. Louis, January/February 1992, pp. 17–30.

STULTZ, RENÉ: "A Model of International Asset Pricing," *Journal of Financial Economics,* December 1981, pp. 383–406.

UPPAL, RAMAN: "A General Equilibrium Model of Portfolio Choice," *The Journal of Finance,* June 1993, pp. 529–553.

CHAPTER 19

Capital Budgeting for Direct Foreign Investment

All the world's a stage.

—WILLIAM SHAKESPEARE
As You Like It, Act 2, Scene 7

CAPITAL BUDGETING: FOREIGN VERSUS DOMESTIC INVESTMENTS

The massive multinational corporations (MNCs), whose names are household words in numerous languages and which have power that is the envy and fear of almost every government, grew by making direct investments overseas. A criterion used for making these direct investments will be presented here as we develop a principle of **capital budgeting** that can be used in evaluating foreign capital investments.

The typical foreign direct investment (FDI) is the building of a plant to manufacture and sell in overseas markets. The choice of building a plant is one of several alternative ways of selling the company's product in a foreign country. Other options include exporting from domestic facilities, licensing a producer in the foreign market to manufacture the good, and producing the good in a facility outside the intended market which the firm already operates. As Exhibit 19.1 explains, the choice is complex and has to be made in a world in which conditions are continually changing. Nevertheless, as is explained in Exhibit 19.2, increasing competition from globalized trade is forcing companies to seriously consider foreign direct investment.

Project evaluations, referred to as capital budgeting, are discussed in a domestic context in almost all introductory finance courses. However, in the international arena, capital budgeting involves complex problems that are not shared in a domestic context. These include, for example, the dependence of cash flows on capital structure because of cheap loans from foreign governments, exchange-rate risks, country risks, multiple tiers of taxation, and restrictions on repatriating income. We will show the conditions under which some of the more complex problems in the evaluation of overseas investments can be reduced to manageable size.

In a matter of than less than a decade, General Electric's rationale for a joint venture to manufacture appliances in Mexico changed several times. As the following excerpt explains, in GE's case the company was fortunate that new developments gave further support for the original choice.

Our major appliance (white goods) business had a mainly domestic focus for many years. In the mid-1980s, [GE Appliances] decided to enter the North American gas range business through a Mexican joint venture with a local partner. They built a plant in Mexico to serve both the export market and eventually, what they foresaw (correctly, as it turns out) as a growing Mexican market for modern domestic appliances. Their initial foreign exchange concern was a 1982-style devaluation and de facto confiscation of . . . financial assets. The solution had two principal elements: one was an offshore sales company, to minimize locally-held . . . assets to the extent possible, the other was careful management of working capital and cash flow exposure to maintain a balanced position. These are classic strategies in devaluation-prone currencies where hedging instruments are either unavailable or prohibitively expensive.

The strategy worked well throughout the 1980s, but within the last two years, the environment has changed. First of all, the local Mexican market for major appliances (including refrigeration and home laundry products, which the joint venture also supplies) has expanded, and GE Appliances is well-positioned to take advantage of the increased local demand. The result, of course, is that we now have more peso assets on the books. Also, financing these assets by borrowing in local currency—a classic hedging technique—remains stubbornly expensive. The business did a lot of homework on the Mexican economic situation and on forecasting cash flows and income statements by currency. Their assessment of the former and their analysis of cash flows and expected returns in the business led them to a greater degree of comfort with an increased level of Mexican asset exposure. The strategy is working well, and Appliances is very enthusiastic about the second stage, as it were, of their Mexican investment.

Less than two years after this item was written, Mexico experienced a serious financial crisis. Between December 1994 and March 1995 the peso lost almost half its foreign exchange value. A strategy of having Mexican asset exposure meant resulting translation or transaction losses; peso assets, such as peso accounts receivable, became worth half their previous value when converted into dollars. However, to the extent that Mexican facilities produced for the U.S. market, the peso devaluation meant increased profitability; see Chapter 14. *A priori,* the net result of the asset versus operating exposures is difficult to discern. Nevertheless, the scale of the 1994–1995 peso crisis helps reinforce the importance of maintaining close scrutiny of foreign direct investments.

Source: Marcia B. Whitaker, "Strategic Management of Foreign Exchange Exposure in an International Firm," in Yakov Amihud and Richard M. Levich (eds.), *Exchange Rates and Corporate Performance,* New York University Salomon Center, 1994, pp. 247–255.

There are a number of approaches to capital budgeting for traditional domestic investments, including **net present value (NPV), adjusted present value (APV), internal rate of return,** and **payback period.** We shall use the APV technique, which has been characterized as a "divide and conquer" approach because it tackles each difficulty as it occurs. This technique involves accounting separately for the complexities found in foreign investments as a result of such factors as subsidized loans and restrictions on repatriating income. Before we show how the difficulties can be handled, we shall give explanations of the difficulties themselves. Our explanations will show why the APV approach has been proposed for the evaluation of overseas projects rather than the traditional NPV approach, which is used extensively in evaluating domestic projects.

Companies in many industries can no longer survive as exclusively domestic operations. Competition from foreign-based firms which have made foreign direct investments and which thereby enjoy economies of large-scale production is forcing previously inward-looking companies to consider investing abroad. In other words, some companies are considering foreign direct investment because *other* companies have made foreign direct investments. The need to keep costs at competitive levels is discussed in the following excerpt. Other developments which are adding to the global level of direct investment and the coordination of the resulting multinational activities are also mentioned.

Multinational corporations (MNCs) today not only participate in most major national markets, but are also increasingly coordinating their activities across these markets to gain advantages of scale, scope, and learning on a global basis. The emergence of global competition represents a major threat, as well as an opportunity, to those European and American companies that gained competitive advantage under an older mode of multinational competition. Labeled "multi-domestic" competition by Michael Porter, this now passing phase in the development of international business was characterized by large MNCs with overseas operations that operated for the most part independently of one another. What centralization existed in this stage of the evo-

lution of the MNC was typically restricted to areas such as R & D and finance. With global competition, a much larger proportion of corporate activities is coordinated globally, including aspects of manufacturing, marketing, and virtually all R & D.

The emergence of global competition reflects the merging of previously segmented national markets caused by a variety of forces, including reductions in trade barriers, a convergence of tastes, and significant advances in product and process technologies. New global strategies also take advantage of changes in information technology and increased organizational sophistication to improve coordination among geographically dispersed operations.

. . .

National financial markets have become increasingly linked into a single global market, as a result of both deregulation and an increase in the market power, global reach, and financial skills of both corporate and institutional users of financial services. At the same time, a significant deepening of financial technology has taken place not only in terms of the information, trading, and document-processing systems, but also in the refinement of analytical techniques that have given rise to new financial instruments, more precise pricing of assets, and new economic risk management approaches.

Source: Donald R. Lessard, "Global Competition and Corporate Finance in the 1990s," *Journal of Applied Corporate Finance,* winter 1991, pp. 59–72.

DIFFICULTIES IN EVALUATING FOREIGN PROJECTS[1]

Introductory textbooks in finance tend to advise the use of the NPV technique. The NPV is defined as follows:

$$\text{NPV} = -C_0 + \sum_{t=1}^{T} \frac{CF_t^*(1 - \tau)}{(1 + \bar{r})^t} \tag{19.1}$$

where

$$C_0 = \text{project cost}$$
$$CF_t^* = \text{expected before-tax cash flow in year } t$$

[1]Our account of the adjusted-present-value technique draws heavily on a paper by Donald Lessard: "Evaluating International Projects: An Adjusted Present Value Approach," in Donald R. Lessard (ed.), *International Financial Management: Theory and Application,* Warren, Gorham & Lamont, Boston, 2d ed., 1985.

$$\tau = \text{tax rate}$$
$$\bar{r} = \text{weighted average cost of capital}$$
$$T = \text{life of the project}$$

The **weighted average cost of capital,** $\bar{r}$, is in turn defined as follows:

$$\bar{r} = \frac{E}{E + D} r^e + \frac{D}{E + D} r(1 - \tau)$$

where

$$r^e = \text{equilibrium cost of equity reflecting only the systematic risk}$$
$$r = \text{before-tax cost of credit}$$
$$E = \text{total market value of equity}$$
$$D = \text{total market value of debt}$$
$$\tau = \text{tax rate}$$

We see that the cost of equity and the cost of debt are weighted by the importance of equity and debt as sources of capital and that an additional adjustment is made to the cost of debt, since interest payments are generally deductible against corporate taxes. The adjustment of $1 - \tau$ gives the effective cost of debt after the fraction τ of interest payments has been saved from taxes. While not universally accepted, this NPV approach has enjoyed a prominent place in finance textbooks.[2]

There are two categories of reasons why it is difficult to apply the traditional NPV technique to overseas projects and why an alternative framework such as the adjusted-present-value technique is required. The first category of reasons involves the difficulties which cause cash flows—the *numerators* in NPVs—to be seen from two different perspectives: that of the investor's home country and that of the country in which the project is located. The correct perspective is that of the investor's home country, which we assume to be the same for all shareholders.[3] The second category of reasons involves the degree of risk of foreign projects and the appropriate discount rate—the *denominator* of the NPV. We shall begin by looking at why cash flows differ between the investor's perspective and the perspective of the country in which the project is located.

CASH FLOWS: HOME VERSUS FOREIGN PERSPECTIVES

Blocked Funds

If funds that are blocked or otherwise restricted can be utilized in a foreign investment, the project cost to the investor may be below the local project construction cost. From the investor's perspective there is a gain from activated funds equal to the

---

[2]For the traditional textbook account of the NPV approach with the weighted average cost of capital, see James C. Van Horne, *Financial Management and Policy,* 8th ed., Prentice-Hall, Englewood Cliffs, N.J., 1988. For an account of the alternative APV approach using an adjusted cost of capital, see Richard Brealey and Stewart Myers, *Principles of Corporate Finance,* 4th ed., McGraw-Hill, New York, 1991.
[3]Michael Adler has tackled the challenging problem of having shareholders from different countries. See Michael Adler, "The Cost of Capital and Valuation of a Two-Country Firm," *Journal of Finance,* March 1974, pp. 119–132.

difference between the face value of those funds and the present value of the funds if the next best thing is done with them. This gain should be deducted from the capital cost of the project to find the cost from the investor's perspective. For example, if the next best thing that can be done is to leave blocked funds idle abroad, the full value of the activated funds should be deducted from the project cost. Alternatively, if half of the blocked funds can be returned to the investor after the investor pays taxes or uses an internal funds transfer system, then half of the value of the blocked funds should be subtracted from the cost of the project.

Effects on the Sales of Other Divisions

From the perspective of the manager of a foreign project, the total value of cash flows generated by the investment is relevant. However, factories are frequently built in countries in which sales have previously taken place. If the multinational corporation exports to the country of the project from the home country or some other preexisting facility, only the increment in the MNC's corporate income is relevant. Sales will often decline or be lost in the absence of a project, and this is why the investment is made. Therefore, we must net out whatever income would have otherwise been earned by the multinational corporation.

Remittance Restrictions

When there are restrictions on the **repatriation** of income, only those flows that are remittable to the parent are relevant from the MNC's perspective. This is true whether or not the income is remitted. When remittances are legally limited, sometimes the restrictions can be circumvented to some extent by using internal transfer prices, overhead payments, and so on. If we include only the income which is remittable via legal and open channels, we will obtain a conservative estimate of the project's value. If this is positive, we need not add any more. If it is negative, we can add income that is remittable via illegal transfers, for example. The availability of this two-step procedure is a major advantage of the APV approach. A two-step procedure can also be applied to taxes.

Different Levels of Taxation

International taxation is an extremely complex subject that is best treated separately, as it is in Appendix 19.1. However, for the purpose of evaluating overseas direct investment, what matters is the total taxes paid, and not which government collects them, the form of taxes collected, the expenditures allowed against taxes, and so on. The essential point is that for a U.S.-based multinational, when the U.S. corporate tax rate is above the foreign rate, the effective tax rate will be the U.S. rate if full credit is given for foreign taxes paid. For example, if the foreign project is located in Singapore and the local tax rate for foreign-based corporations is 27 percent, while the U.S. corporate tax rate is 35 percent, then after the credit for foreign taxes paid is applied, only 8 percent will be payable in the United States. If, however, the project is located in Canada and faces a tax rate of 43 percent, full credit will not be available, and the effective tax rate will be 43 percent. This means that when we deal with foreign projects from the investor's point of view, we should use a tax rate τ which is the higher of the home-country and foreign rates.

Taking τ as the higher of the tax rates at home and abroad is a conservative approach. In reality, taxes are often reduced to a level below τ through the appropriate choice of transfer prices, royalty payments, and so on. These techniques can be used to move income from high-tax countries to low-tax countries and thereby reduce overall corporate taxes. In addition, the payment of taxes can be deferred by leaving remittable income abroad, and so if cash flows are measured as all remittable income whether or not remitted, some adjustment is required, since the actual amount of taxes paid will be less than the cash-flow term suggests. The adjustment can be made to the cost of capital or included as an extra term in an APV calculation.[4]

DISCOUNT RATES: CORPORATE VERSUS SHAREHOLDER PERSPECTIVES

While governments do offer special financial aid or other kinds of help for certain domestic projects, it is very common for foreign investments to carry some sort of assistance. This may come in the form of low-cost land, reduced interest rates, and so on. Low-cost land can merely be reflected in project costs, but concessionary lending is more problematic in the NPV approach. However, with the APV technique we can add a special term to include the subsidy. As we shall see, this is particularly important in that the special concessionary loan will be available to the corporation but not directly to the shareholders. Concessionary financing also makes the appropriate cost of capital for foreign investment projects differ from that for domestic projects, which is what happens in segmented capital markets.[5]

The various difficulties encountered in the evaluation of foreign projects can be incorporated within the APV approach, which we have not yet presented. We need not delay any longer.

The Adjusted-Present-Value Technique

The APV for a foreign project can be written as follows:

$$
\begin{aligned}
APV = &-S_0 K_0 + S_0 AF_0 + \sum_{t=1}^{T} \frac{\left(S_t^* CF_t^* - LS_t^*\right)(1 - \tau)}{\left(1 + DR_e\right)^t} + \sum_{t=1}^{T} \frac{DA_t \tau}{\left(1 + DR_a\right)^t} \\
&+ \sum_{t=1}^{T} \frac{r_g BC_0 \tau}{\left(1 + DR_b\right)^t} + S_0 \left[CL_0 - \sum_{t=1}^{T} \frac{LR_t}{\left(1 + DR_c\right)^t} \right] \\
&+ \sum_{t=1}^{T} \frac{TD_t^*}{\left(1 + DR_d\right)^t} + \sum_{t=1}^{T} \frac{RF_t^*}{\left(1 + DR_f\right)^t}
\end{aligned}
\tag{19.2}
$$

[4]A method for valuing foreign investment that is based on net present value and the weighted average cost of capital that takes care of taxes has been developed by Alan C. Shapiro ("Financial Structure and the Cost of Capital in the Multinational Corporation," *Journal of Financial and Quantitative Analysis,* November 1978, pp. 211–226). In general, the NPV and APV approaches will be equivalent if they take care of all complexities. This has been shown by Lawrence D. Booth ("Capital Budgeting Frameworks for the Multinational Corporation," *Journal of International Business Studies,* fall 1982, pp. 113–123).

[5]Indeed, blocked funds, remittance restrictions, and different levels of taxation are also causes of market segmentation.

where

S_0 = spot exchange rate, period zero

S_t^* = expected spot rate, period t

K_0 = capital cost of project in foreign currency units

AF_0 = restricted funds activated by project

CF_t^* = expected remittable cash flow in foreign currency units

LS_t^* = profit from lost sales, in dollars

τ = the higher of U.S. and foreign corporate tax rates

T = life of the project

DA_t = depreciation allowances in dollar units

BC_0 = contribution of project to borrowing capacity in dollars

CL_0 = face value of concessionary loan in foreign currency

LR_t = loan repayments on concessionary loan in foreign currency

TD_t^* = expected tax savings from deferrals, intersubsidiary transfer pricing

RF_t^* = expected illegal repatriation of income

DR_e = discount rate for cash flows, assuming all-equity financing

DR_a = discount rate for depreciation allowances

DR_b = discount rate for tax saving on interest deduction from contribution to borrowing capacity

DR_c = discount rate for saving via concessionary interest rate

DR_d = discount rate for tax saving via intersubsidiary transfers

DR_f = discount rate for illegally repatriated project flows

r_g = market borrowing rate at home

We can describe each of the terms in the APV equation and show how these terms take care of the difficulties in evaluating foreign investment projects.

$-S_0K_0$: The cost of the project is assumed to be denominated in foreign currency and incurred in year 0 only. It is converted into dollars at S_0.

S_0AF_0: We reduce the project cost by the value, converted into dollars, of the blocked funds activated by the project. AF_0 is the face value of the blocked funds minus their value in the next best use.

$\sum_{t=1}^{T} \dfrac{\left(S_t^*CF_t^* - LS_t^*\right)(1 - \tau)}{\left(1 + DR_e\right)^t}$: CF_t^* represents the expected legally remittable

project cash flows on sales from the new project in year t, beginning after a year.[6] This is measured in foreign currency and converted into dollars at the expected exchange rate, S_t^*. From this is subtracted the lost income on sales from other facilities which are replaced by the new facility, LS_t^*. If the lost income is measured in U.S. dollars, as it will be if sales are lost to the U.S. parent company, we do not multiply the lost income by S_t^*. If the lost income is measured in units of foreign currency, S_t^* applies to LS_t^*. Other funds remitted via intersubsidiary transfer pricing and other illegal means are included in a later term. The cash flows are adjusted for the effective tax rate, τ, which is the higher of the domestic and foreign corporate rates. Any

---

[6]As before in the book, asterisks stand for expected values. Quantities without asterisks are assumed to be known at the time of the investment decision.

reduction from this level that results from moving funds from high-tax countries to low-tax countries can be added later. We assume here that the same tax rate applies to lost income on replaced sales as well as to new income. If the lost income would have faced a different tax rate, LS_t^* must be considered separately from CF_t^*. The discount rate is the all-equity cost of capital that reflects all systematic risk, including unavoidable country risk and exchange-rate risk.[7]

$$\sum_{t=1}^{T} \frac{DA_t \tau}{(1 + DR_a)^t}$$: Depreciation is an allowable expense when determining

corporate taxes for projects located abroad as well as for those at home. The benefits of the depreciation allowances are the amounts of allowances times the corporate tax rates against which they are applied. We have given DA_t in dollar amounts and therefore have not included S_t^*. This will be appropriate if the higher tax rate is the rate in the United States; in this case allowances will be deducted against U.S. taxes. If the higher tax rate is the rate in the foreign country, DA_t will probably be in foreign-currency units, and we need to convert at S_t^*.

$$\sum_{t=1}^{T} \frac{r_g BC_0 \tau}{(1 + DR_b)^t}$$: When debt is used to finance a project at home or abroad, the

interest payments are tax-deductible. Whether or not the project in question fully utilizes its borrowing capacity and consequent tax savings, the tax savings on the amount that *could* be borrowed should be included as a benefit.[8] The annual benefit equals the interest payments that are saved from the tax reduction, the interest rate being the market borrowing rate at home. For example, if the project has a value of $1 million and the firm likes to maintain 50 percent of its value in debt, the project will raise borrowing capacity by $BC_0 = \$500,000$, and the interest payment on this amount, that is, $r_g BC_0$, should be included each year. This will be true even if the actual amount borrowed is larger or smaller than $500,000. For example, if $200,000 is borrowed on the $1 million project, an additional amount of $300,000 can be borrowed elsewhere in the corporation, with consequent tax offsets on the interest on $300,000. If $800,000 is borrowed, the project will reduce the capacity to borrow for other activities by $300,000, and the lower tax deductions elsewhere will offset the tax deductions on $300,000 worth of borrowing for the project. This leaves the interest on only $500,000 appropriate for inclusion as BC_0.

$$S_0 \left[CL_0 - \sum_{t=1}^{T} \frac{LR_t}{(1 + DR_c)^t} \right]$$: The current value of the benefit of a concessionary

loan is the difference between the face value of the loan, CL_0, and the present value of the repayment on the loan discounted at the rate of interest that would have been faced in the absence of the concessionary financing. This overall value must be converted into dollars. For example, if a 10-year loan with a 10 percent interest rate and 10 equal principal repayments is made available when the market rate would have been 15 percent, the present value of the repayment on a £1 million loan is £833,959. This is shown in Table 19.1. The value of the subsidy from the loan con-

---

[7]We are not yet ready to give a full account of country risk, which includes political risk. This will be covered in the next chapter.

[8]Borrowing capacity is not a limit imposed on the firm from outside. It results from the firm's decision on how much debt it wishes to carry.

TABLE 19.1. Value of a £1-Million Concessionary Loan

Year	Loan Outstanding	Principal Repayment	Interest Payment	Total Payment	Present Value of Payment
1	£1,000,000	£100,000	£100,000	£200,000	£173,913
2	900,000	100,000	90,000	190,000	143,667
3	800,000	100,000	80,000	180,000	118,353
4	700,000	100,000	70,000	170,000	97,198
5	600,000	100,000	60,000	160,000	79,548
6	500,000	100,000	50,000	150,000	68,849
7	400,000	100,000	40,000	140,000	52,631
8	300,000	100,000	30,000	130,000	42,497
9	200,000	100,000	20,000	120,000	31,111
10	100,000	100,000	10,000	110,000	27,190
					£833,959

cession is hence £1,000,000 − £833,959 = £166,041. This amount has a current dollar value of \$332,082 if, for example, $S_0 = 2.0$.[9]

$$\sum_{t=1}^{T} \frac{TD_t^*}{\left(1 + DR_d\right)^t}$$: By using the higher of the domestic and foreign tax rates for τ

we have taken a conservative approach. In practice, a multinational is likely to be able to move funds from high-tax locations to low-tax locations and defer the payment of taxes, thereby reducing the effective rate to a level below τ. Cash flows can be moved by adjusting **transfer prices,** head-office overhead, and so on, and the payment of taxes can be deferred by reinvesting in low-tax countries.[10] The APV technique allows us to include these tax savings as a separate term. As we have mentioned, a two-step approach is possible. We can evaluate APV without a TD_t^* and see if it is positive. If it is, we need not do anything else. If it is not, we can see how much of a tax saving will be required to make APV positive and determine whether such a saving can reasonably be expected.

$$\sum_{t=1}^{T} \frac{RF_t^*}{\left(1 + DR_f\right)^t}$$: The cash flow we use for CF_t^* is, like the tax rate, a conservative

estimate. CF_t^* includes only the flows which are remittable when transfer prices, royalties, and so on reflect their appropriate market values. However, a multinational might manipulate transfer prices or royalty payments to repatriate more income (as well as to reduce taxes). Any extra remittable income from additional (and perhaps illegal) channels can be included after the APV from the legal cash flows has been computed, if the APV is negative. This two-step procedure can be applied simultaneously to both the extra remittable income and the extra tax savings that might be obtained through internal price and income tinkering.

---

[9]A general account of the valuation of subsidized financing can be found in Richard Brealey and Stewart Myers, *Principles of Corporate Finance,* 4th ed., McGraw-Hill, New York, 1991.

[10]Transfer prices are those charged for goods and services moving between divisions of a company. They are discussed more fully in the next chapter.

We have described the numerators of the APV formula and shown how they take care of many of the difficulties in evaluating foreign investment projects which we cited earlier. We have not yet said much about the denominators in the APV formula.

Selecting the Appropriate Discount Rates

So far we have said little about the discount rates other than that cash flows should be discounted at an all-equity rate that reflects risk. As we noted in Chapter 18, only the systematic component of total risk matters, and this risk requires a premium in the discount rate to reflect the shareholder's opportunity cost of capital. To some extent the additional risks of doing business abroad are mitigated by the extent to which cash flows from foreign projects are imperfectly correlated and therefore reduce the variance of corporate income. If there is risk reduction from having some independence of cash flows from different countries but the pooling of flows from different countries is not directly available to shareholders, the diversification offered by the MNC should be reflected in discount rates as well as in the market value of the stock.[11] This is because the pooling of cash flows reduces the business risk.

The risks faced with foreign investments that are not explicitly faced with domestic investments are foreign exchange risk and country risk. These risks provide a reason, in addition to those previously cited, why the NPV technique is difficult to apply to foreign capital projects. Both country risk and exchange-rate risk can, for example, make the optimal capital structure change over time. This is difficult to incorporate within the weighted-average cost of capital used in the NPV technique. However, in the APV technique, where we use an all-equity cost of capital (DR_e) to discount cash flows, the capital structure matters only because of the effect on taxes, treated in a separate term.

Country risk and foreign exchange risk, like business risk, can be diversified by holding a portfolio of securities of different countries denominated in many different currencies. This means that the risk premium in the discount rate, which reflects only the systematic risk, need not be very large.[12] It follows from our discussion of the ICAPM in Chapter 18 that knowing the systematic risk requires that we have a covariance for the project with the market portfolio. It is extremely difficult to obtain such a project covariance, because there is no market value of the *project* and no past data to use even if there were a market value. Moreover, the relevant risk premium for the APV approach must be for an all-equity investment. This

[11]As we mentioned in Chapter 18, the ability of the corporation to do what its shareholders cannot requires segmented capital markets that the corporation can circumvent.

[12]Instead of including the country risk in the discount rate, we can incorporate it within the cash-flow term. This procedure, which can also be followed with other types of risk, involves putting cash flows into their "certainty equivalents." A method of dealing with risk that avoids the need to find certainty equivalents or risk premiums is to deduct from cash flows the cost of country risk insurance or a foreign exchange risk management program. This is the recommendation of Arthur I. Stonehill and Leonard Nathanson in "Capital Budgeting and the Multinational Corporation," *California Management Review,* summer 1968, pp. 39–54. The ability of shareholders to diversify foreign exchange risk has been examined by Jeffery A. Frankel ("The Diversifiability of Exchange Risk," *Journal of International Economics,* August 1979, pp. 379–393).

adds even more difficulty when any existing risk premium reflects the company's debt. But these are only some of the problems in selecting appropriate discount rates. We have already mentioned the problem of the shareholder perspective, which is difficult when shareholders are from different countries and capital markets are segmented. Yet another problem is inflation and the connected question of the currency in which cash flows are measured.

Inflation and Discount Rate Choice

A question that arises in all capital-budgeting applications, whether the project being evaluated is foreign or domestic, concerns the choice of the "nominal" versus "real" discount rate. (As mentioned in Chapter 11, the real interest rate is the nominal rate minus the expected inflation rate.) The answer is that the choice does not matter provided we are consistent. That is, we reach the same conclusion whether we discount nominal cash flows (those not adjusted for inflation) by the nominal discount rate or discount real (inflation-adjusted) cash flows by the real discount rate. However, if cash flows are easier to forecast in today's prices so that the forecasts are of real cash flows, as a practical matter it is easier to use these flows and discount at the real rate. (The alternative involves building inflationary expectations into cash flows and then using the nominal discount rate, but this is far more roundabout.)

A related question to that of nominal versus real discount rates concerns the currency of expected cash flows. Should we use foreign-currency cash flows and discount these at the foreign-currency discount rate, or convert foreign-currency cash flows into domestic currency, and discount at the domestic-currency discount rate? Furthermore, do we use nominal or real discount rates? The answer to these questions is that it does not matter which method we use provided everything is consistent. That is, if cash flows are in foreign currency we use the foreign-currency discount rate, and if cash flows are in domestic currency we use the domestic-currency discount rate. Similarly, if we use real cash flows, in terms of either currency, we should use the real discount rate, in the same currency. These conclusions are not obvious, and they are explained in detail in Appendix 19.2. The appendix also shows that despite the theoretical equivalence of methods, when foreign-currency cash flows are predetermined, or **contractual,** we do not have a choice between real and nominal discount rates and between current and future expected exchange rates. Examples of contractual cash flows are revenues from exports sold at fixed prices and depreciation allowances based on historical costs. The contractual amounts are fixed in nominal terms and should therefore be converted into dollars at the expected future exchange rate and discounted at the nominal dollar discount rate. Contractual flows do not lend themselves to simplification through the use of today's cash flows of foreign exchange at today's exchange rates. It is for this reason that in the cash-flow term in equation (19.2) we convert foreign-currency cash flows into U.S. dollars, and discount at the nominal U.S. dollar discount rate. However, as we shall show below, the discount rates for other terms in equation (19.2) take different forms.

Discount Rates for Different Items

Now that the methods for handling inflation with the discount rate have been stated, we are ready to describe the nature of the different discount rates in the APV formula.

DR_e: This should be nominal for contractual cash flows resulting from sales made at fixed future prices. Since the cash flows are converted into dollars at S_t^*, the rate should be the nominal rate for the United States. DR_e should also be the all-equity rate, reflecting the project's systematic risk, including the risk from exchange rates. When the cash flows are noncontractual, we can use a real rate, today's actual exchange rate, and initial-period expected cash flows at today's prices. This is explained in Appendix 19.2.

DR_a: Since in many countries depreciation is based on historical costs, DA_t will be contractual, and DR_a should therefore be the nominal rate. Since we have written DA_t directly in dollar terms, we should use the U.S. rate. The only risk premium should be for the chance that the depreciation allowances will go unused. If the investor feels very confident that the project will yield positive cash flows, this risk is small, and so DR_a should be the riskless nominal rate of the United States. This is true even if DA_t is measured in foreign-currency units, provided we convert them into U.S. dollars.

DR_b: If the project's contribution to borrowing capacity is measured in nominal U.S. dollar terms—and it is very likely that it will be—we should discount at the U.S. nominal rate. The risk is that the tax shield cannot be used, and if this is considered small, we can use the riskless rate.

DR_c: The value of a concessionary loan depends on the interest rate that would otherwise be paid. If the loan repayments will be nominal foreign exchange amounts, we should use the nominal foreign-currency interest rate that would have been paid.

DR_d and DR_f: Tax savings, additional repatriated income via transfer prices, and the deferment of tax payments via reinvestment in low-tax countries could be estimated at either today's prices or future prices. If the estimates of TD_t^* and RF_t^* are at today's prices and are therefore real, we must use a real rate, and if they are at future inflated prices, we must use a nominal rate. If the estimates are in U.S. dollars, as they probably will be, we must use a U.S. rate. Since the risk is that of not being able to find techniques for making these tax savings and additional remittances, the appropriate discount rate requires a risk premium. Donald Lessard advises the use of the same rate used for cash flows, DR_e.[13]

With the nature of the terms in the APV formula carefully defined and the factors influencing the discount rates also explained, we are ready to consider a realistic example of capital budgeting. We consider whether Aviva Corporation should build a jeans-manufacturing factory in Italy.

AN EXAMPLE

Suppose that as a result of the imminent entry of new firms into the Italian jeans market, Aviva is considering opening an Italian factory. Aviva hopes that by being on the spot it can be more responsive to local preferences for style and thereby avoid steadily losing sales to the new entrants. The construction costs of the plant have

---

[13]See Donald R. Lessard, *op. cit.* As we have already mentioned, this paper forms the basis of the APV technique explained here.

been estimated at Lit 2 billion, and it is believed that it will add $1 million to Aviva's borrowing capacity. Because of taxes on remitted earnings from Aviva's previously established sales subsidiary in Italy, the proposed factory can be partially financed with Lit 600 million, which, if it had been returned to the United States, would have faced taxes of Lit 400 million in Italy. Of this amount, a tax credit for only Lit 280 million would have been received in the United States. The funds would have been returned to the United States because nothing better could have been done with them.

Assume for simplicity that the current exchange rate between the lira and the U.S. dollar is Lit 1000/$, and so $S_0 = 0.00100$, and the spot rate is expected to move at a rate given by the relative inflation according to PPP. Italian inflation is expected to proceed at 25 percent, while U.S. inflation is expected to be 10 percent.

Jeans sales, which will begin when the plant is completed after a year, are expected to average 50,000 pairs per year. At the beginning of the year of construction, the jeans have a unit price of Lit 20,000 per pair, and this is expected to rise at the general rate of inflation. The average production cost based on material prices at the time of construction is Lit 15,000 per pair, and this cost is likely to keep in line with general Italian inflation.

The Italian market had previously been supplied by Aviva's main plant in California, and recent sales to the Italian market were 10,000 pairs per year. The most recent profit on U.S.-manufactured jeans was $5 per pair, and this can be expected to keep pace with general U.S. inflation. However, it was expected that in the absence of an Italian factory, Aviva would have lost 9.1 percent per annum of its Italian sales to the new entrants. This is why Aviva is considering opening an Italian plant of its own. It has learned that it must be in touch with local styles when local firms enter the market.

The factory is expected to require little in the way of renovation for 10 years. The market value of the plant in 10 years is extremely difficult to estimate, and Aviva is confident only in the belief that it will have some substantial value.

Aviva has by great art and ingenuity managed to arrive at an all-equity cost of capital that reflects the project's systematic risk (including country risk that is not covered by insurance, the deviation of exchange rates from predicted levels, and so on) of 20 percent. This allows for the fact that much of the risk can be diversified by the shareholders and/or avoided by insurance, forward cover, and so on.

In return for locating the factory in an area of heavy unemployment, Aviva will receive from the Italian government Lit 600 million of the Lit 1400 million it needs in addition to the previously blocked funds, at the subsidized rate of 10 percent. The principal is to be repaid in equal installments over 10 years. If Aviva had been required to borrow competitively in Italy, it could have expected a 35 percent borrowing cost, as opposed to its 15 percent borrowing cost in the United States. This is a little above the U.S. riskless rate of 12 percent. The remaining Lit 800 million that is needed for construction will be provided as equity by Aviva U.S.A. Income on the project is subject to a 25 percent tax in Italy and a 46 percent tax in the United States, and Italian taxes are fully deductible against U.S. taxes.

The U.S. Internal Revenue Service will allow Aviva to write off one-tenth of the dollar equivalent of the historical construction cost each year over 10 years. By using carefully arranged transfer prices and royalties, Aviva thinks it can reduce taxes by deferrals by $5000 in the initial year of operation, and it expects this to hold steady in real terms, but it does not expect to be able to remit more income than the amount declared.

We can show below that in terms of the notation used in defining APV in equation (19.2), Aviva faces the following:

$$K_0 = \text{Lit } 2{,}000{,}000{,}000$$

$$BC_0 = \$1{,}000{,}000$$

$$AF_0 = \text{Lit } 600{,}000{,}000 - (\text{Lit } 600{,}000{,}000 - \text{Lit } 400{,}000{,}000)$$

$$= \text{Lit } 400{,}000{,}000$$

$$S_0 = 0.00100$$

$$S_t^* = 0.00100(1 - 0.12)^t$$

$$CF_t^* = \text{Lit } 50{,}000(20{,}000 - 15{,}000)(1 + 0.25)^t + (\text{scrap value when } t = 10)$$

$$LS_t^* = \$10{,}000(5)(1 + 0.1)^t(1 - 0.091)^t = \$50{,}000$$

$$CL_0 = \text{Lit } 600{,}000{,}000$$

$$LR_t = (\text{see Table 19.2})$$

$$DA_t = \$200{,}000$$

$$TD_t = \$5000(1 + 0.1)^{t-1} \quad \text{for} \quad t > 0$$

$$RF_t = 0$$

$$\tau = 0.46$$

$$DR_e = DR_d = DR_f = 0.20$$

$$DR_a = DR_b = 0.12$$

$$DR_c = 0.35$$

$$r_g = 0.15$$

We will solve the problem by using all nominal values for cash flows and all nominal discount rates.

Many of the values attached to the terms of the APV formula are self-evident. For example, the construction cost is Lit 2,000,000,000, and the borrowing capacity that the plant contributes is $1,000,000. The value of activated funds, AF_0, is their face value minus their value in their next best use. If the next best use is to bring them home and face taxes, the next best value is Lit 600,000,000 – Lit 400,000,000. We exclude the tax credit in the United States *on repatriated restricted funds* because it is smaller than the taxes paid in Italy; thus the effective tax rate is the Italian rate. (If the credit cannot be applied against other income, it has no value.) This means that if the blocked funds had been brought back, Lit 200,000,000 would have been received after taxes. We subtract this from the Lit 600,000,000 used in the project to get Lit 400,000,000 for AF_0.

The expected exchange rates are obtained from the definition $S_t^* \equiv S_0(1 + \dot{S}^*)^t$. We obtain $\dot{S}^*$ from the PPP condition; that is,

TABLE 19.2. Adjusted-Present-Value Magnitudes for Italian Jeans Factory

Year	S_t^*	CF_t^*	$S_t^*CF_t^*$	$S_t^*CF_t^* - LS_t$	$(1-\tau)\dfrac{S_t^*CF_t^* - LS_t^*}{(1+DR_e)^t}$	$\dfrac{DA_t\tau}{(1+DR_a)^t}$
1	$0.0008800/Lit	Lit312,500,000	$275,000	$225,000	$101,250	$82,143
2	0.0007744	390,625,000	302,500	252,500	94,688	73,342
3	0.0006815	488,281,250	332,764	282,764	88,364	65,484
4	0.0005997	610,351,560	366,028	316,028	82,299	48,468
5	0.0005277	762,939,450	402,603	352,603	76,520	52,203
6	0.0004644	953,674,320	442,886	392,886	71,051	46,610
7	0.0004087	1,192,092,900	487,208	437,208	65,889	41,616
8	0.0003596	1,490,116,120	535,846	485,846	61,016	37,157
9	0.0003165	1,862,645,150	589,527	539,527	56,465	33,176
10	0.0002785	2,328,306,440	648,433	598,433	52,191	29,622
					749,733	519,821

Year	$r_g BC_0\tau$	$\dfrac{r_g BC_0\tau}{(1+DR_b)^t}$	TD_t^*	$\dfrac{TD_t^*}{(1+DR_d)^t}$	Outstanding Loan	Loan Interest	LR_t	$\dfrac{LR_t}{(1+DR_c)^t}$
1	$69,000	$61,607	$5,000	$4,167	Lit600,000,000	Lit60,000,000	Lit120,000,000	Lit88,888,889
2	69,000	55,007	5,500	3,819	540,000,000	54,000,000	114,000,000	62,551,440
3	69,000	49,113	6,050	3,501	480,000,000	48,000,000	108,000,000	43,895,748
4	69,000	43,851	6,655	3,209	420,000,000	42,000,000	102,000,000	30,708,959
5	69,000	39,153	7,321	2,942	360,000,000	36,000,000	96,000,000	21,409,296
6	69,000	34,957	8,053	2,697	300,000,000	30,000,000	90,000,000	14,867,567
7	69,000	31,212	8,858	2,472	240,000,000	24,000,000	84,000,000	10,278,812
8	69,000	27,868	9,744	2,266	180,000,000	18,000,000	78,000,000	7,070,082
9	69,000	24,882	10,718	2,077	120,000,000	12,000,000	72,000,000	4,834,244
10	69,000	22,216	11,790	1,904	60,000,000	6,000,000	66,000,000	3,282,511
		389,866		29,054				287,787,548

$$\dot{S}^* = \frac{\dot{P}_{US}^* - \dot{P}_{IT}^*}{\left(1 + \dot{P}_{IT}^*\right)} = \frac{0.10 - 0.25}{1.25} = -0.12$$

The cash flow, CF_t^*, is obtained by multiplying the expected sales of 50,000 pairs of jeans per annum by the expected profit per pair. The profit per pair during the plant construction year, when prices and costs are known, would be Lit 20,000 − Lit 15,000 if production could begin immediately, but by the initial year of operation the profit per pair is expected to rise to (Lit 20,000 − Lit 15,000)(1 + 0.25). The profit is expected to continue to rise at 25 percent per annum, with an expected cash flow by year t of

$$(\text{Lit } 20,000 - \text{Lit } 15,000)(1 + 0.25)^t$$

from each of the 50,000 pairs. The value of this is shown in Table 19.2. The present value of the cash flow at Aviva's chosen cost of capital of $DR_e = 0.20$ is also shown.

The scrap value of the project is uncertain. As a result, we can take a two-step approach to see whether the project is profitable without estimating a scrap value, since if it is, we can save time in our evaluation.

Replaced sales, LS_t^*, have most recently been producing a profit for Aviva U.S.A. of $\$5 \times 10,000 = \$50,000$ per year. With the profit per unit expected to grow at the U.S. inflation rate of 10 percent and the number of units expected to decline by 9.1 percent, expected profits from replaced sales remain at their current level of $\$50,000$ per year; the product of 1.10 and $1 - 0.091$ equals unity.

The amount of the concessionary loan is $CL_0 = \text{Lit } 600,000,000$. The repayments for the principal are at Lit 60,000,000 each year, with interest computed on the unpaid balance at 10 percent per annum. LR_t in Table 19.2 shows the annual loan repayments discounted at the market rate in Italy of $DR_c = 0.35$. The table also gives the values of the discounted net-of-tax depreciation allowances of $\$200,000$ per year. This is 10 percent of the historical cost in dollars, S_0K_0. We use the dollar cost because the depreciation is effectively against U.S. corporate taxes. These are at the rate $\tau = 0.46$. We have discounted depreciation allowances at the riskless dollar rate, $DR_a = 0.12$.

The debt or borrowing capacity of the project is such that Aviva can borrow $\$1,000,000$ (which is half the dollar cost of construction) to obtain tax shields somewhere within its operations. The interest rate Aviva would pay if it took the tax shields by borrowing more at home is $r_g = 0.15$. This will save taxes on $0.15 \times \$1,000,000$ at the tax rate $\tau = 0.46$. We have discounted the saving from the tax shield at the riskless dollar rate, $DR_b = 0.12$.

The extra tax benefits, TD_t^*, of $\$5000$ are assumed to keep pace with U.S. inflation. We have discounted $TD_t^* = \$5000$ at Aviva's cost of equity of 20 percent.

We can form an opinion concerning the feasibility of the jeans factory if we use the values of the terms as we have stated them, including the totals from Table 19.2, in the APV formula, equation (19.2):

$$
\begin{aligned}
\text{APV} =\ & -(0.001 \times 2,000,000,000) + (0.001 \times 4,000,000,000) + 749,733 \\
& + 519,821 + 389,866 + 0.001 \times (600,000,000 - 287,787,548) \\
& + 29,054 + 0 = \$400,686
\end{aligned}
$$

We discover that the APV is positive. This means that the project is worthwhile. Furthermore, the APV does not yet include any estimate for the market value of the factory and land at the end of 10 years. If Aviva feels that while it cannot estimate this value, it should exceed half the original cost in real terms, it can take an even more confident position. Half the original project cost is $1 million, and since this is a real value, it should be discounted at the real interest rate relevant for dollars. Using Aviva's risky rate, this is DR_e minus the U.S. expected inflation rate of 10 percent; that is, $DR_e = 0.20 - 0.10 = 0.10$. At this rate the present value of $1 million in 10 years is $385,543, which makes the APV clearly positive. The $385,543 would be subject to a capital-gain tax if it were to be realized because the entire project has been depreciated, but even after taxes the project would clearly seem to be worthwhile.

ACTUAL PRACTICE OF CAPITAL BUDGETING

The adjusted-present-value approach using the correct discount rate to reflect the contractual or noncontractual nature of cash flows and the systematic risk of the investment project requires management to take a very scientific view. We can expect that constraints on the knowledge of managers and the time available to make decisions will result in approaches that are more pragmatic than the approach we presented. According to a survey of multinational corporations this does appear to be the case. The survey was made of 10 U.S. multinationals by Business International to see how they analyze acquisitions.[14] It showed that only 7 of the 10 corporations used any sort of discounting method at all.

Only one of the respondents in the Business International survey said that it looked at synergy effects, that is, the effects the acquisition would have on other subsidiaries. Five of the ten firms used the same hurdle discount rate for all acquisitions, whatever the country. Projected exchange rates were used by five of the respondents, while two used the projected rate if they considered a currency to be unstable and the current rate if they considered it to be stable. The remainder used current rates to convert all currency flows, but it was not clear from the survey whether these flows were measured in current price terms. At least one company assumed that exchange-rate movements would be reflected in relative interest rates and therefore used the U.S. interest rate on cash flows converted into dollars at the current exchange rate.

A survey of the foreign-investment evaluation practices of 225 U.S. manufacturing MNCs conducted by Marie Wicks Kelly and George Philippatos produced results revealing practices somewhat more in line with theory than those found in the much smaller Business International survey.[15] For example, the majority of companies used cash-flow calculations and costs of capital which, while not exactly the kind explained in this chapter, are approximately in line with appropriate procedures.

[14]See "BIMR Survey Reveals How U.S. Multinationals Analyze Foreign Acquisitions," *Money Report,* Business International, November 28, 1980. See also "Stress on Currency Fluctuations as MNCs Analyze Foreign Acquisitions," *Money Report,* Business International, November 5, 1980.

[15]Marie E. Wicks Kelly and George C. Philippatos, "Comparative Analysis of the Foreign Investment Evaluation Practices by U.S.-Based Manufacturing Multinational Companies," *Journal of International Business Studies,* winter 1982, pp. 19–42.

SUMMARY

1. The net-present-value technique is difficult to use in the case of foreign investment projects. The adjusted-present-value technique is frequently recommended instead.
2. Cash flows from foreign investments can be seen in two different ways: from the investor's perspective and from the perspective of the project managers in the foreign countries. It is the investor's perspective which is relevant. Factors which can make a difference between cash flows from the different perspectives include blocked funds (which reduce project costs to investors), reduced sales from other corporate divisions, restrictions on remitting earnings, extra taxes on repatriated income, and concessionary loans. These factors can be included in the adjusted present value (APV).
3. The APV technique allows a two-step evaluation. The first step involves a conservative estimate that includes only estimated benefits of the project. The second step, including other benefits, is needed only if the first step gives a negative estimate.
4. The calculation of APV includes cash flows net of taxes and reduced earnings elsewhere, depreciation allowances, tax shields, the value of concessionary loans, and other potential benefits. Each item must be discounted at an appropriate discount rate.
5. Discount rates should reflect only the systematic risk of the item being discounted. Doing business abroad can help reduce overall corporate risk when incomes are more independent between countries than between operations within a particular country, and this can mean lower discount rates for foreign projects.
6. Discount rates can, however, be higher on foreign investment projects because of country risk and exchange-rate risk. These risks can be diversified by shareholders if they invest in a number of countries, and this reduces required risk premiums.
7. We must be consistent when we take care of inflation in foreign-project evaluation. We can use either real values of cash flows, and so on, and real interest rates, or nominal cash flows and nominal interest rates.
8. When we are dealing with noncontractual flows, we can choose the method of handling inflation that we prefer. However, with contractual flows, which are nominal amounts, we must use nominal discount rates. The choice of approach with noncontractual flows exists because inflation in cash flows will be offset by movements in exchange rates.

REVIEW QUESTIONS

1. Why might cash flows from a project differ according to whether they are viewed from the perspective of the investor in the investor's country or from the perspective of a project manager in the country where the investment occurs?
2. Which of the two perspectives in question **1** is the correct perspective for judging investments?
3. What does concessionary lending imply for the cost of capital of a corporation enjoying the favorable terms versus the shareholders?
4. If blocked, or nonrepatriable, funds can be activated by a new foreign project, how does this affect the effective capital cost of the new project?
5. What is meant by "borrowing capacity," and how does the APV approach to capital budgeting factor in the implication of a project for any increase in borrowing capacity?
6. How do the levels of corporate tax rates influence whether an investor's home-country rate or the rate in the country of investment is used for calculating after-tax cash flows?
7. What amount of risk—total or only systematic—should be included in the all-equity discount rate used in the APV calculation?
8. What is the nature of the discount rate that is used for cash flows in the APV approach?

9. If cash flows are converted into the investor's domestic currency and are adjusted for inflation so they are real, what discount rate should be used?

10. What is a contractual cash flow?

11. In what way is the handling of contractual foreign-currency cash flows more restrictive in terms of approach than the handling of noncontractual foreign-currency cash flows?

12. What discount rate should be used for calculating the current value of interest payments on a concessionary loan, where the payments are in terms of the foreign currency?

ASSIGNMENT PROBLEMS

1. Will withholding taxes that are at rates below domestic corporate tax rates affect direct investment when full withholding tax credit is available? How will withholding tax rates affect the distribution of total tax revenues between countries?

2. A U.S. automobile manufacturer, National Motors, is considering building a new plant in Britain to produce its sports car, the Sting. The estimated construction cost of the plant is £50,000,000, and construction should be completed in a year. The plant will raise borrowing capacity by about $40,000,000. National Motors can reinvest £20,000,000 already held in Britain. If these funds were repatriated to the United States, they would face an effective tax rate of 46 percent. Inflation in Britain is expected to be at 15 percent; in the United States, at 10 percent. The current exchange rate is $S(\$/£) = 2.00$, and it is believed that PPP is likely to hold.

   National Motors expects to sell the Sting with only minor modifications for 5 years, and after this period the plant will require remodeling. The value of the plant for future use is expected to be £40,000,000 in nominal terms after 5 years. The Sting will have an initial sticker price of about £8000, and it is expected that 10,000 will be sold each year. Production costs are estimated at £6000. These values are expected to move in line with the general price level in Britain.

   National Motors also builds a two-seater car in Germany called the Racer and expects 4000 Racers to be replaced by the Sting. Since Racers are in short supply, 2000 of the 4000 Racers can be sold in Japan at the same profit as in Germany. The expected before-tax profit on the Racer during the initial year of producing the Sting is DM 5000 per car, with $S(DM/£) = 4.00$. This is expected to keep in line with German inflation, and PPP is expected to prevail between Britain and Germany.

   Because National Motors will be building the Sting in Merseyside, an area of heavy unemployment, the British government has offered the company a loan of £20,000,000 at a 10 percent interest rate. The principal is to be repaid in five equal annual installments, with the first installment due at the beginning of the initial year of production. The competitive market rate in Britain is 20 percent, while in the United States, National Motors faces a borrowing rate of 12 percent and a riskless rate of 10 percent. The balance of the capital will be provided as equity. The tax rate in Britain is 50 percent, which is higher than the 46 percent rate in the United States. British tax law allows car plants to be depreciated over 5 years.

   The British and U.S. tax authorities are careful that appropriate transfer prices are used so that no taxes can by saved by using intercompany pricing techniques. National Motors believes a 20 percent discount rate is appropriate for the project.

   Should the Sting be built?

3. Which items in the previous question are contractual and which are noncontractual? Could you discount the cash flows with a real rate of interest?

4. Compare the treatments of tax shields from debt in using the NPV and APV approaches to foreign investments.

5. How would you allow for lost income due to displaced sales from a subsidiary located in

another foreign country, rather than from domestic operations? Consider both exchange-rate and tax problems.

6. How would you include depreciation allowances in the calculation of adjusted present value when the effective corporate income tax is that of the foreign country in which an investment is located? Consider both the exchange-rate issue and the appropriate discount rate.

BIBLIOGRAPHY

ADLER, MICHAEL: "The Cost of Capital and Valuation of a Two-Country Firm," *Journal of Finance,* March 1974, pp. 119–132.

BOOTH, LAWRENCE D.: "Capital Budgeting Frameworks for the Multinational Corporation," *Journal of International Business Studies,* fall 1982, pp. 113–123.

DINWIDDY, CAROLINE, and FRANCIS TEAL: "Project Appraisal Procedures and the Evaluation of Foreign Exchange," *Economics,* February 1986, pp. 97–107.

DOTAN, AMIHUD, and ARIE OVADIA, "A Capital-Budgeting Decision—The Case of a Multinational Corporation Operating in High-Inflation Countries," *Journal of Business Research,* October 1986, pp. 403–410.

EAKER, MARK R.: "Investment/Financing Decisions for Multinational Corporations," in Dennis E. Logue (ed.), *Handbook of Modern Finance,* Warren, Gorham and Lamont, Boston, 1984, pp. 42-1–42-29.

HODDER, JAMES E.: "Evaluation of Manufacturing Investments: A Comparison of U.S. and Japanese Practices," *Financial Management,* spring 1986, pp. 17–24.

LESSARD, DONALD R.: "Evaluating International Projects: An Adjusted Present Value Approach," in Donald Lessard (ed.), *International Financial Management: Theory and Application,* 2d ed., Wiley, New York, 1985.

SHAPIRO, ALAN C.: "Capital Budgeting for the Multinational Corporation," *Financial Management,* spring 1978, pp. 7–16.

STONEHILL, ARTHUR I., and LEONARD NATHANSON: "Capital Budgeting and the Multinational Corporation," *California Management Review,* summer 1968, pp. 39–54.

APPENDIX 19.1
A Survey of International Taxation

International taxation is a complex subject, and we can do little more here than explain variations in the types of taxes encountered and the methods that can be used to help reduce them. We will view taxation questions in the most general terms.

THE DIFFERENT FORMS OF TAXES

Corporate Taxes

Income taxes are the chief source of revenue for the U.S. government, and the corporate income tax is an important although declining component of the total of income taxes. Income taxes are **direct taxes,** and the United States is dependent on direct taxes for a greater proportion of its total revenue than most other countries. Members of the European Union collect direct taxes, but these are augmented by a **value-added tax,** or **VAT,** which is an **indirect tax.**[16] Many poorer countries have a tax on imports as their primary revenue source. Other taxes that are found are based on wealth, sales, turnover, employees, and so on. Despite variations in the proportion of total tax receipts derived from corporate and other income taxes, the corporate tax rates are remarkably similar in industrialized countries. Table 19A.1 shows, for example, that the rates are between 33 and 43 percent in a large number of nations. Outside the industrialized countries the rates that are charged vary considerably, with some tax havens charging no corporate tax at all. Countries with zero rates include the Bahamas and Bermuda. The absence of corporation taxes is designed to encourage multinationals to locate offices for sheltering income from abroad.

The United States considers that it has jurisdiction over all the income of its citizens and residents wherever it is earned. However, credit is given for taxes paid elsewhere as long as the credit does not cause taxes to fall below what would have been paid had the income been earned in the United States.[17] While citizens and residents of the United States are taxed on their full income wherever it is earned, nonresidents are taxed only on their income in the United States. This is the practice in other countries. The resident versus nonresident status of a corporation is determined by where it is incorporated.

Some countries that appear to have low corporate tax rates have more normal rates when local corporate taxes are added. For example, while Switzerland has federal corporate rates below 10 percent, the local authorities, called **cantons,** have tax rates of between 10 and 30 percent. Different provincial rates in Canada can make rates vary up to 5 percent. Further variation and complication are introduced by the fact that some national tax authorities give full credit for local taxes, while others do not. In addition, there is considerable variation

---

[16]By definition, direct taxes cannot be shifted and are borne directly by those on whom they are levied. In contrast, indirect taxes can be shifted in part or in full to somebody who is not directly taxed. For example, corporate and personal income taxes are paid by those on whom they are levied. On the other hand, sales taxes and import duties charged to firms are at least in part paid by consumers. The consumer therefore pays indirectly.

[17]Since the Tax Reform Act of 1986, U.S.-based multinationals have been subject to a minimum corporate tax rate. For the nature of this minimum tax and its consequences, see Andrew Lyon and Gerald Silverstein, "The Alternative Minimum Tax and the Behavior of Multinational Corporations," National Bureau of Economic Research, Paper No. 4783, 1994.

TABLE 19A.1. Corporate Income Tax Rates, 1994*
(Percentages)

Australia	33	Italy	36
Canada	43	Japan	37
Denmark	34	Netherlands	35
Finland	25	New Zealand	33
France	33	Singapore	27
Germany	30	Sweden	28
Hong Kong	17	United Kingdom	33
Ireland	40	United States	35

*Rates are principal corporate levels, rounded to the nearest percent.
Source: Price Waterhouse, *Corporate Taxes: A Worldwide Summary,* 1994 edition.

between countries according to what expenditures are deductible in determining taxable income and the amount of deductions.

Value-Added Tax (VAT)

A value-added tax is similar to a sales tax, but each seller can deduct the taxes paid at previous stages of production. If, for example, the VAT rate is 25 percent and a company cuts trees and sells $100 worth of wood to a furniture manufacturer, the tax is $25, since there are no previous stages of production. If the wood is made into furniture that is sold for $240, the furniture manufacturer must pay $60 minus the already collected VAT. Since the wood producer paid $25, the VAT of the manufacturer is $35. Since the eventual effect is the collection of 25 percent of the final selling price, the VAT is like a sales tax that is collected at each stage of production rather than only at the final retail stage.[18]

Because each payer receives credit for taxes paid at previous stages of production, there is an incentive to get complete records from suppliers. This reduces evasion but can give rise to complaints about burdensome, costly paperwork. The value-added tax has partially replaced income taxes on individuals in the European Union. It has been promoted because it is a tax on spending and not on income. Taxes on income are a disincentive to work and invest, while taxes on spending can be considered a disincentive to spend, that is, an incentive to save. Another advantage of VAT to countries promoting exports is that the rules of the **World Trade Organization** allow rebates of VAT to exporters, while a potential drawback is that VAT can distort patterns of output.

Import Duties

Before income tax and value-added tax became primary sources of revenue, import duties or tariffs (two terms for the same thing) were major sources of fiscal receipts.[19] Since goods entering a country are shipped to specific ports where policing can be intensive, import duties are a good source of revenue when income or sales records are poor. This partly explains why some underdeveloped countries depend on tariffs. Also, tariffs can explain why an automobile or refrigerator can cost 5 times more in some countries than in others. Because tariffs

[18]For more on VAT, see *Value Added Tax,* Price Waterhouse, New York, November 1979.
[19]Tariffs are also called **excise taxes.** They can be based on value *(ad valorem)* or on the weight of imports.

can be levied more heavily on luxuries than on necessities, they do not have to be regressive.[20]

Tariffs explain why some firms move production facilities abroad. For example, if automobiles made in the United States and sold in Britain face a tariff and this can be avoided if the vehicles are produced in Britain, a British plant may be opened. Tariffs are used to protect jobs that are believed to be threatened by cheap foreign imports. For example, if sales of imported footwear or automobiles increase while domestically produced goods face sluggish sales, there may be lobbying to impose tariffs or quantitative restrictions (quotas) on imports. Tariffs tend to distort the pattern of international trade because countries may produce goods and services for which they do not have a comparative advantage but on which they can make profits behind protective barriers. Duties have been imposed by the U.S. government in the form of **countervailing tariffs** when it was believed that foreign competitors were **dumping** (selling at lower prices abroad than at home) or receiving "unfair" export help from their governments.

Withholding Taxes

Withholding taxes are collected from foreign individuals or corporations on income they have received from sources within a country. For example, if a U.S. resident earns dividends in Canada, taxes will be withheld and paid to Revenue Canada. Credit is generally received on taxes withheld, and so the level of withholding primarily affects the amount of taxes received by the respective tax authorities. For example, if the U.S. resident has 15 percent withheld in Canada and is in a 25-percent tax bracket in the United States, the U.S. tax payable will be reduced to 10 percent of the income after credit for the 15 percent is given. Higher withholding rates therefore generally mean that more is collected by the foreign authorities and a smaller amount by the domestic government.

There are some circumstances in which the level of withholding does matter. Clearly, if the rate of withholding exceeds the effective tax rate at home, full credit may not be obtained. This can happen even if the tax *rate* at home is higher than the withholding rate if the definition of income or eligible deductions differs between the countries. For example, if little depreciation is deductible in the foreign country but generous allowances exist at home, the taxable income may differ, and more taxes may be paid abroad than are payable at home. There is an overall limitation on credit for taxes withheld that equals taxes payable in the United States, but when tax returns for a number of countries are combined, full credit may be obtained even when on an individual-country basis there would have been unused credit.[21]

Branch versus Subsidiary Taxes

An important element in corporate tax planning is deciding whether to operate abroad with a **branch** or with a **subsidiary.** A branch is a foreign operation that is incorporated at home, while a subsidiary is incorporated in the foreign country.

If a foreign activity is not expected to be profitable for a number of years, there may be an advantage to starting out with a branch so that negative earnings abroad can be used to offset profits at home in a consolidated tax return. U.S. tax laws and the tax laws of a number of other countries allow branch income to be consolidated. If a company expects positive foreign

---

[20]With a regressive tax, the poor pay a larger *fraction* of their income or spending than do the rich. A tax can be regressive even if the rich pay a larger absolute *amount.*

[21]When high levels of withholding are combined with low levels, the unused credit on the low levels of withholding is utilized by the high levels of withholding within the combined tax return. Even if the combined return does not provide full credit, unused credit can be carried back 2 years or forward 5 years.

income and this income is not to be repatriated, there may be an advantage to a subsidiary. Foreign branches pay taxes on income as it is earned, while subsidiaries do not pay U.S. taxes until the income is repatriated. Whether this is sufficient reason to form an overseas subsidiary depends on relative tax rates and on whether the company wishes to repatriate earnings.[22]

ORGANIZATIONAL STRUCTURES FOR REDUCING TAXES

The Foreign-Sales Corporation (FSC)

The **foreign-sales corporation (FSC)** is a device for encouraging U.S. export sales by giving a tax break on the generated profits. The possibility of establishing a foreign-sales corporation was part of the Tax Reform Act of 1984. Prior to this Act, the U.S. Internal Revenue Service, IRS, offered tax breaks to exporters via the operation of **domestic international-sales corporations (DISCs).** While some DISCs still exist, the FSC has effectively replaced the DISC as the preferred tax-saving vehicle of exporters.

The main advantage offered by an FSC is that the goods or services "bought" by the FSC for subsequent sale do not have to be priced at **arm's length,** that is, at proper market value. Rather the FSC can use an artificial or **administered price** to increase its own profit and consequently reduce the profit—and tax—of the firm producing the U.S. goods or services for export. For example, if Aviva were to establish an FSC, Aviva itself could "sell" its jeans to its FSC for an artificially low price. Aviva's FSC could then sell the jeans abroad. Only a portion of Aviva's FSC's income is then subject to tax, and Aviva's own taxable income is reduced. That is, there is a shifting of income, by using the artificially low prices, from Aviva to its FSC. The tax paid by the FSC is less than the tax saving of Aviva.

There are, however, some limitations on the administrative prices and the portion of an FSC's income which escapes tax, as well as in the structure of an FSC. Some of the more important of the limitations and requirements are as follows:

1. An FSC must have its office in a possession of the United States or in a country with a tax information exchange program with the IRS.[23] This is to ensure the FSC is an "offshore" corporation.
2. Tax and accounting information must nevertheless be available at a location in the United States.
3. At least one director must not be a U.S. resident. This is also to ensure the FSC is "foreign."
4. An FSC may not coexist with a DISC that is controlled by the same corporation(s). An FSC may serve more than one corporation, but must have fewer than 25 shareholders.
5. Qualifying income is generated from the sale of U.S. "property," which essentially means goods or services produced or grown in the United States, including leasing, rental property, and management services unrelated to the FSC.
6. The prices "paid" by the FSC to the producer can be set so that the FSC's income is the largest of the following three amounts:

[22]Withholding tax credits and the taxation of subsidiary income only when it is repatriated have both contributed to foreign direct investment of U.S. firms, according to Alan Auerbach and Kevin Hassett in "Taxation and Foreign Direct Investment in the United States: A Reconsideration of the Evidence," National Bureau of Economic Research, Paper No. 3895, 1992.

[23]The U.S. possessions are Guam, American Samoa, the U.S. Virgin Islands, and the Mariana Islands.

    a. 1.83 percent of the FSC's revenue

    b. 23 percent of the combined taxable income of the FSC and related suppliers associated with the export transactions

    c. The FSC's income that would occur using arm's-length pricing

       The effect of this is that the worst that could happen is that the FSC's income would be as if the goods were priced at arm's length. However, in general the FSC can enjoy higher profits than this. These profits are taxed more favorably than if the profits had been made by the U.S. producer.

7. Only part of the FSC's income is taxed. If pricing is at arm's length, all the FSC's income is called **foreign-trade income,** and 30 percent of this is exempt from tax. If one of the two alternative administrative pricing rules is used, foreign-trade income involves adding the FSC's operating expenses to the taxable income—excluding the cost of goods sold—and $^{15}/_{23}$, or approximately 62.22 percent, of this is exempt. This can be very advantageous if expenses are low.

8. Domestic corporate shareholders of the FSC receive a 100 percent dividend-received deduction when disbursements occur, except for the taxable component of income under arm's-length pricing.[24]

80-20 Subsidiaries

If 80 percent or more of a corporation's income is earned abroad, dividends and interest paid by the corporation are considered foreign-source income by the U.S. Internal Revenue Service. An 80-20 subsidiary is formed to raise capital for the parent, since it is considered foreign by the IRS and therefore does not need to deduct withholding taxes. Payments made to 80-20 corporations may well be taxed by foreign governments, but when the income is consolidated, credit will be obtained. If an 80-20 corporation is incorporated in the Netherlands Antilles or in another country with a treaty with the United States permitting no withholding taxes, then when interest is paid by the U.S. parent to the 80-20 subsidiary, the parent can also avoid having taxes withheld. This means that a company can avoid withholding taxes completely by having an 80-20 corporation in a treaty country. However, since the passage of the Deficit Reduction Act of 1984, which removed the need for U.S. corporations to withhold tax on incomes paid to foreigners, the need for 80-20 subsidiaries has been reduced.

Internal Pricing

It is possible for a corporation to shift profits from high-tax countries to low-tax countries in order to reduce its overall taxes. However, the potential for U.S. corporations to do this is reduced by an important section of the U.S. Internal Revenue Code. Section 482 allows the Treasury to reallocate income and/or expenses to prevent evasion of taxes within commonly owned entities. The IRS requires internal prices to be as if they had been determined competitively. Of course, this does not apply to FSCs.

Tax Havens

Some countries charge extremely low corporate taxes to encourage corporations to locate within their jurisdiction, bring jobs, and so on. These countries include the Bahamas,

---

[24]The alternative minimum tax provisions of the 1986 Tax Reform Act change the incentives and structure of taxes from establishing an FSC. Frequent changes of tax regulations make any summary of taxation, especially international taxation, difficult to keep current.

Bermuda, Cayman Islands, and Grenada, and they are all endowed with delightful climates. The ability of U.S. corporations to take full advantage of tax havens is limited by Section 882 of the U.S. Tax Code. This says that foreign corporations doing business in the United States are taxed at U.S. rates. There is therefore no obvious advantage to locating the corporate headquarters in the tax haven for doing business at home.

APPENDIX 19.2
Currency of Cash Flow and the Choice of Discount Rate

We will concentrate on the expected-cash-flow term of equation (19.2) on page 465 of the text, but our conclusions are valid for any term in the APV formula. The cash-flow term is

$$\sum_{t=1}^{T} \frac{S_t^* CF_t^* (1 - \tau)}{(1 + DR_e)^t}$$

The numerator of this expression consists of the expected cash flow in the foreign currency, CF_t^*, converted into U.S. dollars at the expected spot exchange rate, S_t^*. This is put on an after-tax basis by multiplying by $(1 - \tau)$. What we show in this appendix is that as an alternative to using the nominal foreign-currency cash flow converted into dollars, and then using the nominal dollar discount rate, we can use a simpler alternative: we can use the real initial-period dollar cash flow and the real dollar discount rate. However, we shall also show that this does not work for contractual cash flows.

The exact form of the link between nominal and real interest rates known as the **Fisher equation** can be written as

$$(1 + \rho_{US})^t = \frac{(1 + DR_e)^t}{(1 + \dot{P}_{US}^*)^t}$$

$$\text{or} \quad (1 + DR_e)^t = (1 + \rho_{US})^t (1 + \dot{P}_{US}^*)^t \tag{19A.1}$$

Here, ρ_{US} is the real U.S. discount rate, DR_e is the nominal U.S. discount rate, and $\dot{P}_{US}^*$ is the expected U.S. inflation rate. What the Fisher equation does is define the real discount rate as the nominal rate deflated by the expected inflation rate. We have selected the all-equity U.S. dollar nominal discount rate, DR_e, because that is the one of particular concern. Consequently, ρ_{US} is the all-equity real U.S. dollar discount rate.

If we think that exchange rates will be changing at a steady forecast rate of $\dot{S}^*$, we can write

$$S_t^* \equiv S_0 (1 + \dot{S}^*)^t \qquad t = 1, 2, \ldots, T$$

If, in addition, we believe that cash flows in the foreign currency will grow at the foreign rate of inflation, we can write

$$CF_t^* = CF_1^* (1 + \dot{P}_{UK}^*)^{t-1} \qquad t = 1, 2, \ldots, T$$

where $\dot{P}_{UK}^*$ is the annual rate of inflation and CF_1^* is the initial cash flow, which we assume is unknown. Using this, our definition of S_t^*, and the Fisher equation in equation (19A.1), we have

$$\sum_{t=1}^{T} \frac{S_t^* CF_t^* (1 - \tau)}{(1 + DR_e)^t} = S_0 \frac{CF_1^*}{1 + \dot{P}_{UK}^*} \sum_{t=1}^{T} \frac{(1 + \dot{S}_t^*)^t (1 + \dot{P}_{UK}^*)^t (1 - \tau)}{(1 + \rho_{US})^t (1 + \dot{P}_{US}^*)^t} \tag{19A.2}$$

The magnitudes S_0 and $CF_1^*/(1 + \dot{P}_{UK}^*)$ have been placed in front of the summation because they do not depend on t.[25] We can reduce equation (19A.2) to a straightforward expression if we invoke the PPP condition.

---

[25] We remove $CF_1^*/(1 + \dot{P}_{UK}^*)$ rather than just CF_1^* because we wish to have all expressions in the summation raised to the power t. The interpretation of $CF_1^*/(1 + \dot{P}_{UK}^*)$ is that it is the value of the initial foreign cash flow at today's prices.

We have been writing the precise form of purchasing-power parity as

$$\dot{P}_{US} = \dot{P}_{UK} + \dot{S}\left(1 + \dot{P}_{UK}\right)$$

If the best forecast we can make is that PPP will hold—even though we know that in retrospect we could well be wrong—we can write PPP in the expectations form:

$$\dot{P}_{US}^* = \dot{P}_{UK}^* + \dot{S}^*\left(1 + \dot{P}_{UK}^*\right)$$

By adding unity to both sides, we get

$$1 + \dot{P}_{US}^* = \left(1 + \dot{P}_{UK}^*\right) + \dot{S}^*\left(1 + \dot{P}_{UK}^*\right) = \left(1 + \dot{P}_{UK}^*\right)\left(1 + \dot{S}^*\right)$$

or

$$\frac{\left(1 + \dot{S}^*\right)\left(1 + \dot{P}_{UK}^*\right)}{1 + \dot{P}_{US}^*} = 1$$

By using this in equation (19A.2), we can write the APV cash-flow term in equation (19A.2) in the straightforward form

$$\sum_{t=1}^{T} \frac{S_t^* CF_t^*(1 - \tau)}{\left(1 + DR_e\right)^t} = S_0 \frac{CF_1^*}{1 + \dot{P}_{UK}^*} \sum_{t=1}^{T} \frac{\left(1 + \dot{S}^*\right)^t\left(1 + \dot{P}_{UK}^*\right)^t(1 - \tau)}{\left(1 + \rho_{US}\right)^t\left(1 + \dot{P}_{US}^*\right)^t} \qquad (19A.3)$$

All we need to know to evaluate this expression is the initial exchange rate, S_0; the initial cash flow at today's prices, $CF_1^*/(1 + \dot{P}_{UK}^*)$; the tax rate, τ; and the real discount rate that reflects the systematic risk, ρ_{US}; there is no need to forecast future exchange rates and foreign-currency cash flows. In reaching this conclusion, we assumed only that cash flows can be expected to grow at the overall rate of inflation, that PPP can be expected to hold, and that the Fisher equation does hold. Any noncontractual term can be handled in this straightforward way; we avoid forecasting inflation and exchange rates at which to convert the foreign-currency amounts. Our conclusion is based on the view that inflation and changes in exchange rates are offsetting—requiring PPP—and that local inflation in cash flows and inflation premiums in discount rates are also offsetting—requiring the Fisher equation.

While it is reasonable to *expect* PPP and the Fisher equation to hold, when events are *realized,* it is very unlikely that they will have held. However, the departures from the conditions are as likely to be positive as negative. This is part of the risk of business. The risk is that realized changes in exchange rates might not reflect inflation differentials, and the interest rate might poorly reflect the level of inflation. This risk should be reflected in DR_e or ρ_{US}, which should contain appropriate premiums.

When we are dealing with contractual values, we cannot use the real interest rate with uninflated cash flows. This is because the foreign-currency streams are nominal amounts that must be converted at the exchange rate at the time of payment/receipt and discounted at the nominal rate. What we have if the cash flows are contractual is

$$\sum_{t=1}^{T} \frac{S_t^* CF_t^*(1 - \tau)}{\left(1 + DR_e\right)^t} = \sum_{t=1}^{T} \frac{S_0\left(1 + \dot{S}^*\right)^t CF_t^*(1 - \tau)}{\left(1 + DR_e\right)^t}$$

We cannot expand CF_t^* in order to cancel terms, since all values of CF_t^* are fixed contractually. We are left to discount at the nominal rate of interest, DR_e. We discount the nominal CF_t^* converted into the investor's currency at the forecast exchange rate.

When the profiles of cash flows or incremental effects such as tax shields vary in real terms and do not grow at the inflation rate (perhaps they initially increase in real terms and later decline), we cannot use PPP and the Fisher equation to reduce the complexity of the problem, even for noncontractual cash flows. We must instead use the APV formula—equation (19.2)—with forecasted nominal cash flows and the nominal discount rate.

CHAPTER 20

The Growth and Concerns about Multinationals

"If everybody minded their own business," the Duchess said in a hoarse growl, "the world would go round a deal faster than it does."
—LEWIS CARROLL
Alice's Adventures in Wonderland

Regardless of where you live, chances are you have come across the names of numerous multinational corporations such as those listed in Table 20.1. These mammoth organizations, which measure sales by the tens of billions of dollars and employment by the tens or even hundreds of thousands, have evaluated expected cash flows and risks and decided that foreign direct investment (FDI) is worthwhile. But what makes expected cash flows and risks what they are? Furthermore, can anything be done to influence them? For example, can transfer prices of goods and services moving within a multinational corporation be used to reduce taxes or otherwise increase net cash flows? Can financial structure be used to reduce political risk? Indeed, can an MNC correctly measure the cash flows and political risks of foreign investments? Furthermore, do the matters relating to MNCs apply also to members of transnational alliances—firms in different countries working in cooperation—or are transnational alliances a means of avoiding problems faced by multinational corporations? These questions, which are central to the emergence and management of MNCs and transnational alliances, are a focus of this chapter. In addition, we look at the problems and benefits that have been brought to the world by multinational and transnational forms of industrial organization.

THE GROWTH OF MULTINATIONAL CORPORATIONS

The growth of the multinational corporation has been a result of foreign direct investments which have taken place in the past. In the extensive example in the previous chapter Aviva's overseas direct investment was a result of the movement of indigenous firms into its market. Such strategic overseas investment is especially important in dynamic and changing markets, such as publishing and fashion clothing, where subsidiaries must keep in line with local needs and where shipping time is vital. In addition to strategic reasons for direct investment, numerous other reasons have been put forward, and while these are not strictly financial, they deserve some mention in this book.

Reasons for the Growth of MNCs

Availability of Raw Materials

If there are mills producing denim cloth in other countries and the quality is good and the price is attractive, why should a firm like Aviva Corporation buy the material abroad, ship it to the United States, manufacture the jeans, and then ship the finished garments? Clearly, if the ability exists to manufacture the jeans in the foreign market, the firm can eliminate two-way shipping costs—for denim in one direction and jeans in the other—by directly investing in a manufacturing plant abroad.[1]

Many industrial firms, most particularly mining companies, have little choice but to locate at the site of their raw materials. If copper or iron ore is being smelted, it often does not make sense to ship the ore when a smelter can be built near the mine site. The product of the smelter—the copper or iron bars, which weigh much less than the original ore—can be shipped out to the market. But we still have to ask why it would be a foreign firm rather than an indigenous firm that would carry out the enterprise. With an indigenous firm there would be no foreign direct investment. Thus, to explain FDI, we must explain why a multinational corporate organization can do things better or cheaper than local firms. As we shall see below, there are numerous advantages enjoyed by multinational corporations.

Integrating Operations

When there are advantages to vertical integration in terms of assured delivery between various stages of production and the different stages can be performed better in different locations (as with the smelting of ores), there is good reason to invest abroad. This reason for direct investment has been advanced by Charles Kindleberger, who along with Richard Caves did some of the earlier work on direct investment.[2]

Nontransferable Knowledge

It is often possible for firms to sell their knowledge in the form of patent rights, and to license a foreign producer. This relieves a firm of the need to make foreign direct investment. However, sometimes a firm that has a production process or product patent can make a larger profit by doing the foreign production itself. This is because there are some kinds of knowledge which cannot be sold and which are

---

[1] A model of overseas direct investment that considers transportation costs as well as issues involving stages of production and economies of scale has been developed by Jimmy Weinblatt and Robert E. Lipsey, "A Model of Firms' Decisions to Export or Produce Abroad," National Bureau of Economic Research, Working Paper 511, July 1980.

[2] We refer to Charles P. Kindleberger, *American Business Abroad,* Yale University Press, New Haven, Conn., 1969. See also Richard E. Caves, "International Corporations: The Industrial Economics of Foreign Investment," *Economica,* February 1971, pp. 1–27. A number of papers on direct investment are contained in John H. Dunning (ed.), *International Investment,* Penguin Books, Harmondsworth, England, 1972. For factors affecting the initial decision, the reader may consult J. David Richardson, "On Going Abroad: The Firm's Initial Foreign Investment Decision," *Quarterly Review of Economics and Business,* winter 1971, pp. 7–22.

TABLE 20.1. The 50 Largest Nonfinancial MNCs, Ranked by Total Assets, 1990

Rank	Corporation	Home Country	Industry	Total Assets (Billions $)	Total Sales (Billions $)	Total Employment
1	GM	United States	Motor vehicles & parts	180.2	122.0	767,200
2	Ford	United States	Motor vehicles & parts	173.7	97.7	370,383
3	GE	United States	Electronics	153.9	57.7	298,000
4	Royal Dutch Shell	United Kingdom/Dutch	Petroleum refining	106.4	106.5	137,000
5	Exxon	United States	Petroleum refining	87.7	115.8	104,000
6	IBM	United States	Computers	87.6	69.0	373,816
7	Mitsubishi	Japan	Trading	73.8	129.3	32,417
8	Fiat	Italy	Motor vehicles & parts	66.3	47.5	303,238
9	Matsushita Electric	Japan	Electronics	62.0	46.8	210,848
10	Mitsui	Japan	Trading	60.8	136.2	9,094
11	ENI	Italy	Petroleum refining	60.3	41.8	130,745
12	British Petroleum	United Kingdom	Petroleum refining	59.3	59.3	118,050
13	C. Itoh	Japan	Trading	58.4	151.1	9,643
14	Toyota	Japan	Motor vehicles & parts	55.1	60.1	96,849
15	Marubeni	Japan	Trading	54.9	131.0	9,905
16	ITT	United States	Diversified services	49.0	20.6	114,000
17	B.A.T. Industries	United Kingdom	Tobacco	48.1	22.9	217,373
18	Philip Morris	United States	Food	46.6	51.2	168,000
19	Chrysler	United States	Motor vehicles & parts	46.4	30.6	109,943
20	Daimler Benz	Germany	Transport & communication	45.1	52.9	376,785
21	Siemens	Germany	Electronics	43.1	39.2	373,000
22	Elf Aquitaine	France	Petroleum refining	42.6	32.4	90,000
23	Volkswagen	Germany	Motor vehicles & parts	42.0	42.1	268,744
24	Mobil	United States	Petroleum refining	41.7	57.8	67,300
25	Toshiba	Japan	Electronics	39.2	33.3	162,000

Rank	Corporation	Home Country	Industry	Total Assets (Billions $)	Total Sales (Billions $)	Total Employment
26	Du Pont	United States	Chemicals	38.9	37.8	124,900
27	Nissho Iwai	Japan	Trading	38.8	94.4	7,380
28	Alcatel Alsthom	France	Electronics	38.2	26.6	205,500
29	Xerox	United States	Scientific & photographic	37.5	7.5	110,000
30	Nissan Motor	Japan	Motor vehicles & parts	36.4	35.7	129,546
31	Chevron	United States	Petroleum refining	35.1	38.6	54,208
32	GTE	United States	Telecommunications	33.8	18.4	177,000
33	Sony	Japan	Electronics	32.6	20.9	112,900
34	Amoco	United States	Petroleum refining	32.2	28.0	54,524
35	Verba	Germany	Trading	30.8	32.9	106,877
36	Ferruzzi Montedison	Italy	Food	30.8	14.0	44,949
37	Philips Electronics	Netherlands	Electronics	30.6	30.8	272,800
38	Asea Brown Boveri	Switzerland	Industrial & farm equipment	30.2	26.7	215,154
39	Nestlé	Switzerland	Food	28.0	36.5	199,021
40	Generale Des Eaux	France	Construction	27.7	21.5	173,000
41	Hanson	United Kingdom	Building materials	27.6	13.4	80,000
42	Texaco	United States	Petroleum refining	26.0	40.9	39,199
43	Bayer	Germany	Chemicals	25.4	25.9	171,000
44	Unilever	United Kingdom/Dutch	Food	24.7	39.6	304,000
45	BASF	Germany	Chemicals	24.3	29.0	134,647
46	Eastman Kodak	United States	Scientific & photographic	24.1	18.9	134,450
47	Dow Chemical	United States	Chemicals	24.0	19.8	62,080
48	Renault	France	Motor vehicles & parts	23.5	30.2	157,378
49	Hoechst	Germany	Chemicals	22.9	27.8	172,890
50	Rhone-Poulenc	France	Chemicals	21.3	14.4	91,571

Source: World Investment Report; Transnational Corporations and Integrated International Production, United Nations, New York, 1993.

the result of years of experience. Aviva, for example, might be able to sell patterns and designs, and it can license the use of its name, but it cannot sell a foreign firm its experience in producing and marketing the product. This points to another reason why a firm might wish to do its own foreign production.

Protecting Reputations

Products develop good or bad names, and these are carried across international boundaries. Even people in Russia, for example, know the names of certain brands of jeans. It would not serve the good name of Aviva Corporation to have a foreign licensee to do a shoddy job in producing jeans with the Aviva label. Similarly, it is important for multinational restaurant and hotel chains to maintain homogeneous quality to protect their reputations. We find that there can be valid reasons for direct investment rather than licensing in terms of transferring expertise and ensuring the maintenance of a good name.

Exploiting Reputations

Foreign direct investment may occur to exploit rather than protect a reputation. This motivation is probably of particular importance in foreign direct investment by banks, and it takes the form of opening branches and establishing or buying subsidiaries. One of the reasons why banking has become an industry with mammoth multinationals is that an international reputation can attract deposits; many associate the size of a bank with its safety. For example, a name like Barclays, Chase, or Citibank in a small, less-developed nation is likely to attract deposits away from local banks. Reputation is also important in accounting, as Exhibit 20.1 explains. This is why many large industrial nations such as the United States and Britain have pushed in global trade negotiations for a liberalization of restrictions on services, including accounting and banking. It is also the reason why the majority of less-developed nations have resisted this liberalization.

Protecting Secrecy

Direct investment may be preferred to the granting of a license for a foreign company to produce a product if secrecy is important. This point has been raised by Erich Spitaler, who argues that a firm can be motivated to choose direct investment over licensing by a feeling that, while a licensee will take precautions to protect patent rights, it may be less conscientious than the original owner of the patent.[3]

The Product Life-Cycle Hypothesis

It has been argued, most notably by Raymond Vernon, that opportunities for further gains at home eventually dry up.[4] To maintain the growth of profits, the corporation must venture abroad to where markets are not as well penetrated and where there is perhaps less competition. This makes direct investment the natural consequence of being in business for a long enough time and doing well at home. There is an inevitability in this view that has concerned those who believe that American firms are further along in their life-cycle development than the firms of other nations

[3]See Erich Spitaler, "A Survey of Recent Quantitative Studies of Long-Term Capital Movements," *IMF Staff Papers,* March 1971, pp. 189–217.
[4]Raymond Vernon, "International Investment and International Trade in the Product Life-Cycle," *Quarterly Journal of Economics,* May 1966, pp. 190–207.

EXHIBIT 20.1
Counting on a Good Name

The economics of information suggests that reputation has value when a supplier's reputation is a signal of good quality. Reputation is important when quality is difficult to observe directly, and thus this issue is particularly relevant with services. One service for which reputation has overcome the home-firm advantage of knowing local rules and regulations is accounting. While there are other reasons why accounting has become multinational—including benefits to MNCs of maintaining confidentiality when dealing with the same accounting firm worldwide—the following excerpt from *The Economist* argues that reputation helps to convey information about accountants' quality.

The world's six biggest accountancy firms are in the top rank in virtually every country in the world, except where they are barred by law. Yet auditing and accounting are intensely local affairs, requiring detailed knowledge of local rules and regulations. Arthur Andersen or Price Waterhouse

ought not, in theory, to have an advantage over domestic competitors except with multinational clients—which, though large, are almost always a minority. Why, then, have these firms themselves become such successful multinationals?

One answer may lie in their ancillary businesses such as consulting, in which they have special skills; another may lie in their ability to buy and organise information technology. But these are not enough to explain such widespread dominance. *Reputation, the power of the brand name, must play the biggest part.* The market for accounting and auditing is an imperfect one: buyers lack the information to tell a good accountant from a bad one, or find it costly to find out, which comes to the same thing. They also seek the accountant's brand name as a means to convince others about their own worth, especially investors and creditors, who are similarly short of information.

Source: Multinationals, a supplement in *The Economist,* March 27, 1993, p. 9. Emphasis added. © The Economist Newspaper Group, Inc. Reprinted with permission. Further reproduction prohibited.

---

and are therefore dominant in foreign expansion.[5] However, even when U.S. firms do expand into foreign markets, their activities are often scrutinized by the host governments. Moreover, the spread of U.S. multinationals has been matched by the inroads of foreign firms into the United States, especially since the 1970s. Particularly noticeable have been auto and auto-parts producers such as Toyota, Honda, Nissan, and Michelin Tires. Foreign firms have an even longer history as leaders in the U.S. food and drug industry (Nestlé, Hoffmann-La Roche); in oil and gas (Shell, British Petroleum—as BP—and so on); in insurance, banking, and real-estate development; and in other areas.

Capital Availability

Robert Aliber has suggested that access to capital markets can be a reason why firms themselves move abroad.[6] The smaller one-country licensee does not have the same access to cheaper funds as the larger firm, and so larger firms are able to operate within foreign markets with a lower discount rate. However, Edward Graham and Paul Krugman have questioned this argument on two grounds.[7] First, even if large multinational firms have a lower cost of capital than small, indigenous firms,

---

[5]Inevitable U.S. domination of key businesses in Europe and the world was a popular view in parts of Europe in the 1960s and 1970s. Particularly influential was J. J. Servain-Schreiber's *The American Challenge,* Hamish Hamilton, London, 1968.

[6]Robert Aliber, "A Theory of Direct Foreign Investment," in Charles P. Kindleberger (ed.), *The International Corporation: A Symposium,* M.I.T. Press, Cambridge, Mass., 1970.

[7]Graham, Edward M., and Paul R. Krugman, *Foreign Direct Investment in the United States,* Institute for International Economics, Washington, D.C., 1991.

493

the form of overseas investment does not have to be direct investment. Rather, it can take the form of portfolio investment. Second, the majority of foreign direct investment has been two-way, with, for example, U.S. firms investing in Japan while Japanese firms invest in the United States. This pattern is not an implication of the differential-cost-of-capital argument.

Strategic FDI

As we indicated in the preceding chapter, companies enter foreign markets to preserve market share when this is being threatened by the potential entry of indigenous firms or multinationals from other countries. This strategic motivation for FDI has always existed, but it may have contributed to the multinationalization of business as a result of improved access to capital markets. This is different from the argument concerning the differential cost of capital, given previously. In the case of increased strategic FDI, it is globalization of financial markets that has reduced entry barriers due to large fixed costs. Access to the necessary capital means a wider set of companies with an ability to expand into any given market. This increases the incentive to move and enjoy any potential first-mover advantage.

Organizational Factors

Richard Cyert and James March emphasize reasons given by organization theory, a theme that is extended to direct foreign investment by E. Eugene Carter.[8] The organization-theory view of direct investment emphasizes broad management objectives in terms of the way management attempts to shift risk by operating in many markets, achieve growth in sales, and so on, as opposed to concentrating on the traditional economic goal of profit maximization.

Avoiding Tariffs and Quotas

Another reason for producing abroad instead of producing at home and shipping the product concerns the import tariffs that might have to be paid.[9] If import duties are in place, a firm might produce inside the foreign market in order to avoid them. We must remember, however, that tariffs protect the firm engaged in production in the foreign market, whether it be a foreign firm or an indigenous firm. Tariffs cannot, therefore, explain why foreign firms move abroad, and yet the movement of firms is the essence of direct investment. Nor, along similar lines, can tax writeoffs, subsidized or even free land offerings, and so on, explain direct investment, since foreign firms usually are not helped more than domestic ones. We must rely on our other listed reasons for direct investment and the overriding desire to make a larger profit, even if that means moving abroad rather than into alternative domestic endeavors.

There have been cases where the threat of tariffs or quantitative restrictions on imports in the form of quotas have prompted direct investment overseas. For exam-

---

[8]Richard M. Cyert and James G. March give an account of organization theory in *The Behavioral Theory of the Firm,* Prentice-Hall, Englewood Cliffs, N.J., 1963. E. Eugene Carter extends the theory to direct investment in "The Behavioral Theory of the Firm and Top Level Corporation Decisions," *Administrative Science Quarterly,* December 1971, pp. 413–428.

[9]A geometrical explanation of the effect of tariffs on direct investment has been developed by Richard E. Caves in *Multinational Enterprise and Economic Analysis,* Cambridge University Press, Cambridge, England, 1982, pp. 36–40.

ple, a number of foreign automobile and truck producers considered opening or opened plants in the United States to avoid restrictions on selling foreign-made cars. The restrictions were designed to protect jobs in the U.S. industry. Nissan Motors built a plant in Tennessee, and Honda built a plant in Ohio. For a period of time Volkswagen assembled automobiles and light trucks in the United States and Canada. Other companies making direct investments included Renault, Daimler-Benz, and Fiat.[10]

Avoiding Regulations

As is explained in Chapter 22 in our discussion of the multinationalization of banking, direct investment has been made by banks to avoid regulation. This has also been a motivation for foreign investment by manufacturing firms. For example, a case might be made that some firms have moved to escape standards set by the U.S. Environmental Protection Agency, the Occupational Safety and Health Administration, and other agencies. Some foreign countries with lower environmental and safety standards offer a haven to firms using dirty or dangerous processes. The items produced, such as chemicals and drugs, may even be offered for sale back in the United States.

Production Flexibility

A manifestation of departures from PPP is that there are periods when production costs in one country are particularly low because of a real depreciation of its currency. Multinational firms may be able to relocate production to exploit the opportunities that real depreciations offer. This requires, of course, that necessary technology can be transferred easily between countries and that trade unions or governments do not make the shifting of production too difficult. Small manufactured goods such as computer components and TVs lend themselves to such shuffling of production, whereas automobile production, with its international unions and expensive setup costs, does not.[11]

Symbiotic Relationships

Some firms follow clients who make direct foreign investments. For example, large U.S. accounting firms which have knowledge of parent companies' special needs and practices have opened offices in countries where their clients have opened subsidiaries. These U.S. accounting firms have an advantage over local firms because of their knowledge of the parent and because the client may prefer to engage only one firm in order to reduce the number of people with access to sensi-

---

[10]Offsetting the incentive to produce within a country to avoid import tariffs is the preference that buyers of a product may have for imports. For example, it may be that a German car from Germany will be valued more than if the car were manufactured in the United States.

[11]See Victoria S. Farrell, Dean A. DeRosa, and T. Ashby McCown, "Effects of Exchange Rate Variability on International Trade and Other Economic Variables: A Review of the Literature," *Staff Studies,* no. 130, Board of Governors of the Federal Reserve System, January 1984; Bruce Kogut, "Designing Global Strategies: Comparative and Competitive Value-Added Chains," *Sloan Management Review,* summer 1985, pp. 15–28; John H. Dunning, "Multinational Enterprises and Industrial Restructuring in the U.K.," *Lloyds Bank Review,* October 1985, pp. 1–19; and David de Meza and Frederick van der Ploeg, "Production Flexibility as a Motive for Multinationality," *Journal of Industrial Economics,* March 1987, pp. 343–355.

tive information; see Exhibit 20.1 on page 493. The same factor may apply to consulting, legal, and securities firms, which often follow their home-country clients' direct investments by opening offices in the same foreign locations. Similarly, it has been shown that manufacturing firms may be drawn to where other manufacturing firms from the same country are located. By being in the same region they can work together and benefit from their knowledge of each other. The benefits from being in the same region as other companies are called **agglomeration economies.**[12]

Indirect Diversification

We should not leave our discussion of factors contributing to the growth of MNCs without mentioning the potential for the MNC to indirectly provide portfolio diversification for shareholders.[13] This service will, of course, be valued only if shareholders are unable to diversify themselves. This requires the existence of segmented capital markets that only the MNC can overcome. This argument was mentioned in Chapter 18 in the context of international asset pricing. It is also mentioned in Exhibit 20.2, which argues that all the causes of growth of MNCs, including that relating to diversification, depend on market imperfections.

Empirical Evidence on the Growth of MNCs

It should be apparent from glancing down the list of factors that can be responsible for the growth of MNCs that the relative importance of different factors will depend on the nature of the MNC's business. Partly as a result of this, the empirical evidence we have on MNCs tends to be limited to some stylized facts about the nature of the industries in which most direct investment occurs.

In an investigation of the characteristics of approximately 1000 U.S. publicly owned companies investing abroad, Irving Kravis and Robert Lipsey found a number of characteristics of investing firms vis-à-vis firms not investing abroad.[14] The characteristics were separated into those that could be attributed to the industry of the investor and those distinguishing investing firms from other firms within their industry.

Investing firms spent relatively heavily on research and development (R & D); this was attributable both to the investors' industries and to the firms investing abroad within each industry. That is, the industries with heavy investments abroad spent more on R & D than other industries, and the firms that invested abroad spent more on R & D than the average spending of firms in their industries. (This characteristic of foreign direct investment is consistent with the secrecy-protection explanation given earlier.) Investors were also more capital-intensive than noninvestors, this being mostly attributable to the industries investing overseas. (This is consistent

[12]See Keith Head, John Ries, and Deborah Swenson, "Agglomeration Benefits and Location Choice: Evidence from Manufacturing Investments in the United States," *Journal of International Economics,* 1995, pp. 223–247.

[13]A formal theory of foreign direct investment based on indirect provision of portfolio diversification has been developed by Vihang R. Errunza and Lemma W. Senbet, "The Effects of International Operations on the Market Value of the Firm: Theory and Evidence," *Journal of Finance,* May 1981, pp. 401–417.

[14]Irving B. Kravis and Robert E. Lipsey, "The Location of Overseas Production and Production for Export of U.S. Multinational Firms," *Journal of International Economics,* May 1982, pp. 201–223.

EXHIBIT 20.2
Multinationals: Creatures of Market Imperfections

The long list of reasons given in the text for the growing importance of multinationals are all closely related to market imperfections, which can cause market failures. For example, they are based on transportation costs, tariff barriers, different regulations in different countries, protection of industrial or commercial secrets, and costly information, all of which represent "frictions" causing market failure. This is the theme of the following excerpt from *The Economist*. The article also alludes to the fact that as the market imperfections disappear, the importance of MNCs may diminish.

[M]ultinationals are not exploiters of purity but rather creatures of market imperfections, or failures. The best way to understand their behaviour is to understand those imperfections and how they are developing.

Broadly, two sorts of imperfections are relevant. One is the structural imperfection, which may be natural (transport costs, for example) or manmade. Examples of the latter include government restrictions on investment or imports, taxes and subsidies, inadequate capital markets and monopolistic or oligopolistic markets. Many of these sorts of imperfections have indeed been disappearing in the industrial countries, and are beginning to in developing ones. Not all are going; some industries have become oligopolies, even on a global scale. But, on balance, the imperfections are becoming fewer.

The other sort of imperfection is inherent in transactions and markets themselves and has not, on balance, been disappearing. Examples are the uncertainty that a supplier will deliver on his promise; the volatility of exchange rates; the difficulty that customers face in evaluating unfamiliar products; the costs of negotiating deals; economies of scale in production, purchasing, research and development, distribution or marketing, which give advantages to existing firms and impose barriers against newcomers; concerns about infringement of intellectual property rights; uncertainty about competitors' actions; the opportunity to spread risks through diversification.

It is a long list, yet far from complete. Once there, every item looks obvious, and is. But what matters is this: because of these and other imperfections, firms locate their production and other operations internationally for reasons that are more complex than the simple minimisation of direct costs.

Source: Multinationals, a supplement in *The Economist,* March 27, 1993, p. 9. © The Economist Newspaper Group, Inc. Reprinted with permission. Further reproduction prohibited.

with the capital-availability argument; capital-intensive investors presumably need to raise a relatively large amount of capital.) Other characteristics of investors were that they were large relative to both other industries and other firms within their industries, and that investing firms were more profitable.[15]

Kravis and Lipsey also noted that there appeared to be an order of countries when investing overseas. If an investor had made one foreign investment, it would most likely be in Canada. With two investments, an investor would be in Canada and in Mexico or the United Kingdom. After this, investments were found in Germany, France, and possibly Australia.

Evaluation of direct-investment statistics also suggests that more investment occurs in those countries that have offered investors higher returns.[16] There also appears to be a connection between domestic economic activity and foreign investment, with good conditions at home discouraging investment abroad.

[15]These conclusions are also supported by Irving B. Kravis, Robert E. Lipsey, and Linda O'Connor, "Characteristics of U.S. Manufacturing Companies Investing Abroad and Their Choice of Production Locations," National Bureau of Economic Research, Working Paper 1104, April 1983.

[16]See *International Letter,* Federal Reserve Bank of Chicago, no. 537, October 19, 1984.

SPECIAL ISSUES FACING MULTINATIONAL CORPORATIONS: TRANSFER PRICING

While any firm with multiple divisions must price goods and services transferred between its divisions if it is to be able to judge its profit centers correctly, there are few if any political or tax implications of transfer pricing in the domestic context. The situation is very different for the multinational corporation.

The Measurement of Transfer Prices

If correct measures of prices of goods or services moving between corporate divisions are not available, management will have difficulty making APV calculations for new projects, and will even face difficulties judging past projects and performances of corporate divisions. But how are managers to calculate correct transfer prices?

The prices managers must determine are those of intermediate products moving through vertically integrated firms. The most obvious source for these prices is the market. However, market prices do not always exist for intermediate products. Furthermore, even when there are market prices for the goods and services transferred between divisions within a firm, using these prices may result in incorrect decisions. Let us consider why.[17]

The theoretically correct transfer price is equal to the marginal cost.[18] This is because the price paid then correctly reflects the cost of producing another unit.[19] If a good or service transferred between corporate divisions is available in the marketplace, where it trades in a textbook-type "perfectly competitive" market, the market price will equal the marginal cost, and this market price can then be used as the transfer price. However, goods and services moving between divisions are frequently available only in monopolistic or monopolistically competitive markets. In this case, market prices will typically exceed marginal costs. This means that by setting transfer prices equal to market prices a buying division will be paying above marginal cost for inputs. This will induce the use of too few inputs to achieve the profit-maximizing output from the firm's perspective. The firm's output of its final product will also be less than the profit-maximizing level. In addition, with transfer prices equal to market prices, and these being higher than the firm's marginal costs of the transferred goods and services, input combinations will be inappropriately intensive in products bought from outside the firm. That is, if, instead of setting transfer prices of intermediate products equal to market prices, the firm set them equal to its marginal costs, then buying divisions would correctly use more of the firm's own intermediate products.

While setting transfer prices equal to marginal costs will maximize the firm's

---

[17]The background economic analysis behind the points made here was first provided by Jack Hirschleifer, "On the Economics of Transfer Pricing," *Journal of Business,* July 1956, pp. 172–184, and "Economics of the Divisionalized Firm," *Journal of Business,* April 1957, pp. 96–108.

[18]This assumes constant returns to scale. See Hirschleifer, *op. cit.*

[19]The rationale is the same as for selecting the quantity of any input that maximizes profits: profits are reduced by using less or by using more than the quantity of input at which the marginal revenue product of the input equals the input's marginal cost.

overall profits, it will make it difficult to attribute the company's profit to the correct divisions; marginal costs are typically lower than market prices, so that divisions supplying intermediate products will show losses. This will make bonus allocations and expansion budgets difficult to determine properly. One way around this is to use marginal costs as the transfer prices that are paid, but to calculate divisional profitability at market prices. This requires, of course, that market prices of intermediate products be available, and that marginal costs be known. In reality, neither requirement is likely to be satisfied.

Strategic Considerations in Transfer Pricing

The repatriation of profits by a multinational firm from its overseas operations can be a politically sensitive problem. It is important that host governments do not consider the profit rate too high, or else the multinational is likely to face accusations of price gouging and lose favor with foreign governments. In order to give an appearance of repatriating a lower profit without reducing the actual profit brought home, the multinational can use transfer prices. It can set high transfer prices on what is supplied to a foreign division by the head office or by divisions in environments that are politically less sensitive. For example, it can extract high payments for parts supplied by other divisions or for general overheads. Alternatively, the multinational can lower the transfer prices of products which the foreign division sells to the head office or to other divisions. These methods of reducing foreign profits while repatriating income are particularly advantageous when foreign reinvestment opportunities are limited. Because host governments know these practices occur, it is a good idea to itemize all transfers so as to make it clear that not all flows are profits.

Transfer pricing to reduce overall corporate taxes can be advantageous. The multinational has an incentive to shuffle its income to keep profits low in high-tax countries and relatively high in low-tax countries. There are complications if within a country there are different tax rates on retained versus repatriated income. The gains from profit shuffling via transfer prices are limited by the legal powers of the Internal Revenue Service, and of taxing authorities in some other countries, to reallocate income if it is determined that transfer prices have distorted profits.[20]

A multinational firm is likely to be in a better position to avoid foreign exchange losses than a firm with only local operations. There have been times, especially under fixed exchange rates in the period before 1973, when the devaluation of certain currencies and the revaluation of others were imminent. Because of extensive involvement by central banks, the interest-rate differential between countries did not always reflect the anticipated changes in exchange rates, and so compensation was not offered for expected exchange-rate movements. There were incentives for all corporations to reduce their holdings of the currencies which faced devaluation.

---

[20]For a detailed account of the tax implications of transfer pricing see Donald R. Lessard, "Transfer Prices, Taxes, and Financial Markets: Implications of International Financial Transfers within the Multinational Corporation," *International Business and Finance,* 1979, pp. 101–135, and J. William Petty II and Ernest W. Walker, "Optimal Transfer Pricing for the Multinational Firm," *Financial Management,* winter 1972, pp. 74–87. We might note that if MNCs are in a position to reduce taxes in ways unavailable to local firms, this provides an additional reason for the growth of MNCs. See David Harris, Randall Morck, Joel Slemrod, and Bernard Yeung, "Income Shifting in U.S. Multinational Corporations," National Bureau of Economic Research, Summer Institute's International Taxation Workshop, 1991.

However, an attempt to move from these currencies was viewed as unpatriotic when undertaken by domestic firms and as unfair profiteering when undertaken by multinationals. As a result, considerable constraints were placed on moving funds in overt ways, but multinationals were in a better position than their domestic counterparts to move funds internally.

Transfer prices can be used to reduce import tariffs and to avoid quotas. When tariffs on imports are based on values of transactions, the value of goods moving between divisions can be artificially reduced by keeping down the transfer prices. This puts a multinational firm at an advantage over domestic firms. Similarly, when quotas are based on values of trade, the multinational can keep down prices to maintain the volume. Again, the multinational has an advantage over domestic counterparts, but import authorities frequently adopt their own "value for duty" on goods entering trade to help prevent revenues from being lost through the manipulation of transfer prices.

Large variations in profits may be a concern to shareholders. In order to keep local shareholders happy, fluctuations in local foreign profits can be reduced via transfer prices. By raising the prices of goods and services supplied by foreign operations or lowering prices on sales to foreign operations, unusually high profits can be brought down so that subsequent falls in profits are reduced. Of course, shareholders are normally assumed to be concerned only with systematic risk and not with total risk, so that the premise that profit volatility is of concern to shareholders is open to criticism.

To the extent that transfer prices apply to financial transactions such as credits granted between corporate divisions, the scope for meeting the many strategic objectives we have described, such as reducing host-government criticism over profits and reducing taxes, are substantially enhanced. Indeed, when we add discretion over timing of repayment of credits, the MNC may be at a substantial advantage over nonmultinational competitors.[21]

Practical Considerations in Transfer Pricing

Transfer prices can be used to "window-dress" the profits of certain divisions of a multinational so as to reduce borrowing costs. The gains from having seemingly large profits by paying a subsidiary high transfer prices for its products must, of course, be balanced against the potential scorn of foreign host governments, higher taxes or tariffs that might result, and so on.

For the long-term survival of a multinational, it is important that interdivisional profitability be measured accurately. The record of profitability of different divisions is valuable in allocating overall spending on capital projects and in sharing other corporate resources. In order to discover the correct profitability, the firm should be sure that interdivisional transfer prices are the prices that would have been paid had the transactions been with independent companies, so-called "arm's-length prices." This can be particularly difficult in the international allocation of such items as research and consulting services or headquarters' overheads; there is rarely a market price for research or other services of corporate headquarters. Profit allocation

---

[21]See Lessard, *op. cit.* We recall that to some extent, timing discretion on credits is reduced by leading and lagging restrictions.

will usually be according to the distribution of corporate sales, with the sales valued at the "correct" exchange rate. The advantages of preventing distortions in transfer prices must be balanced against the potential gains from using distorted transfer prices to reduce tariffs, taxes, political risks, and exchange losses. This balance can be a difficult problem for multinational corporations.

SPECIAL ISSUES FACING MULTINATIONAL CORPORATIONS: COUNTRY RISK

As we mentioned in our account of capital budgeting in the previous chapter, when making overseas direct investments it is necessary to allow for risk due to the investment being in a foreign country. In this section we consider both the measurement and the management of this so-called **country risk,** which, as with transfer pricing, takes on special importance in the multinational corporation.

The term "country risk" is often used interchangeably with the terms **political risk** and **sovereign risk.** However, country risk is really a broader concept than either of the other two, including them as special cases. Country risk involves the possibility of losses due to country-specific economic, political, and social events, and therefore all political risk is country risk, but not all country risk is political risk.[22] Sovereign risk involves the possibility of losses on claims to foreign governments or government agencies, whereas political risk involves the additional possibility of losses on private claims as well as on direct investments. Sovereign risk exists on bank loans and bonds and is therefore not of special concern to MNCs—unless they are banks. Since our concern here is with the risk faced on foreign direct investment, we are concerned with country risk and are not particularly interested in the subcomponent of country risk which consists of sovereign risk. Nevertheless, much of what we say about country-risk measurement applies to sovereign risk.

The Measurement of Country Risk

Among the country risks that are faced on an overseas direct investment are those related to the local economy, those due to the possibility of **confiscation** (which refers to a government takeover without any compensation), and those due to the possibility of **expropriation** (which refers to a government takeover with compensation, which at times can be generous[23]). As well as the political risks of confiscation and expropriation, there are political/social risks of wars, revolutions, and insurrections. While these are not the result of action by foreign governments specifically directed at the firm, they can damage or destroy an investment. In addition, there are risks of currency inconvertibility and restrictions on the repatriation of income beyond those already reflected in the cash-flow term of the APV calculation in the previous chapter. The treatment of these risks requires that we make adjustments in the APV calculation and/or allowances for late compensation payments for expropriated capital. The required adjustments can be made to the discount rates by

---

[22]For example, see U.S. Comptroller of the Currency, news release, November 8, 1978.

[23]Clearly, when investors can count on timely and fair compensation at market value, there is no added risk due to expropriation.

adding a risk premium, or to expected cash flows by putting them into their certainty equivalent.[24]

We know that when we view the adjustment for risk in terms of the inclusion of a premium in the discount rate, only systematic risk needs to be considered. Since by investing in a large number of countries it is possible to diversify risk, the systematic component of economic and political/social risk can be very small. Risk diversification requires only a degree of economic and political/social independence between countries. Diversification is made even more effective if the economic and political/social misfortunes from events in some countries provide benefits in other countries. For example, risk on diversified copper investments can be made arbitrarily small if war or revolution in African countries that produce copper raises incomes of South American producers of copper.

Before a company can consider how much of its country risk is systematic, it must be able to determine the risk in each country. Only later can it determine by how much its country risk is reduced by the individual country risks being imperfectly or even negatively correlated. But how can it determine each country's risk? The most obvious method is to obtain country-risk evaluations that have been prepared by specialists. But this merely begs the question how the specialists evaluate country risk. Let us consider a few of the risk-evaluation techniques that have been employed.

One of the best known country-risk evaluations is that prepared by *Euromoney,* a monthly magazine that periodically produces a ranking of country risks. Euromoney's evaluation procedure is summarized in Figure 20.1.[25]

Euromoney consults a cross section of specialists. These specialists are asked to give their opinions on each country with regard to one or more of the factors used in their calculations. There are three broad categories of factors considered. These are analytical indicators (50 percent), credit indicators (30 percent), and market indicators (20 percent). Each of these broad categories is further subdivided into more specific components as shown in Figure 20.1.

The analytical indicators consist of economic and political-risk evaluations. The economic evaluation is based on actual and projected growth in GNP. The political-risk evaluation is provided by a panel of experts consisting of risk analysts, insurance brokers, and bank credit officers. The credit indicator includes measures of the ability of the country to service debt based on debt service versus exports, the size of the current-account deficit or surplus versus GNP, and external debt versus GNP.[26] Market indicators are based on assessments of a country's access to bank loans, short-term credits, syndicated loans, and the bond market, as well as on the premiums occurring on nonrecourse loans made to exporters.[27] Large premiums are a sign of market-perceived risk. Of course, the market also considers the other factors used in Euromoney's ranking, and so there is double-counting; the other factors consid-

---

[24]We have already indicated that the two methods are conceptually equivalent.

[25]Figure 20.1 is based on a description of the *Eurocurrency* method in "Country Risk: Methodology," *Euromoney,* September 1994, p. 380.

[26]While the ratio of debt-service payments to export earnings provides an indication of the foreign exchange earnings that may be available for debt service, it does not reflect the diversity of goods and services that earn foreign exchange. Presumably, a country with a single export is a poorer risk than a country with diversified export earnings, even if the two countries have the same ratio.

[27]Nonrecourse loans to exporters are discussed in Chapter 23 under the heading "Forfaiting: A Form of Medium-Term Finance."

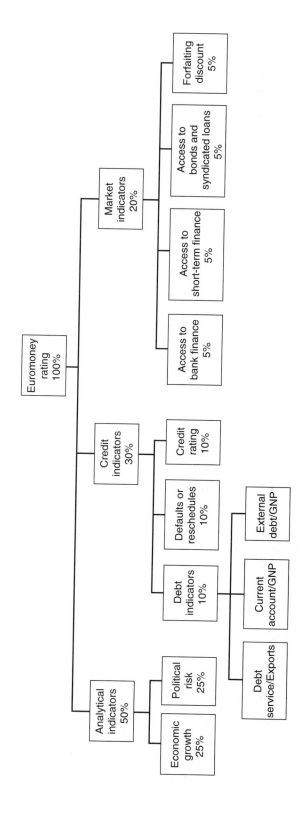

Figure 20.1. Euromoney's Country-Risk Rating Scheme

Euromoney allocates 50 percent of the weight in its country risk evaluation index to analytical indicators, with this 50 percent being divided equally between economic and political factors. The remaining 50 percent of *Euromoney*'s risk evaluation is based on the credit experience and position of a country, and on risk premia set in financial markets.

TABLE 20.2. Euromoney's Country-Risk Ranking, 1994

Top Twenty		Bottom Twenty	
Country	Rating/100	Country	Rating/100
United States	97.93	Antigua & Barbuda	21.85
Switzerland	97.89	Libya	21.60
Luxembourg	97.69	FYR Macedonia	21.41
Singapore	96.92	Mongolia	21.23
Austria	96.52	Georgia	20.22
Japan	96.35	Rwanda	20.07
France	95.61	Azerbaijan	19.65
United Kingdom	95.57	Moldova	19.47
Netherlands	95.38	Tajikistan	19.03
Germany	94.91	Afghanistan	18.88
Denmark	94.69	Sierra Leone	18.78
Canada	94.67	Mozambique	18.12
Belgium	93.00	Sao Tome and Principe	17.72
Norway	92.91	Nicaragua	16.86
Taiwan	92.12	Armenia	16.79
Australia	92.09	Guinea-Bissau	16.75
Spain	91.13	Korea, North	15.55
New Zealand	90.81	Iraq	15.16
Sweden	90.61	Somalia	12.47
Ireland	89.20	Cuba	5.75

Source: Euromoney, September 1994, pp. 376–379.

ered by Euromoney appear directly in the ranking and also indirectly via the premiums on loans. Euromoney's country-risk rankings of the safest and riskiest 20 countries in September 1994 are shown in Table 20.2.

Measures of country risk do not distinguish the different risks facing different *industries;* they measure only the risk of *countries.* Yet a number of studies show that some industries, especially those involving natural resources or utilities, face higher risks than other industries.[28] Indeed, country risk may even differ between firms in the same industry. This potential for different country risks can to some extent be influenced by firms themselves, because there are a number of things firms can do to affect the odds of some political events.

Methods of Reducing Country Risk

Keeping Control of Crucial Elements of Corporate Operations

Some companies making direct foreign investments try to prevent operations from running without their cooperation. This can be achieved if the investor maintains control of a crucial element of operations. For example, food and soft-drink

---

[28]See J. Frederick Truitt, "Expropriation of Foreign Investment: Summary of the Post World War II Experience of American and British Investors in Less Developed Countries," *Journal of International Business Studies,* fall 1970, pp. 21–34; Robert Hawkins, Norman Mintz, and Michael Provissiero, "Government Takeovers of U.S. Foreign Affiliates," *Journal of International Business Studies,* spring 1976, pp. 3–16; and John Calverly, *Country Risk Analysis,* Butterworths, London, 1985.

manufacturers keep secret their special ingredients. Auto companies can produce vital parts, such as engines, in some other country and can refuse to supply these parts if their operations are seized.[29] The multinational oil companies have used refining capacity coupled with alternative sources of oil to reduce the probability that their oil wells will be expropriated. Similarly, many companies have kept key technical operations with their own technicians, who can be recalled in the event of expropriation or confiscation. This has not always been an effective deterrent, as more mercenary technicians can often be found if the salary is sufficient. Moreover, given sufficient time, local people can pick up the important skills.

Programmed Stages of Planned Divestment

An alternative technique for reducing the probability of expropriation is for the owner of a foreign direct investment to promise to turn over ownership and control to local people in the future. This is sometimes required by the host government. For example, the Cartagena Agreement of 1969 requires the foreign owners of enterprises in the Andean countries of South America to lower their ownership, over time, to below 50 percent.

Joint Ventures

Instead of promising shared ownership in the future, an alternative technique for reducing the risk of expropriation is to share ownership with foreign private or official partners from the very beginning. Such shared ownerships, known as **joint ventures,** have been tried by U.S., Canadian, European, and Japanese firms with partners in Africa, Central and South America, and Asia. Joint ventures as a means of reducing expropriation risks rely on the reluctance of local partners, if private, to accept the interference of their own government. When the partner is the government itself, the disincentive to expropriation is the concern over the loss of future investments. Joint ventures with multiple participants from different countries reduce the risk of expropriation, even if there is no local participation, if the government wishes to avoid being isolated simultaneously by numerous foreign powers.

Even if joint ventures with government-controlled enterprises work well while that government remains in power, they can backfire if the government is overthrown by the opposition in a polarized political climate. Extreme changes in governments have been witnessed so many times that the risks of siding with a government that falls are well known. In addition, even when the local partner is a private corporation, if expropriation means more ownership or control for the partner, there is likely to be muted local opposition at best. It is these reasons which may explain the observation that the risk of joint ventures has been greater than that of ventures with total U.S. ownership. A study of U.S. affiliates in the 1960–1976 period showed that joint ventures with host governments were expropriated 10 times more often than fully U.S.-owned ventures and that joint ventures with private firms were expropriated 8 times more often.[30]

---

[29]According to Roy E. Pederson, who cited the case of IBM, the risk can be reduced by keeping all research and development at home. See Roy E. Pedersen, "Political Risk: Corporate Considerations," *Risk Management,* April 1979, pp. 23–32.

[30]See David Bradley, "Managing Against Expropriation," *Harvard Business Review,* July–August 1977, pp. 75–83. For a survey of work on political risks, see Stephen Kobrin, "Political Risks: A Review and Reconsideration," *Journal of International Business Studies,* spring/summer 1979, pp. 67–80.

Local Debt

The risk of expropriation as well as the losses from expropriation can be reduced by borrowing within the countries where investment occurs. If the borrowing is denominated in the local currency, there will often also be a reduction of foreign exchange risk. These obvious gains from engaging in local debt are limited by the opportunities. Those countries where expropriation is most likely tend to be the countries with the least-developed capital markets and host governments unwilling to make loans. The opportunities for reducing risk by having local people hold equity in the firm are also limited by the frequent shortage of middle-class shareholders in the high-risk countries and by the absence of a viable market in which to sell the primary issue.

Despite the techniques for reducing risk, some danger will remain. Fortunately, something can be done to reduce or eliminate the harmful consequences of political developments by purchasing investment insurance.

The Purchase of Investment Insurance

Many countries will insure their companies that invest overseas against losses from political events such as currency inconvertibility, expropriation, war, and revolution. In the United States this insurance is offered by the **Overseas Private Investment Corporation** (OPIC). This corporation has been in operation since the early 1970s, having replaced programs in effect since the Economic Co-operation Act of 1948. OPIC will insure U.S. private investments in developing nations, where there tends to be more risk. Over 60 percent of non-oil-related investments in the underdeveloped countries are covered by OPIC.

In addition to investment insurance, OPIC offers project financing. This involves assistance in finding sources of funds, including OPIC's own sources, and assistance in finding worthwhile projects. Reimbursement for losses on loans is also offered. There is no coverage for losses due to changes in exchange rates, but there is also no need for such coverage because of the private means that are available, such as the forward and futures markets. OPIC charges a fee for complete coverage that is between 1 and 2 percent per annum of the amount covered on the insurance policy. Insurance must generally be approved by host governments and is available only on new projects. Since 1980, OPIC has joined with private insurance companies in the Overseas Investment Insurance Group. This has been done to move the insurance into the private sector of the economy.

In Canada, foreign-investment insurance is provided by the Export Development Corporation (EDC). The Canadian EDC will insure against losses due to war, insurrection, confiscation, expropriation, and events which prevent the repatriating of capital or the transfer of earnings. This role of the EDC is similar to the role of OPIC. The EDC also offers insurance against nonpayment for Canadian exports, a function performed by the **Export-Import Bank** in the United States. The insurance coverage offered in the United Kingdom is very similar to the coverage offered by OPIC and the Canadian EDC, and similar programs exist in many other countries.

If the compensation provided by project insurers (1) is received immediately and (2) covers the full value of the project, the availability of insurance means that the only required adjustment for country risk is a deduction for insurance premiums from cash flows. We can deduct available premiums even if insurance is not actually purchased, since the firm will then be self-insuring and should deduct an appropriate cost for this.

Some of the country risk that MNCs face and that forces them to insure or take other steps is a result of their visibility. This is largely due to their immense size and the difficulty of regulating them. However, there are other factors that have made MNCs the target of criticism and concern. Let us turn our discussion of the growth and special problems of MNCs to these criticisms and concerns, and explain why so much attention has been attracted by MNCs. We shall see that while some of the common concerns over the power and practices of MNCs may be well-founded, there are many benefits that MNCs have brought host countries through the transfer of technology and jobs that can be attributed to their direct investments.

Problems and Benefits from the Growth of MNCs

As we have mentioned, much of the concern about MNCs stems from their size, which can be formidable. Indeed, the profits of some of the larger corporations can exceed the operating budgets of the governments in smaller countries. It is the power that such scale can give that has led to the greatest concern. Can the MNCs push around their host governments to the advantage of the shareholders and the disadvantage of the citizens of the country of operation? This has led several countries and even the United Nations to investigate the influence of MNCs. The issues considered include the following.

It can be difficult to manage economies in which multinationals have extensive investments, such as the economies of Canada and Australia. Since MNCs often have ready access to external sources of finance, they can blunt local monetary policy.[31] When the host government wishes to constrain economic activity, multinationals may nevertheless expand through foreign borrowing. Similarly, efforts at economic expansion may be frustrated if multinationals move funds abroad in search of yield advantages elsewhere. You do not have to be a multinational to frustrate plans for economic expansion—integrated financial markets will always produce this effect—but MNCs are likely to participate in any opportunities to gain profits. Furthermore, as we have seen, multinationals can also shift profits to reduce their total tax burden; they can show larger profits in countries with lower tax rates. This can make the MNC a slippery animal for the tax collector, even though it uses many local public goods provided from general tax revenues.

It has been argued that multinationals can make foreign exchange markets volatile. For example, it has been claimed that when the U.S. dollar is moving rapidly against the European currencies, the Canadian dollar swings even further. In particular, a declining value of the U.S. dollar against, for example, the German mark or sterling has been associated with an average larger decline of the Canadian dollar against the same European currency. Although the existence of this phenomenon has not been formally verified, MNCs have been blamed for such an effect. It has been claimed that when U.S. parent companies are expecting an increase in the

---

[31]While MNCs may reduce the effectiveness of monetary policy, they may also increase the effectiveness of changes in exchange rates on the balance of trade. In particular, they may speed up the increase in exports from countries experiencing depreciations by quickly moving their production to those countries to take advantage of the lower production costs.

value of the mark, sterling, and so on, they buy these foreign currencies and instruct their Canadian subsidiaries to do the same. With a thinner market in the Dominion currency, the effect of this activity could be greater movement in the value of the Canadian dollar than in the value of the U.S. dollar.

Concern has been expressed, especially within the United States, that U.S.-based multinationals can defy foreign policy objectives of the U.S. government through their foreign branches and subsidiaries. A firm might break a blockade and avoid sanctions by operating through overseas subsidiaries. This has caused even greater concern within some host countries. Why should companies operating within their boundaries have to follow orders of the U.S. government or any other foreign government? Multinational corporations present a potential for conflict between national governments. There is even potential for conflict within international/multinational trade unions. For example, in 1980 and 1981 Chrysler Corporation was given loan guarantees to help it continue in operation. The U.S. government insisted on wage and salary rollbacks as a condition. Chrysler workers in Canada did not appreciate the instruction from the U.S. Congress to accept a reduced wage.

Accusations have been made, most notably with regard to the oil industry, that multinationals can use monopoly power to withhold output to effect price increases for their products. Because the multinationals have such extensive operations, much of the data on which the governments must rely are often data collected and reported by the MNCs themselves. There is no guarantee that the data are accurate, and there is no easy way to enforce controls and punish culprits. This became one of the leading political issues of the 1980s and 1990s.

Multinationals tend to concentrate and specialize their "good" and "bad" activities within certain locations. This can mean doing R & D within the home country. Highly trained university and technical-school graduates who find their employment and promotion opportunities diminished would prefer locally owned and managed enterprises in their country to foreign MNCs. This has been a controversial problem in countries that consider themselves "branch plant" economies. Canadian and Australian scientists and engineers have been particularly outspoken.[32]

While MNCs have improved prospects for some better-paid workers in their home countries, it has been argued that they have "exported" lower-wage jobs. The evidence does not support this claim. Indeed, as Exhibit 20.3 explains, the opposite may be true. Direct foreign investment is frequently motivated by strategic considerations, and it can help investing firms retain markets threatened by new entrants. In this way jobs at home—those supplying partly-processed inputs and R & D— are protected.

It is not uncommon to hear the view that because MNCs are so large they have reduced competition. However, the truth may be the opposite. In some industries such as automobiles, computers, steel, and shipbuilding, where a single country might support one or only a few firms in the industry, competition is increased by

---

[32]The data support the claim that multinationals keep a disproportionate share of R & D activity at home. For example, according to the U.S. Department of Commerce, in 1977 only 10 percent of U.S.-based multinationals' R & D was spent by foreign affiliates, and these foreign affiliates employed only 13 percent of the MNCs' scientists and engineers. See U.S. Department of Commerce, Bureau of Economic Analysis, news release, June 2, 1981. See also Irving Kravis and Robert Lipsey, "The Effect of Multinational Firms' Foreign Operations on Their Domestic Employment," National Bureau of Economic Research, Working Paper 2760, March 1989.

EXHIBIT 20.3
Do U.S. Multinationals Export Jobs?

Given that everybody knows American workers earn far, far more than their counterparts in newly industrialized and developing countries, it has not been difficult to convince people that U.S. multinationals have exported Americans' jobs. But do firms make their foreign direct investments to gain access to "cheap labor," or is there more to it than that?

The idea that foreign direct investment by U.S. multinationals has exported jobs has arisen largely from some highly publicized cases, such as the movement of Smith-Corona's typewriter assembly from Connecticut to Mexico and the serious, protracted labor unrest over International Harvester's decision to relocate production. However, the data do not support popular opinion. First, statistics show that 85 percent of manufacturing output by overseas operations of U.S. MNCs are in other relatively high-wage countries such as Canada and Britain. Second, exports from U.S. subsidiaries abroad to the United States are only 12 percent of the subsidiaries' production. The rest is sold abroad. Indeed, the need to supply overseas subsidiaries with partly-processed inputs and capital equipment and to carry out R & D *creates* jobs in the United States. One study convincingly supporting this conclusion, by Robert Lipsey, found that for U.S. multinationals, the higher the share of overseas operations in the firm's total pro-duction, the larger the share of employment at home. The same study suggests that *without* the foreign direct investment, U.S. market share would have been taken by other countries' multinationals. In other words, U.S. foreign investment has a strategic element and has helped the United States retain its share of markets, even though the importance of goods supplied from the United States itself has declined; foreign subsidiaries have helped U.S. *firms* retain markets, and thereby R & D and factor-supply-related jobs at home.

Clearly, there is more to production-location decisions than wages. Overall unit labor costs can be low even when wages are high if workers have high productivity. As long as U.S. workers are more productive, jobs will not be exported. Of course, this requires investment in education as well as in physical capital. Therefore, if there is a danger of losing jobs, it comes from educational and investment levels in the United States versus those levels abroad, not from successful U.S. multinationals.

Source: Based on Robert Lipsey, "Outward Direct Investment and the U.S. Economy," National Bureau of Economic Research, Paper Number 4691, 1994, and M. Blomström and Ari Kokko, "Home Country Effects of Foreign Direct Investment: Evidence from Sweden," National Bureau of Economic Research, Paper Number 4639, 1994.

the presence of foreign MNCs. That is, the MNCs themselves compete in international markets, and without them monopoly powers in some sectors might be even greater.

Also on the positive side, MNCs have transferred technology and capital to less-developed countries (LDCs), and in this way helped accelerate their economic development.[33] U.S.- and Japanese-based MNCs have been particularly active building production facilities in LDCs.[34] For example, U.S. multinationals' influence in Latin America has been particularly strong.[35] The Japanese MNCs' influence has also risen, particularly in Asian LDCs.[36]

---

[33]However, many have argued that the transferred technology is very often inappropriate.
[34]To the extent MNCs provide training, they may also add to the stock of human capital in LDCs.
[35]Magnus Blomstrom, Irving Kravis, and Robert Lipsey, "Multinational Firms and Manufactured Exports from Developing Countries," National Bureau of Economic Research, Working Paper 2493, June 1988.
[36]See Blomstrom, Kravis, and Lipsey, *ibid.*

509

There is little doubt that MNCs spread a common culture. Chain hamburger outlets become the same on Main Street in Iowa and on the Champs-Élysées in Paris. Soft-drink bottles with a familiar shape can wash up on any beach, and there is no obvious way of telling from which country they came. Hotel rooms are alike everywhere. The same corporate names and product names appear in every major Western language. Even architecture shows a common influence—the "international style." Many have decried this development, complaining that it is robbing the world of a good deal of its variety and local interest. Yet the local people demand the products of the MNCs. This is all part of the unending love-hate relationship between concerned people everywhere and the multinational corporation.

TRANSNATIONAL ALLIANCES

Multinational corporations own and control their overseas operations. An alternative to ownership which still allows companies to enjoy some of the benefits of multi-nationalization is the formation of **transnational alliances.** These alliances involve associations of firms in different countries working together to overcome the limitations of working alone. One motivation to form a transnational alliance is cooperation over research where costs and risks may be too high for any one firm, or where different firms may possess different abilities. Such alliances are popular in biotechnology and computers: Quadra Logic of Canada with American Cyanamide in genetic engineering, for example, and IBM with Siemens of Germany in memory-chip development. Cooperation may be between producers and marketers: Chrysler marketed the Colt produced by Mitsubishi; GM marketed the Geo produced in Korea. Other cooperations have involved design, product assembly, component production, and distribution.

The extent and complexity of transnational alliances can be found by writing the names of the global members of any industry in matrix form on a sheet of paper. Lines can then be drawn to represent contacts, whether these be joint ventures, licensing arrangements, production agreements, or research connections. Doing this for computer firms or automobile manufacturers shows an intimate cobweb of tangled connections. Pharmaceutical, aerospace, telecommunications, and defense industry alliances also reveal a highly complex web.

Transnational alliances appear to be formed most frequently for three reasons: to gain access to foreign markets, to exploit complementary technologies, and to reduce the time taken for innovation.[37] The alliances are usually for specific purposes, although once formed, they may be used for further purposes. Typically, ownership connections are limited, unlike the consortia so popular in Japan, called **keiretsu,** and in Korea, called **chaebols.** Keiretsu and chaebols involve ownership cross-holdings not usually present with transnational alliances. Transnational alliances are a compromise between a firm's doing everything itself and dealing with a complete stranger.[38] As such, they are somewhere between independent national operations and multinational corporations.

[37]See *Multinational,* a supplement in *The Economist,* March 27, 1993, pp. 14–17.
[38]*Ibid.*

SUMMARY

1. MNCs have grown by making foreign direct investments.
2. Among the reasons MNCs have made direct investments are to gain access to raw materials, to integrate operations for increased efficiency, to avoid regulations, to protect industrial secrets and patents, to expand when domestic opportunities are exhausted, to avoid tariffs and quotas, to increase production flexibility and thereby profit from fluctuations in real exchange rates, to follow client MNCs, and to increase diversification.
3. MNCs are generally larger and more R & D-intensive than firms in general. These differences are characteristic both of the industries in which MNCs are found, and of the MNCs versus other firms within the same industries.
4. MNCs face two measurement problems to a greater degree than other firms, namely measuring transfer prices and country risks.
5. For maximum overall corporate profits and correct buy-versus-make decisions, transfer prices should be set equal to marginal costs. This means that the use of market prices as transfer prices is appropriate only if the market for intermediate products is competitive.
6. If intermediate-product markets are not perfectly competitive, prices will exceed marginal costs, and so, by using market prices of intermediate products, less than the optimal final output will be produced, and suboptimal use will be made of the MNCs own intermediate products.
7. Even if market prices equal marginal costs, so that transfer prices can be set equal to market prices, if one calculates divisional profits with these transfer prices, then supplying divisions may appear to be unprofitable even when they add to overall corporate profitability.
8. Transfer prices can be used to reduce country risk, taxes, foreign exchange losses, the impact of tariffs and quotas, and shareholder frustration resulting from fluctuating profits. Offsetting the gains from distorting transfer prices is the loss from losing information on divisional profitability.
9. Country risk is a broader concept than either political risk or sovereign risk. Country risk includes economic and social risk, as well as risk faced on private-sector investments.
10. There are a number of published rankings of country risks and political risks which can help in evaluations of direct investments.
11. Political risk can be reduced by keeping control of essential operations, by having a program of planned divestment, or by the use of local debt. Joint ventures can also reduce political risk, but they can backfire with changes in host governments.
12. Losses from political events can be reduced or eliminated by buying investment insurance. In the United States, this is available from the Overseas Private Investment Corporation (OPIC).
13. MNCs have brought numerous problems. They can make it difficult to manage an economy; they may be able to defy the political directions of their own or foreign governments; they can concentrate skilled jobs at home and more menial jobs abroad. MNCs may also be able to manipulate prices and spread a common culture.
14. Transnational alliances are associations of firms from different countries working in cooperation. They are particularly common in the computer, biotechnology, pharmaceutical, defense, and automobile industries, where they give access to foreign markets and/or permit the sharing of technology.

REVIEW QUESTIONS

1. Why might a producer want to own resources located in another country, rather than buy them in the open market?

2. What are the limitations of licenses as an alternative to direct foreign investment?
3. Why are some accounting firms multinationals?
4. What role do market imperfections play in direct foreign investment?
5. What is a transfer price?
6. Can a company set any transfer prices that it wishes?
7. What is meant by "country risk," and how does this risk differ from political risk?
8. How does country risk differ from sovereign risk?
9. How does expropriation differ from confiscation?
10. Why does local debt or equity help reduce country risk?
11. Is country risk the same for all industries and firms?
12. What is a transnational alliance?

ASSIGNMENT PROBLEMS

1. What examples can you list of foreign multinationals operating in the United States?
2. Which of the reasons for the growth of MNCs do you think are the primary reasons for the development of multinationals in the following industries?
   a. Drugs and pharmaceutical manufacturing
   b. Automobile manufacturing
   c. Metal refining
   d. Hotel operation
   e. Commercial banking
   f. Energy development
   g. Fast food
   h. Fashion clothing
3. Which explanation(s) of the growth of MNCs is/are supported by the evidence that MNCs are relatively capital-intensive?
4. What are the pros and cons of setting transfer prices equal to marginal costs?
5. Under what circumstances are market prices appropriate to use as transfer prices?
6. How can conflicts exist when a firm sets transfer prices for maximizing overall profits? Could these conflicts arise from differential tax rates, import tariffs, imminent changes in exchange rates, and political risks?
7. Why are risk premiums on bonds a useful way of ranking risks for direct investments, but not very useful for making bond purchasing decisions?
8. Why might country risk depend on the diversity of exports as well as on the value of exports versus debt-service payments?
9. In what ways might country risk be influenced by a country's political and economic associations and its geography?
10. Do you think the standard of living overseas has been raised by the direct investments of multinationals? Does this provide a reason for offering MNCs concessionary loans?

BIBLIOGRAPHY

ALIBER, ROBERT Z.: *The Multinational Paradigm,* M.I.T. Press, Cambridge, Mass., 1993.
BIRD, GRAHAM: "New Approaches to Country Risk," *Lloyds Bank Review,* October 1986, pp. 1–16.
CALVERLEY, JOHN: *Country Risk Analysis,* Butterworths, London, 1985.
CALVET, A. LOUIS: "A Synthesis of Foreign Direct Investment Theories and Theories of the Multinational Firm," *Journal of International Business Studies,* spring/summer 1981, pp. 43–59.

CASSON, MARK: *The Firm and the Market: Studies on the Multinational Enterprise and the Scope of the Firm,* M.I.T. Press, Cambridge, Mass., 1987.

DAVIDSON, WILLIAM H.: "Location of Foreign Direct Investment Activity: Country Characteristics and Experience Effects," *Journal of International Business Studies,* fall 1980, pp. 9–22.

DUNNING, JOHN H. (ed.): *International Investment,* Penguin, Harmondsworth, U.K., 1972.

————: *Economic Analysis and the Multinational Enterprise,* Praeger, New York, 1975.

The Economist: Multinationals, a supplement, March 27, 1993.

GRANICK, DAVID: "National Differences in the Use of Internal Transfer Prices," *California Management Review,* summer 1975, pp. 28–40.

KOBRIN, STEPHEN J.: "The Environmental Determinants of Foreign Direct Investment: An Ex Post Empirical Analysis," *Journal of International Business Studies,* fall 1976, pp. 29–42.

MAGEE, STEPHEN P.: "Information and the Multinational Corporation: An Appropriability Theory of Direct Foreign Investment," in Jagdish N. Bhagwati (ed.), *The New International Economic Order,* M.I.T. Press, Cambridge, Mass., 1977.

MELVIN, MICHAEL, and DON SCHLAGENHAUF: "A Country Risk Index: Econometric Formulation and an Application to Mexico," *Economic Inquiry,* October 1985, pp. 601–619.

RAGAZZIO, GIORGIO: "Theories of the Determinants of Direct Foreign Investment," *IMF Staff Papers,* July 1973, pp. 471–498.

REICH, ROBERT B.: *The Work of Nations,* Knopf, New York, 1991.

RUMMEL, R. J., and DAVID A. HEENAN: "How Multinationals Analyze Political Risk," *Harvard Business Review,* January/February 1978, pp. 67–76.

VERNON, RAYMOND: *Storm Over the Multinationals: The Real Issues,* Harvard University Press, Cambridge, Mass., 1977.

International Financing

Let us all be happy and live within our means, even if we have to borrow the money to do it with.

—ARTEMUS WARD

The integration and associated globalization of capital markets has opened up a vast array of new sources and forms of project financing. Today's corporate treasurers of large domestic as well as multinational corporations can access foreign capital markets as easily as those at home. This chapter considers these broadened opportunities by explaining the central international financial issues involved in each of the major methods of raising capital. We consider the international aspects of raising capital via stocks, bonds, parallel loans between corporations, credit swaps between banks and corporations, and loans from host governments and development banks. We shall see the importance of exchange-rate risk, taxes, country risk, and issuance costs for the form of financing chosen. The chapter concludes with a discussion of the appropriate relative amounts of each type of financing, that is, the appropriate **financial structure.**

EQUITY FINANCING

The main international financial question concerning equity financing is in which country stocks should be issued. A second question concerns the legal vehicle that should be used for raising equity capital; should this be done by a subsidiary, and if so, where should this subsidiary be registered?

The Country in Which Shares Should Be Issued

Clearly, shares should be issued in the country in which the best price can be received, net of issuing costs. If for the time being we assume the costs of issue to be the same everywhere, the country in which the best price can be received for the shares is the country in which the cost of equity in terms of the expected rate of return is lowest. There is no concern about risk from the equity *issuer's* perspective, other than to the extent that through equity *buyer's* concern for systematic risk, the riskiness of shares issued affects the required expected rate of return and hence the price received for the shares; the required expected rate of return of shareholders is, of course, the expected rate of return paid by the firm.

It should be clear from our discussion of equity investment in Chapter 18 that if capital markets are fully integrated, the expected cost of equity capital will be the same in every country. That is, the expected return on the company's shares will be the same everywhere.[1]

If capital markets are segmented, the expected returns on the same security *could* be different in different markets. A company might then be able to receive more for its shares in some markets than in others. Of course, when a company's shares are listed simultaneously in different countries, the share price will have to be the same everywhere up to transaction costs of arbitrage. However, the cause of segmentation may prevent arbitrage. Furthermore, a company may not be considering simultaneous issue in different countries, but rather, the single country in which to float an issue.

Ceteris paribus, the higher are savings relative to investment in a country, the lower is the cost of capital. This means, for example, that a country like Japan, which has a very high savings rate, should have a lower cost of capital than the United States, which has a very low savings rate, provided investment opportunities are similar. Of course, if markets are integrated, we shall not see these different costs of capital, because those countries which would have had low costs of capital in segmented markets have outflows of capital until the rates of return are the same as elsewhere. Similarly, those countries which would have had high costs of capital with segmentation would have inflows of capital until their rates of return are the same as elsewhere.[2]

Sometimes, as a result of capital-market segmentation, it can be advantageous to issue shares simultaneously in two or more countries' equity markets. Such share issues are called **Euroequity issues.** Since the mid-1980s, the number of Euroequity issues has grown rapidly, with the absolute size and proportion of shares sold in the Euromarkets being substantial. For example, in May 1988, Occidental Petroleum floated $212 million of Euroequities, this being 18 percent of the company's total share issue. In May 1987, U.S. Air floated $90 million of Euroequities, 20 percent of its total issue, and in September 1986 Home Shopping Network sold $56.1 million of shares in the Euromarket, 50 percent of its share offering. What is the source of market segmentation that has prompted so many companies to raise equity in this form? In other words, what is limiting the ability or willingness of foreign investors to buy shares in the U.S. market instead of in the Eurodollar market? As Exhibit 21.2 explains, one possible explanation is the preference of many non-American investors for the anonymity enjoyed with **bearer shares.** (U.S. shares sold in Euromarkets are bearer shares, which means that they do not carry the name of the owner. U.S. shares sold in U.S. markets are all registered in the owners' names, with the registration changed when the shares are exchanged.)

---

[1]The expected return must, of course, be in terms of a given currency. For example, the expected average annual U.S.-dollar rate of return on shares trading in, for example, Britain includes the expected appreciation of the pound as well as the expected change in the pound price of the shares and the expected dividend yield.

[2]Claims have been made that costs of capital in the United States and Japan have not moved together from international financial flows, with Japanese firms facing lower financing costs. However, as Exhibit 21.1 explains, borrowing cost differences may be smaller than many people believe.

Theory suggests that borrowing costs, or more generally, the costs of capital, should be equal in different markets after allowance for exchange rates. Indeed, Chapter 11 was devoted to showing this, in the form of the interest parity principle. Nevertheless, many people have claimed that vital differences in costs of capital exist, especially between Japan and the United States, with Japanese capital costs well below those faced by Americans. Were this to be so, it would give an advantage to Japanese firms, especially in capital-intensive industries. However, as the item below argues, the appearance of a lower cost of capital in Japan than the United States, specifically for bank borrowing, may be due to an incomplete understanding of institutional arrangements in these two countries.

Few subjects in international economics have touched as many political nerves in recent years as the comparison of relative financing costs in different countries. The apparent financing advantage enjoyed by Japanese firms over their U.S. competitors in past decades—short-term real bank loan rates 1 percent to 2.8 percent lower, according to some research—even has been cited as evidence of "unfair trade" that should be redressed by changes in U.S. policy. But a new NBER (National Bureau of Economic Research) study by Richard Marston shows that bank financing costs in Japan were underestimated systematically, and those in the United States overestimated, in the past. In any event, Marston finds, most of the reported gap in financing costs between the two countries can be traced to features of national markets that have largely disappeared.

In "Determinants of Short-Term Real Interest Differentials Between Japan and the United States" (NBER Working Paper No. 4167), Marston focuses on bank loan financing, which continues to be the most important source of external finance for Japanese firms. He finds that interest rates in Japan were governed by market conventions and regulations that often obscured the true cost of funds. Prior to 1989, the most widely reported lending rate was called the "standard rate." This was defined as the rate on loans of "especially high credit standing" and was tied through informal guidelines to the Bank of Japan's discount rate. The cost of borrowing at this rate was understated because Japanese banks typically required that borrowers maintain compensating balances on deposit, raising the effective cost of the loan. For most of the 1970s, the only short-term rate free to reflect monetary conditions was the "gensaki" rate, paid on repurchase agreements. Between 1973 and 1991, the standard rate averaged 5.96 percent while the gensaki rate averaged 6.99 percent: more than one percentage point higher.

Measuring the true cost of bank loans in the United States is also difficult. The meaning of the widely quoted "prime rate" (the rate at which banks traditionally lent to their most creditworthy customers) has changed fundamentally as borrowers gained greater access to direct financing from the 1970s onward. Marston finds that, from 1973 to 1991, the average gap between the prime rate and the rate at which creditworthy firms could borrow on the commercial paper market was 1.57 percent.

With Americans' borrowing rates up to one-and-a-half percent below bank lending costs, and Japanese borrowing at the gensaki rate roughly one percent higher than the standard rate, the 1.0 to 2.8 percent difference some people have claimed is fully closed. However, the *issue* is unlikely to be closed so easily.

Source: "Japan and U.S. Real Interest Rates Converge," *The NBER Digest,* February 1993.

Just as U.S. firms have found it beneficial to sell shares abroad, non-U.S. firms have found it beneficial to sell shares in U.S. stock markets. What is the cause of segmentation that prevents or discourages Americans from buying shares of non-U.S. firms in foreign stock markets? One possible explanation is U.S. reporting requirements that, in accordance with the Securities Exchange Act of 1934, require all companies listing on U.S. exchanges to disclose information conforming to U.S. Generally Accepted Accounting Principles, GAAP. If investors value the security provided by the disclosure requirements, then more shares may be sold by issuing shares in the United States. In other words, it is probably because U.S. reporting

EXHIBIT 21.2
Going Abroad: The Appeal of Euroequities

If capital markets are integrated it does not matter in which country a company issues shares; people will buy them wherever they live. The fact that U.S. companies have sold some of their shares overseas is evidence that markets are not fully integrated, posing the important question of why this is so. In a survey of the Chief Financial Officers (CFOs) of large firms issuing Euroequities during 1985–1988, Wayne Marr, John Trimble, and Raj Varma found an answer. As the excerpt below indicates, they found that the preference for bearer shares by non-U.S. investors and the requirement of the U.S. Securities Exchange Commission (SEC) that U.S.-based shares be registered in the owners' names has encouraged some large U.S. companies to sell shares in the Euromarket.

On more than 200 occasions since 1985, American corporations have raised capital with a new kind of equity offering made available simultaneously to U.S. and foreign investors. Such "Euroequity" issues have also been considerably larger, on average, than traditional domestic equity offerings during the same period. It's true that U.S. companies have long had the option of listing their stock on foreign exchanges, and thus expanding the potential market for their securities. But, for all except a handful of the largest American firms, such listings have not proved a cost-effective method of raising new equity.

What is behind the rise and rapid growth of these overseas equity sales? In an informal survey of the CFOs of U.S. issuers, we found the most common reason for choosing Euroequity was "to take advantage of our good name in overseas markets." But what does this mean? The financing advantages of having a "good name in overseas markets" may be various and thus difficult to quantify. But presumably chief among them is that European investors are willing to pay a higher price for the company's shares—or, alternatively, their added demand enables the issuer to sell a greater quantity of its shares than otherwise without being forced to drop the price.

For financial economists, however, such an alleged financing bargain is puzzling. The existence of a price differential large enough to influence the financing decisions of U.S. corporations appears to run counter to the conventional economic wisdom that international capital markets are becoming progressively more "integrated." And such integration in turn implies that the free flow of capital across international boundaries should erase all but minor and momentary differences in capital costs. How, therefore, does one explain the sudden popularity of Euroequity? And are there genuine equity cost savings for corporate issuers?

[T]he findings of our recently completed study of 32 Euroequity issues by nonfinancial firms between 1985 and 1988 [reveal] market-based evidence of significant savings by issuers. . . . [A]n explanation for these savings—one that centers on recent changes in U.S. tax laws and Treasury Department regulations—[is] that Euroequities allow overseas investors to hold *bearer* shares in U.S. corporations. Thanks to new registration procedures cleared by the SEC, such bearer shares can often be made as liquid as the registered shares traded in U.S. capital markets.

Source: Wayne Marr, John L. Trimble, and Raj Varma, "Innovation in Global Financing: The Case of Euroequity Offerings," *Journal of Applied Corporate Finance*, spring 1992, pp. 50–54.

rules are more stringent than those of some foreign stock exchanges that so many foreign firms have found it necessary to list in the United States to tap the huge U.S. equity market; American and other nationals would otherwise be more wary about buying the stocks.

While some non-U.S. firms have listed on U.S. stock exchanges—mostly the New York Stock Exchange and NASDAQ—the shares of many more foreign firms trade indirectly as **American Depository Receipts** (ADRs). The idea of trading ADRs originated with the Morgan Guarantee Bank, but several other U.S. banks, including Citibank, Chase Manhattan, and the Bank of New York, have become involved. What happens is that the bank holds the foreign shares; receives dividends, reports, and so on; but issues claims against the shares it holds.[3] These claims—the

---

[3]In the terminology of Chapter 18, the bank acts as the global custodian.

ADRs—then generally trade in the relatively unregulated over-the-counter market. This has the advantage for foreign firms of reducing listing fees and the information that they must report.

When we mentioned that the highest price a firm could obtain for its shares, net of issuance costs, is in the market with the lowest required rate of return, we assumed that the costs of issue are the same everywhere. The correct rule for where to issue shares is that they should be sold where the price *net of issue costs* is the highest.

In fact, issue costs do vary and can be an important consideration. The costs of underwriting can be several percent of the value of funds raised and can vary significantly between financial markets. Generally, the lowest costs are faced in large equity markets such as that of the United States. This may explain why a substantial number of foreign companies have sold shares on the New York Stock Exchange and NASDAQ. Indeed, as Figure 21.1 shows, there has been a substantial increase in the number and value of foreign shares listed on the New York Stock Exchange.

The Vehicle of Share Issue

A firm that has decided to issue shares abroad must decide whether to issue them directly, or to do so indirectly via a subsidiary located abroad. There is frequently a motive to use a specially established financing subsidiary to avoid the need to withhold tax on payments made to foreigners. For example, many U.S. firms established

Figure 21.1. Number and Size of Foreign Securities Listed on the NYSE
(*Source:* New York Stock Exchange, *Fact Book,* issues for 1965–1992.)

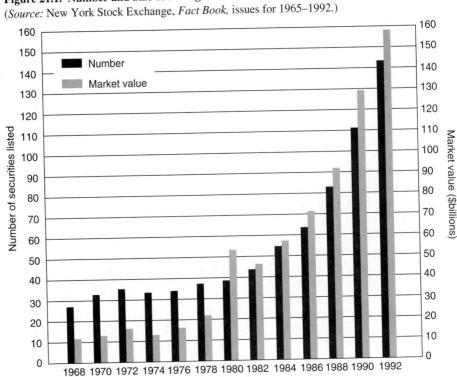

subsidiaries in the Netherlands Antilles and other tax havens to avoid having to withhold 30 percent of dividend or interest income paid to foreigners. As explained in Appendix 19.1, the U.S. financing subsidiaries took advantage of a ruling of the U.S. Internal Revenue Service that if 80 percent or more of a corporation's income is earned abroad, then dividends and interest paid by the corporation are considered foreign and not subject to the need to withhold. To the extent that foreign creditors or shareholders of U.S. companies could not receive full credit for taxes withheld, they would pay more for securities issued by U.S. subsidiaries than for the securities of the parent company in the United States.

BOND FINANCING

The same two issues arise with bond financing as with equity financing, namely, (1) the country of issue and (2) the vehicle of issue. However, an extra issue arises with bond financing: the *currency* of issue.

The currency of issue is not the same as the country of issue, although the two may coincide. For example, if a U.S. company sells a pound-denominated bond in Britain, the currency of issue is that of the country of issue. However, if a U.S. company sells a U.S.-dollar-denominated bond in Britain, the currency of issue is not that of the country of issue. In the former of these situations the bond is called a **foreign bond;** in the latter it is called a **Eurobond.** Let us provide a more general description of foreign bonds and Eurobonds.

Foreign Bonds versus Eurobonds

A foreign bond is a bond sold in a foreign country in the currency of the country of issue. This borrower is foreign to the country of issue, hence the name. For example, a Canadian firm or a provincial government might sell a foreign bond in New York denominated in U.S. dollars. Similarly, a Brazilian company might sell a German-mark-denominated bond in Germany.

A Eurobond is a bond that is denominated in a currency that is not that of the country in which it is issued. For example, a U.S.-dollar-denominated bond sold outside of the United States—in Europe or elsewhere—is a Eurobond, a **Eurodollar bond.** Similarly, a sterling-denominated bond sold outside of Britain is a Eurobond, a **Eurosterling bond.** Table 21.1 shows the sizes of the foreign bond and Eurobond markets, and the dominance of the dollar in the Eurobond market.

Foreign bonds are usually sold by brokers who are located in the country in which the bonds are issued. Eurobonds are sold by international syndicates of brokers, because they are generally sold simultaneously in a number of countries. The syndicates will normally have a lead manager which underwrites the largest proportion of the issue, and a number of smaller members, although some syndicates have co-lead managers. Table 21.2 shows the names of the top 25 lead managers in the market.

Selecting the Currency of Issue

Whether a firm issues a foreign bond, a Eurobond, or an ordinary domestic bond, it must decide on the bond's currency of denomination. Of course, with foreign bonds

TABLE 21.1. The Eurobond and Foreign Bond Markets, 1993

Eurobonds by Currency			Foreign Bonds by Country		
Currency	Amount, Billion U.S.$ Equivalent	Share, %	Country	Amount, Billion U.S.$ Equivalent	Share, %
U.S. dollar	147.7	37.4	U.S.	35.4	41.0
Deutschemark	54.7	13.9	Switzerland	27.0	31.3
Yen	44.4	11.3	Japan	15.2	17.6
Sterling	42.7	10.8	Luxembourg	3.5	4.1
French franc	39.9	10.1	Spain	3.0	3.5
Canadian dollar	29.3	7.4	Netherlands	0.9	0.1
Italian lira	11.5	2.9	Portugal	0.6	0.1
Dutch guilder	11.1	2.8	United Kingdom*	0.0	0.0
ECU	7.1	1.8	Other	0.8	0.1
Australian dollar	3.5	0.9			
Danish kroner	1.1	0.3			
Swedish kroner	0.5	0.1			
Finnish markka	0.1	0.0			
New Zealand dollar	0.1	0.0			
Other	0.9	0.2			
Total	394.6	100.0†			

*Less than $0.05 billion.
†Slight discrepancy from rounding error.
Source: Organization for Economic Cooperation and Development. © OECD, 1994, *Financial Market Trends* No. 57. Reproduced by permission of the OECD.

the currency of denomination is that of the country of issue, so deciding on the currency of denomination is the same as deciding on the country of issue; with Eurobonds the currency and the country or countries of issue must both be decided.

Suppose that Aviva is neutral to exchange-rate risk and is choosing between denominating a bond in pounds and in dollars.[4] For simplicity, let us assume all payments are made at maturity.[5] Writing $r_\$$ for the annual interest cost of a dollar-denominated bond, Aviva's eventual payment on a n-year bond per dollar raised is

$$\$\left(1 + r_\$\right)^n$$

Each $1 raised by selling a pound-denominated bond means raising £$1/S(\$/£)$. Assuming again that all payments are made at maturity, Aviva's payment in terms of pounds per dollar raised on an n-year bond is

$$£\,\frac{1}{S(\$/£)}\left(1 + r_£\right)^n$$

[4]Later we drop the assumption of risk neutrality and show how having pound receivables can make pound borrowing *preferred* on grounds of foreign-exchange exposure and risk reduction.
[5]If we drop this assumption and allow for periodic coupons, the algebra is more complex but the conclusion is the same.

TABLE 21.2. Top 25 Lead Managers in the Eurobond Market, January–June 1994

Rank	Bank/Firm	Amount, Million U.S. $	No. of Issues	Share, %
1	Merrill Lynch	18,598.3	80	9.53
2	Goldman Sachs	13,495.3	52	6.91
3	CS First Boston	12,557.5	44	6.43
4	Union Bank of Switzerland	8,497.5	25	4.35
5	Morgan Stanley	8,473.3	52	4.34
6	Deutsche Bank	8,472.2	37	4.34
7	JP Morgan	7,702.5	31	3.95
8	Lehman Brothers	7,109.6	31	3.64
9	Nomura Securities	6,458.8	42	3.31
10	Swiss Bank Corp	6,275.2	31	3.21
11	Daiwa Securities	6,091.3	29	3.12
12	Société Générale	5,665.5	21	2.90
13	Nikko Securities	5,579.6	28	2.86
14	Salomon Brothers	4,891.8	24	2.51
15	Banque Paribas	4,639.7	23	2.38
16	ABN Amro Bank	4,415.5	29	2.26
17	HSBC Group	3,714.6	19	1.90
18	Dresdner Bank	3,342.2	9	1.71
19	Industrial Bank of Japan	3,305.4	24	1.69
20	Barclays de Zoete Wedd	3,304.7	23	1.69
21	SG Warburg	3,128.0	17	1.60
22	Crédit Commercial de France	3,109.9	13	1.59
23	Kidder Peabody	2,597.3	15	1.33
24	Crédit Lyonnais	2,452.2	10	1.26
25	Citicorp	1,959.4	14	1.00

Source: *Euromoney,* September 1994, p. 292.

where $r_£$ is the annual interest cost on a pound-denominated bond. The expected dollar cost of this payment is

$$\$ \, \frac{S_n^*(\$/£)}{S(\$/£)} \left(1 + r_£\right)^n$$

where $S_n^*(\$/£)$ is the expected exchange rate at the end of year n.[6] Aviva will prefer floating the pound bond if

$$\frac{S_n^*(\$/£)}{S(\$/£)} \left(1 + r_£\right)^n < \left(1 + r_\$\right)^n \tag{21.1}$$

Writing

---

[6]We use the expected future spot rate rather than the forward rate because forward cover may not be available for the maturity of a long-term bond. Of course, so far we have assumed Aviva is neutral to any exchange-rate risk involving the bond.

$$S_n^*(\$/£) \equiv S(\$/£) \cdot \left[1 + \dot{S}^*(\$/£)\right]^n$$

where $\dot{S}^*(\$/£)$ is the expected average annual rate of change of the spot exchange rate, inequality (21.1) becomes

$$\left[1 + \dot{S}^*(\$/£)\right]^n (1 + r_£)^n < (1 + r_\$)^n$$

Taking the nth root of both sides, rearranging, and ignoring the cross-product term $\dot{S}^*(\$/£) \cdot r_£$, we have[7]

$$r_£ + \dot{S}^*(\$/£) < r_\$ \tag{21.2}$$

That is, if inequality (21.2) holds, Aviva should denominate its bond in the pound rather than the dollar. (If Aviva sells a pound bond in Britain, the bond is a foreign bond, and if it sells the pound bond in some country other than Britain, it is a Eurosterling bond.) Alternatively, if interest rates and expected exchange rates are such that

$$r_£ + \dot{S}^*(\$/£) > r_\$ \tag{21.3}$$

Aviva should sell a U.S.-dollar-denominated bond, whether this be sold in the United States, making it an ordinary domestic bond, or outside the United States, making it a Eurodollar bond.

For example, suppose as before that Aviva is risk-neutral and the borrowing costs and Aviva's expected change in the exchange rate are as follows:

$r_\$$	$r_£$	$\dot{S}^*(\$/£)$
10%	14%	−5%

That is, Aviva sees a higher borrowing cost for the firm on pound-denominated bonds, but also expects a decline in the foreign exchange value of the pound against the dollar of 5 percent per annum over the life of the bond. It would be advantageous to denominate in terms of pounds, assuming Aviva is not averse to risk involving exchange rates, because in the example

$$r_\$ > r_£ + \dot{S}^*(\$/£)$$

Ex post, the actual exchange rate will often change by a considerable amount over the life of a bond, creating a potential for sizable gains or losses. In other words, actual changes can deviate markedly from the changes which had been expected by the firm. History is full of examples of currencies which have changed in value against the dollar by substantial amounts. Even some of the major currencies have moved considerably in value over a number of years. Relatively small annual changes in exchange rates build up into very large changes over the life of long-term bonds.

To show how great the mistake can be, we can examine the results of a survey by William R. Folks, Jr., and Josef Follpracht. These results are shown in Table 21.3. Folks and Follpracht examined the cost of a number of foreign-currency-denominated bonds issued by U.S.-based multinational firms over the period July 1969 to December 1972. The table allows us to compare the coupon rates with the

---

[7]As we have noted before, the cross-product term is typically very small.

TABLE 21.3. Costs of Foreign-Currency Bonds

Currency	Issue	Coupon Rate, %/yr	Before-Tax Cost of Borrowing, %/yr
Deutschemark	Studebaker-Worthington	7 1/4	14.69
	International Standard Electric	7	12.31
	TRW	7 1/2	12.38
	Tenneco	7 1/2	12.33
	Tenneco	7 3/4	12.77
	Kraftco	7 1/2	12.27
	Continental Oil	8	15.83
	Transocean Gulf	7 1/2	12.50
	Firestone	7 3/4	11.83
	Philip Morris	6 3/4	9.87
	Goodyear	7 1/4	10.44
	Teledyne	7 1/4	10.44
Swiss franc	Burroughs	6 1/4	12.31
	Standard Oil (California)	6 1/4	12.42
	Goodyear	7	13.69
	American Brands	6 1/2	13.08
	Texaco	6 3/4	13.37
	Cities Services	7 1/4	19.27
Dutch guilder	General Electric	8 1/4	20.08
	GTE	8 1/4	19.44
	IBM	8	16.46
	Cities Service	8	17.65
	International Harvester	8	17.65
	Philip Morris	7 1/2	12.67
	Sperry Rand	6 1/2	10.44
	Holiday Inns	6 1/2	10.62
	Teledyne	6 1/4	10.27
	Standard Brands	6 1/2	10.85
	Textron Atlantic	6 3/4	11.21
Pound sterling	Amoco	8	5.29
Luxembourg franc	International Standard Electric	6 1/2	7.85

Source: William R. Folks, Jr., and Josef Follpracht, "The Currency of Denomination Decision for Offshore Long-Term Debt: The American Experience," working paper, Center for International Business Studies, University of South Carolina, 1976.

eventual effective annual costs computed as of March 1976 or at the bonds' maturities. We can see that the appreciation of the German mark, Swiss franc, Dutch guilder, and Luxembourg franc made the borrowing costs of bonds considerably higher than the rates given by the coupons. We cannot tell whether the costs were high compared with the dollar rates that were available when the bonds were originally sold, but there is good reason to believe that they were. The only foreign-currency bond which turned out to be advantageous as of March 1976 was the pound-sterling bond. The fall in value of the pound reduced the effective dollar repayment cost by over 2.7 percent per annum. The conclusion depends on where

523

the examination ends, but it does show that what may appear to be a cheap debt may end up being expensive.

Because of the potential for large unanticipated costs when borrowing by issuing bonds in currencies that rapidly appreciate, some nontrivial advantage may be required before any added exposure by foreign-currency borrowing is considered worthwhile. In such a case, our criteria (21.2) and (21.3) need some modification. For example, if management determines that any added foreign exchange exposure and risk will be worth taking only with an expected 2 percent saving, we must revise condition (21.2) to the following:

$$r_\$ > r_£ + \dot{S}^*(\$/£) + 0.02 \tag{21.4}$$

Only when (21.4) holds will the expected borrowing cost be sufficiently lower in pounds to warrant borrowing in that currency. For example, if $r_\$$ is 10 percent, $r_£$ is 14 percent, and $\dot{S}^*(\$/£)$ is −5 percent (a 5-percent-per-annum expected depreciation of the pound), then the exposure and risk of borrowing in pounds will not be warranted, for although the criterion (21.2) is met, the revised criterion (21.4) is not.

When foreign-currency bonds do add to exposure and risk, the required risk premiums will have to be established by management. During times of greater economic uncertainty and potential volatility in foreign exchange markets, higher premiums should generally be required to compensate for the greater risk. Borrowing in a foreign currency involves risk because the actual rate of change of the exchange rate, $\dot{S}(\$/£)$ in the dollar-pound case, will in general differ from the *ex ante* expectation, $\dot{S}^*(\$/£)$. If $\dot{S}(\$/£) > \dot{S}^*(\$/£)$, this will make the *ex post* borrowing cost greater than the *ex ante* cost.

For example, if as before we have $r_\$ = 10$ percent, $r_£ = 14$ percent, and $\dot{S}^*(\$/£) = -5$ percent, then by using the straightforward *ex ante* criteria in inequalities (21.2) and (21.3), we know that the U.S. borrower facing these particular conditions should borrow in pounds. Suppose that this is done and that *ex post* we discover that $\dot{S}(\$/£) = -2$ percent. The actual cost of borrowing in pounds will be

$$r_£ + \dot{S}(\$/£) = 0.14 - 0.02 = 0.12, \text{ or } 12 \text{ percent per annum}$$

Having borrowed in pounds will in retrospect turn out to have been a bad idea via-à-vis the 10 percent dollar interest rate.

In general, if it turns out that $\dot{S}(\$/£)$, the actual per annum change in the exchange rate, has been such that

$$r_£ + \dot{S}(\$/£) > r_\$$$

then we know that borrowing in pounds was a mistake. We see that it is necessary to compare the actual, not the expected, per annum change in the exchange rate with the interest differential. A management-determined risk premium such as the 0.02 premium we used in writing the revised criterion in inequality (21.4) will help to ensure that correct decisions are made. The larger the required premiums, the more often the decision will in retrospect appear correct, but larger premiums also mean missing many opportunities, and they will never guarantee *ex post* correct decisions.

Borrowing with Foreign-Source Income

There may be *less* foreign exchange exposure and risk involved in foreign-currency borrowing than in domestic-currency borrowing when the borrower is receiving income in foreign exchange and is facing a long exposure in the foreign currency. That is, foreign-currency receivables can require a *negative* premium when borrowing in foreign exchange because exposure is reduced. We have already pointed out in Chapters 12 and 15 that firms receiving foreign income can hedge by borrowing foreign funds in the money market. The point is even more valid with long-term borrowing and is extremely important for firms which have sizable foreign operations. When a steady and predictable long-term income is received in foreign currency, it makes sense to denominate some long-term payments in that same currency. The amount of debt that should be denominated in each foreign currency will depend on the size of income in that currency, and also on the extent that the firm's income is exposed. As we showed in Chapter 14, the exposure depends on the elasticity of demand, the flexibility of production, the proportion of inputs that are tradable, and so on. That is, it is not simply a matter of borrowing enough in a foreign currency so that debt payments match income in the currency.

An example of a situation where the sale of bonds denominated in foreign exchange will reduce foreign exchange exposure and risk involves a Canadian firm that sells Canadian resources in world markets at contracted amounts in U.S. dollars.[8] If lumber or coal is sold by the Canadian firm to, for example, the U.S. or Japanese market at prices stated in U.S. dollars, then the firm faces a long exposure in U.S. dollars, and it makes good sense for the firm to borrow in New York, Europe, or Canada in U.S. dollars. Then the repayments on the debt can come out of the firm's U.S. dollar revenues. Alternatively, losses on the dollars earned after a U.S. dollar depreciation are matched by a gain in the form of reduced debt when this is translated into Canadian dollars. Similarly, if an Australian manufacturer is selling to Japan in yen, it makes sense to borrow with yen-denominated bonds, or if a Venezuelan oil exporter is selling to Chile in dollars, it makes good sense to borrow by selling U.S.-dollar-denominated bonds in the Eurobond market or in the United States.

Tax Considerations

Bond buyers who pay a lower tax rate on capital gains than on interest income prefer a dollar of capital gain from foreign-currency appreciation to a dollar of interest income. This means that if, for example, the dollar-bond interest rate was equal to the yen-bond rate plus the expected appreciation of the yen, the yen bond would be preferred because it provides expected capital gain from an appreciation of the yen. It follows that bond buyers who pay a lower tax rate on capital gains, *ceteris paribus,* prefer bonds denominated in strong currencies, those that the market expects to appreciate. On the other hand, bond issuers who can deduct the full cost of their bonds as an expense of doing business will be indifferent between interest rates and expected changes in exchange rate. This will lead to borrowing in strong currencies. Let us explain this by an example. The example assume a particular tax situation to illustrate one possibility. Other assumptions will produce different outcomes.

[8]Virtually all natural-resource exports—oil, coal, gas, minerals, and lumber—are sold at U.S. dollar prices. This reduces the foreign exchange problem for U.S.-based firms that sell or buy natural resources.

Suppose that

$$r_\$ = 12\% \qquad r_¥ = 5\% \qquad \dot{S}^*(\$/¥) = 6\%$$

$$\tau_k = 0.2 \qquad \tau_y = 0.4$$

where $\dot{S}^*(\$/¥)$ is the expected appreciation of the Japanese yen by both bond issuers and buyers, $r_¥$ is the interest rate on yen bonds, τ_k is the tax rate on foreign exchange gains of bond buyers, and τ_y is the tax rate on ordinary income, including interest income, of both bond buyers and bond issuers. The after-tax expected returns from U.S. dollar and yen bonds to bond *buyers* are:

Dollar bond : $\quad (1 - \tau_y)r_\$ = (1 - 0.4) \times 0.12 = 7.2$ percent

Yen bond : $\quad (1 - \tau_y)r_¥ + (1 - \tau_k) \times \dot{S}^*(\$/¥) = (1 - 0.4) \times 0.05$

$$+ (1 - 0.2) \times 0.06 = 7.8 \text{ percent}$$

The buyers therefore prefer yen bonds to dollar bonds; they yield more after tax. However, to *borrowers* who can deduct the full cost of bond capital—interest plus exchange-rate movements—against income, the after-tax costs are

Dollar bond : $\quad (1 - \tau_y)r_\$ = (1 - 0.4) \times 0.12 = 7.2$ percent

Yen bond : $\quad (1 - \tau_y)r_¥ + (1 - \tau_y) \times \dot{S}^*(\$/¥) = (1 - 0.4) \times 0.05$

$$+ (1 - 0.4) \times 0.06 = 6.6 \text{ percent}$$

Bond issuers therefore also prefer yen bonds. We see that tax factors can explain the popularity of strong-currency-denominated bonds—those widely expected to appreciate—among bond buyers and bond sellers.

Other Bond-Financing Considerations

Issue Cost

Bond flotation costs are lower in some financial markets than in others. Because flotation costs are nontrivial, the differences in costs between financial markets can influence the country in which bonds are floated.[9] Firms should approach a number of bond underwriters situated in different countries before determining where to issue bonds. With markets in most of the European financial centers, as well as in Asia and North America, and with considerable variation in the flotation costs within and between these financial centers, the benefits of shopping around can be substantial.

Issue Size

Another factor bond issuers should consider when issuing bonds is the size of the issue relative to the sizes of issues handled in different markets. The New York

[9]Rodney Mills and Henry Terrell have shown that front-end fees on Eurobonds on an interest-equivalent basis account for an average of approximately 20 percent of one year's annual return, and vary between 9 percent and 43 percent. See Rodney H. Mills and Henry S. Terrell, "The Determination of Front-End Fees on Syndicated Eurocurrency Credits," International Finance Discussion Paper Number 250, Board of Governors of the Federal Reserve System, Washington, D.C., undated.

and London capital markets can handle very large individual bond issues. In many of the other capital markets of the world, a $200 million bond issue would be considered large, and a $500 million bond issue would be huge. In New York or London, such issues are not uncommon. Indeed, the volume of funds handled by some of the bigger institutions such as the pension funds and insurance companies is such that these institutions can often buy an entire bond issue that is privately placed with them. The bond-issue size that the New York and London markets can handle and the lower costs of issuing bonds under private placement make New York and London attractive markets for large American and foreign borrowers, even when the interest cost of funds is a little higher than elsewhere.[10]

Multicurrency Bonds

Types of Multicurrency Bonds

Not all Eurobonds are denominated in a single currency. Rather, some Eurobonds are **multicurrency bonds.** Some multicurrency bonds give the lender the right to request repayment in one or two or more currencies. The amounts of repayment are often set equal in value at the exchange rates in effect when the bond is issued. If, during the life of the bond, exchange rates change, the lender will demand payments in the currency that has appreciated the most or depreciated the least. This reduces the risk to the lender in that it can help him or her avoid a depreciating currency. It does, however, add to the borrower's risk.

A variant of the multicurrency Eurobond using pre-established fixed exchange rates is the **unit-of-account bond,** such as the European Currency Unit (ECU) bond. As Table 21.1 shows, less than 2 percent of Eurobonds took this form in 1993, compared to 13 percent in 1991. The loss of popularity of ECU bonds coincided with the disintegration of the European Monetary System. The idea of denominating bonds in a "cocktail" of currencies is to reduce the risk from individual exchange-rate changes; the currency unit is a portfolio of currencies and enjoys diversification advantages. Another unit-of-account that can be used is the SDR, which was discussed in Chapter 9.

Currency cocktails can offer significant savings. For example, in January 1981 the rate on a 5-year SDR-denominated bond offered by Nordic Investment Bank was approximately 11.5 percent, while at the same time the rate on a straight 10-year U.S. dollar bond offered by Du Pont of Canada was 13.69 percent, and the rate on a 7-year bond offered by GM's offshore finance subsidiary, General Motors Acceptance Corporation (or GMAC) Overseas Finance N.V., was 12.87 percent. While the rates are not strictly comparable, the lower rate on the SDR bond shows that investors value the diversification of currency cocktails. They will be particularly desirable during unstable times.[11]

---

[10]The importance of transaction costs and the size of borrowing in encouraging Canadian borrowers to look at the United States capital market is examined by Karl A. Stroetmann in "The Theory of Long-Term International Capital Flows and Canadian Corporate Debt Issues in the United States," unpublished Ph.D. dissertation, University of British Columbia, 1974.

[11]For more on SDR bonds, see "Slimmed-Down SDR Makes Comeback: Techniques Include Opening Up Market for Negotiable SDR C.D.'s," *Money Report,* Business International, January 16, 1981.

The Rationale for Multicurrency Bonds

Bond buyers can form their own multicurrency bond portfolios by combining different bonds, each of which is denominated in a single currency. Because this is possible, it is worth asking why some firms have found it advantageous to issue multicurrency bonds. The answer must be that there are limitations faced by some bond buyers in forming their own portfolios. One possible limitation is that the total wealth they have to allocate to bonds is too small to achieve significant diversification, which in turn depends on there being economies of scale when buying bonds; if the costs do not increase as smaller amounts of bonds are bought, the bond buyers can form diversified portfolios of separate bonds as cheaply as buying multicurrency bonds. This size-of-wealth limitation may be a major consideration with bonds, which are frequently sold only in very large minimum denominations.

An example of multicurrency denomination of a lease contract rather than a bond involved the Australian carrier Qantas Airlines. In 1980 Qantas arranged to lease two Boeing 747s from an owner who was willing to accept multicurrency payment. The lease required payment in German marks, Dutch guilders, Australian dollars, and pounds sterling—all currencies that the airline received in its business. With this arrangement, Qantas could match the multicurrency nature of its income with the payments on the lease. If Qantas had bought rather than leased the planes, it could have matched the currencies of incomes and payments by financing the planes with a currency-cocktail Eurobond requiring repayment in the various currencies of income.

The Vehicle of Bond Issue

Whether the bond that is issued is a Eurobond, foreign bond, or domestic bond, and whether it is denominated in a single currency or in several currencies, a decision must be made either to issue the bond directly as a liability of the parent company or to issue it indirectly through a financing subsidiary or some other subsidiary. Companies issue bonds via an overseas subsidiary if they do not want the bonds to be an obligation of the parent company. This has the additional advantage of reducing country risk if some of the subsidiary's bonds are held locally (see Chapter 20). However, because the parent is almost invariably viewed as less risky than subsidiaries, the reduction in the parent's liability and also in country risk must be traded off against the fact that the interest rates that must be paid are generally higher when having a subsidiary issue bonds.

BANK FINANCING, DIRECT LOANS, AND THE LIKE

So far we have examined international aspects of equity and bond financing. We have stated that gains on selling equity in one market rather than another or simultaneously in several markets—Euroequities—depend on the segmentation versus integration of markets. We have also stated that bonds may be sold in a foreign-currency denomination in the country using that currency (foreign bonds) or in countries not using the denomination currency (Eurobonds). The ability to select the currency of issue can lower borrowing costs but can also introduce foreign exchange exposure and risk because forward markets are generally not available for

TABLE 21.4. Sources of Funds for Subsidiaries

	Billions of Dollars			Percentage	
From within the multinational enterprise			6.1		60
Internally generated by affiliate		4.7		46	
Depreciation	2.9			29	
Retained earnings	1.7			17	
From parent		1.4		14	
Equity	1.0			9	
Loans	0.5			5	
From outside the multinational enterprise			4.0		40
Loans		3.9		39	
Equity		0.2		2	
Total			10.1		100

Source: U.S. Department of Commerce, Office of Foreign Direct Investments, *Foreign Affiliate Financial Survey, 1966–1969,* July 1971, p. 34.

hedging on bonds. However, a firm might actually reduce foreign exchange exposure and risk by borrowing in a foreign currency if it has an income in that currency.

A large part of the financing of foreign subsidiaries of MNCs involves neither bonds nor equity. According to a survey of foreign direct investors by the U.S. Department of Commerce, approximately half of the financing of U.S.-based MNCs was generated inside the corporation.[12] The results of the survey are summarized in Table 21.4. If anything, the true percentage of internally generated funds is probably larger than the percentage shown because, according to a different survey by Sidney Robbins and Robert Stobaugh, lending and borrowing by different subsidiaries net out in the Commerce Department's financial survey.[13] Robbins and Stobaugh estimated that the total for outstanding loans was $14 billion. This amount is much larger than the amount quoted for loans outstanding to the parent companies in the Commerce Department's survey. We can note from Table 21.4 that subsidiaries raise little equity. The debt incurred by subsidiaries is almost 20 times the equity they themselves raise.

When a subsidiary borrows from its parent, because this is a transfer within the MNC, there is no increase in the expected cost of bankruptcy which is usually considered to be a factor limiting the debt/equity ratio of a firm. (Firms prefer debt to equity because interest on debt is tax-deductible, but too much debt means a higher chance of bankruptcy.) A subsidiary is able to deduct its interest payments from income when computing corporate tax, while the parent treats the interest as income. This has an advantage if the subsidiary's tax rate is higher than that of the parent. However, the incentive to use all intra-MNC debt to finance a subsidiary is limited by the need to rationalize the interest rate charged to the subsidiary. According to

[12]U.S. Department of Commerce, Office of Foreign Direct Investments, *Foreign Affiliate Financial Survey, 1966–1969,* July 1971. This study has not been revised, because the office that prepared it was eliminated; but the proportion of funds generated within the corporation has probably not changed greatly.
[13]Sidney M. Robbins and Robert B. Stobaugh, "Financing Foreign Affiliates," *Financial Management,* winter 1973, pp. 56–65.

Bhagwan Chowdhry and Vikram Nanda, subsidiaries use some external debt to justify the interest rate charged on internal debt.[14]

According to the survey by Robbins and Stobaugh mentioned above, most MNCs prefer to use intracompany credit rather than discretionary loans. This is because credit requires less documentation than does a discretionary loan and because there are potential gains from avoidance of withholding tax on credit advances, whereas withholding by the foreign government is likely on interdivisional loans.

Some of the earliest work in financing subsidiaries, done by Edith Penrose, revealed a varying financial structure as MNCs' subsidiaries grew larger.[15] Penrose argued that after receiving initial help from the parent company, subsidiaries move onto an independent growth path using funds from retained earnings and local borrowing. James Hines has suggested that the motivation to provide initial help from the parent is limited by the rational expectation that rather than repatriate future income and pay taxes, multinationals will prefer to reinvest subsidiary income in further expansion.[16] This view is consistent with that of Penrose: subsidiary self-financing expands with time. Hines argues that the incentive to minimize initial help in order to preserve future investment opportunities for a subsidiary is highest when foreign corporate income tax rates are low vis-à-vis parent rates.

Some of the debt raised outside companies takes on a character which is peculiarly international. For example, only in the international arena do we find the so-called "back-to-back" or parallel loans.

Parallel Loans

A **parallel loan** involves an exchange of funds between firms in different countries, with the exchange reversed at a later date. For example, Figure 21.2*a* shows a situation in which a U.S. company's subsidiary in Brazil needs Brazilian reals while a Brazilian company's subsidiary in the United States needs dollars. The Brazilian firm can lend reals to the U.S.-owned subsidiary in Brazil while it borrows an approximately equivalent amount of dollars from the U.S. parent in the United States.[17] After an agreed-upon term, the funds can be repaid. There is no exchange-rate risk or exposure for either firm, because each is borrowing and repaying in the same currency. Each side can pay interest within the country where funds are lent according to the going market rates.

The advantages of parallel loans over bank loans are that they can circumvent

---

[14]Bhagwan Chowdhry and Vikram Nanda, "Financing of Multinational Subsidiaries: Parent Debt vs. External Debt," *Journal of Corporate Finance,* August 1994, pp. 259–281.

[15]Edith T. Penrose, "Foreign Investment and the Growth of the Firm," *Economic Journal,* June 1956, pp. 220–235. Reprinted in John H. Dunning (ed.), *International Investment,* Penguin Books, Harmondsworth, England, 1972.

[16]James R. Hines Jr., "Credit and Deferral as International Investment Incentives," *Journal of Public Economics,* forthcoming 1995.

[17]The loan agreement could just as well involve subsidiaries of the Brazilian and U.S. firms in a different country. For example, the U.S. firm might lend the Brazilian firm dollars in New York, while a German subsidiary of the Brazilian firm lends a German subsidiary of the U.S. firm German marks in Germany.

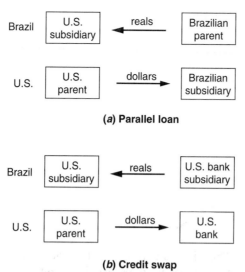

(a) Parallel loan

(b) Credit swap

Figure 21.2. Parallel Loans and Credit Swaps
A parallel loan involves two companies, whereas
a credit swap involves one company and a bank.
In both cases the companies and/or banks are
located in two countries. Both types of financing
avoid money flows between the countries.
Parallel loans are more difficult to arrange than
credit swaps because the parties must find each
other. In the case of a credit swap, all that is
needed is that the parent or its subsidiary
approach a bank.

foreign exchange controls and that they help avoid banks' spreads on borrowing
versus lending and on foreign exchange transactions. The problem with parallel
loans is locating the two sides of the deals. As in other barter deals, the needs of the
parties must be harmonious before a satisfactory contract can be achieved. While
the banks might well know of financing needs which are harmonious, they have little incentive to initiate a deal which avoids their spreads. Consequently, a large portion of parallel loans are arranged by brokerage houses rather than banks.

Credit Swaps

A **credit swap** involves the exchange of currencies between a bank and a firm
rather than between two firms. It is an alternative method of obtaining debt capital
for a foreign subsidiary without sending funds abroad. In a credit swap the parent
makes funds available to a bank at home. For example, a U.S. firm may place U.S.
dollars in an account in New York. The U.S. bank then instructs one of its foreign
subsidiaries to lend foreign currency to a subsidiary of the parent that made the
deposit. For example, an office of the U.S. bank in Rio de Janeiro might lend reals
to a subsidiary of the U.S. firm operating in Brazil: see Figure 21.2*b*. As with par-

allel loans, the major advantage of credit swaps is that they allow firms (and banks) to circumvent foreign exchange controls. In addition, they allow the parent and subsidiary to avoid foreign exchange exposure: the parent deposits and receives U.S. dollars in our example, while the subsidiary borrows and receives Brazilian reals.

GOVERNMENT AND DEVELOPMENT-BANK LENDING

It is not at all uncommon for financing to be provided by governments or development banks. Because government and development-bank financing is generally at favorable terms, many corporations consider these official sources of capital before considering the issue of stock, the sale of bonds, loans from commercial banks, or parallel loans from other corporations.

Host governments of foreign investments provide financing when they believe projects will generate jobs, earn foreign exchange, or provide training for their workers. There are numerous examples of loans being provided to MNCs by the governments of, for example, Australia, Britain, Canada, and Spain, to attract manufacturing firms to make investments in their countries. Sometimes the state or provincial governments also offer financing, perhaps even competing with each other within a country to have plants built in their area. Several U.S. states have provided cheap financing and other concessions to induce Japanese and other foreign firms to establish operations. Canadian provincial and Australian state governments have also used special financing arrangements to attract investors.

Even though the governments of poorer countries do not usually have the means to offer concessionary financing to investors, there are a number of development banks which specialize in providing financing for investment in infrastructure, for irrigation, and for similar projects. While this financing is usually provided to the host government rather than to corporations involved in the construction of the projects, the corporations are indirectly being financed by the development-bank loans to the host governments.

A leading provider of financial assistance is the International Bank for Reconstruction and Development (IBRD), commonly known as the World Bank. The World Bank, which was established in 1944, is not a bank in the sense of accepting deposits and providing payment services between countries. Rather, it is a lending institution that borrows from governments by selling them its bonds, and then uses the proceeds for development in undeveloped (or developing) nations. World Bank or IBRD loans have a maturity of up to 20 years. Interest rates are determined by the (relative low) cost of funds to the bank.

Many developing countries do not meet the conditions for World Bank loans, so in 1960 an affiliated organization, the **International Development Agency (IDA),** was established to help even poorer countries. Credits, as the loans are called, have terms of up to 50 years and carry no interest charges. A second affiliate of the World Bank is the **International Finance Corporation (IFC).** The IFC provides loans for private investments and takes equity positions along with private-sector partners.

OTHER FACTORS AFFECTING THE FINANCING OF SUBSIDIARIES

CHAPTER 21
International
Financing

We have presented a number of international financial considerations affecting bond and equity decisions and decisions involving bank loans, parallel loans, and credit swaps. There are, however, a number of other factors which can affect the financing decision. Frequently these are based on the politically sensitive nature of a large amount of foreign direct investment. Sometimes, however, they are based on concern for exchange-rate risk or on restrictions imposed by host governments. We shall quickly mention some of the more notable factors.

The freezing or seizing of assets by inhospitable governments should not be a worry to those who borrow abroad. Instead, it should be a concern to the investors whose assets are lost. It might therefore be thought that while political risks are important in the investment decision, they are relatively inconsequential in the borrowing decision. However, some firms may borrow abroad in the countries of investment *because* they fear confiscation or expropriation. If assets are seized, these firms can refuse to repay local debts and thereby reduce their losses. Furthermore, the probability of confiscation or expropriation may be reduced by having foreign private bondholders or shareholders. Unfortunately, as we have noted it may be difficult to raise equity or even debt from local private sources.

Generally, the more financing is denominated in local currency, the lower the danger from changing exchange rates. This supports the use of debt. Reinforcing the tendency toward using debt is the greater political sensitivity with regard to repatriating income on equity than with regard to receiving interest on debts. However, offsetting the factors leading to more debt is the fact that if equity is kept small, profits can look unreasonably high on the equity invested in foreign operations. The profit rate on equity can be used in claims of exploitation by foreign governments.

Certain governments require that a minimum equity/debt ratio be maintained, while some banks also set standards to maintain the quality of debt. According to Sidney Robbins and Robert Stobaugh, U.S. firms have generally kept their equity well above that required by local regulations.[18] However, this does not mean that local regulations are not binding. Firms may keep their equity higher than necessary as a cushion against any future need to borrow.

When earnings are retained abroad, U.S. corporations can postpone the payment of U.S. corporate income taxes and foreign withholding taxes on income from subsidiaries. According to Walter Ness, the saving from the deferral of tax payments lowers the cost of equity capital for multinational corporations and induces the corporations to have a lower debt/equity ratio in financing foreign subsidiaries.[19] However, according to Ian Giddy and Alan Shapiro, the alternatives for repatriating income via pricing of intersubsidiary trades, royalties, and interdivisional fees override any advantage from deferred tax payments encouraging the use of equity capital.[20]

[18]Robbins and Stobaugh, *op. cit.*

[19]Walter L. Ness, Jr., "U.S. Corporate Income Taxation and the Dividend Remittance Policy of Multinational Corporations," *Journal of International Business Studies,* spring 1975, pp. 67–77.

[20]Alan C. Shapiro, "Financial Structure and the Cost of Capital in Multinational Corporations," *Journal of Financial and Quantitative Analysis,* June 1979, pp. 211–226; Ian H. Giddy, "The Cost of Capital in the Multinational Firm," unpublished paper, Columbia University, 1976.

Subsidiary or Parent Determination of Financial Structure

If the success or failure of an overseas subsidiary has little or no effect on the ability of the parent or other subsidiaries to raise capital, decisions on financial structure can be left to subsidiaries.[21] A subsidiary can then weigh the various economic and political pros and cons of different sources of funds and adopt a financial structure that is appropriate for its own local circumstances. However, if there are spillovers from the failure of a subsidiary which reduce the financing opportunities of the parent or its other subsidiaries, decisions on subsidiary financial structure should be made by the parent. Full consideration should be given to the implications of a default by one subsidiary for global operations. Because spillovers will exist if the parent is legally or morally bound to support subsidiaries, we should consider the evidence on corporate responsibility for subsidiary debt.

Survey evidence shows clearly that even when not bound by legal guarantees on subsidiary-incurred debt, parent firms rarely if ever admit they will allow a subsidiary to default. For example, in a survey by Robert Stobaugh, all 20 of the large MNCs in the sample, and all but one of the smaller MNCs, said they would not allow a subsidiary to default whatever the circumstances.[22] Similar responses were received in later surveys conducted by *Business International.*[23] This evidence suggests that multinationals realize that a default in a subsidiary will affect operations elsewhere. There is no other explanation for the almost universal willingness to support subsidiaries.

With a parent company having a *de facto* obligation to honor debt incurred by its subsidiaries, the parent must monitor its subsidiaries' debt/equity ratios as well as the corporation's overall debt/equity ratio. This does not, however, mean that a parent should keep its subsidiaries' debt/equity ratios equal to its own overall preferred debt/equity ratio. For example, subsidiaries facing high country risk and no ability to raise local equity capital should be allowed to take on relatively high debt loads. Similarly, subsidiaries in countries with relatively high tax savings from deducting interest but not dividend payments should be allowed to take on relatively large amounts of debt to exploit the tax shield that debt provides. All the time, however, a parent company should make compensating adjustments to the capital structure of itself and its other subsidiaries so that the company's global debt/equity ratio is maintained at the level it deems appropriate.

Capital Structure in Different Countries

Financial structure varies greatly from country to country. This is seen clearly in Figure 21.3. Possible reasons for the variations can be found in explanations of cap-

[21]By financial structure we mean the composition of firm's sources of capital. That is, financial structure involves the amount of equity, versus bond debt, versus bank debt, versus credit swaps, and so on.
[22]Robert B. Stobaugh, "Financing Foreign Subsidiaries of U.S.-Controlled Multinational Enterprises," *Journal of International Business Studies,* summer 1970, pp. 43–64.
[23]Business International, Money Report, "Policies of MNC's in Debt/Equity Mix," 1979, and "Determining Overseas Debt/Equity Ratios," 1986.

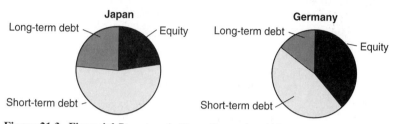

Figure 21.3. Financial Structure in Four Countries, 1985
(*Source:* Provided by Barclays Bank Economics Department, from *Barclays Review,* November 1986.)

ital structure commonly advanced in a domestic context. These explanations hinge on the tax deductability of interest payments but not dividends, and on bankruptcy and agency costs.

Countries in which interest payments are deductible against corporate taxes will, *ceteris paribus,* have relatively high debt/equity ratios. However, if interest rates are particularly high *because* borrowers can deduct interest and lenders must pay tax on interest, this will militate against the advantage of debt.[24]

The risk and expected cost of bankruptcy increase with the amount of debt.[25] If expected costs of bankruptcy are lower in some countries than others, debt/equity ratios will, *ceteris paribus,* be higher in the countries with low expected bankruptcy costs. In countries where banks are both providers of debt and holders of companies' equity, the probability of bankruptcy is relatively low because the banks are likely to help in times of trouble. It follows that in countries such as Japan and Germany, where banks hold considerable amounts of equity, debt/equity ratios are higher than in countries such as the United States and Canada, where banks provide debt but little or no equity.

Lenders know that once they have made loans to firms, the managers of the

---

[24]An account of the effect of differential tax shields that considers the role of both corporate and individual income tax rates has been provided by Moon H. Lee and Josef Zechner, "Debt, Taxes, and International Equilibrium," *Journal of International Money and Finance,* December 1984, pp. 343–355. Lee and Zechner point out that for there to be an advantage in debt, corporate relative to individual tax rates must be higher in one country than in other countries. This is because high individual tax rates on interest earnings push up interest rates and thereby reduce the attractiveness of debt. For debt to be attractive the corporate deductibility needs to be high relative to the extent interest rates are pushed higher by individual tax rates.

[25]The expected cost of bankruptcy depends on the probability that bankruptcy will occur as well as on legal and other costs if it does occur.

firms will be more concerned with taking care of their own and their shareholders' well-being than with protecting the lenders' interests. This is one of the **agency costs** of debt, and because lenders are aware of this cost, they demand corresponding high interest rates on their loans. These high interest rates reduce typical debt/equity ratios. The greater is the agency cost of debt, the lower is the typical debt/equity ratio. Agency costs are reduced when banks hold directorships in firms, because they can then very directly represent their interests as creditors when attending board meetings. The high degree of horizontal integration in Japan, where banks and manufacturers are frequently subdivisions of the same giant MNC, has greatly reduced agency costs, and this, combined with reduced expected bankruptcy costs, probably explains Japan's high debt-to-equity ratio.

SUMMARY

1. If capital markets are internationally integrated, the cost of capital should be the same wherever the capital is raised.
2. If capital markets are segmented, it pays to raise equity in the country in which the firm can sell its shares for the highest price. It may also pay to consider selling equity simultaneously in several countries; such shares are called Euroequities.
3. Low issuance costs may make some markets better than others for selling shares. Generally, the costs of selling shares are lowest in big financial markets such as New York.
4. Firms must decide on the best vehicle for issuing equity and raising other forms of capital. Should capital be raised by the parent company or a financing subsidiary?
5. A foreign bond is a bond sold in a foreign country and in the currency of that country. A Eurobond is a bond in a currency other than that of the country in which it is sold.
6. Firms must decide on the currency of issue of bonds. All foreign-pay bonds are by definition in a foreign currency for the firm, and many Eurobonds are also in a foreign currency for the firm.
7. Large gains or losses are possible from denominating bonds in currencies that are not part of a firm's income. For this reason a risk premium may be demanded before speculating by issuing foreign-currency-denominated bonds.
8. When a firm has foreign-currency income, foreign-currency borrowing reduces exchange-rate exposure. Therefore, a firm may be prepared to pay higher interest on a foreign-currency-denominated bond than on a bond denominated in domestic currency.
9. When bond buyers face lower tax rates on foreign exchange gains than on interest income, it may pay to issue strong-currency bonds. These will have relatively low interest rates because they offer bond buyers part of their return as capital gain.
10. Bond issuers should consider costs and sizes of bond issues when determining the country of issue.
11. Bonds denominated in two or more different currencies, called multicurrency or currency-cocktail bonds, will appeal to lenders if there are costs associated with forming portfolios of bonds denominated in single currencies.
12. A substantial proportion of financing of overseas subsidiaries is provided from within multinational corporations.
13. Parallel loans are made between firms. They are particularly useful when there are foreign exchange controls.
14. Credit swaps are made between banks and firms. They are also a way of avoiding foreign exchange controls.
15. Political risk can be reduced by borrowing in countries in which investment occurs; this tends to increase debt/equity ratios of subsidiaries.

16. Because parent companies tend to honor subsidiaries' debts whether legally obligated to do so or not, a parent company should monitor subsidiaries' debt/equity ratios as well as its own global debt/equity ratio. Nevertheless, parent companies should allow variations in debt/equity ratios between subsidiaries to take advantage of local situations.

17. If a country has a high debt/equity ratio, this can be because of high tax shields on debt or low bankruptcy or agency cost.

18. The links between banks and corporations in Japan, Germany, and some other countries may explain the high debt/equity ratios in these countries.

REVIEW QUESTIONS

1. What do integrated capital markets imply for the decision of where to raise capital?
2. What is a Euroequity?
3. What is an American Depository Receipt?
4. What is a foreign bond?
5. What is a Eurobond?
6. Under what condition will a risk-neutral borrower borrow pounds?
7. Why might some borrowers pay *more* to borrow foreign rather than domestic currency?
8. Why are strong-currency bonds preferred by lenders facing lower tax rates on capital gains than on interest income?
9. What is the advantage of a multicurrency bond to lenders?
10. What is a parallel loan?
11. What is a credit swap?
12. How does country risk affect parent versus subsidiary borrowing?
13. How does liability for debt affect parent versus subsidiary borrowing?
14. How might the extent of equity ownership by banks in different countries affect financial structure differences between countries?

ASSIGNMENT PROBLEMS

1. Why might a firm want to issue shares simultaneously in a number of financial centers?
2. How can the availability of savings and the opportunities for investment influence the cost of capital in different countries?
3. Is a U.S. dollar bond sold by a British firm in the United States a foreign bond or a Eurobond? How about a pound bond sold by a British firm in the United States?
4. Why do Canadian firms borrow so heavily in U.S. dollars?
5. When lenders are more optimistic about the future value of a currency than borrowers, what do you think this implies about the likelihood of debt denomination in that currency?
6. How is the tax shield on debt mitigated by a high tax rate on interest earnings, thereby making debt/equity ratios in different countries depend on individual income versus corporate tax rates?
7. With $r_\$ = 12.50$ percent, $r_£ = 14.00$ percent, $S(\$/£) = 2.25$, and $S_{10}^*(\$/£) = 1.50$, in which currency would you borrow? What is the total gain on each $1 million borrowed from making the correct choice?
8. If $r_\$ = 12.50$ percent, $r_£ = 14.00$ percent, and $S(\$/£) = 2.25$, what must the actual exchange rate after 10 years, $S_{10}(\$/£)$, be in order to make borrowing in pounds a good idea?
9. Why does having an income in foreign currency reduce required borrowing risk premiums? What type of risk—translation/transaction risk or operating risk—is reduced?

10. What determines whether you would issue a Eurosterling bond or a sterling bond (that is, a foreign bond) in Britain?

BIBLIOGRAPHY

BROWN, ROBERT L.: "Some Simple Conditions for Determining Swap Feasibility," unpublished, Monash University, Australia, 1986.

CHOWDHRY, BHAGWAN, and VIKRAM NANDA: "Financing of Multinational Subsidiaries: Parent Debt vs. External Debt," *Journal of Corporate Finance,* August 1994, pp. 259–281.

EDWARDS, FRANKLIN R.: "Listing of Foreign Securities on U.S. Exchanges," *Journal of Applied Corporate Finance,* winter 1993, pp. 28–36.

HODDER, JAMES E.: "Hedging International Exposure: Capital Structure Under Flexible Exchange Rates and Expropriation Risk," unpublished, Stanford University, 1982.

——— and LEMMA W. SENBET: "International Capital Structure Equilibrium," unpublished, Stanford University, 1988.

LEE, MOON H., and JOSEF ZECHNER: "Debt, Taxes, and International Equilibrium," *Journal of International Money and Finance,* December 1984, pp. 343–355.

LESSARD, DONALD R., and ALAN C. SHAPIRO: "Guidelines for Global Financing Choices," *Midland Corporate Finance Journal,* winter 1983, pp. 68–80.

MARR, WAYNE, JOHN L. TRIMBLE, and RAJ VARMA: "Innovation in Global Financing: The Case of Euroequity Offerings," *Journal of Applied Corporate Finance,* spring 1992, pp. 50–54.

NAUMAN-ETIENNE, RUDIGER: "A Framework for Financial Decisions in Multinational Corporations—A Summary of Recent Research," *Journal of Financial and Quantitative Analysis,* November 1974, pp. 859–875.

NESS, WALTER L., JR., "A Linear Approach to Financing the Multinational Corporation," *Financial Management,* winter 1972, pp. 88–100.

REMMERS, LEE, "A Note on Foreign Borrowing Costs," *Journal of International Business Studies,* fall 1980, pp. 123–134.

SHAPIRO, ALAN C., "Financial Structure and the Cost of Capital in the Multinational Corporation," *Journal of Financial and Quantitative Analysis,* June 1978, pp. 211–226.

———, "The Impact of Taxation on the Currency-of-Denomination Decision for Long-Term Foreign Borrowing and Lending," *Journal of International Business Studies,* spring 1984, pp. 15–25.

STONEHILL, ARTHUR, THEO BEEKHUISEN, RICHARD WRIGHT, LEE REMMERS, NORMAN TOY, ANTONIO PARES, DOUGLAS EGAN, and THOMAS BATES: "Financial Goals and Debt Ratio Determinants: A Survey of Practice in Five Countries," *Financial Management,* autumn 1975, pp. 27–41.

TOY, NORMAN, ARTHUR STONEHILL, LEE REMMERS, RICHARD WRIGHT, and THEO BEEKHUISEN: "A Comparative International Study of Growth, Profitability, and Risk as Determinants of Corporate Debt Ratios in the Manufacturing Sector," *Journal of Financial and Quantitative Analysis,* November 1974, pp. 875–886.

WIHLBORG, CLAS: "Economics of Exposure Management of Foreign Subsidiaries of Multinational Corporations," *Journal of International Business Studies,* winter 1980, pp. 9–18.

Institutional Structure of International Trade and Finance

The theory and practice of international finance described in the preceding chapters are built on an institutional framework which is shaped and defined by important private and government institutions. This final part of the book describes these institutions and the functions they serve.

The first of the two chapters in Part Six deals with multinational banking. While banks are frequently ignored when considering multinational corporations—for example, Table 20.1, which is a standard table of MNCs, lists only *nonfinancial corporations*—banking is the epitome of an industry that is multinational in nature. When we focus on, for example, the countries in which operations occur and where foreign direct investments have been made, banks are more widely spread than firms from just about any other industry, and their effects are as pervasive as their territorial coverage.

An important activity of banks is the acceptance of deposits, and here the multinational dimension is both fascinating and controversial. Chapter 22 begins by looking at "offshore deposits," often simply but inaccurately called

"Eurodollars," and explains what they are, where they come from, and what they imply for regulatory agencies. After describing the controversy over the creation of offshore deposits, the chapter deals with the organization of international banking. We then explain why banking has become multinational, and conclude with a discussion of anxieties that have been expressed about the fragility of international banking due to "derivatives" trading and a discussion of the "deregulation wars" that have radically changed the activities in which banks are engaged.

Chapter 23 looks at the structure, instruments, and institutions of international trade. No course in international finance is complete without an explanation of the nature and role of letters of credit, bills of exchange, payments drafts, bills of lading, waybills, and other such documents. The chapter explains how methods of payment and trade credit have evolved to meet the special needs of international trade. Several forms of export financing are explained, including short-term credits involving delayed payment dates on bills of exchange, and medium-term credits involving forfaiting. We also discuss a form of trade called countertrade and why it is used.

Chapter 23 ends with a description of the institutions that monitor and regulate international trade, such as the World Trade Organization (WTO), which replaced the General Agreement on Tariffs and Trade (GATT) in January 1995. Since a substantial portion of international trade is between partners of free-trade pacts such as the members of the European Union and the NAFTA, a brief overview of free-trade arrangements is given.

Multinational Banking

Think global, act local.

—THEODORE LEVITT

Currencies have leaped beyond their traditional boundaries, so that today it is possible to write checks in U.S. dollars against bank accounts in Tokyo, or to write checks in Japanese yen against bank accounts in New York. Indeed, bank accounts in different currencies exist side by side in just about every financial center, so that in, for example, London, we find bank accounts in dollars, yen, marks, francs, and every other major currency. Similarly, it has become possible to arrange loans in U.S. dollars in Hong Kong or in marks in Madrid. The growth rate of these so-called **Eurocurrency** deposits and loans has been nothing short of startling and is part of the increased globalization of financial markets in general and of the banking industry in particular.[1]

Spearheading the growth of Eurocurrencies was the appearance of **Eurodollars** in the 1950s. Despite several decades of study of the causes and consequences of the emergence of Eurodollars, there are few topics in international finance that have attracted as much controversy and disagreement. The most important parts of this disagreement center on the extent banks can create Eurodollars and the danger Eurodollar creation involves. We shall attempt to give a balanced view of these issues and shall also explain the many aspects of Eurodollars and Eurocurrencies on which there is consensus. Then we shall describe the nature of the banks which deal in the Eurocurrency market. However, before we begin, we should define what we mean by "Eurodollars" and "Eurocurrencies."

THE EURODOLLAR AND EUROCURRENCY MARKETS

What Are Eurodollars and Eurocurrencies?

Here is a short, accurate definition:

> A Eurodollar deposit is a U.S.-dollar-denominated bank deposit outside the United States.

---

[1]The existence of foreign-currency bank deposits and loans outside of Europe in such centers as Singapore, Sydney, Tokyo, Manila, and Hong Kong has prompted some to use the more general term **offshore currencies** rather than Eurocurrencies. We will stay with the latter term, which is still commonly used.

542

*PART SIX
Institutional
Structure of
International Trade
and Finance*

Hence, a dollar-denominated bank deposit in Barclays Bank in London or in Citibank in Singapore is a Eurodollar deposit, while a dollar deposit in Barclays or Citibank in New York is not.[2] Eurocurrency deposits are a generalization of Eurodollars and include other externally held currencies. For example, a Euromark deposit is a mark-denominated bank deposit held outside Germany, and a Eurosterling deposit is a sterling deposit held outside Britain.

The existence of the Eurocurrency market means that in making hedged or covered investment and borrowing decisions such as those described in Chapter 11, there is no need to go to the different currency centers to arrange deals. For example, an American investor could compare covered 3-month yields on dollars, sterling, marks, yen, and various other currencies in London and arrange for investment or borrowing in the currency of his or her choice in that market. Moreover, as we shall see later in this chapter, the multinational nature of banks means that this American, dealing in London in foreign currencies, could easily be trading with an American bank. The larger U.S., British, Japanese, French, German, and Swiss banks, along with many others, maintain sizable operations in the larger money-market Eurocurrency centers. As we explained in Chapter 11, the ease of comparing yields on different currency-denominated deposits with banks and their deposits side-by-side in many centers has resulted in covered yields being very similar: see Table 11.1, page 262.

Why Did Eurodollar Deposits Develop?

In order to explain why Eurodollars developed and why later other Eurocurrencies developed, we must explain why holders of U.S. dollars preferred to keep them in banks located outside the United States rather than in banks in the United States. We must also explain why borrowers of U.S. dollars arranged their loans with banks located outside the United States rather than with banks in the United States.

The original establishment of Eurodollar accounts is usually credited to the former Soviet Union, although in reality its role was probably rather small.[3] During the 1950s, the Soviet Union found itself selling gold and some other products in order to earn U.S. dollars. These dollars were to be used to purchase grain and other western products, many of which came from the United States. What were the Moscow Narodny bank and its fellow financial institutions to do with dollars between the time they were received and the time they would be needed? Of course, banks in New York were willing to take them on deposit. This, however, was generally unacceptable to the Soviets because of the risk that the dollars might be frozen if the cold war became hotter. Also, placing dollars in New York banks would have meant that the Soviet government was "making loans" to capitalist banks, which would channel the funds to other capitalist enterprises. So instead of using New York banks as the place of deposit for their dollars, the Soviets made their dollars available to banks in Britain and France. The British and French banks took the Soviet-earned dollars and invested them at interest. This partly involved making

---

[2]The Singapore market is also referred to as the Asiadollar market. Currencies other than dollars are not heavily traded in Asia.
[3]See especially Gunter Dufey and Ian Giddy, *The International Money Market,* Prentice-Hall, Inc., Englewood Cliffs, N.J., 1978.

loans in the United States by buying U.S. treasury bills, private commercial and financial paper, and so on.[4] With the interest earned on these investments, the banks in Europe were able to pay interest on the Soviet deposits.

As intriguing as the covert Soviet role in the creation of Eurodollars may sound, in reality the development and expansion of the Eurocurrency market had its roots in more overt events. We can classify these events as affecting the supply of deposits moving to the Eurodollar market or affecting the demand for loans from Eurodollar banks.

The Supply of Eurodollar Deposits

During the 1960s and 1970s, U.S. banks and other deposit-taking institutions were subject to limitations on the maximum interest rates they could offer on deposits. The most notable of these limitations came from the U.S. Federal Reserve Board's Regulation Q. Banks in London and other centers were not subject to such interest limitations, and so were able to pay more on U.S. dollar deposits than U.S.-based banks could. With higher interest rates offered on dollars deposited in London and other financial centers than in the United States, there was an obvious incentive to deposit dollars outside the United States. Many U.S. banks opened overseas offices to receive these funds. Most U.S. interest rate restrictions were removed after the mid-1970s, but to the extent that limitations were effective before that time, they contributed to the flow of dollars abroad. The dollars placed abroad to avoid U.S. interest ceilings on deposits were reinvested, often back in the United States.

The supply or availability of Eurodollar deposits also grew from the advantage for U.S. banks in moving operations overseas to avoid Federal Reserve Regulation M. This regulation required the keeping of reserves against deposits. Until 1969, this regulation did not apply to deposits of overseas branches of U.S. banks (and since 1978 this regulation has not applied to such deposits). Since reserves mean idle funds, the cost of operations overseas was reduced vis-à-vis the cost of operations in the United States. This encouraged U.S. banks to move some of their depositors' accounts, including the accounts of many Americans, to the relatively unregulated overseas market, principally to London and other large European financial centers. Also, the absence of reserve requirements and other troublesome Federal Reserve regulations, such as the need to pay for deposit insurance on deposits held in the United States, has allowed U.S. banks operating overseas to offer higher interest rates on dollar deposits.[5]

Since the late 1960s, growth in Eurodollars has come from sources other than Federal Reserve and U.S. government regulations. For example, Eurodollars are more convenient than dollars that are in the United States. Europeans and other non-Americans have uneven cash flows in U.S. dollars. On some occasions they have inflows of dollars, and on others they have outflows. They could, of course, sell the dollars for their home currency when their inflows are large and repurchase dollars with the home currency when outflows are large. However, this involves transaction

---

[4]The truth, therefore, is that the Soviet government was, via British and French banks, making loans to the U.S. government, defense manufacturers, and so on.

[5]Banks operating in tax havens such as the Cayman Islands and Netherlands Antilles had an additional advantage of paying low corporate income taxes. This allowed them to cover operating costs with a lower spread between deposit and lending rates.

costs, and there is the potential for exchange risk. Alternatively, these non-Americans could leave their dollars in banks in the United States. However, this means dealing with bankers who are thousands of miles away and unfamiliar with the customers' problems. It is easier to keep the dollars in a bank with offices close by which can respond quickly to the customers' needs. Therefore, the Eurocurrency market has expanded at a rapid rate. The convenience of Eurodollars is, of course, augmented by the higher yields on them.

The Demand for Eurodollar Loans

Eurodollars could have developed without a local desire to borrow the funds left on deposit, but the banks would have been required to recycle their Eurodollar holdings back into the U.S. money market. However, as a result of limitations in the 1960s and 1970s on obtaining loans within the United States that did not apply overseas, a demand for U.S. funds outside the United States was created. This encouraged the growth of Eurodollars on the asset side of banks' balance sheets. The controls and restrictions on borrowing funds in the United States for reinvestment abroad began with a voluntary restraint program in 1965. This was followed by mandatory controls in 1968. These controls forced many borrowers to seek sources of loans in the Eurodollar market, and the loans were often arranged with U.S. banks.

Another regulation affecting foreign demand for Eurodollar loans was the U.S. interest equalization tax, introduced in 1963 and in effect until 1974. This was a tax on U.S. residents' earnings on foreign securities. To encourage U.S. residents to lend to foreign borrowers, the foreigners were forced to offer higher yields in order to cover this tax. By channeling funds via Eurodollars, the interest equalization tax was avoided, and this allowed lower interest rates to be offered.

With deposits going abroad to escape Regulation Q, banks going abroad to escape Regulation M and the U.S. Federal Reserve, and borrowing going abroad to escape the interest equalization tax and credit and direct investment controls, the Eurodollar market expanded very rapidly. Furthermore, despite the removal of most of the regulations, taxes, and controls in the 1970s, the Eurodollar market continued to grow rapidly.

Considerations of convenience affected the demand for Eurodollars as well as the supply of Eurodollars. Taking Eurodollar loans is often more convenient than taking loans in the United States. The same is true for other currency loans; it is more convenient to arrange for them locally instead of in a currency's home market. Local bankers know the creditworthiness and talents of local borrowers in a way that is rarely possible for distant bankers. Consequently, instead of taking dollar loans in New York, sterling loans in London, and so on, borrowers take loans in the different currencies in their local market.

The Role of Narrow Spreads

In the final analysis, the most important factor affecting the supply of and demand for Eurodollars is the desire of dollar depositors to receive the highest yield and the desire of dollar borrowers to pay the lowest cost. Because of the absence of reserve requirements, deposit-insurance requirements, and other costly regulations, the Eurobanks can offer higher yields on dollar deposits than can U.S. banks. At the same time, the Eurobanks can charge lower borrowing costs. The lower interest rates on loans are made possible by the absence of severe regulations and by the sheer size and number of informal contacts among the Eurobanks. These factors are important advantages in making large loans. Higher rates to depositors and lower costs to borrowers mean operating on narrower spreads. Nevertheless, the Eurobanks are left with profits because of their lower costs. While the growth of the Eurodollar market is best attributed to the ability of the Eurobanks to operate on a narrow spread, this has not always been the accepted explanation.

The Role of U.S. Deficits

During the early period of development of the Eurodollar market, the market's growth was often attributed to the U.S. trade deficits occurring at the time. A trade deficit means that dollars are being received and accumulated by non-Americans. This did not, however, have much to do with the expansion of Eurodollar deposits. The dollars being held by non-Americans could have been placed in banks within the United States or invested in U.S. financial securities. Eurodollar deposits will grow only if the dollars are kept in overseas banks. Similarly, the Eurodollar market will not disappear if the United States runs trade surpluses. We need the reasons given above, such as convenience and liberal offshore regulations, for the Eurodollar market to exist. As long as banks located outside the United States offer greater convenience and smaller spreads than banks within the United States, they will continue to prosper.

The same factors that are behind the emergence and growth of the Eurodollar market are behind the emergence and growth of the markets in other Eurocurrencies. For example, Japanese-yen deposits and loans are found in London and New York because British and American businesses have found it more convenient to make yen deposits and arrange yen loans locally than in Japan, and because banks in London and New York can avoid restrictions faced by banks in Tokyo. The restrictions that are avoided by operating overseas vary from country to country and have generally become less important in recent years with the global trend toward the deregulation of banking. The role of convenience has increased as a result of the growth in importance of international trade versus domestic trade. As more trade comes to be denominated in the Japanese and European currencies, we can expect more deposits and loans to be denominated in these currencies in the Eurocurrency market.

Determination of Eurocurrency Interest Rates

Eurocurrency interest rates cannot differ much from rates offered on similar deposits in the home country. For example, as we have indicated, the rate offered to Eurodollar depositors is slightly higher than in the United States, and the rate charged to borrowers is slightly lower. Each country's market interest rates influence the Eurocurrency interest rates, and vice versa, as they are all part of the global money market. The total supply of each currency in this global market, together with the total demand, determines the rate of interest. As a practical matter, however, each individual bank bases its rates on the rates it observes in the market.

The interest rates charged to borrowers of Eurocurrencies are based on **London Interbank Offer Rates (LIBOR)** in the particular currencies. LIBOR rates are those charged in interbank transactions (that is, when banks borrow from each other)

546

PART SIX
Institutional
Structure of
International Trade
and Finance

and are the base rates for nonbank customers. LIBOR rates are calculated as the averages of the lending rates in the respective currencies of six leading London banks. Borrowers are charged on a "LIBOR-plus" basis, with the premium based on the creditworthiness of the borrower. With borrowing maturities of over 6 months, a floating interest rate is charged. Every 6 months or so, the loan is rolled over, and the interest rate is based on the current LIBOR rate. This reduces the risk to both the borrower and the lender (the bank) in that neither will be left with a long-term contract that does not reflect the current interest costs. For example, if interest rates rise after the credit is extended, the lender will lose the opportunity to earn more interest for only 6 months. If interest rates fall after a loan is arranged, the borrower will lose the opportunity to borrow more cheaply for only 6 months. With the lower interest-rate risk, credit terms frequently reach 10 years.

Different Types of Eurocurrency Instruments

Eurocurrency deposits are primarily conventional term deposits, which are bank deposits with a fixed term, such as 30 days or 90 days. The interest rate is fixed for the term of a deposit, and this keeps the maturity of deposits short.

Not as important as any of the individual Eurocurrency denominations, but nevertheless of some importance, are the Eurocurrency deposits denominated in Special Drawing Rights (SDRs). SDRs were originally introduced as central-bank reserve assets by the International Monetary Fund, and they have already been briefly described in Chapter 9. SDR term deposits were first offered by Chemical Bank in London. Like the bulk of other Eurodeposits, SDR-denominated deposits are mostly nonnegotiable term deposits.

A relatively small proportion of the liabilities of Eurobanks are not term deposits, but instead take the form of **certificates of deposit (CDs).** Unlike Eurocurrencies in the form of term deposits, the CDs are negotiable instruments that can be traded in a secondary market. This makes the CDs more liquid than term deposits, which have a penalty on early withdrawal. In the case of Eurodollars approximately 20 percent of Eurobank liabilities are CDs, the balance being conventional term deposits. Since 1981, some London-based banks have offered SDR-denominated CDs as well as conventional deposits. The banks that first offered the SDR-denominated CDs were Barclays Bank International, Chemical Bank, Hong Kong and Shanghai Bank, Midland Bank International, National Westminster Bank, and Standard Chartered Bank.[6]

An expansion of Eurocurrency operations within the United States has been made possible by rules allowing the establishment of **international banking facilities** (IBFs). The IBFs are, in effect, a different set of accounts within an existing bank; they date back to late 1981. The facilities can accept foreign-currency deposits and are exempt from both U.S. reserve requirements and insurance premiums on deposits as long as the deposits are used exclusively for making loans to foreigners. Two days' notice for withdrawals is required. These facilities compete with the Eurocurrency banks operating within Europe and have brought some of the offshore business back to the United States.

---

[6]See Business International, "Slimmed-Down SDR Makes Comeback; Techniques Include Opening Up Market for Negotiable SDR CDs," *Money Report,* January 16, 1981.

Eurobanks generally remain well hedged. They accept deposits in many different currencies, and they also have assets in these same currencies. When they balance the two sides of their accounts with equal volumes and maturities of assets and liabilities in each denomination, they are perfectly hedged and therefore unaffected by changes in exchange rates. Sometimes it is difficult to balance the maturities of assets and liabilities, and until 1981 this situation involved the Eurobanks in risk. However, since 1981 the Eurobanks have been able to avoid risk from unbalanced maturities by using the Eurodollar futures market at the International Monetary Market operated by the Chicago Mercantile Exchange. Since the early 1980s banks have also been able to use the Eurodollar futures markets of the Chicago Board of Trade, the New York Futures Exchange, the London International Financial Futures Exchange, and the Singapore Monetary Exchange. It is worthwhile to explain the risk from unbalanced maturities and the way this can be avoided with Eurodollar futures.

Suppose that a bank accepts a 3-month Eurodollar deposit of $1 million on March 1 at 9 percent and at the same time makes a Eurodollar loan for 6 months at 10 percent. In June, when the 3-month deposit matures, the Eurobank must refinance the 6-month loan for the remaining 3 months. If by June the deposit rate on 3 month Eurodollars has risen above 10 percent, the spread on the remaining period of the loan will become negative. To avoid this risk, on March 1, when making the 6-month loan, the bank could sell a 3-month Eurodollar future for June. (On the International Monetary Market in Chicago, contracts are traded in $1 million denominations for March, June, September, and December.) If by June the Eurodollar rates have gone up, the bank will find that it has made money on the sale of its Eurodollar future. This follows because, as in the bond market, purchases of interest-rate futures (long positions) provide a profit when interest rates fall, and sales (short positions) provide a profit when interest rates rise. The profit made by the Eurobank in selling the Eurodollar future will offset the extra cost of refinancing the 6-month Eurodollar loan for the remaining 3 months.

Eurobanks perform "intermediation" when they convert Eurocurrency deposits into, for example, commercial loans. This term is used because the banks are intermediaries between the depositors and the borrowers. If the two sides of the Eurobankers' accounts are equally liquid—that is, if the IOUs they purchase are as marketable as their Eurocurrency deposits—then according to the view of some researchers, the Eurobanks have not created any extra liquidity or "money."[7] However, it could happen that the original foreign currency that was deposited in a Eurobank is redeposited in other Eurobanks before finding its way back to the home country. In this way we can have a total of Eurocurrency deposits that is a multiple of the original deposit. Before demonstrating how we can have a **Eurocurrency multiplier** we should state that this remains a topic of considerable controversy, and there is even some dispute over whether Eurodollar multipliers can be defined at all.[8]

---

[7]This is the view in Jurg Niehans and John Hewson, "The Euro-Dollar Market and Monetary Theory," *Journal of Money, Credit and Banking,* February 1976, pp. 1–27.

[8]The controversy began after the publication of Milton Friedman's article "The Euro-Dollar Market: Some First Principles" (*Morgan Guarantee Survey,* October 1969, pp. 4–14, reprinted with clarifications in *Review,* Federal Reserve Bank of St. Louis, July 1971, pp. 16–24). Friedman treated the Eurodollar mul-

548

PART SIX
Institutional
Structure of
International Trade
and Finance

TABLE 22.1. Change in Balance Sheets from $100 of Primary Deposits

Bank	Assets			Liabilities	
British	Deposit in U.S. bank	+$ 2.00		Term deposit of	
	Loan to Britfirm B	+$ 98.00		Britfirm A	+$100.00
		+$100.00			+$100.00
Italian	Deposit in U.S. bank	+$ 1.96		Term deposit of	
	Loan to Italfirm B	+$ 96.04		Italfirm A	+$ 98.00
		+$ 98.00			+$ 98.00
Dutch	Deposit in U.S. bank	+$ 1.92		Term deposit of	
	Loan to Dutchfirm B	+$ 94.12		Dutchfirm A	+$ 96.04
		+$ 96.04			+$ 96.04
Canadian	Deposit in U.S. bank	+$ 1.88		Term deposit of	
	Loan to Canafirm B	+$ 92.24		Canafirm A	+$ 94.12
		+$ 94.12			+$ 94.12

Redepositing and Multiple Eurocurrency Expansion

Let us construct a situation in which multiple expansion of Eurodollars does occur. Assume that a British exporter, Britfirm A, receives a $100 check from an American purchaser of its products and that this check is drawn against a U.S. bank. This is an original receipt of dollars in Europe. Assume that Britfirm A does not need the dollars immediately but that it will need them in 90 days. The $100 is held in Britfirm A's account in a British bank as a dollar term deposit—a Eurodollar. The British bank will, after accepting the check from Britfirm A, send the check to the U.S. bank with which it deals. The British bank will be credited with $100.

The $100 deposit in the British bank probably will not be removed during the term of the deposit, since removing it would involve a substantial interest penalty for Britfirm A. The British bank will therefore look for an investment vehicle that approximately matches the term of Britfirm A's deposit. Suppose that the British bank decides to maintain a cash reserve of 2 percent with an American bank and discovers a British firm, Britfirm B, which wishes to borrow the remaining $98 for 90 days to settle a payment with an Italian supplier, Italfirm A. The British bank will give to Britfirm B a check for $98 drawn against the British bank's account at the U.S. bank and payable to Italfirm A. We have the situation in the top part of Table 22.1. (If the dollars are loaned to a U.S. borrower, as they could well be, the effects end here with the British bank merely intermediating, that is, serving as go-between for the depositor and the borrower.)

On receiving the check from Britfirm B, Italfirm A will deposit it in its account

---

tiplier as a conventional domestic banking multiplier, and this prompted a criticism from Fred H. Klopstock ("Money Creation in the Euro-Dollar Market—A Note on Professor Friedman's Views," *Monthly Review,* Federal Reserve Bank of New York, January 1970, pp. 12–15). The controversy expanded with the publication of Niehans and Hewson's paper (see note 7 above). Gunter Dufey and Ian H. Giddy have introduced a variety of multipliers (*The International Money Market,* Prentice-Hall, Englewood Cliffs, N.J. 1978). We will use the conventional multiplier and treat the question in the conventional way.

at an Italian bank, which will in turn send it for collection to the United States. If the Italian bank deals with the same U.S. bank as the British bank, all that will happen in the United States is that $98 will be removed from the British bank's account and credited to the Italian bank's account. The British bank's account with the U.S. bank will be reduced to $2. The British bank's account will have the entries shown in Table 22.1; it will show the $100 Eurodollar deposit offset by a $2 reserve and a $98 IOU. (If the British and Italian banks maintain reserves at different U.S. banks, the outcome will be the same after U.S. interbank clearing.) We see that the clearing of Eurodollars takes place in New York, with the banks in the United States merely showing different names of depositors after Eurodollars have been transferred. Originally, they showed the owner of the dollars who paid Britfirm A. Afterward, the U.S. banks showed the British bank and then the Italian bank as the depositor. Since only the names change, nothing happens inside the United States to increase or decrease the number of loans.

After Italfirm A deposits the check in the Italian bank, the Italian bank will have a $98 deposit at the U.S. bank to offset its Eurodollar liability to Italfirm A. Like its British counterpart, it will not leave the funds idle. Let us suppose that it maintains 2 percent, or $1.96, in the U.S. bank, and lends the balance of $96.04 to Italfirm B. The loan will be effected by the Italian bank's drawing a check for $96.04 against its U.S. bank account on behalf of Italfirm B. We assume that this check is made payable to Dutchfirm A.

If Dutchfirm A deposits the check in a Dutch Eurodollar term account, the Italian bank will be left with $1.96 in reserves in the U.S. bank. The Dutch bank will be credited with $96.04. We now assume that the Dutch bank keeps 2 percent of the $96.04 deposit, that is, $1.92, as a cash reserve, and lends the balance of $94.12 to Dutchfirm B by drawing a check on Dutchfirm B's behalf to Canafirm A. After Canafirm A deposits the check, the Dutch bank will have $1.92 in reserves, and the Canadian bank with which the check is deposited will have $94.12. If the Canadian bank lends Canafirm B 98 percent of this, or $92.24, and Canafirm B pays an American company that banks in the United States, then the process of Eurodollar creation will end. The Canadian bank will have its account in its U.S. bank reduced by $92.24 and will be left with 2 percent, or $1.88, against its Eurodollar deposit of $94.12. The books are balanced, and every bank is in its desired position of having a 2-percent reserve backing its Eurodollar deposit, with the remaining 98 percent out as loans. By the time the Eurodollar creation comes to an end, there is a total of $100.00 + $98 + $96.04 + $94.12, or $388.16, in Eurodollars. The original deposit of $100 has grown 3.8816 times, and this might be called the Eurodollar multiplier vis-à-vis the original $100 base. However, the $388.16 in Eurodollars vis-à-vis *the reserves still remaining in Eurobanks*—that is, $2 + $1.96 + $1.92 + $1.88, or $7.76, gives a **deposit ratio** of 50. That is, $388.16 is 50 times the remaining dollar reserves of $7.76. This is what we would expect with a reserve ratio of 0.02, since each $1 of reserves supports $50 of deposits.

The interesting magnitude is not the deposit ratio but rather the multiplier, which is the expansion on the base of the original deposit. Only if there are no leakages back to the United States will the multiplier be as large as the deposit ratio. If funds deposited in the Euromarket are loaned back in the United States at the outset, the leakage is immediate and the Eurobank is merely intermediating. The rate of leakage depends on how extensively U.S. dollars are used for settling payments

550

PART SIX
*Institutional
Structure of
International Trade
and Finance*

between parties outside the United States. The more any currency is used between offshore parties, the larger the multiplier is likely to be.

When dollar loans offered by commercial banks outside the United States are made to central banks, a leakage back to the United States is almost certain to occur. Central banks tend to hold their dollars in U.S. banks or place them in U.S. treasury bills. This will drain any extra dollar reserves back into the U.S. banking system. However, when many central banks kept dollars at the Bank for International Settlements (BIS) in Basle, Switzerland, in the 1960s, the leakage back to the United States did not occur. The BIS frequently reinvested in the Eurodollar market and thus contributed to the expansion of Eurodollars.

Estimates of the value of the Eurodollar multiplier vary. As we have seen, the value of the multiplier depends on the definition and on the speed with which funds return to the United States. Fred Klopstock estimates that the leakage back to the United States is so rapid that the multiplier is about 1.05 to 1.09. Alexander Swoboda gives a value of about 2.00, which is close to the estimates of Boyden Lee. John Hewson and Eisuke Sakakibara find a range of 3 to 7, whereas John Makin has produced estimates from 10.31 to 18.45.[9] Clearly, the larger estimates must refer to deposits-to-reserve ratios rather than to the Eurodollar multiplier and are incorrect as multiplier estimates.

MULTINATIONAL BANKING

The Multinationalization of Banking

Offices of foreign-owned banks are becoming commonplace in financial districts of larger cities and towns. In the United States, for example, 299 foreign banks had 740 offices in 1991, with 10 countries each with more than a dozen offices (see Table 22.2). Banks are competing in each others' markets for deposits and loans, taking bigger and bigger shares of activity according to just about every measure. For example, as Figure 22.1 shows, foreign banks' share of U.S. deposits grew from 6.6 percent to 16.2 percent between 1980 and 1991, while the share of assets grew from 11.9 percent to 22.6 during the same period. Measured by loans to businesses, the presence of foreign banks is even more pronounced, with more than one-third of such loans in the United States in 1991 coming from foreign banks, double the relative importance in 1980 (see Figure 22.2).

International banks are linked together in various formal and informal ways, from simply holding accounts with each other—correspondent accounts—to common ownership. As we shall see, the types of connections affect the nature of the business that the banks conduct.

---

[9]These estimates are found in Boyden E. Lee, "The Eurodollar Multiplier," *Journal of Finance,* September 1973, pp. 867–874; John Hewson and Eisuke Sakakibara, "The Eurodollar Multiplier: A Portfolio Approach," *IMF Staff Papers,* July 1974, pp. 307–328; Fred H. Klopstock, "Money Creation in the Euro-Dollar Market—A Note on Professor Friedman's Views," *Monthly Review,* Federal Reserve Bank of New York, January 1970, pp. 12–15; John H. Makin, "Demand and Supply Functions for Stocks of Eurodollar Deposits: An Empirical Study," *Review of Economics and Statistics,* November 1972, pp. 381–391; and Alexander K. Swoboda, *The Eurodollar Market: An Interpretation,* Essays in International Finance, no. 64, Princeton University Press, Princeton, N.J., 1968.

TABLE 22.2. U.S. Banking Offices of Foreign Banks, 1991

Country	Banks with U.S. Offices	Number of U.S. Offices
Japan	52	149
Canada	6	51
Britain	10	39
Italy	13	26
France	16	37
Netherlands	3	25
Hong Kong	10	30
Switzerland	7	18
Israel	4	25
Mexico	6	13
Other	172	327
Total	299	740

Source: U.S. Department of Commerce, Bureau of the Census, *Statistical Abstract of the United States,* 1993.

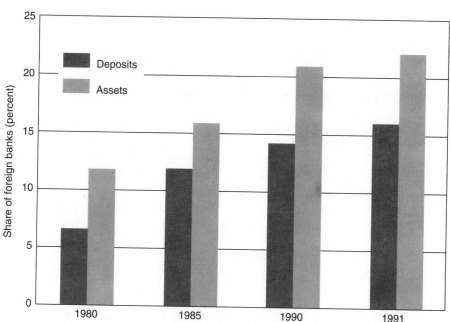

Figure 22.1. Deposit and Asset Shares of Foreign Banks in the United States, 1980–1991
(*Source:* U.S. Department of Commerce, Bureau of the Census, *Statistical Abstract of the United States,* 1993.)

552

PART SIX
Institutional
Structure of
International Trade
and Finance

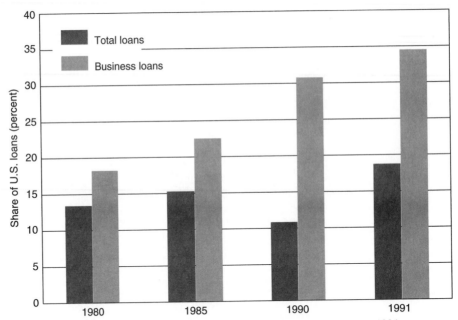

Figure 22.2. Share of Loans by Foreign Banks in the United States, 1980–1991
(*Source:* U.S. Department of Commerce, Bureau of the Census, *Statistical Abstract of the United States*, 1993.)

Organizational Features of Multinational Banking

Figure 22.3 shows the relative importance of different forms of banking offices in the United States. These and other forms of banking organization are described below.

Correspondent Banking

An informal linkage between banks in different countries is set up when banks maintain correspondent accounts with each other. Large banks have correspondent relationships with banks in almost every country in which they do not have an office of their own. The purpose of maintaining foreign correspondents is to facilitate international payments and collections for customers. The term "correspondent" comes from the mail or cable communications that the banks used to use for settling customer accounts. Today, these communications have largely been replaced by SWIFT messages, and the settling between banks occurs via CHIPS.[10] For example, if Aviva wants to pay a Canadian supplier, it will ask its U.S. bank, which will communicate with its Canadian correspondent bank via SWIFT. The Canadian bank credits the account of the Canadian firm, while Aviva's bank debits Aviva's account. The U.S. and Canadian banks then settle through CHIPS.

Correspondent banking allows banks to help their customers who are doing

---

[10]SWIFT and CHIPS were discussed in Chapter 2. For more on how correspondent banking has been rationalized and reorganized through these message and bank-settlement systems see "On Correspondent Banking," *Euromoney*, December 1988, p. 115.

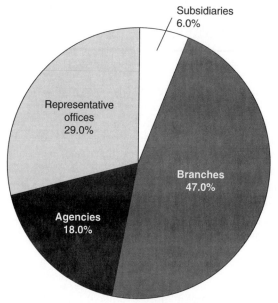

**Figure 22.3. The Forms of Foreign-Bank Operations
in New York**
(*Source:* Computed from *International Bankers'
Directory*, first 1986 edition, Rand-McNally, Chicago,
1986.)

business abroad, without having to maintain any personnel or offices overseas. This
relationship is primarily for settling customer payments, but it can extend to providing limited credit for each other's customers and to setting up contacts between
local businesspeople and the clients of the correspondent banks.

Resident Representatives

In order to provide their customers with help from their own personnel on the
spot in foreign countries, banks open overseas business offices. These are not banking offices in the sense of accepting local deposits or providing loans. The primary
purpose of these offices is to provide information about local business practices and
conditions, including the creditworthiness of potential customers and the bank's
clients. The resident representatives will keep in contact with local correspondent
banks and provide help when needed. Representative offices are generally small;
they have the appearance of an ordinary commercial office rather than a bank.

Bank Agencies

An agency is like a full-fledged bank in every respect except that it does not
handle ordinary retail deposits. The agencies deal in the local money markets and in
the foreign exchange markets, arrange loans, clear bank drafts and checks, and channel foreign funds into financial markets. Agencies are common in New York; for
example, Canadian and European banks keep busy offices there, with perhaps
dozens of personnel dealing in the short-term credit markets and in foreign

554

PART SIX
Institutional
Structure of
International Trade
and Finance

exchange. Agencies also often arrange long-term loans for customers and act on behalf of the home office to keep it directly involved in the important foreign financial markets.

Foreign Branches

Foreign branches are operating banks like local banks, except that the directors and owners tend to reside elsewhere. Generally, foreign branches are subject to both local banking rules and the rules at home, but because they can benefit from loopholes, the extra tier of regulations is not necessarily onerous. The books of a foreign branch are incorporated with those of the parent bank, although the foreign branch will also maintain separate books for revealing separate performance, for tax purposes, and so on. The existence of foreign branches can mean very rapid check clearing for customers in different countries, because the debit and credit operations are internal and can be initiated by fax or electronic mail. This can offer a great advantage over the lengthy clearing that can occur via correspondents. The foreign branch also offers bank customers in small countries all the service and safety advantages of a large bank, which the local market might not be able to support.

There would probably be far more extensive foreign branch networks of the large international banks were it not for legal limitations imposed by local governments to protect local banks from aggressive foreign competition. Britain has traditionally been liberal in allowing foreign banks to operate and has gained in return from the reciprocal rules that are frequently offered. On the other hand, until the 1980 Bank Act was passed, the opening of foreign bank subsidiaries within Canada was prohibited, and branches of foreign banks are still not allowed. The United States selectively allows foreign banks to operate. The regulation and supervision of foreign banks within the United States is provided for in the International Banking Act of 1978. This act allows the U.S. Comptroller of the Currency to grant foreign banks a license to open branches (or agencies). The foreign banks can open wherever state banking laws allow them to. The banks are restricted to their declared "home state" and are subject to federally imposed reserve requirements when they are federally chartered.[11] They have access to services of the Federal Reserve and can borrow from its discount window. Since 1980, the foreign banks that accept retail deposits have been required to provide deposit insurance for customers. The foreign banks are relatively more important in providing commercial and industrial loans than in other investment activities.

Foreign Subsidiaries and Affiliates

A foreign branch is part of a parent organization that is incorporated elsewhere. A **foreign subsidiary** is a locally incorporated bank that happens to be owned either completely or partially by a foreign parent. Foreign subsidiaries do all types of banking, and it may be very difficult to distinguish them from an ordinary locally owned bank.

Foreign *subsidiaries* are controlled by foreign owners, even if the foreign ownership is partial. **Foreign affiliates** are similar to subsidiaries in being locally incor-

---

[11]Foreign as well as domestic banks can, however, operate outside their declared home states by establishing Edge Act subsidiaries. These are discussed later in this chapter.

porated and so on, but they are joint ventures, and no individual foreign owner has control (even though a *group* of foreign owners might have control).

CHAPTER *22*
Multinational
Banking

Consortium Banks

Consortium banks are joint ventures of the larger commercial banks. They can involve a half dozen or more partners from numerous countries. They are primarily concerned with investment, and they arrange large loans and underwrite stocks and bonds. Consortium banks are not concerned with taking deposits, and they deal only with large corporations or perhaps governments. They will take equity positions— part ownership of an investment—as well as make loans, and they are frequently busy arranging takeovers and mergers.

Edge Act and Agreement Corporations

While U.S. banks can participate in investment-bank consortia and may operate branches overseas, they cannot themselves have equity—direct ownership—in foreign banking subsidiaries. However, because of a 1919 amendment to the Federal Reserve Act initiated by Senator Walter Edge, U.S. banks are able to establish subsidiaries for doing business "abroad." These subsidiaries, which are federally chartered, can have equity in foreign banks and are known as **Edge Act corporations.** They profit both from holding stock in subsidiaries overseas and by engaging in **investment banking,** that is, borrowing and investing. Edge Act corporations engage in almost all the activities of banking: accepting deposits, making loans, exchanging currencies, selling government and corporate securities, and so on. They can invest in equity, while domestic banks are not allowed to.[12] A major impetus to the growth of Edge Act corporations has been that they enable a bank to open an office outside of its home state. The International Banking Act of 1978 allows *foreign* banks to open Edge Act corporations and accept deposits directly related to international transactions. There is no longer a rule that states that foreign-bank-owned Edge Act corporations will be permitted only if the directors of these corporations are U.S. citizens. These changes in the International Banking Act were made to put foreign and U.S. banks on a more equal footing.

Agreement corporations are a little different from Edge Act corporations. The authority to establish agreement corporations dates from a 1916 amendment to the Federal Reserve Act. This allows banks which are members of the Federal Reserve System to enter into an agreement with that organization to engage in international banking. Agreement corporations, unlike Edge Act corporations, can be chartered by a state government, and they can only engage in international banking, not in general investment activities. There are only a handful of agreement corporations.

U.S. International Banking Facilities (IBFs)

We have already mentioned international banking facilities (IBFs) in connection with the Eurodollar market. Since 1981, U.S. banks, Edge Act corporations, foreign commercial banks through branches and agencies in the United States, savings and loan associations, and mutual savings banks have been allowed by the Board of

---

[12]In February 1988, the Federal Reserve Board made an exception when it allowed U.S. banks to swap loans to governments of heavily indebted developing countries into equity investments. This was done to help the debtor countries and the U.S. banks deal with the third-world debt crisis.

556

PART SIX
Institutional
Structure of
International Trade
and Finance

Governors of the Federal Reserve System to establish IBFs as adjunct operations.[13] The motive for this permission is to allow banks in the United States to participate in the lucrative Eurocurrency market. IBFs are not subject to domestic banking regulations, including reserve requirements and interest ceilings, and escape some local and state taxes. IBFs can accept deposits only from non-Americans and with a minimum size of $100,000. Withdrawals are also subject to a $100,000 minimum. Deposits cannot be withdrawn without at least 2 days' notice. However, overnight deposits can be offered to overseas banks, other IBFs, and the IBF's parent bank. Funds obtained by IBFs cannot be used domestically; they must be used overseas. To ensure that U.S.-based companies and individuals satisfy this requirement, borrowers must sign a statement when they begin taking loans. Over 500 IBFs had been established, the majority in New York and California.

Why Banking Has Become Multinational

Through the opening of representative offices, agencies, and branches and through the acquisition or establishment of subsidiaries, banking has become a truly multinational enterprise. While reputation, regulation, and other factors contributing to the multinationalization of business in general apply to banking, there are special factors that apply to banking alone. These include market information, borrower information, serving clients, custodial services, and regulation, all of which are discussed below.[14]

Market Information

It might seem that with the rapid dissemination of information via modern subscription services such as Reuters and Dow Jones Telerate Services, which flash up prices and news developments on video screens at the speed of light, there is no need to have operations in expensive money centers such as London and New York. However, it is one thing to be plugged into the latest developments, but quite another to be able to interpret or even anticipate events. For being able to interpret what is happening and to get a sense of where markets are going there is nothing like having personnel on the spot where the big markets and events are unfolding. For this reason we find a vast number of foreign banks with offices in the large money-market centers, especially London and New York. Many of these offices may not be profitable on their own, but by acting as eyes and ears for their parent banks, they improve the profitability of overall operations.

Borrower Information

When making loans abroad, banks could in theory take the word of a foreign bank such as a correspondent about the financial stability of a borrower, or send

---

[13]For more on IBFs see K. Alec Chrystal, "International Banking Facilities," *Review,* Federal Reserve Bank of St. Louis, April 1984, pp. 5–11.

[14]For empirical evidence on the importance of some different factors for the evolution of multinational banking see Michael A. Goldberg, Robert W. Helsley, and Maurice D. Levi, "On the Development of International Financial Centers," *The Annals of Regional Science,* February 1988, pp. 81–94. For the evolution of the structure of international banking see Robert L. Heinkel and Maurice D. Levi, "The Structure of International Banking," *Journal of International Money and Finance,* June 1992, pp. 251–272.

bank personnel to the borrower's country and review the borrower's finances on the spot. It can, however, be cheaper and more efficient to maintain local offices to gather "street talk," not only at the time of making a loan, but afterward when the borrower's circumstances may suddenly deteriorate.

The importance of reliable information about borrowers has played a significant role in banking history and, in particular, in the relative success of early family banking houses. For example, it was no accident that the Rothschild bank did so well in the nineteenth century, after the founder, Mayer Rothschild of Frankfurt, posted his sons in the capitals of Europe. Mayer Rothschild could trust the reports coming from his sons about the quality of sovereign borrowers in a way that banks without "in house" overseas representation could not. Thus, in competition with banks with less reliable information, family banking houses such as the Rothschilds, Warburgs, and others did extremely well. Indeed, we can meaningfully consider the family banking houses of Europe as the precursors of today's multinational banks, their success being based on the same factors.[15]

Serving Clients

Profit-maximizing banks do not open overseas offices merely to provide services for clients. Usually, correspondents could do most of what an overseas office can do to serve customers. However, it may be better for a bank to serve its domestic customers in their foreign operations than to allow its customers to develop strong ties with foreign banks or competing domestic banks that do have overseas offices. Some overseas banking offices may therefore follow the trade of domestic clients for strategic reasons rather than to earn from the services provided to clients.

Of course, it may be that the services that are provided by overseas banking offices *are* profitable. For example, the handling of collections and payments for domestic clients engaged in foreign trade can be lucrative and serve as reason for having an office, such as a representative office, in a country in which important clients are doing business. Indeed, for many banks the fees from services provided to customers that are connected to international trade have become an increasingly important component of their earnings. For example, the sale of letters of credit, the discounting of bills of exchange, the provision of collection services, and the conversion of currencies have become increasingly important in comparison with accepting deposits and making loans.

Custodial Services

One fee-for-service activity of multinational banks that was mentioned in Chapter 18 is the provision of custodial services. These services are provided to clients who invest in securities overseas. As we have seen, global custodians take possession of foreign securities for safekeeping, collect dividends or offer up coupons, and

---

[15]The House of Rothschild in particular knew the value not just of information about borrowers, but also about events which could affect financial markets. For example, by using pigeons, runners, horsemen, and rowers, Nathan Rothschild, the London-based member of the Rothschild family, knew before others that the Duke of Wellington had defeated Napoleon in the fields of Waterloo in 1815. Rothschild capitalized on his superior information by *selling* British bonds. This triggered panic selling, because it was known that Rothschild was the first in London to know the outcome of the battle. Rothschild profited by employing others to buy the heavily discounted bonds before word finally arrived that Wellington had won.

558

*PART SIX
Institutional
Structure of
International Trade
and Finance*

handle stock splits, rights issues, tax reclamation, and so on. The custodians are typically banks. It is clear that custodial services require that banks have overseas offices, that is, that they be multinational.

Avoiding Regulations

In the list of reasons banks have become so multinational we should not overlook the role of regulations. As we saw in our discussion of the evolution of the Eurocurrency market, banks have frequently moved abroad to avoid reserve requirements, deposit insurance, onerous reporting requirements, corporate taxes, interest-rate ceilings, and other hindrances to their operations. For example, many U.S. banks opened offices in London and in tax-havens to avoid U.S. regulations and taxes. Similarly, many Japanese banks have opened offices in New York and London to avoid domestic restrictions and to exploit special opportunities. Indeed, over the years, the activities which are open to foreign banks have become more and more similar to those open to domestic banks. This is made clear in Table 22.3, which shows by the similarity of the "yes" and "no" entries for functions in different centers that, with a few exceptions, there remains little discrimination between foreign and domestic banks in the important financial centers—New York, London, and Tokyo.

While overseas offices may make banks more profitable by avoiding domestic regulations, at the same time they make banks and the banking industry more vulnerable and subject to crisis. It is worthwhile considering the problems that have accompanied the multinationalization of banking.

The Problems of Multinational Banking

"Deregulation Wars"

Banking can be risky business. Evidence of the risk of multinational banking has been provided by a string of failures and other crises including the failure of Franklin National Bank and Bankhaus Herstatt; major losses by the Union Bank of Switzerland, Westdeutsche Landesbank, Lloyds International and Barings; the upheaval at the Banco Ambrosiano; and the banking crisis of the 1980s, which occurred after Mexico, Brazil, Argentina, and over 20 other borrowers announced they were unable to meet scheduled repayments on their debts.

The major cause of the risk of multinational banking is also a major cause of the development of multinational banking. In particular, the opening of overseas offices to avoid domestic regulations such as reserve requirements, reporting of asset positions, and payment for deposit insurance has at the same time made banks more vulnerable to deposit withdrawals. Furthermore, the acceptance of default and other risks from overseas lending has made banks' domestic depositors subject to greater risks. While there has been some easing of anxiety of depositors in the 1990s, it is worthwhile considering why the problem developed.

Banking provides a country with jobs and prestige. Consequently, each country has an incentive to make its regulations just a little more liberal than other countries' and thereby attract banks from other locations. For example, if London can be a little less regulated than New York, it can gain at New York's expense. Then, if the Cayman Islands, Bermuda, the Netherlands Antilles, or Liechtenstein can be less regulated than London, they can gain at London's expense. The attractiveness of

TABLE 22.3. Activities Open to Different Institutions in Different Centers

Activity	Location*	Permitted to†					
		U.S. Bank Holding Co.	Japanese City Bank	U.K. Clearing Bank	U.S. Securities Firm	Japanese Securities Firm	U.K. Merchant Bank
Banking license	NY	YES	YES	YES	S	S	S
	LO	YES	YES	YES	YES	YES	YES
	TO	YES	YES	YES	NO	NO	NO
Dealing in corporate securities	NY	NO	NO	NO	YES	YES	YES
	LO	YES	YES	YES	YES	YES	YES
	TO	S	NO	S	YES	YES	YES
Foreign-exchange dealing	NY	YES	YES	YES	YES	YES	YES
	LO	YES	YES	YES	YES	YES	YES
	TO	YES	YES	YES	NO	NO	NO
Dealing in U.S. treasuries	NY	YES	YES	YES	YES	YES	YES
	LO	YES	YES	YES	YES	YES	YES
	TO	NO	NO	NO	YES	YES	YES
Dealing in U.K. gilts	NY	NO	NO	NO	YES	YES	YES
	LO	YES	YES	YES	YES	YES	YES
	TO	NO	NO	NO	YES	YES	YES
Dealing in Japanese govt. bonds	NY	NO	NO	NO	YES	YES	YES
	LO	YES	YES	YES	YES	YES	YES
	TO	YES	YES	YES	YES	YES	YES
Trust bank	NY	YES	YES	YES	S	S	S
	LO	YES	YES	YES	YES	YES	YES
	TO	YES	NO	YES	NO	NO	NO
Account at the central bank	NY	YES	YES	YES	S	S	S
	LO	YES	YES	YES	YES	YES	YES
	TO	YES	YES	YES	YES	YES	YES

*NY = New York; LO = London; TO = Tokyo.

†YES = full license permitted; NO = not generally permitted; S = permitted only through special-purpose companies, such as a 50-percent-owned affiliate or a "near bank."

Source: E. Gerald Corrigan, "A Perspective on the Globalization of Financial Markets and Institutions," *Quarterly Review,* Federal Reserve Bank of New York, spring 1987, pp. 1–9.

banking in this way drew more and more countries into competitive deregulation, with special advantages being offered by Cyprus, Jersey, Gernsey, Malta, Madeira, Gibraltar, Monaco, the Isle of Man, and other new entrants. Traditional centers like London and New York were forced to respond to avoid losing their niche, creating a wave of financial deregulations in the 1980s that left more than a few regulators feeling extremely uneasy.

What is needed to prevent "deregulation wars" is international cooperation. Some efforts have been made in this regard. For example, the **Basle Committee** was established after the Herstatt and Franklin Bank failures for the purpose of "better co-ordination of the surveillance exercised by national authorities over the international banking system. . . ." This committee has had some success in sharing

EXHIBIT 22.1

EXHIBIT 22.1
Derivatives: Differentiating the Hyperbole

Debate over the benefits and dangers of the explosive growth in derivatives trading has been raging without any resolution. Do banks that buy and sell currency or interest futures and options put themselves, their depositors, and even taxpayers at risk, or are they reducing risk by hedging their business exposures? The following from *The Economist*'s special survey on international banking looks at both sides of the issue. The excerpt suggests that we can expect to hear more on the matter and to eventually see tighter regulation of bank trading in derivatives, and certainly more disclosure of derivatives positions taken by banks.

Given the growing political concern about derivatives, it is sometimes easy to forget that they are supposedly a method for reducing risk rather than for increasing it. A firm that does not want to be exposed to a change in the price of a foreign currency, say, or of some commodity, can cover itself against that exposure by buying forwards or puts or calls or caps or some other kinds of exotically named but often quite simple derivative contract. Indeed, central bankers and regulators routinely praise the risk-reducing benefits that derivatives have conferred on the financial system. David Mullins, a former Fed vice-chairman, recently called derivatives "one of the most dramatic success stories in modern economic history" (and later quit the Fed to work for a derivatives house).

Even so, closer regulation of derivatives activities seems inevitable, if only because of their immense volume (their notional values stands at about $7 trillion), apparent complexity, and the fact that they straddle and link so many markets. These factors are enough on their own to prompt legitimate fears about the possibility that derivatives might cause an accident in the financial system. Most worrying of all is counterparty risk: should one party to a complex derivatives contract be unable to pay, there is a theoretical possibility of a domino effect as one institution after another loses liquidity and the whole system seizes up.

Regulators and politicians around the world are struggling to catch up with the implications of all this. In mid-April Henry Gonzalez, chairman of the American Congress's House banking committee, introduced a bill that would require banks (but not securities houses) to make a fuller disclosure of their derivatives activities. He was goaded into action in part by Jim Leach, the committee's senior Republican, who has already tabled a bill that would create a new federal agency to oversee derivatives activities. Derivatives are also increasingly a matter of concern to the Basle committee. It recently issued controversial proposals to extend capital-adequacy regulations from credit risks (i.e., the risk of default on a loan) to market risks (i.e., the risk of a change in prices). Part of the intention was to reduce the risk from derivatives.

Source: "A Survey of International Banking," *The Economist,* April 30, 1994, p. 40. © The Economist Newspaper Group, Inc. Reprinted with permission. Further reproduction prohibited.

information on banks and their subsidiaries so that national regulators can learn more quickly about difficulties occurring outside the country that could adversely affect bank safety at home. For example, for the situation of a subsidiary experiencing serious loan losses, the 1975 and 1983 **Concordat Agreements** among the Basle Committee members provide a procedure for relaying this information to the parent bank's regulators.

With the world's financial system so intricately connected and with deregulation's having taken on a competitive element, those responsible for overseeing the international banking system have sounded the alarm and swung into action. The leading role has been taken by the Bank for International Settlements (BIS), which has set new global standards for bank safety.[16] The most important step has been the establishment of a capital requirement of 8 percent. This means that banks must maintain a net worth, or equity, of at least 8 percent of deposits and other liabili-

[16]The Bank for International Settlements is discussed in Chapter 9. See especially Exhibit 9.3 on page 222.

ties. While banks in many countries were already at or above this capital standard, other banks, especially in Japan, were below it. This required banks with inadequate capital to issue shares and reduce their liabilities to move toward the new BIS standard.

561

CHAPTER 22
Multinational
Banking

Derivatives Trading

One problem which has occupied the attention of the BIS and the G-7 members during meetings in 1994 is the increased activity of banks in the **derivatives markets.** The concern is the risk that some banks face that is not reflected in traditional measures of bank safety, such as reserve-deposit and capital-deposit ratios. Concern over bank trading in derivatives reached crisis proportions after the massive losses of Barings from trading in Japanese stock market index futures by a 28-year-old trader at the bank's Singapore office. (Losses revealed in 1995 exceeded $1 billion.) While it is true that trading derivatives such as currency and interest-rate futures and options can be risky, as Exhibit 22.1 points out, derivatives can be used to *reduce* risk as well as to *take* risk. It all depends on other business exposures that are faced. This is what makes the issue of derivatives so difficult for regulators to resolve. The matter is still a burning issue for policymakers, and we can expect new standards, especially of disclosure of derivative positions of banks, in the future.

SUMMARY

1. Eurodollars are U.S.-dollar bank deposits held outside the United States. Included within the Eurodollar market are the Asiadollar market and other markets outside Europe.
2. Eurocurrencies are bank deposits held outside the home countries of the currencies. The Eurocurrency market is also known as the offshore currency market.
3. Eurocurrency markets allow investors and borrowers to choose among different currencies of denomination at the same location.
4. The commonly held view is that Eurodollars came into existence initially as the result of the preferences of Soviet holders of dollar balances. For safety and ideological reasons, they preferred to hold their dollars in Europe. Perhaps more important were the U.S. Federal Reserve System regulations on interest rates on deposits, and on holding reserves. These regulations encouraged a flow of dollars to Europe. The borrowing of these dollars was stimulated by credit and capital-flow restrictions in the United States.
5. The convenience of holding deposits in and negotiating loans with local banks, as well as the lower spreads on Eurocurrencies from the absence of severe regulation, resulted in the later expansion of Eurodollars and other Eurocurrencies.
6. Eurocurrencies result in potential multiple expansions of bank deposits. The size of the multiplier depends on the speed with which funds leak to a currency's home market.
7. Banks can do business abroad via correspondents. They can also post representatives abroad to help clients. If they wish even greater involvement overseas, they can consider opening an agency, which does not solicit deposits; opening a foreign branch; or buying or establishing a subsidiary. Banks can venture abroad as part of a consortium. In the United States, banks can establish an Edge Act subsidiary to invest in foreign subsidiary banks or otherwise invest outside the home state or abroad, or they can establish an international banking facility.
8. Banks are among the most multinational of firms. The benefits of being multinational include more timely and meaningful information on financial markets and events, better

562

PART SIX
Institutional
Structure of
International Trade
and Finance

information on borrower quality, keeping clients from using other banks, earning fees from custodial and other services, and avoiding onerous regulations.

9. The opening of overseas offices to avoid domestic regulations on required reserves, reporting assets, and paying deposit insurance premiums has increased the riskiness of banks. That is, the major factors making banks multinational are also the major factors contributing to their riskiness.

10. Countries have to some extent competed with each other by progressively deregulating banking. Banking regulators have tended to match the deregulations of other countries to avoid losing banks, but as a result, banking has become more risky.

REVIEW QUESTIONS

1. What is a Eurodollar?
2. What is a Eurocurrency?
3. How did the U.S. Federal Reserve contribute to the supply of Eurodollar deposits?
4. What contributed to the demand for Eurodollar loans?
5. Did U.S. trade deficits contribute to the growth of Eurodollars?
6. What is meant by "LIBOR"?
7. Why do banks trade Eurocurrency futures?
8. What is the Eurodollar multiplier?
9. How do leakages of dollars back to the United States affect the size of the Eurodollar multiplier?
10. Why do banks have correspondent relationships with other banks?
11. How does a foreign bank agency differ from a branch?
12. Why have some banks set up Edge Act corporations?
13. What is an IBF?
14. In what ways has information contributed to the multinationalization of the banking industry?

ASSIGNMENT PROBLEMS

1. Since a person can open a Eurosterling account with dollars—by converting the dollars into pounds—or open a Eurodollar account with sterling, what yield differences can exist between different (forward-hedged) Eurocurrencies?
2. Why do you think Eurodollars are the major Eurocurrency? Does it have to do with the amount of business transacted in U.S. dollars?
3. Given the relatively extensive use of dollars in denominating sales contracts in international trade, are Eurodollar multipliers likely to be larger than multipliers for other Eurocurrencies? [Hint: Recall that the value of a multiplier has to do with the speed with which funds return to their home.]
4. a. What is the Eurodollar creation from a deposit of $2 million when the Eurocurrency banks maintain a 5 percent reserve? Assume that the $2 million is deposited in a London office of Barclays Bank, which makes a loan to British Holdings Ltd., which uses the funds to pay for goods from British Auto Ltd., which in turn places the proceeds in Citibank in London. Assume that Citibank uses its extra dollars to make a loan to Aviva Corporation, which uses the dollars back in the United States.
   b. Recompute the change in Eurodollars in a above, assuming instead that a 10 percent reserve is maintained.
   c. Recompute the change in Eurodollars in a above with the 5 percent reserve, assuming that five banks are involved before leakage occurs.

    d. What do you think is more important in affecting the size of the Eurodollar multiplier—the size of reserves or the time before a leakage occurs?

5. Give a reason (or reasons) why each of the following might open a Eurodollar account:

    a. The government of Iraq

    b. A U.S. private citizen

    c. A Canadian university professor

    d. A European-based corporation

    e. A U.S.-based corporation

6. Does it make any difference to the individual bank that makes a loan whether the loaned funds will leak to the United States? In other words, does the individual bank lose the funds no matter who borrows the dollars?

7. What is the difference between a foreign branch, a foreign subsidiary, a foreign affiliate, and a foreign agency? Which types of foreign banking will make banks multinational?

8. If the object of U.S. banks moving overseas had been purely to help customers, could they have used only correspondent relationships and representative offices? Why then do you believe they have opened branches and purchased subsidiaries?

9. In what way does Table 22.3 suggest little discrimination against foreign financial firms? Can you find any apparent examples of discrimination?

10. Empirical evidence suggests that banks tend to locate near importers rather than exporters. What do you think is responsible for this?

BIBLIOGRAPHY

ALIBER, ROBERT Z.: "International Banking: A Survey," *Journal of Money, Credit and Banking,* Part 2, November 1984, pp. 661–678.

BAKER, JAMES C., and M. GERALD BRADFORD: *American Banks Abroad, Edge Act Companies and Multinational Banking,* Frederick A. Praeger, New York, 1974.

BHATTACHARYA, ANINDYA: *The Asian Dollar Market,* Frederick A. Praeger, New York, 1977.

CORRIGAN, E. GERALD: "Coping with Globally Integrated Financial Markets," *Quarterly Review,* Federal Reserve Bank of New York, winter 1987, pp. 1–5.

DEBS, RICHARD A.: "International Banking," *Monthly Review,* Federal Reserve Bank of New York, June 1975, pp. 122–129.

DUFEY, GUNTER, and IAN GIDDY: *The International Money Market,* Prentice-Hall, Englewood Cliffs, N.J., 1978.

EINZIG, PAUL A.: *The Euro-Dollar System,* 5th ed., St. Martin's Press, New York, 1973.

FREEDMAN, CHARLES: "A Model of the Eurodollar Market," *Journal of Monetary Economics,* April 1977, pp. 139–161.

FRIEDMAN, MILTON: "The Euro-Dollar Market: Some First Principles," *Morgan Guarantee Survey,* October 1969, pp. 4–44.

GOLDBERG, MICHAEL A., ROBERT W. HELSLEY, and MAURICE D. LEVI: "On the Development of International Financial Centers," *The Annals of Regional Science,* February 1988, pp. 81–94.

HEINKEL, ROBERT L., and MAURICE D. LEVI: "The Structure of International Banking," *Journal of International Money and Finance,* June 1992, pp. 251–272.

HENNING, CHARLES N., WILLIAM PIGOTT, and ROBERT H. SCOTT: *International Financial Management,* McGraw-Hill, New York, 1977.

KLOPSTOCK, FRED H.: "Money Creation in the Euro-Dollar Market—A Note on Professor Friedman's Views," *Monthly Review,* Federal Reserve Bank of New York, January 1970, pp. 12–15.

LEES, FRANCIS A.: *International Banking and Finance,* John Wiley & Sons, New York, 1974.

MCKENZIE, GEORGE W.: *The Economics of the Euro-Currency System,* John Wiley & Sons, New York, 1976.

564

McKinnon, Ronald I.: *The Eurocurrency Market,* Essays in International Finance, no. 125, Princeton University Press, Princeton, N.J., 1977.

Ricks, David A., and Jeffrey S. Arpan: "Foreign Banking in the United States," *Business Horizons,* February 1976, pp. 84–87.

Robinson, Stuart W., Jr.: *Multinational Banking,* A. W. Sijthoff International, Leiden, The Netherlands, 1972.

CHAPTER 23

Instruments and Institutions of International Trade

In war as in love, to bring matters to a close, you must get close together.
—NAPOLEON

EXTRA DIMENSIONS OF INTERNATIONAL TRADE

In ordinary domestic commercial transactions, there are reasonably simple, well-prescribed means of recourse in the event of nonpayment or other causes of disagreement between parties. For example, the courts can be used to reclaim goods when buyers refuse to pay or are unable to pay. The situation is substantially more complex with international commercial transactions, which by necessity involve more than one legal jurisdiction. In addition, a seller might not receive payment, not because the buyer does not want to pay, but because, for example, the buyer's country has an insurrection, revolution, war, or civil unrest and decides to make its currency inconvertible into foreign exchange. In order to handle these and other difficulties faced in international transactions, a number of practices and institutional arrangements have been developed, and these are explained in this chapter.

In addition to different practices and institutions for ensuring payment and delivery in international versus domestic trade, national and international institutions have been established to finance and monitor international trade. This chapter will describe the roles of these institutions as well as explain practices such as forfaiting and countertrade that are unique to the international arena.

INTERNATIONAL TRADE INVOLVING LETTERS OF CREDIT: AN OVERVIEW OF A TYPICAL TRANSACTION

In order to give a general introductory overview of the documentation and procedures of international trade, let us suppose that after considering costs of alternative suppliers of cloth, Aviva has decided to buy cloth from the British denim manufacturer British Cotton Mills Ltd. An order is placed for 1 million yards at £4 per yard, with Aviva to receive the shipment in 10 months, and pay 2 months after delivery.

566

*PART SIX
Institutional
Structure of
International Trade
and Finance*

Assume that after having made the agreement with British Cotton Mills, Aviva goes to its bank, Citibank, N.A., in New York and buys forward (12 months ahead) the £4 million. Assume that at the same time Aviva requests a **letter of credit,** which is frequently referred to as an **L/C,** or simply as a **credit.**[1] An example of a letter of credit application and agreement issued by Citibank, N.A., in New York is shown in Figure 23.1.[2] The letter of credit is a guarantee by Aviva's bank that if all the relevant documents are presented in exact conformity with the terms of the letter of credit, the British exporter will be paid. Aviva Corporation will have to pay Citibank, N.A., a fee for the letter of credit. Citibank will issue the letter only if it is satisfied with the creditworthiness of Aviva Corporation. If it is unsure, it will require some collateral.

A copy of the letter of credit will be sent to Citibank, N.A., in London. That bank will inform the British exporter's bank, Britbank Ltd., which will in turn inform British Cotton Mills of the credit advice. In our example, Citibank is both the "opening bank" and the "paying bank," as shown by the "drawn on" entry in the letter, while Britbank is the "advising bank." On receiving the credit advice, British Cotton Mills Ltd. can begin producing the denim cloth, confident that even if Aviva Corporation is unable to pay, payment will nevertheless be forthcoming from Citibank, N.A. The actual payment will be made by means of a **draft** (also called a **bill of exchange**), and this will be drawn up by the exporter or the exporter's bank after the receipt of the credit advice. The draft will stipulate that payment is to be made to the exporter at the exporter's bank, and therefore it is different from conventional checks, which are drawn up by those making the payment rather than by those who are to receive payment.

The draft corresponding to the letter of credit in Figure 23.1 is shown in part *a* of Figure 23.2. It was drawn up by the exporter, British Cotton Mills Ltd., and specifies that £4,000,000 is to be paid at the exporter's bank, Britbank. This is a **time** or **usance draft,** because the exporter, British Cotton Mills, is allowing a 60-day credit period.[3] The draft will be sent directly or via Britbank Ltd. to Citibank, N.A., in London, and that bank will **accept** the draft if the draft and other relevant documents that are presented to the bank are in exact conformity with the letter of credit. If the draft is stamped and signed by an officer of Citibank, it becomes a **banker's acceptance.** A banker's acceptance looks like the specimen in part *b* of Figure 23.2.[4]

British Cotton Mills Ltd. can sell the accepted draft at a discount which reflects the interest cost of the money advanced but not any risk associated with payment by Aviva Corporation because the draft has been guaranteed. The draft is sold in the banker's acceptance market at a discount related to the quality of the accepting bank, Citibank. Since the draft is in pounds, it will be discounted at a pound rate of inter-

---

[1]If Aviva frequently does business with British Cotton Mills, or if Aviva has had problems paying in the past, some other procedure is likely to be used. Such procedures are described later in the chapter.

[2]The format of the letter of credit application and agreement shown in Figure 23.1 follows the standard recommended by the International Chamber of Commerce. The letter in Figure 23.1 was kindly provided by Citibank, N.A. Examples of letters of credit and other documents can be found in *An Introduction to Letters of Credit,* Citibank, New York 1991. The letter of credit we have presented is for a straightforward situation.

[3]The maturity of a time or usance draft is also sometimes referred to as its **tenor.**

[4]Citibank in London is the accepting bank because the draft is in pounds. If the draft were denominated in dollars, it would be accepted by Citibank in New York.

Application and Agreement For Documentary Letter of Credit

Citibank, N.A. 111 Wall Street
North American Trade Finance

16th Floor, New York, N.Y. 10005
Credit Number:

Advising Bank (Name and Address)
Britbank Ltd,
1 Floor Street,
London, England

Applicant (Name and Address)
Aviva (Denim Clothing) Corp.
New York, New York

Beneficiary (Name and Address)
British Cotton Mills Ltd.
London, England

Amount   (Four Million British
(in specific currency of Credit) pounds sterling)
L4,000,000

Expiry Date and Place
(for negotiation)   June 30, (next year)

Subject to the following terms and conditions, please issue your Irrevocable Letter of Credit (hereinafter called the "Credit") to be available by the beneficiary's draft(s):

Drawn at ☐ Sight, ☒ 60 Days Sight, ☐ _____ Days Date, ☐ other _____

Drawn on ☐ Citibank, N.A. New York, N.Y. for _____% invoice cost.

Drawn on ☒ Citibank, N.A. London, England for _____% invoice cost.
(Name and Address of paying bank if any).

Accompanied by the following documents which are indicated by an "X".

☒ Commercial Invoice(s) _____ original(s) and __2__ copies.

☒ Customs Invoice(s) _____ original(s) and __0__ copies.

☐ Insurance Policy and/or Certificate (to be effected by shipper, unless otherwise indicated below)

☐ Insurance to include: (list coverage) _____

☒ Transport Document: ☒ Marine, ☐ Multimodal, ☐ Air, ☐ Other (define) _____

issued in full set consigned: ☐ to, or ☐ to the order of __Citibank, N.A.__

marked Freight ☐ Collect or ☐ Paid and notify __Aviva Corporation, New York, New York__

_____ Dated Latest: June 20, (current year)

☐ Other documents _____

Covering: Merchandise described in the invoice(s) as: (Brief Description) 1,000.000 yards of denim cloth

Terms:
☐ FAS _____ , ☐ FOB _____ , ☒ CFR _____ , ☐ CIF _____

☐ CPT _____ , ☐ CIP _____ , ☐ Other _____

Shipment from __London, England__ to __New York, New York__

For Multimodal Transport Document only:
Place of Receipt/Taking in Charge _____ Place of Final Destination _____

Partial Shipment ☒ Permitted, ☐ Prohibited   Transhipment ☒ Permitted, ☐ Prohibited

Draft(s) and documents must be presented to the negotiating or paying bank within __15__ days after the date of issuance of the Bill(s) of Lading or other shipping documents, but not later than the expiry date of the Credit.

☐ All banking charges other than issuing bank's charges are for account ☐ Beneficiary, ☐ Applicant.

☐ Negotiation fees are for account ☐ Beneficiary, ☐ Applicant.

☐ Discount charges are for account ☐ Beneficiary, ☐ Applicant.

☐ Acceptance fees are for account ☐ Beneficiary, ☐ Applicant.

☒ Insurance effected by the Applicant.

Attachments hereto impose additional terms and conditions on Applicant and/or Citibank and are incorporated into this Application and Agreement as if fully set forth herein.

Transmit the Credit through your correspondent, or directly to the beneficiary, or to: _____

_____ , by ☐ Cable/Swift, ☐ Airmail, ☐ Courier Service, ☐ Pre-Advice by Cable/Swift.

All drafts and documents called for under the Credit are to be delivered by the negotiating or paying bank to Citibank, N.A., New York by Airmail in a single mailing.

Shipping documents for custom house entry are to be sent by you to _____

To induce the establishment of the Credit, Applicant agrees to the terms and conditions of the Agreement as set forth hereinafter.

Figure 23.1. Application and Agreement for Documentary Letter of Credit   **567**
(*Source:* Citibank, N.A. Reproduced by permission.)

568

PART SIX
Institutional
Structure of
International Trade
and Finance

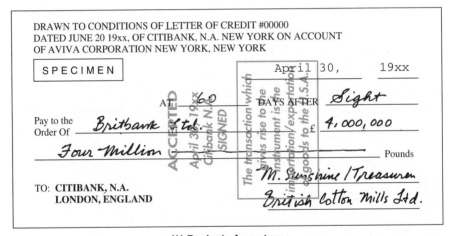

(a) Bank draft

(b) Banker's Acceptance

Figure 23.2. The Draft and Banker's Acceptance
(*Source:* Citibank, N.A. Reproduced by permission.)

est and sold in the London money market. Alternatively, instead of selling the draft, British Cotton Mills Ltd. can wait until payment is made to Britbank Ltd. and its account with the bank is credited. This will occur on June 30—2 months after the date on which the draft was accepted (April 30) and a year after the date of the sales contract.

Citibank in London will forward the documents to New York. Citibank in New York will require payment from Aviva Corporation on June 30 of the dollar amount in the forward contract agreed to in the previous year for the purchase of £4 million. At the same time that Aviva's account is debited by Citibank in New York, Citibank will give the documents to Aviva. The New York and London offices of Citibank will then settle their accounts with each other. British Cotton Mills will have been paid via Britbank; Aviva will have paid Citibank in New York; Citibank in New York will have paid Citibank in London; and Citibank in London will have

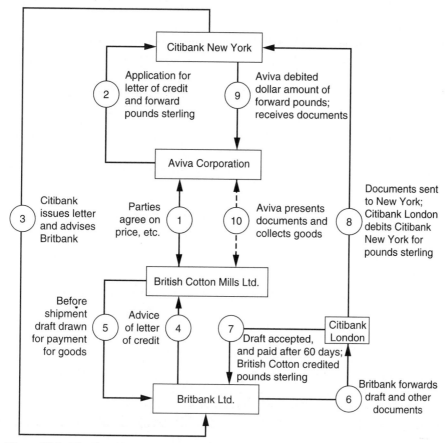

Figure 23.3. The Steps in International Trade
(Adapted from Leonard A. Back, *Introduction to Commercial Letters of Credit*, Citicorp, New York, undated.)

paid Britbank. Aviva will have the papers to receive the cloth. The transaction is complete. The steps are summarized in Figure 23.3.

Because the letter of credit in Figure 23.1 requires that certain documents be presented, it is a **documentary credit.** This is shown at the top of the letter. The accompanying draft (Figure 23.2a) is referred to as a **documentary draft. A clean draft** does not require a letter of credit or other supporting documents and is used only when there is complete trust—for example, when goods are shipped between subsidiaries of the same multinational. If the documents are delivered upon the *acceptance* of a draft, the draft is an **acceptance draft,** and if the documents are delivered upon the *payment* of a draft, the draft is a **payment draft.**[5]

The most important document that is required before a bank will accept a draft is the **bill of lading.** The bill of lading, or **B/L,** is issued by the carrier and shows that the carrier has originated the shipment of merchandise. The B/L can serve as the

[5]When payment is made upon the presentation of a draft, the draft is a **sight draft.** When payment is made after sight, the draft is a time draft (as in part *a* of Figure 23.2)

570

*PART SIX
Institutional
Structure of
International Trade
and Finance*

title to the goods, which are owned by the exporter until payment is made. Then, via the participating banks, the bill of lading is sent to the importer to be used for claiming the merchandise. An **order bill of lading** is a bill which gives title to a stated party. It can be used by that party as collateral for loans.

When goods are sent by air, the equivalent of the bill of lading is called an **air waybill.** This serves the same purpose as a bill of lading, being required for release of the goods and transferring ownership from seller to shipper to final buyer. A logistical difficulty with air waybills is ensuring they reach buyers before the goods which are to be claimed. The waybill may accompany the goods, but for reasons of safety—to ensure the right party receives the goods—waybills are better sent separately. Today, consideration is being given to sending waybills electronically.

ALTERNATIVE PAYMENT AND GUARANTEEING PROCEDURES

Open-Account and Consignment Sales

If Aviva and British Cotton Mills have been doing business with each other for many years and Aviva has established a reputation for prompt payment, Aviva may try to avoid the expense of a letter of credit, for which banks charge a fee according to the credit rating of the importer and the value of the credit. Instead, Aviva might ask British Cotton Mills if it can order cloth on an **open account** basis, whereby the value of cloth shipped is added to the account Aviva keeps at British Cotton Mills. An invoice might be sent at the end of each month or after each shipment, allowing Aviva to pay by buying a clean draft, or simply by writing a check on an account denominated in the invoice currency. This saves collection fees as well as the cost of the letter of credit.

In situations of trust, goods are sometimes supplied on a **consignment** basis. In this case, payment is not made until after the buyer has sold the goods, and in the meantime the goods remain the property of the supplier.

Cash in Advance and Confirmed Credits

When there is no trust, as after a firm has developed a bad reputation for settling its accounts, perhaps having been late settling previous transactions with the supplier, payment may be required in advance. In this situation, cash is sent to the supplier's bank before the goods are shipped.

When an exporter's lack of trust concerns the importer's bank or the importer's government—perhaps the importer's bank is poorly capitalized, or the importer's government might freeze foreign exchange payments—and when the importer cannot pay cash in advance, the exporter can ensure payment by having a letter of credit guaranteed by a domestic bank. What happens in this situation is that the exporter asks the importer for a letter of credit, even though this will be issued by a bank in the importer's country. The exporter takes this letter to a bank at home and pays the domestic bank to guarantee, or **confirm,** the letter of credit. The result will be a foreign letter of credit with a domestic confirmation. The exporter will then be paid regardless of what happens to the importer's bank or in the importer's country. Nonpayment due to the failure of the importer's bank or action taken by the importer's government is the problem of the confirming bank and not the exporter, provided that the exporter has delivered the goods.

Export Insurance

Letters of credit must be purchased by the importer, and while the cost is not high—a mere fraction of a percent if the importer's credit is good—obtaining the letter may be inconvenient, and will reduce the importer's available credit for other purposes. For these reasons, an exporter may find that a sale is contingent upon not asking for a letter of credit. Indeed, pressure from other exporters who are not requiring letters of credit frequently means exporters can assume that any talk of letters of credit will mean no sale. In such a case exporters can buy export credit insurance. This insurance is arranged and paid for by the exporter and can cover a variety of risks.

It is possible to buy credit insurance against commercial risk only, or against both commercial and political risk. Insurance against both commercial and political risk serves rather like a confirmed letter of credit in that the exporter will be paid whether the importer pays or not, and whether the importer's country allows payment or not. Insurance against commercial risk alone serves rather like an unconfirmed letter of credit in that the exporter will not be paid if the importer's government prevents payment. However, there are some important differences between letters of credit and export credit insurance. One of these differences is the presence of a deductible portion on insurance, whereas letters of credit typically cover 100 percent of credit.[6] The deductible means the exporter loses something if the importer does not pay. The uninsured portion of a credit is a contingent liability of the exporter. Clearly, the presence of a deductible makes credit insurance less desirable to exporters than confirmed letters of credit. So, of course, does the need to pay for credit insurance; the importer pays for a letter of credit, while the exporter has to pay for export credit insurance.[7]

Typically there are two forms of export credit insurance. One form provides automatic coverage up to a stated limit on exporters' receivables from buyers whose credit the insurers have approved. This type of insurance is well suited to exporters who must quote commodity prices over the telephone and accept orders if the buyers agree to these prices. For example, exporters selling lumber or wheat can buy credit insurance which covers all sales to approved buyers. This type of credit insurance is variously called **continuous, whole-turnover,** or **rollover** insurance.

A second form of credit insurance covers only specific contracts and specific risks. For this, an exporter must apply for coverage of the specific export credit. For example, if a firm receives an order for six large passenger planes, the exporter will have to apply to the credit insurer and state the specifics of the sale. This type of insurance is usually called **specific export credit insurance.**

---

[6]The deductible may be 10 percent or more of the amount insured. There are also other differences between letters of credit and credit insurance when an exporter is unable to deliver goods, when goods are damaged or lost in transit, and so on: credit insurance typically provides broader coverage than a letter of credit.

[7]For a more detailed treatment of the pros and cons of letters of credit and credit insurance see Dick Briggs and Burt Edwards, *Credit Insurance: How to Reduce the Risks of Trade Credit,* Woodhead-Faulkner, Cambridge, England, 1988.

572

PART SIX
Institutional
Structure of
International Trade
and Finance

The Rationale for Government-Provided Credit Insurance

Even though export credit insurance can be purchased from private-sector insurance companies such as the large British-based insurance company Trade Indemnity, most governments sell export credit insurance themselves, usually through an especially established agency. For example, in the United States export credit insurance can be purchased from the Export-Import Bank ("Ex-Im Bank"), in Britain from the Export Credits Guarantee Department, and in Canada from the Export Development Corporation. Since governments do not typically provide fire, life, disability, automobile, and accident insurance, it is worth asking why in the case of insurance of export credits it has become the norm for governments to arrange coverage. That is, why do governments step in to insure export credits rather than allowing private insurance companies to provide the insurance at a competitively determined premium? Even apart from trying to subsidize exports because of the jobs and incomes they generate, there are "market failures" which might warrant government involvement. There are also arguments that the government may be able to provide the insurance more cheaply. Let us consider these arguments.

Credit insurance requires the insurer to keep current on the situation in different companies in a number of countries. A government can do this through its existing trade representatives stationed at its embassies and consular offices abroad. For private insurance companies to assess risks they all need to maintain overseas offices in different countries.[8] Indeed, it might be that the market in each country could support only one credit insurer. Then the government might have to regulate the industry if it did not provide the credit insurance itself. That is, from the economies of scale insurers face, credit insurance may be a **natural monopoly.**

Another reason why governments might argue that they are better suited to provide export credit insurance than private insurance companies is that a government insurer can use other branches of government to provide muscle and thereby reduce country risk. For example, if a country decided it would no longer allow payment to foreign creditors, a government export credit agency might ask its government to threaten withdrawal of aid to the delinquent country. Unlike the previous reason given, this relies on an **economy of scope,** not an economy of scale. Economies of scope are a result of the range of activities performed or products produced, not the level of activity or production. In this case, governments enjoy an economy of scope by being in different activities, specifically, credit insurance and foreign aid.

A factor which supports official against private credit insurance, and which applies to export financing as well as to export insurance, is that there may be benefits to other firms in the exporting country if one of that country's companies makes an export sale. For example, if a U.S. engineering company wins a contract to supply machinery to China, there may be improved prospects for other U.S. companies to sell to China. That is, there may be **positive externalities** or spillovers that derive from an export contract. These positive externalities will not be considered by private export credit insurers in a competitive market, but a government agency can take them into account when deciding whether to provide export insur-

---

[8]Alternatively, the insurance companies might buy information from a country-risk-evaluating company. However, the risk-evaluating company would need to maintain offices abroad if it were to be current on the situations in different countries.

ance or financing. That is, export insurance and financing have elements of a **public good,** and as is generally the case for public goods, they will be underprovided by profit-maximizing firms.

THE FINANCING OF INTERNATIONAL TRADE

Short-Term Financing: Banker's Acceptances

When an exporter gives credit to a foreign buyer by issuing a draft for some date in the future, the draft itself can be used by the exporter for short-term financing. As we explained earlier, when the draft is stamped "accepted" by a bank and signed by an officer of the bank, it becomes a banker's acceptance. The exporter can sell the banker's acceptance in the money market at a discount that is related to the riskiness of the accepting bank. If the exporter's draft is drawn without an importer's letter of credit, the draft is a **trade draft.** This can be sold in the money market, but because it is only a commercial rather than a bank obligation, the draft will face a higher discount than would a banker's acceptance. However, the exporter can pay a bank to accept the draft, and then sell this at a lower discount. The acceptance charge can be compared to the extra value received on the discounted draft. All documents, including shipping documents, will normally be provided to the bank accepting the draft.

When an exporter draws up a time draft, the exporter is granting the importer credit which the exporter may finance by selling the signed draft. When an exporter draws up a sight rather than a time draft, the exporter is not granting credit to the importer; there is no delay in payment. Nevertheless, a banker's acceptance may be created in this situation. This will happen if the importer draws up a time draft in favor of a bank, signs the draft, and has it accepted by the bank. The banker will immediately pay the importer the discounted value of the draft. The bank will then either sell the draft or hold it for collection. An importer might take this step to finance goods purchased from abroad before they are sold.[9]

The time after sight on a banker's acceptance, whether created by the exporter or by the importer, is typically 30, 90, or 180 days. Consequently, bankers' acceptances are only a mechanism for short-term trade financing.

Forfaiting: A Form of Medium-Term Finance

Forfaiting Explained

Forfaiting is a form of medium-term financing of international trade.[10] It involves the purchase by a bank, the forfaiter, of a series of promissory notes, usually due at 6-month intervals for 3 to 5 years, signed by an importer in favor of an exporter.[11] These notes are frequently **avalled,** or guaranteed, by the importer's bank. The promissory notes are sold by the exporter to the forfaiting bank at a dis-

---

[9]These means of financing trade and providing payment guarantees are an alternative to earlier procedures such as those used by the Merchant of Venice. See Exhibit 23.1.

[10]In French it is called *a forfait,* and in German, *Forfaitierung.*

[11]Of course, the language of these promissory notes must be in accordance with legal requirements. These requirements are spelled out in the Geneva Convention of 1930, which has been signed by numerous countries, and the Bill of Exchange Act of 1882, which governs practice in Britain.

The Merchant of Venice in Shakespeare's play with the same title faced a trade-financing problem. For merchants of his day, goods would arrive from afar in large loads, in fact shiploads. Paying immediately for imported goods was difficult because of the sheer size of the amount that would arrive by ship, perhaps once or twice in a year, and because sales from the large inventories occurred continually through the year. Financing was needed to bridge the gap between lumpy arrival and steady sales, that is, financing was needed for the inventory stocks that the nature of trade forced upon merchants.

A just-in-time inventory system, were this to have been possible in the merchant's Venice, would have avoided the trade-financing problem. If goods could have arrived at the same rate as they were sold to customers in the area, the cash flow from sales would have paid for the imports. Clearly, the nature of ships, which cannot be made small enough to deliver one day's worth of sales, prevented the use of just-in-time inventories at that time, just as it does

today. Better predictions of arrival of goods and of sales can reduce the required inventory levels, but they cannot eliminate inventories of imports and the need to finance them. However, instruments such as letters of credit have been developed to ensure payment, allowing trade to be based on more acceptable collateral than the Merchant's pound of flesh. That is, if the Merchant of Venice had had at his disposal a bank that could guarantee his credit for an L/C fee, he could have guaranteed his payment for imports with paper instead of blood. Late arrival of payment for the imported product would have forced the L/C-issuing bank to pay Shylock, lifting the merchant's burden but stealing Portia's poetic appeal for all-round compassion:

The quality of mercy is not strain'd;
It droppeth as the gentle rain from heaven
Upon the place beneath. It is twice blest:
It blesseth him that gives and him that takes.
   —*The Merchant of Venice,* Act 4, Scene 1

count. The bank pays the exporter immediately, allowing the exporter to finance the production of the goods for export, and the importer to pay later. The notes are held by the forfaiter for collection as they come due, without recourse to the exporter in whose favor the notes were originally drawn before being assigned. This absence of recourse distinguishes the forfaiting of promissory notes from the discounting of trade drafts, for which the exporter is open to recourse in the case of nonpayment.[12] This can all be summarized in the following short definition:

> Forfaiting is medium-term nonrecourse exporter-arranged financing of importers' credits.

The nature of forfaiting is also summarized in Figure 23.4. The figure shows what happens, and the order of events, when a U.S. jeans-machine manufacturer sells its machines to a Russian jeans manufacturer. The lightly shaded arrows show the exchanges occurring at the time the export deal is made, while the dark arrows show subsequent settlements.

Many forfaiting banks hold the promissory notes themselves and collect payments as they come due. Others buy notes for investors who have expressed interest

---

[12]The lack of recourse explains the origin of the term "forfaiting"; the buyer of the promissory notes forefeits the right of recourse.

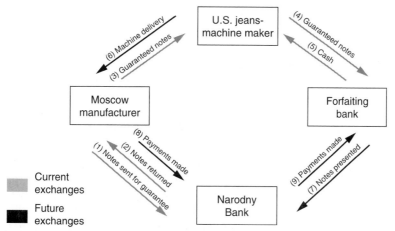

Figure 23.4. The Steps Involved in Forfaiting

Forfaiting is a means of providing medium-term import credits. The importer prepares promissory notes that are guaranteed by a bank. These are sent to the exporter, who then sells them for cash to a forfaiting bank. The bank may then sell the notes. The holder of the notes has no recourse to the exporter. The credit risk is entirely borne by the noteholder.

in taking up the high-yielding paper, and still others arrange forfaiting and then trade the notes in the secondary market.[13]

The discount rates that apply to forfaiting depend on the terms of the notes, the currencies in which they are denominated, the credit ratings of the banks avalling the notes, and the country risks of the importing entities. The spreads between forfaiting rates and Eurocurrency deposit rates, with which forfaiting rates move, are typically about one-and-a-half times the spreads between straight Eurocurrency loans and deposits.[14] The higher spreads reflect the lack of recourse and interest-rate risk; the typical 5-year term of forfaiting deals means forfaiters have difficulty matching credit maturities with the typically much shorter-maturity Eurocurrency deposits and futures contracts. Although there have been some floating-rate agreements which have reduced interest-rate risk, fixed-interest-rate deals still predominate.

Forfaiting banks have shown considerable flexibility and often quote rates over the telephone once they know the name of the importer or the avalling bank.[15] This allows exporters to quote their selling prices after working out what they will net from their sales after forfaiting costs. Another advantage to the exporter is that because there is no recourse, the promissory notes are not carried on the exporter's books as a contingent liability. Yet another is that there is no need to arrange credit insurance. Of course, the advantage of forfaiting to importers is that they receive credit when it might not otherwise be offered or not be offered on the same terms.

---

[13]Forfaiting yields are relatively high because there is no recourse in the event the goods are not delivered, the importer does not pay, and so on.

[14]See Donald Curtin, "The Unchartered $4 Billion World of Forfaiting," *Euromoney,* August 1980, pp. 62–70.

[15]The forfaiter may charge a **commitment fee** for this service.

576

*PART SIX
Institutional
Structure of
International Trade
and Finance*

The History of Forfaiting

As with the introduction of Eurodollars, the development of forfaiting probably owes its origins, but not its subsequent popularity, to the difficulties faced in east-west trade. (We recall that it has been argued that the Eurodollar market started because the former Soviet Union wanted to hold U.S. dollars, but not to hold them in the United States.) The practice of forfaiting dates back to the early 1960s and the placing of orders by the eastern-bloc Comecon countries for capital equipment and grain. Many of these orders were placed with West German firms which were not in a position to supply credit themselves, or to arrange financing with banks or official lending agencies. That is, the exporters were unable to offer **supplier credits,** and they were unable to arrange **buyer credits** through lending institutions. Instead, they found banks which were willing to purchase the importers' promissory notes at a discount. One of the first banks to recognize the opportunity was Credit Suisse through its subsidiary Finance A.G. Zurich.[16] The original deals involved the sale of U.S. grain to West Germany, which resold the grain to eastern European countries. Forfaiting allowed the U.S. exporters to be paid immediately and the eastern European buyers to receive medium-term credit.[17]

While originally viewed as "lending of last resort," forfaiting grew in popularity, spreading from Switzerland and Germany, where it began, to London, later to Scandinavia and the rest of Europe, and eventually to the United States. Forfaiting is still not as important as payment by traditional time or usance bills of exchange or credit from official export financing agencies, but it has nevertheless become an important source of financing, especially for the medium-term maturities.[18]

Financing by Government Export Agencies

Because of the jobs and income that derive from a healthy export sector, it has become standard practice for governments around the world to help their exporters win contracts by offering export financing. This financing can be of short-, medium-, or long-term maturity, and takes a number of different forms.

A large part of official export financing takes the form of loan guarantees to exporters. For example, the U.S. Export-Import Bank ("Ex-Im Bank") helps small businesses obtain working capital to finance exports. The bank does this by guaranteeing the principal and interest on working capital loans by commercial lenders to eligible U.S. exporters. The funds can be used for producing the goods for export, buying raw materials, holding inventory, or marketing. The guarantees help companies raise supplier credits. Buyer credits, that is, loans or loan guarantees to the buyers of a country's exports, are also offered in many countries. For example, the Export Credits Guarantee Department offers buyer credits to purchasers of British exports, and the Export Development Corporation provides buyer credits to buyers of Canadian exports.

---

[16]See Werner R. Rentzman and Thomas Teichman, "Forfaiting: An Alternative Technique for Export Financing," *Euromoney,* December 1975, pp. 58–63.

[17]See Donald Curtin, *op. cit.*

[18]As we have seen, time drafts typically provide only short-term financing. Clearly, time drafts are a form of supplier credit.

Official export financing also takes the form of loans to domestic or foreign financial institutions, which in turn make loans to the importers. Sometimes only a portion of the funds required by the importers is made available to the financial institutions, the balance being provided by other lenders. In some countries, the export finance agency provides its component of the shared financing on a "first in, last out" basis. This means that the export agency commits its money before the private financial institution makes its contribution, and that the export agency gives the private financial institution the first claim on repayments. This and other financing practices have given rise to claims of hidden assistance and subsidies to exporters and to a number of disputes. Accusations that financing constitutes a subsidy have been especially common over interest rates charged on buyer credits. Some countries have tried to hide their subsidies by offering **mixed credits,** which are a combination of export credits at market interest rates and what the export agencies call "foreign aid." That is, some export agencies say that they are able to offer very low interest rates on export credits as a result of contributions by their countries' development aid agencies.[19]

It is not uncommon for official export agencies to offer guarantees to banks in the exporter's country if the banks offer buyer credits. This substantially reduces the risk to the banks, thereby reducing the interest rates they charge. In the United States, the Ex-Im Bank guarantees export credits that are offered by the **Private Export Funding Corporation** (**PEFCO**). PEFCO is a private lending organization that was started in 1970 by a group of commercial banks and large export manufacturers. PEFCO raises its funds through the sale of the foreign repayment obligations which it has arranged and which have been guaranteed by the Ex-Im Bank. PEFCO also sells secured notes on the securities market.

The need for export financing, the need for special trade documents, such as letters of credit and trade drafts, and the need for export insurance, are all greatly reduced or eliminated when international trade takes the form of countertrade. There are different variants to countertrade, and it is well worthwhile considering what these variants are and why countertrade occurs.

COUNTERTRADE

The Various Forms of Countertrade

Countertrade involves a reciprocal agreement for the exchange of goods or services. The parties involved may be firms or governments, and the reciprocal agreements can take a number of forms.

Barter

The simplest form of countertrade involves the direct exchange of goods or services from one country for the goods or services of another. No money changes hands, so that there is no need for letters of credit or drafts. Furthermore, since the

---

[19]The bickering over interest rates on export credits was reduced in 1983 when the OECD countries agreed to link interest rates to a weighted average of government-bond yields and to all charge the same rate. See *International Letter,* no. 515, Federal Reserve Bank of Chicago, December 16, 1983.

578

*PART SIX
Institutional
Structure of
International Trade
and Finance*

goods or services are exchanged at the same time, there is no need for trade financing or credit insurance. An example of a barter deal was the trading of the Polish soccer star Kazimierz Deyna for photocopiers and French lingerie.[20]

Counterpurchase

Barter requires a "double coincidence of wants" in that the two parties in the transaction must each want what the other party has to provide, and want it at the same time. Because such a coincidence is unlikely, a form of countertrade called **counterpurchase** is substantially more common than barter. With counterpurchase the seller agrees with the buyer either to

1. make purchases from a company nominated by the buyer (the buyer then settles up with the company it has nominated), or
2. take products from the buyer in the future (that is, the seller accepts credits in terms of products).

Counterpurchase can also involve a combination of these two possibilities. That is, the seller agrees to receive products at a future date from a company nominated by the buyer.

Counterpurchase frequently involves only partial compensation with products, and the balance in cash. These types of countertrade deals are called **compensation agreements.**

Industrial Offset

A large portion of countertrade involves reciprocal agreements to buy materials or components from the buying company or country. For example, an aircraft manufacturer might agree to buy engines or fuselage materials from a buyer of its aircraft. The materials or components may not be only for the aircraft sold to the company or country. For example, a military aircraft manufacturer might agree to buy engines for all its planes from a foreign producer if the engine manufacturer's country agrees to buy a large number of aircraft.

Buyback

This form of countertrade is common with capital equipment used in mining and manufacturing. In a **buyback agreement** the seller of the capital equipment agrees to buy the products made with the equipment it supplies. For example, the maker of mining equipment might agree to buy the output of the mine for a given period, perhaps 10 or 15 years. This is a guarantee to the equipment buyer that it can pay for the capital equipment whatever happens to the price of what it produces, provided, of course, it can ensure continued production. When the equipment buyer pays partly in terms of its product and partly in cash, then, as in the case of other counterpurchase agreements of this kind, the arrangement is called a compensation agreement.

Switch Trading

Switch trading occurs when the importer has received credit for selling something to another country at a previous time and this credit cannot be converted into

---

[20]See *Euromoney,* September 1988, p. 54.

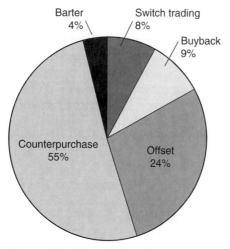

Figure 23.5. The Different Forms of Countertrade
(*Source:* Willis A. Bussard, in Christopher M. Korth (ed.), *International Countertrade*, Quorum Books, New York, 1987, p. 18.)

financial payment, but has to be used for purchases in the country where the credit is held. The owner of the credit switches title to its credit to the company or country from which it is making a purchase. For example, a British firm might have a credit in Poland for manufacturing equipment it has delivered. If a firm finds a product in France that it wishes to purchase, the British firm might pay the French firm with its Polish credit. The French firm might agree to this if it wishes to buy something from Poland. Because it is difficult for the various parties to locate each other for a switch deal, most of them are arranged by brokers. Many of these brokers are based in Austria.

The relative importance of the different forms of countertrade that we have described is shown in Figure 23.5. The figure shows clearly that counterpurchase is the dominant form and that barter is relatively unimportant.

Before leaving a description of the forms of countertrade we might mention that in the 1980s, in response to the deepening third-world debt crisis, some countries began to substitute commodities for debt payments. For example, in 1985 Peru repaid part of its foreign debt with broiler chickens, shoes, and a variety of other products. Mexico also tried to arrange an oil-for-debt swap. These arrangements are a form of countertrade in that they circumvent the use of convertible currencies.

Reasons Why Countertrade Occurs

Given that countertrade is estimated to make up about 10 to 20 percent of world trade, we might ask why trading agreements that are so difficult to arrange have assumed such importance.[21] That is, why do so many firms and countries decide

---

[21]See the surveys of countertrade summarized in Christopher Korth (ed.), *International Countertrade,* Quorum, New York, 1985.

580

*PART SIX
Institutional
Structure of
International Trade
and Finance*

against selling their products for a convertible currency and using this convertible currency to pay for what they buy?

A common reason for circumventing the use of a convertible currency and instead practicing countertrade is that a buyer in the countertrade does not have access to convertible currency. It is no accident that countertrade often occurs where at least one party cannot obtain convertible currency to make payments. If one party cannot pay with convertible currency, then it must pay with goods, which is barter; with other companies' goods, which is counterpurchase; with credits, which could be a switch trade or a counterpurchase; and so on. Many LDCs (less-developed countries), restrict access to convertible currency, and therefore many of the countertrades that occur involve an LDC.[22]

Countertrade is also encouraged when prices are kept artificially high or low. For example, if the official OPEC oil price is above the market price, an oil seller might arrange a countertrade in which the oil is implicitly valued at the market price. The alternative of selling the oil at market price and using the proceeds for purchases is more likely to cause anger among other members of the OPEC cartel. More generally, countertrade allows goods to be exchanged internationally in specific transactions at relative prices which reflect genuine market values, while allowing nonmarket prices to be charged domestically. That is, countertrade is a way of circumventing problems caused by mispriced goods or currencies.[23]

It has been argued that countertrade can promote exports. Rolf Mirus and Bernard Yeung have suggested that countertrade transactions constitute a sale of domestic goods for a "bundle" consisting of foreign goods plus marketing services.[24] The foreign firm will not "shirk" in its marketing effort because it stands to benefit fully; it takes ownership of the goods. The alternative of finding an independent firm to market the product on behalf of the producer offers a weaker incentive to work hard. By aligning the marketing firm's interest with that of the exporter, it is possible that exports are larger than they would have been otherwise.[25]

THE INSTITUTIONS REGULATING INTERNATIONAL TRADE

A glance along the shelves at the vast range of goods we purchase from abroad, and a moment's reflection on the number of jobs which depend on export sales, should amply convince us that international trade is vital to our well-being and that protectionism could do more to harm that well-being than almost any other development. Recognition of the potential damage that protectionism can bring has resulted in a number of post-World War II institutional arrangements designed to reduce protectionism and allow us to more fully exploit the benefits of trade. We shall

[22]See Rolf Mirus and Bernard Yeung, "Countertrade and Foreign Exchange Shortages: A Preliminary Investigation," *Weltwirtschaftliches Archiv,* vol. 123, no. 3, 1987, pp. 535–544.
[23]A denial of access to foreign currency can be considered a mispricing, in this case of the exchange rate; implicitly, the price of foreign currency is infinite if it cannot be purchased at any exchange rate.
[24]Rolf Mirus and Bernard Yeung, "Economic Incentives for Countertrade," *Journal of International Business Studies,* fall 1986, pp. 27–39.
[25]See Jean-Francis Hennart, "The Transaction-Cost Rationale for Countertrade," *Journal of Law, Economics and Organization,* spring 1989, pp. 127–153.

quickly review the more important of these institutional arrangements in concluding our discussion of the organization of international trade. The two most important arrangements involve the regulation of the conduct of trade by the **World Trade Organization, WTO** (and formerly by the General Agreement on Tariffs and Trade, GATT), and by the establishment of **free-trade areas.**

The World Trade Organization and GATT

The World Trade Organization, which began operation in 1995, was created to replace the General Agreement on Tariffs and Trade. The WTO differs from GATT in that:

1. The WTO is a chartered trade *organization,* not just a secretariat as was GATT.
2. The WTO has enhanced coverage vis-à-vis GATT. Most important, the WTO covers services, including trade-related aspects of intellectual property rights (TRIPs).
3. The WTO has a more compelling dispute settlement function than GATT because agreement cannot be blocked by a failure to achieve consensus.

However, despite these differences, the WTO continues the work of GATT to limit harmful trade practices, just as the IMF was to limit harmful financial practices such as competitive devaluations. In its role as trade regulator, GATT had some notable successes in reducing the level of damaging trade practices.

The two central principles of GATT were:

1. Trade relations could not be discriminatory.
2. Export subsidies were not permitted.

The nondiscriminatory principle was effected via the **most favored nation** clause, which disallowed offering better trade treatment to any country than was given to other GATT signatories. This meant that all GATT members were treated in the same way as the most favored nation was treated. An exception was made to allow free-trade areas, or **customs unions,** to exist, whereby members of the area or union could *all* be treated more favorably than nonmembers. The prohibition on export subsidies meant that no benefits could be offered to domestic producers which would give them an advantage in foreign markets. Again, an exception was made, this time for agricultural products. Where subsidies were shown to exist outside agriculture, countries were permitted to apply discriminatory tariffs to counteract trade subsidies; these are referred to as countervailing tariffs.

GATT managed to broker some general reductions in tariffs under the so-called **Kennedy–, Tokyo–,** and **Uraguay rounds.** Completed in 1994, the Uraguay round represented major progress in dealing with services and various nontariff trade barriers. GATT's success can be measured by the fact that compared to the situation when it was created, developed-country tariffs fell from an average of approximately 40 percent to 4 percent. Also, the proportion of industrial products entering developed countries duty-free has more than doubled, increasing from 20 percent to 43 percent.[26]

---

[26]See Don Macnamara, "Peter Sutherland's GATT," *Acumen,* September/October 1994, pp. 18–24.

EXHIBIT 23.2
U.S. Free-Trade Zones

The United States has had free-trade zones (FTZs), also called "foreign trade zones," since 1934. However, little use was made of them until the 1980s, which is the same time that other nations from Britain to China opened such zones within their borders. As the excerpt below explains, while the motivation for FTZs is to improve international trading competitiveness, the benefits of FTZs are largely financial, stemming from less money being tied up in duties, defective products, and so on.

Foreign trade zones (FTZ) are areas located within U.S. boundaries, but outside of its customs territory. Foreign goods can be imported duty-free into an FTZ and then either re-exported without duties or formally imported into the U.S. market accompanied by payment of U.S. import duty. . . .

Foreign trade zones consist of two types of zones: general purpose zones and subzones. In practice, general purpose zones and subzones are used for different activities. The general purpose zone is created before any of its subzones and is normally located at a port of entry such as a shipping port, border crossing, or airport. A general purpose zone usually consists of a distribution facility or industrial park.

Space is leased in a manner similar to any other industrial park or shared warehousing facility. Activities in general purpose zones typically consist of inspecting, storing, repackaging, and distributing merchandise, and destroying defective merchandise, prior to re-export. For example, the Miami FTZ acts as a distribution center for European and Asian companies exporting into South America and the Caribbean. Manufacturing activities take place in only a few general purpose zones.

Subzones are areas that are physically separate from the general purpose zone but are legally and administratively attached. Subzones allow new or existing facilities that are located outside of the general purpose zone to take advantage of FTZ benefits. For example, subzones allow space-intensive facilities, such as assembly plants, to become part of an FTZ without using expensive port space. A subzone is used by a single company and is typically created around a manufacturing plant.

FTZs potentially provide firms with a wide array of benefits. Firms can re-package or assemble imported merchandise along with domestic components for re-export without having to pay a customs duty on the imported components. This benefit makes it competitive for exporters to operate within U.S. boundaries and was the original goal of the FTZs. However, many firms have found it to be more convenient and cost effective to avoid duties on re-exported goods by alternative means such as bonded warehouses or duty drawback programs, which return tariffs on re-exported goods.

Another benefit of FTZs is that custom duties and taxes on goods for domestic consumption are not paid until the merchandise leaves a foreign trade zone and enters U.S. customs territory. In fact, while in a zone, merchandise is not subject to taxes of any kind. Furthermore, defective imports can be discarded before tariffs are paid, so that tariffs are not paid on unusable products. In practice, the deferral of both tariffs and domestic taxes until the imported merchandise leaves the trade zone is the major benefit enjoyed by current users of general purpose zones. Most of these establishments are repackaging and distribution centers.

A third benefit of FTZs is that firms may keep merchandise in a zone indefinitely. This allows firms to weather periods of poor sales without paying import duties and to defer import quotas. If import quotas have been met for the year, the merchandise can be stored in the FTZ until the next year so that it will not be included in the current year's quota.

Source: David Weiss, "Foreign Trade Zones: Growth Amid Controversy," *Chicago Fed Letter,* Federal Reserve Bank of Chicago no. 48, August 1991.

Free-Trade Areas and Customs Unions

A free-trade agreement is in some ways the lowest level of economic integration.[27] While tariffs are removed on trade among members, each nation retains the freedom to set its own tariffs to outsiders. The North American Free Trade Agreement,

[27]While not multilateral in nature, **free-trade zones,** which are sometimes called *foreign* trade zones, are a step below free-trade agreements in their importance for freer trade. Exhibit 23.2 discusses the economics of U.S. free-trade zones.

NAFTA, has this characteristic. The next level of economic integration is a customs union. Customs unions have no tariffs among members and common tariff rates for outsiders. The European Union (EU), previously known as the European Community (EC), has been a customs union since January 1993. A customs union has operational advantages because outside goods can be traded freely between members once the tariffs have been collected for the goods to enter the union. The level of integration above the customs union involves zero tariffs between members, common tariffs to outsiders, and the integration of trade policy, fiscal policy, monetary policy, and perhaps even political policy to outside bodies. Such economic and political integration within the European Union is the goal of the Maastricht Treaty.

Since its establishment in the 1950s, the European Union has swollen in size to include Belgium, Britain, Denmark, France, Greece, Italy, Ireland, Luxembourg, The Netherlands, Portugal, Spain, and Germany. Trade being an important component of economic activity within and between these nations, the EU is the largest customs union that exists. As a customs union, companies operating outside the EU have to face competition from firms inside the EU that have favorable terms within the union. For example, U.S. car makers selling in Britain have to face tariffs, whereas German, Italian, and French car makers do not.

The United States, which has traditionally been a staunch supporter of freer trade even if its rhetoric has sometimes been sharper than its actions, made its own entry into trading agreements when, in January 1989, it signed the Free Trade Agreement (FTA) with Canada. Although often overlooked, the fact is that U.S. trade with Canada is larger than U.S. trade with Japan, Germany, or any other nation, and indeed, U.S.-Canadian trade is the largest bilateral trading relationship on earth. The comprehensive and detailed arrangement of the U.S.-Canadian FTA therefore meant that each country gained improved access to its largest foreign market. Tariffs were scheduled to be removed on a large range of products over a 10-year period from the original signing of the FTA in 1989. In addition, each country obtained greater freedom to invest in the other. For the United States, one of the most important features of the FTA is Canada's agreement to give U.S. energy producers and consumers the same treatment given to Canadians. The FTA operates within the rules of GATT. Procedures have been put in place to resolve disputes, with the United States retaining its right to levy countervailing tariffs when it believes U.S. industry is being damaged by unfair trading practices.

The U.S.-Canadian FTA was the precurser to the much more widely discussed North American Free Trade Agreement (NAFTA), which since 1994 has begun the process of removing tariffs in trade between the United States, Mexico, and Canada. With a combined population of over 350 million, the NAFTA provides a market even slightly larger than the EU. Tariffs are being reduced over a 15-year period in an effort to create a borderless trading area, at least as far as tariffs and other explicit trade restrictions are concerned. Fear of job losses and environmental damage hindered acceptance of the NAFTA in the United States even though at the agreement's inception the United States enjoyed a large trade surplus with Mexico, and even though many people felt that if Mexico were a signatory of the NAFTA Mexico's environmental standards could be more easily raised than if the country were left outside the agreement. Subsequent supplementary arrangements concerning the environment as well as labor standards in Mexico are designed to increase accep-

584

PART SIX
Institutional
Structure of
International Trade
and Finance

tance of the NAFTA in the United States and Canada. A timetable and outline agreement for Chile to join the NAFTA countries was signed in Miami in 1994.

With trading agreements existing in North America, Europe, and Asia (in the form of the Association of South East Asian Nations, ASEAN), some people have come to fear the consequences of a world that is divided into three trading blocs. The pattern of localized freer-trading arrangements with unchanged or even increased protectionism against outsiders does not correspond to the principles envisioned by those who established GATT and its successor, the WTO. The danger is that the large trading blocs have constituencies which would prefer restricted trade. The bigger the bloc, the more types of constituencies that are present, and the less they need to trade with outsiders. Big trading blocs could therefore ultimately threaten globally free trade.

SUMMARY

1. Special procedures have evolved for dealing with the extra risks of international trade, and national and international institutions have been established to finance and regulate international trade.

2. Before shipping goods to foreign buyers, many exporters require buyers to provide a letter of credit from a reputable bank. This is a guarantee that the exporter will be paid if the goods are supplied in good order.

3. Payment is made by a bill of exchange, or draft, which is sent by the exporter to the importer or to the importer's bank. The importer or the importer's bank signs the draft. If the draft is payable on presentation, it is a sight draft. If it is payable at a future date, it is a time draft.

4. The shipper gives the exporter a bill of lading, the original copy of which is required for collection of the goods. The bill of lading is forwarded to the importer for the goods to be released.

5. When an exporter is confident an importer will pay, goods may be sold on an open account, and a bill presented after shipment. When an exporter suspects that an importer may not pay, cash may be demanded before shipment occurs.

6. When an exporter lacks trust in the importer's bank or country, the exporter can have the importer's letter of credit confirmed. A confirmed letter of credit is one way of avoiding country risk.

7. Export credit insurance is an alternative to letters of credit for avoiding commercial and/or country risks. Export insurance, however, typically involves a deductible portion of coverage and differs from letters of credit in other ways that are sometimes important.

8. Credit insurance may be a natural monopoly and be more effectively offered by an official rather than a private institution, because a government may have more success avoiding nonpayment and because a government may consider positive spillovers of trade deals.

9. Official export financing agencies often provide direct buyer credits, as well as guarantees on credits to buyers granted by domestic or foreign financial institutions.

10. When an exporter's time draft is accepted by a bank, the resulting accepted draft is called a banker's acceptance.

11. Banker's acceptances are a means of short-term trade financing, typically up to 6 months. Forfaiting is a means of medium-term trade financing, with a typical term of 5 years.

12. Forfaiting involves the sale by an exporter of promissory notes issued by an importer and usually avalled by the importer's bank. The forfaiter has no recourse to the exporter in the event that, for whatever reason, the forfaiter is not paid.

13. Forfaiting is a particularly useful means of financing the sale of capital goods. The exporter is paid immediately, while the importer can make payments out of revenue generated by the products of the capital goods.
14. A substantial portion of trade is countertrade. This may involve barter, an agreement to purchase products at a later date or from a designated supplier, an agreement to provide parts or to buy goods produced with capital equipment that has been supplied, or an agreement to switch credits.
15. Countertrade is motivated by foreign exchange controls and mispricing of products, and often involves LDCs.
16. The conduct of international trade is governed by the World Trade Organization (WTO), which has succeeded GATT. Members of the WTO agree to have nondiscriminatory tariffs by accepting the "most favored nation" principle, and they agree to not subsidize exports.
17. GATT was forced to grant exceptions to its tariff policy. These exceptions were to permit the establishment of free-trade areas and customs unions and to exempt agriculture from the prohibition on export subsidies.
18. The majority of trade occurs between countries which are members of customs unions or free-trade agreements. The trend toward the establishment of trading blocs could threaten globally free trade.

REVIEW QUESTIONS

1. What purpose is served by a letter of credit?
2. What purpose is served by a bill of exchange?
3. How does a time draft differ from a sight draft?
4. What is a banker's acceptance?
5. What is a "clean draft"?
6. What purpose is served by a bill of lading or air waybill?
7. Why might a company have a letter of credit confirmed?
8. Are letters of credit and export credit insurance perfect substitutes?
9. List the market failures that support government export credit insurance.
10. What is forfeited with forfaiting?
11. What forms does countertrade take?
12. Why does countertrade occur?
13. How does the World Trade Organization differ from its predecessor, the GATT?
14. What is the difference between a free-trade agreement and a customs union?

ASSIGNMENT PROBLEMS

1. Why are letters of credit not used in domestic trade?
2. Why does the exporter provide the importer with the check for payment that the importer signs, rather than just allow the importer to send a check?
3. Why are banks willing to accept time drafts, making them bills of exchange, and why do importers and exporters arrange for banks to accept drafts?
4. Are cash terms likely when an importer can arrange a letter of credit?
5. Why is export credit insurance typically offered by government agencies?
6. Why do you think promissory notes used in forfaiting deals are avalled by the importer's bank?
7. What is the similarity between an aval and an acceptance?

586

PART SIX
Institutional
Structure of
International Trade
and Finance

8. Is forfaiting a form of factoring?

9. What form of trade financing is an exporter likely to seek first, and how would the choice depend on the export deal?

10. Why is counterpurchase so much more common than barter in countertrade?

11. How can a customs union or common market such as the EU hurt a U.S. exporter?

12. Under what conditions might the emergence of a limited number of free-trade blocs lower standards of living?

BIBLIOGRAPHY

CITIBANK: *An Introduction to Letters of Credit,* Citibank, New York, 1991.

HARRINGTON, J.A.: *Specifics on Commercial Letters of Credit and Bankers' Acceptances,* Scott Printing Corp., Jersey City, N.J., 1974.

HENNART, JEAN FRANCIS: "Some Empirical Dimensions of Countertrade," *Journal of International Business Studies,* summer 1990, pp. 243–270.

KORTH, CHRISTOPHER (ed.): *International Countertrade,* Quorum, New York, 1985.

KRUGMAN, PAUL R., and MAURICE OBSTFELD, *International Economics: Theory and Policy,* Scott-Foresman, Glenview, Ill., 1988, Chapter 9.

LECRAW, DONALD: "The Management of Countertrade: Factors Influencing Success," *Journal of International Business Studies,* spring 1989, pp. 41–60.

RENTZMANN, WERNER F., and THOMAS TEICHMAN: "Forfaiting: An Alternative Technique of Export Financing," *Euromoney,* December 1975, pp. 58–63.

SÖDERSTEN, BO: *International Economics,* 2d ed., Macmillan, London, 1980, Chapter 17.

WATSON, ALASDAIR: *Finance of International Trade,* Institute of Bankers, London, 1976.

Glossary

80-20 subsidiary A specially established wholly owned company used to raise capital for a U.S.-based corporation. The subsidiary must earn 80 percent or more of its income abroad. Up to 20 percent of income may be earned in the United States. 80-20 subsidiaries do not need to withhold tax (see **withholding tax**) and therefore are useful for raising funds from foreigners who would not receive full credit for tax withheld.

absolute advantage A country has an absolute advantage in products it can produce at lower cost than other countries. See **comparative advantage.**

absolute form of the purchasing-power parity principle The form of the **purchasing-power parity principle** stated in terms of *levels* of prices and *levels* of exchange rates, rather than in terms of inflation and changes in exchange rates. See **relative form of the purchasing-power parity principle.**

absorption approach Interpretation of the **balance of trade** in terms of the value of goods and services produced and the value of goods and services "absorbed" by consumption, investment, or the government. The absorption approach views the **balance of payments** from the perspective of the **national-income accounting identity.**

accelerator model Theory which links the demand for capital goods to the level of GDP, and hence the rate of investment in capital goods to the growth rate of the GDP.

accept Willingness of a bank to guarantee a **draft** for payment of goods and services.

acceptance draft Check or **draft** for which documents such as the **bill of lading** are delivered upon acceptance of the draft by the payee's bank. See **clean draft, documentary draft, payment draft.**

accommodation Situation in which a central bank expands the money supply to prevent a reduction in spending after a jump in the price level, thereby supporting the higher price level.

accounting exposure The amount of **foreign exchange exposure** reflected in a company's financial statements.

adjusted present value (APV) A technique for capital budgeting that is similar to **net present value** but which considers difficult matters, if necessary, after dealing with easy-to-handle matters.

administered prices   Prices set by firms, often for internal purposes or to reduce taxes, not by the market. See **arm's-length pricing.**

agency cost   The cost that may be faced by shareholders, and perhaps also by the economy at large, when managers do not own the corporations they manage. The cost occurs when managers pursue their own interests instead of the interests of shareholders.

agglomeration economies   Mutual benefits firms enjoy from being in the same location.

agreement corporation   A means for a U.S.-based bank to engage in international banking. Can be established with permission of the Federal Reserve Board or a state government.

air waybill   The document issued by a carrier showing details of the merchandise being transported by air. See **bill of lading.**

American Depository Receipts (ADRs)   Claims issued against foreign shares and traded in the over-the-counter market. ADRs are used so that the foreign shares can trade in their home market but nevertheless be sold in the United States.

American options   Options contracts that can be exercised on any date up to and including the maturity date of the option. See **European options.**

appreciation   An increase in the foreign exchange value of a currency when exchange rates are **flexible.** See **depreciation, devaluation,** and **revaluation.**

arbitrage   Simultaneously buying and selling for the purpose of profiting from price differences.

arbitrager   A person or institution engaging in **arbitrage.**

arbitrage profit   The profit from simultaneously buying and selling the same item.

arm's-length pricing   Prices set according to proper market values. See **administered prices** and **transfer prices.**

Articles of Agreement (Bretton Woods)   The principles signed at the Bretton Woods conference which helped define the **Bretton Woods system.**

ask rate   The price at which a bank or broker is willing to sell. See **bid rate.**

asset approach to exchange rates   A theory which emphasizes that monies are assets and therefore have values according to what market participants think the monies will be worth in the future.

Association of South East Asian Nations (ASEAN)   The economic membership organization between countries of South East Asia working toward tariff reductions and easier access of members to each others' markets. The ASEAN is less formalized and covers a narrower range of concerns than does the **European Union** or the **North American Free Trade Agreement.**

at-the-money option   An option with a **strike price** or **exercise price** equal to the current market price of the underlying asset. For example, an option on spot pounds is "at the money" if the U.S. dollar strike price equals the U.S. dollar spot value of the pound. See **in-the-money options** and **out-of-the-money options.**

autocorrelation   The situation in which successive regression errors are systematically related, indicating, for example, that relevant variables may be missing from a **regression equation.** Also called **serial correlation,** autocorrelation causes a bias toward finding that included variables are significant.

automatic price-adjustment mechanism   The built-in way that deficits and surpluses in the **balance-of-payments account** are self-correcting via changes in countries' price levels, with the price-level changes caused by changes in money supplies. Money supplies are changed by central-bank responses to **balance-of-payments surpluses** and **deficits.** See **price-specie automatic adjustment mechanism.**

avalled Guaranteed **time drafts** provided by an importer's bank in association with **forfaiting.**

Baker initiative Arrangement organized by James Baker, the U.S. Secretary of the Treasury in 1985, to help deal with the **third-world debt crisis.**

balance-of-payments account A statistical record of the flow of payments into and out of a country during an interval of time. Provides a record of the sources of supply of and demand for a country's currency.

balance of payments on capital account The difference between the value of a country's assets *sold to* nonresidents and the value of assets *bought from* nonresidents during an interval of time.

balance of payments on current account The **balance on goods, services, and income,** plus net **unilateral transfers.**

balance of trade A commonly used abbreviation for the **balance on (merchandise) trade,** and equal to **merchandise exports** minus **merchandise imports.**

balance-of-trade deficit The extent to which the value of **merchandise imports** exceeds the value of **merchandise exports** during an interval of time. See **balance-of-trade surplus** and **balance on (merchandise) trade.**

balance-of-trade surplus The extent to which the value of **merchandise exports** exceeds the value of **merchandise imports** during an interval of time. See **balance-of-trade deficit** and **balance on (merchandise) trade.**

balance on goods, services, and income The difference between the value of exports of merchandise, services, and investment income *received from* abroad and the value of imports of merchandise, services, and investment income *paid* abroad.

balance on (merchandise) trade The difference between the value of **merchandise exports** and the value of **merchandise imports** during an interval of time.

Bancor Name given by John Maynard Keynes to a proposed form of international money which was to be used for international settlements.

bank agency A bank's operation in a foreign country which is like a full-fledged bank except that it does not handle retail deposits.

bank draft A check issued by a bank promising to pay the stated amount of a currency. See **draft** and **time draft.**

banker's acceptance A **time draft** which has been guaranteed by a bank stamping it as **accepted** so that the draft can be sold at a bank-related discount rate, not at a rate related to the risk of the issuer of the draft.

Bank for International Settlements (BIS) An organization of central bankers and bank regulators, located in Basle, Switzerland. The BIS is a "bank for central banks" and serves as a forum for central bankers to discuss international banking regulatory standards and coordinate central-bank policies.

bank note The paper currency of a nation, such as the U.S. "greenback" or Bank of England paper money. Bank notes are frequently referred to as "cash."

bank-note wholesaler A company that buys currency in the form of **bank notes** from banks or currency dealers and sells the notes to other banks or currency dealers, usually in the home country of the currency.

Basle Committee A bank-safety surveillance organization which provides information to bank regulators about the financial condition of banks and their subsidiaries.

bearer shares Equities which are not registered in an owner's name. This is the form of many equities sold in the **Euroequity** market.

beggar-thy-neighbor policy   Policy of **devaluation** that attempts to help exporters and create jobs but which hurts other countries whose exports compete with those of the devaluing country. Therefore, the policy shifts unemployment to other countries.

bid rate   The price which a bank or broker is willing to pay. See **ask rate.**

bilateral trade   Trade between two nations.

bill of exchange   A check used for payment between countries, that is, an intercountry form of **bank draft.**

bill of lading (B/L)   Document issued by a shipper (or carrier) to show the details of merchandise that is to be transported. The bill of lading can serve as title to the merchandise and is needed to obtain the merchandise when it arrives at its destination.

bimetallic standard   An exchange rate system in which exchange rates are faced by central banks exchanging their currencies for either of two precious metals, gold and silver.

blocked funds   Funds that cannot be **repatriated.**

Brady plan   A scheme devised in 1989 by U.S. Secretary of the Treasury Nicholas Brady (with bank and government approval) providing debtor nations with three options for handling their debts: reduced principal, reduced interest rates, or new loans.

branch   A foreign office of a bank or other company that is domestically incorporated and integrated with domestic operations. See **foreign (bank) branch.**

Bretton Woods system   The procedure for fixing exchange rates and managing the international financial system, worked out in Bretton Woods, New Hampshire, in 1944. The system involved fixing foreign currencies to the U.S. dollar, and the U.S. dollar to gold. The Bretton Woods system was in effect until the early 1970s. Also called the **gold-exchange standard.**

brokers   Agents who help arrange the trading of currencies between banks by assembling buy and sell orders and showing the **inside spread,** which is the lowest selling **(ask)** rate and highest buying **(bid)** rate.

Buffer Stock Facility   **International Monetary Fund** provision out of which loans are made to countries to finance crucial inventory.

buyback agreements   **Countertrade** where the seller of equipment agrees to buy some or all of the products made with the equipment.

buyer credits   Loans to buyers, especially importers, from banks. See **supplier credits.**

call option   Gives the buyer the right, but not the obligation, to buy an asset such as a foreign currency at the stated **strike price** or **exercise price.** See **put option.**

calling (margin)   Situation in which a bank or broker demands that additional funds be placed in a **margin** account.

canton   Local area in Switzerland which collects taxes from residents and provides services.

Capital Asset Pricing Model (CAPM)   An economic model which gives the equilibrium expected return on an asset or a portfolio of assets in terms of the risk-free interest rate and a risk premium representing the **systematic risk** of the asset or asset portfolio.

capital budgeting   A technique for deciding whether to incur capital expenditures such as building a new plant or purchasing equipment.

capital gains tax   A tax paid on the increase in value of an asset between its purchase and sale.

capital market line   The line tracing the expected returns and risks associated with different combinations of a risk-free asset (treasury bills) and the market portfolio (the portfolio of all securities existing in the market).

central-bank swaps   Arrangements between central banks for exchanging currency reserves to assist in supporting a country's exchange rate, where reserve exchanges are reversed later.

certificate of deposit (CD)   A negotiable claim against a deposit at a bank.

chaebol   Consortium of Korean companies.

CHIPS   See **Clearing House Interbank Payments System.**

clean draft   A check providing payment without the need to present any other documents.

clearing corporation   A corporation that pairs orders to buy futures or options contracts with orders to sell, and which guarantees all resulting two-sided contracts.

clearing house   An institution at which banks keep funds that can be moved from one bank's account to another bank's account in order to settle interbank transactions.

Clearing House Interbank Payments System (CHIPS)   The **clearing house** used to settle interbank transactions which arise from foreign exchange purchases and sales settled in U.S. dollars. CHIPS is located in New York and is owned by its members.

closed economy   An economy without trade of goods or capital with other nations. The assumption of a closed economy is used as a means of simplifying economic models.

coefficient of variation   A statistical measure of volatility consisting of the standard deviation divided by the mean. Can be used to compare the volatility of exchange rates in different time periods.

cointegration techniques   Statistical procedures involving the comparison of the path followed by the difference between two economic variables over time and the paths followed by the variables themselves.

commitment fee   A charge by a **forfaiting** bank for quoting a rate for accepting (buying) payments from an exporter.

commodity arbitragers   Those who attempt to profit from differences in prices in different locations, buying commodities where they are cheap and selling them where they are more expensive. Their actions help bring about the **law of one price.**

common currency   Situation, as in the United States, where the same currency is used everywhere. The **European Union** has declared its intention to work toward a common currency.

comparative advantage   A relative efficiency in producing something, indicated by having a lower opportunity cost of one product versus another product than occurs in some other country. Countries gain from international trade by producing products for which they have a comparative advantage. See **absolute advantage.**

Compensating Financing Facility   A means by which the **International Monetary Fund** provides foreign exchange reserves to countries facing short-term difficulties.

compensation agreement   **Countertrade** in which some payment is in cash.

competitive advantage   A term coined by Michael Porter to reflect the edge a country enjoys from dynamic factors affecting international competitiveness. Factors contributing to a competitive advantage include well-motivated managers, discriminating and demanding consumers, and the existence of service and other supportive industries, as well as the necessary factor endowments.

composite currency unit   A unit formed by combining a number of different currencies. Examples are **Special Drawing Rights** and the **European Currency Unit.** Composite currency units are also called **currency baskets** and **currency cocktails.**

Concordat Agreements   1975 and 1983 agreements for host countries to provide information to a parent bank's home regulators when an overseas subsidiary of the parent bank is experiencing serious loan losses.

confirm (letter of credit)   Occurs when an exporter obtains a guarantee from a local bank of a **letter of credit** issued by a foreign bank.

confiscation   The seizure of assets without compensation. See **expropriation.**

consignment sales   The basis of payment whereby the producer is paid by an intermediary only after the intermediary has sold the goods.

consortium banks   Joint ventures of large banks.

constant returns to scale   The situation where average cost of production remains the same when all factors of production are varied in amount to produce more or less of a product. For this to occur, output must change in the same proportion as the inputs employed, and input prices must remain constant. See **increasing returns to scale.**

consumption function   A relationship between consumption and the value of national income. See **marginal propensity to consume.**

continuous (export) insurance   Insurance of credits granted by exporters where exporters do not have to inform the insurer of each credit that is to be insured. Also called **whole turnover** and **rollover** insurance.

continuous market   A market in which quotations of prices are continuously available.

contractual assets or cash flows   Assets or cash flows with a fixed face value. See **noncontractual assets** and **contractual liabilities.**

contractual liabilities   Payment obligations with a fixed face value. See **contractual assets or cash flows, noncontractual assets.**

cooperative intervention   Situations whereby **G-7** central banks work together to stabilize exchange rates. Agreement to cooperate reached in the **Plaza Agreement,** 1985, and effected after the **Louvre Accord,** 1987.

correspondents   Banks which maintain accounts with each other against which checks can be drawn on behalf of customers.

counterpurchase   **Countertrade** in which the return exchange is delayed, or in which some other party is nominated to receive the return exchange.

countertrade   A reciprocal agreement for the exchange of goods or services.

countervailing tariffs   Taxes applied to offset measures that other countries have taken to make their goods artificially cheap, such as **export subsidies** or **dumping.**

country risk   Uncertainty surrounding payment from abroad or assets held abroad due to the possibility of war, revolution, asset seizure, or other similar political, social, or economic event. See **political risk** and **sovereign risk.**

cover   To take steps to isolate assets, liabilities, or income streams from the consequences of changes in exchange rates. See **hedge.**

covered interest arbitrage   Borrowing and investing with **foreign exchange exposure hedged** in order to profit from differences in yields/borrowing costs on securities denominated in different currencies.

covered interest parity condition   An aspect of the **law of one price** that occurs in financial markets, namely, that if **foreign exchange exposure** is **covered** by a **forward contract,** yields and borrowing costs are the same irrespective of the currency of investment or borrowing. Takes the form of a mathematical condition that the difference between interest rates on different currency-denominated securities equals the **forward premium** or **discount** between the currencies.

covered margin   The advantage, if any, from engaging in **covered interest arbitrage.**

crawling peg   An automatic system for revising the **parity** (par) exchange rate, typically basing the par value on recent experience of the actual exchange rate within its **support**

points. The crawling peg allows exchange rates to move toward equilibrium levels in the long run while reducing fluctuations in the short run.

credit   Short form of **letter of credit.**

credit swap   An exchange of currencies between a bank and a firm, with the exchange reversed at a later date. See **parallel loan.**

cross forwards   A **forward contract** between two currencies, neither of which is the U.S. dollar.

cross rate   An exchange rate between two currencies, neither of which is the U.S. dollar.

currency area   An area, consisting of a country or set of countries, in which exchange rates are fixed.

currency basket   A unit of measurement for international transactions formed by combining a number of different currencies, such as **Special Drawing Rights** and the **European Currency Unit.** Also called a **composite currency unit** and a **currency cocktail.**

currency center   The central location where a **multinational corporation** manages cash flows.

currency cocktail   A unit of measurement for international transactions formed from a combination of different currencies, such as **Special Drawing Rights** and the **European Currency Unit.** Also called a **composite currency unit** and a **currency basket.**

currency futures   Standardized contracts for the purchase or sale of foreign currencies that trade like conventional commodity futures on the floor of a futures exchange. Unlike **forward contracts,** currency futures are for standardized amounts, they trade for a limited number of **maturity dates,** and gains or losses are settled every day between the contract holder and the futures exchange. See **marking to market.**

currency option   A contract which gives the buyer the opportunity, but not the obligation, to buy or sell at a preagreed price, the **strike price** or **exercise price.**

currency per U.S. dollar   The method of quoting exchange rates as the amount of foreign currency per U.S. dollar. See **U.S. dollar equivalent** and **European terms.**

currency pool   In Britain after the Exchange Control Act of 1947, those wishing to make foreign investments were required to buy foreign currency out of a pool of currencies. The amount in the pool was limited by the British government.

customs union   An association between countries in which **tariffs** are low or zero between members of the association, and in which all members impose common tariff levels on outsiders. See **free-trade area.**

debtors' cartel   Title given to a feared collusion of debtor countries collectively refusing to repay loans.

debt-service exports   Investment income earned from abroad during an interval of time. See **debt-service imports.**

debt-service imports   Investment income paid to nonresidents during an interval of time. See **debt-service exports.**

decentralized, continuous, open-bid, double-auction market   The organizational form of the **interbank market** for foreign exchange. See **decentralized market, open-bid market** and **double-auction market.**

decentralized market   A market which does not have a centralized location but which instead involves buyers and sellers linked by telephone or similar means.

defect   To opt for a noncooperative action, usually involving cheating.

deposit ratio   The ratio of bank deposits to bank reserves.

depreciation A decline in the foreign exchange value of a currency when exchange rates are **flexible.** See **appreciation, devaluation,** and **revaluation.**

derivative A financial asset such as a futures or options contract, the value of which is derived from the claim it makes against some underlying asset, such as a foreign currency.

derivatives markets Markets in which assets whose values derive from underlying securities are traded. Examples are options and future markets.

Deutschemark (DM) The currency of the united Germany (formally the currency of West Germany only).

devaluation A decline in the foreign exchange value of a currency on **fixed exchange rates.** It occurs when the **parity** rate is set at a lower level. See **appreciation, depreciation,** and **revaluation.**

direct investment Short version of **foreign direct investment,** which is overseas investment where the investor has a measure of control. For accounting purposes, control is defined as holding 10 percent or more of a company's shares.

direct taxes Taxes, such as income taxes, paid directly by the persons or companies taxed. See **indirect tax.**

dirty float Occurs when governments attempt to influence exchange rates which are otherwise **flexible** and allowed to **float.** Also called a **managed float.**

discount rate The percentage interest rate used for converting future incomes and costs into current, or present, values. Usually set equal to the opportunity cost of funds, which is what shareholders could otherwise earn on an alternative investment of equal risk.

divergence indicator A mechanism based on the **European Currency Unit** for determining which country is at fault for a currency being at the upper or lower support of its permissible range within the **Exchange Rate Mechanism** of the **European Monetary System.**

divest Selling off past investments.

documentary credit A credit guarantee which requires that certain documents be presented before settlement. **Letters of credit** are documentary credits.

documentary draft A check providing payment subject to certain documents being presented and usually associated with a **documentary credit.** See **acceptance draft, clean draft, payment draft.**

dollar standard The exchange-rate system in effect during 1968–1973 when foreign currencies were fixed to the U.S. dollar as they were with the **Bretton Woods system,** but the U.S. dollar was no longer freely convertible into gold.

domestic international sales corporation (DISC) A device for encouraging U.S. firms to export by offering low corporate income tax rates. Since 1984, DISCs have largely been replaced by **foreign sales corporations.**

domestic reporting currency The currency in which a firm reports its income and in which it produces its financial statements. Usually the currency of the country in which a corporation's head office is located.

Dornbusch sticky-price theory Explanation advanced by Rudiger Dornbusch as to why exchange rates might **overshoot.** The theory emphasizes that because some goods' prices change slowly, exchange rates must overadjust to keep the demands and supplies of monies in balance throughout the adjustment process.

double-auction market A market in which the participants on both sides of a transaction could be either buyers or sellers. For example, when two banks are in contact with each other about trading currency, both banks may show prices at which they are willing to buy or sell.

double-entry bookkeeping Accounting procedure in which every debit is matched by a credit elsewhere in the account.

draft A check used for payment, also called a **bill of exchange** when the payment is between countries.

dumping Selling goods or services abroad at a lower price than at home. Done to attract customers away from local producers.

Durbin-Watson statistic (D-W) A statistical measure indicating whether **serial correlation** is present in a **regression equation**.

Dutch disease Problem associated with **flexible exchange rates** and originally identified after the discovery of natural gas off the Dutch coast, and the associated appreciation of the Dutch guilder. The increase in the value of the guilder hurt traditional Dutch exporters and employment in the traditional industries.

EC See **European Community.**

economic exposure A more complete title for **exposure,** with the word "economic" added to distinguish true *economic* effects of exchange rates from effects which appear in financial statements. Effects in financial statements involve **accounting exposure.**

economic risk An alternative title for **exchange-rate risk,** with the word "economic" added to distinguish true *economic* risk from risk that might be evident upon evaluation of financial statements.

economy of scope Cost savings associated with the range of items being produced.

Edge Act corporations A means by which U.S. banks can engage in overseas **investment banking.**

EEC See **European Economic Community.**

efficient market A market in which prices reflect available information. See **weak-form efficiency, semi-strong-form efficiency,** and **strong-form efficiency.**

efficient markets form of the purchasing-power parity principle The statement of the **purchasing-power parity principle** in terms of *expected* inflation in two countries and the *expected* change in the exchange rate between their currencies. Also called the **expectations form of the purchasing-power parity principle.**

efficient portfolio A collection of assets, the amounts of which are designed to have maximum expected return for a given volatility, or minimum volatility for a given expected return.

envelope (of efficient portfolios) The upward-sloping part of the curve giving the best combinations of expected return and risk that can be achieved with different portfolios.

escrow account An account which a bank holds at a **clearing house** for settling interbank transactions.

EU See **European Union.**

Eurobond A bond denominated in a currency that is not that of the country in which it is issued; often sold in several countries simultaneously. See **foreign bond** and **Eurodollar bond.**

Eurocurrency deposits Deposits at financial institutions denominated in currencies other than those of the countries in which the deposits are located. A generalization of **Eurodollar deposits.**

Eurocurrency multiplier The multiple by which **Eurocurrency deposits** increase from an original increase in foreign exchange reserves.

Eurodollar bond   A U.S.-dollar-denominated bond sold outside of the United States. A particular type of **Eurobond.**

Eurodollars   A commonly used abbreviation for funds held in the form of **Eurodollar deposits.**

Eurodollar deposit   A U.S.-dollar-denominated bank deposit at a financial institution located outside the United States. See **Eurocurrency deposits.**

Eurodollar market   The market outside of the United States in which U.S.-dollar-denominated loans are made and in which U.S. dollars are deposited in financial institutions.

Euroequity (issues)   Shares sold simultaneously in two or more countries' stock markets.

European Community (EC)   The successor of the **European Economic Community** and predecessor of the **European Union.**

European Currency Unit (ECU)   An artificial unit defined as a weighted average of each of the **European Monetary System** currencies and used as a **divergence indicator** as well as for denominating loans.

European Economic Community (EEC)   The association of European countries which limited its activities largely to economic matters, mainly tariffs and trade conditions, and which became the **European Community** and eventually the **European Union** as its domain of interest expanded beyond economic concerns.

European Monetary Cooperation Fund (EMCF)   A central pool of money and source of help, advice, and policy coordination for the members of the **European Monetary System.**

European Monetary System (EMS)   The procedure involving the **Exchange Rate Mechanism** for fixing exchange rates among the **European Union** countries. The EMS was intended to be a precursor to a **common currency.**

European options   Options contracts that can be exercised only on the maturity date of the option and not before this date. See **American options.**

European terms   The quotation of exchange rates as the amount of foreign currency per U.S. dollar. See **U.S. dollar equivalent** and **currency per U.S. dollar.**

European Union (EU)   The association of countries formerly called the **European Community (EC),** and prior to that known as the **European Economic Community (EEC).** The EEC became the EC when the issues handled in common moved from solely economic matters to social and political matters. The EC became the EU when common **tariff** levels were applied by all members to outside countries. The EU is a **customs union.**

Eurosterling bond   A British-pound-denominated bond sold outside of Britain.

even-dated contracts   Standard-length forward contracts with, for example, 3-month maturity, 1-year maturity, etc.

event study   A statistical approach examining the situation before, after, and at the same time something happens. The purpose is to check if conditions are normal or unusual surrounding the event.

Exchange Rate Mechanism (ERM)   The procedure used for fixing exchange rates within the **European Monetary System** from 1979 to 1993. The ERM involved establishing a **grid** which provided upper and lower **support points** for each member's currency versus each other member's currency. When an exchange rate between two currencies approached a support point, the central banks of both countries were required to take action. Assistance to maintain exchange rates was also available from the **European Monetary Cooperation Fund.**

exchange-rate risk   The variance of the domestic-currency value of an asset, liability, or operating income attributable to unanticipated changes in exchange rates.

excise tax   Another word for a **tariff.** A tax on imports, usually based on value, *ad valorem,* or on weight.

exercise price   The price at which an options contract buyer has the right to purchase or sell. See **strike price** and **currency option.**

expectations form of the purchasing-power parity principle   The form of the **purchasing-power parity principle** stated in terms of the *expected* inflation in two countries and the *expected* change in exchange rate between the countries' currencies. Also called the **efficient markets form of the purchasing-power parity principle.**

Export-Import (Ex-Im) Bank   U.S. export promotion agency which guarantees loans by private banks to U.S. exporting firms.

export insurance   Guarantee of payment to an exporter when credit has been extended to a foreign buyer.

export subsidy   An action designed to make a country's exports artificially inexpensive.

exposure   A commonly used abbreviation for **foreign exchange exposure.**

exposure line   A plot of the systematic relationship between changes in values of assets, liabilities, or operating incomes, and unanticipated changes in exchange rates.

expropriation   The seizure of assets with compensation. See **confiscation.**

Extended Fund Facility   Procedure introduced in 1974 for the **International Monetary Fund** to provide medium- and long-term loans to countries facing structural difficulties.

FAS 8   The now-abandoned reporting system of the U.S. Financial Accounting Standards Board which required companies to show all foreign exchange **translation** gains or losses in the current-period income statement. Replaced by **FAS 52.**

FAS 52   The reporting system of the U.S. Financial Accounting Standards Board which replaced **FAS 8** and which allows companies to include foreign exchange **translation** gains and losses in a separate shareholder-equity account. This reduces income volatility and allows income tax to be deferred on translation gains.

fiat money   Money, the acceptability of which is required by an order or edict of government. Paper money is fiat money.

filter   A selection rule for decision making.

financial engineering   A technique that uses **payoff profiles** to show the consequences of different financial strategies. The profiles can be combined to show the outcomes of different strategies.

financial structure   Composition of capital raised by a firm—for example, the mix between debt and equity.

Fisher equation   An equation which states that interest rates observed in the market consist of the **real interest rate** plus the expected rate of inflation.

Fisher-open condition   The mathematical condition that **real interest rates** are equal in different countries.

fixed asset   As asset such as real estate or plant and equipment. Fixed assets are often called **real assets.**

fixed exchange rates   A system of exchange-rate determination in which governments try to maintain exchange rates at selected official levels. See **flexible exchange rates, floating exchange rates,** and **pegged exchange rates.**

flat   The situation where the **forward exchange** rate equals the **spot exchange rate.**

flexible exchange rates   A system of exchange rates in which exchange rates are determined by the forces of supply and demand without any interference by governments or official bodies. See **fixed exchange rates, floating exchange rates,** and **pegged exchange rates.**

floating exchange rates   Another way of referring to **flexible exchange rates.**

flow   Value per period of time. See **stock.**

foreign (bank) affiliate   Similar to a **foreign (bank) subsidiary** in being locally incorporated and managed, but a foreign (bank) affiliate is a joint venture in which no individual owner has control.

foreign (bank) branch   A bank similar to local banks in appearance and operations except that incorporation and ownership are in the parent bank's country. Operations of foreign branches are integrated with those of the parent bank.

foreign (bank) subsidiary   Locally incorporated bank owned completely or partially by a foreign parent.

foreign bond   A bond sold by a foreign issuer and denominated in the currency of the country of issue. For example, a U.S.-dollar-denominated bond of a Canadian firm issued in the United States is a foreign bond. See **Eurobond.**

foreign direct investment (FDI)   Investment in a foreign country in which the investor has a measure of control of the investment, usually taken as holding 10 percent or more of voting shares of a public company. See **direct investment.**

foreign exchange exposure   The sensitivity of changes in the real domestic-currency value of assets, liabilities, or operating incomes to unanticipated changes in exchange rates. Exposure can be measured by the slope of a **regression equation** which relates changes in values of assets, liabilities, or operating incomes to unanticipated changes in exchange rates.

foreign-pay bond   A bond denominated in a foreign currency.

foreign resident withholding tax   A tax applied to nonresidents at the source of their earnings. See **withholding tax credit.**

foreign sales corporation (FSC)   A device made available in 1984 for promoting U.S. exports by offering low corporate tax rates to companies primarily engaged in exporting. Replaced **domestic international sales corporations.**

foreign-trade income   The income of a **foreign sales corporation** that is subject to a preferred tax rate.

forfaiting   A form of medium-term nonrecourse export financing. Involves a series of **avalled** time drafts.

forward bias   A systematic difference between the **forward exchange** rate and the expected future **spot exchange** rate.

forward (exchange) contract   An agreement to exchange currencies at a specified exchange rate on a future date. See **outright forward contract.**

forward discount   The extent that the forward price of a currency is below the spot price. See **forward premium.**

forward exchange rate   The rate that is contracted today for the exchange of currencies at a specified date in the future. See **forward contract.**

forward-forward swap   Purchase/sale of a currency offset by a subsequent sale/purchase of the same currency, where both transactions are forward transactions.

forward premium   The extent that the forward price of a currency exceeds the spot price. See **forward discount.**

Four Tigers   The rapid-growth economies of South East Asia: Hong Kong, Singapore, Taiwan, and South Korea.

free-trade area   An area within which trade is not subject to **tariffs.** However, member countries can have their own tariff levels against outsiders. See **customs union.**

free-trade zone   An area within a country in which import tariffs are not paid. Often used as a device for reexporting products.

functional currency   The primary currency in which a subsidiary operates. This is the currency in which a subsidiary reports its income; such reporting may involve translating foreign-currency amounts into the functional currency. U.S. parent companies convert functional currency magnitudes into U.S. dollars.

futures contract   A standardized agreement to buy or sell a given amount of a commodity or financial asset, including currencies, at a given date in the future.

futures option   An option to buy a **futures contract** at a stated price. See **spot option.**

G-7   See **Group of Seven.**

game theory   The paradigm that views actions in terms of each player's or agent's expectations about the actions of other players or agents.

GATT   See **General Agreement on Tariffs and Trade.**

General Agreement on Tariffs and Trade (GATT)   A multicountry framework dating back to the 1940s to restrict tariffs and other impediments to international trade. Replaced by the **World Trade Organization** in 1995.

General Arrangements to Borrow   1990 extension of the **International Monetary Fund's** lending authority to permit loans to nonmember countries.

global custodians   Financial firms, typically banks, which hold and handle transactions involving securities on behalf of overseas owners of these securities.

globalization   The movement from local, **segmented** markets to multinational, **integrated** markets.

gold-exchange standard   Also known as the **Bretton Woods system,** the gold-exchange standard involved fixing exchange rates of foreign currencies to the U.S. dollar, and the U.S. dollar to gold. The gold-exchange standard was in effect from 1944 to 1968, after which time it became the **dollar standard.**

gold points   The upper and lower limits on the range within which exchange rates can move when currencies are fixed to gold. The size of the range within the gold points depends on the costs of shipping gold and of exchanging currencies for gold. See **lower gold point** and **upper gold point.**

gold standard   The system of fixing exchange rates between currencies by fixing the price of the currencies to gold. The gold standard lasted well into the twentieth century.

gold tranche   The part of the original contributions that countries made to the **International Monetary Fund (IMF)** that took the form of gold and against which IMF members could borrow without conditions.

grid   The matrix of upper and lower **support points** of the exchange rates among the **European Monetary System** currencies.

Group of Five (G-5)   The United States, Japan, Germany, Britain, and France; subsequently expanded to the **Group of Seven** by the addition of Canada and Italy.

Group of Seven (G-7)   Grew from **Group of Five** and consists of government leaders from the United States, Japan, Germany, Britain, France, Canada, and Italy. Holds "summit" meetings at least once each year to discuss economic matters of mutual interest.

hedge   The action of reducing or eliminating effects from, for example, changes in exchange rates. See **cover.**

home-country bias   Holding a disproportionately large fraction of domestic assets vis-à-vis an efficiently diversified international asset portfolio.

hot money   Short-term funds which move easily between countries or currencies in response to small changes in interest rates.

IMF   See **International Monetary Fund.**

imperfect competition   The situation in which there are a large number of firms with free entry into and out of an industry but different firms' products are not exactly the same.

import duty   A tax or **tariff** on imported products.

import quota   A limit on the quantity of a good that can be imported.

import substitutes   Goods or services produced at home that may be purchased instead of similar foreign goods or services.

increasing returns to scale   The situation where average cost of production decreases when inputs of all factors of production are increased to produce more of a product. For this to occur, output must increase by a greater proportion than the inputs employed. See **constant returns to scale.**

indirect barriers   Factors, such as difficulties in obtaining information on foreign firms, that cause capital markets to be **segmented.**

indirect tax   A tax which is ultimately paid by somebody other than the person or firm being taxed. For example, a sales tax is remitted by a firm, but if the tax is fully added to the amount paid by the consumer, it is actually paid by the consumer, not the firm.

industrial offset   **Countertrade** involving reciprocal agreements to buy materials or components from the buying company or country.

inflation risk   The result of uncertainty in the buying power of an asset in the future due to uncertainty about the future price level.

inside spread   The lowest selling **(ask)** price and the highest buying **(bid)** price on the books of a broker. These are the best prices available, constituting the smallest difference between buying and selling prices.

integrated capital market   Situation when the connection between countries' capital markets is seamless. Occurs when markets are not **segmented.**

interbank   Between banks. Term used to distinguish the part of the foreign exchange market in which banks deal directly with each other from the part involving **brokers.**

interbank market   The currency market in which banks trade with each other over the telephone or via other electronic means. Central banks as well as commercial banks trade currencies in the interbank market.

interest arbitrage   Simultaneously borrowing and lending for the purpose of gaining from **(covered)** interest rate differences.

interest-rate adjustment mechanism   Automatic tendency for deficits and surpluses in the **balance-of-payments account** to be self-correcting under **fixed exchange rates,** and operating via changes in interest rates. For example, deficits cause declines in money supplies, higher interest rates, and improvements in the **balance of payments on capital account** and **the balance of payments on current account.**

internal rate of return   The **discount rate** that makes the **net present value** equal zero.

International Bank for Reconstruction and Development (IBRD)   Also known as the **World Bank,** the IBRD assists developing nations by granting loans and providing economic advice. Origin dates to the start of the **Bretton Woods system.**

international banking facilities (IBFs)   Adjunct operations of U.S. banks which raise funds and make loans outside the United States but which operate in the United States without having to meet normal regulatory requirements of U.S. banks.

international capital asset pricing model (ICAPM)   An extension of the **capital asset pricing model** to the international context.

International Development Agency (IDA)   An organization (affiliated with the **World Bank**) that provides very long-term loans at a zero interest rate to poor countries.

International Finance Corporation (IFC)   An organization (affiliated with the **World Bank**) that provides loans for private investments and sometimes takes equity positions along with private-sector partners.

International Monetary Fund (IMF)   Membership organization of over 160 countries, originally established as part of the **Bretton Woods system** in 1944. The IMF holds foreign exchange reserves of members, makes loans, provides assistance and advice, and serves as a forum for discussion of important international financial issues.

international-investment-position account   The record of a country's foreign assets and its liabilities to nonresidents.

in-the-money option   An option which, if exercised immediately, would provide the holder of the option with some value. For example, a **call** option on **spot** pounds is "in the money" if the spot value of the pound is above the **strike price.** See **intrinsic value, out-of-the-money option,** and **at-the-money option.**

intrinsic value   The extent to which an option is **in the money.** See **time value.**

investment banks   Institutions which raise funds in capital markets and then provide financing, often in the form of equity. **Edge Act corporations** are established by U.S. commercial banks to engage in investment banking.

invisibles   Service imports and exports including tourism, royalties, licences, consulting fees, and business services.

J-curve effect   The path of the **balance of trade** over time after a change in exchange rates. The path of the balance of trade after a devaluation may have the appearance of the letter J.

joint venture   Shared ownership of an investment, instituted because of need for a large amount of capital or to reduce the risk of **confiscation** or **expropriation.**

keiretsu   Consortium of Japanese companies.

Kennedy round   General tariff reductions arranged by the **General Agreement on Tariffs and Trade** in the 1960s.

Kingston Agreement   Agreement among **International Monetary Fund** (IMF) member countries reached in Kingston, Jamaica, in 1976 to, among other things, sell the IMF's gold holdings and make the funds available as development loans. See **Trust Fund.**

law of one price   The rule resulting from actions of **arbitragers** that a given item will cost the same everywhere, whether this be a commodity or a financial asset. The law of one price means that prices of the same item in different currencies reflect the exchange rates between the currencies. See **covered interest parity principle** and **purchasing-power parity principle.**

leading and lagging   The practice of **netting** receivables and payables over a period of time forward, called leading, and backward, called lagging.

"leaning against the wind"   The practice of some central banks to try to reduce fluctuations in the value of their currency by raising interest rates to prevent depreciations and lowering interest rates to prevent appreciations.

letter of credit (L/C)   An irrevocable guarantee from a bank that a seller's credit to a buyer will be honored provided the seller fulfils her or his part of a specified agreement, such as the delivery of goods on time and in good condition. Also called a **credit.**

limit orders   Orders given to brokers to buy or sell limited, specified amounts of currency at specified prices on behalf of clients.

liquidity preference   The value asset holders attach to being able to cash in assets cheaply and at a predictable value. Liquidity preference may induce investors to hold domestic-currency assets instead of hedged foreign-currency assets.

liquidity trap   Situation where increasing the money supply does not reduce interest rates.

London interbank offer rate (LIBOR)   Interest rate charged on interbank loans in London. The average of rates charged by large, London banks on a given currency is often used as the basis for adjusting interest rates on floating-rate loans.

long   Having agreed to buy more of a currency than one has agreed to sell. Alternatively, holding more of a currency than is needed. See **short, long position,** and **short position.**

long exposure   Situation when, for example, a company or individual gains when the foreign exchange value of a currency increases. See **short exposure.**

long position   Having contracted to buy a currency on the **forward** market or on a **futures** exchange. See **long, short, short position.**

Louvre Accord   An agreement reached at the Louvre Museum in Paris in 1987 for the leading industrial powers to cooperate in stabilizing exchange rates. The Louvre Accord followed the **Plaza Agreement,** which accepted the need to periodically intervene in foreign exchange markets.

lower gold point   The lowest possible value of an exchange rate when currencies are fixed to gold. See **gold points** and **upper gold point.**

Maastricht Agreement   An agreement between **European Union** countries, signed in Maastricht, Holland, to work toward common economic, social, and political policies, including achievement of a **common currency.**

maintenance level   The minimum amount in a margin account below which the account must be supplemented by buyers and sellers of **futures** or options contracts.

managed float   **Flexible-exchange-rate** system in which central banks occasionally intervene in the foreign exchange markets to prevent extreme changes in exchange rates. Also called a **dirty float.**

margin   Money posted at a brokerage house, bank, or clearing corporation to help ensure that contracts are honored.

marginal efficiency of investment   The rate of return enjoyed on an additional, or incremental, investment. It is the return from increasing the amount of capital formation during a given interval by a small amount.

marginal propensity to consume   The percent of extra, or incremental, income spent on consumption, representing the slope of the **consumption function.**

marginal propensity to import   The percentage of extra, or incremental, income spent on imports.

marginal utility   The increase in utility, or satisfaction, from a small, incremental increase in the rate of consumption.

market-makers   Agents who continuously stand ready to buy and to sell assets, including currencies.

marking to market   Adjustment of margin accounts to reflect daily changes in the values of contracts against which **margins** are held.

marking-to-marking risk   Risk from variability in interest rates on funds in a **margin** account. Risk is due to a possible difference between funds in a margin account and the gain or loss on an asset or liability.

Marshall-Lerner condition   The requirement concerning the elasticities of demand for imports and exports in order for foreign exchange markets to be stable. Named after the co-discoverers of the condition, Alfred Marshall and Abba Lerner.

maturity date   The date of expiry of a bond, option, or forward contract.

merchandise exports   Sales of tangible items to foreign buyers.

merchandise imports   Purchases of tangible items from abroad.

mercantilists   Adherents to the view that the objective of international trade is to earn gold and run balance-of-trade surpluses. Mercantilism was popular from the sixteenth century to the eighteenth century.

mixed credits   A procedure used to calculate an interest rate for credit provided to an importer, where the interest rate is an average of rates on different credit sources.

monetary theory of exchange rates   The theory that bases the value of a country's currency in foreign exchange markets on the supply of that currency (money supply) relative to the demand to hold the currency (money demand).

money market   The market in which short-term borrowing and investment occur (with "short term" usually meaning less than one year).

most favored nation (clause)   The clause in the **General Agreement on Tariffs and Trade** which disallowed offering better trade terms to any country than those terms given to the most favored country.

multicurrency bond   A bond which gives the owner repayment in two or more currencies. Also called a **currency cocktail** bond. See **unit-of-account bond.**

multinational corporation   A company which has made **direct investments** overseas and which thereby has operations in many countries.

multiple regression equation   The fitted relationship between three or more variables. See **regression equation.**

multiplier   The change in the national income relative to the size of the underlying, original cause of this change.

NAFTA   See **North American Free Trade Agreement.**

Nash equilibrium   The situation in **game theory** where expectations of different players are consistent and where the expectations are borne out.

national-income accounting identity   A statement of national income divided into four components: consumption, investment, government spending, and exports minus imports.

natural monopoly   A situation in which a supplier faces a declining average cost over a very large range of output relative to market demand, and thereby becomes the sole supplier of a good or service.

net present value (NPV)   The income from a capital project minus the cost of the project stated in terms of the current (or present) value of the income and project cost. A technique for **capital budgeting.** See **adjusted present value** and **internal rate of return.**

netting   Calculating the overall situation for payables and receivables in a currency that faces a firm. Amounts to be paid are subtracted from amounts to be received so that **hedging** can be limited to the net amount of the currency coming in or going out. See **leading and lagging.**

neutralization policy   A policy of not allowing changes in foreign exchange reserves to affect a country's money supply, frustrating the **automatic price-adjustment mechanism.** Also called **sterilization policy.**

nominal anchor   Something linked to the money supply, such as gold, which serves to maintain a stable price level.

nominal interest rate   The interest rate observed in the market. See **real interest rate.**

noncontractual assets   Assets without a fixed face value, such as real estate or equities. See **contractual assets** and **contractual liabilities.**

nontariff trade barriers   Restrictions on imports, such as size restrictions and red tape, that interfere with international trade. Nontariff barriers are often less obvious but just as harmful as explicit import restrictions such as tariffs and quotas.

North American Free Trade Agreement (NAFTA)   The 1993 treaty between the United States, Canada, and Mexico containing provisions for the reduction or elimination of trade barriers between the countries. In late 1994, Chile signed its intent to join the NAFTA.

OECD   See **Organization for Economic Cooperation and Development.**

offshore currencies   Bank deposits which are denominated in a currency different from that of the country in which the deposits are held. A generalization of **Eurodollar deposits.**

Oil Facility   **International Monetary Fund** provision, established in 1974 after a rapid increase in oil prices, to provide credits (loans) to countries facing difficulties due to high-priced imported oil. Became the **Supplementary Financing Facility** in 1976.

one-way arbitrage   The process of choosing the best way to exchange one currency for another or choosing the best currency in which to invest or borrow. See **arbitrage, round-trip arbitrage,** and **triangular arbitrage.**

open account (sales)   The basis of sales where the amount due is added to the buyer's account, and the balance owed is settled periodically. A payment method used when the seller trusts the buyer's credit.

open-bid market   A market in which participants quote both buying (**bid**) and selling (**ask**) prices.

open economy   An economy with trade of goods and capital with other nations. See **closed economy.**

open interest   The number of outstanding two-sided futures or options contracts at any given time.

operating exposure   The sensitivity of changes in the real domestic-currency value of operating incomes to unanticipated changes in exchange rates. Also called **residual foreign exchange exposure.**

operating risk   Related to the volatility of real domestic-currency operating incomes due to unanticipated changes in exchange rates. Usually measured by the variance in operating incomes from unanticipated changes in exchange rates.

optimum currency area   An area within which exchange rates *should* be fixed. Coverage of area depends on the mobility of factors of production and the similarity of the economies of component countries. See **region.**

option premium   The amount paid per unit of foreign currency when buying an options contract.

order bill of lading   A **bill of lading** which gives title (ownership) of goods that are being shipped to a stated party and which may be used as collateral against loans.

Organization for Economic Cooperation and Development (OECD) A Paris-based government-level organization providing information and advice on the economies of its 24 member nations, which include the United States and most of Western Europe.

out-of-the-money option An option which, if exercised immediately, would not provide the holder with any value. For example, a **call option** on **spot** pounds is "out of the money" if the spot value of the pound is below the **strike price.** See **in-the-money option** and **at-the-money option.**

outright forward contract An agreement to exchange currencies at an agreed exchange rate at a future date. See **swap.**

over-the-counter (OTC) option Right to buy or sell sold by banks to customers, rather than on an options exchange.

Overseas Private Investment Corporation (OPIC) Insures U.S. private investments in developing nations.

overshooting of exchange rates The situation whereby exchange-rate changes are larger in the short run than in the long run. Occurs when exchange rates go beyond their eventual equilibrium level. See **Dornbusch sticky-price theory.**

parallel loan An exchange of funds between firms in different countries, with the exchange reversed at a later date. See **credit swap.**

parity (exchange rate) The officially determined exchange rate under fixed exchange rates.

payback period The length of time before the capital cost of an investment project has been recovered.

payment draft Check or **draft** for which documents such as the **bill of lading** are delivered upon payment of the draft by the payee's bank. See **acceptance draft** and **clean draft.**

payoff profile A plot of the gains or losses on an asset against unexpected changes in price. For example, a forward exchange contract payoff profile shows the gains or losses on the forward contract against unexpected changes in the spot exchange rate.

pegged exchange rates Another term for **fixed exchange rates,** which are rates set by governments at selected, official levels.

perfectly competitive market A market in which there are so many buyers and sellers that each buyer and seller can take the price of a given, homogeneous product as given. Also involves free entry and exit of new firms and perfect information on prices.

perfectly substitutable (monies) The situation in which people are equally as prepared to hold one country's currency as to hold that of another country.

permanent A change in an economic variable that persists, such as a long-lasting increase in income or an exchange rate. See **transitory.**

peso problem Problem of having high interest rates when there is a strong possibility of a **devaluation,** with interest rates remaining high while the devaluation is delayed.

Plaza Agreement An agreement among the **G-7** leaders reached at the Plaza Hotel in New York in 1985 that accepted the need to intervene in foreign exchange markets. Led to the **Louvre Accord** of 1987 which involved cooperative intervention.

point The last digit in traditional exchange rate quotations.

political risk Uncertainty surrounding payment from abroad or assets held abroad because of political events. A special case of **country risk,** which includes economic and socially based uncertainty as well as political uncertainty.

pooling The practice of holding (and managing) cash in a single location.

portfolio-balance approach to exchange rates A theory basing exchange rates on the supply of and demand for money and bonds. The situation for money/bond supply and demand in one country versus another country determines the exchange rate between the two countries' currencies. People are assumed to hold both countries' money and bonds but prefer to hold their own. Exchange rates are such that all money and bonds are held.

portfolio investment Investment in bonds, and in equities where the investor's holding is too small to provide effective control.

positive externalities Benefits or cost savings enjoyed by others which are in addition to benefits or cost savings of those taking an action.

price-specie automatic adjustment mechanism The built-in way that deficits and surpluses are self-correcting via movements of precious metals between countries and consequent changes in money supplies and price levels. The **gold standard** is said to exhibit the price-specie automatic adjustment mechanism.

Private Export Funding Corporation (PEFCO) A private U.S. organization providing loans to U.S. exporters.

probability distribution The relationship between possible outcomes and their probability of occurrence.

product life-cycle hypothesis Theory that companies follow a similar evolutionary path, going from domestic to multinational orientation.

public good Something that nonpayers cannot be excluded from enjoying.

purchasing-power parity (PPP) principle The idea that exchange rates are determined by the amounts of different currencies required to purchase a representative bundle of goods.

pure exchange gain That part of the overall gain from trade which arises from the exchange of products without any specialization of production.

put option A put option gives the buyer the right to sell an asset such as a foreign currency at the stated **strike price** or **exercise price.** See **call option.**

quantity theory of money The view that inflation is caused by money supply growth being in excess of the growth rate of output.

quasi-centralized market A market in which brokers in several different locations help to facilitate transactions.

quasi-centralized, continuous limit-book, single-auction market A market in which brokers in several locations take **limit orders** and show the resulting **inside spread** occurring at any time to prospective clients.

quota (import) A restriction on the quantity of a good that can be imported.

ratchet effect Effect attributed to **flexible exchange rates** concerning the impact they have on inflation. The ratchet refers to jumps in prices from **depreciations** without fully offsetting declines in prices during **appreciations.**

rational forecasts Forecasts which are on average correct and which do not reveal persistent errors.

real asset As asset such as real estate for which the market price tends to go up and down with inflation. Sometimes called **fixed assets.**

real change in exchange rates A change that produces a difference between the overall rate of return on domestic versus foreign assets/liabilities or in the profitability of export-oriented, import-using, or import-competing firms.

real interest rate The **nominal interest rate** minus expected inflation.

reference currency The official currency of measurement of values of assets, liabilities, or operating incomes.

regime   A period during which a particular policy, for example, toward regulating exchange rates, is in effect.

region   Term used by Robert Mundell to describe an **optimum currency area,** being an area within which factors of production are mobile and from which they are not mobile.

regression coefficient   An estimate of the magnitude of the impact of a variable on some other variable. An element of a **regression equation.**

regression equation   A statistically calculated relationship between two or more variables. See **multiple regression equation.**

regression error   The difference between the actual value of a variable and the value predicted from a **regression equation.**

relative form of the purchasing-power parity principle   The form of the **purchasing-power parity principle** stated in terms of inflation and changes in exchange rates: a country's currency depreciates by the excess of its inflation over that of another country. See **absolute form of the purchasing-power parity principle.**

relative-price risk   Risk due to the possibility of changes in the price of an individual asset vis-à-vis asset prices in general.

repatriation   Bringing funds home from abroad.

representative (bank) office   An office maintained by a bank in a foreign country to facilitate contact with local banks and businesses and to provide services for clients.

rescheduling   Arranging for delay in the repayment of interest or principal on loans. Occurred frequently during the **third-world debt crisis.**

residual foreign exchange exposure   Another term for **operating exposure** which reflects the difficulty companies have hedging their operating exposure.

revaluation   An increase in the foreign exchange value of a currency on fixed exchange rates. It occurs when the **parity** rate is set at a higher level. See **appreciation, depreciation,** and **devaluation.**

risk premium (forward)   The difference between the **forward exchange rate** and the expected future **spot foreign exchange** rate.

rollover (swap)   A **swap** where the purchase/sale and subsequent sale/purchase of a currency are separated by 1 business day.

rollover insurance   **Export insurance** where sellers do not have to inform the insurer of each credit that is to be insured. Also called **continuous** and **whole-turnover** insurance.

round-trip arbitrage   Borrowing in one currency, lending in another, and then selling the second currency back into the first so as to end up back in the first currency. See **arbitrage, one-way arbitrage,** and **triangular arbitrage.**

segmented capital market   Situation where different countries' capital markets are not **integrated** because of implicit or explicit factors inhibiting the free movement of capital between the countries.

seigniorage   The profit from creating money. Said to have occurred from the need for countries to hold U.S. dollar foreign exchange reserves under the **Bretton Woods system.**

semi-strong-form efficiency   The situation where all publicly available information is reflected in market prices. See **efficient market, weak-form efficiency,** and **strong-form efficiency.**

serial correlation   A situation in which successive **regression errors** are systematically related, indicating, for example, that relevant variables may be missing from a **regression equation.** Also called **autocorrelation.**

short   Having agreed to sell more of a currency than one has agreed to purchase. Alternately, holding less of a currency than is needed. See **long, long position,** and **short position.**

short exposure   Situation where, for example, a company or individual faces a loss when the foreign exchange value of a currency increases. See **long exposure.**

short position   Having contracted to sell a currency on the **forward** market or on a **futures** exchange. See **long, long position,** and **short.**

sight draft   A draft payable not on some stated future date, as with a **time draft,** but rather payable on presentation to the issuing bank. It can be cashed immediately.

signal   An action which indicates credibility to others. Credibility is usually achieved by taking an action which is costly and which therefore would not be taken unless the agent was in the situation implied by the signal.

single-auction market   A market where the agent being approached, but not the person making the approach, quotes buying and selling prices.

Smithsonian Agreement   Agreement of **International Monetary Fund** members reached in December 1971 to raise the U.S. dollar price of gold and to create a **wider band** within which exchange rates could **float** before central bank intervention.

snake   The **fixed-exchange-rate system** designed to keep the **European Community** (EC) countries' exchange rates with a narrower band vis-à-vis each other's currencies rather than vis-à-vis non-EC currencies, such as the U.S. dollar.

Society for Worldwide International Financial Telecommunications (SWIFT)   Satellite-based international communications system for the exchange of information between banks, used, for example, to convey instructions for the transfer of deposits.

sourcing   A **hedging** technique involving the invoicing of input prices and other cost items in the currency of sales.

sovereign loans   Loans to governments or guaranteed by governments.

sovereign risk   Uncertainty involving loans to foreign governments or government agencies.

Special Drawing Rights (SDRs)   Reserves at, and created by, the **International Monetary Fund** (IMF) and allocated by making ledger entries in countries' accounts at the IMF. Used for meeting imbalances in the balance of payments and assisting developing nations.

specific export credit insurance   **Export insurance** for a particular stated item.

speculation   Taking an **exposed** position, consciously or unconsciously.

spot exchange rate   The exchange rate between two currencies where the exchange is to occur "immediately," meaning usually the next business day or after 2 business days.

spot foreign exchange market   The market in which currencies are traded and where delivery is "immediate," meaning usually the next business day or after 2 business days.

spot option   An option to buy or sell **spot exchange.** See **futures option.**

spread   The difference between the buying (**bid**) and selling (**ask**) prices of a currency, or the difference between borrowing and lending interest rates.

stationary   The situation where the process, or model, generating data is not changing over time.

statistical discrepancy   The adjustment required to balance the balance-of-payments account due to errors in the measurement of items included in the account.

sterilization policy   A policy of not allowing changes in foreign exchange reserves to affect a country's money supply, frustrating the **automatic price-adjustment mechanism.** Also called **neutralization policy.**

sterling   Another name for the British pound, written as £.

stock   Value or quantity at a point in time. See **flow.**

straddle   The purchase of a **put option** and a **call option** at the same **strike price.** Used as a means of speculating on high volatility.

strike price   The price at which an option can be exercised. For example, the exchange rate at which a **call option** buyer can purchase a foreign currency. See **currency option** and **exercise price.**

strong-form efficiency   The situation where all information, including that available to insiders, is reflected in market prices. See **efficient market, weak-form efficiency,** and **semi-strong-form efficiency.**

subsidiary   A foreign operation that is incorporated in the foreign country but owned by a parent company.

Supplementary Financing Facility   **International Monetary Fund** provision established in 1976 out of which standby credits could be granted to countries needing loans. Also known as the **Witteveen Facility,** the Supplementary Financing Facility replaced the **Oil Facility** of 1976.

supplier credits   Financing provided by the seller, usually by issuing **time drafts.**

supply-side economics   A economic philosophy popular after the 1980 U.S. presidential election, based on the view that production (supply) in the economy would be increased by lower tax rates.

support points   The upper and lower limits of an exchange rate band at which central banks step in to prevent the exchange rate from going outside the band. Central banks buy at the lower support point and sell at the upper support point in a **fixed-exchange-rate** system.

swap (currency)   A sale/purchase of a currency combined with an offsetting purchase/sale for a later time, or borrowing and lending in the same currency. The initial purchase/sale might be a **spot** transaction, with the offsetting sale/purchase being a **forward** transaction. This is a spot-forward swap. However there are also **forward-forward swaps** involving offsetting purchases and sales where all transactions occur in the future. See **outright forward contract, swap-in,** and **swap-out.**

swap-in   Term used to indicate the currency being purchased and subsequently sold in a **swap** transaction. See **swap-out.**

swap-out   Term used to indicate the currency being sold and subsequently bought back in a **swap** transaction. See **swap-in.**

swap points   The number of **points** to be added to or subtracted from the spot exchange rate in order to calculate the **forward exchange rate.**

SWIFT   See **Society for Worldwide International Financial Telecommunications.**

switch trading   **Countertrade** where a title to a credit is transferred to another party.

symbiotic relationship   Connection of mutual benefit, for example, between firms which move together into a foreign market.

systematic relationship   Situation where two variables change in more or less predictable ways vis-à-vis each other. For example, if on average dollar values of assets go up with the foreign exchange value of the dollar, there is a (positive) systematic relationship.

systematic risk   The part of risk that cannot be diversified away.

target zone   The range within which an exchange rate is to be kept.

tariff   A tax on imports. See **excise tax.**

tax arbitrage   Attempt to profit from pricing or interest rate situations due to the existence of taxes. For example, borrowing in one currency and investing in another currency which is at a forward exchange premium. This can be profitable when **forward (exchange) premiums** face a low **capital gains tax** rate.

tax haven   A country with low tax rates that attracts companies or individuals fleeing higher tax rates elsewhere.

technical forecasts   Forecasts of a variable based on the pattern of past values of the variable.

temporal distinction   Different accounting treatment of operating income and expenses than of **fixed assets** and liabilities.

tenor   The maturity of a **time draft** or **usance draft.**

terms of trade   The price of exports in terms of imports determining the amount of imports a country can receive per unit of exports. An improvement in terms of trade occurs when a country can obtain more imports per unit of its exports.

thinness   A market is thin when the volume of transaction is low, that is, when transactions are relatively infrequent.

third-world debt crisis   Serious concern in financial markets during 1982–1989 that developing nations would be unable to meet scheduled payments on loans from developed-country-based banks. See **rescheduling.**

tick   The minimum price change on a futures or options contract.

time draft   A check, or **draft,** payable at a future date and used as a form of credit. Also called a **usance draft.**

time value   The part of an **option premium** that comes from the possibility that an option might have higher intrinsic value in the future than at the moment.

Tokyo round   General tariff reductions arranged by the **General Agreement on Tariffs and Trade** in the 1970s.

tradable inputs   Inputs that are traded internationally or could be traded internationally.

trade draft   An exporter's **draft** that is drawn without an importer's **letter of credit** and which is therefore a commercial rather than a bank obligation.

trading pit   The floor of an exchange where traders call out prices and make transactions.

transaction cost   The amount paid in brokerage or similar charges when making a transaction. On currencies, transaction costs are represented by the **spread** between the **bid** and **ask** exchange rates.

transaction exposure   The sensitivity of changes in realized domestic-currency values of assets or liabilities when assets or liabilities are liquidated with respect to unanticipated changes in exchange rates.

transaction risk   The uncertainty of realized domestic-currency asset or liability values when the assets or liabilities are liquidated due to unanticipated changes in exchange rates.

transfer prices   Prices used for goods and services moving within a **multinational corporation** from one division to another. Rules typically require that transfer prices be **arm's-length prices.**

transitory   A change in an economic variable that is short-lived, such as a once-and-for-all increase in income or an exchange rate. See **permanent.**

translated value   The value of an asset, liability, or income after it has been converted into another currency. For example, the value of a foreign-currency asset converted into the owner's domestic currency.

translation   Conversion of the value of an asset, liability, or income from one currency to another.

translation exposure The sensitivity of changes in real domestic-currency asset or liability values appearing in financial statements with respect to unanticipated changes in exchange rates.

translation risk The uncertainty appearing in financial statements due to unanticipated changes in exchange rates.

transnational alliance Separately owned corporations from different countries working in cooperation for such purposes as research and development or marketing.

triangular arbitrage Simultaneously buying and selling for the purpose of profiting from differences between **cross rates** and direct exchange rates vis-à-vis the U.S. dollar. Such arbitrage involves three currencies and transactions.

Triffin paradox Problem identified by Robert Triffin that for the **Bretton Woods system** to work, the United States would have to run **balance-of-payments deficits,** thereby providing the other countries with dollar reserves. However, if the United States did run deficits, the Bretton Woods system would fail because countries would not want to hold U.S. dollars as reserves due to fear of a dollar **devaluation.**

Trust Fund Money at the **International Monetary Fund** resulting from the sale of gold and used for development loans. Established in 1976 as part of the **Kingston Agreement.**

U.S. dollar equivalent The quotation of the price of a currency in terms of its value in U.S. dollars. See **European terms** and **currency per U.S. dollar.**

U.S. official reserve assets Liquid foreign assets held by the U.S. Federal Reserve or Department of the Treasury. Includes gold, foreign currencies, and short-term investments.

uncovered interest parity condition The situation, analogous to the **covered interest parity condition,** in which **foreign exchange exposure** is not **covered** with a **forward (exchange) contract.** Takes the form of a mathematical condition that the difference between interest rates on different currency-denominated securities equals the expected rate of change of the exchange rate between the two currencies.

unilateral transfers Payments from one country to another in the form of gifts and foreign aid.

unit-of-account bond A bond making payments based on pre-established **fixed exchange rates.**

upper gold point The highest possible value of an exchange rate when currencies are fixed to gold. See **gold points** and **lower gold point.**

Uraguay round General tariff reductions agreed to in 1994 resulting from many years of negotiation centered in Uraguay and under the auspices the **General Agreement on Tariffs and Trade.**

usance draft Another term for a **time draft.** A check payable at a future date and used as a form of **supplier credit.**

value date The date on which currency is to be received. See **maturity date.**

value-added tax (VAT) A tax on the difference between the amount received from the sale of an item and the cost of acquiring or making it.

vector auto regression A statistical technique which selects variables and combinations of variables for inclusion in a **regression equation** according to how strong a statistical relationship they provide.

waybill (air) Another term for **bill of lading,** used particularly for goods being transported by air cargo or courier.

weak-form efficiency   The situation when information only on historical prices or returns on a particular asset are reflected in market prices. See **efficient market, semi-strong-form efficiency,** and **strong-form efficiency.**

weighted-average cost of capital   The per annum cost of funds raised via debt (bank borrowing, bonds) and equity (selling shares), where the two items are weighted by their relative importance.

whole-turnover insurance   **Export insurance** where sellers do not have to inform the insurer of each credit that is to be insured. Also called **continuous** and **rollover** insurance.

wider band   A compromise between fixed and flexible exchange rates which allows exchange rates to fluctuate by a relatively large amount on either side of an official value. Tried during 1971–1973 after approval by **International Monetary Fund** members as part of the **Smithsonian Agreement.**

wire transfer   The movement of money with instructions being sent by electronic means, such as via **SWIFT.**

withholding tax   A tax applied to nonresidents at the source of their earnings. See **withholding tax credit.**

withholding tax credit   Allowance made for taxes withheld by foreign governments in order to avoid double taxation.

Witteveen Facility   A fund at the **International Monetary Fund** from which countries can be given loans to help with temporary difficulties. Also known as the **Supplementary Financing Facility.**

World Bank   Also known as the **International Bank for Reconstruction and Development,** the World Bank assists developing nations by granting loans and providing economic advice. Origin dates back to the early 1940s.

World Trade Organization (WTO)   The World Trade Organization took over from the **General Agreement on Tariffs and Trade** in 1995. The WTO's objective is to expand international trade and resolve trade disputes.

writer (option)   The person selling an option, who must stand ready to buy (when selling a **put option**) or to sell (when selling a **call option**).

Name Index

Subject Index

619